KT-510-395

Romania
& Moldova

Nicola Williams
Kim Wildman

Bucureşt

LONELY PLANET PUBLICATIONS
Melbourne • Oakland • London • Paris

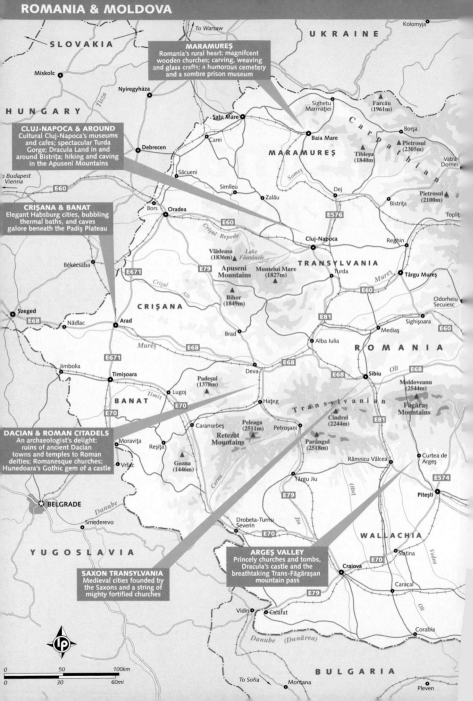

ROMANIA & MOLDOVA

To Warsaw

SLOVAKIA

UKRAINE

Kolomyja

MARAMUREŞ
Romania's rural heart: magnificent wooden churches; carving, weaving and glass crafts; a humorous cemetery and a sombre prison museum

Miskolc

Nyiregyháza

Satu Mare

Sighetu Marmaţiei

Farcău (1961m)

Borşa

HUNGARY

Carei

Baia Mare

MARAMUREŞ

Tibleşu (1840m)

Pietrosul (2305m)

Vatra Dornei

CLUJ-NAPOCA & AROUND
Cultural Cluj-Napoca's museums and cafes; spectacular Turda Gorge; Dracula Land in and around Bistriţa; hiking and caving in the Apuseni Mountains

Debrecen

Săcueni

Simlleu

Zalău

Dej

Bistriţa

Pietrosul (2100m)

Topliţ

To Budapest Vienna

E60

Bors

Oradea

CRIŞANA & BANAT
Elegant Habsburg cities, bubbling thermal baths, and caves galore beneath the Padiş Plateau

Crişul Repede

E60

Cluj-Napoca

E576

Reghin

Vlădeasa (1836m)

Lake Fântânele

Apuseni Mountains

Muntelui Mare (1827m)

TRANSYLVANIA

Turda

Mureş

Târgu Mureş

Békéscsaba

E671

E79

Bihor (1849m)

Odorheiu Secuiesc

Crişul Alb

CRIŞANA

Szeged

E68

Nădlac

Arad

Brad

E81

Sighişoara

Mediaş

E60

Alba Iulia

ROMANIA

Mureş

E68

Jimbolia

E671

Deva

E68

Sibiu

Olt

E68

Moldoveanu (2544m)

Timişoara

Padeşul (1378m)

Lugoj

E70

Haţeg

Transylvanian

Făgăraş Mountains

DACIAN & ROMAN CITADELS
An archaeologist's delight: ruins of ancient Dacian towns and temples to Roman deities; Romanesque churches; Hunedoara's Gothic gem of a castle

BANAT

Timiş

Caransebeş

Peleaga (2511m)

Petroşani

Cindrel (2244m)

E81

Moraviţa

Reşiţa

Retezat Mountains

Parângul (2518m)

Râmnicu Vâlcea

Curtea de Argeş

Vršac

Gozna (1446m)

E574

★ BELGRADE

Cerna

Piteşti

Smederevo

Danube

Târgu Jiu

Olteţ

Jiu

WALLACHIA

Drobeta-Turnu Severin

E70

YUGOSLAVIA

ARGEŞ VALLEY
Princely churches and tombs, Dracula's castle and the breathtaking Trans-Făgăraşan mountain pass

E79

Slatina

Vedea

SAXON TRANSYLVANIA
Medieval cities founded by the Saxons and a string of mighty fortified churches

Craiova

E70

Caracal

E79

Olt

Vidin

Calafat

Corabia

Danube (Dunărea)

0   50   100km
0   30   60mi

To Sofia

Montana

BULGARIA

Pleven

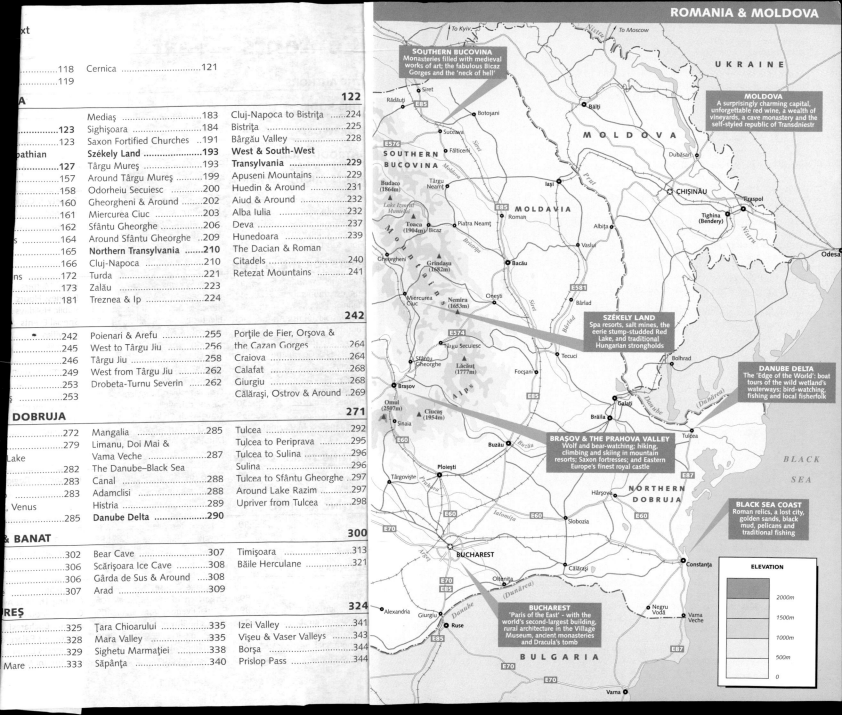

Romania & Moldova
2nd edition – May 2001
First published – May 1998

Published by
Lonely Planet Publications Pty Ltd ABN 36 005 607 983
90 Maribyrnong St, Footscray, Victoria 3011, Australia

Lonely Planet Offices
Australia Locked Bag 1, Footscray, Victoria 3011
USA 150 Linden St, Oakland, CA 94607
UK 10a Spring Place, London NW5 3BH
France 1 rue du Dahomey, 75011 Paris

Photographs
All of the images in this guide are available for licensing from
Lonely Planet Images.
email: lpi@lonelyplanet.com.au

Front cover photograph
Road signs near Bucharest (Nicola Williams)

Romanian title page photograph
Old Clock Tower, Sighişoara (Dave Greedy)

Moldovan title page photograph
Soviet monument, Piaţa Libertăţii, Chişinău (Dan Herrick)

ISBN 1 86450 058 1

text & maps © Lonely Planet 2001
photos © photographers as indicated 2001

Printed by Craft Print International Ltd, Singapore

Although the authors and Lonely Planet try to make the information as accurate as possible, we accept no responsibility for any loss, injury or inconvenience sustained by anyone using this book.

Contents – Text

MOLDAVIA

MOLDOVA

LANGUAGE

GLOSSARY

INDEX

MAP LEGEND

METRIC CONVERSION

Contents – Maps

ROMANIA & MOLDOVA MAP INDEX

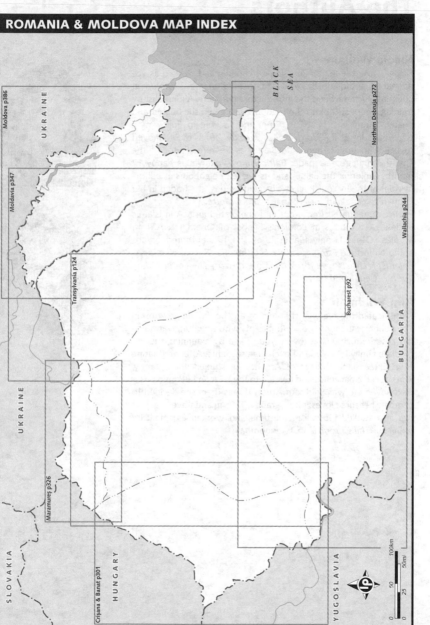

UKRAINE

BLACK SEA

SLOVAKIA

HUNGARY

YUGOSLAVIA

BULGARIA

0   50   100km
0   25   50mi

The Authors

Nicola Williams

Nicola wrote the 1st edition single-handedly and worked as co-ordinating author on the 2nd edition of *Romania & Moldova*, updating Bucharest and the introductory chapters. A journalist by training, she first took to the road in 1990 when she bussed and boated it from Jakarta to East Timor and back again. Following a two-year stint at the *North Wales Weekly News*, Nicola moved to Latvia to bus it round the Baltics as Features Editor of the English-language newspaper *Baltic Times*. Following a happy 12 months exploring the Baltics and its big red neighbours as editor-in-chief of the In Your Pocket city-guide series, she traded in her Lithuanian *cepelinai* for Lyonnaise *andouillette*.

Nicola graduated from Kent and completed an MA in Islamic Societies & Cultures at London's School of Oriental & African Studies. Other Lonely Planet titles she has authored or co-authored include *Estonia, Latvia & Lithuania*, *Russia, Ukraine & Belarus*, *France*, *Provence & the Côte d'Azur*, *The Loire*, *Milan, Turin & Genoa* and *Italy*.

Kim Wildman

Kim updated the regional chapters of this book. She grew up in Toowoomba, Queensland, with parents who unwittingly instilled her a desire to travel at a very young age by extending the immediate family to include 11 exchange students. After graduating from Queensland College of Art, having studied photography, Kim packed a backpack and headed to the USA and Bermuda. Her next adventure was Southern Africa. It was there she decided to combine her three loves: photography, writing and travelling. Kim has also studied journalism full-time and worked as a feature writer for *The Chronicle* in Toowoomba.

FROM THE AUTHORS

Nicola Williams In Bucharest, sincere thanks to George Roman from Salvaţi Copii (Save the Children) for taking time out from his invaluable work to talk to me; Nicolae Păduraru for revealing some Transylvanian Society of Dracula's ghoulish secrets; Cristina Ion from the UNDP; Corina Popescu and Liviu Plop at Romania's National Authority for Tourism; Steven Wright and Tim Johnson from *Bucharest Business Week*; Adrian Dascălu from Reuters; Maria Popescu of the Cultural Tourism Initiative; Jeroen van Marle; Craig Turp; and last but far from least, Oana Sav who proofread the Romanian in this guide, sent me a wad of updated train schedules after I left Romania; and never failed to give me an answer quick-smart to every question I had. Elsewhere in the land of monasteries and mountains, a sweet thank you to my dear friend Laura Vesa from Braşov, to the Orleanus from Casa Orleanu in Moeciu de Sus and to Colin Shaw of Roving Romania.

Kim Wildman In Romania, many thanks to Laura Vesa, Sorin Fînăţan, Sorin Bibicioiu, Salvamont's Nagy Alexandru and Vintilă Florin, and AGMR's Iulian Cozma (Braşov); Maria Stioan and all the Antrec staff (Bran); Mihai Serengeu and Bobby from Bobby's Hostel (Sighişoara); Ruxandra Sinci, Richard Sterner, Radu Mititean and all the guys from the Transylvanian Ecological Club (Cluj); Lăcrămioara Beilic (Suceava); Sanda Bitere (Iaşi); Mirela Anghel (Arad); the excellent staff at OVR-Art-Tur (Vadu Izei); Florentina Dumitru (Constanţa); Florentina Dospinescu (Mangalia); Christoph Promberger and Andrei Blumer of the Carpathian Large Carnivore Project; Colin Shaw of Roving Romania and IYP's Jeroen van Marle.

Special thanks to Andrei Mahalnischi for all your patience and driving skills; and Tom Haberman for the warm beer, language lessons and skiing pointers.

In Moldova my deepest gratitude goes to Corina Cepoi and all the staff and students at the Centrul Independent de Jurnalism, in particular: Sirbu Angela; Aurel Ciobanu; Emil Dediu; Iulian Robu; Diana Acristinii for truly loving your country and for the chocolates; Maxim Anmeghichean; Adrian Covalciuc; and Vlad Bolocan for your packed lunch and good humour. Many thanks also to the Transdniestr border guards for being impressed by Australian coins; Glen Puckets for helping a complete stranger; Barbara Martinez; Anna Morgen; and finally to Tony Hawks for writing the funniest book I've read this year!

Back home I owe the greatest debt to my dear friend Donnita White for her endless cups of tea, proofreading and nit-picking.

This Book

The 1st edition of *Romania & Moldova* was written by Nicola Williams. This 2nd edition has been coordinated by Nicola, who also updated the introductory and Bucharest chapters. The rest of the book was updated by Kim Williams.

From the Publisher

This 2nd edition of *Romania & Moldova* was edited in Lonely Planet's Melbourne office by Shelley Muir, with assistance from Carolyn Bain, Melanie Dankel and Susannah Farfor. Celia Wood was responsible for mapping, design and layout, assisted by Gus Poó y Balbontin and Sally Morgan. Quentin Frayne prepared the Language chapter, Csanád Csutoros produced the climate charts, Margaret Jung designed the cover and Mark Germanchis provided Quark support.

Martin Harris supplied the new illustrations, and photographs were supplied by Lonely Planet Images.

Acknowledgments

Many thanks to the travellers who used the last edition and wrote to us with helpful hints, useful advice and interesting anecdotes:

Peter H Allan, Uta Allanson, Brendan Allen, Nicholas Anchen, Paolo Attanasio, Jerry Azevedo, Melangell Bakker, Silye Barnabas, John Bedford, Jenny Bolger, Deborah Braddock, Nicky Bridges, Rachel Bridges, Sabine Brinker, Martin Bronner, Hans J Buhrmester, Karen Carlsen, Scott Catey, Chris & Malcolm Clark, Pauline Clark, Jennifer Cook, Elizabeth Cosgrove, Christena Coutsoubos, Budescu Cristu, Karen Davies, John Dixon, Patrick Doering, Craig Dreves, Stephanie Dufrene, Wes Eichenwald, Anthony Elgort, Caroline Elliot, Gerhard Eshuis, Jean Eustache, Claire Farrelly, Jon Fox, Rokos Frangus, Michael Frost, Peter Fyllgraf, Ines Gawehn, Constantin Gheorghiu, Lucian Giambasu, Marc Gonzalez, Gerhard Goochwill, Jodie Goulden, Carlos Griell, Massimo Gugnoni, Sally Haldane, Pasi Hannonen, Vasile Hanzu, Amanda Harvey, Phil Hayward, Eoghan Hicks, Tim Hill, Susanne Hrinkov, Leonard & Judith Hyman, Jens Jakob de Place Hansen, Martha D Jones, Gregers Jorgensen, Tobias Kamer, Bernhard Kasparek, Neil Klemp, Andrew Knoght, Gottfried Knott, Tina Knox, Werner Koch, Agnieszka Koltonik, Rolf Korzonnek, Jon Kujawa, Evelyn Kwak, Trevor Landers, Elizabeth Lane, Juliette Lelieur, Bas Leurs, Johnny Lonut Gorganeanu, Nicholas Lustry, Roberto Manfredi, Amy Marsh, Jose Luis Martin Mas, Raffaella Mascia, Neal-Douglas Messier, Marita Mircea, J Morton, Doru Munteanu, Roman Mycka, Al Nedelea, Alexandru Nedelea, Margaret Nichols, Richard Noakes, Prunea Ovidiu, Rolf Palmberg, J S Parrish, Magnus Perlestam, Billie L Porter, Carmel Posea, Kevin Presto, Artur Radziwill, Mark Ricketts, Harvey Shaw, Jan Smith, Zoe Smith, Carolyn Snell, Maaike Stomp, Richard Sudborough, Zoltan Szilagyi, Keith Thoresz, Kyle Thorson, Cezar Tipa, Jaume Tort, Andreea Totescu, Pedro Vale, Mike Wallace, Coryn Weigle, Will Werley, Barry Wijnandts, Joel Wilson, Astrid van der Wis, Quentin A Wood, Phillip Wright, Jose Zimmermann, Michael Ziser

Foreword

ABOUT LONELY PLANET GUIDEBOOKS

The story begins with a classic travel adventure: Tony and Maureen Wheeler's 1972 journey across Europe and Asia to Australia. Useful information about the overland trail did not exist at that time, so Tony and Maureen published the first Lonely Planet guidebook to meet a growing need.

From a kitchen table, then from a tiny office in Melbourne (Australia), Lonely Planet has become the largest independent travel publisher in the world, an international company with offices in Melbourne, Oakland (USA), London (UK) and Paris (France).

Today Lonely Planet guidebooks cover the globe. There is an ever-growing list of books and there's information in a variety of forms and media. Some things haven't changed. The main aim is still to help make it possible for adventurous travellers to get out there – to explore and better understand the world.

At Lonely Planet we believe travellers can make a positive contribution to the countries they visit – if they respect their host communities and spend their money wisely. Since 1986 a percentage of the income from each book has been donated to aid projects and human rights campaigns.

Updates Lonely Planet thoroughly updates each guidebook as often as possible. This usually means there are around two years between editions, although for more unusual or more stable destinations the gap can be longer. Check the imprint page (following the colour map at the beginning of the book) for publication dates.

Between editions up-to-date information is available in two free newsletters – the paper *Planet Talk* and email *Comet* (to subscribe, contact any Lonely Planet office) – and on our Web site at www.lonelyplanet.com. The *Upgrades* section of the Web site covers a number of important and volatile destinations and is regularly updated by Lonely Planet authors. *Scoop* covers news and current affairs relevant to travellers. And, lastly, the *Thorn Tree* bulletin board and *Postcards* section of the site carry unverified, but fascinating, reports from travellers.

Correspondence The process of creating new editions begins with the letters, postcards and emails received from travellers. This correspondence often includes suggestions, criticisms and comments about the current editions. Interesting excerpts are immediately passed on via newsletters and the Web site, and everything goes to our authors to be verified when they're researching on the road. We're keen to get more feedback from organisations or individuals who represent communities visited by travellers.

> Lonely Planet gathers information for everyone who's curious about the planet – and especially for those who explore it first-hand. Through guidebooks, phrasebooks, activity guides, maps, literature, newsletters, image library, TV series and Web site we act as an information exchange for a worldwide community of travellers.

Research Authors aim to gather sufficient practical information to enable travellers to make informed choices and to make the mechanics of a journey run smoothly. They also research historical and cultural background to help enrich the travel experience and allow travellers to understand and respond appropriately to cultural and environmental issues.

Authors don't stay in every hotel because that would mean spending a couple of months in each medium-sized city and, no, they don't eat at every restaurant because that would mean stretching belts beyond capacity. They do visit hotels and restaurants to check standards and prices, but feedback based on readers' direct experiences can be very helpful.

Many of our authors work undercover, others aren't so secretive. None of them accept freebies in exchange for positive write-ups. And none of our guidebooks contain any advertising.

Production Authors submit their raw manuscripts and maps to offices in Australia, USA, UK or France. Editors and cartographers – all experienced travellers themselves – then begin the process of assembling the pieces. When the book finally hits the shops, some things are already out of date, we start getting feedback from readers and the process begins again ...

WARNING & REQUEST

Things change – prices go up, schedules change, good places go bad and bad places go bankrupt – nothing stays the same. So, if you find things better or worse, recently opened or long since closed, please tell us and help make the next edition even more accurate and useful. We genuinely value all the feedback we receive. A well travelled team reads and acknowledges every letter, postcard and email and ensures that every morsel of information finds its way to the appropriate authors, editors and cartographers for verification.

Everyone who writes to us will find their name in the next edition of the appropriate guidebook. They will also receive the latest issue of *Planet Talk*, our quarterly printed newsletter, or *Comet*, our monthly email newsletter. Subscriptions to both newsletters are free. The very best contributions will be rewarded with a free guidebook.

Excerpts from your correspondence may appear in new editions of Lonely Planet guidebooks, the Lonely Planet Web site, *Planet Talk* or *Comet*, so please let us know if you *don't* want your letter published or your name acknowledged.

Send all correspondence to the Lonely Planet office closest to you:

Australia: Locked Bag 1, Footscray, Victoria 3011
USA: 150 Linden St, Oakland, CA 94607
UK: 10A Spring Place, London NW5 3BH
France: 1 rue du Dahomey, 75011 Paris

Or email us at: talk2us@lonelyplanet.com.au

For news, views and updates see our Web site: www.lonelyplanet.com

HOW TO USE A LONELY PLANET GUIDEBOOK

The best way to use a Lonely Planet guidebook is any way you choose. At Lonely Planet we believe the most memorable travel experiences are often those that are unexpected, and the finest discoveries are those you make yourself. Guidebooks are not intended to be used as if they provide a detailed set of infallible instructions!

Contents All Lonely Planet guidebooks follow roughly the same format. The Facts about the Destination chapters or sections give background information ranging from history to weather. Facts for the Visitor gives practical information on issues like visas and health. Getting There & Away gives a brief starting point for researching travel to and from the destination. Getting Around gives an overview of the transport options when you arrive.

The peculiar demands of each destination determine how subsequent chapters are broken up, but some things remain constant. We always start with background, then proceed to sights, places to stay, places to eat, entertainment, getting there and away, and getting around information – in that order.

Heading Hierarchy Lonely Planet headings are used in a strict hierarchical structure that can be visualised as a set of Russian dolls. Each heading (and its following text) is encompassed by any preceding heading that is higher on the hierarchical ladder.

Entry Points We do not assume guidebooks will be read from beginning to end, but that people will dip into them. The traditional entry points are the list of contents and the index. In addition, however, some books have a complete list of maps and an index map illustrating map coverage.

There may also be a colour map that shows highlights. These highlights are dealt with in greater detail in the Facts for the Visitor chapter, along with planning questions and suggested itineraries. Each chapter covering a geographical region usually begins with a locator map and another list of highlights. Once you find something of interest in a list of highlights, turn to the index.

Maps Maps play a crucial role in Lonely Planet guidebooks and include a huge amount of information. A legend is printed on the back page. We seek to have complete consistency between maps and text, and to have every important place in the text captured on a map. Map key numbers usually start in the top left corner.

Although inclusion in a guidebook usually implies a recommendation we cannot list every good place. Exclusion does not necessarily imply criticism. In fact there are a number of reasons why we might exclude a place – sometimes it is simply inappropriate to encourage an influx of travellers.

Introduction

Romania is a country of crazy superstitions and fantastic legends. With its dramatic castles and medieval towns where mass tourism means you, a horse and cart and a handful of farmers, Romania *is* the Wild West of Eastern Europe.

Dracula fiends flock to this land of alpine peaks, Black Sea beaches and castles in the Carpathian Mountains. Ghoulish appetites feed on Romania's rich pageant of medieval princes, about whom heroic and horrific stories abound. These noble spirits live in the country's ruined or restored palaces and monasteries.

Bird, bear and wolf-watching, hiking, skiing and snowboarding are among the bounty of outdoor activities for those seeking to immerse themselves in nature, adventure or both.

Few Eastern European nations feature such a kaleidoscope of cultures: Transylvania's towns are straight out of medieval Hungary or Germany while the exotic Orthodox monasteries of Moldavia and Bucovina evoke Byzantium. Western Romania bears the imprint of the Austro-Hungarian empire, while Roman and Turkish influences colour Constanţa and Dobruja. Bucharest, dubbed by travellers either 'the Paris of the East' or 'Hell on Earth', has a Franco-Romanian character all its own.

Romania's modern history is equally legendary. In 1989 the world watched with bated breath as revolutionaries rid themselves of one of the most ruthless dictators Europe has seen this century. Since then Romania has been grappling to recover from its communist past, with reform-minded governments bringing new hope to a people haunted by modern-day Draculas for far too long.

The country's new goal is entry into the European Union, which is expected to be achieved by 2007–10.

Next door to Romania is Moldova, a former Soviet republic sharing roughly the same history and language with Romania.

This country, which has been independent since 1991, comprises part of historic Bessarabia and has been heavily Russified and sovietised over the past century. Still largely unexplored today, Moldova produces some extraordinary wine and shelters what many dub the last bastion of Soviet socialism in Europe – the self-styled republic of Transdniestr created by Russian-speaking separatists.

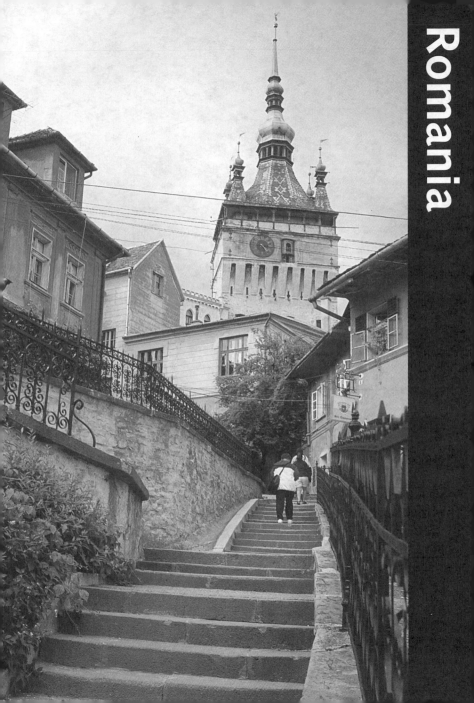

Romania

Facts about Romania

HISTORY
Antiquity

Ancient Romania was inhabited by Thracian tribes. The Greeks called them the Getae, the Romans called them Dacians, but they were actually a single Geto-Dacian people. Their principal religion was the cult of Zalmoxis, based on the fundamental belief that believers did not die but went to the god Zalmoxis. The Geto-Dacians communicated with their god through meditation and ritual sacrifice. The ultimate communion with Zalmoxis could only be achieved through shunning all bodily desires.

From the 7th century BC the Greeks established trading colonies along the Black Sea at Callatis (Mangalia), Tomis (Constanţa) and Histria. In the 1st century BC, a Dacian state was established by King Burebista to counter the Roman threat. During the Roman civil wars, Burebista lent his backing to Pompey in his struggle against Julius Caesar, prompting Caesar to plot an attack against the Dacians. Caesar was murdered before he could carry out his plans.

The last Dacian king, Decebal (ruled AD 87–106), consolidated this state but was unable to stave off attacks led by the Roman emperor Trajan in 101–102. Further attacks ensued in 105–106, leading to the Roman victory at the Dacian capital of Sarmizegetusa and the final Roman conquest of the region. Rather than fall captive to Trajan's army, King Decebal committed suicide. Dacia thus became a province of the Roman Empire.

The Romans recorded their expansion north of the Danube (most of present Romania, including the Transylvanian plateau, came under their rule) on two famous monuments: Trajan's Column in Rome, and the 'Tropaeum Trajani' at Adamclisi, on the site of their victory in Dobruja. The slave-owning Romans brought with them a superior civilisation and mixed with the conquered tribes to form a Daco-Roman people speaking Latin. A noted visitor during the Roman period was the Latin poet Ovid, who was exiled to Tomis (Constanţa) on the Black Sea by the Roman emperor, Augustus, in AD 9. In the works that he wrote during his banishment, Ovid complained of barbarians who attacked Tomis inhabitants with poisoned arrows, of wild tribes whose hairy faces were covered with icicles in winter, of regular sword fights between neighbours in the city forum, and of the horrific human sacrifices that the Tomisans practised.

Little is known of what became of the traditional Geto-Dacian god Zalmoxis. The Romans destroyed all the Dacian sanctuaries, replacing them with temples to their own deities. Any elements of Zalmoxian beliefs surviving the Roman occupation were rapidly absorbed by the spread of Christianity in the Roman province in the 2nd and 3rd centuries.

Faced with Goth attacks in AD 271, Emperor Aurelian (r. 270–275) decided to withdraw the Roman legions south of the Danube. But the Romanised Vlach peasants remained in Dacia – hence the formation of a Romanian people.

The Middle Ages

Waves of migrating peoples, including the Goths, Huns, Avars, Slavs, Bulgars and Magyars (Hungarians), swept across this territory from the 4th to the 10th centuries. The Romanians survived in village communities and gradually assimilated the Slavs and other peoples who settled there. By the 10th century a fragmented feudal system ruled by a military class had appeared. Small Romanian state formations emerged, developing first as *cnezats* (clusters of villages) and later evolving as *voievodats* (princely states) and *ţări* (literally 'land'). The eventual consolidation of these *ţări* led to the formation of the principalities of Moldavia, Wallachia and Transylvania.

From the 10th century the Magyars expanded into Transylvania, north and west of the Carpathian Mountains, and by the 13th century all of Transylvania was an autonomous principality under the Hungarian crown. This marked the first division of the Romanian population, thus preventing the formation of a united medieval Romanian state.

Following devastating Tartar raids on Transylvania in 1241 and 1242, King Bela IV of Hungary invited German Saxons to Transylvania to defend the crown's southeastern flank. He offered the Saxons free lands and tax incentives to persuade them to settle in the region. The Hungarian king also coerced the Székelys – a Hungarian ethnic group who had earlier migrated to the region with the Magyars – into a defensive role. Renowned for their remarkable warrior qualities, the Székelys were granted autonomy by the crown in return for services rendered.

In the 14th century, Prince Basarab I (r. 1310–52) united various political formations in the region south of the Carpathians to create the first Romanian principality – Wallachia. Hungarian forces almost immediately attacked the newly created principality in an attempt to force it to accept the suzerainty of the Hungarian crown. From 9 to 12 November 1330, Basarab's forces won an outstanding victory at the Battle of Posada, thus confirming Wallachian independence. The principality was dubbed Ţara Românească (Romanian Land).

The state formations led by dukes and princes in the region east of the Carpathians were united into the principality of Moldavia by Bogdan of Cuhea in 1359. Hungarian king Louis I sent an army to force Romania's second independent land into submission. Again, his forces were defeated.

Peasants dominated the populations of these medieval principalities. In Wallachia and Moldavia peasants were subjugated as serfs to the landed aristocracy (*boyars*), a hereditary class. There were some free, land-owning peasants (*moşneni*) too. The two principalities were ruled by a prince (*voievod*) who was also the military leader of the principality.

The feudal setup in Transylvania differed to the extent that feudal lords – noblemen – could only be recognised by the Hungarian crown. Most noblemen were Hungarian. The peasants were Romanians. In 1437 Transylvanian peasants staged an uprising against the nobles which was quickly crushed. Afterwards the Transylvanian nobles formed a political alliance with the Székely and Saxon leaders. This Union of the Three Nations became the constitutional basis for government in Transylvania in the 16th century.

Ottoman Expansion

Throughout the 14th and 15th centuries the Romanian-speaking principalities of Wallachia and Moldavia offered strong resistance to the Ottoman's northward expansion. Mircea cel Bătrân (Mircea the Old; r. 1386–1418), Vlad Ţepeş ('The Impaler'; r. 1448, 1456–62, 1476), and Ştefan cel Mare (Stephen the Great; r. 1457–1504) were legendary figures in this struggle.

When the Turks conquered Hungary in the 16th century, Transylvania became a vassal of the Ottoman Empire, retaining its autonomy by paying tribute to the sultan. The threefold medieval nation which embraced the Hungarian nobility, the Saxons and the Székelys – and discounted the Romanians – was immediately reinforced by the new Transylvanian Diet (legislative assembly). Semi-independence also meant that Hungarians and Saxons in Transylvania were able to convert from Catholicism – formerly imposed on them by medieval Hungary – to Protestantism. The Diet consequently recognised the Catholic and Protestant faiths as official state religions. The Orthodox faith of many Romanians by this time remained an unofficial, 'non-national' religion.

After the Ottoman victory in Transylvania, Wallachia and Moldavia also paid tribute to the Turks but maintained their autonomy (this indirect control explains why the only Ottoman buildings seen in Romania today are in Dobruja, the area between the Danube and the Black Sea).

In 1600 the three Romanian states were briefly united under Mihai Viteazul (Michael the Brave; 1593–1601) at Alba Iulia. Viteazul came to the Wallachian throne in 1593 and pursued a staunchly anti-Ottoman policy. In

November 1594 he joined forces with the ruling princes of Moldavia and Transylvania against the Turks, attacking Ottoman strongholds on the Danube and ordering the massacre of all Turks in Wallachia. In Giurgiu on 28 October 1595 the three Romanian armies attacked Turkish troops, prompting the Turks to call a truce with Viteazul.

The Transylvanian prince, Andrew Báthory, consequently turned against the Wallachia prince and, on 28 October 1599, Mihai Viteazul defeated Báthory's troops near Sibiu. Báthory fled the battle scene only to be captured by Székely troops who beheaded him and presented his head on a plate to Viteazul. To show disapproval for the Székelys' ruthlessness, Viteazul staged an elaborate funeral for Báthory and then marched straight to Alba Iulia to declare himself the new prince of Transylvania. In spring 1600 he invaded Moldavia and within three weeks was crowned prince of Moldavia too. This first political union of the three Romanian principalities lasted but a year: Viteazul was defeated by a joint Habsburg-Transylvanian noble army just months later and in August 1601 was captured and beheaded on the orders of Habsburg general George Basta.

In 1683 the Turks were defeated at the gates of Vienna and in 1687 Transylvania came under Habsburg rule. Great attempts were made during this period to convert Orthodox Romanians – whose faith remained unrecognised – to Catholicism, and between 1703 and 1711 the Austrian Habsburgs suppressed an independence struggle led by the Transylvanian prince, Francis (Ferenc) Rákóczi II.

The 18th century marked the start of Transylvanian Romanians' fight for political emancipation. Romanian peasants constituted 60% of the population yet continued to be excluded from political life. In 1784 three serfs called Horea, Cloşca and Crişan led a peasant uprising. It was quashed, and its leaders were imprisoned and crushed to death (Crişan killed himself in prison). But on 22 August 1785 the Habsburg emperor, Joseph II, abolished serfdom in Transylvania.

Turkish suzerainty persisted in Wallachia and the rest of Moldavia well into the 19th century. The 17th century in Wallachia was marked by the lengthy reign of Constantin Brâncoveanu (r. 1688–1714), a period of relative peace and prosperity characterised by a great cultural and artistic renaissance. The Turks called Brâncoveanu *Altân-bey* (Golden Prince) and his reign went down in history as the golden age of Romanian art and literature. The 18th century saw the imposition of a Phanariot regime in both Wallachia (from 1716) and Moldavia (from 1711), under which local rulers were removed and replaced by Greek *hospodars*, known as Phanariots, appointed by and subservient to the Ottoman Turks. Moreover, in 1775 part of Moldavia's northern territory – Bucovina – was annexed by Austria-Hungary. This was followed in 1812 by the loss of its eastern territory – Bessarabia – to Russia.

Following the national uprising led by Tudor Vladimirescu in 1821, native princes were returned to the Wallachian and Moldavian thrones. After the Russo-Turkish War of 1828–29 Ottoman domination over the principalities finally came to an end.

Nationalism

The year 1848 saw revolutions in Wallachia, Moldavia and Transylvania as well as the rest of Europe. The uprisings in all three principalities were unsuccessful but they gave impetus to a growing national movement that culminated in the creation of the national state of Romania in 1862.

Severe droughts in Wallachia and Moldavia followed by a cholera epidemic preempted the revolutions in these two principalities. The Wallachian nationalist movement's manifesto called for the abolition of serfdom and boyar privileges, freedom of the press and a democratically elected assembly. Russian troops intervened to squash revolutionary troops. In Moldavia ruling prince Mihai Sturdza initially conducted talks with the revolutionaries who were demanding reforms. Fearing tsarist intervention, however, he almost immediately arrested revolutionary leaders.

In Transylvania the revolution was entangled with the Hungarian revolution, which was led in Transylvania by Hungarian poet Sándor Petőfi. Hungarian revolutionaries sought an end to Habsburg domination of Hungary. Romanian revolutionaries demanded their political emancipation, equality and the abolition of serfdom.

Meanwhile in Budapest Hungarian revolutionaries had succeeded in briefly overthrowing the government, but in October 1848 Austrian rule was restored. The Austrian authorities then struck a deal with Transylvania's Romanians, promising them national recognition in return for joining forces with them against the Hungarian revolutionaries in Transylvania. Thus, in a twist of fate, Transylvanian Romanians fought against Transylvanian Hungarians. Russian intervention finally quashed the Hungarian revolutionaries, ending a revolution that had shocked all sides by its escalation into civil war.

In its aftermath the Transylvanian Diet was abolished and the region fell under direct rule of Austria-Hungary from Budapest. Ruthless 'Magyarisation' then followed: Hungarian was established as the official language and any Romanians who dared oppose the regime – such as the Memorandumists of 1892, a group of intellectual and political figures who voiced their opposition to the Austro-Hungarian rule in a memorandum – were severely punished.

By contrast Wallachia and Moldavia prospered. Romanian nationalism was accelerated further by Russian defeat in the Crimean War (1853–56), and in 1859, with French support, Alexandru Ioan Cuza was elected to the thrones of Moldavia and Wallachia, creating a national state known as the United Romanian Principalities on 11 December 1861 (renamed Romania in 1862).

The reform-minded Cuza was forced to abdicate in 1866, by mutinous army officers, and his place was taken by the Prussian prince Carol I. With Russian assistance, Romania declared independence from the Ottoman Empire in 1877. After the 1877–78 War of Independence, Dobruja – up to now part of the Ottoman Empire – became part of Romania. Under the consequent Treaty of San Stefano and the Congress of Berlin in 1878, Romanian independence was recognised. In 1881 it was declared a kingdom and on 22 May 1881 Carol I was crowned king of Romania.

WWI

Despite Romania forming a secret alliance with the Triple Entente (Britain, France and Russia) in 1883, Romania did not enter WWI immediately. In an equally secret agreement made with the Central Powers (Germany and Austria-Hungary), Carol I traded Romania's neutrality for recognition of part of Transylvania and Bucovina. However the king died in 1914. He was succeeded by his nephew Ferdinand I who, in 1916, gave his blessing for Romania to join WWI on the side of the Triple Entente. Its objective was to liberate Transylvania – where 60% of the population was Romanian – from Austria-Hungary. During the fighting, the Central Powers occupied Wallachia, but Moldavia was staunchly defended by Romanian and Russian troops.

The defeat of Austria-Hungary in 1918 paved the way for the formation of modern Romania. Bessarabia, the area east of the Prut River which had been part of Moldavia until 1812 when it was taken by the Russians, was joined to Romania. Likewise Bucovina, which had been in Austrian-Hungarian hands since 1775, was also reunited with Romania. Part of the Austrian-Hungarian Banat which had been incorporated in Romania, was also handed over. Furthermore, Transylvania was finally united with Romania. Hence, at the end of WWI Romania – now known as Greater Romania – more than doubled its territory (from 120,000 sq km to 295,000 sq km) and its population (from 7.5 to 16 million). The acquisition of this new territory was ratified by the Triple Entente powers in 1920 under the Treaty of Trianon.

WWII

In the years leading up to WWII, Romania, under the able guidance of foreign minister Nicolae Titulescu, sought security in

The Four Kings

Romania had four kings. **Carol I** (1839–1914), Prussian cousin of Kaiser Wilhelm I, was the first. He entered Romania incognito in 1866, and proposed to his future queen, Elizabeth of Wied, on their second meeting (said to be the peak of their relationship, after which it degenerated rapidly). He was crowned king of Romania in 1881. His last act before dying in 1914 was to refuse to enter WWI on the side of his German cousin.

His widowed queen (1836–1916) was a cranky poet who wrote under the pen name Carmen Sylva and decreed that everyone in the royal court should wear folk costume. As a child she had been regularly taken to lunatic asylums to observe the inmates. Elizabeth and Carol failed to produce an heir – the couple's only daughter died at the age of four.

Carol I's nephew, **Ferdinand I** (1865–1927), was Romania's second monarch. Beckoned from Germany to the Balkans to prepare for his regal role, he promptly fell in love with his Aunt Elizabeth's favourite lady-in-waiting, Helene Vacaresco. King Carol, horrified at this, banished his wife and her lady-in-waiting to Germany, then packed Ferdinand off to Europe, armed with a list of eligible young princesses. The best move Ferdinand – renowned for his weak character and protruding ears – ever made was to wed Marie, Queen Victoria's granddaughter, under whose shrewd guidance he successfully ruled the country from 1916 until his death from cancer in 1927.

Ferdinand and Marie's son, **Carol II** (1893–1953), was Romania's third king. The notorious playboy was said to be great in bed and the only man in town able to satisfy the 'crow', an infamous Bucharest prostitute of the 1930s. In 1918 the 24-year-old Carol deserted his military unit to elope with a commoner called Jeanne Lambrino or Zizi. The lovestruck pair crossed the Romanian border incognito and wed in Odesa. The marriage was later annulled although the couple remained together in exile for some time in France. In 1919, following his parents' refusal to allow him to remarry the pregnant Zizi, Carol renounced his right to the throne. Soon after, however, he returned to Romania and in 1921 married Princess Helene of Greece, only to elope two years later with the promiscuous Jewish divorcee Elena Lupescu.

In 1930 Carol II returned to Romania to resume his role as king. His 10-year rule was abruptly terminated in 1940 after the convulsions of WWII, and he fled the country with Lupescu, taking nine railway carriages of stolen state treasures as bounty. The couple wandered aimlessly through Europe until the end of WWII when they finally wed and settled in Brazil, then Portugal. After Carol's death in 1953, Lupescu, who lived another 25 years, moved in with one of Carol's former prime ministers.

Carol and Princess Helene's son, **Michael** (1921–), became king for the first time following Ferdinand's death in 1927. The knickerbockered King Michael (Mihai) was five years old at the time. Following his father's shock return to Romania in 1930 the nine-year-old was forced to abdicate. Following King Michael's second forced abdication in 1947 when the monarchy was abolished, the entire royal family was exiled from their homeland.

Michael married Princess Ana de Bourbon Parma in 1948 and subsequently settled in Versoix, Switzerland, where he still lives today. The eldest of his two daughters, Marguerite, who is married to the actor Radu Duda, is alleged to have had a five-year affair with Britain's Chancellor of the Exchequer, Gordon Brown.

The exiled king, a former test pilot and technical consultant, returned to Romania for the first time in 1990 but was not reissued with a Romanian passport until 1997. Following an April 2000 court ruling, royal properties seized by the communists in 1945, including three residences in Bucharest and a 17th-century castle in northern Romania, were officially returned to Michael.

GREATER ROMANIA (AFTER WWI)

POLAND
HUNGARY
USSR
Northern Bucovina
Moldavia
Bessarabia
Iaşi
Transylvania
YUGO-SLAVIA
Wallachia
Bucharest
BLACK SEA
Acquired by Romania (1918-20)
Southern Dobruja
BULGARIA

ROMANIA (DURING WWII)

Northern Bucovina (to USSR)
USSR
HUNGARY
Transylvania (to Hungary)
Iaşi
Bessarabia (to USSR)
Timişoara
Braşov
YUGO-SLAVIA
Bucharest
BLACK SEA
Ceded from Romania (1940)
Southern Dobruja (to Bulgaria)
BULGARIA

an alliance with France and Britain, and joined Yugoslavia and Czechoslovakia in the Little Entente. Romania also signed a Balkan Pact with Yugoslavia, Turkey and Greece, and later established diplomatic relations with the USSR. These efforts were weakened by the Western powers' appeasement of Hitler and by Romania's own King Carol II.

Carol II succeeded his father Ferdinand I to the throne. Under Ferdinand I, numerous political parties had emerged, of which the National Liberal Party led initially by Ion C Brătianu (from 1909 to 1927) and the National Peasant Party headed by Iuliu Maniu (from 1926 to 1933) played key roles in governing the country. Extreme right-wing parties opposed to a democratic regime also emerged, notably the anti-Semitic League of the National Christian Defence which consequently gave birth to the Legion of the Archangel Michael in 1927. This notorious breakaway faction, better known as the

fascist Iron Guard, was led by Corneliu Codreanu and by 1935 dominated the political scene.

Finding himself unable to manipulate the political parties, Carol II declared a royal dictatorship in February 1938. All political parties were dissolved and in May 1939 electoral laws were passed to halve the size of the electorate. Carol II had the right to dissolve parliament. Between 1939 and 1940 alone, Romania had no less than nine different governments.

In 1939 Carol II clamped down on the anti-Semitic Iron Guard, which until 1937 he had supported. Codreanu and 13 other legionaries were arrested, sentenced to 10 years imprisonment, then assassinated. In revenge for their leader's death, Iron Guard members murdered Carol II's prime minister, Armand Călinescu, leading to the murder of 252 Iron Guard members by Carol II. In accordance with the king's wishes, the corpses were strung up in public squares.

Romania was isolated after the fall of France in May 1940, and in June 1940 Greater Romania collapsed in accordance with the Molotov-Ribbentrop Pact. The USSR occupied Bessarabia (which had been taken from Russia after WWI). On 30 August 1940 Romania was forced to cede northern Transylvania (which covers 43,493 sq km) and its 2.6 million inhabitants to Hungary by order of Nazi Germany and Fascist Italy. In September 1940 southern Dobruja was given to Bulgaria.

Not surprisingly, these setbacks sparked widespread popular demonstrations. Even Carol II realised he could not squash the increasing mass hysteria and on the advice of one of his councillors, the king called in General Marshall Ion Antonescu. To defend the interests of the ruling classes, Ion Antonescu forced King Carol II to abdicate in favour of the king's 19-year-old son Michael. Antonescu then imposed a fascist dictatorship with himself as *conducător* (supreme leader). German troops were allowed to enter Romania in October 1940, and in June 1941 Antonescu joined Hitler's anti-Soviet war. One of Antonescu's aims in joining forces with Hitler was to recover

Bessarabia and this was achieved in August 1941. The results of this Romanian-Nazi alliance were gruesome, with at least 400,000 Romanian Jews – mainly from newly regained Bessarabia – and 40,000 Roma (Gypsies) deported to transit camps in Transdniestr and murdered in Auschwitz. After the war, Antonescu was tried as a war criminal: King Michael ordered his arrest on 23 August 1944 then turned him over to the Soviet authorities who condemned him to death in a show trial in Moscow two years later. Following the war, Bessarabia fell back into the hands of the USSR.

Throughout WWII, anti-Nazi resentment smouldered among the Romanian soldiers and people. As the war went badly and the Soviet army approached Romania's borders, a rare national consensus was achieved. On 23 August 1944 Romania suddenly changed sides, captured 53,159 German soldiers who were in Romania at the time, and declared war on Nazi Germany. By this dramatic act, Romania salvaged its independence and shortened the war. By 25 October the Romanian and Soviet armies had driven the Hungarian and German forces from Transylvania. The Romanian army went on to fight in Hungary and Czechoslovakia. The costs, however, were appalling: 500,000 Romanian soldiers died fighting for the Axis powers, and another 170,000 died after Romania joined the Allies.

The Communist Era

Prior to 1945 Romania's Communist Party had no more than 1000 members and had little influence. Its post-war ascendancy, which saw membership soar to over one million, was a consequence of backing from Moscow. The Soviet-engineered return of Transylvania greatly enhanced the prestige of the left-wing parties, which won the parliamentary elections in November 1946. A year later Prime Minister Petru Groza forced King Michael to abdicate (allegedly by holding the queen mother at gunpoint), the monarchy was abolished, and a Romanian People's Republic proclaimed.

A period of terror ensued in which all the prewar leaders, prominent intellectuals and suspected dissidents were imprisoned or interned in hard-labour camps. Peasants who opposed collectivisation of agriculture – integral to communist plans for a national economy – were imprisoned. The most notorious prisons were in Piteşti, Gherla, Sighetu Marmaţiei and Aiud. Psychiatric hospitals were also used for political purposes.

In 1948 the Communist and Social Democratic Parties united as the Romanian Workers' Party (in 1965 the name was changed back to the Romanian Communist Party). On 11 June 1948 a law on nationalisation was passed, paving the way for state control of the country's industrial factories, mines and businesses – representing 90% of the country's production – by 1950. A new constitution based on the USSR model was introduced, pre-empting the intense period of the Russification of Romania. In 1953 a new Slavicised orthography was introduced to obliterate all Latin roots of the Romanian language, while street and town names were changed to honour Soviet figures. The town of Braşov was renamed Staline.

Romania's loyalty to Moscow continued until the late 1950s. It then started to distance itself from the Soviet Union. Soviet troops were withdrawn from Romania in 1958, and street and town names were changed once more to emphasise the country's Roman heritage. After 1960 Romania adopted an independent foreign policy under two 'national' communist leaders, Gheorghe Gheorghiu-Dej (leader from 1952 to 1965) and his protégé Nicolae Ceauşescu (from 1965 to 1989), both of whom had been imprisoned during WWII. Under these figures the concept of a great Romanian socialist state was flaunted. Ceauşescu's first move was to change the Stalinist Romînia back to România.

Unlike other Warsaw Pact countries, Romania was allowed to deviate from the official Soviet line. While it remained a member of the Warsaw Pact, Romania did not participate in joint military manoeuvres after 1962. Romania never broke with the USSR, as did Tito's Yugoslavia and Mao's China, but Ceauşescu did refuse to assist the Soviets in their 1968 'intervention' in Czechoslovakia. He even condemned the invasion publicly as a 'shameful moment in the history of the revolutionary movement', earning him praise and economic aid from the West and turning him into an international hero. In the late 1960s Ceauşescu received British prime minister Harold Wilson, US president Richard Nixon, and French president Charles de Gaulle. In 1975 Romania was granted 'most favoured nation' status by the USA, which yielded more than US$1 billion in US-backed credits in the decade that followed. And when Romania condemned the Soviet invasion in Afghanistan and participated in the 1984 Los Angeles Olympic Games despite a Soviet-bloc boycott, Ceauşescu was officially decorated by Britain's Queen Elizabeth II. Abroad, Western publishing houses such as Robert Maxwell's Pergamon Press reprinted books written by Ceauşescu.

In contrast to its skilful foreign policy, Romania suffered from increasingly inept

ANN JEFFREE

During the Cold War, Ceauşescu's foreign policy earned him hero status in the West.

government at home during the 25-year reign of Nicolae Ceauşescu. In 1974 the post of president was created for Ceauşescu, who went on to place members of his immediate family in high office during the 1980s. His wife, Elena, became first deputy prime minister; his son, Nicu, became head of a communist youth organisation; and three brothers were assigned to key posts in Bucharest.

Ceauşescu's domestic policy was chaotic at best, megalomaniacal at worst. Of the many grandiose projects he conceived, only two can be considered successes: the Trans-Făgăraşan Highway and the Bucharest metro (which opened in 1985). Others were expensive failures.

Ordinary Romanians were kept in check by the Ministry of Interior's security police, better known as the Securitate. The Securitate was an offspring of the secret police organisation, Siguranţa, set up in 1924 and responsible for Corneliu Codreanu's assassination under the orders of Carol II in 1939. The Siguranţa was renamed the General Direction of Popular Security (Direcţia Generală a Securităţii Poporului, DGSP) – Securitate in short – in 1948.

By the late 1980s, with the Soviet bloc quickly disintegrating, the USA no longer required an independent Romania and withdrew Romania's 'most favoured nation' trading status. Undaunted, Ceauşescu continued spending millions of dollars to build the House of the People and transform Bucharest into a showcase socialist capital. But his greatest blunder was the decision in the 1980s to export Romania's food to help pay off the country's mounting debt.

Bread rationing was introduced in 1981. Rationing of eggs, oil, salt, sugar, beef, flour and even potatoes quickly followed. By the mid-1980s meat was completely unobtainable.

When Ceauşescu arranged lavish public celebrations in March 1989 to mark the final payment of Romania's US$10 billion foreign debt, few Romanians were in the mood to celebrate. In November 1987 a few thousand workers had rioted in Braşov to demand better conditions, and during the

Big Brother Ceauşescu

There were eyes and ears everywhere in Ceauşescu's Romania. While the Securitate was estimated to have 20,000 full-time personnel by the 1980s, its real terror lay in its vast network of informers (over one million), recruited from the ordinary population. Phone lines were tapped, mail intercepted, all conversations reported. Teenagers who dared grow their hair long or sing Bob Dylan songs were 'called in' for interrogation by the Securitate.

The Securitate was backed up by militia forces responsible for keeping tabs on people's whereabouts: no-one was allowed to change dwellings without gaining permission from the militia and anyone who, for more than 24 hours, visited a town where they did not live had to report to the militia forces.

The liberty of Romanians was further infringed on by a 1966 law which made abortion illegal. Childbirth became nothing more than another of the nation's great industries. Women were required to have at least five children and the use of contraceptives was forbidden. Routine gynaecological checks were carried out on women in an attempt to stop illegal abortions.

winter of 1988–89 the country suffered its worst food shortages in decades. Ethnic tensions simmered as the population endured prolonged scarcities of almost everything.

In late 1989, as the world watched the collapse of one communist regime after another, it seemed a matter of time before Romania's turn would come. However, on 20 November 1989, during a six-hour address to the 14th Congress of the Romanian Communist Party, Ceauşescu denounced the political changes sweeping across Eastern Europe and vowed to resist them. His speech was interrupted by 60 standing ovations. The Congress went on to re-elect Ceauşescu as general secretary.

The 1989 Revolution

The Romanian revolution was carried out with Latin passion and intensity. The spark that ignited Romania came on 15 December 1989, when Father László Tökés publicly condemned the dictator from his Hungarian church in Timişoara, prompting the Reformed Church of Romania to remove him from his post. Police attempts to arrest demonstrating parishioners failed and within days the unrest had spread across the town. Ceauşescu proclaimed martial law in Timiş County and dispatched trainloads of troops to crush the rebellion. The turning point came on 19 December, when the army in Timişoara went over to the side of the demonstrators.

On 21 December in Bucharest, an address made by Ceauşescu during a mass rally was cut short by anti-Ceauşescu demonstrators in the 100,000-strong crowd who booed the dictator and shouted 'Murderer', 'Timişoara' and other provocations. These demonstrators later retreated to the wide boulevard between Piaţa Universităţii and Piaţa Romană – only to be brutally crushed hours later by police gunfire and armoured cars. Drenched by ice-cold water from fire hoses, the demonstrators refused to submit and began erecting barricades under the eyes of Western journalists in the adjacent Hotel Inter-Continental. At 11 pm the police began their assault on Piaţa Universităţii, using a tank to smash the barricades. By dawn the square had been cleared and the bodies of those killed removed.

The following morning thousands more demonstrators took to the streets, and a state of emergency was announced. At noon Ceauşescu reappeared on the balcony of the Central Committee building to try to speak again, only to be forced to flee by helicopter from the roof of the building. Ceauşescu and his wife, Elena, were arrested in Târgovişte, taken to a military base and, on 25 December, condemned by an anonymous court and executed by a firing squad. Footage of the Ceauşescu family's luxury apartments broadcast on TV showed pure gold food scales in the kitchen and rows of diamond-studded shoes in Elena's bedroom. No wonder Romanians were prepared to believe unsubstantiated rumours that their 'great' leader renourished his bloodstream once a year with the blood of children.

Reports of the 1989 casualties were wildly exaggerated. At the Ceauşescus' trial it was claimed that 64,000 people died in the revolution; after a week this number was reduced to 7000, and later still, to 1033. In Timişoara, it is believed 115 people (as opposed to the 4000 reported) died.

Democracy or Neocommunism?

It is widely believed that the Communist Party had been preparing a coup d'etat against Ceauşescu and his family for at least six months before demonstrations forced them to shift their schedule forward in December 1989. The National Salvation Front (FSN) took immediate control on the country. In May 1990, it won the country's first democratic elections, placing Ion Iliescu at the helm as president and Petre Roman as prime minister.

In Bucharest, student protests against the FSN's ex-Communist Party leadership were ruthlessly squashed by 20,000 coal miners from the Jiu Valley near Târgu Jiu, shipped to the capital courtesy of Iliescu. Many injuries were sustained, and it was later revealed that secret police had infiltrated the miners and provoked the worst violence.

Ironically, when the miners returned to Bucharest in September 1991, it was to force the resignation of Roman whose free-market economic reforms, it was believed, had led to worsening living conditions. Despite Roman's departure and the re-election of Iliescu in 1992 at the head of a coalition government under the banner of the Party of Social Democracy (PDSR, successor of the FSN), market reforms remained nowhere in sight. In 1993 subsidies on food, transportation and energy were scrapped, prompting prices to spiral sky-high and unemployment to plummet to a new all-time low.

Iliescu was finally ousted in the 1996 presidential elections by an even more embittered, impoverished and desperate populace who – in a last-ditch attempt to win a democracy sought, but not established, in 1989 – ushered in Emil Constantinescu, leader of the right-of-centre election alliance Democratic Convention of Romania (CDR) and former geology professor, as president.

Constantinescu's Romania

Constantinescu's reform-minded government made entry into NATO and the European Union (EU) its top priorities, together with fast-paced structural economic reform and the fight against corruption. Despite internal party bickering over the pace of reforms, the alliance survived two no-confidence votes in mid-1997.

Following the forced resignation of Prime Minister Victor Ciorba and subsequent appointment of Radul Vasile in 1998, some harsh – yet effective – free-market reforms were executed. Among them was the controversial closure of Romania's loss-making coal mines in the Jiu Valley. Unlike the previous year, when miners agreed to pit closures in return for lucrative redundancy packages, 10,000 striking miners threatened to storm Bucharest in response to government attempts to close 37 pits in early 1999. Militant miners managed to smash through police barricades to reach within 170km of the capital, forcing Prime Minister Vasile to submit to a 35% wage hike and stall the closure of two mines in exchange for peace.

Emil Constantinescu was elected president on a promise of economic reform.

Miron Cozma, leader of rampaging miners in 1990 and 1991, was arrested and imprisoned for 18 years.

Under Constantinescu, relations with Hungary were markedly improved. Romania's 1.8 million-strong Hungarian minority was represented in parliament (for the first time since 1918) by the Hungarian Democratic Union of Romania (UDMR), one of the political parties to form a governing coalition with the CDR. While the previous government had already signed a basic treaty with Hungary in 1996, burying centuries of mistrust, Constantinescu agreed to grant more rights to the Hungarian minority (despite protests from Romanian nationalists who accused the Hungarian community of plotting secession). By 1998 ethnic relations had sufficiently improved for the Council of Europe (of which Romania has been a member since 1993) to lift council monitoring.

Romania has likewise made peace with its other neighbours. In 1997 it relinquished all territorial claims to northern Bucovina and southern Bessarabia in exchange for respect of minority rights of Romanians in Ukraine. An April 2000 basic treaty establishing post-communist bilateral relations with the republic of Moldova was pending approval by parliament at the start of 2001. With Bulgaria, a long-standing dispute over the location of a new bridge across the Danube was resolved in March 2000. The two countries agreed to build the US$185 million road and rail bridge near the Romanian port town of Calafat and Vidin in Bulgaria. Partially funded by the EU, bridge construction will start in May 2001 and be completed by 2003.

Despite NATO's rejection in 1996 of Romania's application for full membership into the defensive alliance, hopes remain for entry by 2002. Accession talks with the EU kicked off in March 2000. Privatisation is but one of a plethora of social and economic reforms required to meet criteria set by the EU for full membership (which Romania expects to achieve by 2007–10). At the start of 2000, some 50% of land remained in state hands, along with the majority of commercial firms, banks and medical services. As a direct result of the huge public debt incurred by these state enterprises, government spending on health and education is both minimal (3.6% and 3.3% of GDP respectively in 1998) – and worryingly ineffective.

Poverty remains an enormous gripe – and an immense problem that is getting worse, not better. The percentage of those living in poverty rose from 19.85% in 1996 to more than 30% in 1999. The number of Bucharestians struggling to survive below the poverty line has more than doubled in recent years, while the number of children squatting on streets and/or infected with the HIV virus is rising. More than one-fifth of the national population is not expected to reach the age of 60, only 7% of rural homes have running water and the average monthly salary is US$95.

The darker side of Romania's recovery from five decades of communist rule is also reflected in the corruption that continues to plague the government. In December 1999 Constantinescu dismissed Prime Minister Vasile and replaced him with Mugur Isărescu. Yet by mid-2000 Isărescu was fighting for his political life after opposition parliamentarians accused the former National Bank of Romania governor of failing to weed out irregularities in the management of the State Property Fund. This was followed in May 2000 by the collapse of the National Fund for Investment (NFI) which saw thousands of investors – mainly pensioners who'd deposited their life savings into the government fund – take to the streets to demand their cash back (US$47.4 million, long squandered by the NFI). Police used tear gas to dispel rioters in Bucharest. Another bank, the Fortune Popular Bank, created another round of penniless victims when it crashed a month later.

Scandal and corruption surrounded the November 2000 electoral race. Opposition PDSR candidate and former president Ion Iliescu was almost forced to pull out after a money-laundering scandal suggested that Iliescu's 1996 presidential campaign had been funded illegally. Meanwhile, incumbent president Constantinescu did pull out, announcing on national television in July 2000 that he would not run for a second term of office in such a 'Mafia-type system'.

The final shockwave came in late November 2000 when a disquieting 28.3% of Romania's disgruntled electorate backed extreme-right politician Corneliu Vadim Tudor of the Greater Romania Party (PRM). Huge sighs of relief were let out across Europe when the alarming far-righter was pipped at the post by social democrat Iliescu in run-off elections held the following month (for more details, see Government & Politics later in this chapter).

GEOGRAPHY

Covering 237,500 sq km, oval-shaped Romania is the largest Eastern European country after Russia and Ukraine. The Danube River drains the whole of Romania (except the Black Sea coast) and completes its 2850km course through nine countries in Romania's Danube Delta. Romania's rivers are mainly tributaries of the Danube.

Most of central and northern Romania is taken up by the U-shaped Carpathian Mountains, which hoop north from Romania into western Ukraine, southern Poland, and Slovakia, ending in Bratislava. The centre of the U is occupied by the Transylvanian plain (Câmpia Transilvaniei), an eroded plateau with hills and valleys, while the Moldavian plateau lies to the east. Earthquakes are common in the south and south-west.

The Carpathians (see the Exploring the Carpathian Mountains special section for more details) account for about a third of the country's area, with alpine pastures above and thick beech, fir, spruce and oak forests below. Another third of Romania is covered by hills and tablelands full of orchards and vineyards. The final third is a fertile plain where cereals, vegetables, herbs and other crops are grown.

CLIMATE

Romania's average annual temperature is 11°C in the south and on the coast, but only 2°C in the mountains. Romanian winters can be extremely cold and foggy with lots of snow from mid-December to mid-April.

In summer there's usually hot, sunny weather on the Black Sea coast. Annual rainfall is 600mm to 700mm, much of it in spring. The mountains get the most rain and the Danube Delta the least.

ECOLOGY & ENVIRONMENT

Romania has an appalling environmental track record – a legacy of five decades of communist rule when a policy of reckless industrial expansion was pursued. Yet supposed clean-up measures taken since 1990 – cleaning up a chemical and nuclear waste-pit at Sulina, where European countries dumped waste in exchange for hard currency; building new smoke stacks at Baia Mare, Romania's largest non-ferrous metal centre, to alleviate air pollution; closing industrial plants in Giurgiu and Copşa Mică – have only exacerbated a boom in industrial

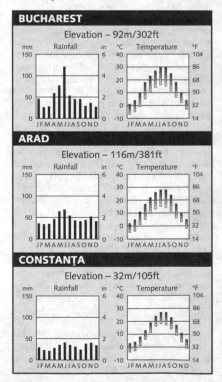

and domestic waste. Uncontrolled and/or non-existent waste storage is one of Romania's greatest environmental problems, and one that multiplies daily. Walk down any street or in the countryside and you'll see all types of garbage dumped everywhere.

Romania's health record speaks volumes, with Romanian health conditions deteriorating in the past five years. Average life expectancy is falling (73 years for women and 66 for men in 1998), tuberculosis remains a common illness (about 100 cases per 100,000 inhabitants), respiratory diseases are on the rise (44% of all new disease cases) and state-funded medical care remains woefully inadequate (12.1/1.7 hospital beds per 1000 inhabitants in urban/rural communities). Air pollution exceeds maximum allowable levels more than 50% of the time in 11 of Romania's 41 counties, and nitrate levels exceed safety levels in 14 counties' water supply. Not surprisingly, Romania has the highest infant mortality rate in Europe after Albania.

Ecological disaster struck Romania in January 2000 when a tailings dam burst at a Romanian- and Australian-owned gold mine in Baia Mare, prompting 100,000 cubic metres of cyanide-contaminated water to spill into the Tisa and Danube Rivers and subsequently kill thousands of fish and birds in Romania, Hungary and Yugoslavia. Two months later another dam burst at a state-run lead and zinc plant in Baia Borsa that, just weeks before, had been warned by the Ministry of Environment to step up security at the dam. An estimated 20,000 tonnes of pollutive waste again gushed into the Tisa, upping its lead content to 2.7 times above the permitted level. Thus, residents in towns along the contaminated river stretch were again warned to keep well clear of the toxic water.

Experts say it will take 10 years for the affected habitat to fully recover, although 95% of river life should return by 2004. Neighbouring Hungary, the worst hit by the spills, estimates its clean-up costs to be US$10 million. Meanwhile, the big question is what Romania can do, given its limited funds, to avoid another such disaster. In northern Romania alone, there are 50 similar dams considered to be ecological time bombs.

The ecological ills of the Black Sea and Danube Delta have long been a thorn in Romania's side. Since 1991 the Danube Delta Biosphere Reserve (DDBR) has 'ecologically reconstructed' large areas of land in the Delta, removing dikes and reflooding what was originally natural marshland. Romania continues to be involved in various joint projects with the World Bank to protect Black Sea ecosystems, although the Danube (one of the four big international rivers that flow into it) is the sea's biggest pollutant. Since the 1960s, the Black Sea has been practically devoid of fish.

Natural disasters to have befallen an already-troubled Romania in 2000 include snowstorms and avalanches in January that killed six people, a minor earthquake in south-eastern Romania in March which hit 3.5 on the Richter scale, floods in April which claimed seven lives and damaged 94,000 hectares of farmland, followed by droughts in June which devastated 40% of farmland.

Romania's only nuclear power plant is at Cernavodă in Dobruja.

FLORA & FAUNA

Pre-WWII Romania was a predominantly agrarian society with 85% of its population leading a rural, peasant existence. Despite the environmental catastrophe that ensued, much of the country's rich natural heritage was untouched. Forest and agricultural land accounts for 28.1% and 39.% of Romania's total land area respectively, while the Carpathians remain among the least-spoilt mountains in Europe; see the Exploring the Carpathian Mountains special section for information on its varied flora and fauna.

Birdlife in the Danube Delta is unmatched. It is a major migration hub for numerous bird species and is home to 60% of the world's small pygmy cormorant population. Half the world's red-breasted goose population winters here. Protected species typical to the Delta include the great white egret, bee-eater and white-tailed eagle. This region also shelters Europe's largest white pelican and Dalmatian pelican colonies, and constitutes the largest unbroken reed bed in the world.

National Parks

Romania has 13 national parks and 586 protected areas, most of which are in the Carpathians – see the Exploring the Carpathian Mountains special section. In south-eastern Romania, the Danube Delta has been protected as a biosphere reserve on Unesco's World Heritage list since 1991. Some 50,000 hectares of the Danube Delta Biosphere Reserve (DDBR) are strictly off-limits to tourists and locals alike.

Except for the DDBR, none of the reserves or national parks have organised visitor facilities. Some are accessible by public transport; others not. Detailed information on many reserves and parks are included in the relevant regional chapters.

GOVERNMENT & POLITICS

Romania's 1991 constitution provides for a parliamentary system of government. Its two-chamber parliament – comprising the Chamber of Deputies (lower house) and Senate (upper house) – is elected every four years. Political parties currently have to gain at least 3% of national votes to enter parliament, although there is talk of upping the threshold to 5%. The head of the state, the president, is also elected by popular vote for a four-year term. The prime minister is nominated by the president but approved by the parliament. The next parliamentary and presidential elections will be in 2004.

Romania has a handful of leading parties, split between the ruling centrists, spearheaded by Emil Constantinescu's Democratic Convention of Romania (CDR), and the leftist opposition led by Ion Iliescu's Party of Social Democracy (PDSR). In the November 2000 presidential and parliamentary elections, incumbent president Constantinescu had already won the backing of the coalition National Peasant Party Christian Democratic (PNTCD) and Union of Rightist Forces – until he withdrew from the race.

Romania's coat of arms

This left the major players in the field to be former president and PDSR leader Ion Iliescu, shown to be backed by 31% of the electorate in August 2000 opinion polls; incumbent prime minister Mugur Isărescu of a newly formed centre-right CDR (an electoral alliance between the PNTCD, the Union of Rightist Forces and the Ecologist Federation); Theodor Stolojan of the National Liberal Party (PNL), who served as prime minister in 1991–92; Teodor Melescanu of the Alliance of Romania (APR); and Petre Roman (prime minister in 1989 and incumbent foreign minister) of the Democratic Party (PD). Prince Paul of Romania also ran (see the boxed text 'Prince Turned President').

Increasing poverty and hardship prompted the electorate to lean heavily towards in the right in presidential elections held in November 2000. Extreme right-wing Corneliu Vadim Tudor of the Greater Romania Party (PRM) gained a startling 28.3% of votes (compared to 4.72% in the 1996 elections). But run-off elections in mid-December saw the notoriously nationalist, anti-Semitic and xenophobic politician crushed by Ion Iliescu of the leftist PDSR. The 70-year-old Iliescu, who won 36.4% of the first-round vote, secured 66% of nationwide votes and secured a second term in office. The former communist served as president of Romania between 1990 and 1996. Integration into Europe and economic reform top his political agenda.

ECONOMY

The legacy of Romania's post-communist shift from a centrally planned to market economy continues to haunt most of the population, more than 30% of which lives below the poverty line. Living standards continue to decline, the average monthly salary remains at an inadequate US$95 and unemployment continued its climb from 11.8% in February 1999 to 12.2% in March 2000. The cost of services, food and non-food products rose by 94.7%, 60.2% and 36.7% respectively in 1999.

Despite the promise of future EU membership by 2007–10, the years leading up to it are expected to be as economically painful as the past, as the government continues its shock-therapy program to overhaul an economy still mired in post-communist stagnation. Analysts nevertheless believe that the fall in industrial and grain output of 17% and 30% registered in 1998 compared with the previous year, would have been stronger if the government had rigorously implemented the closure of loss-making companies. The closure and sell-off of industrial giants – such as the Sidex steel plant which reported debts of US$1 billion at the close of 1999 – remains vital for the pursuit of economic reforms in Romania, despite its inevitable creation of further unemployment. Equally integral to the whole process is privatisation, yet in 1990–98 the sluggish State Ownership Fund – the governmental body in charge of privatisation – only privatised 20% of state companies. In 2000 it plans to sell 2366 and liquidate 292.

It was not until early 2000 that the Romanian parliament approved a bill allowing for 1.6 million Romanians to reclaim family land that had been confiscated by the

Prince Turned President

Paul of Romania (born 1948) is the grandson of Jeanne 'Zizi' Lambrino and Romania's playboy king Carol II (1893–1953) who eloped to Odesa, wed, annulled their marriage, then had a son called Mircea – Paul's father. Although Paul calls himself prince and claims a right to the throne, the Paris-born Romanian was raised in England, lived in the US and says he has no intention of restoring his country's monarchy. Rather, the self-styled prince of Romania wants to be president. In the 2000 presidential race he ran as a candidate for the National Reconciliation Party, the political party he has presided over since 1999. His charity, the Prince Paul Foundation for Romania, has raised US$3 million since 1990. Both are online at http://prn.kappa.ro.

A court ruling in Lisbon in 1955 recognised Paul's father, Mircea, as the son of King Carol II. But it did not declare him – or his offspring – to be a prince. In April 1999 the ruling was upheld by an appeals court in Bucharest. In August 2000 Paul was back in court quibbling with Carol II's youngest son Michael (who, in fact, usurped Mircea to the throne in 1927) over his legal right to some of the royal properties, currently being returned by the Romanian courts to their rightful heirs.

communists in the 1950s. The law was hailed as the first step in the break-up of state farms.

Upon assuming office in late 1999, Prime Minister Mugur Isărescu announced his intention to slash annual inflation – a criterion for EU membership – from 54% in 1999 to 27% in 2000 and 12% in 2002; and to increase Romania's GDP per capita from US$3500 in 2000 to US$10,000 by 2010. Additionally, he hopes to achieve a 1.3% GDP growth in 2000 after three consecutive years of negative growth; in 1999 GDP fell 3.2%. To this end, his austere budget for 2000 slashed corporate tax from 38% to 25% and imposed a highly unpopular 19% VAT on food in January, followed by electricity, gas and water in April. The country's

25 utilities companies, all state-owned still, account for some of the biggest losses in the economy. Isărescu's tough budget was aimed primarily at persuading the International Monetary Fund (IMF) to extend a US$547 million loan until February 2001.

Romania's largest foreign trading partners are the Netherlands, Germany, Italy, USA, France, Turkey and the UK. In 1999, US$256.2 million in foreign investment was ploughed into Romania – a US$28 million increase on 1998 but a mere drop in the ocean compared with the foreign investment attracted by Romania in the early 1990s. In mid-1999 Renault bought a 51% stake in Piteşti-based Dacia, pledging to invest US$220 million in the car manufacturing company by 2004.

Romanian trade along the Danube River was brought to a halt by the NATO bombings of Yugoslavia in 1999. The EU agreed to pay US$20.5 million to remove the rubble from bombed bridges that blocked the channel, although the river is not expected to be navigable again until spring 2001. An estimated 80% of Romanian river boats are currently grounded as a result; prior to the bombings, Galaţi-based Navrom was the biggest shipping operator on the Danube, transporting more than 700,000 tonnes of cargo per month.

Foreign companies who have invested over US$2.5 billion in Romania include Daewoo Corporation (which holds a controlling share in Romanian car maker Oltcit), Shell, Coca-Cola, ABN Amro Bank, ING Bank, McDonald's, British American Tobacco, Krafts Jacobs and Nestlé.

POPULATION & PEOPLE

Romania has a population of 22.4 million, more than 55% of whom live in towns and cities. Population density is 98 people per square kilometre. Bucharest (two million inhabitants) is by far the largest city, followed by Constanţa, Braşov, Timişoara and Iaşi.

Romania's population is 89.7% Romanian, 6.9% Hungarian, 1.8% Roma, 0.4% German and 0.3% Ukrainian. Other nationalities include Croats, Serbs and Turks. Romania's multiethnicity is most obvious in Transylvania, which historically was dominated by Hungarians and Saxons (Germans). In May 1999, the government passed a bill to ensure that civil servants who work in communities where an ethnic minority counts 20% are able to speak the minority language.

Romanians consider themselves the direct heirs of ancient Rome and thus on a higher plain than the descendants of barbaric Slav and Hungarian tribes. Many bear a fierce hatred towards Russians, who they blame for Romania's economic situation. Many believe if it were not for the former Soviet Union's interference during WWII, Romania would still be the economic superpower it was before 1940. Russia's reluctance to see NATO expand is perceived by Romanians as a Russian conspiracy aimed at stalling their economic growth and so maintaining Romania as a buffer zone.

Germans

The German population in Romania peaked in the 1930s when there were 800,000 Saxons in Transylvania. Numbers have dwindled to no more than 65,000 today. Their future looks equally gloomy: the remaining German population is elderly and most yearn for a better life in Germany.

Saxons from Rheinfranken settled in Romania between 1141 and 1181 upon the invitation of the Hungarian king, Geza II, who appointed them as guardians of Transylvania's mountain passes. After the Banat became an Austrian colony in 1718, Swabians from different parts of Germany colonised towns in the Banat while others from Württemberg in Germany settled in Bucovina. Only the Saxons had a political voice in Romania, making up a quarter of Transylvania's population by the 18th century and contributing more than 60% of total taxes paid to the state.

During WWII, 175,000 Romanian Germans were killed or left the country. After Romania switched sides to join the Allies against Hitler's Nazi Germany, 70,000 Germans were accused of Nazi collaboration and sentenced to five years hard labour in the Soviet Union. The survivors returned to

ETHNIC MINORITIES IN ROMANIA & MOLDOVA

find their land and properties confiscated by the newly installed communist regime.

Under Ceauşescu, Germans, like all other inhabitants, were not allowed to freely leave Romania. Instead Ceauşescu granted them exit permits in exchange for vast amounts of cash from the West German government. In the 1980s, West Germany 'bought' exit permits for some 70,000 people. One exit permit was alleged to have cost around US$8000. Not surprisingly, between 1989 and 1995 an estimated 100,000 Germans left the country.

The Saxon community in Transylvania totals around 20,000 today. It is served by state-run German schools and represented politically by the German Democratic Forum (Demokratisches Forum der Deutschen).

Roma

The government estimates that only 420,000 Roma (Gypsies) live in Romania, although the community itself and the Budapest-based European Roma Rights Centre (http://errc.org) believes it to be at least 1.8 million, making it the largest such community in the world. It's Romania's second-largest minority group.

The Mongols and Tartars brought the first enslaved Roma to Romania in 1242. Nomadic Roma *(corturari)* from India settled in Romania from the 15th century onwards.

Around 50% of the world's Roma population was wiped out by the Holocaust; during WWII 40,000 Roma were deported from Romania to Auschwitz. They were persecuted under communism and still are today, the authorities robbing these traditionally nomadic people of their nonconformist lifestyle. The remaining nomadic Roma number around 2000. They are split between 40 different clans comprising 21 castes, each of which has its own traditional costume, superstitions and taboos.

Despite two-thirds of Romania's Roma population being assimilated with the broader Romanian culture *(vătraşi*, literally 'settled'), they remain an unwanted people. Roma villages are burnt by Romanian nationalists with official complicity and most Roma children are considered 'problem children' by local authorities, thus forced out of state school. A quarter of those aged 12 to 20 are estimated to be illiterate. Police brutality against Roma is systematic and in August 2000 Amnesty International lodged an official complaint against the Romanian force after police shot two Roma suspects (in separate incidents).

Politically, Roma are represented by the Alliance for Romany Unity, the Romany Christian Centre, the Community of Roma Ethnicity and the Roma Party (Partida Romilor), headed by Madalin Voicu, son of one of Romania's top violin virtuosos and a symphony orchestra conductor. In the November 2000 parliamentary elections, Voicu received 0.7% of votes, maintaining his seat in parliament.

In April 2000 the first national Roma bank opened its doors in Craiova. The bank, set up partly in response to the refusal of many mainstream banks to give credit to Roma, aims to encourage the economic and social life of Roma.

For information on Romania's Roma king and emperor, see the boxed text 'Battle for the Roma Crown' in the Sibiu section of the Transylvania chapter.

Hungarians

Under Ceauşescu, all Hungarian-language newspapers and magazines in Romania were closed down, and official plans to systemise some 8000 villages, many of them in Transylvania, threatened Romania's Hungarians with cultural assimilation.

Since 1989, however, the rights of Romania's 1.7 million Hungarians have been recognised. They are represented politically by the UDMR (see Constantinescu's Romania, earlier) and have their own Hungarian-language newspaper. Despite losing the fight for their own university, Hungarians can study in their own mother tongue. Cluj-Napoca university runs 32 courses in Hungarian (compared with 77 in Romanian and 10 in German) and operates branch colleges, also with Hungarian-taught courses, in Sfântu Gheorghe, Satu Mare and Gheorgheni.

Most accounts of ethnic conflicts in Romania published in the West showed justified concern for the Hungarian minority, yet tended to ignore the fact that the Romanian majority in Transylvania was subjected to forced 'Magyarisation' under Hungarian rule prior to WWI.

EDUCATION

Education in Romania is free from preschool to university graduation. Children legally have to attend school from the age of seven although, in reality, only those whose parents can afford to send them do. In most rural villages parents need their children to help work the fields.

Some private secondary schools and universities have opened since 1989, with 32% of those able to afford an education opting for the private path. The number of students attending secondary school dropped from 90.7% in 1990 to no more than 68% in 1999, although those staying on for university has increased (from 10% of the respective age group in 1990 to 25.4% in 1998). Romania's leading universities are in Bucharest, Iaşi, Cluj-Napoca and Timişoara.

State education is woefully underfunded, prompting 400,000 teachers across the country to strike in February 2000 and force the government to submit to their demands: an increase in the state education budget (they requested 4% of GDP) to cover the cost of increasing their monthly salaries from US$40 to US$80.

English and French are the first foreign languages taught in all Romanian schools. Hungarian, German, Serbian and Ukrainian are also taught in some schools. Where minority groups comprise a class, they can be taught in their mother tongue.

ARTS
Folk & Roma Music & Dance

Traditional Romanian folk instruments include the *bucium* (alphorn), the *cimpoi* (bagpipes), the *cobză* (a pear-shaped lute) and the *nai* (a panpipe of about 20 cane tubes). Many kinds of flute are used, including the *ocarina* (a ceramic flute) and the *tilinca* (a flute without finger holes). The violin, which is of more recent origin, is today the most common folk instrument. Romania's best known composer, George Enescu (1881–1955), was a virtuoso violinist and used Romanian folk themes in his work.

The *doină* is an individual, improvised love song, a sort of Romanian blues with a social or romantic theme. The *baladă*

Romania's Unwanted Children

Providing better state protection for Romania's unwanted children – on whom the country's communist past weighs most heavily – is among the stiff membership criteria set by the EU. The number of children living in orphanages or state institutions has decreased significantly – from 98,872 in early 1997 to 30,069 at the end of 1999 – yet Romania still remains a long way behind the EU in its childcare.

On the streets, an estimated 700 to 1000 youngsters live permanently in Bucharest's red-hot heating ducts beneath manhole covers. Another 1000 to 1300 squat in Constanţa, Craiova, Iaşi, Braşov, Timişoara and other large towns. Many more children beg on the streets by day but do have a roof to return to come nightfall. For the 20% of Romania's street-kid population – aged four to 18 and 80% male – that has lived on the streets for five years or more, the chances of reintegration into a family is remote. At least 70% of street children have tried sniffing glue; 20% sniff daily. Tuberculosis, skin and lung diseases are rife.

The government has taken steps to overhaul the childcare system. In March 2000 plans were announced to decentralise orphanages and place childcare responsibility in local-authority hands instead. Child benefit in 2000 stood at US$10 per month (compared with US$1.50 in 1996) – sufficient to persuade impoverished parents not to abandon their children. Benefits were only paid if parents could prove their children (of school-going age) attended school regularly.

It took Romania until 1997 to crack down on illegal adoptions and baby trafficking to the West by passing a law placing adoption procedures in the hands of the Romanian Adoption Committee (CRA). Of the 4323 adoptions the committee approved in 1999, 3041 children were adopted by foreigners. Children's rights groups believe some 10,000 children were illegally sold to Westerners between 1990 and 1997.

The abortion rate in Romania remains among the highest in Europe (1.5 for every live birth), despite contraceptives being available to those who can afford them. Almost 10% of newborn babies are born underweight and have a 10% greater chance of dying in the first 12 months of their life. Romania has the second-highest infant mortality rate in Europe.

All this is a legacy of Ceauşescu's ban on contraception and abortion in 1966, coupled with his ruling that women under 45 should have at least five children. Following communism's collapse, international aid organisations and individuals on 'mercy missions' flooded Romania with aid. The flood has long receded, however, leaving aid to be handled by a focused network of larger organisations committed to working with local non-governmental organisations and aid groups as part of a longer-term solution to help Romanians help themselves.

(ballad), on the other hand, is a collective narrative song steeped with feeling.

Couples may dance in a circle, a semicircle or a line. In the *sârbă* males and females dance quickly in a closed circle with their hands on each other's shoulders. The *hora* is another fast circle dance. In the *brâu* (belt dance), dancers form a chain by grasping their neighbour's belt.

Modern Roma or 'Tzigane' (Gypsy) music has absorbed many influences. Roma *lăutari* (musicians) circulate through the village inviting neighbours to join in weddings, births, baptisms, funerals and harvest festivals. Improvised songs *(cântec)* are often directed at a specific individual and are designed to elicit an emotional response (and a tip). To appeal to older people, the lăutari sing traditional baladă or epic songs *(cântece epice)* in verse, often recounting the exploits of Robin Hood-style *haiduci* (outlaws) who apply justice through their actions. Violin-players inspire villagers to perform the *cingăresc* dance.

Professional Roma ensembles or *tarafs*, such as the famous Taraf de Haiduci (The Outlaws' Ensemble) from Clejani, southwest of Bucharest, use the violin, accordion, guitar, double bass, *ţambal* (hammered dulcimer), *fluier* (flute) and other instruments.

Under communism, an urbanised folk music was promoted by the state to bolster Romanian national identity. In this genre virtuoso *nai* and *ţambal mare* (concert cymbalum or dulcimer) players are backed by large orchestras seldom seen in Romanian villages. You'll either love or hate the music of Gheorghe Zamfir, self-proclaimed 'Master of the Panpipe'.

Classical Music & Opera

The Romanian Philharmonic orchestra was established in Bucharest in 1868 and in the 1880s the Ateneul Român (Romanian Athenaeum) was built. It was here that the 'great genius' of Romanian music, George Enescu, made his debut in 1898. His first major work *Oedip*, performed in Paris in 1936, evoked the soul and passion of the Romanian people through elements of Romanian folk music.

Romania's first opera *Crai Nou* (New Moon) was composed by Moldavian-born Ciprian Porumbescu (1853–83). It made its debut in Braşov in 1882. Porumbescu's best known love-ballad, *Ballad of Ciprian*, was inspired by his thwarted love for a rich vicar's daughter who he was considered too poor to marry. He spent several years in prison for alleged anti-state activities and died in Braşov at the age of 30.

Romania's best-known contemporary opera star is soprano Angela Gheorghiu, daughter of a train conductor and a graduate of the Bucharest Conservatory. She has made recordings with tenor Placido Domingo among others.

Literature

Romanian literature draws heavily on the country's rich folkloric heritage coupled with its turbulent history as an occupied country inhabited by a persecuted people. In 15th-century medieval society, when writings were still scripted in Slavonic, an oral epic folk literature emerged. These fairy tales, legends and ballads were firmly rooted in traditional pastoral life and lamented on the great themes of birth, marriage and death.

It was in this way that the Romanian *mioriţa* emerged, originally spread orally and later written down. The *mioriţa* was a simple folk tale featuring life in the fields or on the mountainside. Behind its colourful images of nature and folk culture, there would be a sting in the tale. Every region created its own version, adapted to the local philosophy of life. An oral literature also developed in the courts, in which the heroics of the great medieval princes and warriors were recounted.

Writings in the Romanian language, initially religious, took shape around 1420. Modern literature emerged in the mid-19th century in the shape of romantic poet Mihai Eminescu (1850–89), who captured the spirituality of the Romanian people in his work. Only one volume of his work, *Poesii* (Poems), was published during his lifetime (1883) but it served to create a new language in literature. Eminescu's grand disillusionment with love, interwoven with folk myths and historical elements, characterised his major works. Many of Eminescu's poems have been translated into English, including his most famous work *Luceafărul* (Evening Star), which appeared in *Poesii. Poems & Prose of Mihai Eminescu* (Centre of Romanian Studies), edited by Kurt Treptow, was published in 2000 to mark the 150th anniversary of his birth.

During the latter half of the 19th century the influential Junimea literary society (1863), of which Eminescu was a member, was founded by Titu Maiorescu (1840–1917) in Iaşi. Maiorescu was a literary critic who condemned the growing influence of foreign literature on Romanian writers. The upshot of this in the period that followed was the emergence of a more realist genre in which daily life in Romania was depicted. In his plays, satirist Ion Luca Caragiale (1852–1912) decried the impact of precipitous modernisation on city life and showed the comic irony of social and political change. His first play *O noapte furtunoasă* (Stormy Night) was a comedy based on his observations of middle-class life in Bucharest. Perhaps the Romanian writer best known internationally is the playwright Eugene Ionesco (1912–94), a leading exponent of the 'theatre of the absurd', who lived in France after 1938.

The quest for 'national values' ensued in the prewar period. Novelists Cezar Petrescu (1892–1961), Liviu Rebreanu (1885–1944), and Mihail Sadoveanu (1880–1961) all produced their best works during this time. The traditional lives of Carpathian shepherds are unravelled in a Moldavian dialect, distinctive of Sadoveanu's novels, in *Baltagul* (The Hatchet), published in 1930.

Romanian literature became a tool of the Communist Party from 1947 onwards, with few works of note emerging. In 1971 Ceauşescu passed a law forbidding the publication abroad of Romanian works prejudicing the state, thereby removing many writers' only means of expression. Paul Goma, born in 1935, was one of a handful of dissident writers who dared express his thoughts publicly in the 1970s. Goma had already spent two years in prison and four years in solitary confinement in the 1950s for his outspoken views. In 1977 he was exiled to France where all his major works, including his 10th novel *My Childhood at the Gate of Unrest* (the first to be translated in English), were published.

Feminist poet Nina Cassian (born 1924 in Galaţi), whose works were also published abroad, sought political asylum in the USA in 1985 after her poems were discovered in a friend's diary by the Securitate. Her volumes *Cheerleader for a Funeral* and *Call Yourself Alive?* are both available in English, as is *Silent Voices: An Anthology of Romanian Women Poets*, which also features her work.

Another literary voice who found his feet in the USA is Andrei Codescru, born in Sibiu in 1946 and exiled to the USA from 1966. The poet, novelist, journalist and radio commentator returned to Romania to cover the events of 1989 for a US television network. *The Hole in the Flag* (1991), in which he recounted his return, was voted Book of the Year by the *New York Times*. More titles addressing communism and other Romania-related issues include *Zombifications* (1995) and *The Dog with the Chip in his Neck* (1997), which includes, among

other things, cyberspace dreams, tales of Sibiu and dogs with their own Web sites. Codrescu's is at www.codrescu.com.

Since 1989 several works have been published attesting to the horrors of the communist era, almost all of them translated into English. The story of Lena Constante – arrested in 1950 for her friendship with the wife of Lucreţiu Pătrăscanu, a communist leader purged in one of the period's 'show trials' – unfolds in her autobiography *The Silent Escape – 3000 Days in Romanian Prisons*.

Don't Harm Thy Neighbour by Nicholas Radoui is an autobiographical account of a Transylvanian doctor arrested by the Securitate in 1948. He escaped, sought refuge for three months in the mountains, then fled to Yugoslavia submerged in the water tank of a train, only to be arrested again. The author of *Hell Moved its Border*, Dumitru Nimigeanu, was a peasant farmer until he was deported to Siberia in 1939.

On Clowns – the Dictator and the Artist by Norman Manea is a cutting, philosophical rant on Romanian dictatorship as seen through the eyes of an author who was deported to a Transdniestr concentration camp when he was five years old.

Equally angst-ridden is *On the Heights of Despair*, a musing on the Romanian struggle by Romanian-born Emil Cioran 'under the constraints of suicidal insomnia'. The giant autobiography of US-exiled Romanian writer Mircea Eliade – published in two volumes entitled *Journey East, Journey West 1907–37* and *Exile's Odyssey 1937–60* – is translated into English.

Volumes of poems available in English translation include *Demon in Brackets* by Romanian poet Maria Banuş; *The Error of Being* by deportee Ion Caraion; *Let's Talk About the Weather* by satirist Marin Sorescu; the savage *Exile on a Peppercorn* by Mircea Dinescu, today's president of the Bucharest Writers' Union and a leading light in the 1989 revolution; and *As I came to London one Midsummer's Day* by Ion Stoica, director of Bucharest's Central University Library destroyed in 1989. The poems in *A Juicier Way* were written in English in the 1960s by

Romanian poet Mihai Rădoi, but were not published until after the revolution.

Contemporary Romanian literature looks to the future as much as the past. The energy of today's writers is epitomised in the two poetry volumes, *Young Poets of a New Romania* translated by Brenda Walker, and *An Anthology of Contemporary Romanian Poetry* translated by Andrea Deletant. The voice of Romania's minorities is also slowly being heard in this genre: *Pied Poets – A German Minority of Romanian Poets*, translated by Robert Elsie, features contemporary verse by Transylvanian Saxons and German-Danube poets. Paul Celan (1920–70), a pseudonym for Paul Antschel, is Romania's most notable German-speaking poet. He is of Jewish origins and both his parents died in death camps during WWII; his best-known poem *Todesfugue* addresses the Holocaust. *Breathturn-Atemwende* (1995) is an English-German collection of his poems.

Folk Art

Painting on glass and wood remains a popular folk art today. Considered to be of Byzantine origin, this traditional peasant art was widespread in Romania from the 17th century onwards.

Superstition and strong religious beliefs surrounded these icons which were painted, not for decorative reasons but to protect a household from evil spirits – St Dimitru protected the cattle from wolves, St Peter held the keys to heaven, while the archangels Michael and Gabriel cared for the souls of the deceased.

Well-known 19th-century icon painters include Dionisie Iuga, Maria Chifor and Tudor Tocariu. The glass icons of contemporary artist Georgeta Maria Uiga from Baia Mare are exhibited worldwide.

Painting

Medieval painting was marked by a strong Byzantine influence. It expressed itself through frescoes depicting scenes from the Bible on outside walls as a means of educating peasants, on the iconostasis inside churches, and in miniature form as a decorative frame for religious manuscripts.

The reign of Ştefan cel Mare in Moldavia in the 16th century marked a watershed in Romanian art. The outside walls of churches and monasteries were adorned with frescoes. These churches were the first in the world to be painted in this way. A definite anti-Ottoman message dominated many of the frescoes tattooed on the church walls.

The paintings of Nicolae Grigorescu (1838–1907) absorbed French impressionism and created canvasses alive with the colour of the Romanian peasantry. He broke the prevailing strict academic mould, heralding the emergence of modern Romanian painting. Grigorescu's work is exhibited in art galleries in Bucharest, Iaşi, Craiova and Constanţa, and the Nicolae Grigorescu Museum is in Câmpina.

Modernism was further embraced by Gheorghe Petraşcu (1872–1949), whose paintings also drew on the world around him.

The symbolist movement was represented by Ion Ţuculescu (1910–1962), who incorporated elements of Romanian folk art such as the decorative motifs of Moldavian carpets in his work.

Film

Romanian cinema blossomed in 1994 with Lucian Pintilie's *O Vara de Neuitat* (Unforgettable Summer), which made a small splash at Cannes that year. Other notable films to look out for include Mircea Daneliuc's *Senatorul Melcilor* (Senator of the Snails) and Radu Gabrea's *Rosenemil, o Tragica Lubire* (The Tragic Love Story of Rosenemil).

Several big names have made an appearance at the Castel Films studios in Snagov, just outside Bucharest. In mid-2000 the line-up included Jane March and Roger Daltrey, who were set to star in a US-produced film on Vlad 'the Impaler' Ţepeş. Castel Films also shot scenes from *Highlander IV (Endgame)*, released late 2000/early 2001, in Snagov and Bucharest.

SOCIETY & CONDUCT

Romania is a jigsaw of economics and attitude as much as of ethnicity. While politicians refuse to play the game in fixing ethnic relations, the nationality of one's neighbour no longer matters for most people who find themselves united in a common battle for survival. Many of the older generation hark back to the 'great' days of communism when prices were low, pensions comparatively high and state benefits abundant. By contrast, Romania's younger generation is full of beans. A sizable chunk of it drives fast cars and sports mobile phones; the remaining chunk is driven by the dream of doing the same.

Being late is not a concept for most Romanians, particularly in the countryside where many have no job, nowhere to rush to and are happy to spend hours waiting in line at a post office or in shops. The upside is that most Romanians will go out of their way to help travellers, spending hours talking to you. These egocentric people have a Latin temperament and are typically strong-minded, stubbornly proud and staunchly aware of their roots. Most take great pride in their country's rich natural heritage and folk culture. Befriend any Romanian and within hours an expedition to the mountains will be mapped out for you.

Dos & Don'ts

Romanian hospitality is formidable. These people spill their hearts to you, welcome you with open arms into their modest homes, feed you until you burst, and expect *nothing* in return except simple friendship. Don't rebuff it.

Romanians are generally tactile. Men and women both greet each other with a kiss. Women walk down the street linking arms or holding hands, while menfolk offer a hearty handshake to practically every man they meet, regardless of whether they're only vaguely acquainted or saw each other just five minutes previously. Wild gesticulations are common.

When discussing prices with Romanians be tactful. Express sympathy with their situation rather than raving about the bargains you've found. Carrying your belongings in a tatty plastic bag is the first sign of adapting to local life. When you go shopping always take a bag with you. Take an egg box too if you don't want your eggs scrambled.

Visiting a Romanian Home

Superstitions abound in Romania. The arrival of a guest is signified by a spider in the home. The bigger the spider, the more important the guest. If you happen to be that lucky guest, take a small gift for your host – flowers, a watermelon, but never money.

Don't kiss or shake hands across the threshold and take your shoes off when you enter the house. Your host will usually offer you a pair of oversized slippers or beach shoes to wear. Don't expect your glass to be topped up during dinner until you have drained the last drop; if you do have the misfortune to have your glass filled by your host while it is half-full, it means she/he wants to kill you. Traditionally, your inner power and strength is derived from alcohol. Maybe this is the reason why most Romanians drink a lot, at any time of day.

On the streets, expect good luck if someone crosses your path with a pail of water (it does happen!).

In Bucharest prostitution is rife. So is child prostitution and the HIV virus. For your own safety and the sake of the young girls at hand, restrain yourself. Don't even dabble in this activity.

Treatment of Animals

Between 1976 and 1989 brown bears were protected for only one reason – so Nicolae Ceauşescu could hunt them. Since then, trophy hunting has become a big business. A bear yields up to US$20,000 for the Romanian forest administration authorities and they therefore encourage foreign trophy-hunters to stalk prey in their forests. On average, 300 of Romania's brown bears are killed by hunters each year.

Wolves have been protected by law since 1996, but the forest administration authorities still issue permits to hunt them.

RELIGION

Romania is the only country with a Romance language that does not have a Roman Catholic background. Its ethnic diversity is reflected in its religious mix – 86% of the population is Romanian Orthodox, 5% Roman Catholic, 3.5% Protestant, 1% Greco Catholic, 0.3% Muslim and 0.2% Jewish.

Romania's ethnic Saxon and Hungarian communities form the mainstay of Romania's Protestant church today. Traditionally, Transylvanian Saxons are Lutherans and many Hungarians belong to the Hungarian Reformed Church (also known as Calvinist). The Roman Catholic church was brought to Romania by the Habsburgs. Today it comprises Hungarians and Romanians whose ancestors converted during the great Habsburg drive to catholicise Transylvania in the 17th century.

Most Muslim mosques are in Dobruja, serving small Turkish communities centred in Constanța and Mangalia. The few Jewish synagogues still in use today serve an elderly congregation of around 14,000.

Romanian Orthodoxy

Unlike other ex-communist countries where the church was a leading opposition voice to the dictatorial regime, Romania's leading Orthodox Church remained subservient to, and a tool of, the Romanian communist government. Yet immediately after the collapse of the Ceaușescu regime, Orthodox heads asked forgiveness for sinning against the church through their 'compromises'.

The Romanian Orthodox Church fell under the patriarchy of Constantinople until 1864 when a free Romanian church was established. During the Habsburg domination of Transylvania and later Hungarian occupation of northern Transylvania, Orthodox churches were burnt and congregations forced to adopt the Roman Catholic faith.

Today Romania's leading church is hierarchical, dogmatic and wealthy. It condemns abortion and homosexuality.

Greco Catholicism

Unlike Romanian Orthodoxy, Greco Catholicism (also known as Uniate) allows its congregation freedom of thought. The church, legally established in Romania in 1699, was seen as dangerous by the post-WWII government and in 1948 the Greco Catholic Church was outlawed. Greco Catholics remained a persecuted minority until 1990 when the post-communist Romanian government legalised the church again.

The Greco Catholic Church is an offspring of Orthodoxy. It established itself in Romania in the 17th century when Romanian Orthodox believers were persuaded to accept the authority of the Vatican as opposed to that of Constantinople. It adheres to the same Byzantine rite as the Romanian Orthodox Church but looks to the Pope for authority. Unlike in Roman-Catholicism, priests are allowed to marry. The Greco Catholic church is strongest in Maramureș.

LANGUAGE

Romanian is the official national language. English and French are the first foreign languages taught in schools; coupled with the fact that most films at cinemas and on TV are screened in their original language with subtitles in Romanian, this means that most younger Romanians are practically fluent in one, if not two, foreign languages. Some Hungarian is spoken in Transylvania.

See the Language chapter at the back of the book for a short guide to Romanian pronunciation and a list of useful words and phrases.

Facts for the Visitor

HIGHLIGHTS

Romania's greatest asset is its diversity, offering as much to do and see to tourists who want to stray off the beaten tourist track as those who want to stay well and truly on it. Scale mountain peaks. Share fresh cheese and milk with a local shepherd. Slam shots of fiery ţuica with new-found friends. Shiver in an ice cave. Explore the Danube Delta's wild waterways. Climb 1480 steps to Dracula's castle in Poienari. Visit the Saxons' mighty fortified churches in Transylvania. Snowboard in Poiana Braşov. Watch brown bears in the Carpathians. Boogie the night away on the Black Sea coast...

Typical highlights on most people's 'must-see' list are incorporated in the following Suggested Itineraries section. Other people's 'must-see' lists might include: Bucharest's Belu and Ghencea Cemeteries; a few nights in a rural home around Bran; a mountain hike to 2000m in Sinaia (or take the cable car); the ancient Greek and Roman remains at Histria; Maramureş' villages (try the homemade cheese); and the Danube Delta (for bird-watching and fish).

For those following in the footsteps of Dracula (tons do), Curtea de Argeş, Sighişoara, Bran, Bistriţa, Poienari, Arefu, and Târgovişte are key points. Those interested in tracking the 1989 revolution should spend time in Bucharest, Timişoara, Scorniceşti and Târgovişte.

More highlights are listed at the start of each regional chapter.

SUGGESTED ITINERARIES

Whether you have a few days or a month, the following suggested itineraries may help you plan your trip.

Two days Visit medieval Braşov, and Sinaia (home to Eastern Europe's finest royal pad).
One week Visit Braşov, Sinaia, Bran and its castle (Count Dracula never actually slept there), and the medieval towns of Sighişoara and (perhaps) Cluj-Napoca. If you're southbound, add at least a day in the capital, if only

to visit Bucharest's Palace of Parliament and Village Museum.
Two weeks To the above add Sibiu, and at least one hike in the Carpathian Mountains. Or skip Cluj-Napoca and visit Bucovina's painted monasteries. Then head west to traditional Maramureş.
One month You'll have time to explore Bucharest, Transylvania and Bucovina more fully, as well as the Danube Delta and the Black Sea coast.

PLANNING
When to Go

May and June are by far the best months to visit, followed by September and early October. Spring in Romania is a pastiche of wildflowers, melting snow and melodious bird song. At higher elevations, snow lingers as late as mid-May, and the hiking season doesn't begin in earnest until mid-June. The resorts along the Black Sea coast start filling up in late June and stay packed until mid-August. Romania is famous for its harsh winters, when tourism focuses on ski resorts such as Poiana Braşov.

Visiting southern Bucovina's monasteries off-season invariably means you'll have more chance than in July and August of having these medieval works of art all to yourself; and also more chance of being offered shelter, providing a unique opportunity to see these world-famed monasteries from the 'inside'.

Bird-watchers flock to the Danube Delta in spring and autumn.

Maps

Maps in Romania range from the adequate to downright useless. Minor roads and villages are not marked on many road maps and road hierarchies can be right up the creek.

In towns and cities, street names are constantly changing, meaning the most recently published of city maps can feature out-of-date street names. Always check a map's publication date before parting with any cash. Those printed before 1994 feature Russified spellings (since changed to pre-communist 'Latinised' spellings).

Country & Regional Maps The only map you need before arriving is a country map. Quality regional maps available abroad include Marco Polo's 1999 edition of *România* (1:750,000), an excellent bet for Romania-bound travellers; Kümmerly & Frey's *Romania & Bulgaria* (1:750,000), which includes Moldova, Bulgaria and decent-sized areas of Ukraine and Hungary; and Geocenter's *Romania-Moldavia* map (1:750,000).

In-country, *Romania 2000* (1:700,000) published by Bucharest-based Editura JIF (☎ 01-232 2897) is a road map worth buying. Romania's leading map-maker, Amco Press (☎/fax 01-340 3109, e amco@mail.kappa.ro), Blvd Nicolae Grigorescu 29A, Bucharest, publishes an unbeatable range of country and city maps, which are cheap and widely available in bookshops in Bucharest, Braşov and other larger cities. Its Romanian road map *România Harta Rutieră* (1:850,000), published in 2000, includes a place-name index and costs US$2.50. Its 1999 equivalent for neighbouring Moldova, the *Moldova Road Map* (1:650,000), costs US$2.

Amco Press also produces thematic country maps, including the *România Harta Mânǎstirilor* (Monasteries Map; 1:400,000) which features 265 monasteries (US$2). The only Romanian road atlas is Top-Gráf's 52-page *Road Atlas România* (1:500,000), which also features maps of Central Europe (1:350,000) and city maps (1:10,000 to 1:18,000).

Some excellent maps of the region are published by map-makers in Hungary. Dimap publishes the useful country road map *România* (1:700,000). Those intent on exploring Transylvania in depth should invest in the outstanding *Erdély-Transilvania-Siebenbürgen* (1:500,000). This 1998 map features almost every forest road, dirt track and village in Transylvania, Crişana, Banat and Maramureş and an exhaustive listing of place names in Romanian and Hungarian.

Equally invaluable is *Ţara Secuilor-Székelyföld-Székely Land* (1:250,000) by Hungary's largest map-maker, Cartographia. The map covers eastern Transylvania and includes an index of place names (in Romanian, Hungarian and German).

All three maps are sold in selected bookshops in Bucharest and Transylvania. In Hungary contact Dimap (☎ 01-377 7908, e dimap@elender.hu), Báthory út 104, H-1196 Budapest; or Cartographia (☎ 01-363 3639, e mail@cartographia.hu), Bosynák tér 5, H-1149 Budapest. In the UK try Stanfords (☎ 020-7836 1321, e sales@stanfords.co.uk), 12–14 Long Acre, London WC2, with its Web site at www.stanfords.co.uk. In the US contact the US-based electronic map shop OMNI Resources (☎ 336-227 8300, e custserv@omnimap.com), with its Web site at www.omnimap.com.

City Maps Amco Press (mentioned earlier) publishes quality city maps of a clutch of cities – including Bucharest, Braşov, Constanţa, Iaşi and Ploieşti. Bookshops in the capital, and in the respective cities, sell them (US$1.50). Further details of maps are listed in cities' or regions' Orientation sections throughout this book.

What to Bring

Most forgotten items can easily be picked up in Bucharest or other larger cities. Bring your own gear if you plan to hike or camp. If you intend travelling around, take a backpack.

Basic necessities include a water bottle, small first-aid kit, a Swiss army knife, and a small torch (flashlight). A universal sink plug is useful as is an adaptor plug for electrical appliances. Always carry a good wad of tissues or toilet paper in your pocket. If you intend visiting caves, bring a larger torch, and if you'll be visiting the Danube Delta binoculars and vast amounts of insect repellent come in handy.

In early and late summer, bring a light waterproof garment. In spring and autumn there are cold snaps so bring warm headgear, gloves and a coat. In winter, bring thermals and snow gear. In the mountains it can be nippy year-round. Indestructible footwear is recommended for all seasons. Bring spare tapes for your video camera, contact lens solution and any special medicines you need. In Bucharest and larger cities tampons, sanitary towels and condoms are widely available; elsewhere not.

RESPONSIBLE TOURISM

Environmental protection was not a legacy inherited by Romania in the aftermath of communist rule. And from the shocking amount of litter that scars most rivers, villages and the open countryside – a factor exacerbated by the lack of any organised rubbish collection – Romania clearly has a long way to go before any real inroads are made to protect the region's fragile ecosystems, biological diversity and natural treasures. In 1997 just 6% of rural areas (compared to 94% of urban areas) had any sewerage system.

Visitors can avoid placing pressure on the environment by conserving water and electricity, not littering or burying rubbish, and taking care with wildlife. In the Danube Delta, only pitch your tent in designated areas and be sure to purchase the required permit (US$1) before setting foot in the protected wetland. Do not light fires or discard cigarette butts in the countryside and keep to assigned paths. Staying in Romanian homes rather than hotels gives locals a bigger share of the money you spend, as does buying produce from the farm or marketplace rather than the supermarket or shop.

Medieval Sighişoara, the Danube Delta, many of the fortified Saxon churches in Transylvania, the painted monasteries of southern Bucovina, Horezu Monastery and the wooden churches of Maramureş star on Unesco's list of 'cultural and natural treasures of the world's heritage'. Pay these precious sights the due respect they deserve.

TOURIST OFFICES
Local Tourist Offices

Romania has no national tourist office network, making information tough to track down. The former ONT Carpaţi government agency that controlled tourism under communism is defunct today, although a handful of these former state-run offices – since privatised but still adhering to the same dinosaur-age philosophy – continue to trade under their ONT title. Staff in these offices rarely speak English and have absolutely no comprehension of customer service.

A handful of efficient, independently run tourist centres – such as those in Arad, Predeal and Poiana Braşov – have sprung up in the past couple of years. Elsewhere, private travel agencies double as tourist offices, although their quality, usefulness and attitude varies dramatically.

Touring ACR, the travel agency of the Automobil Clubul Român (ACR), has desks in several hotels around Romania. These are useful for reserving accommodation at upmarket hotels and providing general information for visiting motorists.

Tourist Offices Abroad

Contrary to the disheartening lack of information locally, Romania runs a string of efficient tourist offices abroad, coordinated by Romania's National Authority for Tourism (☎ 01-410 1262, e turism@kappa.ro), Str Apolodor 17, RO-70663 Bucharest; Web site: www.turism.ro.

Belgium (☎/fax 02-502 46 42, e tourisme.roumain@wanadoo.be) 17 Ave de la Toison d'Or, B-1050 Brussels
Web site: www.ibelgique.com/romania
France (☎ 01 40 20 99 33, fax 01 40 20 99 43, e roumanie@office-tourisme-roumanie.com) 12 rue des Pyramides, F-75001 Paris
Germany (☎ 030-241 9041, fax 247 25020, e romaniatour@t-online.de) Budapester-strasse 20A, D-10787 Berlin
(☎ 069-295 278, fax 292 947, e ro-touramt@t-online.de) Zeil 13, D-60313 Frankfurt
Moldova (☎/fax 22-273 555, e optro@mdl.net) Blvd Ştefan cel Mare 4, Chişinău
Netherlands (☎ 020-623 90 44, fax 626 26 60, e romaniantourist@site.nl) Weteringschans 183, NL-1017 XE Amsterdam
Turkey (☎ 212-238 2588, fax 256 8417, e info@romaniantravel.org) 7 Lamartin Cad. Kat 1, 8090 Taksim, Istanbul
UK (☎ 020-7224 3692, fax 7935 6435, e uktourff@romania.freeserve.co.uk) 22 New Cavendish Street, London W1M 7LH

USA (☎ 212-545 8484, fax 251 0429,
ⓔ ronto@erols.com) 14 East 38th St, 12th
Floor, New York, NY 10016
Web site: www.rezq.com/ronto

VISAS & DOCUMENTS

Rumour has it that, since this guide was
researched, Romania has ditched its archaic
talon de intrare (entry card) and *talon de
ieşire* (exit card), a positively scrappy piece
of paper which everyone, except Romanian
citizens, had to fill in upon entering the country and resubmit when exiting. Should you,
for some bizarre reason, be confronted by a
border official who still insists on practising
this ridiculously Soviet habit, simply smile;
fill in your name, date of birth and passport
details, and retain the exit part of the slip in
a safe place (just in case you encounter that
same sour-faced official when leaving!).

Passport

Your number one document is your passport. Its validity must extend to at least six
months beyond the date you enter the country in order to obtain a visa. Never *ever* part
with your passport (see Dangers & Annoyances later in this chapter).

Visas

American citizens and (from 1 January
2001) EU citizens may travel visa-free for
30 days in Romania. All other foreign visitors require a visa to enter, except residents
of many Eastern Europe countries.

Romania issues two types of visas to
tourists: transit or single-entry. (With the
exception of American citizens, multiple-
entry visas are only issued to business travellers and must be supported by a letter of
invitation from a company in Romania.)

To apply for a visa you need a passport,
one recent passport photograph and the completed visa application form accompanied by
the appropriate fee. If you are applying for a
visa by post you have to enclose a stamped,
self-addressed envelope too. The cost of a
visa varies from embassy to embassy.

Transit visas can be either single-entry
(US$35 to US$38) – valid for three days
and allowing you to enter Romania once –

or double-entry (US$35 to US$50), allowing you to enter the country twice and stay
for three days each time. Transit visas must
be used within one month of the date they
were issued.

Regular single-entry visas (US$35 to
US$50) are valid for 30 days from the day
you enter the country. Single-entry visas are
issued the same day or, at the most, within
24 hours by most embassies; the visa must
usually be used within three months of the
issue date.

Multiple-entry visas (US$70 to US$90),
valid for six months, allow you to stay up to
30 days at a time.

Cut-price single-entry visas (about $20)
are also issued to people travelling to Romania under the umbrella of an officially
registered charity. To obtain a charity visa
you need all the documents listed above
plus a letter from your home organisation
confirming the purpose and role of your
visit. You also need an official letter of invitation from the relevant charity in Romania. Charity visas must be used within three
months of the issue date. Multiple-entry
charity visas are *not* issued.

Canadian citizens can buy a single-entry
30-day visa at the border, including Bucharest's Otopeni airport which charges US$33
(payable in any currency). At all other borders you are liable to get ripped off and it is
better to get a visa before leaving home.

Visa Extensions In Romania, you can extend your stay by reporting to a passport office such as the one at Str Nicolae Iorga 2
in Bucharest. You must apply before your
current visa expires.

Visas for Neighbouring Countries All
foreigners, except residents of many Eastern
Europe countries, need a visa to enter Moldova (see the Moldova chapter for details),
Yugoslavia and Ukraine. Contact the respective embassy in Bucharest for details. If
you are taking the Bucharest–St Petersburg
train you need Ukrainian, Belarusian and
(depending on your nationality) Baltic transit visas on top of the Russian visa. Most
Europeans do not need a Baltic transit visa,

but check. EU nationals don't need a visa for Hungary or Bulgaria.

Travel Insurance

A fully comprehensive travel insurance policy to cover theft, loss and medical problems in all situations is strongly advisable, especially if you intend to do a lot of travelling. A policy which covers the costs of being flown out of the country for treatment is a definite bonus, given the still limited local facilities.

Driving Licence & Permits

If you are planning to drive in the region, an International Driving Permit (IDP) will be useful, though if you don't have one, your own national licence (if from a EU country) should suffice. An IDP is obtainable, usually cheaply, from your local automobile association. British driving-licence holders should note that licences not bearing a photograph of the holder have been known to upset traffic police: get an IDP before you arrive. You also need your vehicle's registration document. In Romania accident insurance is compulsory.

Hostel Cards

A Hostelling International (HI) card yields a token discount in some hostels. You can become a member by joining your own national Youth Hostel Association (YHA) or IYHF; see the Web site www.iyhf.org/index.html for details. Alternatively, you can buy an annual card for $5 at two HI-affiliated hostels, Villa Helga in Bucharest or Do-Re-Mi in Cluj-Napoca. One-night membership is not yet available.

Student & Youth Cards

Of use in the region are the International Student Identity Card (ISIC) and the Euro<26 card (the international youth card of the Federation of International Youth Travel Organisation, available to people 26 or under but not a student). Both cards are issued by student travel agencies. ISIC has a Web site at www.istc.org.

Although neither card is officially recognised in Romania, flashing one often gets you into museums, cinemas and theatres at reduced rates. It also comes in handy if you are booking a flight with airlines which offer student or youth discounts – see the Getting There & Away chapter.

Seniors Cards

Few discounts are available for elderly foreigners.

EMBASSIES & CONSULATES
Romanian Embassies & Consulates

Romanian embassies and consulates abroad include:

Australia (☎ 02-6286 2343, 6290 2442, fax 6286 2433, e roembcbr@cyberone.com.au) 4 Dalman Crescent, O'Malley ACT 2606

Bulgaria (☎ 02-973 2858, fax 973 3412, e ambsofro@exco.net) Sitnjakovo 4, Sofia

Canada (☎ 613-789 5345, fax 789 4365, e romania@cyberus.ca) 655 Rideau St, Ottawa, Ontario K1N 6A3
Web site: www.cyberus.ca/~romania
Consulates: (☎ 416-585 5802/9177, fax 585 4798) 111 Peter St, Suite 530, Toronto, Ont M5V 2H1
(☎ 514-876 1792, fax 876 1797) 1111 St Urbain, Suite M01-04, Montreal, Quebec H2Z 1Y6

France (☎ 01 40 62 22 02, fax 01 45 56 97 47, e ambparis.roumanie@free.fr) 3–5 rue de l'Exposition, F-75007 Paris

Germany (☎ 030-803 30 18, fax 803 16 84, e ro-amb.berlin@t-online.de) Matterhornstrasse 79, D-14129 Berlin

Hungary (☎ 01-352 0271, 343 6035, fax 343 6035, e roembbud@mail.datanet.hu) Thököly út 72, H-1146 Budapest XIV

Ireland (☎ 031-269 2852, fax 269 2122, e ambrom@eircom.net) 47 Ailesbury Rd, Ballsbridge, Dublin 4

Moldova (☎ 02-233 434, 224 118, fax 228 129, e ambrom@ch.moldpac.md) Str Bucureşti 66/1, Chişinău
Consulate: (☎ 2-237 622) Str Vlaicu Parcalab 39, Chişinău

UK (☎ 020-7937 9666, ☎/fax 7937 4675, e romania@roemb.demon.co.uk) 4 Palace Green, Kensington Gardens, London W8 4QD

Ukraine (☎ 044-224 52 61, fax 224 20 25, e romania@iptelecom.net.ua) ul Mihaia Kotziubinskogo 8, UA-252030 Kyiv

USA (☎ 202-232 4846/4848, fax 232 4748, @ office@roembus.org) 1607 23rd St NW, Washington DC 20008
Web site: www.roembus.org
(☎ 212-682 9120/9121, fax 972 8463, @ mail@romconsny.org) 200 East 38th St, New York, NY-10016
Web site: www.romconsny.org
Consulate: (☎ 310-444 0043, fax 445 0043, @ consulat@romanian.org) 11766 Wilshire Blvd, Suite 1230, Los Angeles, CA-90025
Web site: www.romanian.org/consulat
Yugoslavia *Consulate:* (☎ 011-646 151, fax 646 267, @ ambelgro@infosky.net) Kneza Miloša 70, YU-11000 Belgrade

Embassies & Consulates in Romania

Unless stated otherwise, the following foreign embassies are in Bucharest (city code ☎ 01):

Australia *Consulate:* (☎ 320 9802, fax 320 9823, @ don.cairns@austrade.gov.au) Blvd Unirii 74
Bulgaria (☎ 230 2150, fax 230 7645) Str Rabat 5
Consulate: (☎ 211 1106, fax 210 5248) Str Vasile Lascăr 32
Canada (☎ 222 9845, fax 312 0366, @ bucst@dfait-maeci.gc.ca) Str Nicolae Iorga 36
France (☎ 312 0217, fax 312 0200, @ presse@ambafrance.ro) Str Biserica Amzei 13–15
Web site: www.ambafrance.ro
Consulate: (☎ 312 0991, fax 312 3381) Intrarea Cristian Tell 6
Germany (☎ 230 2580, fax 230 5846) Str Rabat 21
(☎ 069-211 133, fax 214 180) Str Lucian Blaga 15–17, Sibiu
(☎ 056-220 796, fax 220 798) Hotel Continental, Blvd Revoluției 1989 3, Timişoara
Consulates: (☎ 230 0357, fax 230 2155) Str Rabat 19
(☎ 069-214 442, fax 214 177) Str Hegel 3, Sibiu
(☎ 056-190 495, fax 190 487) Blvd Republicii 6, Timişoara
Hungary (☎ 312 0073, fax 312 0467, @ hunemb@ines.ro) Str Jean Louis Calderon 63–65
Consulates: (☎ 312 0468, fax 312 7470) Str Henri Coandă 5
(☎ 064-196 300, fax 194 109, @ huconkol@codec.ro) Piaţa Unirii 23, Cluj-Napoca
Ireland *Consulate:* (☎ 211 3967, fax 211 4384) Str Vasile Lascăr 42–44
Moldova (☎ 230 0474, fax 230 7790, @ moldova@customers.digiro.net) Aleea Alexandru 40

Consulate: (☎ 410 9827, fax 410 9826) Blvd Eroilor 8
Russia (☎ 222 3168/3170, fax 222 9450) Şoseaua Kiseleff 6
Consulates: (☎ 222 1556, fax 222 6405) Str Tuberozelor 4
(☎ 041-611 106, ☎/fax 615 168) Str Mihai Viteazul 5, Constanţa
Turkey (☎ 210 0279, fax 211 0407) Calea Dorobanţilor 72
Consulate: (☎ 041-611 135, fax 615 367) Blvd Ferdinand 82, Constanţa
UK (☎ 312 0303/0304/0305, fax 312 0229, @ britemb@dnt.ro) Str Jules Michelet 24
Honorary Consulate: (☎ 041-638 282, 638 283, fax 638 285) Blvd Tomis 143A, Constanţa
Ukraine (☎ 211 6986, fax 211 6949) Calea Dorobanţilor 16
Consulate: (☎ 222 3162, ☎/fax 223 2702) Str Tuberozelor 5
USA (☎ 210 4042, fax 210 0395, @ usvisa@state.gov) Str Tudor Arghezi 7–9
Consulate: (☎ 210 4042, fax 211 3360, @ usvisa@state.gov) Str Nicolae Filipescu 26
Information Bureau (☎ 042-439 121) Str Universităţii 79, Cluj-Napoca
Web site: www.usembassy.ro
Yugoslavia (☎ 211 9871, consulate section ☎ 211 4980, fax 210 0175) Calea Dorobanţilor 34
Consulate: (☎ 056-190 334, 193 467, fax 190 425) Str Remus 4, Timişoara

CUSTOMS

Romanian customs regulations are complicated but not often enforced. Gifts worth up to a total of US$100 may be imported duty-free. For foreigners, duty-free allowances are 4L of wine, 1L of spirits and 200 cigarettes.

Officially, you're allowed to import hard currency up to a maximum of US$10,000. Valuable goods and foreign currency over US$1000 should be declared upon arrival.

MONEY
Currency

The currency in Romania is the leu (plural lei). Since the collapse of the Romanian leu, valued at nine to US$1 in 1989, Romania has become an inexpensive country for foreigners – most of whom walk out of currency exchanges a millionaire. For ease of comparison, prices in this book are listed in

US$, converted from lei at the official rate and abbreviated to $.

There are coins of 100 and 500 lei and banknotes of 1000, 2000, 5000, 10,000, 50,000 and 100,000 lei.

Exchange Rates

Currency exchange rates are posted daily online at www.xe.net/ucc. At the time of printing, official exchange rates included:

country	unit		Lei
Australia	A$1	=	14,524 Lei
Bulgaria	1 leva	=	12,524 Lei
Canada	C$1	=	17,368 Lei
euro	€1	=	24,531 Lei
France	1FF	=	3740 Lei
Germany	DM1	=	12,542 Lei
Hungary	100Ft	=	9260 Lei
Ireland	IR£1	=	31,148 Lei
Japan	¥100	=	22,083 Lei
Moldova	1 Lei	=	1957 Lei
Netherlands	f1	=	11,132 Lei
New Zealand	NZ$1	=	11,692 Lei
UK	UK£1	=	38,665 Lei
Ukraine	1 hv	=	4829 Lei
USA	US$1	=	26,238 Lei

Exchanging Money

Currency exchanges – a handful of which open 24 hours – and banks dot almost every street corner in Bucharest and major cities. By contrast, changing your foreign currency into lei in the countryside can present huge challenges (always keep a secret stash of cash at hand for such moments).

Whether you change money at a bank or currency exchange, you need your passport. Keep any receipts you are given: they are needed to change excess lei back into hard currency, which you can do at main branches of the banks listed and at the exchange desk at Bucharest's Otopeni airport ($50 maximum).

When changing $10 or more, ask if you can have 100,000 or 50,000 lei notes. If not you will end up with inches of banknotes.

Cash All major currencies are accepted in exchanges and banks, but marked or torn banknotes are often refused. US dollar notes issued before 1990 are not accepted.

Travellers Cheques Travellers cheques offer protection against theft and are easy to exchange in the capital and cities in Romania – but impossible to trade in for cold hard cash elsewhere. Most branches of Banca Comercială Română and Banca Comercială Ion Țiriac change travellers cheques for a 1.5% to 3% commission. American Express has a representative in Bucharest.

ATMs ATM machines giving 24-hour advances (Cirrus, Plus, Visa, MasterCard, Eurocard) are rife in the capital and major cities. There are a couple at Otopeni airport and at Gara de Nord in Bucharest. The maximum withdrawal per transaction (in lei only) is $70 (from Banca Comercială Română) or $95 (from Société Générale).

Credit Cards Credit cards are accepted in upmarket hotels, restaurants and shops in most towns and cities. By contrast, plastic is pretty useless in rural areas. Credit cards are essential for hiring a car, unless you are willing to pay in cash up-front.

You can get a cash advance on Visa and MasterCard (in lei only) from banks in most towns, including branches of Banca Comercială Română and Banca Ion Țiriac (1.5% to 3% commission).

International Transfers Direct bank-to-bank transfer is possible – but slow. Commission (usually 5%) is charged on the amount you transfer; the service takes at least five days. Western Union's Money Transfer system is available at post offices in Bucharest.

Black Market Changing money on the street is illegal, risky and the quickest way to get ripped off. Most black marketeers who change money on the street are professional thieves. Counting out your roll of money in front of you then switching it with a dud roll at the last instant is a common trick (which works).

Another is for the moneychanger to take your dollars and give you the correct amount, only for the trickster to shout 'not good, not good' as you walk off, and insist on giving 'your' money back in exchange for theirs.

Despite warnings, numerous travellers think they know what they are doing and end up cheated. See Dangers & Annoyances later in this chapter for other scams.

Security

Any Westerner will stick out like a sore thumb. And for Bucharest's skilled pickpockets, that bulging wallet in your back pocket will stick out even more. Of all Eastern Europe's capitals, Bucharest suffers the worst reputation for petty theft against foreigners (all Westerners are wealthy as far as Romanians are concerned).

Always store the bulk of your cash and all other important travel documents in a moneybelt beneath your clothing. Keep sufficient cash for the day in a separate, easily accessible (to you) wallet. Leaving a secret stash of cash in your hotel room is not a good idea.

Costs

Romania is relatively inexpensive for Western travellers. Accommodation is the biggest expense. In Bucharest, rock-bottom rates for a shared room with communal bath in the train station area start at $10 per person a night, without breakfast. For a dormitory bed in a city-centre hostel you'll pay $12 a night, including breakfast. Expect to pay at least $30 for a double room with shared bath in any hotel within walking distance of the centre. Accommodation in private homes starts at $10 a night.

Restaurant meals, drinks, public transport, museum admissions and theatre tickets are cheap. While in Bucharest it is tough to eat for less than $5 a head, excluding alcohol, elsewhere filling your tummy is cheaper and a bottle of fine Romanian wine can cost as little as $1.50.

You pay no more than $1 to see a film or play, while museum admission fees average $0.30 in the capital (less elsewhere). Some places – such as the Palace of Parliament, Peleş Castle and the Bucovina monasteries – command a fee (about $1/2.50) for taking in a camera/video.

A public-transport ticket good for two journeys costs no more than $0.15. About $3 will take you approximately 100km by bus or comfortable express train.

Some museums offer concession prices for children, students and those aged over 60 years.

Tipping & Bargaining

In flashier restaurants in Bucharest, waiters will not hesitate to ask where their tip is if you fail to leave one. Elsewhere tipping is a rarity – and often undeserved. Tips and bribes should not be offered to officials, including train conductors.

Some bargaining, but not much, goes on in flea markets. Countrywide, taxi drivers drive the hardest bargain; haggle.

POST & COMMUNICATIONS
Post

Mail in and out of Romania is still unreliable. Letters and postcards take four to six days to Western Europe and seven to 10 days to North America. Expect to pay $0.35/0.50 to send a postcard/letter up to 20g to Western Europe, and $0.50/0.75 to Australia and the USA. Post offices (*poştă*)

Romanian Addresses

Bl 5, Sc C, Int D, Et 2, Ap 16 – most Romanian addresses comprise what can appear to be a jumble of incomprehensible letters and numbers. Decoded, those sneaky little numbers and letters actually mean:

Strada Ştefan cel Mare 62	62 Ştefan cel Mare Street
Bl 5	Block (*bloc*) No 5
Sc C	Staircase (*scară*) C
Int D	Entrance (*intrarea*) D
Et 2	2nd floor (*etaj*)
Ap 16	Apartment No 16

In this book we have abbreviated Strada to Str and Bulevardul to Blvd. Aleea means 'drive' or 'avenue', Şoseaua means 'highway', Piaţa is 'square' and Splaiul is 'embankment'.

WAP, Mobiles & No Phone At All

Nowhere is Romania's 'great divide' between urban and rural more evident than in its telephone technologies.

Mobile telephones are all the rage in cosmopolitan Bucharest where most Romanians in the 20- to 30-something age group strut around with a ringing device glued firmly to their hip. A select few dial up the Internet for everything from the weather forecast to nightclub listings, with Romania's first WAP portals (www.wapnet.ro, www.connex.ro) both live since 2000.

Regular mobile telephones can be rented easily in Bucharest, at Otopeni airport and from network providers such as Connex and Mobil Rom (Dialog) in town. Mobil Rom has a Web site at www.mobil-rom.com. A SIM card credited with an initial 40 units (40/20 minutes of national calls within the same/other network) typically costs $30. Subsequent prepaid cards will set you back $20/30 for 60/130 units. An international call made from a mobile to Europe/USA-Canada/Australia averages $0.50/0.95/1.25 per minute. Mobile telephone numbers comprise six digits and a three-digit code – ☎ 092, 093, 094, 095 or 098 – which must always be dialled.

Take a tiger leap from cosmopolitan Romania to the countryside – and you're back in the Stone Age. In some rural areas, particularly in Maramureş and southern Bucovina, telephone calls still have to be made via an operator (☎ 191) or through a central switchboard. Other areas – including some places to eat and drink that we include in this guide – quite simply have no phone at all.

are often signposted with the letters PTTR, an abbreviation for Poştă-Telegraf-Telefon-Radio. All post offices sell stamps *(timbre)*. Mail boxes – labelled *Poştă Romană* – in Bucharest are red, elsewhere they are usually yellow. The mail-box slot marked *Pentru Bucureşti* is for letters for Bucharest. Mail for other destinations in Romania and abroad has to be posted in the slot marked *alte localităti* (other localities).

Post offices open until 8 pm Monday to Saturday. When mailing parcels home, you may be asked to pay an export duty of 20% of their value. Recommended mail *(postală recomandată)* can be sent from any post office, and gives confirmation of delivery, within Romania.

Collect post-restante mail (addressed c/o Poste Restante, Poştă Romană Oficiul Bucureşti 1, Str Matei Millo 10, RO-70700 Bucureşti, Romania) at Bucharest's main post office at Str Matei Millo 10 between 7.30 am and 8 pm weekdays, 7.30 am to 1 pm Saturday. Mail is held for you for one month.

Telephone

Direct local, national and international calls can be made/received from most private phones and all public cardphones – bright orange in colour and abundant in most towns and cities.

Magnetic phonecards *(cartela telefonică)* are sold at the telephone building in Bucharest, on the corner of Calea Victoriei and Str Matei Millo, and at any telex-fax office or post office in other towns and cities. At the time of writing, only phonecards worth 50,000 lei (about $2.50) were available, meaning you need a clutch of cards to make anything but the briefest of calls to Western Europe and the USA. If you need to exchange a spent card midway through a call, press the button on the telephone labelled 'K'. This allows your remaining credit to be stored, giving you the time to insert a new card without being rudely cut off. Incoming calls (limited to three minutes) can also be received on these cardphones.

As with street names, telephone numbers are also prone to change. In Bucharest, seven-digit numbers kicking off with 611, 612, 613, 614 or 615 have been changed to 311, 312, 313 etc *or* – to confuse the issue – 211, 212 etc.

Romania's international operator can be reached by dialling ☎ 971. For an English-speaking operator abroad, dial ☎ 01-800 4444 (British Telecom), ☎ 01-800 4288

(AT&T USA Direct), ☎ 01-800 1800 (MCI Worldwide) or ☎ 01-800 0877 (Sprint).

To call other cities in Romania, dial the city/area code (listed at the start of the relevant sections in this book), followed by the recipient's number.

To call Romania from abroad dial your international access code, Romania's country code (☎ 40), then the city code (minus the first 0) and the recipient's number.

Fax

Sending an international fax from any telex-fax office in Bucharest or main post office elsewhere is easy and costs around $2 per A4 page; to receive a fax should cost no more than $1 a page.

Email & Internet Access

There's an easy explanation for the dozens of cybercafes – many of which are open 24 hours – you'll find in Bucharest: it's because few Romanians have computers at home (0.25% of the population in 1998) or at work (2% in 1998). In mid-2000 Romania estimated its Internet hosts to number no more than 32,500 (compared to over 2 million in the UK and 38 million in the US).

The upside of this slow technological progress means travellers will find plenty of places to log-on. Expect to pay $1.50 to $2 per hour in the capital and $0.50 to $0.75 in other towns.

INTERNET RESOURCES

Email account holders can subscribe for free to Radio Free Europe/Radio Liberty (RFE/RL; ℮ newsline-request@list.rferl .org) which mails out daily news reports on the region, including Romania and Moldova. Archived stories are on its Web site at www.rferl.org.

Addresses for many handy Romanian-related Web sites are listed throughout this guide. General sites, loaded with practical information about the country and worth a surf prior to departure, include the following:

www.turism.ro – Romania's National Authority for Tourism's site; a good introduction to the country's attractions

www.romaniatravel.com – the Romanian Tourism Promotion Office's site; a wealth of information for visitors to Romania

www.rotravel.com – Romanian Travel Guide; another useful site covering all aspects of travelling around Romania

www.inyourpocket.com – the entire contents of the locally published city guide *Bucharest In Your Pocket* posted for free

www.centraleurope.com/romaniatoday – Romania's latest breaking news, views and local press digests, courtesy of the *Central European Review* journal, updated daily

www.romaniabynet.com – RomaniaByNET touts the most interactive site around: chat rooms, e-cards, hyperlinks to Romanian radio and TV stations with Internet relay, the best of Romanian rock and pop music etc

BOOKS

Literature by Romanian writers is discussed under Arts in the Facts about Romania chapter.

Foreign-language books can be found in many bookshops in Romania; those in Bucharest and Iaşi offer the widest selection. Many titles listed here can only be found in bookshops in Western Europe or via Internet booksellers.

Those published by the Iaşi-based Center for Romanian Studies (CRS; ☎ 032-219 000, fax 219 010, ℮ csr@romanianstudies.ro), Str Poligon 11A, 6600 Iaşi, can be ordered online at www.romanianstudies.ro. Editura Humanitas (☎ 01-222 8546, ℮ editors@ agora.humanitas.ro) is another Romanian publisher offering English-language titles.

Lonely Planet

If you're travelling elsewhere in Eastern Europe, *Eastern Europe* and the *Eastern Europe phrasebook* are the guides for you. Eastbound travellers should consider Lonely Planet's *Russia, Ukraine & Belarus*.

Travel

Back Door to Byzantium (1997) by Bill & Laurel Cooper. Detailed account of an eastbound voyage in 1995 from northern France to the Black Sea, with a good chunk dedicated to the 'bureau-crass-y' encountered at border crossings in Romania.

Clear Waters Rising (1996) by Nicholas Crane. A lone hiker tramps from Cape Finisterre

(Spain) across the Sierras, Pyrenees, Alps and the Carpathians to Istanbul.

Looking for George – Love & Death in Romania (1995) by Helena Drysdale. Hard-hitting account of the author's search for a Romanian tour guide and defrocked monk she met at Putna monastery in 1979. Psychiatric abuse in communist Romania is the main issue she tackles.

Bury Me Standing – The Gypsies and their Journey (1996) by Isabel Fonseca. The author spent several months travelling with Roma in Eastern Europe between 1991 and 1995. The chapter covering Romania looks at racial attacks against Roma in Transylvania.

Exit into History (1993) by Eva Hoffman. Part of this lamenting travelogue of the Polish-American author's travels across Eastern Europe in 1990 and 1991 takes place in Romania. Told from an exasperating 'nice, middle-class woman' perspective but highlight the 'aesthetic torment' a first-time traveller to Romania could suffer.

Balkan Ghosts (1993) by Robert Kaplan. This insightful title recounts a journalist's investigative travels across Eastern Europe and Romania in the 1990s.

Between the Woods and the Water (1986) by Patrick Leigh Fermor. Fermor's book, the second in a trilogy, describes Transylvania in the 1930s.

Balkan Trilogy (1987, reprinted 1998) by Olivia Manning. This colourful portrait of Bucharest at the outbreak of WWII has long been considered *the* classic work on Romania, gaining a new lease of life since being serialised on British TV as *The Fortunes of War*.

Stalin's Nose (1993) by Rory Mclean tackles his journey across Eastern Europe with his nutty old aunt and her pet pig.

Romania Revisited: On the Trail of English Travellers 1602–1941 (CRS, 2000) by Alan Ogden. Dacian, Byzantine and Saxon Romania are beautifully evoked in this collection of tales by the author who in 1998 followed in the footsteps of previous travellers, from the first motorists to the Romantics like Leigh Fermor.

The Gypsy in Me (1997) by Ted Simon. A Romanian Jew traces his roots.

Romanian Journey (republished 1992) by Sicheverell Sitwell. The journey of an Englishman abroad, travelling from London to Bucharest by train and spending four weeks exploring Romania and its tribes; first published in 1938.

History & Politics

Kiss the Hand You Cannot Bite: The Rise and Fall of the Ceauşescus by Edward Behr, and *Transylvania: Its Products & its People* by Charles Boner are two classics in their fields which, though out of print, are well worth scouring bookshops for. The first title provides fascinating background on the 1989 revolution; the latter is an authority on Saxons in Transylvania from the 12th century onwards. Titles more readily available include:

Ceauşescu and the Securitate – Coercion and Dissent in Romania 1965–89 (1996) by Denis Deletant is a detailed analysis of the Securitate by Britain's leading authority on Romanian history and politics. Another Deletant title worth reading is *Romania under Communist Rule* (CRS, 1999) which focuses on the history of the Communist Party in Romania, from its formation in 1921 through to 1989.

The Red Army in Romania (CRS, 2000) by Constantin Hlihor & Ioan Scurtu focuses on the USSR occupation of Bessarabia in 1940–41 and subsequent military presence in Romania until the final withdrawal of Soviet troops in 1958.

Byzantium after Byzantium (CRS, 2000) by Nicolae Iorga. Originally published in French in 1935, this in-depth history by the renowned Romanian historian analyses Byzantium's influences on south-eastern Europe. Iorga fans can also read *Nicolae Iorga: A Biography* (CRS, 1998) by Nicholas Nagy-Talavera.

The Green Shirts & the Others (CRS, 2000) by Nicholas Nagy-Talavera. The unsettling subject of this detailed history is the rise and fall of fascist movements in Romania and neighbouring Hungary from 1918 to 1945. First published in 1970.

Romanian Politics 1859–71 (CRS, 1998) by Paul Michelson. Covers from Alexandru Ioan Cuza to Carol I.

The Land of Green Plums (1996) by Herta Müller, first published in German in 1993. The Romanian-born novelist tells the tale of a group of students in Ceauşescu's Romania and examines the cancer of betrayal and suicide that infests their friendships.

John Hunyadi – Defender of Christendom (CRS, 2000) by Camil Muresanu. Biography of 15th-century Transylvanian prince Iancu de Hunedoara (János Hunyadi in Hungarian).

Marie, Queen of Romania (1984) by Hannah Paluka. In-depth biography of the half-English, half-Russian granddaughter of Queen Victoria whose persuasive charm at the 1919 Paris Peace Conference helped Romania obtain Transylvania. *Americans and Queen Marie of Romania*

(CRS, 1998) edited by Diana Fotescu is another regal title.

A History of Romania (CRS, 1997) edited by Kurt W Treptow. The most comprehensive history book around, combining a clear account of events, Stone Age to present-day, with biographies, photos and maps. Also available on CD-ROM.

Vlad III Dracula: The Life & Times of the Historical Dracula (CRS, 2000) by Kurt W Treptow. A study of the extraordinary cult following that has sprung up around Bram Stoker's *Dracula* novel and its association with the historical figure Prince Vlad Ţepeş.

Athene Palace (CRS, 1998) by Rosie G Waldeck is a memoir, written by a German-Jewish countess and journalist, of Bucharest's grand hotel and the political intrigues which filled its atmospheric lobby prior to WWII. First published in 1942.

Autobiographies

Out of Romania (1995) by Dan Antal. An autobiography of a youth existing on the 'wrong side' of the Securitate. Brilliant for its wit, deadpan humour and startling insights into the hardships and cruelties encountered.

The Anti-Humans (1971) by former political prisoner Dimitru Bacu. A disturbing account of life inside communist prisons in the 1950s; first published in Romanian in Spain in 1963.

Assignment: Bucharest – An American Diplomat's View of the Communist Takeover of Romania (CRS, 2000) by Donald Dunham. The author served as an American diplomat in Bucharest from 1947 to 1950, subsequently publishing his semi-autobiographical account of his Romanian posting in German under the pseudonym Ray Stanley.

Red Horizons (1990) by Ion Mihai Pacepa. One of the highest ranking officials of any communist secret service to defect to the West, Pacepa, the head of the foreign intelligence service of the Securitate, defected to the US in 1978 and promptly published a behind-the-scenes account of his work in Romania.

Flying Against the Arrows: An Intellectual in Ceauşescu's Romania (2000) by Horia Roman Patapievici. The autobiographical account of an intellectual striving to be ideologically 'free' under 1980s communism.

Women Behind Bars in Romania (1997) by Annie Samuelli. Tells the story of the Samuelli sisters and the women they were imprisoned with in communist Romania between 1947 and 1961.

Art & Architecture

Superb B&W photographs illustrate both these books:

The Wooden Architecture of Maramureş (1997) by Ana Bârcă (text) and Dan Dinescu (photographs). A sociological and architectural study of life in a Maramureş village, with a heavy emphasis on how Romania's most unique architectural form evolved and what its motifs and ornamentations symbolise.

Fortresses of Faith (CRS, 2000) by Alan Ogden. The fascinating and tragic history of Transylvania's Saxon community and the fortress-churches they built.

Cookbooks

The first two titles listed are published by the Romanian Cultural Foundation Publishing House (☎ 01-230 2543, fax 230 7559, e fcr@algoritma.fr), Aleea Alexandru 38, 71273 Bucharest, and are only available in bookshops in Romania.

The Story of Romanian Gastronomy (1999) by Matei Cazacu. Crammed with colourful anecdotes and facts, eg, a Romanian peasant's diet comprised beans and *mămăligă* for 133 to 200 days a year at the start of the 20th century.

Savoury Romanian Dishes and Choice Wines (1999) is a reproduction of a 1939 recipe book, featuring scores of easy (predominantly vegetarian) recipes.

Taste of Romania: Its Cookery & Glimpses of its History, Folklore, Art, Literature & Poetry (1999) by Nicolae Klepper. Over 140 traditional recipes, including a staggering seven for Romania's infamous *mămăligă*.

The Balkan Cookbook: Traditional Cooking from Romania, Bulgaria & the Balkan Countries (2000) edited by Lesley Chamberlain. Regional cuisine.

NEWSPAPERS & MAGAZINES

The most popular Romanian daily papers are *Adevărul* (The Truth) which favours the PDSR; *România Libera*, an opposition voice; *Evenimentul Zilei* (Daily Events), a popular mainstream paper; and *Ziua* (The Day), the hottest tabloid choice. In a former life *Adevărul* was, in fact, the communist newspaper *Scânteia* (The Spark) which the entire populace was compelled to read (and use as toilet paper). The weekly journal *Academia*

Caţaremcu is a satirical paper established by former dissident Mircea Dinescu.

Româniai Magyar Szo is the main daily in Hungarian. *A Hét* (Hungarian) and *Deutsche Zeitung* (German) are published weekly.

Local foreign-language publications are abundant and, in the main, free: *România Liberă* publishes a weekly English-language edition on Friday, available in major hotels in Bucharest. *Nine O'Clock* (http://9.eforie .ro) is Bucharest's free daily English-language newspaper, likewise found on most hotel reception desks. *Bucarest Matin* (www.bucarest-matin.ro) is the French-language equivalent. The leading English-language business newspapers are the weekly *Bucharest Business Week* (www.bbw.ro) and rival *The Business Review*. *Romanian Economic Daily* (www.romanian-daily.ro) and *Romanian Business Journal* (www.sta rnets.ro/RBJ) are two others.

Numerous free magazines pop up and disappear all the time. Those of sufficient quality to command a cover price include the glossy business-orientated *Invest Romania* (www.investromania.ro), published quarterly ($5); and *Vivid*, a bold, social and cultural magazine published fortnightly ($2). The authoritative city guide *Bucharest In Your Pocket* is handy (www.inyourpocket.com); it comes out five times a year ($1).

Invaluable for gaining deeper insight into Romanian culture are the informative journals published three times a year by the Center for Romanian Studies in its *Romanian Civilization* series. In Romania, back issues, which cover every cultural topic imaginable, cost around US$2 in bookshops ($15 by mail order).

Newsstands and hotels in larger cities sell *Newsweek, Time, Economist, International Herald Tribune, Wall Street Journal* and other international papers.

RADIO & TV

All mid-range and top-end hotels, and some budget ones too, have a colour TV. Regardless of its decrepit state, if you fiddle with the knobs enough you should be able to pick up various cable channels, including MTV,

Euronews and Eurosport in English. Numerous English-language films and American sitcoms (in their original language with Romanian subtitles) are screened on Pro TV, Romania's main private TV channel which has had a cult following since its launch by Romanian tennis star and business tycoon Ion Ţiriac. Launched in 1999, Atomic TV – Romania's equivalent of MTV – targets a 15- to 30-something age group and presents the latest on the Romanian band scene and pop culture. Heavy-going documentaries and the like (in Romanian) are the mainstay of TVR and TV2, Romania's two public channels.

Tune into Radio Hit on 94.9 FM to pick up Voice of America (VOA) or try Radio France International on 93.5 FM. The BBC World Service can only be picked up in Romania on short wave.

Other popular radio stations include Radio Contact which has Internet relay at www.radiocontact.ro and can be picked up on 96.1 FM in Bucharest, 92 FM in Iaşi, 89.8 FM in Cluj-Napoca and on 91.8 FM in Sibiu, and Radio Delta on the Danube Delta.

On the coast, tune into Radio Vacanţa on 100.1 FM.

VIDEO SYSTEMS

PAL is the main video system used in the region.

PHOTOGRAPHY & VIDEO

Kodak, Agfa and Fuji colour films and basic accessories such as batteries are widely available except in remote villages with few shops. Slide and black-and-white film is not so widespread. Stock up before leaving Romania for Moldova.

In both countries you are not allowed to photograph military installations, including army barracks, border posts, hydroelectric power plants, dams, and often coal and gold mines. If in doubt, look for a sign featuring a crossed-out camera – no photographs allowed.

TIME

Romanian time is GMT/UTC plus two hours, which means there's a one-hour difference between Romania/Moldova and Hungary/Yugoslavia, but no difference between Romania/Moldova and Bulgaria. Romania and Moldova start daylight saving at the end of March, when clocks are turned forward an hour. At the end of October, they're turned back an hour.

The 24-hour clock is used for all transport schedules, which are always listed in local time. Dates are listed the American way: the month comes first, followed by the day and year, ie, 03/08/01 refers to 8 March 2001 as opposed to 3 August 2001.

ELECTRICITY

Romania runs on 220V, 50Hz AC. Most appliances that are set up for 240V will handle this happily. Sockets require a European plug with two round pins.

WEIGHTS & MEASURES

Romania uses the metric system, often to a ridiculous degree. In most restaurants the Soviet practise of listing on menus the precise gram weight of each ingredient incorporated in the final dish is still alive and well. Prices are often listed per 100g.

Outdated it might seem, but Romanians are not stupid: listing items this way provides the perfect opportunity to rip diners off. See the later Food section for details.

LAUNDRY

Self-service laundrettes simply do not exist in Romania, with the exception of Nuf Nuf in Bucharest where you can wash your socks 'n smocks for $2 a kilo. Failing that, make use of the washing machine at Bucharest's Villa Helga (free to guests) – or hand-wash.

Most mid-range and top-end hotels offer a pricey laundry service.

TOILETS

The cleanest toilet is behind a bush. Unfortunately bush-squatting is not allowed in towns and cities, where you'll be arrested should you pull your pants down in public.

Public toilets in towns and cities come in three grades. Bottom of the pile are those smelly holes in the ground at train and bus stations. These are stinking, vile pits that will leave you gasping for fresh air as you attempt to race in, pee and race out again without inhaling the stench. Grade two toilets are those touting a cracked seat and a flushing system – marginally less smelly and with a babushka at the entrance doling out squares of coarse toilet paper for a nominal fee. Grade three toilets: McDonald's (in most big cities). Most homes in rural areas only have an outside toilet.

Many toilets have a plastic bin by their side. This is intended for used toilet paper. Women's toilets are marked with the letter F (femei) or with a ▲. Men's are marked B (bărbaţi) or ▼.

HEALTH

Romania is a pretty healthy place to travel around. While the potential dangers can seem quite frightening, in reality few travellers experience anything more than an upset stomach. There are plenty of private Western-run clinics in Bucharest staffed with English-speaking doctors. Elsewhere, medical care is *not* up to Western standards.

Predeparture planning

Immunisations No immunisations are required for Romania or Moldova but some vaccinations are strongly advisable, particularly if you intend exploring remote areas. Check that routine vaccinations recommended are up-to-date. These include diphtheria, tetanus, polio and measles.

You should then consider a rabies, typhoid and encephalitis vaccination. Stray dogs are rife in Romanian cities, especially Bucharest. A rabies vaccination is particularly recommended for those cycling, handling animals, caving, travelling to remote areas, or for children (who may not report a bite). Pretravel rabies vaccination involves having three injections over 21 to 28 days. If someone who has been vaccinated is bitten or scratched by an animal they will require two booster injections of vaccine, those not vaccinated require more.

Typhoid is an important vaccination to have if you really intend to be roughing it in remote areas. A vaccination against encephalitis, a disease transmitted by forest ticks, has to be administered in advance. Other considerations should be vaccinations against Hepatitis A, a common travel-acquired illness, and Hepatitis B which is spread by blood or by sexual activity.

All vaccinations should be recorded on an International Health Certificate. Don't leave vaccinations until the last minute; they often have to be spread out over a few weeks.

Health Insurance Make sure that you have adequate health insurance. See Travel Insurance in the Documents section earlier in this chapter.

Other Preparations Make sure you're healthy before you start travelling. If you are going on a long trip make sure your teeth are OK. If you wear glasses take a spare pair and your prescription. You cannot replace lost contact lenses in Romania or Moldova. If you require a particular medication take an adequate supply, as it may not be available locally.

Basic Rules

Food & Nutrition Vegetables and fruit should be washed with purified water or peeled where possible. Beware of ice cream which is sold in the street or anywhere it might have melted and been refrozen.

Mushroom and berry picking is a national pastime in Romania. Feel free to join in the fun but don't eat anything until it has been positively identified as safe by someone whose judgement can be relied on.

Milk should be treated with suspicion as it is often unpasteurised, though boiled milk is fine if it is kept hygienically. Tea or coffee should also be OK, since the water should have been boiled.

In summer make sure you drink enough liquid – don't rely on feeling thirsty to indicate when you should drink. Not needing to urinate or small amounts of very dark yellow urine is a danger sign. Always carry a water bottle with you on long trips.

Water You won't die if you drink the tap water, but it is advisable to treat it with

---

Medical Kit Check List

Following is a list of items you should consider including in your medical kit – consult your pharmacist for brands available in your country.

☐ **Aspirin or paracetamol (acetaminophen in the USA)** – for pain or fever

☐ **Antihistamine** – for allergies, eg, hay fever; to ease the itch from insect bites or stings; and to prevent motion sickness

☐ **Cold and flu tablets, throat lozenges and nasal decongestant**

☐ **Multivitamins** – consider for long trips, when dietary vitamin intake may be inadequate

☐ **Antibiotics** – consider including these if you're travelling well off the beaten track; see your doctor, as they must be prescribed, and carry the prescription with you

☐ **Loperamide or diphenoxylate** –'blockers' for diarrhoea

☐ **Prochlorperazine or metaclopramide** – for nausea and vomiting

☐ **Rehydration mixture** – to prevent dehydration, which may occur, for example, during bouts of diarrhoea; particularly important when travelling with children

☐ **Insect repellent, sunscreen, lip balm and eye drops**

☐ **Calamine lotion, sting relief spray or aloe vera** – to ease irritation from sunburn and insect bites or stings

☐ **Antifungal cream or powder** – for fungal skin infections and thrush

☐ **Antiseptic (such as povidone-iodine)** – for cuts and grazes

☐ **Bandages, Band-Aids (plasters) and other wound dressings**

☐ **Water purification tablets or iodine**

☐ **Scissors, tweezers and a thermometer** – note that mercury thermometers are prohibited by airlines

---

caution. Although Romanians tend to drink it straight, travellers and foreigners should boil it first. If you don't know for certain that the water is safe assume the worst; only 38% of rural areas and 62% of the urban populace have access to a drinking water supply. In many towns, the water supply covers less than half the length of every street. Only 7% of rural residences have running water.

Water fountains on train station platforms and water drawn from wells in villages could give you a stomach upset.

Medical Problems & Treatment

Self-diagnosis and treatment can be risky, so you should always seek medical help.

Pharmacies in towns and cities stock basic Western items such as aspirin, insect repellent (a definite must for travellers who intend visiting the Danube Delta), and insect bite reliefs. Many pharmacies sell antibiotics over the counter too. These should ideally be administered only under medical supervision.

There are few alternatives to the dismal local medical system, which is short on both facilities and equipment, if you do need serious attention. Medical treatment in state-run hospitals (*spital*) and clinics is free for Romanians and foreigners alike. Some private clinics do offer Western-standard medical care in Bucharest but they are expensive. In an emergency seek your hotel's help first (if you're in one) – the bigger hotels may have doctors on call. Emergency care is free in Romania. Secondly, your embassy or consulate can recommend an English-speaking doctor or hospital, but if things are serious be prepared to go straight home. Romanian doctors are paid $90 a month.

To call an ambulance (in Romanian) dial ☎ 961.

Diarrhoea Simple things like a change of water, food or climate can all cause a mild bout of diarrhoea, but a few rushed toilet trips with no other symptoms is not indicative of a major problem.

Dehydration is the main danger with any diarrhoea, particularly in children or the elderly as dehydration can occur quite quickly. Under all circumstances fluid replacement (at least equal to the volume being lost) is the most important thing to remember. Weak black tea with a little sugar, soda water, or soft drinks allowed to go flat and diluted

50% with clean water are all good. With severe diarrhoea a rehydrating solution is preferable to replace lost minerals and salts. Commercially available oral rehydration salts (ORS) are very useful; add them to boiled or bottled water. In an emergency you can make up a solution of six teaspoons of sugar and a half teaspoon of salt to a litre of boiled or bottled water. You need to drink at least the same volume of fluid that you are losing in bowel movements and vomiting. Urine is the best guide to the adequacy of replacement – if you have small amounts of concentrated urine, you need to drink more. Keep drinking small amounts often. Stick to a bland diet as you recover.

Lomotil or Imodium can be used to bring relief from the symptoms, although they do not actually cure the problem. Only use these drugs if you do not have access to toilets. Lomotil and Imodium are not recommended for children under 12. Do not use these drugs if the person has a high fever or is severely dehydrated.

Hepatitis Hepatitis is a general term for inflammation of the liver. It is a common disease worldwide. There are several different viruses that cause hepatitis, and they differ in the way that they are transmitted. The symptoms are similar in all forms of the illness, and include fever, chills, headache, fatigue, feelings of weakness and aches and pains, followed by loss of appetite, nausea, vomiting, abdominal pain, dark urine, light-coloured faeces, jaundiced (yellow) skin and yellowing of the whites of the eyes. People who have had hepatitis should avoid alcohol for some time after the illness, as the liver needs time to recover.

Hepatitis A is transmitted by contaminated food and drinking water. You should seek medical advice, but there is not much you can do apart from resting, drinking lots of fluids, eating lightly and avoiding fatty foods.

There are almost 300 million chronic carriers of hepatitis B in the world. It is spread through contact with infected blood, blood products or body fluids – for example through sexual contact, unsterilised needles and blood transfusions, or contact with blood via small breaks in the skin. Other risk situations include having a shave, tattoo or body piercing with contaminated equipment. The symptoms of hepatitis B may be more severe than type A and the disease can lead to long term problems such as chronic liver damage, liver cancer or a long term carrier state. There are vaccines against hepatitis A and B.

HIV & AIDS Infection with the human immunodeficiency virus (HIV) may lead to acquired immune deficiency syndrome (AIDS), which is a fatal disease. Any exposure to blood, blood products or body fluids may put the individual at risk. The disease is often transmitted through sexual contact or dirty needles – vaccinations, acupuncture, tattooing and body piercing can be potentially as dangerous as intravenous drug use. HIV/AIDS can also be spread through infected blood transfusions. If you do need an injection, ask to see the syringe unwrapped in front of you, or take a needle and syringe pack with you. Fear of HIV infection should never preclude treatment for serious medical conditions.

Romania bears more than half of all Europe's known juvenile AIDS (SIDA in Romanian) cases; 90% of AIDS cases in Romania affect children aged under 15.

Romania's national AIDS information and advice, ARAS (Asociaţia România Anti-SIDA; ☎ 01-324 5680, e aras@kappa.ro), Şoseaua Mihai Bravu 285, Bucharest, runs a 24-hour hotline on ☎ 01-252 4141.

Sexually Transmitted Diseases Gonorrhoea, herpes and syphilis are all painfully common in this region. Many syphilis sufferers are street children.

Sores, blisters or rashes around the genitals, discharges or pain when urinating are common symptoms. In some STDs, such as wart virus or chlamydia, symptoms may be less marked or not observed at all especially in women. Syphilis symptoms eventually disappear completely but the disease continues and can cause severe problems in later years. While abstinence from sexual contact is the only 100% effective prevention, using condoms is also effective. The treatment of gonorrhoea and syphilis is with antibiotics. The different sexually transmitted diseases each require specific antibiotics.

Tick-Borne Encephalitis From May to September there is a risk of tick-borne encephalitis in forested areas. Encephalitis is inflammation of the brain tissue. Symptoms include fever, headache, vomiting, neck stiffness, pain in the eyes when looking at light, alteration in consciousness, seizures and paralysis or muscle weakness. Correct diagnosis and treatment require hospitalisation. Ticks may be found on the edge of forests and in clearing, long grass and hedgerows. A vaccine is available (see the Immunisations details earlier).

Always check your body if you have been walking through a potentially tick-infested area. If found, press down around the tick's head with tweezers, grab the head and gently pull upwards. Avoid pulling the rear of the body as this may squeeze the tick's gut contents through the attached mouth parts into the skin, increasing the risk of infection and disease. Smearing chemicals on the tick will not make it let go and is not recommended.

Rabies This fatal viral infection is found in many countries. Many animals can be infected (such as dogs, cats, bats and monkeys) and it is their saliva which is infectious. Any bite, scratch or even lick from an animal should be cleaned immediately and thoroughly. Scrub with soap and running water, and then apply alcohol or iodine solution. Medical help should be sought promptly to receive a course of injections to prevent the onset of symptoms and death.

Lyme Disease This is a tick-transmitted infection which may be acquired throughout North America, Europe and Asia. The illness usually begins with a spreading rash at the site of the tick bite and is accompanied by fever, headache, extreme fatigue, aching joints and muscles and mild neck stiffness. If left untreated, these symptoms usually resolve over several weeks but over subsequent weeks or months disorders of the nervous system, heart and joints may develop. Treatment works best early in the illness. Medical help should be sought.

Bedbugs & Lice Bedbugs live in various places, but particularly in dirty mattresses and bedding, evidenced by spots of blood on bedclothes or on the wall. Bedbugs leave itchy bites in neat rows. Calamine lotion or a sting relief spray may help.

All lice cause itching and discomfort. They make themselves at home in your hair (head lice), your clothing (body lice) or in your pubic hair (crabs). You catch lice through direct contact with infected people or by sharing combs, clothing and the like. Powder or shampoo treatment will kill the lice and infected clothing should then be washed in very hot, soapy water and left in the sun to dry.

Hypothermia Too much cold can be just as dangerous as too much heat. Whether you're hiking, hitching or simply taking a long bus trip over mountains, particularly at night, always be prepared for cold, wet or windy conditions.

Hypothermia occurs when the body loses heat faster than it can produce it and the core temperature of the body falls. It is surprisingly easy to progress from very cold to dangerously cold due to a combination of wind, wet clothing, fatigue and hunger, even if the air temperature is above freezing. It is best to dress in layers; silk, wool and some of the new artificial fibres are all good insulating materials. A hat is important, as a lot of heat is lost through the head. A strong, waterproof outer layer (and a 'space' blanket for emergencies) is essential. Carry basic supplies, including food containing simple sugars to generate heat quickly and fluid to drink.

Symptoms of hypothermia are exhaustion, numb skin (particularly toes and fingers), shivering, slurred speech, irrational or violent behaviour, lethargy, stumbling, dizzy spells, muscle cramps and violent bursts of energy. Irrationality may take the form of sufferers claiming they are warm and trying to take off their clothes.

To treat mild hypothermia, first get the person out of the wind and/or rain, remove their clothing if it's wet and replace it with dry, warm clothing. Give them hot liquids - not alcohol - and some high-kilojoule, easily digestible food. Do not rub victims: instead, allow them to slowly warm themselves. This should be enough to treat the early stages of hypothermia. The early recognition and treatment of mild hypothermia is the only way to prevent severe hypothermia, which is a critical condition.

Gynaecological Problems Antibiotic use, synthetic underwear, sweating and contraceptive pills can lead to fungal vaginal infections, especially when travelling in hot climates. Fungal infections are characterised by a rash, itch and discharge and can be treated with a vinegar or lemon-juice douche, or with yogurt. Nystatin, miconazole or clotrimazole pessaries or vaginal cream are the usual treatment. Maintaining good personal hygiene and wearing loose-fitting clothes and cotton underwear may help prevent these infections.

Sexually transmitted diseases are a major cause of vaginal problems. Symptoms include a smelly discharge, painful intercourse and sometimes a burning sensation when urinating. Medical attention should be sought and male sexual partners must also be treated. For more details see the section on Sexually Transmitted Diseases earlier. Besides abstinence, the best thing is to practise safer sex using condoms.

Pregnancy It is not advisable to travel to some places while pregnant as some vaccinations normally used to prevent serious diseases are not advisable during pregnancy. In addition, some diseases are much more serious for the mother (and may increase the risk of a stillborn child) in pregnancy.

Most miscarriages occur during the first three months of pregnancy. Miscarriage is not uncommon and can occasionally lead to severe bleeding. The last three months should also be spent within reasonable proximity of good medical care. A baby born as early as 24 weeks stands a chance of survival, but only in a good modern hospital.

Pregnant women should avoid all unnecessary medication, although vaccinations and malarial prophylactics should still be taken where needed. Additional care should be taken to prevent illness and particular attention should be paid to diet and nutrition. Alcohol and nicotine, for example, should be avoided.

WOMEN TRAVELLERS

Traditional gender roles are firmly intact. Romania has one of the lowest percentages (5.3%) of women in parliament in Europe and few vocal women's groups exist. Male chivalry plays a vital role in daily life. Many older Romanian women expect their menfolk to carry their bags and kiss their hands upon meeting, while the vast majority of Romanian men cannot comprehend that a woman is able to step off a bus or train unaided.

Romania is as safe a place for women travellers as anywhere else in the world; just don't wander about alone late at night, avoid sitting in empty compartments on long-distance and overnight trains, and don't appear unnerved.

Some Romanian men have the revolting habit of hissing but, beyond that, they'll leave you alone. The only exception is Constanţa and the Black Sea coastal resorts which teem with Romanian *and* Western men on the pull. If things get desperate, shout '*Poliţia!*'

GAY & LESBIAN TRAVELLERS

Until mid-2000, homosexual acts in private, gay bars, clubs and newspapers, and all 'attempts to convert' were illegal in Romania under Article 200 of its penal code. At the start of 2001, Romania's small but tenacious gay and lesbian community was waiting with bated breath to see if the Romanian Senate would axe this draconian law – already repealed by the lower Chamber of Deputies in June 2000. Assuming it did, this would decriminalise homosexuality, but still leave homosexual behaviour in public punishable by five years imprisonment.

Not surprisingly, few gay and lesbian Romanians show affection in public. The Orthodox Church still considers homosexuality a sin. Hotel managers will turn away openly gay couples, so be discreet if you're travelling with a same-sex partner.

Organisations

Romania's capital is the only place with an active gay and lesbian community, represented by Bucharest-based Accept (☎ 01-252 1637, fax 252 5620, ✉ accept@fx.ro), Str Lirei 10, which has a Web site at http://accept.ong.ro. It holds regular meetings and social events, screens films on Friday at 6 pm, and publishes a Romanian- and English-language newsletter.

Romania Action at www.raglb.org.uk is a British-based Web site which campaigns for gay and lesbian equality in Romania. Its press clippings archive makes fascinating reading.

DISABLED TRAVELLERS

Disabled travellers will find it difficult, if not downright impossible, to conquer Romania. Street surfaces are woefully uneven, ramps and specially equipped toilets and hotel rooms virtually unheard of. Consider joining a package tour that will cater to your specific needs – some hotels on the Black Sea coast have wheelchair access from the hotel to the beach. Bucharest's Gara de Nord train station has ramps for wheelchairs but offers no solution to the problem of actually getting on the train.

TRAVEL WITH CHILDREN

If you intend travelling across the region by public transport with young children, take every opportunity to break up the journey. Bus and train journeys between regional cities can be long and arduous with little to make the journey pass quickly. Take sufficient food and drink supplies as none are available on buses and most trains.

Many of the larger hotels have family rooms or will put an extra bed in the room. See Lonely Planet's *Travel with Children* for some useful tips.

USEFUL ORGANISATIONS

Abroad, the following Romanian cultural centres supply country-wide information:

France (☎ 01 40 62 22 70/71, fax 01 40 62 22 72) 1 rue de l'Exposition, 75005 Paris
Hungary (☎ 01-122 62 93, 142 25 24) Iszto út 5, 1146 Budapest XIV
UK (☎ 020-7439 4052, 7437 0015, fax 7437 5908, e romaniancentre@rhplondon.freeserve .co.uk) 7th floor, 54–62 Regent St, London WIR 5PJ
Web site: www.radur.demon.co.uk/RCC.html
USA (☎/fax 212-687 0181, e roculture@ aol.com) 200 East 38th St, New York NY-10016
Web site: www.roculture.org

DANGERS & ANNOYANCES
Street Crime

Crime has soared in the region since the collapse of communism, primarily because daily survival for an increasing number of people is so damn difficult. But we're not talking gangland murders, gruesome rapes and protection rackets though. Most crime stems from simple economics – pickpocketing, muggings, theft from hotel rooms etc.

Be on guard if walking late at night, keep to well-lit streets and look purposeful. If you are attacked, don't expect much help from bystanders or the police. Never leave valuables unattended, including in hotel rooms, camp sites and in the boot of your car. Motorists should lock their vehicle at night and leave not so much as a tourist map on the dashboard.

Beggars can be a nuisance in Romania. Be wary of professional beggars, colourfully dressed women with babies in their arms, or gangs of sweetly smiling beggar children. On the streets, scams are rife. New scams – all designed to extract cash from you and each more inventive than the last – crop up daily.

To call the (Romanian-speaking only) police dial ☎ 955.

Stray Dogs

Bucharest has a serious stray dog problem – a bizarre legacy of Ceauşescu's systemisation in the 1980s when scores of city-

Street Scams

Tourist Police A man stops you on the street and asks if you want to change money. You refuse. Seconds later, another man appears, arrests the first man, and demands to see your passport and wallet, explaining he is from the tourist police squad. Simply walk away. If he flashes an ID badge, still do not hand over your passport and/or money. As a last resort, insist on being accompanied to the nearest police station – on foot. Taking a taxi with a thief is not a good idea.

Stupid Tourist A man stops you on the street, explains that he is from a foreign country, has never seen a 100,000 lei banknote before, and asks you to show him one. If you pull out your wallet, it – and the 'stupid tourist' – will have disappeared before you can say Jack Robinson.

Fake Taxi Driver A man greets you off the train at Gara de Nord train station, explains he is a member of staff from the Villa Helga youth hostel, and offers to drive you there. En route he asks for payment for your accommodation in advance. Anyone at Gara de Nord who says they are from the hostel is a dud. Villa Helga staff *never* meet guests at the station. Insist on making your own way there (see Places to Stay in the Bucharest chapter for details).

centre and countryside homes were demolished. Replacement tower blocks proved so cramped that many dog-owners faced no alternative but to let their pets loose on the streets.

These dogs (estimated at one per every 10 people) have since multiplied – and continue to multiply, despite sporadic attempts by the authorities to rid the city of its unnerving canine presence. Most dogs roaming the city centre are harmless if left alone, but bitches with puppies can be snappy. Keep well clear. At night, most dogs are a barking nuisance; ear plugs are your best defence.

Should you be bitten by a dog, seek medical advice. Bucharest hospitals and English-speaking doctors which handle rabies vaccinations are listed under Medical Services in that chapter.

Other Nuisances

Hay fever sufferers will sneeze their way around the region in May and June when the pollen count is at its highest. Blood-sucking mosquitoes are rife in summer, particularly in the Danube Delta. Water pressure is low and hot water is restricted to certain hours in many middle and bottom-end hotels – a pathetic dribble of lukewarm water from the shower head is common.

LEGAL MATTERS

If you are arrested you can insist on seeing an embassy or consular officer straight away. Be polite and respectful towards officials.

BUSINESS HOURS

Banking hours are 9 am to 2 or 3 pm weekdays. Most shops and markets close on Sunday. Many museums close on Monday. Theatrical performances and concerts usually begin at 7 pm, except on Monday and in summer when most theatres are closed.

PUBLIC HOLIDAYS & SPECIAL EVENTS

Public holidays in Romania are New Year (1 and 2 January), Easter Monday (in March/April), National Unity Day (1 December) and Christmas (25 and 26 December).

Romania enjoys a juicy calendar of folk-lore festivals, many of which remain un-publicised, preserving their authenticity but making them difficult for the traveller to attend. Many festivals are detailed in the relevant regional chapters. Annual festivals include:

May
Tânjaua de pe Mara Festival – 1–14 May; traditional folk festival to celebrate the first ploughing of spring, Hoteni, Maramureş
Juni Pageant – mid-May; traditional folk festival in Schei district, Braşov
Bucharest Carnival – last weekend in May; street carnival in the capital

Whit Sunday
Székely Pilgrimage – the largest traditional Székely folk and religious festival of the year, Miercurea Ciuc

June
Fundata Fair – traditional folklore fair originally held for people to get together and shepherds to meet their future wives, Fundata near Bran
Sârbătoare – (Midsummer) 23/24 June; celebrated most in Maramureş

July
Girls' Fair – Sunday around 20 July; traditional wife-arranging festival, Mount Găina, Avram Iancu

August
Hora de la Prislop – mid-August; wild dancing festival on the Prislop Pass
Medieval Days – two-week medieval arts, crafts and music festival in the streets of Sighişoara

September
Golden Stag – international pop music festival, Braşov
Sâmbra Oilor – a major pastoral festival to mark the coming down of the sheep from the mountains, Bran and around

ACTIVITIES

Romania is rich in things to do, be it bird- and bear-watching or sheer self-pampering.

Many outdoor activities – skiing and snowboarding, hiking, climbing, caving, mountain biking, horse riding, mountain railway tours – revolve around Romania's greatest natural treasure, the Carpathians; see the Exploring the Carpathian Mountains special section for details.

Information on touring Romania by 4WD or by motorcycle is listed under Car &

Emergency

Nationwide toll-free 24-hour emergency numbers include:

Police	☎ 955
Ambulance	☎ 961
Fire	☎ 981
Roadside assistance	☎ 927

Consider yourself lucky if you hook up with an operator who speaks anything other than Romanian, though.

Motorcycle and Organised Tours, respectively, in the Getting Around chapter.

Agro-tourism organisations (see Accommodation, later) offer a unique choice of activities to help you discover the countryside, learn about local folklore and witness firsthand the traditional occupations – such as cheese-making, shepherdry, weaving – of Romania's rural population. The three valleys – Vâlsanului, Argeşului and Topologului – north of Curtea de Argeş have local agro-tourism groups which organise these and other activities (see the Curtea de Argeş section in the Wallachia chapter). Many more are listed in other regional chapters.

Bird-Watching
The Danube Delta and the part of Dobruja immediately south of it offer some of Europe's most spectacular bird-watching. Most bird-watchers watch during the migratory seasons in mid-April to mid-May and late October. Large bird colonies are protected by the Danube Delta Biosphere Reserve where white clouds of pelicans overhead are a common sight. Some 65 observation towers stud the wetland and it is easy to pick up a local guide or join a birding tour. Details are listed in the Northern Dobruja chapter.

Elsewhere, the Romanian Ornithological Society arranges day trips and can provide professional guides. It has its headquarters at Str Gheorghe Dima 49/2 in Cluj-Napoca.

Where to Watch Birds in Europe by John Gooders (considered the birders' bible) is worth bringing along: local guides only know Romanian names for species.

Spas
One-third of all European sources of mineral or thermal waters are concentrated in Romania, which has more than 160 spas. The mud baths on Lake Techirghiol at Eforie Nord go well with the salty lake water and the nearby Black Sea. Other important spas are Băile Felix (near Oradea) and Băile Herculane (known since Roman times).

Mara Tours organises Romanian spa tours; see Organised Tours in the Getting Around chapter.

COURSES
Universities in Bucharest, Iaşi and Timişoara offer foreigners two- or three-week summer courses in Romanian language and civilisation. Tuition includes about 20 hours of instruction per week, accommodation in student halls of residence, meals at student cafeterias, cultural events and other activities.

Numerous private language schools run courses year-round. In Bucharest, FiaTest Centre Educationnel (☎ 01-313 1880, fax 312 2106, ⓔ fiatest@itcnet.ro), Str General Berthelot 24, charges around $10 per hour for groups up to five people; private and larger-group courses are also available. The school has branches in Sibiu (☎ 069-213 446), Str General Vasile Milea; in Baia Mare (☎ 062-222 165), Blvd Bucureşti 6, 3rd floor, apartment 41; and Braşov (☎ 068-410 152) at Str Gheorghe Dima 2.

Prosper-Transilvania Language Centre (☎ 068-151 553), Str Iuliu Maniu 32, is another school, charging from $15 per hour.

Cluj-Napoca is another centre of learning. Hungarian-run ILS Heltai International Language School (☎ 064-190 096, fax 190 811, ⓔ heltai@mail.soroscj.ro), Str Clinicilor 18, runs Romanian, Hungarian and German language courses costing from $5 per person for a one-day course (six hours).

In Iaşi, contact the International Language Centre (☎ 031-252 936, fax 252 933, ⓔ info@dntis.ro), 8th floor, DNT Iaşi, Str Moara de Foc 35.

The Romanian Cultural Foundation (Fundaţia Culturală Română; ☎ 01-230 2854, fax 230 7559, ⓔ fcr@algoritma.ro), Aleea Alexandru 38, 71273 Bucharest, runs summer workshops in Baia Mare, Maramureş. It runs three-week intensive Romanian language courses for all levels and summer courses in traditional song, dance, folk art and cuisine.

WORK
Romania has enough difficulty keeping its own people employed so there is little work for foreigners. What work exists is usually in specialist fields (on a local salary) and requires previous work experience and formal qualifications in that field.

There are plenty of opportunities, however, to be had in the realm of charity work, providing you are prepared to fund the trip yourself.

Many mainstream charities such as UK-based CRY Romania (with a Web site at www.cry.org.uk) place volunteers with work experience or qualifications in a certain field. The Partnership for Growth (☎ 01903-529 333, fax 529 007, e info@pfg-charity.org), 59-61 Lyndhurst Road, Worthing, West Sussex, BN11 2DB, was among the first to make an impact on Romania after 1989. Information on how to donate, assist or subscribe to its newsletter is on its Web site, www.p4g.org.

ACCOMMODATION

Even if a hotel lists its prices in $, you still have to pay in lei. Top-end and many mid-range hotels accept credit cards. When checking in, you have to show your passport. Many will try to keep it for the duration of your stay; tell staff at reception you need it to change money and they will happily return it to you. Floors are numbered the American way; the ground floor is the first floor. Reservations are only necessary for hotels on the Black Sea coast which can get packed in July and August.

Staying in a family home in rural Romania will bring you closer to the 'real' Romania than any number of nights in a hotel.

Camping

Camping grounds (popas turistic) have little wooden huts (căsuţe) which sleep two or four people. Bare mattresses are usually provided but you have to bring your own sleeping bag. Some upmarket huts tout beds with sheets and even washbasins. Communal showers in most sites are basic, and hot water rarely flows. Space is usually allocated for tents in these grounds.

Freelance/wild camping on beaches and in fields along the Black Sea coast is fairly common, as in lower-lying areas in the mountains. It is forbidden in the Danube Delta, where you need a camping permit ($1) to pitch your tent in allocated camping grounds.

Mountain Huts

In mountain regions, accommodation in cabane – isolated cabins with few comforts but plenty of cheer – is the norm; see the Exploring the Carpathian Mountains special section for details.

Homes & Farmstays

Paying to stay in someone's private home is the most down-to-earth type of accommodation anyone wanting to get to the roots of Romanian home life, tradition and cuisine can find. A paying guest you might well be, but that will not deter your host family from welcoming you with open arms. Their spontaneous friendship is free – and not optional. An evening meal costs extra.

Finding a private room is difficult in Bucharest, but a doddle in most towns and tourist spots, where you will be accosted by a gaggle of babushkas (portly women with headscarves) the moment you set foot off the train. Make sure you understand exactly where the room is before you take up their offer, and don't part with any cash until you have checked the room is habitable. Expect to pay $6 to $20 a night.

A more pleasing alternative is agro-tourism (B&B in the countryside), which has blossomed in recent years. The leading organisations are the National Association of Rural, Ecological and Cultural Tourism (Antrec) and Opération Villages Roumains (OVR), both of which offer a choice of rural activities as well as B&B. Several smaller groups likewise exist.

Belgian-based OVR, with a Web site (French) at www.citeweb.net/ovro, was established in 1989 in response to Ceauşescu's systemisation scheme. Today it operates an excellent network of village offices in Romania through which accommodation in rural homes (from $12 for B&B and $15/17 for half/full board), folklore evenings, local guides ($10 per day) and various cultural activities can be arranged. Details are listed in the regional chapters. Agro-Tur-Art in Vadu Izei in Maramureş is among the most active OVR affiliates.

Abroad, you can book OVR accommodation through:

Belgium (☎ 02-7128 4082, fax 7128 4083,
ⓔ ovr@win.be) Espace Santé, Blvd Zoé Drion
1/2, 6000 Belgium
France (☎ 01 40 15 71 51, fax 01 40 15 72 30)
18bis rue Alexis Duparchy, 91600 Savigny
sur Orge
UK (☎ 01373-466 555, fax 454 442) The Old
Dye House, Spring Gardens, Frome, Somerset
BA11 2NZ

Antrec has its headquarters in Bucharest
(☎ 01-222 8001, 311 2845, ☎/fax 223 7024,
ⓔ office@antrec.ro, antrec@mirabilis.ro),
Str Maica Alexandra 7, 78178 Bucharest,
and a Web site at www.antrec.ro which lists
its countrywide representatives and properties. It charges $15 to $20 per person a night
for B&B and $7 or $8 extra for an evening
meal. Abroad, bookings can be made
through the Eurogîtes country holiday
reservation system, which has a Web site at
www.eurogites.com. Representatives abroad
include:

France Gîtes de France (☎ 03 88 75 56 50, fax
03 88 23 00 97, ⓔ alsace-gites@alsace-gites-
de-france.com), 7 place des Meuniers,
67000 Strasbourg
Web site: www.alsace-gites-de-france.com
Germany (☎ 069-247 880, fax 247 88110)
Eschborner Landstrasse 122, 60489 Frankfurt
(☎ 0228-819 8220, fax 371 870) Godesberger
Allee 142–148, 53175 Bonn
Hungary (☎/fax 01-268 0592) Klauzal Tér 5,
1072 Budapest
Ireland Irish Country Holidays (☎ 1-475 1257,
fax 475 1258, ⓔ info@country-holidays.ie), 5
Lord Edward Court, Bride Street, Dublin 8

Hostels

Romania has five accredited Hostelling International (HI) hostels, two of which are in
Bucharest and open year-round. They charge
$12 a night for a bed in a two- to 10-bed
room, including breakfast and laundry. The
other hostels – Do-Re-Mi in Cluj-Napoca,
Bobby's in Sighişoara and the Piatra Neamţ
hostel – are in student dorms and only open
in summer. They charge $5 to $7 per night.

These hostels offer discounts to HI card
holders. Villa Helga in Bucharest and
Cluj's Do-Re-Mi both issue HI cards, valid

for one year and costing $10 – amongst the
cheapest in the world. Alternatively, head
for the headquarters of Romania's hostelling association, Youth Hostels Romania
(YHR; ☎ 064-198 067, ☎/fax 186 616,
ⓔ yhr@mail.dntcj.ro), Piaţa Ştefan cel
Mare 5, 3400 Cluj-Napoca, with a Web site
at www.dntcj.ro/yhr.

In addition to these hostels, a handful of
hotels and cabanas across the country – including Hotel Continental in Cluj-Napoca,
Vila Lunca Ilvei in Lunca Ilvei, BTT in
Baişoara and Motel West near Suceava –
are affiliated to the hostelling association.
While not hostels, these places offer cheap
beds ($6 to $9, including breakfast) in basic
doubles or four- to six-bed rooms.

Hotels

Romanian hotels are rated by a government
star system. At the top of the scale (three to
five stars) you're guaranteed hot water, a
phone, private bathroom and cable TV.
Prices at these places range from $100 to
$300 per night for a double room in the cap-
ital and $60 to $100 elsewhere. Breakfast
(mic dejun) is usually included in the price.

Not much separates one- and two-star hotels. Hot water *(apă caldă)* is common (but
not guaranteed). In more rural towns, it can
be restricted to a few hours in the morning
and evening; the schedule is normally pinned
up at reception. Occasionally cold water
(apă rece) will be programmed too. You can
usually choose between a more expensive
room with private bath or a cheaper one with
shared bath. Both charge $30 to $60 for a
double in Bucharest and $20 to $40 in
provincial Romania. At these joints, the sig-
nature breakfast of stale bread and tasteless
jam is not usually included, so check first.

Except for the grottiest hotels, most supply guests with a ration of crisp pink toilet
paper neatly rolled up in the bathroom or on
your bedside table. Towels (often as rough
as sand paper) and soap are usually included in private bathrooms (even in one-
and two-star hotels).

Double rooms – even in four- and sometimes five-star hotels – do not sport real double beds. Rather, two single beds are either

Ceauşescu's Private Villas

Travellers keen to sleep in Ceauşescu's bed can do so. The former dictator had two or three private residences in all 41 of Romania's counties. He spent lavish amounts of money on them, decking them out with extravagant furnishings and elaborate mechanisms, only to decide he didn't like the final result.

Since 1989 some of these properties have been transformed into restaurants, hotels or villas. Many remain in state hands, serving as guesthouses for state VIPs, visiting rock stars and the like. Others – in Olăneşti, Lacu Roşu, Neptun, Predeal, Sfântu Gheorghe and Sinaia – are open to humble tourists. Some are castles, others are former hunting lodges; and they all command about $80 a night for a double. Details of most of these are listed in the regional chapters.

pushed together to create the false impression of a double room, or simply left apart as in a standard twin. Rooms with genuine double beds are usually called 'matrimonial rooms' and are always more expensive than a regular 'double'; but few hotels, even at the top end of the bracket, offer them.

FOOD

Restaurants in Romania range from elegant, upmarket places in Bucharest, offering a choice of numerous ethnic cuisines, to those hangovers from a bygone era which serve, with unnerving consistency, communism's trademark grilled pork, tripe soup and greasy potatoes. In between these two extremes there's a whole range of budgets, cuisines and attitudes to choose from.

Beware of being ripped off in city restaurants. A common trick is to price items per 100g on the menu, leading diners to believe this is the final price. When the bill comes, the amount will have doubled or tripled, leaving you wondering how on earth you can prove that the slab of mystery meat happily nestling in your stomach did not in fact weigh 200g. Garnishes, such as potatoes, bread – never served with butter except in the most upmarket restaurants – and salads, can also bump up the final bill beyond belief. Fries are often served with a sprinkling of grated cheese on top.

Gangs of restaurant staff sitting round a table smoking and watching TV is a norm in many older establishments. Despite the horror that crosses their face when customers dare to walk in wanting to eat, they do offer quite nippy service once they get going. In some more remote towns, hotel restaurants are still the only ones serving proper meals from regular menus.

Romanian Cuisine

Mămăligă is Romania's most novel dish. In short, it is a hard or soft cornmeal mush, which is boiled, baked or fried (a Romanian version of Italian polenta) Traditionally it is served with nothing more than a sprinkling of *brânză*, a very salty sheep cheese. Mămăligă is so bland-tasting that it pretty much goes with – and *is* served with – practically everything. In many Romanian households it is served as a main dish.

Ciorbă (soup) is the other mainstay of the Romanian diet. It is tart, deliciously warming on cold winter days and often served with a welcome dollop of *smântână* (sour cream). Favourites include *ciorbă de perişoare* (spicy soup with meatballs and vegetables), *ciorbă de burtă* (a garlicky tripe soup) and *ciorbă de legume* (vegetable soup cooked with meat stock). The leftovers are transformed into *ghiveci* (vegetable stew) or *tocană* (onion and meat stew) for the following day's dinner.

Restaurants and beer gardens typically offer *mititei* or *mici* (grilled meatballs), pronounced 'meech'. Other common dishes are *muşchi de vacă/porc/miel* (cutlet of beef/pork/lamb), *ficat* (liver), *piept de pui* (chicken breast) and *cabanos prajit* (fried sausages). Cooking styles include grilled *(la grătar)*, fried *(prăjit)*, boiled *(fiert)* and roasted on a spit *(la frigare)*. Almost every dish comes with *cartofi* (potatoes) and *pâine* (bread).

Typical desserts include *plăcintă* (turnovers), *clătite* (crêpes) and *cozonac* (a brioche). *Saraillie* is a yummy almond cake soaked in syrup.

Folk dishes are hard to find but worth the search, especially *ardei umpluti* (stuffed peppers), *sarmale* (cabbage or vine leaves stuffed with spiced meat and rice) and *creier pane cu suncă* (breaded brains with ham). Another goodie is *tochitură moldovenească*, a Moldavian speciality comprising pan-fried pork in a spicy pepper sauce served with mămăligă and topped with a fried egg. *Crap kebab* (carp kebab) is typical of the Danube Delta, as are most fish dishes. Fish is *peşte*, herring is *scrumbie*, pike is *ştuică*, salmon is *somon*, shrimp is *crevete*, sardine is *sardele* and tuna is *ton*.

Coajă is a unique type of cheese found only in the villages around Bran, which comes wrapped in (and tasting of) tree bark.

Fast Food

Fast food has stormed its way across the country since 1989, with McDonald's running sit-down restaurants and drive-ins in every big city (open 24 hours in Bucharest) and most larger towns. Pizza Hut and KFC have outlets in Bucharest. Countrywide a variety of locally run outlets offer a cheap feed for as little as $1.

For a Romanian snack attack while on the move, munch on *covrigi*, rings of hard bread speckled with salt crystals. Everything is generally doused with ketchup, be it a burger, toasted sandwich or pizza. 'Nu vreau ketchup' means 'I do not want ketchup'.

Vegetarian

Thanks to the Orthodox diet (see the boxed text), there are vegetarian dishes to be had, unexciting as they may be. If a plate of mămăligă does not turn you on, try *caşcaval pâine* (cheese covered in breadcrumbs and fried), *salată roşii* (tomato salad), *salată castraveţi* (cucumber salad) and *salată asortată* (mixed salad, alias a mix of tomatoes and cucumbers). Peppers are *ardei* in Romanian, mushrooms are *ciuperci* and eggs are *ouă*. Rice is *orez*. Beyond this staggering choice, dishes are generally meat-based.

Self-Catering

Every town has a central market (*piaţa centrală*), piled high with fresh fruits and vegetables, sometimes fish and dried products. Pastries and cakes are sold everywhere for no more than $0.10 a piece, with bread about $0.10 a loaf. In Bucharest and some other towns there are 24-hour shops and Western-style supermarkets. In smaller towns the old, 'don't touch – point at what you want' style of shopping still rules. Here you'll find row upon row of uninspiring pickled peas, cucumbers etc.

The Orthodox Diet

Devout Orthodox Romanians fast on Wednesday or Friday, for seven weeks before Easter, four weeks before Christmas and for two weeks before religious holidays such as the Feast of Saints Peter and Paul on 29 June and Assumption on 15 August.

Fasters adhere to a set of stringent rules: namely, that they only eat *post* (kosher) products – anything that comes directly from the soil, such as fruit, vegetables and honey. Forbidden products, categorised as *de dulce* (literally 'sweet'), include meat, milk products and eggs. During fasting periods, many restaurants in Bucharest (including Pizza Hut!) advertise *post* dishes on their menus.

Easter is the most important feast of the year in the Orthodox calendar. Traditionally a kosher lamb (a lamb that has not eaten grass) is slaughtered, every part being used in the great culinary celebration that ensues. *Drob de miel* (haggis) is made from its heart, liver, lungs and stomach. A *ciorbă de miel* (lamb soup) is made from its shoulder or leg, while *stufat de miel* (braised lamb), made with the most succulent meat, is served as the main course. The equivalent is done to a pig at Christmas.

Following a death, a *colivă* – a ring-shaped wheat cake with nuts, honey, vanilla and cinnamon – is baked to honour the deceased.

DRINKS

The region is noted for its wine, while local beer is notable for its price (about $0.50 for a half-litre). Among the best Romanian wines are Cotnari, Murfatlar, Odobeşti, Târnave and Valea Călugărească. Red wines are called *negru* and *roşu*, white wine is *vin alb*, while *sec* means dry, *dulce* is sweet and *spumos* translates as sparkling. Sweeter wines are automatically mixed with sparkling mineral water: if you want it neat ask for it *sec*. A bottle of wine in a restaurant should cost no more than $5, and substantially less in a wine shop or cellar *(vin* or *vinuri)* – the cheapest and most fun way to sample local wine. Bring your own mug or plastic bottle.

In Romania, *must* is a fresh unfermented wine available during the wine harvest. *Ţuică*, a plum brandy called *palincă* (from the Hungarian *pálinka*) in parts of Transylvania, is a fiery liqueur knocked back at the start of a meal. *Crama* refers to a wine cellar, and a *berărie* is a pub or beer hall.

In a land where wine rules, nonalcoholic drinks are unvaried. Coke, Fanta etc are sold everywhere. In May and June locals wander in the forests to collect the young green branches from fir trees, from which they make *sirop de brad*. The pines, fermented in sugar to make the syrup which is then drunk with water, are believed to contain healing properties.

Ness is an awful instant coffee made from vegetable extracts, served supersweet, tepid or cold; some nightclubs serve *Ness-coke* (Ness and Coke mixed). Many cafes also serve *cafea naturală*, coffee made the Turkish way with a thick sludge of ground coffee beans at the bottom and a generous spoonful of sugar. Unless you specifically ask, coffee and *ceai* (tea) are served black and with sugar. If you want it white ask for it *cu lapte* (with milk); without sugar, *fără zahăr*. *Apă minerală* (mineral water) is cheap and widely available in Romania.

ENTERTAINMENT

Funky bars and clubs abound in Bucharest, but outside the capital nightlife remains low-key. For most Romanians a 'night on the town' is a ţuică-fuelled sing-song around a campfire which, for travellers from the West, can be an enlightening experience and a refreshing change from life in the fast track back home.

One of Romania's unique joys lies in its folk festival calendar, some of which are listed under Public Holidays & Special Events, earlier. Classical music concerts, opera and ballet feature strongly on the arts agenda, all of them cheap and easily accessible. In cinemas, foreign films are usually screened in their original language (with Romanian sub-titles); even in Bucharest, films are rarely shown after 9 pm.

Free weekly entertainment magazines such as *Şapte Seri* (Seven Evenings) and *Timpul Libera*, the *România Libera* newspaper's free Friday pull-out, run extensive listings of what's on in the capital.

SPECTATOR SPORTS

Romanians are football (soccer) crazy. Their national team reached the quarterfinals of the 1994 World Cup, and glided through the European qualifiers for the 1998 World Cup, not losing any of its 10 matches. In Euro 2000 the Romanian side got through to the quarter finals, the final international match for soccer star Gheorghe Hagi who retired from the game after a glowing career which saw him score 35 times since 1983. Hagi was voted Romanian 'player of the century' in 1999.

Top club Steaua Bucharest forged itself a formidable international reputation by winning the European Champions' Cup in 1986. Since then, it has suffered from bribery scandals and match-fixing allegations. In 1999 and 2000 numerous 1st- and 2nd-division players' contracts were cancelled by the Romanian Soccer Federation because clubs could not afford to pay their wages. Steaua Bucharest's home ground is Steaua Stadium (☎ 01-410 7710), Blvd Ghencea 35. Dinamo Stadium (☎ 01-210 3519), Şoseaua Ştefan cel Mare 18–22, and Rapid Stadium (☎ 01-220 2149) on Calea Giuleşti, are other notable stadiums in the capital. Tickets are sold at the stadium gates.

Gold-Medal Gymnasts

Never was there such a hoo-haa in Romanian gymnastics as during the 2000 Sydney Olympic Games when **Andreea Răducan** was stripped of the much-coveted gold medal in the women's all-round competition after testing positive for pseudoephedrine (a drug inadvertently taken in a cold relief medication, according to the 16-year-old). Despite appealing, her gold was re-awarded to retiring team-mate **Simona Amânar** (the world's greatest vaulter, who landed four medals at the 1996 Olympics), while **Maria Olaru** (1999 overall world champion, also Romanian) got silver instead of bronze. Răducan, who lives and trains in Deva, was allowed to keep her other medals – a gold (team) and a silver (vault).

The last Romanian gymnast to land a gold in the coveted all-round championship was 14-year-old **Nadia Comăneci** (left) who wiped the floor at the 1976 Montreal Olympic Games, landing an unprecedented seven 10-out-of-10 scores and waltzing off with three golds, a silver and a bronze. She subsequently became the only woman to win three consecutive European Championship all-round titles and, at home, was the youngest Romanian to be awarded Ceauşescu's Hero of Socialist Labour gold medal.

Tucked double-back somersaults, 'Comăneci flips' and 'toe-on half-twists tucked-back to dismount' were all new moves pioneered by the fearless Comăneci as she flip-flopped her way to success. She retired, aged 22, in 1984 and defected five years later to the US where she was granted political asylum. In 1995 Comăneci returned to Romania to wed American gymnast Bart Conner in Ceauşescu's Palace of Parliament and exchange religious vows at Casin Monastery. In 1993 she posed in her underwear for a Times Square poster to raise cash for Romania's orphans. Today she runs a gymnastics school in Oklahoma.

MARTIN HARRIS

The Romanian Gymnastics Federation, of which Comăneci is honorary president, has a Web site at www.romaniangymnastics.ro.

Romania's women gymnasts are among the world's best, but you are unlikely to see them in action within the country.

SHOPPING

Traditional purchases in Romania include plum brandy (*ţuică*), embroidered blouses, ceramics, wooden sculptures, tablecloths and handwoven carpets. The latter are easiest to find at major tourist sights, particularly Bran Castle and Bucovina's monasteries.

Romarta stores sell glassware, textiles, women's clothing and ceramics. Pirated rock music cassettes are cheap.

Always take a plastic carrier bag with you on any shopping spree; most shops don't provide them.

Getting There & Away

AIR

Tarom (Transporturile Aeriene Române), Romania's state-owned carrier, plus scores of other airlines link Bucharest with most European cities. Most long-haul destinations still require a change of plane in another European capital.

Airports & Airlines

Tarom operates weekly flights between Bucharest's Otopeni airport and many European cities, including Amsterdam, Berlin, Budapest, Chişinău, Düsseldorf, Frankfurt, Milan, Prague, Sofia, Warsaw and Zagreb.

Additionally, it operates a handful of international flights into and out of airports in Arad in the Banat (to/from Frankfurt and Stuttgart), Constanţa on the Black Sea coast (to/from Istanbul), Satu Mare (to/from Montreal), Sibiu (to/from Munich) and Timişoara (to/from Chicago, Düsseldorf, Frankfurt,

London and New York). Year-round, Tarom runs charter flights from Arad, Bucharest, Cluj-Napoca and Timişoara to a handful of cities in Italy; flights are operated in conjunction with Viaclub (see Travel Agencies in the Bucharest chapter).

For more information contact Tarom offices:

France (☎ 01 47 42 25 42, fax 01 42 56 43 67) 38 ave de l'Opéra, F-75002 Paris
UK (☎ 020-7935 3600, fax 7487 2913, e taromlon@talk21.com) 27 New Cavendish Street, London, W1M 7RL
USA (☎ 212-687 6013/6014, fax 661 6056) 342 Madison Ave, Suite 168, New York 10173

It has many other offices or sales representatives worldwide, including in Vienna, Belgrade, Brussels, Copenhagen, Berlin, Frankfurt, Budapest, Rome, Amsterdam, Warsaw, Moscow, Stockholm and Zürich. Contact details are posted on the Tarom Web site at http://tarom.digiro.net.

Numerous other airlines fly to/from Otopeni airport, including Air France, Alitalia, Austrian Airlines, British Airways, Czech Airlines, Delta Air Lines, JAT-Yugoslavia, KLM-Royal Dutch Airlines, LOT Polish Airlines, Lufthansa Airlines, Malev-Hungarian Airlines, Olympic Airways, Swissair and Turkish Airlines.

Flights between Bucharest and Chişinău in Moldova use Bucharest's Băneasa airport, primarily a domestic airport.

For details on how to travel from the airport to/from the city centres, see Getting Around in the relevant chapters.

Buying Tickets

An air ticket alone can gouge a great slice out of anyone's budget, but stiff competition has resulted in widespread discounting. Before parting with any cash, always check the total fare, stopovers required (or allowed), the journey duration, the period of validity, cancellation penalties and any

Air Travel Glossary

Cancellation Penalties If you have to cancel or change a discounted ticket, there are often heavy penalties involved; insurance can sometimes be taken out against these penalties. Some airlines impose penalties on regular tickets as well, particularly against 'no-show' passengers.

Courier Fares Businesses often need to send urgent documents or freight securely and quickly. Courier companies hire people to accompany the package through customs and, in return, offer a discount ticket which is sometimes a phenomenal bargain. However, you may have to surrender all your baggage allowance and take only carry-on luggage.

Full Fares Airlines traditionally offer 1st class (coded F), business class (coded J) and economy class (coded Y) tickets. These days there are so many promotional and discounted fares available that few passengers pay full economy fare.

Lost Tickets If you lose your airline ticket an airline will usually treat it like a travellers cheque and, after inquiries, issue you with another one. Legally, however, an airline is entitled to treat it like cash and if you lose it then it's gone forever. Take good care of your tickets.

Onward Tickets An entry requirement for many countries is that you have a ticket out of the country. If you're unsure of your next move, the easiest solution is to buy the cheapest onward ticket to a neighbouring country or a ticket from a reliable airline which can later be refunded if you do not use it.

Open-Jaw Tickets These are return tickets where you fly out to one place but return from another. If available, this can save you backtracking to your arrival point.

Overbooking Since every flight has some passengers who fail to show up, airlines often book more passengers than they have seats. Usually excess passengers make up for the no-shows, but occasionally somebody gets 'bumped' onto the next available flight. Guess who it is most likely to be? The passengers who check in late.

Promotional Fares These are officially discounted fares, available from travel agencies or direct from the airline.

Reconfirmation If you don't reconfirm your flight at least 72 hours prior to departure, the airline may delete your name from the passenger list. Ring to find out if your airline requires reconfirmation.

Restrictions Discounted tickets often have various restrictions on them – such as needing to be paid for in advance and incurring a penalty to be altered. Others are restrictions on the minimum and maximum period you must be away.

Round-the-World Tickets RTW tickets give you a limited period (usually a year) in which to circumnavigate the globe. You can go anywhere the carrying airlines go, as long as you don't backtrack. The number of stopovers or total number of separate flights is decided before you set off and they usually cost a bit more than a basic return flight.

Transferred Tickets Airline tickets cannot be transferred from one person to another. Travellers sometimes try to sell the return half of their ticket, but officials can ask you to prove that you are the person named on the ticket. On an international flight tickets are compared with passports.

Travel Periods Ticket prices vary with the time of year. There is a low (off-peak) season and a high (peak) season, and often a low-shoulder season and a high-shoulder season as well. Usually the fare depends on your outward flight – if you depart in the high season and return in the low season, you pay the high-season fare.

other restrictions. Better-known travel agents where you may pay slightly more than a rock-bottom fare in return for security and peace of mind include US-based Council Travel (www.counciltravel.com), STA Travel (www.sta-travel.com), Canada-based Travel CUTS (www.travelcuts.com), Irish-based USIT (www.usit.ie) and the French/Belgian-based Wasteels (www.voyages-wasteels.fr), which has offices in Bucharest and Braşov.

Student & Youth Fares Tarom offers special youth fares to people aged under 25 on its European and transatlantic flights, and aged under 24 on its weekly flights to/from Tel Aviv. Youth tickets, though often more expensive than a standard return, are valid for one year and subject to no restrictions. Students aged 24 to 31 years are likewise eligible for youth fares. You have to show a document proving your date of birth or a valid International Student Identity Card (ISIC) when buying your ticket.

Courier Flights Courier flights are a bargain if you're lucky enough to find one. Air-freight companies expedite delivery of urgent items by sending them with you as your baggage allowance. You can bring along a carry-on bag, but that's all. In return, you get a steeply discounted ticket.

These flights are occasionally advertised in the newspapers, or you could contact air-freight companies listed in the phone book. *Travel Unlimited* (PO Box 1058, Allston, MA 02134, USA) is a monthly travel newsletter ($25 per year) based in the USA that publishes many courier flight deals from destinations worldwide. Another possibility (for US residents) is the International Association of Air Travel Couriers (IAATC; ☎ 561-582 8320) with a Web site at www.courier.org.

Travellers with Special Needs
Most international airlines can cater to people with special needs – travellers with disabilities, people with young children and even children travelling alone. Travellers with special dietary preferences (such as vegetarian or kosher) can request appropriate meals with advance notice. If you are travelling in a wheelchair, most international airports can provide an escort from check-in desk to plane where needed; ramps, lifts and toilets are available.

Many airlines – including Tarom – allow babies aged up to two to fly for 10% of an adult fare. International airlines often provide nappies (diapers), tissues, talcum and all the other paraphernalia needed to keep babies clean, dry and half-happy.

Children aged between two and 12 years pay 50% of the standard adult fare on Tarom flights.

Central & Eastern Europe
Tarom flies six times weekly between Bucharest and Budapest. A single/return fare (maximum stay one month) is $198/211. A youth fare (under 25) with no restrictions (valid for one year) is $102/210. Malev-Hungarian Airlines runs a daily flight to/from Bucharest and the Hungarian capital.

Other Central and Eastern European cities on Tarom's flight schedule include Warsaw ($204/269 single/return, daily except Saturday), Sofia (three times weekly) and Prague (twice weekly).

Czech Airlines and LOT Polish Airlines also fly to their home capitals.

Tarom and Aeroflot code-share on a twice-weekly flight to/from Moscow.

Turkey
Tarom operates a daily Bucharest-Istanbul flight that stops in Constanţa on Wednesday and Sunday, May to mid-September. Single/return fares from either city are $131/188. Turkish Airlines also flies this route.

The UK & Ireland
There are numerous ways of getting to Bucharest from the UK and a continuous price war rages between the major airlines. The cheapest options include flying from London's Heathrow or Gatwick to Bucharest with Air France via Paris, Austrian Airlines via Vienna, KLM-Royal Dutch Airlines via Amsterdam, Lufthansa Airlines via Frankfurt or Swissair via Zürich. A return (with

Saturday night stay) usually costs between UK£210 and UK£310.

British Airways and Tarom both have direct London-Bucharest flights. Single/return fares fluctuate wildly. At the time of research a return fare with Tarom was UK£189/169 for a weekday/weekend departure, including a Saturday night stay (maximum stay one month). Its full flexible youth fare equivalent (valid one year) was a pricey UK£330.

Tarom also runs a twice-weekly London-Timişoara flight and a flight once a week between Bucharest and Dublin.

Continental Europe
Bucharest is well linked with all the major European capitals. Western European destinations are also served by regional airports in Arad in the Banat (to/from Frankfurt and Stuttgart twice weekly), Sibiu (to/from Munich four times a week) and Timişoara (to/from Düsseldorf and Frankfurt twice weekly).

Tarom and Viaclub operate charter flights year-round between Romania's regional airports and Italy's Ancona (from Bucharest and Arad), Bologna (Bucharest and Cluj-Napoca), Treviso (Bucharest, Arad and Timişoara) and Verona (Bucharest, Arad, Oradea and Timişoara). All these flights run once or twice weekly and single/return fares for flights originating in Bucharest cost $220/290 (maximum stay three months) or $310/382 (maximum stay six months). Departures from Arad, Oradea and Timişoara are about $10/20 higher. No youth or student fares are available, but children aged two to 12 get a 50% discount.

The USA & Canada
The flight options across the North Atlantic, the world's busiest long-haul air corridor, are bewildering. The *New York Times, LA Times, Chicago Tribune* and *San Francisco Chronicle* all have weekly travel sections where you can find travel agents' ads galore. Council Travel (toll-free ☎ 800-226 8624), with a Web site at www.counciltravel.com, and STA (toll-free ☎ 800-777 0112), online at www.sta-travel.com, both have

offices in major cities. The best bargain-hunting agency in Canada is Travel CUTS (☎ 888-835 2887), which has offices in major Canadian cities and a Web site at www.travelcuts.com.

Tarom operates twice-weekly direct flights between Bucharest and Chicago, and three times weekly (four in summer) between Bucharest and New York. The latter route cost as little as $500 return at the time of research. Once a week, the New York flight stops in Satu Mare, as does one of the national airline's twice-weekly flights to/from Montreal in Canada.

Australia & New Zealand
STA Travel (☎ 131 776 Australia-wide, ☎ 09-309 0458 in New Zealand), with a Web site at www.statravel.com.au, and Flight Centre (☎ 131 600 Australia-wide, ☎ 09-309 6171 in New Zealand), with a Web site at www.flightcentre.com.au, are major dealers in cheap air fares.

From Australia, expect to pay from A$1499 to A$1699 for a return fare during the low season. High-season fares range from A$1949 to A$2279. Swissair, Lauda Air and Qantas all have some good fare deals. From New Zealand, count on around NZ$2399 for a return low-season fare from Auckland with either Swissair or Qantas.

LAND
Train
Travelling by train is one of the most interesting ways of reaching Romania. This applies even more so with Moldova, where train travel is the most economical means of getting there. Most travellers fly or take a train to Bucharest, from where you can take an overnight sleeper to Chişinău in Moldova.

If you intend to do a lot of train travel around Europe, consider purchasing the Thomas Cook European Timetable, updated monthly with a listing of schedules. It covers destinations as far east as Moscow. Single issues cost about UK£11 from Thomas Cook Publishing (☎ 01733-503571, fax 503596, ℮ publishing-sales@thomascook.com) in the UK.

Rail Passes

When considering a rail pass, bear in mind that travel in Romania is cheap – depending how far and frequently you intend travelling, buying train tickets while in the country can be more economical than a pass.

Romania is included in the Wasteels/BIJ (Billets Internationales de Jeunesse) ticket network too. Student and youth travel offices abroad and some travel agencies sell tickets and can provide you with further information. Train passes and onward discounted tickets are sold at offices of Wasteels at Gara de Nord in Bucharest and Braşov train station. Information is online at www.wasteelstravel.ro.

The Euro-Domino and Inter-Rail passes are only available to those who have been residents in Europe for at least six consecutive months immediately prior to date of purchase. Anyone can invest in a Balkan Flexipass.

No rail passes or discounted youth fares are available for Moldova.

Euro-Domino Pass

This pass can be used within Romania for three to eight consecutive days or non-consecutive over a one-month period in 2nd class. Adult versions cost UK£29/37/53/69 for three/four/six/eight days and passes for those aged under 26 cost UK£21/27/39/51. Travellers who intend railing it around neighbouring countries can buy individual, country-specific passes to add on to the Romanian version. A Hungarian equivalent, for example, for three to eight consecutive days of travel within Hungary costs UK£32/40/57/75 (UK£24/30/42/54 for those aged under 26). Passes do not include seat or couchette reservations.

A Euro-Domino pass for use in Romania *must* be bought prior to your departure; it cannot be bought in Romania, although passes for use in other countries (eg, Hungary, Yugoslavia or Bulgaria) can.

Inter-Rail Pass

This pass allows you to travel in 29 European countries organised into eight zones; Romania is grouped in zone H with Bulgaria, Yugoslavia and Macedonia. Hungary is grouped together with the Czech and Slovak Republics, Poland and Croatia in zone D; and Turkey is in zone G with Italy, Greece and Slovenia. For 22 days of unlimited 2nd-class travel in one zone, the cost is UK£129/179 for those aged under/over 26. More expensive two-zone passes are valid for one month and cost UK£169/235 (UK£195/269 for three zones). You also get 50% off rail travel from your home country to your zone(s) and between adjacent zones.

Balkan Flexipass

The regional Balkan Flexipass scheme – available to all ages and nationalities – offers unlimited travel for five, 10 or 15 days in a one-month period around Romania, Bulgaria, Yugoslavia, Greece, Macedonia and Turkey. Passes include 1st-class travel and can be bought upon arrival in any of the specified countries. In Bucharest you can purchase a Balkan Flexipass at the central CFR office (☎ 314 5528), Str Domniţa Anastasia 10–14. At the time of research a five/10/15-day pass cost $161/280/336. Passes do not include couchette reservations.

Ticket Reservations International train tickets are rarely sold at train stations, but rather at CFR (Romanian State Railways) offices in town (look for the Agenţie de Voiaj CFR signs) or Wasteels offices. Tickets must be bought at least two hours prior to departure.

Those travelling on an Inter-Rail pass still need to make seat reservations ($2 to $4) on express trains within Romania. Even if you're not travelling with a rail pass, practically all international trains require a reservation (automatically included in tickets purchased in Romania). If you already have a ticket, you may be able to make reservations at the station an hour before departure, though it's preferable to do so at a CFR office at least one day in advance.

Western Europe The overnight *Pannonia Expres* train links Munich with Vienna, Budapest and Bucharest, stopping en route at Arad in Banat; Deva, Alba Iulia, Mediaş, Sighişoara, Braşov, Predeal and Sinaia in Transylvania; Ploieşti in Wallachia; and Buzău, Brăila and Galaţi in Moldavia. It departs Munich at 11.15 pm and Vienna at 4.29 am, arriving in Budapest-Keleti (714km) at 8.30 am and in Bucharest at 11.15 pm.

On the return journey, the *Pannonia Expres* departs from Bucharest every morning at 7.05 am. In Budapest, a couple of carriages are unhitched and attached to a Prague-bound train which stops in Bratislava en route; this train departs Budapest at 8.40 pm, Bratislava at 11.55 pm, and arrives in Prague the next morning at 5.31 am.

The daily Bucharest-Venice service (32 hours) stops in Zagreb and Ljubljana en route to Italy. Another great rail journey is Bucharest-Paris. Each week on Wednesday and Thursday, a luxurious sleeping car is attached to the *Muntenia*, which departs Bucharest at 12.20 am. In Budapest, the car is transferred to the *Orient Express* to continue its westbound voyage via Munich and Stuttgart. The train pulls into Paris 34 hours later at 10.22 am.

To get between Romania and other Western European cities, change trains in Budapest.

Hungary The Budapest-Bucharest train journey (873km) takes around 12 hours. To/from Arad in Romania's Banat, it is a mere 28km to the Hungarian border town of Lököshaza, from where it is a further 225km (4½ hours) to Budapest. It is not cheap to travel between the two countries. At the time of research a 1st/2nd-class Bucharest-Budapest single fare was $44/30 ($58/40 return) on an express international train. A single 2nd-class Arad-Budapest fare was $21, Oradea-Budapest $20.

The cheapest way to do this journey is to cross Romania or Hungary on a local train to the nearest border town, then get another local train over the border. Two daily local Hungarian trains shuttle between Oradea and Budapest's Nyugati train station (four hours, 249km). Reservations aren't required, but in Romania try to buy an open Oradea-Budapest ticket ($20) at a CFR office well in advance. If this is impossible, board the train at Episcopia Bihor, following the instructions given in the Oradea section of the Crişana & Banat chapter. Arad is also served by local trains to/from Hungary.

International daily trains between Bucharest and Budapest include the *Dacia Expres*; the *Pannonia Expres* which continues to Munich and Vienna; and the *Ister* and *Traianus*. In addition, there is the daily *Muntenia* between Galaţi and Budapest.

There are also direct Budapest trains from Baia Mare and Satu Mare in Maramureş; Cluj-Napoca and Târgu Mureş in northern Transylvania; and Constanţa on the Black Sea coast. The daily *Ovidius* from Constanţa stops at Bucharest and then takes a southern route via Craiova, Drobeta-Turnu Severin and Băile Herculane. See the individual chapters for details of departures for all these trains.

Yugoslavia The *Bucureşti* express train runs daily between Belgrade-Dunav and Bucharest (12 to 13 hours, 693km) via Timişoara, Băile Herculane, Drobeta-Turnu Severin and Craiova. If you can't get a ticket or reservation for this train, you can get an unreserved early morning train from Timişoara Nord to Jimbolia (39km), where you change to another local train to Kikinda, Yugoslavia.

The daily *Bucureşti* leaves Bucharest at 3.42 pm and arrives in Belgrade at 5.45 am. Eastbound, it departs at 11.20 pm, arriving in Bucharest the following morning at 11.32 am. At the time of writing, the 2nd-class single fare was $14 (plus $9.50/16 for a couchette in a six/three-bunk carriage). Travel in a 1st-class sleeper with two bunks costs $44.

Bulgaria & Turkey The train service between Romania and Bulgaria is slow and crowded but cheap. Between Sofia and Bucharest (509km) there are two daily nameless trains, both of which stop in Ruse. The daytime/overnight train departs from Bucharest at 12.10/7.45 pm, arriving in Sofia at 11.23 pm/5.48 am. A 1st/2nd-class fare costs about $30/21. Sleepers are only available on the overnight train; buy your ticket ($39/27 in 1st/2nd class) well in advance to guarantee yourself a bunk for the night.

The overnight train journey from Bucharest to Istanbul (803km) on the daily *Bosfor* (previously called the *Bucureşti-Istanbul Expres*) theoretically takes around 17¼ hours. It does not go via Sofia but rather via eastern Bulgaria. A single 2nd-class fare in a seat/six-bunk couchette costs $21/25, and a sweet night's sleep in a 1st/2nd-class three-bunk sleeper is $40/28. The train leaves from Bucharest at 2.45 pm and is scheduled to arrive in Istanbul at 7 am the following morning (but has been known to arrive as late as noon).

Moldova, Ukraine & Beyond From Bucharest, the overnight *Prietenia* (literally 'friendship') trundles its way to Chişinău. This Soviet-built train is the most economical method of getting to Moldova. It departs from Bucharest at 9.46 pm daily and arrives in Chişinău (591km) the following morning at 10.38 am. Westbound, it pulls out of Chişinău at 5.30 pm, pulling into Bucharest at 5.46 am. A single fare in a 1st/2nd-class sleeper costs $22/11.

In both directions, the train stops at the Romanian-Moldovan border at Ungheni for a two-hour bogie change. Waking up is no problem. The train lurches, vibrates and clanks while the under-carriages are changed to fit the broader gauge tracks of the former Soviet Union. Every carriage is lifted 2m off the ground by a crane so rail workers can change each bogie by hand. Passengers are forbidden to get off the train during this bizarre operation.

Between Romania and Ukraine, there is a daily Bucharest-Moscow train which goes via Kyiv. A second train, the Sofia-Moscow

Bulgaria Expres takes a different route through western Ukraine to Chernivtsi (Cernăuţi in Romanian), departing Bucharest at 8.05 am, Chernivtsi at 9.22 pm, then continuing to Kyiv and Moscow. Total Bucharest-Moscow journey time is 46 hours and a single 2nd-class fare in a sleeper is $46 (no 1st-class carriages). At Chernivtsi some carriages of this train are unhitched to take an alternative route along the eastern realm of Eastern Europe. This route goes via Lviv, Baranovici and Lida (Belarus), Vilnius (Lithuania) and Daugavpils (Latvia) to St Petersburg. Travelling time between Bucharest and St Petersburg (2608km) is 55 hours.

Poland The aptly named Bucharest-Warsaw *Carpaţi* crosses the Carpathians twice; first in Romania between Bucharest (departing 8.35 pm) and Arad (5.38 am). The train then continues through eastern Hungary to Kosice, Slovakia, where it crosses the Carpathians (Tatra Mountains) into Kraków (7.55 pm). It arrives in Warsaw (1645km) 26½ hours later at 11.04 pm. A 1st/2nd-class fare is $84/56 ($113/75 in a 1st/2nd-class sleeper).

Bus

With an unbeatable train service linking Romania to Western Europe and Russia, there is little reason to travel to/from Romania by bus. A number of private bus companies operate daily buses between Romania and Germany (from where there are connections to the rest of Western Europe), but fares rarely compete with the inexpensive comfort offered by trains.

The exception is the trip to Istanbul, where the bus is marginally cheaper ($20/40 single/return) but usually substantially faster (taking 11 to 14 hours) than the train. There are four to eight daily buses between Bucharest and Istanbul.

Tickets are sold from ticketing agencies in Romania's larger cities; see the relevant Getting There & Away sections.

Western Europe Eurolines, with a Web site at www.eurolines.ro, is an association of companies that together form Europe's largest international bus network, linking cities such as Bucharest, Braşov and Sighişoara with points all over Western and Central Europe and Scandinavia. In Romania, Eurolines is represented by Touring, which has its head office in Bucharest (☎ 01-210 0890, 210 0812, ⓔ office@touring.ro), Blvd Alexandru Ioan Cuza 5a, and 15 offices across the country that sell tickets and make reservations for Eurolines buses, including:

Arad
(☎ 057-281 403) Str Unirii 5–7
(☎ 057-250 397, ⓔ arad@eurolines.ro) Blvd Revoluţiei 39-41

Braşov
(☎ 068-474 008, ⓔ brasov@eurolines.ro) Piaţa Sfatului 18

Bucharest
(☎ 01-230 3661, ⓔ touring.rez@eurolines.ro) Str Sofia 26
(☎/fax 01-230 0370, ⓔ touring.ankara@eurolines.ro) Str Ankara 6
(☎ 01-211 7193, ⓔ turism@touring.ro) Calea Dorobanţilor 35–37

Cluj-Napoca
(☎/fax 064-431 961) Blvd 21 Decembrie 54–56

Constanţa
(☎/fax 041-662 704) Str Ştefan cel Mare 71

Iaşi
(☎/fax 032-217 822, ⓔ iasi@eurolines.ro) Piaţa Unirii 2

Sibiu
(☎/fax 069-212 248, ⓔ sibiu@eurolines.ro) Str Fratii Grachi 20

Timişoara
(☎ 056-190 931, ⓔ timisoara@eurolines.ro) Blvd Republicii 6

Touring operates a daily Eurolines bus to Frankfurt and numerous other cities in Germany, from where there are numerous and frequent connections to all the European capitals. Straight-through tickets for your final destination are sold in Romania. Some routes offer a 10% to 15% discount for those aged under 26 or over 60, although many only offer a discount on tickets from Germany onwards – making it cheaper to buy a ticket from Romania only as far as Germany, where you can then pick up a discounted fare. Children aged four to 12 get a 50% discount and those aged under four pay just 20% of the full adult fare. Returns cost substantially less than two one-way tickets.

At the time of research the daily Frankfurt/ Hamburg bus departed from Bucharest at 3 am; picked up passengers en route in Ploieşti, Braşov, Târgu Mureş, Sighişoara, Mediaş, Sibiu, Bistriţa, Cluj-Napoca, Deva, Timişoara and Arad; and arrived in Frankfurt/ Hamburg the following day at 1.30/8.30 pm. Several days a week, the bus originates in Constanţa (departing at 10.30 pm and arriving in Bucharest at 3 am). A single/return Bucharest-Frankfurt fare costs DM190/345 ($95/170) including 40kg of luggage. Every kilogram over this limit costs an additional DM2 ($1).

The Eurolines Pass covering bus travel between 48 European cities can be used to get to/from Romania. A 30-day pass in mid/high season costs €290/370 (€232/ 296 for those aged four to 25).

Other bus companies operating daily services between Romania and Germany include TransEuropa, with a Web site at www.transeuropa.ro, and Double T, which operates additional buses to/from Italy ($120/190 single/return, five times weekly) and Switzerland ($120/190, twice a week). Ticketing agencies for these and other companies are listed in the relevant chapters of this book.

Hungary To/from Hungary, the cheapest option is the Hungarian public system, known as Volánbusz (☎ 1-317 2562 in Budapest). There are weekly services between Budapest's Népstadion bus station and Oradea, Cluj-Napoca, Arad, Bucharest, Timişoara, Târgu Secuiesc, Miercurea Ciuc and Târgu Mureş. Sample one-way fares to Budapest include: from Braşov ($15), Oradea ($5), Târgu Mureş ($6.50) and Bucharest ($20, 18 hours). Fares originating in Hungary are more expensive.

Other cities in Romania which are served by cheaper public buses to Hungary include Arad, Braşov, Cluj-Napoca, Deva, Gheorgheni, Miercurea Ciuc, Satu Mare, Târgu Mureş and Timişoara. A single fare is no more than $10.

Private bus companies – about 30% more expensive – operate buses to Budapest and other cities from various towns in Romania. Ticketing agencies and schedules are listed in the relevant chapters in this book.

Yugoslavia Cheap private buses aimed more at local traders than foreign tourists operate daily from Drobeta-Turnu Severin to Negotin and Pojarevat in Yugoslavia. A single fare costs $7. See the Drobeta-Turnu Severin section in the Wallachia chapter for details.

Turkey Buses galore trundle the 804km between Bucharest and Istanbul in 11 to 14 hours. Coaches tend to be of the modern Mercedes variety these days, but border crossings remain tiresome.

The leading bus companies, including Toros Trans and Ortadoğu Tur, have offices in Bucharest as well as other large Romanian cities like Braşov, Piteşti and Craiova. From Bucharest, all these companies operate four to eight buses daily to/from Istanbul. A single/return fare costs $20/40. Buses are less frequent from other cities (see relevant chapters for details).

Moldova & Ukraine There is a daily bus from Bucharest via Ploieşti to Chişinău (Kishinev in Russian; 591km), departing from Gara de Nord at 6 am daily. A single/return ticket costs $10/20; journey time is around 12 hours. A weekly bus departs from Bucharest's Gara de Nord to Chernivtsi in Ukraine (called Cernăuţi in Romanian) at 4 pm Wednesday. A single fare is $20.

From Moldavia, there are regular Suceava-Chernivtsi and Rădăuţi-Chernivtsi buses. There is a daily bus from Suceava to Chişinău in Moldova and daily buses between Iaşi and Chişinău. See the regional chapters for details.

Car & Motorcycle

For information and tips on driving once you're in Romania and Moldova, see the Getting Around chapter. Drivers and motorcyclists need the vehicle's registration papers, liability insurance and a driving licence. Contact your local automobile association for details about all documentation, or alternatively contact the national motoring association in Romania, the Automobil Clubul Român (ACR; ☎ 01-222 1553, fax 222 1552, ℮ acr@acr.ro), Str Tache Ionescu 27, 70154 Bucharest 22. It has a Web site at www.acr.ro.

In Romania liability insurance for drivers is compulsory, but payouts are low, while in Moldova it is not needed at all. So, either way, you really need comprehensive insurance in case of damage done by another driver. The Green Card (a routine extension of domestic motor insurance to cover most European countries) is valid in Romania, but *not* in Moldova, so you must organise insurance separately. Insurance policies with limited compensation rates can be bought at the Romanian borders.

Border Crossings When crossing the border by car, expect long queues at Romanian checkpoints, particularly on weekends. Carry food and water for the wait. Don't even consider trying to bribe a Romanian official and beware of unauthorised people charging dubious 'ecology', 'disinfectant' or other dodgy taxes at the border. Ask for a receipt if you are unsure.

All the following border crossings are open 24 hours, with the exception of those to/from Ukraine and Moldova, which open 8 am to 8 pm.

Hungary Romania shares border crossings with Hungary at Petea (11km north-west of Satu Mare), Borş (14km north-west of Oradea), Vărşand (66km north of Arad) and Nădlac (between Szeged and Arad). The borders at Petea, Borş and Nădlac are generally the busiest as they connect with major highways to Budapest.

Yugoslavia From Romania, you can cross into Yugoslavia at Jimbolia (45km west of Timişoara), Moraviţa (mid-way between Timişoara and Belgrade), Naidăş (120km east of Belgrade) and at Porţile de Fier (10km west of Drobeta-Turnu Severin).

Bulgaria You can cross at Calafat (opposite Vidin), Giurgiu (opposite Ruse), at the Ostrov-Silistra crossing (opposite Călăraşi in Romania), Negru Vodă (37km north-east of Tolbuhin) and at Vama Veche (10km south of Mangalia).

Giurgiu is the main border crossing with a 4km-long toll bridge across the Danube (inaccessible to pedestrians) and ferries that plough their way across the Danube every half-hour or so. The border crossing at Calafat also involves a short ferry trip, with car ferries crossing the Danube hourly year-round.

The Ostrov border is on the southern bank of the Danube and practically adjoins the Bulgarian border town of Silistra. To get to Ostrov, you have to cross the Danube by ferry at the small port 8km south of Călăraşi. Details on all these crossing are listed under Getting There & Away in the relevant city section of the Wallachia chapter.

Moldova To get to/from Moldova, cross the border at Albiţa (65km south-east of Iaşi), Sculeni (24km north of Ungheni), Sânca Costeşti (60km east of Botoşani) or at Oancea (50km north of Galaţi).

Most commercial traffic uses the Albiţa crossing. Public buses between Romania and Moldova pass through the Sculeni border. Sânca Costeşti and Oancea are very small borders where foreigners might get hassled by bureaucratic border guards. For more information, see Getting There & Away in the Moldova chapter.

Ukraine From Romania, there is one border crossing into Ukraine at Siret (45km north of Suceava on the main road to Chernivtsi). Expect to queue.

From Moldova, there are several border crossings into Ukraine. The Pervomaisc border, 30km south-east of Tiraspol in Transdniestr, is the main Chişinău-Odesa (183km) crossing. Volume of traffic coupled with border guards makes crossing here a nightmare; expect to wait.

The border 20km north-east of Dubăsari on the main road to Kyiv attracts less traffic

since the direct M21 route from Chişinău was shut (see the Getting Around section of the Moldova chapter). The border crossing 11km north of Soroca is closed to foreigners. Cross the border at Otaci, 50km northwest of Soroca. Neither of these borders involves passing through Transdniestr.

SEA & RIVER

There are passenger and car ferries year-round into Bulgaria from Calafat and Giurgiu in Romania. See the Border Crossings section earlier.

To get from Ostrov, Romania, to Silistra in Bulgaria, you have to make a 20-minute ferry crossing from Călăraşi. See the Crişana & Banat chapter for details.

ORGANISED TOURS

Travel agencies abroad specialising in tours to Romania include:

Australia & New Zealand
Eastern Europe Travel Bureau
(☎ 02-9262 1144, fax 9262 4479) 75 King St, Sydney, NSW 2000
(☎ 03-9600 0299, fax 9670 1793) 343 Little Collins St, Melbourne 3000 – Eastern Europe specialists and agents for Tarom, with offices in other state capitals too
Adventures Abroad (☎ 09-273 9366, fax 273 3265, e adventures-abroad@xtra.co.nz) 6 Glassonby Road, Howick, Auckland 1705 – grand four-week Eastern European tours taking in Romania and its neighbouring countries; offices in the UK and USA too
Web site: www.adventures-abroad.com

UK
Discover Transylvania (☎ 01704-823 442, fax 822 915, e travel@enzia.com) 67 Highsands Ave, Rufford, Lancs L40 1TE – offers activity-based tours including hiking, kayaking, caving and photo safaris
Web site: www.enzia.com
Explore Worldwide (☎ 01252-760 000, fax 760 001, e info@exploreworldwide.com) 1 Frederick Street, Aldershot, Hants GU11 1LQ – 12-day 'village folklore' walking tour of Romania, taking in Transylvania, Maramureş, Bucovina's painted monasteries and the natural wonders of the Danube Delta wetland, costing UK£625/645 in low/high season
Web site: www.exploreworldwide.com

Footloose Adventure Travel (☎ 01943-604 030, fax 604 070) 105 Leeds Rd, Ilkley, West Yorkshire, LS29 8EG – organises walking tours through Transylvania and the Carpathian Mountains, among others
Web site: www.footlooseadventure.co.uk

Over the Wall (☎ 01903-529 333, fax 529 007, ⓔ info@otwtravel.co.uk) 59/61 Lyndhurst Rd, Worthing, West Sussex, BN11 2DB – offers small cause-related tours such as mountain hikes and minibus tours, with a large percentage of tour profits going to Romanian charities
Web site: www.otwtravel.co.uk

Romania Travel Centre (☎ 01892-515 524, fax 540 727, ⓔ romania@packyourbags.com) Pack Your Bags, 39 Mount Pleasant, Tunbridge Wells, Kent TN1 1PN – discount centre for flights to Romania; spa tours, horse-riding in the Carpathians and one-week 'Wolves & Bears of Transylvania' expeditions costing UK£646
Web site: www.packyourbags.com/romania

USA

Quest Tours (☎ 800-621 8687, fax 503-777 0224, ⓔ tours@romtour.com) 8455 SE Foster Road, Portland, OR-97266 – Dracula tours, monastery trips and spa accommodation
Web sites: www.romtour.com

Transylvania (☎ 925-229 4810, ⓔ info@undiscoveredlands.com) 1350 Arnold Dr, Suit 102-T, Martinez, CA – offering spooky Dracula tours
Web site: www.draculatours.com

LEAVING THE REGION

There is no departure tax when leaving Romania or Moldova.

Although the old 'exit card' *(talon de iesire)* check has reputedly been scrapped, there's still a chance you may be asked to show this card on departure – see Visas & Documents in the Facts for the Visitor chapter for details.

Getting Around

Getting around Romania is fairly painless, Moldova less so.

In both countries, travelling is traditionally viewed as a joyous yet hazardous occupation, be it by horse-drawn cart, ferry or on foot. Romanians frequently bless themselves with a holy Sign of the Cross as a bus or train pulls out of the station. Romanians are also the first to wish foreign travellers a cheery *Drum Bun!* (Good Road!).

AIR

State-owned carrier Tarom, with a Web site at http://tarom.digiro.net, has an extensive network of domestic flights to/from Bucharest. Many flights to Constanţa only operate in July and August, but you can fly out of Bucharest's Băneasa domestic airport to most other parts of the country year-round. Flights (three to 12 weekly) include to/from Arad, Baia Mare, Cluj-Napoca, Constanţa, Iaşi via Suceava, Oradea, Satu Mare, Sibiu, Târgu Mureş and Timişoara. To many cities there is an early morning and evening flight.

Airfares are expensive, with both foreigners and Romanians paying the same price. At the time of research, a one-way Bucharest–Cluj-Napoca fare was $33; Bucharest-Constanţa was $50. Other fares are quoted in the relevant sections of the regional chapters. Return fares offer no saving; they are double the price of a single. Children aged two to 12 years get a 50% reduction; those aged under two pay 10% of a full adult fare. Tarom does not offer any youth discounts on domestic flights.

Flights are rarely full and you can usually buy a ticket just hours before departure. Tarom offices at regional airports and in city centres sell tickets. Only 10kg of luggage is carried free, after which you pay 1% of your air fare for each kilogram overweight.

TRAIN

Rail has long been the most popular way of travelling around Romania. Căile Ferate Române (CFR; Romanian State Railways) runs trains over 11,106km of track, providing a frequent service to most cities, towns and larger villages in the country. By the end of 2001, high-speed trains will travel at 200km/h on some segments of track, thanks to an EU and EBRD (European Bank for Reconstruction and Development) grant awarded to Romania in 2000 for it to upgrade its rail infrastructure.

The national train timetable *(mersul trenurilor)* is published in book form each May and is sold for $1.50 from CFR offices. Before setting foot in Romania, you can view the complete schedule on the CFR Web site at www.cfr.ro.

Sosire means arrivals and *plecare* is departures. On posted timetables, the number of the platform from which each train departs is listed under *linia*.

Types of Train

In Romania there are five different types of train, all of which travel at different speeds, offer varying levels of comfort and charge different fares for the same destination.

The cheapest trains are local *personal* trains. These trains are slow – so slow that they travel with their doors open enabling passengers to leap on or off while the train is still in motion. Personal trains serve rural routes, stopping at every imaginable station en route – fantastic if you want to enjoy the scenery but a pain in the neck if you want to get somewhere fast. Seats on these trains are not numbered, meaning it is a free-for-all to grab a seat when the train pulls into the station. Personal trains are always crowded and offer the cheapest tickets. Bring your own food and water.

Accelerat trains are faster, hence more expensive and less crowded. Seat reservations are obligatory and automatic when you buy your ticket.

There is little difference between *rapid* and *expres* trains. Both travel at a fair speed and serve international routes as well as

ROMANIAN & MOLDOVAN RAILWAYS

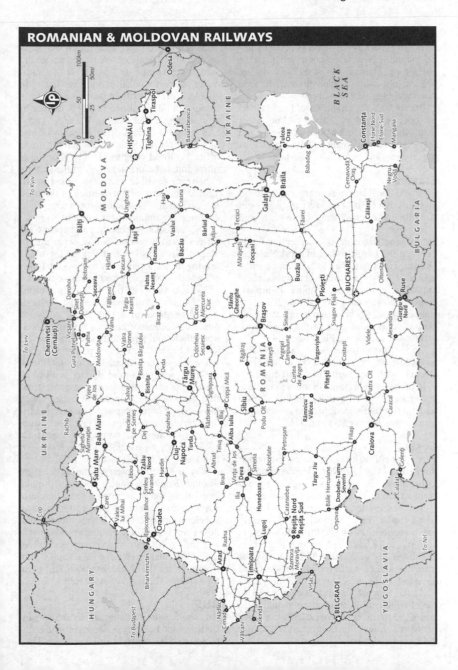

cities within Romania. Their speeds and fares are generally the same as those of accelerat trains. Seat reservations are likewise obligatory. These trains often have dining cars; a meal with a main meat dish, side salad and beer will cost about $4.

Pricier *Inter-City* trains should be avoided by those on a budget. They travel no faster than other trains (other than personal) and serve the same destinations but are twice as expensive – and twice as comfortable.

Classes

First and 2nd-class tickets are available on all trains. Inter-City 1st-class passengers get complimentary chocolates, clean seats and free coffee.

Sleepers *(vagon de dormit)* are available between Bucharest and Arad, Cluj-Napoca, Oradea, Timişoara, Tulcea and other points, and are a good way to cut accommodation expenses. First-class sleeping compartments generally have two berths, 2nd-class sleepers generally have four berths and 2nd-class couchettes have six berths. Book these well in advance at a CFR office.

On overnight trains between Bucharest and Chişinău in Moldova, only 2nd-class sleepers with four berths are available.

If you're caught riding in the wrong class you must pay a $6 penalty. Riding a train with no ticket at all warrants an on-the-spot fine costing between $8 and $11.

Costs

Fares for all Romanian trains comprise three parts – the basic fare, calculated on the kilometres you are travelling; a speed/comfort supplement; and a seat reservation.

Seat reservations are obligatory for all trains (apart from personal). You usually pay a supplement of $0.50 to $3, which is automatically included in the total fare when you buy your ticket. If you miss your train the ticket is valid for 24 hours but you have to buy a new seat reservation.

At the time of research it cost $0.85 to travel 100km in 1st class on a personal train and $2.95 to travel the equivalent on a rapid or expres. Inter-City trains cost $5.60 per 100km in 2nd class.

Buying Tickets

Tickets are sold in advance for all trains except local personal ones. Advance tickets are sold at an Agenţie de Voiaj CFR – a train-ticket office found in every city centre. In smaller towns the office is often at the train station. In this book we list CFR offices in city sections under Getting There & Away.

Most CFR offices open weekdays only; the odd few open Saturday. When the ticket office is closed you have to buy your ticket immediately before departure at the station. Whenever possible, buy your ticket in advance. This saves time queuing at the train station and also guarantees you a seat. Tickets for some trains do get sold out.

Theoretically you can buy tickets at CFR offices up to two hours before departure. In reality many do not sell tickets for trains leaving the same day so try to buy your ticket at least the day before you intend to travel.

You can only buy tickets at train stations two hours – and in some cases just one hour – before departure. Get there early as queues can be horrendous. At major stations there are separate ticket lines for 1st and 2nd class; you may opt for 1st class when you see how much shorter that line is.

Often several trains depart within 30 minutes of each other for the same destination, so note your train number, then check the carriage number (posted on metal signs on every train carriage). Your reservation ticket lists the code number of your train along with your assigned carriage *(vagon)* and seat *(locul)*.

If you have an international ticket right through Romania, you're allowed to make stops along the route but you must purchase a reservation ticket each time you reboard an accelerat or rapid train. If the international ticket was issued in Romania, you must also pay the expres train supplement each time.

For information on rail passes valid within Romania, see the boxed text 'Rail Passes' in the Getting There & Away chapter.

BUS

Bus services in Romania are snail-slow, infrequent and horribly underdeveloped compared to the country's rail network. They are generally used for serving outlying villages in more rural areas and are also handy to hop between resorts along the Black Sea coast. Many buses embark on their return journey immediately, rendering many services useless for day trips.

Heating systems that function or can be moderated and windows that do not leak in rainy weather are rare commodities on long-distance buses. Unless you are a masochist, opt for one of the numerous private buses that have sprung up in recent years to travel between cities.

The handwritten schedules posted in bus stations are often incomplete or out of date, so always ask at the ticket window for details. Buses in transit are written on the timetable in a different colour (usually red). Many services do not run on weekends so check the timetable carefully.

You usually have to purchase your ticket before boarding at a bus station (autogară). You can reserve a seat by buying a ticket the day before and arriving early at the station.

Travelling by bus is cheap although fares (calculated per kilometre) are upped slightly each month. A list of some destinations, their distance in kilometres, and price can be found in most bus stations. Look for a scrappy piece of A4 paper – handwritten – stuck on the wall. At the time of research, it cost approximately $0.25/0.50 to travel 6/15km and $2/3 to travel 100/200km.

CAR & MOTORCYCLE

Don't attempt to drive in Romania unless your car is in good shape and has been serviced recently. Repair shops are common but, unless you're driving a Renault (the same as Romania's Dacia) or a Citroën (the basis of Romania's Oltcit model), parts are hard to come by. Most Romanian roads are best suited for 4WD vehicles.

Romania has only a few short stretches of motorway (autostrada), including between Bucharest and Piteşti (114km), and crossing the Balta Ialomiţei from Cernavodă to Fiteşti (15km), west of Constanţa; the latter is a toll road, meaning motorists must pay a small fee to enjoy its smooth surface. Some major roads (drum naţional) have been

resurfaced, but many remain in a poor (understatement!), pot-holed condition. Secondary roads (drum judeţean) can become dirt tracks, and mountain and forestry roads (drum forestier) can be impassable after heavy rain. Concrete roads (such as the Bucharest ring road) were shoddily constructed and are quickly deteriorating. Level crossings over railway lines should be approached with caution, as the roads can become very rough at these points. Open manhole covers are a hazard in cities such as Bucharest and Constanţa.

Even more hazardous than the dire state of the roads are the obstacles moving about on them. Many drivers are aggressive and lack discipline. Horse-drawn carts piled high with hay, playing children, drunkards, cows, pigs and other moving objects dart in and out without warning, making driving here a downright displeasure. Avoid driving at night. Some roads have no markings and are unlit – as are many vehicles.

Breakdowns

Members of foreign automobile clubs (such as AA and AA) are covered by Romania's Automobil Clubul Român (ACR) which has a Web site at www.acr.ro. Of course, you must still pay: emergency road service costs upwards of $10 to $13, and towing is $0.57 per kilometre. In the event of a breakdown, call Car's 24-hour emergency service number (☎ 927). The ACR has an office in most cities, listed in the relevant sections of this book.

Check the pressure of your tyres before entering Romania because it's often impossible to do so at Romanian petrol stations. Punctures can be repaired at workshops signposted vulcaniser, abundant in Romania and found even in the tiniest village in the middle of nowhere.

If you intend hiring a car (see Rental later), consider a Dacia. Romania's national car might well be the butt of endless jokes but in the event of a breakdown you'll be glad you're not driving a Mercedes. Romanians are adept at dismantling/reassembling Dacia engines and take great pride in showing off their engineering skills. If you break

Road Distances (km)

	Arad	Baia Mare	Braşov	Bucharest	Chişinău	Cluj-Napoca	Constanţa	Craiova	Drobeta-T. Severin	Iaşi	Oradea	Ploieşti	Piteşti	Satu Mare	Sibiu	Suceava	Târgu Mureş	Timişoara
Arad	---																	
Baia Mare	318	---																
Braşov	416	399	---															
Bucharest	528	399	171	---														
Chişinău	846	640	429	467	---													
Cluj-Napoca	271	152	271	426	548	---												
Constanţa	812	781	382	265	491	653	---											
Craiova	386	557	261	244	710	405	495	---										
Drobeta-T. Severin	270	546	372	354	801	393	606	111	---									
Iaşi	716	510	299	391	130	418	477	580	671	---								
Oradea	119	199	423	592	700	152	805	441	394	570	---							
Ploieşti	528	511	112	60	415	383	274	242	353	350	535	---						
Piteşti	433	481	139	113	568	329	379	122	233	438	467	120	---					
Satu Mare	251	67	440	611	707	169	822	573	526	577	132	552	498	---				
Sibiu	274	322	142	260	571	170	538	226	296	441	308	254	159	339	---			
Suceava	589	318	329	436	276	318	562	590	701	146	470	395	468	385	410	---		
Târgu Mureş	378	227	172	341	457	108	554	351	421	327	260	284	284	277	125	285	---	
Timişoara	52	370	427	577	856	323	829	334	223	726	171	539	444	303	285	641	389	---

down, flag down the first passing car. It will be a Dacia and its driver will be able to make yours go again. And they'll have all the necessary tools too.

Fuel
Petrol is widely available in Romania: Shell, Lukoil, Petrom and Agip have sparkling, Western-style stations across the country, with at least one 24-hour station in every major city. Most accept Visa and/or MasterCard. Western-grade petrol (*benzină*) and diesel (*motorină*) are the norm, including unleaded 95-octane (*fără plumb* or *benzină verde*), premium and superplus (96–98 octane). Expect to pay about $0.50 per litre for premium/superplus, $0.45 for unleaded and $0.30 for diesel in Bucharest and a little less in provincial cities.

Road Rules
The whole region drives on the right. The speed limit for cars is 60km/h in built-up areas or 70km/h on the open road. Motorcycles are limited to 40km/h in built-up areas and 50km/h on the open road. Drink-driving is severely punished in Romania; the blood-alcohol limit is 0.01%.

If you are issued a fine for a traffic violation, insist on a receipt before parting with any money. Don't accept a written statement that doesn't specify the exact amount, or the money may go straight into the police officer's pocket.

Rental
Avis, Budget, Hertz and Europcar have offices in most cities and at Otopeni airport in Bucharest. Car rental is geared solely towards business travellers, however, and is therefore expensive. If coming from abroad, it is often cheaper to book (and pay) for a car in advance through any Avis, Budget, Europcar or Hertz office overseas, and collect it upon arrival at Otopeni airport. To hire a small car in Romania costs upwards of $75

(unlimited kilometres) or $35 (plus $0.35 per kilometre) per day. Check if prices quoted include the required 19% VAT.

In some cities there are small private car-rental companies that rent out Dacias and undercut the larger rental firms. Daily rental, including 200km per day, starts at about $45.

BICYCLE

Providing you are well equipped and prepared for some hard cycling, travelling around Romania on two wheels is one of the most rewarding ways of seeing the country. In many parts of the country you will have the road all to yourself. However, the pot-holed state of Romania's roads makes the going tough for anything less than a robust touring or mountain bike.

Bicycles can be taken on trains. Most trains have a baggage car *(vagon de bagaje)*, marked by a suitcase symbol on train timetables. Bicycles stored here have to be labelled with your name, destination and the bicycle's weight. But it is easier and safer to simply take your bicycle on the train with you. On local and express trains there is plenty of room at either end of the carriage next to the toilet. You might be charged a minimal 'bulky luggage' fee.

The flashier your bicycle, the more chance there is of it being stolen.

Cycling Organisations

There are cycling clubs and shops in Sibiu, Cluj-Napoca and Oradea. In Timişoara, EnduRoMania (see the boxed text 'Motorcycle Tours') runs country-wide mountain-biking tours. In Bucharest, a good starting point for information on two-wheeling around the country is the Romanian Cycling Federation (Federaţia Româna de Ciclism; ☎ 01-312 7042, fax 210 0161), Str Academiei 2.

For its members, the Cyclists' Touring Club in the UK (CTC; ☎ 01483-417 217, fax 426 994, ⓔ cycling@ctc.org.uk), Cotterell House, 69 Meadrow, Godalming, Surrey GU7 3HS, publishes a free booklet on cycling in Romania, plus free touring notes and itineraries for several routes around the country. The CTC also offers tips on bikes,

---

Motorcycle Tours

EnduRoMania (☎/fax 056-191 457, mobile ☎ 094-841 015, ⓔ sergio@mail.dnttm.ro), Str George Enescu 6, 1900 Timişoara, is a member of the International Motorcycle Federation and organises touring, off-road and discovery trips throughout Romania for motorcyclists with their own bikes. It also arranges several competitive off-road motorcycle events each summer.

During tours and events EnduRoMania offers motorcyclists guarded parking for their bikes at night, special access to forest roads otherwise off-limits to the public, and can arrange accommodation in camping grounds, private homes, monasteries or hotels.

It runs a regular free email forum that anyone can subscribe to via email (ⓔ enduromania-subscribe@onelist.com) and has a Web site at www.enduromania.ro. EnduRoMania can also be contacted in Germany (☎ 069-670 2652, fax 676 017), Im Mainfeld 23, 60528 Frankfurt am Main.

---

spares and insurance; it sells maps and cycling guides by mail order. See the Web site at www.ctc.org.uk.

See Mountain Biking in the Exploring the Carpathian Mountains special section for more two-wheeling information.

Rental

You can hire road or mountain bikes in Bucharest for $10 per day and in Braşov, Târgu Mureş and the mountain resorts of Poiana Braşov and Sinaia in Transylvania for $5 to $8 per day ($1.50 to $2 per hour). The afore-mentioned cycling clubs also arrange bike rentals.

HITCHING

Hitching is never entirely safe in any country in the world. Travellers who decide to hitch should understand that they are taking a small but potentially serious risk. People who do choose to hitch will be safer if they travel in pairs and let someone know where they are planning to go.

Hitchhiking in Romania is a common way of getting from A to B and as a Westerner you have a greater chance of being picked up. It is common practice in Romania and Moldova to pay the equivalent of the bus fare to the driver. Many local motorists solicit business at bus and train stations as a way of covering their fuel costs.

Horse, Donkey & Wagon

In many rural parts, the only vehicle that passes will be horse-powered. Horse and cart is the most popular form of transport in Romania and you will see numerous carts, even in cities (although some downtown areas are off-limits to them). Many carts will stop and give you a ride, the driver expecting no more than a cigarette in payment.

BOAT

Boat is the only way of getting around much of the Danube Delta. Navrom, with a Web site at www.navrom.ro, operates passenger ferries along the three main channels from Tulcea to Sulina and Sfântu Gheorghe on the Black Sea and to Periprava just south of Romania's border with Ukraine. You can easily hire private motorboats, rowing boats and kayaks in Tulcea and all the Delta villages to explore the smaller waterways. Local fishermen and boatmen double as guides.

To get to Ostrov, the Romanian border town connecting to Silistra in Bulgaria, you have to cross the Danube on a shoddy ferry that does not meet international safety standards. It is 'suitable' for cars and foot passengers. Ferries also cross the Danube River at Calafat and Giurgiu. See the Wallachia chapter for details on all three crossings.

LOCAL TRANSPORT
Bus, Tram & Trolleybus

Buses, trams and trolleybuses (buses run by electricity with wires overhead) provide transport within most towns and cities in Romania – although boarding can be a feat in itself. Expect at least two or three battles before you succeed in clambering aboard one of the infrequent sardine cans that pass by. Shoving, pushing, elbowing and stamping on toes are allowed.

Buses, trams and trolleybuses usually run from about 5 am to midnight, although services can get thin on the ground after 7 pm in more remote areas. Purchase tickets at street kiosks marked *bilete* or *casă de bilete* before boarding, and validate them once aboard. Some tickets are good for one trip *(calatori)*; others are for two trips, each end of the ticket being valid for one ride. Tickets cost less than $0.30. Travellers staying any length of time in Bucharest or another large city should invest in a weekly or monthly travel pass; see the respective regional chapters for details.

Ticket kiosks, which also sell public transport maps, close around 5 pm and also without warning for sporadic intervals during the day. Buy a handful of tickets when you first arrive in town. Drivers don't sell tickets.

If you travel without a validated ticket or with no ticket at all you risk a $5 on-the-spot fine. Spot checks are carried out on all modes of public transport by plain-clothed ticket inspectors who have no qualms about making a spectacle of the 'stupid foreigner' before physically removing you from the vehicle. The best option in these cases is to just shut up and pay.

Metro

Bucharest is the only city in Romania to sport a metro; see Getting Around in that chapter for details.

Taxi

Romanian taxi drivers, as in many places across the globe, are notorious rip-off merchants who have no scruples in charging you over the odds or driving you around in circles.

In Bucharest, cabs with functioning meters and reasonably honest drivers – identifiable by the yellow pyramid attached to their roofs – do exist. Their fixed meter rate is $0.45 per kilometre, compared to $0.10 per kilometre in Braşov and other provincial towns. You are also charged 'waiting time' (up to $2 per hour in the capital).

If a taxi has no meter – invariably the case outside Bucharest – then bargain before roaring off. Some taxis still tout old prerevolution meters which clock up fares in tens of lei rather than thousands. In these cases the driver will multiply the digits on the meter by 100. These meters are not reliable and are tantamount to a rip-off.

It is always cheaper to telephone for a taxi than to hail one in the street. Numbers for local taxi firms are listed in the regional chapters of this book.

ORGANISED TOURS

Practically every travel agency in the capital (listed under Information in the Bucharest chapter) offers a seemingly impressive array of guided tours around Romania, enabling visitors to see the prime sites in a minimum amount of time. Unfortunately, few agencies seem to acknowledge the existence of independent travellers and it can be difficult to sign up for a tour unless you are part of a group of 20.

The following are among the more imaginative companies, offering tours designed with the independent traveller in mind.

Company of Mysterious Journeys (☎/fax 01-231 4022, mobile ☎ 092-599 099, e cdt@art .ro) Str George Călinescu 20, Bucharest – offers fabulous (and fabulously scary) tours of Romania organised by the official tour operator for the Transylvanian Society of Dracula, a serious cultural and academic society despite its seemingly jesting nature. Eight-day itineraries include a steam-engine ride 'between Hell & Heaven', Count Dracula Treasures and a Classic Dracula Tour. Tours cost about $800 per person including meals, accommodation and lots of ghoulish entertainment. One-day tailor-made trips can also be organised.

Cultural Tourism Initiative (☎/fax 01-223 2619, 230 2292, e cti@com.pcnet.ro) 50 Blvd Primă-verii, Bucharest – heritage tours for two to 25 people organised by the nonprofit academic association of Bucharest's European Cultural Centre. Tours on offer include the best of Transylvania and Wallachia in two/four days ($150/375 per person), study tours of Transylvania (four days, from $225 per person for groups of six) and the Bucovina monasteries (five days, $345 per person for groups of six). Staff can also arrange wine tours.
Web site: www.cti@rotravel.com

Green Mountain Holidays (☎/fax 064-257 142, e gmh@mail.dntcj.ro) Str Principală 305, Izvorul Crişului – offers activity-based tours including hiking, kayaking, caving and photo safaris.
Web site: www.dntcj.ro/gmh

Kron-Tur (☎ 068-410 615/515, ☎/fax 410 715) Str Gheorghe Bariţul, Braşov – offers similar deals to Suntours (see following) and is an agent for most private German bus companies.

Mara Tours (☎/fax 01-310 4152, 324 5626) Calea Victoriei 214, Bucharest – travel agency specialising in spa tours around Romania. Wallow in everything from mud to bubbling warm waters from $20 per day for hotel accommodation, plus $15/4 per day for meals/treatments.

Micomis Agenţie de Turism (☎ 068-470 472, 475 658, fax 410 321, e micomis@brasovia .ro) Str Republicii 35, Braşov – offers cheap skiing packages and regional tours, including an eight-day Dracula Classical Tour.
Web site: www.canad.ro/~micomis

Roving Romania (☎ 094-212 065, e roving@ mic.ro) – specialises in tailor-made and off-the-beaten-track tours, by 4WD Landrover, bike or foot, including thematic tours such as photography, bird-watching, botany, rural traditions and customs, painted monasteries and Dracula tours, as well as mainstream outdoor activities (hiking, skiing etc).
Web site: www.roving-romania.co.uk

Suntours (☎ 068-474 179, fax 417 639) Piaţa Sfatului 19, Braşov – arranges ski packages to Poiana Braşov ($220 per week including accommodation and lift passes).

Bucharest

☎ 01 • pop 2.2 million

Tree-lined boulevards, park-girdled lakes, pompous public monuments and its very own Arc de Triomphe give Bucharest (Bucureşti in Romanian) a smooth Parisian flavour. The city is at its best in spring and summer, when relaxed crowds fill the beer gardens and parks. As well as having the usual complement of museums, Bucharest has a gentle Latin air that goes well with the mysticism of its Orthodox churches.

On the other hand, few travellers fall in love with Romania's capital, largely thanks to its petulant street hustlers and expensive restaurants which spur far too many travellers to leave as quickly as possible. Bucharest can be fascinating if you approach it with patience and humble expectations. Back streets bustle with hawkers and artists, 18th-century monasteries and churches hide behind pretty walled gardens (or monumental apartment blocks), while the decaying elegance of the city's historic quarter is riddled with a charm of its very own.

During the 1980s southern Bucharest was transformed by Nicolae Ceauşescu's attempt to recast Bucharest as a grandiloquent socialist capital, with the behemoth House of the People as its centrepiece. The 1989 revolution put an end to the city's Stalinist make-over, yet reminders of the Ceauşescu era remain – the turn of every corner unveils a bullet-pocked building, a candle quietly burning by a memorial statue, or a marble-covered apartment that once housed Communist Party elite.

HISTORY

Bucharest derives its name from a legendary shepherd named Bucur (*bucurie*; literally 'joy') who founded the city and built a church on the right bank of the Dâmboviţa River.

The city, which lies on the Wallachian plains between the Carpathian foothills and the Danube River, was settled by Geto-

Highlights

- Gaze in awe at the lavish interior of the Palace of Parliament, the world's second-largest building

- Stroll through rural Romania at the Village Museum, admiring the architecture and mingling with the elite along Şoseaua Kiseleff en route

- Discover historical Bucharest through its churches: don't miss Stavropoleos Church, Patriarchal Cathedral or the hidden gems of the Prince Mihai Monastery, Princess Bălaşa Church and St Apostles' Church

- Watch a movie on the 4th floor of the National Theatre

- Flee the city heat: row your sweetheart across Snagov Lake to Dracula's grave

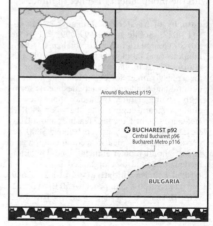

Around Bucharest p119

✪ BUCHAREST p92
Central Bucharest p96
Bucharest Metro p116

BULGARIA

Dacians as early as 70 BC. By 1459 a princely residence and military citadel had been established under the chancellery of Prince Vlad Ţepeş. By the end of the 17th century, the city was the capital of Wallachia and ranked among south-eastern Europe's wealthiest cities. Bucharest became the national capital in 1862.

The early 20th century was Bucharest's golden age. The city's narrow streets were replaced with wide, tree-lined boulevards as Romania looked to France for its cultural and architectural inspiration. Large neoclassical buildings sprang up, fashionable parks were laid out and landscaped on Parisian models and, by the end of the 1930s, Bucharest was known throughout Europe as 'Little Paris' or the 'Paris of the Balkans'.

Bombing by the Allies during WWII, coupled with a 1940 earthquake measuring 7.4 on the Richter scale, destroyed much of Bucharest's prewar beauty. In March 1977 a second major earthquake claimed 1391 lives and flattened countless buildings. Ceauşescu's criminal redevelopment of the city marked the final death knell of Romania as the 'Paris' of Eastern Europe.

ORIENTATION

Bucharest's main train station, Gara de Nord, is a couple of kilometres north-west of central Bucharest and conveniently connected to the centre by metro; otherwise it's 20 minutes' walk.

Blvd General Magheru, the southern foot of which is called Blvd Nicolae Bălcescu, is the main street in central Bucharest. It links Piaţa Romană (north) with Piaţa Universităţii (south), a central focal point close to the National Theatre and Hotel Inter-Continental. Bucharest's historic heart lies immediately south and west of here. Forming the eastern edge of the historic centre, Blvd IC Brătianu runs south from Piaţa Universităţii to Piaţa Unirii, the Civic Centre and the Palace of Parliament.

Parallel Calea Victoriei links Piaţa Victoriei (north) with the Romanian Athenaeum on Piaţa Revoluţiei (south). From Piaţa Victoriei, Şoseaua Kiseleff leads north past Herăstrău Park to the airports at Băneasa (8km) and Otopeni (17km).

Most embassies (listed in Facts for the Visitor) are on and around Blvd Dacia, east of Piaţa Romană.

Maps & Guides

Amco Press' bilingual *Bucharest City Plan* (1:15,000) is the only quality map available ($2.50 from bookshops). Their *Bucharest Public Ground Transport* map ($0.15 from bus ticket kiosks) is an essential publication for anyone intent on exploring the city by public transport.

Bucharest in your Pocket touts a centrefold twin set of city centre maps. Lonely Planet guides are sold in newspaper kiosks in the Athénée Palace Hilton and Inter-Continental hotels (see Places to Stay).

INFORMATION
Tourist Offices

Bucharest has no tourist office. Some travel agencies (see that section) organise tours and offer limited tourist information. Motoring information is available from Automobil Clubul Român (ACR; ☎ 222 1553, fax 222 1552, ℮ acr@acr.ro), Str Tache Ionescu 27.

The European Union Information Centre (☎/fax 315 3470, ℮ contact@infoeuropa.ro), in the Central University Library, overlooking Piaţa Revoluţiei at Calea Victoriei 88, is a handy, English-speaking source of information.

Money

Currency exchanges are all over the city, including along the length of Blvd General Magheru and Blvd Nicolae Bălcescu. Capitol Exchange at Blvd Nicolae Bălcescu 34 opens 24 hours, as does Alliance Exchange at No 30 on the same street and OK Exchange Nonstop, around the corner from McDonald's on Str George Enescu.

There are ATMs in the baggage claim area at Otopeni airport; next to IDM Exchange at Gara de Nord; outside the CFR office at Str Domniţa Anastasia 10–14; next to the Union International Centre on Str Ion Câmpineanu (Société Générale ATM); outside the Blue Moon nightclub at Blvd General Magheru 1–3; and inside the World Trade Plaza & Shopping Gallery at Blvd Expoziţiei 2.

Banca Comercială Română, Blvd Regina Elisabeta 5, cashes travellers cheques and gives cash advances on credit card; open 9 am to 5 pm Monday to Thursday, 9 am to 4 pm Friday. It has a couple of ATMs outside, as does its branch office at Calea Victoriei 155 (open 8 am to 1 pm weekdays).

Bank Austria Creditanstalt, next to the European Union Information Centre at Calea Victoriei 88, cashes American Express travellers cheques and gives cash advances on MasterCard. Lost AmEx cards/cheques can be replaced at Marshal Turism (☎ 659 6812, fax 223 1203, ⓔ amex@marshal.ro), Blvd General Magheru 43, open 9 am to 5 pm weekdays, 10 am to 1 pm Saturday.

Post

The central post office (Poştă Română Oficiul Bucureşti 1) is just off Calea Victoriei at Str Matei Millo 10. It opens 7.30 am to 8 pm weekdays and 7.30 am to 2 pm Saturday. Poste-restante mail can be collected here. Branch post offices next to the telex-fax office on Str Tache Ionescu, at Str Ion Câmpineanu 21, and close to Gara de Nord at Str Gării de Nord 6–8, are open 7 am to 8 pm weekdays and 7 am to 2 pm Saturday.

Telephone

Orange, card-operated public phones bespeckle the streets and many hotel lobbies. RomTelecom phonecards cost 50,000 lei ($2.50) and are sold at post offices or a telex-fax office such as the one on Str Tache Ionescu. Alternatively, feed a crisp 50,000 lei note into one of the automatic phonecard dispensers found at the airports and the train station.

The central telephone office, on the corner of Calea Victoriei and Str Matei Millo, opens 24 hours.

You can rent a mobile telephone (see Telephone in the Facts for the Visitor chapter) from Mobil Rom's Dialog shop (☎ 203 3000, ⓔ info@mobil-rom.com), Calea Dorobanţilor 135–145; open 9 am to 6 pm weekdays, 9 am to 1 pm Saturday.

Email & Internet Access

Villa Helga (see Hostels under Places to Stay) charges $2.50 per hour to log on. Internet Café (☎ 650 4214), Calea Victoriei 136, sports a genuine cafe as well as Internet access ($1.85 per hour). The same team has another outlet, also called Internet Café (☎ 313 1048, ⓔ eugen@icafe.ro), at Blvd Carol I 25. Both open 24 hours.

PC-Net Data Network (☎ 311 2682, ⓔ florina@pcnet.ro), Calea Victoriei 25, has several computers with speedy connection costing $0.50/0.75/1.50 for 15/30/60 minutes; open 10 am to 10 pm Monday to Saturday. Its second branch at Str Jean Louis Calderon 1–5 charges $1 per hour; open 24 hours.

The French Institute (see Libraries & Cultural Centres) operates a cybercafe.

Travel Agencies

With the painful absence of a national tourist office, travel agencies offering a moderate range of services have mushroomed in the city. Some are better than others.

CMB Travel (☎ 210 6071/4901, 211 1458, ⓔ office@cmbtravel.ro) Blvd Nicolae Bălcescu 20 – efficient agency; takes accommodation bookings for several hotels

Contact Tour (☎ 211 0979, fax 211 0920, ⓔ contour@fx.ro) Blvd Dacia 45 – sightseeing tours in Bucharest, fishing and cruises in the Danube Delta, weekend escapes to Sinaia

Dacia Tours (☎ 310 2547, 315 4558, fax 310 2514, ⓔ daciatour@mail.com) Blvd General Magheru 1–3 – an agent for most airlines including Tarom, Air Moldova and Ion Ţiriac Air

European Travel Services (☎/fax 323 6187, ⓔ ets.dobre@xnet.ro) Str Orzari 5 – English-managed agency; accommodation bookings, tailor-made tours, weekend breaks
Web site: www.europeantravelservices.com

Lar Tours (☎ 315 3206/3276, fax 312 0148, ⓔ lartours@webline.ro) Str Ştirbei Vodă 2–4 – hosts an information desk for agro-tourism agent Antrec

Marshal Turism (☎ 659 6812, 650 2347, fax 223 1203, ⓔ incoming@marshal.ro) Blvd General Magheru 43 – member of the American Society of Travel Agents and Romania's only representative for American Express (see Money, earlier). Its head office (☎ 410 5304, fax 312 4657) is at Blvd Unirii 20

Nova Tours (☎ 315 1357/1358, fax 312 1041, ⓔ nova.tour@snmail.softnet.ro) Blvd Nicolae Bălcescu 21 – huge variety of organised tours, including Bucharest city tours by car ($20); book at least three days in advance

Viaclub (☎ 311 2398/239, fax 311 1806, ⓔ viaclub@customers.digiro.net) Blvd Regina Elisabeta 3 – tickets for charter flights to Italy can be purchased here

Bookshops

The best (and almost only) bet for English-language novels, dictionaries and guidebooks about Romania is Librăria Noi (☎ 314 3786), Blvd Nicolae Bălcescu 18; open 10 am to 8 pm Monday to Saturday, 11 am to 7 pm Sunday.

There's a fair selection of French-, German- and English-language novels to be found at Librăria Mircea Nedelciu, Str Franceză 44. Humanitas (☎ 313 5035), Calea Victoriei 120, sells a good range of reference books published by Editura Humanitas (see Books in the Facts for the Visitor chapter).

Libraries & Cultural Centres

The British Council Library (☎ 210 0314, ℮ bc.library@bc-bucharest.bcouncil.org), Calea Dorobanţilor 14, opens 10 am to 6 pm weekdays, 10 am to 1 pm Saturday (closed August).

The American Information Resource Centre (☎ 210 1602, ℮ infobuch@usia.gov), Str Jean Louis Calderon 7–9, stocks English-language journals, magazines and newspapers for digestion in its reading room and has a CD-ROM database; open 2 to 4 pm Tuesday and Thursday.

The French Institute (☎ 210 0224), Blvd Dacia 77, arranges numerous festivals and cultural events and has a cinema (see under Entertainment).

The Hungarian Cultural Centre (☎ 210 4884) at Str Batiştei 39 and the German Institute (Goethe Institut; ☎ 312 0231) at No 15 on the same street both have libraries.

Laundry

Bucharest has one self-service laundrette, Nuf Nuf, at Calea Şerban Vodă 76–78. Washing and drying costs $2 per kilogram; open 24 hours. Guests staying at the Villa Helga hostel can machine-wash their clothes for free.

Immaculate Cleaners (☎ 211 4413) is a dry-cleaners offering a 24-hour dry-cleaning or laundry, door-to-door service. Branches at Str Polonă 113a and Str Cotroceni 10 open 7.30 am to 8.30 pm weekdays, 9 am to 4 pm Saturday.

Medical Services

Recommended by several embassies is Centrul Medical Unirea (☎ 327 1188/1190, fax 327 1195), on the ground floor at Blvd Unirii 57, block E. Doctors speak English and German; in an emergency call ☎ 092-286 770 (mobile). Medicover (☎ 310 4066/4040), Calea Plevnei 96, is another private, embassy-recommended clinic with English-speaking staff and a 24-hour emergency service.

There is a 24-hour pharmacy on the corner of Calea Victoriei and Str Stavropoleos. Farmacia Magheru, on the corner of Blvd General Magheru and Str Pictor Verona, opens 8 am to 8 pm daily and has a list of other pharmacies open late and/or on Sunday posted in its window.

Dent-a-America (☎ 230 2608), Str Varşovia 4, has English-speaking staff; open 8 am to 8 pm weekdays.

Emergency

To call (Romanian only) an ambulance dial ☎ 961; police ☎ 955; fire brigade ☎ 981.

For general emergencies go to the 24-hour Emergency Hospital (Spitalul de Urgenţă; ☎ 230 0106/4953/0179), Calea Floreasca 8. Colentina Hospital (☎ 210 5485), close to Circus Park on Şoseaua Ştefan cel Mare, specialises in rabies treatments.

Dangers & Annoyances

Scams and snarling street dogs are rife in Bucharest. To safeguard your wallet and ankles, see Dangers & Annoyances in the Facts for the Visitor chapter.

CENTRAL BUCHAREST
The Historic Heart & West of Calea Victoriei

Bucharest's historic heart – flanked by Splaiul Independenţei to the south, Blvd Regina Elisabeta to the north, Blvd IC Brătianu to the east and Calea Victoriei to the west – sprang up around the **Old Princely Court** (Curtea Veche) in the 15th century. Artisans and traders – whose occupations are still reflected in street names like Str Covaci (trough-makers street) and Str Şelari (saddle-makers street) – settled here in the 14th

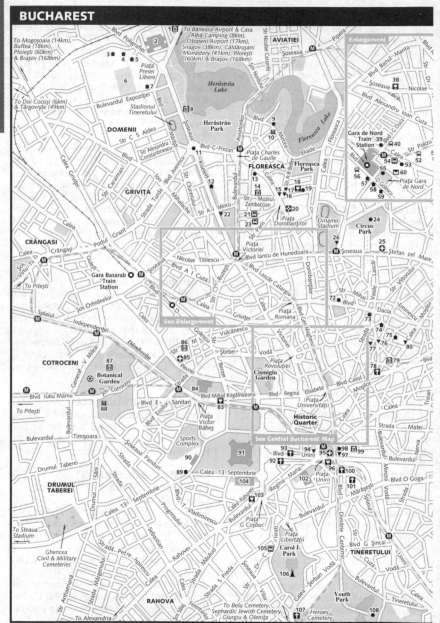

BUCHAREST

To Băneasa Airport & Casa
Alba Camping (8km),
Otopeni Airport (17km),
Snagov (38km), Căldăruşani
Monastery (41km), Ploieşti
(60km) & Braşov (168km)

To Mogoşoaia (14km),
Buftea (18km),
Ploieşti (60km)
& Braşov (168km)

To Doi Cocoşi (6km)
& Târgovişte (49km)

Blvd Poligrafiei

Piaţa
Presei
Libere

Herăstrău
Lake

AVIAȚIEI

Bulevardul Expoziţiei

Stadionul
Tineretului

Herăstrău
Park

DOMENII

Str C S Aldea

Str Alexandru
Constantinescu

Blvd C-Prezan

Piaţa Charles
de Gaulle

FLOREASCA

Floreasca
Park

GRIVIȚA

Muzeul
Zambaccian

Piaţa
Dorobanţilor

CRÂNGAŞI

Piaţa
Victoriei

Dinamo
Stadium

Circus
Park

Ştefan cel Mare

Nicolae Titilescu

Blvd Iancu de Hunedoara

Gara Basarab
Train
Station

Şos Orhideelor

Piaţa
Romana

Splaiul

Independenței

Vulcănescu

COTROCENI

Botanical
Garden

Ştirbei

Piaţa
Revoluţiei

Cişmigiu
Garden

Blvd Mihail Kogălniceanu

Piaţa
Universităţii

To Piteşti

Blvd Iuliu Maniu

Blvd Erolor Sanitari

Piaţa
Victor
Babeş

Historic
Quarter

See Central Bucharest Map

Bulevardul Timişoara

Sports
Complex

DRUMUL
TABEREI

Piaţa
Unirii

Calea 13 Septembrie

Piaţa
G Coşbuc

Piaţa
Libertăţii

To Steaua
Stadium

Ghencea
Civil & Military
Cemeteries

Carol I
Park

TINERETULUI

RAHOVA

To Alexandria

To Belu Cemetery,
Sephardic Jewish Cemetery,
Giurgiu & Oleniţa

Heroes
Cemetery

Youth
Park

Enlargement

Gara de Nord
Train
Station

Piaţa Gara
de Nord

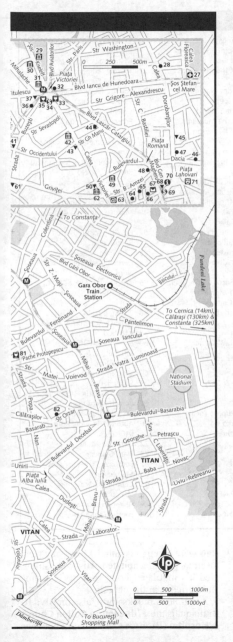

century, but it was not until the reigning prince of Wallachia, the notorious Vlad Ţepeş, fortified the settlement and built a **Prince's Palace** (Palatul Voievodal) that it flourished as a commercial centre. The palace was the official residence of the Wallachian princes until the end of the 18th century, when, heavily damaged by earthquakes and fires over the years, it was auctioned off to local merchants. Ruins are all that remain today. To enter the court on Str Franceză from the north-western side of Piaţa Unirii, cross the river, and a little west along Splaiul Independenţei you'll find Str Şelari. Cut along this narrow street to Str Franceză.

The **Old Court Church** (Biserica Curtea Veche), built in 1546–59 during the reign of Mircea Ciobanul (Mircea the Shepherd), is Bucharest's oldest church. Much of the interior has blackened with time, but the original 16th-century frescoes next to the altar, and the unusual horizontal strips of alternating plaster mouldings and brick which adorn the spire, remain well preserved. The carved stone portal was added in 1715. South-east of the church stands **Manuc's Inn** (Hanul lui Manuc), built to shelter travelling merchants in the 19th century.

Head west on Str Franceză a few blocks, and when you see a large white church turn right on to Str Poştei and then make your way to **Stavropoleos Church**, on the corner of Str Stavropoleos (literally 'town of the cross'). It was built by the Greek monk Ioanichie Stratonikeas in 1724 in a typical Brâncoveanu style, characterised by a harmonious blend of Renaissance and baroque elements with traditional Romanian architectural forms. Inside are richly ornate wood and stone carvings, coloured with paintings and frescoes. Those in the church porch are particularly well preserved. The votive inscription carved in stone above the entrance is written in Greek and Romanian (in the Cyrillic alphabet). Tombstones engraved in Romanian, Greek and Serbian lie behind the church alongside the tomb of Metropolitan Grigorie I of Wallachia (1627–37). A song-filled service is held on Sunday at 10.30 am with additional services during the week.

BUCHAREST

PLACES TO STAY
3 Crowne Plaza Bucharest
    Flora
4 Parc Hotel
5 Hotel Turist
7 Hotel Sofitel; World Trade
    Plaza & Shopping Gallery
12 Hotel Triumf
44 Hotel Minerva
51 Hotel Marna
57 Hotel Bucegi
58 Hotel Cerna
59 Hotel Astoria
74 Villa Helga
75 YMCA Hostel
89 Grand Hotel Marriott

PLACES TO EAT
15 Cafe Einstein; Brutăria
    Deutschland
16 Dunkin' Donuts
17 Ana; Supermarket Unic
22 Casa Doina
26 La Mama
37 Springtime
41 McDrive
43 Casa Vernescu
45 Diplomat
50 Il Gattopardo
61 Hong Kong
68 McDonald's
76 Nicoreşti
77 Smart's
80 Bureibista
94 Dunkin' Donuts
97 McDonald's

THINGS TO SEE
1 Minovici Museum of Ancient
    Western Arts
2 Press House
8 Village Museum
9 Former Residence of
    Gheorghe Gheorghiu-Dej
10 Primăverii Palace & Cultural
    Tourism Institute
11 Triumphal Arch
13 Romanian TV Headquarters

14 Zambaccian Museum
24 'Wooden Spirits' Sculptures
29 Museum of Geology
30 Museum of the Romanian
    Peasant
31 Grigore Antipa Natural
    History Museum
32 Government Building
42 George Enescu Museum
49 Museum of Romanian
    Literature
62 Art Collection Museum
78 Museum of the Armenian
    Community
79 Theodor Pallady Museum
86 National Military Museum
87 Botanical Museum &
    Greenhouse
88 Cotroceni Palace
90 Ministry of Defence
91 Palace of Parliament
92 Antim Monastery
93 St Apostles' Church
99 Jewish History Museum
100 Church of Bucur the Shepherd
101 Prince Radu Monastery
102 Patriarchal Cathedral & Palace
104 National Institute for Science
    & Technology
106 Mausoleum
107 Martyr Heroes' Church

ENTERTAINMENT
18 White Horse
33 Sydney Bar & Grill
35 Vox Maris
38 Dubliner
71 Ţăndărică Puppet Theatre
81 Opium Studio
83 Sherlock Holmes
84 Opera House
96 The Harp
103 Becker Bräu

OTHER
6 Exhibition Pavilion &
    Conference Centre (EXPO);
    World Trade Centre

19 Company of Mysterious
    Journeys
20 Mario Plaza
21 Touring (Eurolines Buses to
    Western Europe)
23 Touring (Eurolines Buses to
    Western Europe)
25 Colentina Hospital
27 Emergency Hospital
28 Dialog
34 Banca Comercială Română
36 Tarom
39 Kidik Tour (Buses to Istanbul)
40 Bus Stop for No 79 to Villa
    Helga
46 Contact Tour
47 British Council Library
48 Marshal Turism & American
    Express
52 Bus Stop for No 86 to Piață
    Romană
53 CFR Train Ticket Office
54 Central Bus Station & Hotel
    Nord
55 Autotrans & Ortadoğu Tur
    (Buses to Moldova, Ukraine &
    Turkey)
56 Bus Stop for No 133 to Villa
    Helga & Star Turism (Buses to
    Istanbul)
60 Branch Post Office
63 Internet Café
64 Piață Amzei
65 Unic & Vox Maris
    Supermarkets
66 Telex-Fax Office
67 Branch Post Office
69 OK Exchange Nonstop
70 Automobil Clubul Român
    (ACR)
72 French Institute
73 Piață Gemeni
82 European Travel Services
85 Medicover
95 Centrul Medical Unirea
98 La Fourmi
105 Filaret Bus Station
108 Sports & Culture Palace

The Wallachian prince Constantin Brâncoveanu (ruled 1688–1714) is buried in **New St George's Church** (Biserica Sfântul Gheorghe-Nou; built 1699) on Str Lipscani. Brâncoveanu was captured by the Turks in 1714 following his refusal to take part in the Russo-Turkish War (1711). He and his four sons were taken to Istanbul where they were tortured then decapitated. His wife smuggled his mutilated body back to Romania and buried it in the church.

A couple of blocks north, also on Blvd IC Brătianu, is the 17th-century **Colţea Church & Hospital** (Biserica Colţea), built between

1699 and 1704. From Colţea Church walk back south past New St George's Church, then head west along **Str Lipscani**, a pedestrianised street. Dreams of transforming it into the fashionable, Parisian-style mall it was in the 1930s remain unrealised.

At its western end, Str Lipscani crosses **Calea Victoriei**, Bucharest's most historic street, built under Brâncoveanu's orders in 1692 to link his summer palace in Mogoşoaia, 14km north-west of Bucharest, with the heart of his capital city. In the interwar years, this was where the fashion-conscious would promenade to see and be seen.

Bucharest's financial houses moved to the historic heart in the 19th century after the princely residence was moved to the north of the city. On the corner of Str Lipscani and Calea Victoria stands the **Bucharest Financial Plaza**, a mirrored building. Next door is the **Economic Consortium Palace** (Casa de Economii şi Consemnaţiuni, CEC), designed by French architect Paul Gottereau in 1894–1900.

Opposite, at Calea Victoriei 12, is Bucharest's **National History Museum** (☎ 315 7056), in the former Post Office Palace built in a neoclassical style between 1894 and 1900. The 600,000 exhibits tell Romania's story from prehistoric times to WWI, the highlight being a treasury crammed with gold objects and precious stones. Information in English and French is posted in most rooms; open 10 am to 6 pm Wednesday to Sunday ($1.50).

Heading north along Calea Victoriei, you pass **Casa Capşa** at No 36, a historic cafe dating from 1852, and renowned as the meeting place of a glittering crowd of Romania's most eminent artists, literary figures and politicians of the 1930s. At the time of writing, it was closed for renovation.

Piaţa Revoluţiei to Piaţa Victoriei

Continue north on Calea Victoriei towards Piaţa Revoluţiei. After four or five long blocks, just south of the square, stands **Creţulescu Church** (1722), a red-brick structure damaged in the 1989 revolution and still under renovation. To the side of it

stands a **memorial bust** of Corneliu Coposu who spent 17 years in prison for his anti-communist activities and, prior to his death in 1995, was awarded the Légion d'Honneur by the French government. Behind the church is a statue of a headless human form in **memorial** to those who died in 1989.

Ceauşescu made his fateful speech from the balcony of the former **Central Committee of the Communist Party building** (1950), the long stone edifice on the opposite side of **Piaţa Revoluţiei**. It houses the Senate today. On the front facade next to the entrance is a plaque dedicated to the 'young and courageous people' who 'drove out the dictator', thus 'giving the Romanian people back their freedom and dignity'. A bold **statue** of a man, broken but put back together again, dominates the small green area in front.

The **Central University Library** (1895) houses the European Union Information Centre, an Austrian bank and a new university library today. The **shell of a building**, another revolution victim, on the corner of Str Dobrescu and Str Boteanu will be left charred and bullet-riddled in honour of those who died in 1989.

Dominating the square to the west at Calea Victoriei 49–53 is the massive **Royal Palace**. Each spring, a handful of monarchists keen to see Romania's monarchy re-established gather outside to celebrate Romania's former national day (10 May). Built in 1812–15 by Prince Dinicu Golescu, the Royal Palace became the official royal residence in 1834 during the reign of Prince Alexandru Ghica (r. 1834–42). The current facade dates from the 1930s. Until 1989 it was the seat of the State Council and was called the Palace of the Republic. Today it displays an extensive collection of Romanian and European art in the four-storey **National Art Museum** (Muzeul Naţional de Artă; ☎ 315 5193, 312 4327, e national .art@art.museum.ro), open 10 am to 6 pm Wednesday to Sunday ($0.50/0.25). Several branch museums of the National Art Museum are dotted around town.

One block north is the neoclassical **Romanian Athenaeum** (Ateneul Român), a

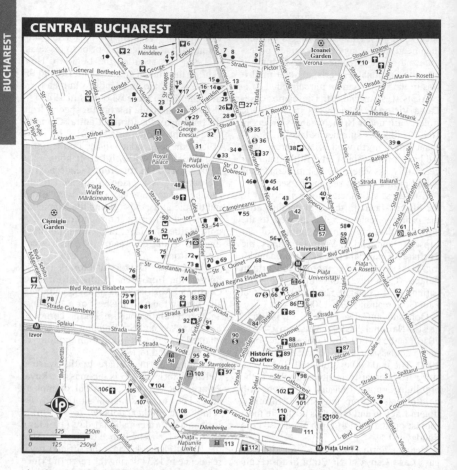

CENTRAL BUCHAREST

circular, temple-style building with a 41m-high dome. Scenes from Romanian history are featured on the interior fresco inside the Big Hall on the 1st floor. The peristyle is adorned with mosaics of five Romanian rulers, including Moldavian prince Vasile Lupu (r. 1512–21), Wallachian Matei Basarab (r. 1632–54) and King Carol I (r. 1881–1914). The Romanian Athenaeum was built in 1888 as a culture house for the Athenaeum academic and literary circle. George Enescu made his debut here in 1898, followed five years later by the first performance of his masterpiece *Romanian Rhapsody*. Today the Athenaeum is a concert hall for the **George Enescu Philharmonic Orchestra**.

Adjacent to the Athenaeum on the northern side of Piaţa Revoluţiei is the prestigious **Athénée Palace**, Bucharest's fanciest hotel in the 1930s. The building, designed and built in 1914 by French architect Téophile Bradeau, was heavily bombing during WWII and consequently rebuilt in 1945. A new wing was added in 1966. The hotel was notorious for being a den of iniquity and cradle of high-class prostitution in the interwar years.

CENTRAL BUCHAREST

PLACES TO STAY
13 Hotel Ambasador
19 Hotel Bucureşti
23 Athénée Palace Hilton
25 Hotel Lido
42 Hotel Inter-Continental
51 Hotel Carpaţi
53 Hotel Continental; Cofetăria Continental
54 Hotel Muntenia
73 Hotel Capitol
78 Hotel Dâmboviţa
80 Hotel Central
111 Hanul lui Manuc (Manuc's Inn)

PLACES TO EAT
4 Café Olé
5 Casa Veche
10 Mediterraneo
16 Menuet
17 Bistro Atheneu
18 La Taifas
29 Cina
32 Boema
40 La Premiera
55 Da Vinci
56 Planet Diner
60 McMoni's
62 Golden Falcon
65 Café de la Joie
72 Simplon Fast Food
75 Maxim Club
79 McDonald's
96 Caru cu Bere
98 Mes Amis
104 Count Dracula Club
105 Springtime

THINGS TO SEE
11 Church of the Icon
12 St Slujbă's Monastery
21 German Lutheran Church
24 Romanian Athenaeum
30 Royal Palace (National Art Museum)
33 Shell of Building

37 Italian Church
47 Senate (Former Central Committee of Communist Party Building)
48 Memorial Bust of Corneliu Coposu
49 Creţulescu Church
63 Colţea Church & Hospital
64 History & Art Museum
68 University
84 Romanian National Library
85 Student Church
87 New St George's Church
88 Bulgarian Church
93 Bucharest Financial Plaza
94 Economic Consortium Palace
97 Stavropoleos Church
99 Choral Temple
103 National History Museum
106 Prince Mihai Monastery
110 Old Princely Court Church
112 Princess Bălaşa Church
113 Justice Palace

ENTERTAINMENT
2 Green Hours 22 Jazz Club; Humanitas Bookshop
3 Terminus
6 Planter's Club
20 Salsa, You & Me II; Galeriile Lutherana
26 Blue Moon Nightclub
27 Cinema Scala
57 Ion Luca Caragiale National Theatre & Lăptăria Enache
77 Tipsy
82 Cinemateca Română & Café Indigo
86 Cinema Luceafărul
89 Club A
101 Swing House; Gulaş
102 Backstage

OTHER
1 Pâtisserie Parisienne Valerie
7 Farmacia Magheru

8 Lufthansa; Swiss Airlines
9 Telex-Fax Office
14 Air Ukraine
15 Europcar Car Rental
22 Lar Tours
28 Dacia Tours
31 Central University Library; Bank Austria Creditanstalt
34 Unic Supermarket
35 Capitol Exchange
36 Alliance Exchange
38 US Embassy
39 Hungarian Cultural Centre
41 US Consulate
43 Air Moldova
44 Librăria Noi
45 CMB Travel
46 Nova Tours
50 Branch Post Office
52 Central Post Office
58 American Information Resource Centre
59 PC-Net Data Network
61 Internet Café
66 Viaclub
67 Banca Comercială Română
69 Brutăria Deutschland
70 Casa Capşa
71 Central Telephone Office
74 Cercul Militar
76 Steaua Bucureşti Club Shop
81 Main CFR Train Ticket Office
83 PC-Net Data Network
90 National Bank of Romania
91 Pasajul Villacros (Covered Passage)
92 Police Station
95 24-Hour Pharmacy
100 Cocor Department Store
107 Tarom
108 Double T (Buses to Western Europe)
109 Librăria Mircea Nedelciu

West of Piaţa Revoluţiei is the **German Lutheran Church**, behind Hotel Bucureşti on Str Luterană. Services are held in German. The Roman-Catholic red-brick **Italian Church** at Blvd Nicolae Bălcescu 28 holds services in Italian.

North again at Calea Victoriei 111 is the excellent **Art Collection Museum** (Muzeul Colecţiilor de Artă; ☎ 650 6132), formed from several private art collections and today part of the National Art Museum. Note the many fine works by 19th-century Romanian painter Nicolae Grigorescu; open 10 am to 6 pm Wednesday to Sunday ($1/0.50; free admission first Wednesday of the month). Don't miss the acclaimed contemporary art gallery, **Galeria Cata-comba**, hidden in the catacombs of the art museum building.

National composer George Enescu (1881–1955) lived for a short time in the former Cantacuzino Palace at Calea Victoriei 141. The building, built in the early 1900s in a French baroque style, features a fantastic clam-shaped porte-cochere above the main entrance. The **George Enescu Museum** (Muzeul George Enescu; ☎ 659 7596), now occupying the building, exhibits the musician's manuscripts and personal belongings. A collection of Bach belonging to Queen Elizabeth of Romania is on display; open 10 am to 5 pm Tuesday to Sunday ($0.50).

Piaţa Victoriei, at the northern end of Calea Victoriei, is dominated by the massive, heavily guarded **Government Building** (1938). On the north-western side of the square is the worthwhile **Grigore Antipa Natural History Museum** (Muzeul de Istorie Naturală Grigore Antipa; ☎ 650 4710). The museum's showpiece is a 4.5m reconstruction of a fossil mammoth skeleton (Deinotherium Gigantissimum), found in the Bârlad Valley in Moldavia and the only surviving skeleton of its type in the world; open 10 am to 5 pm (6 pm in summer) Tuesday to Sunday ($0.30/0.15).

A short walk south-east of Piaţa Victoriei, down Blvd Lascăr Catargui, is **Piaţa Romană**. It has a statue of **Lupoaica Romei** (the wolf of Rome) and the abandoned children **Romulus and Remus**, whom the wolf fed and cared for, enabling them to found the city of Rome. West of the square at Blvd Dacia 12 is the **Museum of Romanian Literature** (Muzeul Literaturii Române), open 10 am to 4 pm daily (free). Close by on Str Icoanei is the **Church of the Icon** (Biserica Icoanei), built by monk and former privy secretary Mihail Babreanu in 1745–50. Around the corner at Str Schitul Darvari 3 is pretty **St Slujbă's Monastery** (Mănăstirea Sfânta Slujbă), surrounded by a lush walled garden.

Piaţa Universităţii & Around

From Piaţa Romană, the centre's other main artery – Blvd General Magheru leading into Blvd Nicolae Bălcescu – runs parallel to Calea Victoriei. It leads south to Piaţa Universităţii, the hub of Bucharest's intellectual and political life. The main **university** building – built in 1856–68 and inaugurated in 1869 – is on the north-western corner of Piaţa Universităţii, adjoining Blvd Regina Elisabeta.

The onion domes of the **Student Church** peep out at the university from the south-eastern side of the square on Blvd Regina Elisabeta. To get to this Russian Orthodox church dating from 1905–09, cut down the street next to the Romanian Commercial Bank on to Str Ion Ghica. One block south, in a small yard at Str Doamnei 18, is Bucharest's small **Bulgarian Church**.

On the south-western corner of Piaţa Universităţii is the **History & Art Museum** (☎ 313 8515), Blvd IC Brătianu 2. Designed by two Austrian architects, the neo-Gothic palace was built in 1832–34 for the Şuţu family, notorious for their high-society parties. The museum has displays on 19th- and 20th-century Bucharest. The document, issued by Vlad Ţepeş in 1459, in which the city of Bucharest was chronicled for the first time, is also here; open 9 am to 5 pm Tuesday to Sunday ($0.75).

Heading east from Piaţa Universităţii along Blvd Regina Elisabeta and its continuation, Blvd Carol I, you come to the **Museum of the Armenian Community** (Muzeul Comunitaţii Armene), inside the Armenian Orthodox Church at Blvd Carol I 43; open 10 am to 4 pm Tuesday to Sunday.

A couple of blocks north-east along Str Spătarului (the street parallel to Str Armenească) is Bucharest's **Theodor Pallady Museum** (Muzeul Theodor Pallady; ☎ 211 4979), housed inside the exquisite 18th-century Casa Melik at Str Spătarului 22. A former merchant's house, Casa Melik exhibits the private art collection of the Raut family (part of the National Art Museum today) and includes several works by the Romanian artist Pallady; open 11 am to 6 pm Wednesday to Sunday.

The Civic Centre

In the last years of Ceauşescu's reign, the southern section of central Bucharest around **Piaţa Unirii** was 'systemised' to create a new civic centre. Some 26 churches, two synagogues and a monastery in the city's most historic quarter were bulldozed, and about 70,000 people made homeless, to accommodate the megalomaniac leader's grandiose building plans.

From Piaţa Unirii metro station walk over to the large ornamental **fountain** (dry for years) in the middle of the square to get your bearings. On the north-eastern side of the square is the **Unirea Department Store**; the main **city market** is a long block behind it – shop here for fresh fruit and vegetables. The **Dâmboviţa River** snakes up to the north-eastern corner of Piaţa Unirii before disappearing underground, beneath the square, on its journey to the south-west of the city. The natural twists and turns of the river were canalised between 1880 and 1883 and further enhanced with concrete in the 1980s.

Theoretically, the centre of Piaţa Unirii could be filled one day by the hulk of an Orthodox cathedral. In a bid to boost flagging morale, the foundation stone of the **Cathedral of National Salvation** (Catedrala Mântuirii Neamului) was laid with great pomp and ceremony in January 1999. Yet any sane Bucharestian knows that the Romanian Orthodox Church will never raise sufficient cash to build their pipe-dream edifice.

East from the fountain on Piaţa Unirii runs **Blvd Unirii**, a wide boulevard intended to replicate the Champs Élysées. Exactly 3.2km in length, the 'boulevard of the Victory of Socialism', as it was originally named, is flanked by towering concrete blocks and leads to a square at its western end, large enough to hold 300,000 people. Government ministries, the state prosecution office and the Romanian Intelligence Service (the successor to the Securitate) are housed in the vast civic centre buildings bordering the square to the north-east and south-east. The converging streets are lined with towering apartment buildings once intended to house privileged bureaucrats employed in nearby ministries.

South-west of Piaţa Unirii, atop Patriarchy Hill, is the majestic **Patriarchal Cathedral** (Catedrala Patriahală), wedged

between Blvd Regina Maria and Str Dealul Mitropoliei. During the 15th century a small wooden church surrounded by copious vineyards stood on the hill. The cathedral consecrated the metropolitan centre of Wallachia in 1868, and was built in 1656–58 by Wallachian prince Şerban Basarab. None of the original interior paintings or icons remains bar a single icon (1665) depicting Constantin and Helen, the cathedral's patron saints. The present-day frescoes were painted by Dimitrie Belizarie in 1923. The icons embedded in the gold iconostasis were wrought in iron in the Romanian Patriarchy's workshops in 1965. To the west of the cathedral is a small **chapel**, linked by a balcony to the **Patriarchal Palace**, the south wings of which date to 1932. Three beautifully carved, 16th- and 17th-century **stone crosses** flank the northern wall of the cathedral. Alongside is a belfry (1698) and a former parliament building dating from 1907.

Other surviving churches include the 16th-century **Prince Radu Monastery** (Mânăstirea Radu Vodă), south-east of Piaţa Unirii at Str Radu Vodă 24; and the nearby **Church of Bucur the Shepherd** (Biserica Bucur Ciobanul), dating from 1743 and dedicated to the city's legendary founder.

Tiny **St Apostles' Church** (Biserica Sfintii Apostoli), built in 1636 at Str Apostoli 33a, west of the square, survived systemisation to a degree. It was not moved but the surrounding parkland was ripped up and replanted with blocks of flats. Cut through one of the alleyways at the western end of Blvd Unirii. South of Blvd Unirii on Str Antim is the surviving **Antim Monastery** (Mănăstirea Antim), a beautiful walled complex built in 1715 by the metropolitan bishop Antim Ivireanu.

Another impressive church to survive systemisation is the candy-striped **Princess Bălaşa Church** (Biserica Domniţa Bălaşa), whose orange and red bricks provide a dramatic contrast to the grey, concrete apartment blocks which surround the edifice today. The church, just north of Piaţa Unirii, is named after Brâncoveanu's sixth daughter who had a small wooden church built here in 1744. Widowed from 1745, the princess replaced the church with a stone structure in 1751 and set up a school and asylum. Damaged by an earthquake, the second church was replaced by a third church in 1838–42, which was subsequently damaged by floods and replaced by a fourth church in 1881–85. It is this church which still stands today. The princess' grave lies in front and the church remains famous for its choir, established in 1868 and still performing today. It's just off Splaiul Independenţei, near the Justice Palace.

The fortified **Văcăreşti Monastery**, built by Prince Ioan and Nicolae Mavrocordat on the south bank of the river between 1718 and 1722, was destroyed in 1985. The neighbouring 16th-century **Prince Mihai Monastery** (Mânăstirea Mihai Vodă), built in 1589–91 under the orders of Mihai Viteazul (r. 1593–1601), was moved 279m east in 1985 to a patch of wasteland between apartment blocks at Str Sapienţei. To reach the church – one of the last remaining architectural treasures from pre-Ceauşescu Romania – head west along Splaiul Independenţei, and cut down the alleyway next to Springtime fast food at Splaiul Independenţei 7.

Towering above Piaţa Unirii to the west is Bucharest's star tourist attraction, the **Palace of Parliament** (Palatul Parlamentului; ☎ 311 3611, ⓔ cic@cic.camera.ro), which ranks as the world's second-largest building in terms of surface (third-largest by volume). Following Ceauşescu's overthrow in 1989, a reluctant Chamber of Deputies moved into the Stalinist monstrosity, then called the House of the People (Casa Poporului). Seven of its 3000-plus rooms can be visited today with a guided tour (45 minutes) in English, departing about every 10 minutes between 10 am to 4 pm ($1.50, plus $1.50/2 per camera/video). To enter the building, it's the second entrance on the right, heading west along Calea 12 Septembrie.

On the southern side of the Palace of Parliament is the huge, half-built **National Institute for Science & Technology** of which Elena Ceauşescu was president. West is the new **Ministry of Defence**. Ceauşescu planned to have the remodelling

of Bucharest complete by the end of 1990 and literally hundreds of gigantic, almost-finished buildings can be seen around the city, especially in this southern part.

WESTERN BUCHAREST

In order to make Bucharest as great a capital as Paris or Moscow, Ceauşescu decided his new city needed a river. So the Dâmboviţa was rechannelled through southern Bucharest in a tremendous engineering project.

To ensure a regular supply of water for the Dâmboviţa, he had a massive dam built across the river on the western side of Bucharest, creating **Dâmboviţa Lake**. The Crângaşi metro station is about 500m from the dam, visible from the station.

From the dam or metro station, board a southbound No 41 tram to the end of the line. From here it's two stops east on tram No 8 to the **Ghencea Civil & Military Cemeteries** on Blvd Ghencea. See the 'City Cemeteries' boxed text for details of these.

Heading north from here, Blvd Geniului snakes along the high wall of the 19th-century **Cotroceni Palace**, home to the royal court from 1893 until 1947. It was built in 1891–93 as a gift from King Ferdinand to his wife, Marie. Today the palace houses the **National Cotroceni Museum** (Muzeul Naţional Cotroceni; ☎ 222 1200) and the **Presidency of Romania** in its wings. Visits to the museum have to be booked in advance ($2.50 for an English-language tour; no visits Monday).

The entrance to Bucharest's **Botanical Garden** is on the northern side of Şoseaua Cotroceni, a little farther east. Originally part of the palace's park, the gardens were replanted in the university grounds in the 1870s and relocated to the present site in 1884. The garden – spread across 17 hectares and home to some 20,000 plant species from all over Romania – opens daily, but the **Botanical Museum & Greenhouse** only opens 9 am to 1 pm Tuesday, Thursday and Sunday ($0.15).

Heading back east towards the centre along Şoseaua Cotroceni/Str Mircea Vulcănescu, you pass the **National Military Museum** (Muzeul Militar Naţional; ☎ 637 3830,

BUCHAREST

Palace of Parliament: Vital Statistics

- Built in 1984 as the centrepiece of Ceauşescu's Civic Centre, to house the Central Committee, the presidential office and the state ministries, it's home today to the chamber of deputies, constitutional court and an international conference centre.
- One-sixth of Bucharest – including 12 churches, three monasteries, two synagogues and 7000 homes – was bulldozed to accommodate the monstrous building, which stands 85m tall and has a surface area of 330,000 sq metres.
- Ceauşescu intended it to be the largest building in the world. It is, in fact, the world's second-largest in surface (after the USA's Pentagon) and the third-largest in volume.
- Over 700 architects and three shifts of 20,000 workers laboured on it 24 hours a day for five years.
- It has three tiers, 12 storeys and 3100 furnished rooms (cleaned by a wholly female army of cleaners). Two of its 60-plus galleries are 150m long and 18m wide. Forty of its 64 reception halls are 600 sq metres. Union Hall is 3000 sq metres in size and large enough to land a helicopter in.
- Beneath the edifice is a vast nuclear bunker, plummeting 20m deep.
- In the 1980s, when lit, the building consumed a day's electricity supply for the whole of Bucharest in four hours.
- When Ceauşescu was toppled, building work was not complete. He had not yet quite decided on the final roof design. All the present-day furnishings were installed in 1992–96.
- The carpet once coating the floor of Union Hall weighs 14 tonnes; it's rolled up today and hidden behind screens at one end of the hall. The crystal chandelier in the Human Rights Hall weighs 2½ tonnes.
- It was renamed Palace of Parliament (Palatul Parlamentului) after Romania's first postcommunist parliament moved in, but is often still known locally by its former name, the House of the People (Casa Poporului).
- Locals have a love-hate relationship with the house – it's among the world's worst eyesores yet its interior is a fantastic showpiece of Romanian craftsmanship.
- Estimated building costs range from US$760 million to US$3.3 billion.

JEROEN VAN MARLE

638 7630), Str Mircea Vulcănescu 125–127, which recounts the history of the Romanian army. The rooms to the left of the ticket desk house an exhibition on the 1989 revolution; the names of 939 people who died during the bloodshed are engraved on a marble memorial cross here. The museum is open 9 am to 5 pm Tuesday to Sunday ($0.30). From here, if you bear south along

Calea Plevnei, you eventually come to the **Opera House** (Opera Română). A **statue** of George Enescu, whose opera *Oedipus* was premiered here, stands in front of the opera building.

NORTHERN BUCHAREST

Pleasant, tree-lined **Şoseaua Kiseleff**, with its elegant mansions and beautifully tended

City Cemeteries

Romanian dictator Nicolae Ceauşescu and his wife-in-crime, Elena, are buried at **Ghencea Civil Cemetery** (Cimitirul Civil Ghencea), west of the city centre. Following their secret burial here on 30 December 1989, the couple's graves were marked with wooden crosses bearing the pseudonyms of two reserve colonels – 'Colonel Popa Dan 1920–89' and 'Colonel Enescu Vasile 1921–89' – in an attempt to prevent their graves becoming a place of pilgrimage. Today, nonetheless, fresh flowers adorn Ceauşescu's grave and candles burn around the clock thanks to a handful of disgruntled pensioners who tend his grave and pay homage to the man who granted them an adequate monthly pension, rent-free apartments and free medical treatment – none of which they receive today.

Small, elaborate tombstones replaced the wooden crosses marking the tombs in May 1990. Nicolae's grave bears three crosses – a heavy cross made from stone bearing no name; a black steel cross inscribed with his name, date of birth and death (26 January 1918 – 24 December 1989); and a more ornate, marble cross erected in May 1996 by the Romanian Workers' Party. Elena's more modest grave is flagged by a wooden cross, on which her name is scrawled with a black pen. The Ceauşescus lie on opposite sides of the main avenue that leads to the church in the cemetery's centre; Nicolae to the left and Elena to the right. The flamboyant grave of their son Nicu (1951–96) – a notorious playboy, womaniser and drunkard who died in Vienna of liver cirrhosis – lies to the left of the church.

The **Ghencea Military Cemetery** (Cimitirul Militar Ghencea) adjoins this civil cemetery. Most tombstones bear a photograph of the deceased. Propeller blades stand upright amid the sea of graves. A silver-domed, white church stands in the centre of the cemetery. Both cemeteries are a straight 2.5km trek along Calea 13 Septembrie from the Palace of Parliament.

Bucharest's other graveyards lie south of the city centre, on the south-western fringe of Youth Park. Amid the vast sea of graves in **Belu Cemetery** (Cimitirul Belu), the main city cemetery, are the tombs of Romania's most notable writers and poets, including comic playwright and humorist Ion Luca Caragiale (1852–1912), novelist Ion Liviu Rebreanu (1885–1944), Moldavian-born writer and historian Mihail Sadoveanu (1880–1961) and national poet Mihai Eminescu (1850–89). Eminescu's grave is on the northern side of plot No 9 – sadly, his dying wish to be buried under a lime tree did not come to pass. A plan of the cemetery and a list of some of the people buried in it is posted on a board at the main entrance on Calea Şerban Vodă. The postwar communist leader Gheorghe Gheorghiu-Dej, who died in 1965 after ruling Romania for two decades, is buried in the modest **military section** of Belu cemetery.

Heroes' Cemetery (Cimitirul Eroii Revoluţiei), at Belu's northern end, pays homage to the heroes of the 1989 revolution. A sea of identical graves frames **Martyr Heroes' Church** (Biserica Eroilor Martiri), raised in the late 1990s by the Romanian Orthodox Church.

On the opposite side of Calea Şerban Vodă is the city's **Sephardic Jewish Cemetery** (see the boxed text 'Jewish Bucharest' later in this chapter).

---

lawns and flower beds, stretches north from Piaţa Victoriei to Herăstrău Park. At its most southern end is the **Museum of the Romanian Peasant** (Muzeul Ţăranului Român; ☎ 650 5360, e mtr@itcgate.itc.ro), Şoseaua Kiseleff 3. Built on the site of Bucharest's former mint and Mavrogheni Palace, the building was, in 1953–90, a museum dedicated to the history of the Communist Party. Today's museum displays Romania's largest collection of folklore treasures, including an 18,000-piece pottery collection; open 10 am to 6 pm Tuesday to Sunday ($1/0.25). Taking photographs inside costs an additional $5 and you can hire an English-speaking guide ($2.50) to explain the Romanian-only captions to you. The **Museum of Geology** (Muzeul de Geologie; ☎ 650 5094) is opposite; open 10 am to 3 pm weekdays ($0.75/0.50).

A further 1.5km north on Şoseaua Kiseleff is the **Triumphal Arch** (Arcul de Triumf). Its resemblance to the Arc de Triomphe in Paris was intentional and gives some evidence of the strength of French-Romanian cultural ties prior to WWI. The 11m-tall arch, constructed from reinforced concrete and granite mined in Deva, was built in 1935–36 to commemorate the reunification of Romania in 1918.

The sites of the WWI battles in which the Romanian front fought are inscribed inside the arch and King Ferdinand and Queen Marie feature on its southern facade. A makeshift triumphal monument allegedly made from cardboard and wood had been erected on the site in 1878 to mark the achievement of Romanian independence the previous year. In 1922 a new wooden structure was hastily thrown up in time for King Ferdinand's triumphant entry into the city as the first king of a united Greater Romania. The arch was so equally ludicrous that composer George Enescu was motivated to write to the city mayor, demanding to know when, in fact, a 'real' triumphal arch would be erected.

East of here, beyond Piaţa Charles de Gaulle, is the headquarters of **Romanian Television**, on Calea Dorobanţilor. In the late 1980s, the TV was reduced to a mere two hours air-time a day, one devoted to presidential activities. In December 1989 revolutionaries broke into the television building and announced the collapse of the government on air. In front of the building is a small **memorial** to those killed here.

From Calea Dorobanţilor, a short walk south along Str Emil Pangratti or parallel Str Grigore Mora brings you to the **Zambaccian Museum** (Muzeul Zambaccian; ☎ 230 1920) at Str Muzeul Zambaccian 21a. This small but fascinating house museum displays the private art collection of Krikor Zambaccian (1889–1962), an Armenian businessman who collected works by Cézanne, Matisse and Picasso as well as all the Romanian greats during his lifetime; open 10 am to 6 pm Tuesday to Sunday.

During the communist era Şoseaua Kiseleff was the most prestigious residential area

in the city, parts of it reserved strictly for Communist Party officials *(nomenklatura)*. Nicolae and Elena Ceauşescu had their private residence, **Primăverii Palace**, at Blvd Primăverii 50 (on the corner of Blvd Mircea Eliade), north-east of Piaţa Charles de Gaulle. The palace is heavily guarded and off-limits to everyone except state guests and personnel from the European cultural centre that is also here. Just across the entrance to Ceauşescu's mansion on Blvd Mircea Eliade is the **former residence** of Gheorghe Gheorghiu-Dej, Romania's communist ruler until Ceauşescu took over in 1965.

A short walk north from the Triumphal Arch along Şoseaua Kiseleff is one of Bucharest's best sights, the **Village Museum** (Muzeul Satului; ☎ 222 9103/9106), which contains full-scale displays of nearly 300 churches, wooden houses, windmills, roadside crosses and farm buildings. Established in 1936, it is one of Europe's largest and oldest outdoor museums, and should *not* be missed if you don't plan to travel to Romania's more rural regions; open 9 am to 5 pm (closed Monday October to May). Admission costs $1.50. The main entrance to the museum is at Şoseaua Kiseleff 28–30; the northern entrance opens into Herăstrău Park (see the later Parks & Lakes section). To get here from the centre, take bus No 131 or 331 from Blvd General Magheru or Piaţa Romană to the 'Muzeul Satului' stop.

North-west of the Village Museum, at Blvd Expoziţiei 2, is the **Exhibition Pavilion & Conference Centre**, home to the Romanian EXPO. The modern **World Trade Centre**, housing a fashionable shopping mall and five-star hotel, stands on the same site.

At its northern end, Şoseaua Kiseleff splays out into Piaţa Presei Libere, on the northern side of which is Bucharest's giant **Press House** (Casa Presei Libere), a 1956 Stalinist, wedding-cake structure. Until 1990 the house was called the 'House of the Sparks' (Casa Scânteii); behind closed doors it was known as the 'House of Lies'. A **statue of Lenin** which stood on the red marble pedestal in front of the building was levelled in 1989 and dumped in Mogoşoaia (see Around Bucharest later in this chapter).

North-east of the square at Str Dr Nicolae Minovici 3 is the **Minovici Museum of Ancient Western Arts** (Muzeul de Artă Veche Apuseană Minovici; ☎ 657 1505), housed in an English-style castle; open 9 am to 5 pm Thursday to Sunday ($0.10).

PARKS & LAKES

The lush, well-kept parks and not-so-clear-blue lakes in Bucharest's suburbs provide a welcome escape from the hustle and bustle of the city.

To the north of the city centre is **Herăstrău Lake** (Lacu Herăstrău), which stretches almost the entire width of the city from east to west, north of Piaţa Charles de Gaulle (metro Piaţa Aviatorilor). The surrounding 200-hectare pleasure park, Bucharest's largest, opened in 1936. You can hire boats and swim in the lake. On the lake's western shores, there are two small landings, from where you can cross or circle the lake in a cruising boat. Two boats sail daily between May and October. To take the return crossing ($0.75, 10 minutes), go to the landing marked 'traversări cu vaporul'. The circular cruise ($1.50, 30 minutes) leaves from the central landing ('debarcaderul centrul').

Ten kilometres north of Bucharest is **Băneasa Park** (Parcul Băneasa), surrounded by deep forest. Fast-food kiosks and huts cooking traditional Romanian spicy sausages *(mititei)* are plentiful here. To reach the park from the centre, take bus No 301 from Piaţa Romană.

Just north-east of the centre is **Circus Park** (Parcul Circului), 10 minutes' walk from the Obor or Ştefan cel Mare metro stations or a short ride by tram No 34 along Şoseaua Ştefan cel Mare.

Scattered throughout this quiet park is a unique collection of **sculpted wooden caricatures** entitled 'Wooden Spirits' (Spirite în Lemn). The totem-pole-style sculptures, the work of local sculptor Titi Teodorescu, are carved from the trunks of trees that have died in the park. A peasant *(ţăran)*, a mother and child *(mamă şi copii)*, lovers *(îndrăgostiţi)*, a monkey *(maimuţă)* and an elephant *(elefant)*, along with Pinocchio, Superman and opera tenor Luciano

Pavarotti, are just some of the 'spirits' to haunt the park.

Also central is the historic **Cişmigiu Garden** (Grădina Cişmigiu), close to Piaţa Universităţii. Bucharest's oldest park, it dates from the early 19th century and is dubbed 'lovers' park'. The pretty gardens were landscaped in classical English style by a gardener from Berlin. You can rent rowing boats here.

Youth Park (Parcul Tineretului; metro Tineretului), at the southern limits of the city centre, is a popular haunt for city dwellers in summer. You can rent rowing boats from the small boathouse on the north-eastern shores of the lake in the centre of the park, which, despite its murky waters, people still swim in. Cycling paths circle the lake. Sporting events, fashion shows, conferences and open-air concerts take place in the **Sports & Culture Palace** (Palatul Sporturilor şi Culturii) in the centre of the park.

Carol I Park, five minutes' walk north-east of Youth Park on Calea Şerban Vodă, was inaugurated in 1906. An eternal flame burns in memory of the unknown soldier and bands play in the bandstand. Its centre-piece is a 20m-tall **mausoleum**, built in 1958 from black Norwegian granite and topped with five arches of red Swedish granite. It was put up in memory of 'the Heroes of the Struggle for the People's and the Homeland's Liberty, for Socialism'. Until 1991, when the mausoleum was dis-interned, Gheorghe Gheorghiu-Dej was buried beneath the arches along with other early Romanian communists.

Since 1991, indecision has surrounded the future of the communist monstrosity which remains guarded by police today. The Romanian Orthodox Church has played with the idea of building Romania's largest Orthodox cathedral in the park, the bell of which would hang from the arches. In April 2000, meanwhile, the mausoleum was used by the government as an auction hall to auction off a load of Ceauşescu's unwanted possessions.

From the mausoleum, stairs lead north through the park to a square where you get to tree-lined Str 11 Iunie; this brings you into Blvd Regina Maria and Piaţa Unirii.

Jewish Bucharest

Jewish merchants and traders first settled in Bucharest in the 16th century. By 1861 more than 6000 Jews – mainly from Russia, Turkey and Balkan regions south of the Danube – lived in the capital. There were around 30 synagogues at this time. Mounting anti-Semitism in the latter part of the 19th century, coupled with increasing internal conflicts within the Jewish community, prompted many Jews to leave Bucharest. As early as 1801, an estimated 100 Jews died during anti-Semitic riots. Nevertheless, on the eve of WWII there were an estimated 95,000 Jews in Bucharest and 80 working synagogues.

Little remains of the old **Jewish quarter** of Văcărești, north-east of Piața Unirii in Bucharest's historic heart. During the Iron Guard's fascist pogrom in 1941, entire streets of houses were burnt to the ground, synagogues looted and Jewish-run businesses razed. What remained of the quarter's narrow cobblestone streets, small wooden houses, synagogues and schools was levelled by Ceaușescu in the mid-1980s.

The **Jewish History Museum** (Muzeul de Istorie al Comunitaților Evreiești din România) is housed in the former tailors' synagogue at Str Mămulari 3. It dates from 1850 and is one of three pre-WWII synagogues to survive. Its centrepiece is a sculpture of a mourning woman, in memory of the estimated 100,000 to 150,000 Jews who were deported to hard-labour camps in Transdniestr, Moldova, and the 200,000 from Transylvania who died in Auschwitz. Candles burn in tribute to the six million Jews killed during the Holocaust. The museum opens 9.30 am to 1 pm Wednesday and Sunday ($0.75).

Close by at Str Vineri 9 is the **Choral Temple**, built in 1857 and still serving Bucharest's remaining Jewish community of 8000. Its magnificent Moorish turrets, choir loft and organ remain intact. A **memorial** to the victims of the Holocaust, put up in 1991, fronts the temple. The third, smaller synagogue close to Piața Amzei on Str Tache Ionescu is no longer used.

The **Sephardic Jewish Cemetery** (Cimitirul Evreisc de rit Sefard) lies opposite Belu Cemetery on Calea Șerban Vodă, in the south of the city (metro Eroii Revoluției). Two rows of graves dated 21–23 January 1941 mark the Iron Guard's pogrom against the Jewish community in Bucharest, during which at least 170 Jews were murdered.

LANGUAGE COURSES
See Courses in the Facts for the Visitor chapter.

ORGANISED TOURS
Most travel agencies organise city tours and day trips around Bucharest (see Travel Agencies, under Information earlier in this chapter).

The Cultural Tourism Institute (☎/fax 223 2619/2292, e cti@com.pcnet.ro), Blvd Primăverii 50, organises cultural and academic tours in English, French, German and other languages of the city and surrounds. It has an office in Primăverii Palace (closed to the public); tours must be booked in advance by email or telephone.

Spooky tours are the speciality of the Company of Mysterious Journeys, the official tour operator for the Transylvanian Society of Dracula; see Organised Tours in the Getting Around chapter for details.

SPECIAL EVENTS
Bucharest plays host to numerous theatre and music festivals. Annual events worth attending include:

Bucharest Carnival – late May/early June: a week-long carnival with street dancers, street theatre, folk dancers dressed in 1900 period costume and live bands performing in Bucharest's historic heart
Dreher Beer Festival – mid-June: four-day beer festival with live bands, drinking contests and the like in Herăstrău Park
Fête de la Musique – 21st June: annual French music festival organised by the French Institute
Hora Festival – 1st August: three-day dance festival attracting traditional folk dance troupes from all over the country; held in the Village Museum

Craftsman's Fair – 15th August: local craft fair hosted by the Village Museum with guest craftspeople from all over Romania

International George Enescu Music Festival – September: held every odd-numbered year, attracting musicians from all over the world

National Theatre Festival – October: a week-long theatre festival held every year in the National Theatre

St Dumitru Day – last week of October: a two-day carnival celebrating Bucharest's patron saint, Dumitru

PLACES TO STAY – BUDGET

Budget accommodation can get fully booked in summer.

Camping

In Băneasa, *Casa Albă* (☎ 230 5203, ☎/fax 230 6255, Aleea Privighetorilor 1–3) is a restaurant with adjoining camping ground, open mid-April to October. A two-bed wooden hut *(căsuţe)* in the well-maintained grounds costs $15; or negotiate a fee to pitch your tent. To get here, take bus No 301 from Piaţa Romană to Şoseaua Bucureşti-Ploieşti; get off at the stop after Băneasa airport and head east along Aleea Privighetorilor to the Casa Albă complex. Bus No 783 to/from Otopeni airport also stops here.

Hostels

Backpackers should head to *Villa Helga* (☎/fax 610 2214, 🅴 helga@rotravel.com, Str Salcâmilor 2), five minutes' walk from Piaţa Romană. Housed in a villa with a vine-covered terrace, the 32-bed HI hostel is run by a young, dynamic team who go out of their way to make travellers feel at home. It has a washing machine, cable TV, tons of tourist guides/reference books, Internet access, bicycles to rent and free, locally produced Carpaţi cigarettes. A bed in a two- to 10-bed room costs $12 a night (or $72/198 a week/month), including breakfast. From Gara de Nord, don't take a taxi here (see the boxed text 'Street Scams' in the Facts for the Visitor chapter). Take bus No 79 or 133 to Piaţa Gemeni (the sixth stop) instead; or bus No 783 from Otopeni airport to Piaţa Romană, then bus No 79, 86, 133 or 226 two stops along Blvd Dacia to Piaţa Gemeni.

Nearby is *YMCA Hostel* (☎/fax 210 0909, Str Silvestu 23), a smaller and less-appealing place which charges the same rate for a bed in a two-, three- or four-bed room. Reception hours are theoretically 2 pm to 6 pm; call in advance to check it's open. From Gara de Nord take bus No 133 or 123, or trolleybus No 26 to Moşilor station.

At the time of writing, a third hostel, *Villa 11* (mobile ☎ 092-495 900, 🅴 villa11 bb@hotmail.com, Str Institutul Medic Militar 11), was expected to open near Gara de Nord. Run by a Romanian and American team, the hostel has six rooms. A bed costs $12.50 a night and advance reservations are required.

Hotels – City Centre

Hotel Carpaţi (☎ 315 0140, fax 312 1857, Str Matei Millo 16) is Bucharest's most aesthetically pleasing budget option. A sparkling reception area leads to renovated singles with shared bathroom costing $11. Doubles with private shower *or* toilet (make your choice clear when checking in) cost $27; some have a balcony (again, request one when checking in).

The entrance to downtrodden but quiet *Hotel Dâmboviţa* (☎ 315 6244, Blvd Schitu Măgureanu 6) is on Str Gutemberg. Single/double rooms with shared showers cost $10/16 and singles with private shower are $16.

Hotel Muntenia (☎ 314 6010/1784, fax 314 1782, Str Academiei 19–21) is noisy but has a great location near the university. It costs $14.50/24/40/43 for a single/double/triple/quad with shared bath, and $32 for doubles with private shower.

Hotels – Around Gara de Nord

Around Gara de Nord, just north-west of the city centre, is a cluster of cheap hotels. Exit the station and walk 30m right to noisy but surprisingly clean *Hotel Bucegi* (☎ 637 5225/5030, fax 637 5115, Str Witing 2). Single rooms with shared bath cost $10, and doubles without/with bath cost $13/20. Triples/quads with private bathroom are exceptionally good value at $15/20. Breakfast costs an additional $2.50 per person.

Across the street, renovated *Hotel Cerna* (☎ *637 4087, Blvd Dinicu Golescu 29*) charges $12/16 for a single/double with shared bath ($20/32 with bath). It also has apartments for $43 a night. For breakfast, the adjoining *Cofetărie Ema* serves tasty pastries from 8 am to 8 pm.

Cheerful, 30-room *Hotel Marna* (☎ *650 6820, fax 312 9455, Str Buzeşti 3*) is perhaps the best of the station bunch, with a welcoming reception that has actually been renovated. Singles/doubles with shared bath cost $14/19, and doubles with private bathroom cost $32.50. Prices include breakfast.

PLACES TO STAY – MID-RANGE
City Centre

One of the most historic places to stay is two-star *Hanul lui Manuc* (*Manuc's Inn; ☎ 313 1415, fax 312 2811, Str Franceză 62–64*), housed in a 19th-century merchants' inn. Singles/doubles with private bath cost upwards of $45/53. Unfortunately, its restaurant is a rip-off and its staff surly.

In the centre, the aptly named *Hotel Central* (☎ *312 5636/5637, Str Brezoianu 13*) has 60 quite good-value renovated rooms with private bathroom costing $63/79.

Around Gara de Nord

Around Gara de Nord, the two-star *Hotel Astoria* (☎ *637 7640, ☎/fax 638 2690, Blvd Dinicu Golescu 27*) has the dimmest-lit reception hall in the city. Gloom apart, this hotel lures business travellers with its $36/53 singles/doubles with private bath. Rates include breakfast.

By mid-2001 *Hotel Nord* (*Calea Griviţei 143*) next to the bus station, under renovation at the time of writing, will reopen as an Ibis chain hotel.

North of the Centre

To the north, towards the Triumphal Arch, is elegant *Hotel Triumf* (☎ *222 3172, fax 223 2411, Şoseaua Kiseleff 12*) with single/double rooms costing $35/47. The hotel grounds are superb.

East of the Press House is *Parc Hotel* (☎ *224 4460/2000*, e *rdm@parc-hotel.ro, Blvd Poligrafiei 3–5*), a concrete block

adopted by the Best Western hotel chain. Plain rooms cost $59/69; their renovated counterparts go for $90/110. Behind its brightly painted blue-and-yellow facade is grey *Hotel Turist* (☎ *222 4462, ☎/fax 224 2984, Blvd Poligrafiei 3–5*, e *parchtl@ fx.ro*). Singles/doubles/triples here are a steal at $25/33/42.

PLACES TO STAY – TOP END
City Centre

Attractive *Hotel Minerva* (☎ *650 6010, 311 1551, fax 312 2734*, e *reservation@miner va.ro, Str Gheorghe Manu 2–4*) has singles/doubles warranting no complaints for $120/150. Its *Nan Jing Restaurant* is known for its exquisite (but pricey) Chinese food.

Four-star *Hotel Lido* (☎ *314 4930, fax 312 1414, Blvd General Magheru 5–7*) is a 1930s building with every conceivable mod-con inside. Rooms cost $180/195.

Not as historic, but showing its age, is *Hotel Ambasador* (☎ *315 9080, fax 312 3595, Blvd General Magheru 8–10*), another business-traveller favourite with doubles costing $120/135 in the low/high season.

Along Calea Victoriei, there are several top-end choices, including *Hotel Bucureşti* (☎ *312 7070/7047, fax 312 0927*) at No 63–68, said to be the haunt of local parliamentarians (and prostitutes), and *Hotel Continental* (☎ *312 0132, 638 5022, fax 312 0134*, e *continen@kappa.ro*) at No 56, both of which charge around $180/200. *Hotel Capitol* (☎ *315 8030, fax 312 4169*) at No 29 has cheaper $80/100/125 single/double/triple rooms.

The southern foot of Blvd Nicolae Bălcescu is dominated by towering *Hotel Inter-Continental* (☎ *310 2020, fax 312 0486*, e *inter@starnets.ro*), a handy landmark at No 4. Its 22 floors host single/double rooms costing $294/320. Its *restaurants* – including Balada on the 21st floor – sport a decor of the prerevolution variety.

Five-star *Athénée Palace Hilton* (☎ *303 3777, fax 315 2121*, e *hilton@hilton.com, sa@hilton.ro, Str Episcopiei 1–3*) is steeped in history. It has a beautiful *restaurant* serving Sunday brunch ($19), a bistro, English Bar, casino and banquet hall with an exquisite glass-dome ceiling. Rooms cost upwards of $300/340.

Behind the Palace of Parliament on Str Izvor is a half-built monstrosity which will house the five-star *Grand Hotel Marriott* by the end of 2001. A costly facelift will likewise transform, by mid-2001, the grim block at Calea Dorobanţilor 1–7 into the sparkling, multistarred *Howard Johnson Plaza Hotel*.

North of the Centre
American presidents and other suitably powerful people grace *Hotel Sofitel* (☎ 224 3000/2683, fax 211 5688, ⓔ business@sofit el.net.ro, Blvd Expoziţiei 2), adjoining the World Trade Centre, with their presence when in town. Expensive, elegant single/ double rooms start at $258/283, including breakfast and excluding 19% VAT.

Farther north off Piaţa Presei Libere is *Crowne Plaza Bucharest Flora* (☎ 224 0034, fax 224 1126, ⓔ cplaza@fx.ro, Blvd Poligrafiei 1), a sparkling haven of peace and luxury. Rooms theoretically cost upwards of $240/260, but reception staff make no bones about discounts being available.

PLACES TO EAT
Restaurants
Dining out in Bucharest is not cheap. There has been a rapid influx of flashy, upmarket restaurants offering a dazzling array of international cuisine with prices to match. However, it is still easy to track down traditional Romanian cooking – generally at a less painful price. Even places which purport to be French, Turkish or Greek will generally have at least one local dish on the menu.

Reservations are not needed in most restaurants. Most upmarket places accept Visa/MasterCard.

Historic Quarter In Bucharest's historic heart, *Mes Amis* is an intimate restaurant tucked down narrow Str Zarafi (off Str Lipscani) where you can dine by candlelight. Local art is displayed for purchase on its ochre walls and wine is served by the glass ($0.50) as well as bottle, a rarity in Bucharest. Don't miss its house speciality – apple-packed pancakes.

A hop away is *Caru cu Bere* (☎ 313 7560, Str Stavropoleos 3), Bucharest's oldest beer hall dating from 1875 and worth a visit for its lavish, Gothic-style decor. Traditional Romanian dishes appear dirt cheap – until you realise prices are per 100g. A 240g portion of *sarmale* (stuffed cabbage or vine leaves), accompanied by 200g of *mămăligă* (Romanian polenta), costs $2. Roma bands play most days from noon.

Hop again and you arrive at *Hanul lui Manuc* (Manuc's Inn; ☎ 313 1415, Str Franceză 62–64), a historic inn dating from 1812. It touts an old-world atmosphere, a beautiful terrace overlooking a courtyard, and bolshy waiters yet to understand the concept of customer service. Legend has it that the original 19th-century owner was poisoned by a fortune-teller who had to murder him to make his prophecy – that the inn-keeper would die – come true. It costs around $10 a head to dine here; dishes on the menu are priced per 100g.

Impossible to find, but an absolute gem once found, is French *Café de la Joie* (☎ 315 0937, Str Bibliotecii 4), hidden in the basement of a soulless concrete office block off Piaţa Universităţii. The candlelit bistro oozes soul, with jazzy French classics spinning on the turntable and a changing menu chalked up on the blackboard. You'll pay around $6 a head, including wine. Don't confuse this Café de la Joie with the inferior establishment of the same name at Str Băcani 3–5.

Another interior worth a peep is that of the ghoulish *Count Dracula Club* (☎ 312 1353, ⓔ romantic@fx.ro, Splaiul Independenţei 8a), which – despite the human skulls, pickled bats, blood-dripping walls etc – is surprisingly civilised. A wholly traditional, Romanian menu is enlivened with game dishes such as pheasant, venison and wild boar. Dine in the coffin-clad chapel if you want the full house-of-horror experience.

No guessing what's served at *Gulaş* (pronounced 'goulash'; Str Gabroveni 20), a Hungarian restaurant at the same address as Swing House bar.

Some distance west of the historic centre is *Tipsy*, serving hearty portions of munchworthy Romanian cuisine for delicious prices (see Pub & Bars in the later Entertainment section).

Piaţa Revoluţiei & Around Opposite the Romanian Athenaeum, *Bistro Atheneu* (☎ 313 4900, Str Episcopiei 3) is an old favourite. Its high-quality food and friendly, French-inspired atmosphere draws large crowds, as does its serenading musicians who play most evenings. Salads/mains average $2.50/5. Around the corner, *La Taifas* (☎ 313 4900, 311 3204, Str Georges Clemenceau 6) is run by the same team and touts an almost-identical menu.

The southern side of the Romanian Athenaeum faces *Cina* (☎ 310 1017, Str Franklin 12), whose sun-filled *terasa* (terrace) overlooking Piaţa Revoluţiei more than compensates for its less tasteful interior. Pre-WWII Cina, featured in Manning's *Balkan Trilogy*, lured an illustrious set.

Jars of pickled gherkins, furry wall rugs and vibrant Transylvanian fabrics lend *Boema* (☎ 315 7298, 313 3783, Str CA Rosetti 10) a suitably rustic feel. Somewhat more subtle is nearby *Menuet* (☎ 312 0143, Str Nicolae Golescu 14), which – despite its heavy, old-style furnishings – dishes up excellent Romanian cuisine, including the crispiest, gooiest and tastiest *caşcaval pâine* (fried breaded cheese) around.

More upmarket choices include *Maxim Club* (☎ 315 9260, Str Oteteleşanu 3), where you feast on traditional Romanian dancing, music and folklore entertainment while you dine.

For Italian fare, try *Casa Veche* (☎ 615 7897, Str George Enescu 15–17), known for its excellent pizzas, astonishingly slow service and fabulous walled summer garden. Its adjoining cafe-cum-bakery is a good spot to breakfast from 7 am. Those seeking more than a pizza should head next door to *Café Olé* (☎ 310 1722, Str George Enescu 11a), an upmarket restaurant serving authentic and delicious Italian fare (but no pizza), kicked off by a 'complimentary' serve of bruschetta in exchange for the $1 cover charge.

East of the Historic Quarter Cheap and cheerful spots, ideal for a backpacking budget and within walking distance of the Villa Helga and YMCA hostels, are *Bureibista* (☎ 210 9704, Calea Moşilor 26) and *Nicoreşti* (☎ 211 2480, Str Maria Rosetti 40). Dine at either for $2.

Sun-inspired cuisine from the shores of the Mediterranean is served at *Mediterraneo* (☎ 211 5308, Str Icoanei 18–20).

Nearby, *Smart's* (☎ 211 9035, Str Alex Donici 14) serves European bar-style food like meaty beef steaks doused in a choice of sauces ($8.50) and well-dressed, giant-sized salads ($5.50). This place gets busy so book a table in advance to avoid disappointment.

La Premiera (☎ 312 4397, Str Tudor Arghezi 16), behind the National Theatre, has an Aladdin's Cave-style interior which is crammed with historical knick-knacks, black-and-white prints of 1920s Bucharest – and expats. A piano-cello-violin trio plays most nights. Mains cost around $8, plus $1 per garnish.

Just south-east of Piaţa Universităţii is Bucharest's only Turkish restaurant: the *Golden Falcon* (Casa Chebab; ☎ 314 2825, Str Histro Botev 18–20) serves delicious Turkish dishes, accompanied by pitta bread so large it won't fit on your plate.

North of the Centre Italian *Il Gattopardo* (☎ 659 7428, Calea Victoriei 115), near Piaţa Romană, is named after the famous Visconti film, *The Leopard*. It's favoured for its unique and historical setting inside the Writers' Union house (Uniunea Scriitorilor).

La Mama (☎ 212 4086, Str Barbu Văcărescu 3), a convivial, contemporary spot farther north of the centre, serves delicious Romanian cuisine at great prices. Salads/main dishes cost around $1/2.50 and advance reservations are essential.

Transit passengers seeking a decent munch between trains should consider *Hong Kong* (☎ 659 5025), two minutes' walk from the train station on Calea Griviţei. Sizzling meat platters average $3 and fish dishes swim in around $8.

Casa Vernescu (☎ 231 0220, Calea Victoriei 129–133), adjoining Bucharest's most popular casino where limousines hover outside, is lavishly decorated and highly atmospheric.

Elegant *Casa Doina* (☎ *222 3179/6717,* e *casadoina@meganet.ro, Şoseaua Kiseleff 4)* dates from 1892. Expensive but exquisite Romanian dishes are served in a beautiful terrace garden, adorned with tinkling fountains, serenading musicians and waiters dressed in penguin suits. Farther north out of town, there's another lovely summer garden at *Doi Cocoşi* (☎ *667 1998, Şoseaua Bucureşti-Târgovişte 6)* where traditional folk bands play most evenings. It's pricey and attracts a wanna-be-seen set.

Cafes
Da Vinci (☎ *312 2494, Str Ion Câmpineanu 11),* inside the Union Business Centre, is one of the few places in the city to serve strong espresso, hearty sandwiches, filled baguettes and tasty salads costing upwards of $2. Don't confuse the cafe with the restaurant of the same name, directly opposite.

Diplomat (Calea Dorobanţilor 20–28) is a spacious but spartan, indoor cafe which serves freshly made cakes, pastries and other sweet-tooth temptations. Semi-smiling service is at the counter. Farther north, just off Calea Dorobanţilor on the corner of Str Radu Beller and Str George Călinescu, is *Ana*, an old-world cake-filled shop where you can consume thousands of calories sitting down or standing up.

A stone's throw away on Piaţa Dorobanţilor is *Brutăria Deutschland* and *Café Einstein*, a German-style bakery which bakes the best bread in Bucharest. Soft drinks in its pricey cafe cost $1.75.

A great place on busy Calea Victoriei for sampling rich cakes in a nonsmoking environment is *Cofetăria Continental*, adjoining Hotel Continental at No 56. Its huge windows overlooking the street make it a great people-watching spot.

Fast Food
Bucharest is plastered with fast-food outlets and 24-hour kiosks selling hot dogs, burgers, popcorn, *covrigi* (rings of hard bread speckled with salt crystals) and other munch-while-you-walk snacks.

Planet Diner (Blvd Nicolae Bălcescu 3–5), opposite Hotel Inter-Continental, is a vast, modern diner with counters specialising in pizza, pasta, meat dishes, coffee and cakes etc. Its outside terrace is among Bucharest's best-placed.

Simplon Fast Food, opposite Hotel Majestic on Calea Victoriei, serves healthy salads, burgers and hot dogs. Farther south along Calea Victoriei is Pasajul Victoriei, an alleyway crammed with fast-food kiosks.

McMoni's (Piaţa Rosetti 3), two minutes' walk from Piaţa Universităţii, is always packed, as is *Springtime*, a chain with outlets at Splaiul Independenţei 7 and on Piaţa Universitaţii and Piaţa Victoriei.

McDonald's has countless outlets in central Bucharest; its McDrive on the corner of Str Buzeşti and Str Polizu is five minutes' walk from Gara de Nord and opens 24 hours. *Dunkin' Donuts*, at the south end of Str Radu Beller and on Piaţa Unirii, also opens nonstop.

Self-Catering
Piaţa Amzei (Amzei Market), just off Calea Victoriei on Piaţa Amzei, opens daily from sunrise to sunset and has the juiciest selection of fresh fruit and veg in Bucharest. Another open-air market, *Piaţa Gemeni*, is within spitting distance of the Villa Helga hostel, off Blvd Dacia on Piaţa Gemeni.

The *Nic* (open 8 am to 8.30 pm Monday to Saturday, 9 am to 2.30 pm Sunday) and *Vox Maris* (open 24 hours) supermarket chains both have branches on Piaţa Amzei. Vox Maris also has a 24-hour shop on Piaţa Victoriei. *Unic*, another chain, has a branch at Blvd Nicolae Bălcescu 33.

La Fourmi (The Ant), on the eastern side of Piaţa Unirii, is Bucharest's most advanced (and expensive) supermarket, complete with trolleys and every imaginable imported food product money can buy.

Pâtisserie Parisienne Valerie, a French-style bakery selling delicious cakes and pastries, has branches close to Hotel Bucureşti at the northern end of Calea Victoriei, and on the corner of Piaţa Romană and Blvd Dacia. For Schwarzbrot, Nussbrot and other nutty German breads, look no further than

Brutăria Deutschland at Str Edgar Quinet 5 and on Piaţa Dorobanţilor.

ENTERTAINMENT

For a weekly listing of what's on where, pick up a copy of *Şapte Seri* (Seven Evenings), a free entertainment magazine crammed with cinema, theatre and opera programs; details of the week's sporting events; and information on live gigs and concerts in Bucharest's bars and clubs.

The Romanian daily newspaper *România Libera* publishes the weekly events listing *Timpul Liber* – a free pull-out – with its Friday (English-language) edition.

Cinemas

Most films are shown in their original language with Romanian subtitles and cost around $1. Mainstream cinemas are clustered on the section of Blvd Nicolae Bălcescu between Hotel Inter-Continental and Piaţa Romană, and on Blvd Regina Elisabeta. Popular downtown cinemas include *Cinemateca Română* (☎ 313 0483, Str Eforie 2), *Cinema Scala* (☎ 211 0372, Blvd General Magheru 2–4), *Cinema Luceafărul* (☎ 315 8767, Str IC Brătianu 6) and *Cinema Cotroceni* (☎ 638 4045, Şoseaua Cotroceni 9).

Alternative films are screened in summer at hip *Lăptăria Enache* (see Pubs & Bars following). The French Institute (see Libraries & Cultural Centres under Information, earlier) screens a variety of foreign films (including in English) in its adjoining *Elvire Popescu* cinema.

Pubs & Bars

Becker (☎ 335 5648/5650, Bräu Calea Rahovei 155) – authentic German beer bar adjoining a brewery. Metres of filtered or unfiltered beer, German beer snacks and summer terrace overlooking Ceauşescu's half-built Science & Technology Institute; open 11.30 to 1 am
Dubliner (☎ 222 9473, Blvd Titulescu 18) – ask the taxi driver for 'Bar Irlandez'. A handful of chairs and a couple of tables on the street outside. Guinness costs $3; open 9 to 2 am
The Harp (☎ 335 6508, Piaţa Unirii 1) – quintessential Irish-pub-abroad with bacon-and-egg breakfasts, toasted sandwiches and other pub grub costing no more than $3; open 9 to 2 am

Lăptăria Enache (Blvd Nicolae Bălcescu 2) – trendy, rooftop bar (also called Prima Club) on the 4th floor of the National Theatre (in its old lighting ducts, in fact); live jazz on weekends and summer film screenings on the roof terrace. Enter via the unmarked entrance at the northern side of the theatre, to the side of Dominusart Gallery
Opium Studio (☎ mobile 094-386 760, Str Horei 5) – cool, collected and outrageously eclectic is the name of the game at this cellar bar, furnished in the most fabulously theatrical of manners; open 7 pm to 4 am
Planter's Club (☎ 659 2184, Str Mendeleev 35) – Bucharest's most popular mainstream drinking hole with small dance floor, just off Piaţa Amzei; always crammed with expats and open 6 pm to 5 am
Sydney Bar & Grill (☎ 312 9670, Calea Victoriei 224) – Australian-inspired terrace bar which was *the* expat place to be seen – until the city mayor ordered its fabulous summer terrace to be bulldozed. Popular nonetheless with an 'all-hours-drinking' clientele. Pub-grub-type menu and $3 to $5 breakfasts; open 24 hours
Terminus (Str George Enescu 5) – warm wine-red walls, wooden furnishings and a maze of red-brick cellar bars makes this Bucharest's hippest bar. Guinness, Murphy's Irish Stout as well as local beers. By day, sip the creamiest hot chocolate in town; open 10 to 5 am
Tipsy (Blvd Schitu Măgureanu 13) – simple but soulful bar which markets itself as Bucharest's only plub (pub-cum-club), opposite the western entrance to Cişmigiu Garden. Sunny summer terrace and great food; open 3 pm to 4 am
White Horse (☎ 679 7796, Str George Călinescu 4) – British pub with typical pub grub; call a black London cab from its red phone-box to take you home; open noon to 3 am

Clubs

Good places to listen to live music or dance the night away include:

Backstage (☎ 315 0812, Str Gabroveni 14) – hard, live rock with prerecorded rock in a red-brick vaulted cellar; open 8 pm to 5 am
Café Indigo (☎ 312 6336, Str Eforie 2) – hip jazz club in the basement of Cinemateca Română. Live bands most nights, 116 sexily named cocktails and an exotic range of natural juices; open 8 to 2 am
Club A (☎ 315 6853, Str Blănari 14) – 'A' stands for the architecture students who run this cellar bar-cum-disco; open until 5 am

Green Hours 22 Jazz Club (☎ *211 9592, Calea Victoriei 120*) – hip cellar bar with live jazz concerts every Thursday, a disco Friday and Saturday evening, and short theatre performances each Monday. By day mellow out in the cool outside cafe to the sound of Beethoven, Brahms and Enescu; open 10 to 2 or 3 am

Salsa, You & Me II (☎ *335 5640*) on Str Luterană – bongos, steel drums and lots of body-beat dancing in the Galeriile Lutherană shopping mall, behind Hotel Bucureşti; open 11 pm to 5 am

Swing House (*Str Gabroveni 20*) – trendy, smoke-filled cellar bar in the historic quarter, just around the corner from Backstage. Jazz concerts most evenings from 9.30 pm; open 3 pm to 6 am

Vox Maris (☎ *311 1994, Calea Victoriei 155*) – among the 'biggest-and-the-best' of Bucharest nightclubs, with lots of slot machines and one-armed bandits; open 10 pm to 4 am

Why Not? (☎ *323 1450, Str Turturelelor 11*) – wholly mainstream nightclub frequented by wild young things; open 10 pm to 5 am

Gay & Lesbian Venues
Sherlock Holmes (*Blvd Mihail Kogălniceanu 49*), near the opera, is a simple cellar bar which plays host to the city's gay and lesbian populace; open 24 hours.

Classical Music
Attending a performance at the **Romanian Athenaeum** (*Ateneul Român;* ☎ *315 6875, Str Benjamin Franklin 1*), home to the George Enescu philharmonic orchestra, is a must. Tickets ($2) are sold in the box office (via the side door on Str Constantin Exarcu); open noon to 7 pm and before performances (Thursday, Friday and occasionally weekend evenings) which start at 6.30 or 7 pm.

Opera & Ballet
At Bucharest's **Opera House** (*Opera Română;* ☎ *313 1857, 314 6980, Blvd Mihail Kogălniceanu 70*), west of Cişmigiu Garden, you can enjoy a full-scale opera for $1; the box office opens 10 am to 1 pm and 5 to 7.30 pm Tuesday to Sunday.

Theatre
Bucharest has countless theatres, offering a lively mix of comedy, farce, satire and straight contemporary plays in a variety of languages. Tickets cost no more than $3. Theatres close in July and August.

The most sought-after tickets are those for performances at the **Ion Luca Caragiale National Theatre** (*Teatrul Naţional Ion Luca Caragiale;* ☎ *614 7171, 615 4746, Blvd Nicolae Bălcescu 2*), opposite Hotel Inter-Continental. The theatre, named after the 20th-century playwright who kicked off his career here as a prompter, was built in the 1970s. The original theatre dating from 1852 was destroyed during WWII. The box office, on the southern side of the building facing Blvd Regina Elisabeta, opens 10 am to 7 pm. Tickets cost $0.30 to $2.50.

The **Ţăndărică Puppet Theatre** (*Teatrul de Marionete şi Păpuşi Ţăndărică;* ☎ *211 0829, Str Eremia Grigorescu 26*) presents innovative, amusing puppet shows ($0.75). Its box office opens 2 to 5 pm weekdays, 9 am to noon and 2 to 5 pm Saturday, 9 am to 3 pm Sunday.

Plays in Hebrew and Yiddish are held at the **Jewish State Theatre** (*Teatrul Evreiesc de Stat;* ☎ *323 4530, Str Iuliu Barasch 15*).

SPECTATOR SPORTS
When at home, Steaua Bucureşti play at Steaua Stadium; fans can get kitted out in all the red-white-and-blue Steaua paraphernalia at the side's club shop (mobile ☎ 094-299 037), just off Blvd Regina Elisabeta on the corner of Str Ion Zalomit and Str Ion Brezioanu. Rival side Dinamo Bucureşti plays at Dinamo Stadium, also home to a club shop. For contact and ticketing details, see Spectator Sports in the Facts for the Visitor chapter.

SHOPPING
For beautifully made woven rugs, table runners, national Romanian costumes, ceramics and other local crafts, don't miss the excellent folk art shop inside the Romanian Peasant Museum at Şoseaua Kiseleff 3. There is a similar, but substantially smaller, shop inside the Village Museum at Şoseaua Kiseleff 28–30.

Interesting art galleries and antique shops are clustered in 'embassy land' around Str

Piaţa Amzei, a bustling fruit and vegetable market in Bucharest

National Theatre, opposite Hotel Inter-Continental

Pasajul Victoriei Mall in Bucharest

Antim Monastery, Bucharest

Piaţa Unirii fountains in front of communist-era apartment blocks, Bucharest

Roman Orthodox Cathedral, Bucharest

Statue, Palace of the Parliament

Central University Library, Piaţa Revoluţiei, Bucharest

Off-Court Tennis Stars

Nasty by name. Nasty by nature. That's what sport critics said about **Ilie Năstăse**, Romania's first tennis player to achieve stardom in the West. At the peak of his career between 1971 and 1975, Năstăse – who sacrificed a promising football career with Steaua Bucharest to pursue tennis – was ranked the world's No 1. During his 26-year career he won 57 singles titles, including the US Open in 1972 and the French Open in 1973. He married Alexandra King (his second marriage), a US model and soap-opera actor, in 1984 with whom he set up home in Manhattan. After failing at local Romanian politics (he ran for Bucharest's mayorship in 1996), a not-so-nasty Năstăse agreed in early 2000 to partly fund and lend his name to a 12-court tennis academy in Bucharest to train Eastern Europe's stars of the future. The complex, expected to cost \$10 million, will open in 2003.

Năstăse's doubles partner was Romanian **Ion Țiriac**. Together they took Romania to the 1972 Davis Cup final in Bucharest, but the home country lost to the US. Țiriac subsequently settled in Germany where he managed German tennis champion Boris Becker. Since 1990 Țiriac has promoted foreign investment in Romania: he owns the Ion Țiriac Commercial Bank (Banca Comercială Ion Țiriac; BCIT); is a major shareholder in Pro TV, the country's first private TV channel; established Mercedes-Benz in Romania; set up his own private airline; and opened Romania's first cash-and-carry, Metro, in Bucharest. In his home town of Brașov, Țiriac 'adopted' 100 children and set up the Waldorf school for orphans. Ion Țiriac, president of the Romanian Olympic Committee during the 2000 Sydney Games, remains a national hero in Romania today.

Jean Louis Calderon; and north of Hotel București along Calea Victoriei. Don't miss Pasajul Villacros, a covered passage topped with an ornate yellow glass roof at Calea Victoriei 20. The narrow alleys and passages winding off Str Lipscani in the old part of the city are equally delightful to explore; wrought iron gates from here lead to Str Hanul cu Tei, a alley passage filled with tiny craft shops.

Cocor at Blvd IC Brătianu 29–33 and Unirea at Piața Unirii 3 are Bucharest's two department stores. Mario Plaza at Calea Dorobanților 172–178, București Mall at Calea Vitan 55–59 and Galeriile Lutherană behind Hotel București on Str Luterană are indoor shopping malls.

GETTING THERE & AWAY

This section concentrates on transport between Bucharest and other places in Romania and Moldova. See the earlier Getting There & Away chapter for details on air, bus and train links with other countries.

Air

Most international flights use Otopeni airport (Aeroportul Otopeni; ☎ 230 1602/0042/0022), 17km north of Bucharest on the road to Ploiești. Arrivals use prerevolution terminal A and departures leave from newer terminal B. The Otopeni airport information desk (☎ 204 1000) in terminal B opens 24 hours.

Domestic flights use Băneasa airport (☎ 201 4976), 8km north of the centre at Șoseaua București-Ploiești 42. The information number is ☎ 9361/9371.

Romania's national airline Tarom has its main office (☎ 337 0220/0400, fax 337 2036) at Spaiul Independenței 17, block 101, open 9 am to 7 pm weekdays and 9 am to 2 pm Saturday. It has a useful branch office (☎ 659 4185/4125), just off Piața Victoriei at Str Buzești 59–61; and another on the 1st floor of the CFR office at Str Domnița Anastasia 10–14. Both open 8 am to 7 or 7.30 pm weekdays and 8 am to noon or 1 pm Saturday.

From Băneasa airport there are daily flights to Cluj-Napoca; five weekly flights to Arad, Constanța (summer only), Oradea and Timișoara; and two or three flights a week to Baia Mare, Satu Mare, Sibiu, Suceava and Târgu Mureș.

Fares are discussed in the introductory Getting Around chapter and in the Getting There & Away sections in the relevant chapters in this book. Don't expect any bargains.

Moldova Air Moldova (☎ 312 1258, ☎/fax 312 0822), Str Batiştei 5, sells tickets for its flights to/from Chişinău (three times weekly) in the republic of Moldova. Flights arrive/depart from Băneasa airport. A return fare costs $140.

Train

Bucharest is served by a comprehensive train network linking the capital to most towns. The central train station – from which all international and most national trains arrive/depart – is Gara de Nord (☎ 223 0880), Blvd Gării de Nord 2. To enter the station, flash your valid train ticket or buy a platform ticket ($0.10) at the entrance. The left-luggage counter, on the right side of the central hall if your back is towards the tracks, charges around $0.50/1 per day to store a small/big bag; open 24 hours.

Some local trains to/from Cernica and Constanţa use Gara Obor station, east of the centre. Local trains to/from Snagov and a couple of seasonal *accelerat* trains to/from Mangalia on the Black Sea coast and Cluj-Napoca sometimes use Gara Băneasa, on the northern edge of town on Şoseaua Bucureşti-Ploieşti. All local trains to/from Giurgiu use Gara Progresul (☎ 685 6385l), on the far southern side of Bucharest (take tram No 12).

Tickets for all trains can be bought in advance from the Agenţie de Voiaj CFR office in Bucharest. You have to pay a nominal reservation fee (no more than $1) but this is well worth it, if only to avoid queuing for hours at the train station. A seat reservation is mandatory if you are travelling with an Inter-Rail pass. International tickets must be bought in advance.

The main CFR office (☎ 314 5528 for information on train schedules and fares) is at Str Domniţa Anastasia 10–14. Domestic tickets are sold on the ground (1st) floor, international tickets and rail passes on the 2nd floor. Train timetables ($0.75) are sold at the ticket desks in the domestic ticket hall. Some staff speak English. Both halls open 7.30 am to 7.30 pm weekdays, 8 am to noon Saturday.

Tickets for local and national trains are only sold at the train station one hour before departure. At Gara de Nord, there are separate ticket halls for 1st and 2nd class. The ticket hall for international destinations, 1st-class tickets and sleeping compartments – marked *casele de bilete Cl. 1* – is on the right as you enter the station's main entrance. Window No 1 *(casa internaţionala)* is for international tickets; window Nos 2 to 7 are for other 1st-class tickets; and window Nos 8 and 9 are for sleepers and couchettes on national trains *(vagon de dormit şi cuseta)*. To get to the 2nd-class ticket hall – marked *casa II* – walk past the 1st-class hall and turn right when you reach the tracks.

Timetables are in the main aisle of the station building opposite the 1st-class ticket hall. Notice boards listing ticket prices are displayed in the 2nd-class ticket office. Prices change every month. Timetables are sold at the information desk, at the end of the main aisle opposite the tracks.

Wasteels (☎ 222 7844, fax 222 7863, e sales@wasteelstravel.ro), which sells discounted tickets to Western Europe for under-26s, is on the right as you enter the main station building; open 10 am to 6 pm weekdays.

Bus

Bucharest is served by a poor domestic bus system, so much so that if you ask someone where the central bus station *(autogară)* is, they'll look at you in astonishment. Many claim Bucharest has no such station.

The central bus station – a stop rather than a fully fledged station – is, in fact, outside Hotel Nord on Calea Griviţei. Services change regularly and it is wise to check the timetables stuck on the lamp posts at the bus stop first. There is no ticket office; hop aboard the bus you intend travelling on and buy a ticket from the driver.

At the time of writing, daily bus services included to/from Ploieşti (59km, one daily), Curtea de Argeş (140km), Râmnicu Vâlcea (171km) and Târgu Jiu (257km), as well as Piteşti (108km, five daily) and Târgovişte (78km, 13 daily). See Getting There & Away in the relevant regional chapters.

Moldova & Ukraine Tickets for a daily bus to Chişinău ($10, about 12 hours) in

Moldova, departing from Gara de Nord at 6 am, are sold at the Autotrans kiosk (☎ 638 2798), next to the Ortadoğu Tur office on Piaţa Gara de Nord. Tickets are also sold here for Autotrans' weekly Ukraine-bound bus to Chernivtsi (Cernăuţi in Romanian), which departs at 4 pm on Wednesday ($12.50 one way).

Turkey Daily buses to Istanbul ($20/40 single/return, 11 to 15 hours) depart from Filaret bus station (☎ 641 0692), Piaţa Gării Filaret 1; or from Militari bus station (☎ 769 7042) at Blvd Păcii 141. The companies operating these buses have kiosks opposite the train station on Piaţa Gara de Nord, which sell tickets and run a shuttle service, 30 minutes before departure, from Gara de Nord to the bus station.

Companies include Kidik Tour (☎ 223 2925, ☎/fax 222 3389), Str Gheorghe Duca 1–3, departing at 2 and 4 pm Sunday to Friday, 2 pm Saturday; Toros Trans (☎ 223 1898), Str Gării de Nord, departing noon and 4 pm Sunday to Friday, 2 pm Saturday; Ortadoğu Tur (☎ 312 2423, 637 6778), Piaţa Gara de Nord 1, departing 10 am, noon, 3 and 4 pm daily; and Star Turism (☎ 637 6723, 638 7050), Blvd Dinicu Golescu 31, daily departure 4 pm.

Western Europe Daily buses to Germany (from where there are connecting services to the rest of Western Europe; see the introductory Getting There & Away chapter for details) depart from Piaţa Dorobanţilor. Most companies which operate these buses have a ticketing office on nearby Str Ankara or parallel Str Sofia. Double T (☎ 313 3642, fax 315 8166, ℮ doublet@fx.ro) is at Calea Victoriei 2.

For information on Eurolines buses and offices see the introductory Getting There & Away chapter.

Car & Motorcycle

There are plenty of 24-hour petrol stations around the city which sell a great array of imported junk food as well as petrol, oils, accessories etc. Handily placed stations in downtown Bucharest include the Inter-Continental at Str Tudor Arghezi 7; the Dorobanţi at Calea Dorobanţilor 180; and the Cotroceni station west of the centre on Splaiul Independenţei. Heading north to the airports, there is the Băneasa Service at Şoseaua Bucureşti-Ploieşti 2; Shell Otopeni 13km north of the centre along the same road; and AGIP at Otopeni airport.

Car Rental Car rental is geared solely towards the business traveller, thus is expensive. Many travel agents and hotels act as agents for the major car-rental companies. Check if prices quoted include the required 19% VAT.

If coming from abroad, it is often cheaper to book (and pay) for a car in advance through any Avis, Budget, Europcar or Hertz office overseas, and collect it on arrival at Otopeni airport.

Avis (☎ 230 0054) Otopeni airport; (☎ 210 4333/4344, fax 210 6912) Str Rafael Sanzio 1; (☎ 312 2043) Athénée Palace Hilton; (☎ 314 1837) Hotel Inter-Continental; (☎ 312 2738) Hotel Minerva
Budget (☎ 210 2867) Str Mihai Eminescu 50–54, Apartment 2; (☎ 312 7070, extension 1015) Hotel Bucureşti; (☎ 315 9080) Hotel Ambasador
Europcar (☎ 312 7078) Otopeni airport; (☎ 313 1540) Blvd General Magheru 7
Hertz (☎ 201 4954) Otopeni airport; (☎ 337 2910, ℮ reservations–hertz@fx.ro) Blvd Regina Maria 1

GETTING AROUND
To/From the Airports

To get to Otopeni or Băneasa airport take bus No 783 from the city centre, which departs every 15 minutes between 6.30 am and 9 pm from Piaţa Unirii and various bus stops on the eastern side of Blvd Brătianu, Blvd Nicolae Bălcescu and Blvd General Magheru. An easy stop to find is the one outside KFC on Blvd General Magheru.

Double-journey tickets cost $0.90 and are sold at ticket booths, marked *bilete şi cartele magnetice*, next to bus stops. Feed your ticket into the green machine next to the driver inside the bus. Single-journey tickets are not available.

BUCHAREST

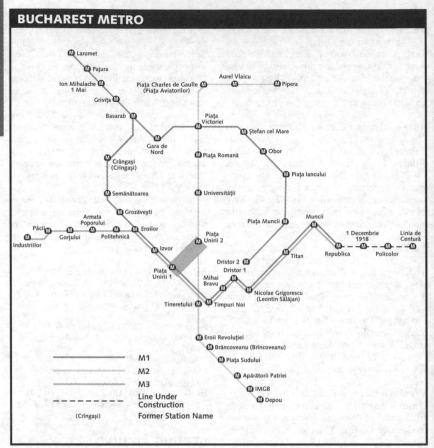

BUCHAREST METRO

Bǎneasa is 20 minutes from the centre; get off at the *aeroportul Bǎneasa* stop. Buses also link Bǎneasa with Piaţa Romană and Gara de Nord.

Otopeni is about 30 minutes from the city centre. The bus stops outside the departures hall (terminal B) then continues to arrivals (terminal A). To get to the centre from Otopeni, catch bus No 783 from the stop in front of terminal A. Tickets are sold at the booth next to the stop, or direct from the driver (the easier option).

Avoid the taxi drivers at both airports at all costs, unless you are happy to pay an outrageous $25 to $40 for the 20 to 35 minutes' ride.

Bus, Tram & Trolleybus

For buses, trams and trolleybuses buy tickets ($0.15) at any RATB (Régie Autonome de Transport de Bucureşti) street kiosk, painted yellow or silver and marked *casa de bilete* or simply *bilete*. Punch your ticket on board or risk a $5 on-the-spot fine if caught by an inspector without a validated ticket. Single- and two-journey tickets are available as well as a handy one-day/weekly pass ($0.65/2.20) which entitles you to unlimited travel on buses, trams and trolley-buses. A two-week/one-month pass costs $4.30/6.30. Students get a 50% discount on day and monthly passes.

Public transport runs from 5 am to midnight (reduced service on Sunday).

Metro

Bucharest's metro dates from 1985 and has three lines. Trains run every five to seven minutes during peak periods and about every 20 minutes off-peak.

To use the metro buy a magnetic-strip ticket at the subterranean kiosks inside the main entrance to the metro station. Tickets valid for either two or 10 journeys cost $0.30 or $1.50 respectively, and a one-day metro pass is available for $0.50. For routes see the Bucharest metro map included in this book.

Metro stations are poorly signposted so sit near the front of the train to give yourself a better chance of seeing the station names. At platform level, the name of the station where you are is the one with a box around it. The others indicate the direction the train is going.

Taxi

Opt for a cab with a meter and seemingly honest driver; Cris Taxi (☎ 9421/9461) and Eurotaxi (☎ 9851) are among the cab companies that fit into this category. Flag one down on the street (identifiable by the yellow pyramid fixed to its roof) or call one from any phone on the street. The fixed metered rate usually works out at $0.45 per kilometre.

Practically every taxi driver that hangs around either of the airports and Gara de Nord is unscrupulous and should be avoided at all costs.

Bicycle

Villa Helga (see Places to Stay) has bicycles to rent in summer for $10 a day.

Around Bucharest

Dracula's tomb, 'Lenin's graveyard' and acres of unspoilt forests and lakes are among the varied sights within an easy day's reach of Bucharest. Who said Bucharest was dull?

MOGOŞOAIA PALACE & BUCHAREST'S LENIN

One of Romania's most remarkable palaces lies just 14km north-west of Bucharest in Mogoşoaia (literally, Mogoş' wife). Mogoşoaia Palace was built by Wallachian prince Constantin Brâncoveanu between 1698 and 1702 as a summer residence for his family and an inheritance for his son Ştefan. It is considered to be among the country's finest examples of Brâncoveanu architecture. Built within a large court and surrounded by a lake and oak forests, the palace's main feature is a traditional balcony that winds around the front facade.

Following the death of Ştefan, his three brothers and his father at the hands of the Turks in Istanbul in 1714, the palace was turned into an inn. It was then plundered and made into a warehouse by occupying Russian forces in 1853. At the end of the 19th century, the estate was handed down to the Bibescu family, descendants of the Brâncoveanus through the female line. A large guesthouse was built and, in 1912, Prince George Valentin Bibescu (1880–1941) relinquished Mogoşoaia to his wife, Martha (1886–1973). Under her guidance, Italian architect Domenico Rupolo restored the estate, laying a black and white chequered marble floor in the main palace and restoring the ornate gilded arched doorways. The guesthouse was rebuilt, taking the fish market in Venice as its model. State-owned since 1956, the palace served as a museum until the 1970s when Ceauşescu closed it and took the furniture for his own use.

Prince George Valentin Bibescu is buried in the small, white 1688 church on the estate. A path from the main entrance to the palace leads to the **Bibescu family tomb** where Elizabeth Asquith (1898–1945), the daughter of former British prime minister Henry Herbert Asquith, lies. She married Prince Antoine Bibescu in London in 1919.

The **grave of 'Lenin'** is also located at Mogoşoaia. Following the 1989 downfall

MATTHIAS LÜFKENS

Mogoşoaia's fallen Lenin

CĂLDĂRUŞANI MONASTERY

Swedish tennis champion Björn Borg married Romanian player Mariana Simionescu at the picturesque Căldăruşani Monastery, some 27km farther north-east of Mogoşoaia. The monastery, built in 1638 under the guidance of Wallachian prince Matei Basarab (r. 1632–54), gained recognition during the 18th century as home to one of Romania's most distinguished icon-painting schools. The 17-year-old Nicolae Grigorescu spent some months at the monastery in 1854–55, painting several icons for the church. These are displayed in a small museum in the compound ($0.15), signposted 'spre muzeul'; ask a monk for the key if it's locked.

Getting There & Away

Some Bucharest-Galaţi trains, departing from Gara de Nord, stop at Greci (50 minutes, five daily) where you alight for Căldăruşani. The monastery is a 2km hike north from the train station.

BUFTEA

Ştirbei Palace (Palat Ştirbei), 18km north of Bucharest, was a Communist Party hotel until 1989. Built by Wallachian prince Barbu Ştirbei in 1855–64, it was here that the Romanian government signed a preliminary WWI peace treaty with Germany on 5 March 1918. After WWII, the palace – also known as Buftea Castle – was turned into a guesthouse for important state guests.

Today the pretty castle, enclosed in lush parkland at Str Ştirbei Vodă 36, is a three-star *hotel* (☎ 01-313 1500/1510, ☎/fax 311 2417) and *restaurant* oozing old-style grandeur. Anyone can stay here. Singles/doubles in the main building cost upwards of $30/37 and excellent-value rooms in *Vila Parc*, a small villa in the wooded grounds, start at $6/19.

of Romanian communism, the statue of Lenin which stood outside Bucharest's Press House was removed from its pedestal and dumped on wasteground behind the palace kitchens on the Mogoşoaia estate. The head of Lenin's 5m-tall bronze body lies peacefully against that of **Petru Groza**, the communist prime minister at the head of the 1945 government which forced King Michael to abdicate in 1947.

Entering the main enclosure, turn right into the field after the **palace kitchens**, the unusual building of archways on the right as you pass under the guards tower.

The complex (☎ 01-312 8894), Str Valea Parcului, opens 10 am to 6 pm Tuesday to Sunday ($0.25). Guided tours of the furnitureless palace are free.

Getting There & Away

The only way of getting to Mogoşoaia by public transport is to take tram No 20 or 31 from the centre of Bucharest to the last stop on the line (in the Laromet district), from where bus No 460 trundles to/from Mogoşoaia.

Getting There & Away

From Bucharest's Gara de Nord, there are 17 local trains to Ploieşti daily, some of which stop at Buftea (34 minutes). Bus No 460 links Laromet and Buftea (see this section under Mogoşoaia Palace, earlier).

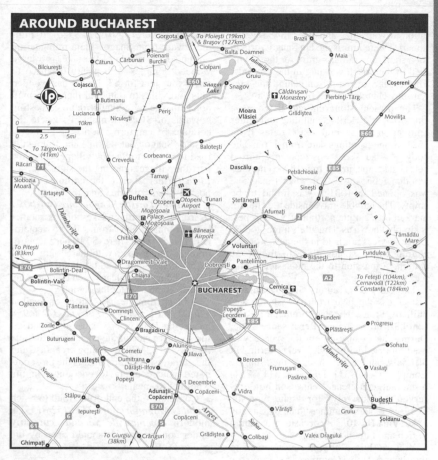

AROUND BUCHAREST

Entering Buftea from the south, bear north along the Bucharest-Ploieşti road (the main road through the village), pass the post office and immediately turn left onto Str Otului. At the end of Str Otului, turn right.

SNAGOV

Snagov, 38km north of Bucharest, is a favourite picnic spot for city dwellers, with a famous 16th-century **church and monastery** tucked away on an island in Snagov Lake, inhabited by no-one bar an elderly abbot and nun who take care of the monastery. Deep forest surrounds the lake, which

is estimated to be 576 hectares large and an impressive 18km long.

A simple wooden church was built on the island in the 11th century by Mircea cel Bătrân. A monastery was added in the late 14th century during the reign of King Dan I (r. 1383–86), and in 1453 the wooden church was replaced by a stone edifice which later sank in the lake.

In 1456 Vlad Ţepeş (the Impaler) built fortifications around the monastery. He also built a bridge from the lake to the mainland, a bell tower, a new church, an escape tunnel, and a prison and torture chamber.

Nicolae Bălcescu, leader of the 1848 revolution in Wallachia, and other 1848 revolutionaries were imprisoned in Snagov prison for a short time. A mass grave for those who died in the prison was dug in the grounds. The remains of the prison behind the present-day church can still be seen today.

The present stone church, listed as a Unesco World Heritage building and under renovation for several years, dates from 1521. Some paintings date from 1563. The body of Vlad Ţepeş was reputedly buried below the dome, just in front of the church's wooden iconostasis, but when the grave was opened in 1931 it was found to be empty. The humble grave inside the church, marked by a simple portrait of Vlad Ţepeş, is simply known as 'Dracula's tomb' today. Daily services are held in the new wooden church which stands close to the stone church. Admission to the monastery complex is $0.25.

The early-20th-century **Snagov Palace**, just across the lake from the island, was built by Prince Nicolae, brother of King Carol II, in the Italian Renaissance style. During the Ceauşescu era the palace was used for meetings of high-level government officials, and today houses the Snagov Complex (☎ 01-311 3782, fax 311 3781) restaurant, conference centre and hotel reserved exclusively for state guests. Ceauşescu had a summer home on Snagov Lake, **Villa No 10**, now occasionally rented to rich and famous tourists.

You can **hire a boat** to row yourself to the island from Complex Astoria (see Places to Stay & Eat). It costs $1.30 an hour. Alternatively, you can call upon the services of the burly Ana who will row you there and back for $1.30 per person from the village of Silestru on the northern lakeshore – go to the end of the small wooden jetty next to house No 324 in Silestru (at the foot of the radio mast) and shout 'Ana'. To get to Silestru, continue north along the D1 past the 'Snagav Sat. 11km' turn-off and turn right in Ciolpani.

Some winters, in December and January, it is often possible to walk or ice skate across the frozen lake to the monastery.

Places to Stay & Eat

Complex Astoria (☎ 01-314 8320), 10 minutes' walk from Snagov Plajă train station on the southern side of the lake, is a large wooded complex with plenty of space to pitch your tent for $3. It also has wooden huts and villas to rent, and there's a small hotel on site with singles/doubles costing upwards of $10/20 a night. To get to the complex by car, turn east off the D1 (signposted 'Snagov Sat. 11km') and follow the road for 11km to Snagov village. Continue past the village, ignoring the sign 'centru', for a further 2km to the complex (signposted 'Baza Turistică Snagov').

Complex Turistic Snagov Parc (☎ 01-794 0236), on the northern lakeshore, is another large complex, open from May to September. You can camp here ($0.10 per sq metre) or rent a double room with shared shower for $7.50. There are paddle boats to hire ($2.50/hour) and a clean beach to lounge on. It costs $0.50 to enter the complex.

A blast from the past can be enjoyed at *Vila 23* (☎ 01-315 1410/1107, fax 312 4695), an ageing hotel near Ceauşescu's pad on the southern side of the lake. Single/double rooms cost $24/30, including breakfast, and the grandiose reception hall is the most outdated you're likely to encounter in the whole of Romania.

Continue to the end of the road to reach *Holiday Magnum* (☎ 01-232 8152/8153), a modern *complex de vacantă* currently under construction. It should open by the end of 2001.

Getting There & Away

One train daily departs from Bucharest's Gara de Nord at 7.50 am and arrives in Snagov Plajă at 8.52 am. Returning, it departs from Snagov Plajă at 8.22 pm and pulls into Bucharest by 9.26 pm. Snagov Plajă – a stop in the middle of oak forest – is 10 minutes' walk from Complex Astoria.

The Villa Helga hostel in Bucharest (see under Bucharest – Places to Stay) arranges informal guided tours to Snagov; it charges $10 per person, which includes Ana's rowing services as well as admission to the monastery.

CERNICA

The 19th-century monastic complex of Cernica (Sfânta Mănăstire Cernica), nestled on a small island in the middle of Cernica Lake 14km east of Bucharest, is one of Romania's most idyllic – yet least visited – monasteries. Two churches, some chapels, a cemetery, seminary and a **religious art & typography museum** are contained within the fortified complex, founded on the site of a former 17th-century church in 1781. A smaller church, **St Nicolae's Church** (Biserica Sfântul Nicolae din Ostrov) was built in 1815, but it was not until the mid-1800s, under the guidance of St Calinic of Cernica,

that the monastery really flourished. Between 1831 and 1838 **St Gheorghe's Church** (Biserica Sfântul Gheorghe) was built, a library and seminary was opened and a school for religious painting set up. After WWII the monastery was closed, not reopening until 1995. Some 80 monks live on the island complex – joined by a causeway to the mainland. The graves of Romanian painter Ion Ţuculescu, and writer and priest Gala Galaction, are in the cemetery on the lake shores, in front of St Gheorghe's Church.

Cernica is unfortunately inaccessible by public transport.

Transylvania

To most people, the name Transylvania conjures up images of haunted castles, werewolves and vampires. Certainly, the 14th-century castles at Râşnov and Bran could be straight out of a Count Dracula movie.

Yet the charms of Transylvania are far more diverse – mountain scenery, some of Romania's best hiking and skiing, glimpses of ancient Roman and Dacian settlements, plus scores of rural villages that haven't changed much since the 18th century.

For lovers of medieval art and history, it's an unparalleled chance to see an over-looked corner of the old Austro-Hungarian empire. Most travellers head straight up the Prahova Valley to the old Saxon merchant town of Braşov and the citadel of Sighi-şoara. Move on!

Transylvania forms the central region of Romania, bordered to the east, south and west by the Carpathian Mountains. South-eastern Transylvania, most accessible by public transport from Bucharest, is dominated by the Prahova Valley with Romania's leading ski resorts. The Făgăraş Mountains and a string of medieval cities founded in the 12th century are within easy reach. Just north and east of here is Romania's Hungarian enclave, known as Székely Land and stretching as far Târgu Mureş, the cradle of Magyar culture.

Transylvania's ethnic diversity is most prevalent in Cluj-Napoca in the north, a lively potpourri of Romanians, Saxons and Hungarians.

The south-west of the region is home to a string of awe-inspiring Dacian and Roman citadels, including the fantastic remains of the Roman capital of Sarmizegetusa.

History

For a thousand years, up to WWI, Transylvania was associated with Hungary. In the 10th century a Magyar (Hungarian) tribe, the Székelys, settled in what it called Erdély ('beyond the forest' – the literal meaning of 'Transylvania'). In the 12th century, Saxon

Highlights

- Watch wild wolves in the Carpathians near Piatra Craiului
- Eat homemade cheese and bread in a family home around Bran
- Stroll through the medieval streets of Braşov, Sighişoara & Sibiu
- Explore Roman ruins at Sarmizegetusa
- See how the royals lived at Peleş Castle in Sinaia
- Sleep in Ceauşescu's bed in a Sfântu Gheorghe castle
- Marvel at the Saxon fortified churches in the Târnave plateau

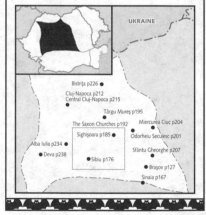

merchants arrived to help defend the eastern frontiers of Hungary. The seven towns they founded – Bistriţa (Bistritz), Braşov (Kronstadt), Cluj-Napoca (Klausenburg), Mediaş (Mediasch), Sebeş (Mühlbach), Sibiu (Hermannstadt) and Sighişoara (Schässburg) – gave Transylvania its German name, Siebenbürgen ('seven boroughs').

Medieval Transylvania was an autonomous unit ruled by a prince responsible to the Hungarian crown. The indigenous Romanians were serfs. After the 1526 Turkish defeat of Hungary the region became semi-independent, recognising Turkish suzerainty.

In 1683 Turkish power was broken and Transylvania came under Habsburg rule in 1687. The Catholic Habsburg governors sought to control the territory by favouring first the Protestant Hungarians and Saxons and then the Orthodox Romanians. In 1848, when the Hungarians revolted against the Habsburgs, Romania sided with the Austrians. After 1867, Transylvania was fully absorbed into Hungary. In 1918, Romanians gathered at Alba Iulia to demand Transylvania's union with Romania.

This has never been fully accepted by Hungary and from 1940 to 1944 it re-annexed much of the region. After the war, Romanian communists quashed Hungarian nationalist sentiments. Today, however, feelings of resentment have quelled and Romania's relations with its western neighbour continue to strengthen.

Saxon Land & the Prahova Valley

The area colonised by Saxons from the 12th century onwards lies north of Bucharest. Attacks by Tartars and Turks prompted them to fortify their churches and towns with sturdy walls.

The Prahova Valley snakes its way north along the Prahova River from Sinaia, to Predeal, just south of Braşov. Romania's kings, queens and dictators had summer residences along this 48km stretch renowned today for skiing and hiking. The Bucegi Mountains lie to the west, straddled by the Făgăraş chain which dominates the southern region between Braşov and Sibiu.

BRAŞOV
☎ 068 • postcode 2200 • pop 320,000
Braşov is a pleasant medieval town flanked by verdant hills. Established on an ancient Dacian site at the beginning of the 13th century, today it is one of Romania's most visited cities. Piaţa Sfatului, the central square, is the finest in the country, lined with baroque facades and pleasant outdoor cafes. Within easy reach by public transport are the ski resorts of Sinaia and Poiana Braşov, the castles of Bran and Râşnov, and trails that lead into the dramatic Bucegi Mountains.

Braşov started as a German mercantile colony named Kronstadt (Brassó in Hungarian). Located at the juncture of three principalities, it became a major medieval trading centre. The Saxons built ornate churches and townhouses, protected by a massive wall that still remains. The Romanians lived at Schei, just outside the walls to the south-west. During the Stalinist era, Braşov was renamed 'Staline', with the name carved in bold letters on the side of Mount Tâmpa.

One of the first public oppositions to the Ceauşescu government flared here in 1987. Thousands of disgruntled workers took to the streets demanding basic foodstuffs. Ceauşescu called in the troops and three people were killed.

Street protests in 1997 were followed by more protests in November 1999 which turned ugly as some 7000 workers, from the state-owned Roman SA Tractor Factory, raided the offices of the local prefecture in response to threats of redundancy and unfulfilled promises of wage increases. During the riots 17 police officers were injured as workers hurled petrol bombs. In an attempt to defuse the labour conflict, the Romanian government agreed to purchase some 320 vehicles in part payment of the company's debt to the state budget.

Orientation
Str Republicii, Braşov's pedestrian-only promenade, is crowded with shops and cafes. The train station is 2km north-east of the town centre.

Braşov has three bus stations: bus station No 1 (Autogară 1) is next to the train station on Blvd Gării. Buses to Târgu Mureş, Târgovişte and international buses arrive/depart from here. Buses to/from Curtea de Argeş, Făgăraş and Câmpulung depart from bus station No 2 (Autogară 2), west of the train station at Str Avram Iancu 114. Few buses use bus station No 3 (Autogară 3) in the east of the town.

TRANSYLVANIA

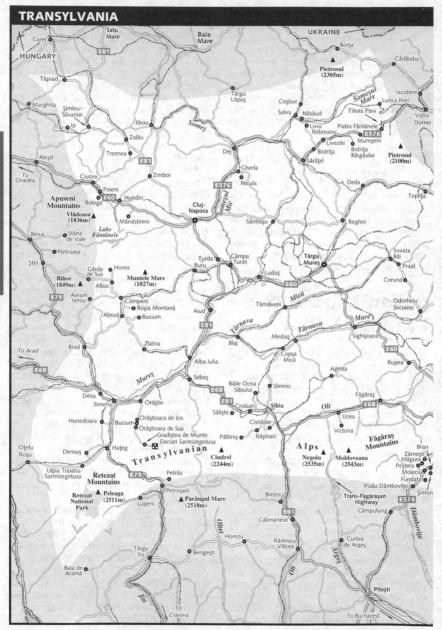

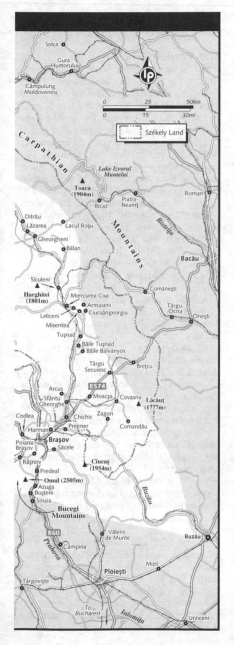

Mount Tâmpa towers over the town to the south-east.

Maps The best map of Braşov is the *Braşov* city map (Amco Press, 1999) which includes maps of Poiana Braşov and Predeal and costs $1.50. The fold-up *Braşov Ghid Turistic şi Comercial* contains a detailed map of the city and costs $0.70.

Also worth picking up is the *Travel Guidebook-Ghid Turistic* which includes piste maps of Poiana Braşov and Predeal and a hiking map of Mount Postăvarul. All are widely available in the city's major bookshops.

The multilingual *What, Where, When Braşov* city guide is published every two months and is available free from most hotels.

For an online map and tourist guide to Braşov go to www.brasov.ro.

Information

Tourist Offices The best on offer is the tourist desk in the lobby of Hotel Aro Palace at Blvd Eroilor 27. It sells maps and can book overpriced excursions to Sibiu ($20), the Bicaz Gorges ($26), Sighişoara ($20), Bran ($10) and Sinaia ($16).

The Automobil Clubul Român office (ACR; ☎ 412 345, 419 297) is farther from the centre, at Str Bucureşti 68.

Money The IDM currency exchange, Blvd Eroilor, cashes Eurocheques; open 7.30 am to 9 pm weekdays, 9 am to 4 pm Saturday, and 9 am to 5 pm Sunday. The BAM Exchange International on Str Apollonia Hirscher offers good rates; open 10 am to 6 pm weekdays, and 10 am to 2 pm Saturday.

Banca Comercială Română, Piaţa Sfatului 14, changes travellers cheques, gives cash advances on Visa/MasterCard and has an ATM; open 8.30 am to 5 pm weekdays, and 8.30 am to noon Saturday. BCIT (Banca Comercială Ion Ţiriac), Str Weiss 20, gives cash advances and cashes travellers cheques 9 am to 2.30 pm weekdays.

There are also ATMs outside the restaurant of Hotel Aro Palace on Blvd Eroilor and opposite McDonald's on Str Republicii.

TRANSYLVANIA

Post & Telephone The central post office is opposite the Heroes' Cemetery on Blvd Eroilor; open 7 am to 8 pm weekdays, and 8 am to noon Saturday.

Braşov has a number of telephone centres: Str Republicii 12, open 7 am to 7 pm weekdays; Blvd Eroilor, between the Capitol and Aro Palace Hotels, open 7 am to 7 pm daily; and one street farther east off Blvd Eroilor, open 7 am to 1.30 pm and 2 to 7 pm weekdays.

Email & Internet Access Hercules (☎ 410 164, e her@hercules.ro), Piaţa Sfatului 7, in Discul de Aur's cellar, charges $0.75 per hour for Internet access; open 24 hours.

Café Internet, on the top floor of the International Trade Centre, Str Alexandru Vlahuţă 10, also charges $0.75 per hour for Internet access; open 10 am to 10 pm daily.

One of the hippest, and possibly the cheapest, places to log on is Café Art Internet (☎ 472 535, e cafe@prosum.ro), in the Casa Schei building at Str Republicii 48. Internet access is $0.50 per hour; open 24 hours. There's also an adjoining bookshop and upstairs cafe/bar.

Bookshops The Librărie Unirea on Str Politehnicii, the Librărie George Coşbuc at Str Republicii 29, the Librărie Universitas on the northern side of Piaţa Sfatului, and the Librărie Sfântu Iosif at Str Mureşenilor 14 all sell a small selection of English-language novels.

The best bookshop for maps and guidebooks is the Librărie Aldus at Str Apollonia Hirscher 4; open 7.30 am to 4 pm Monday to Saturday.

Cultural Centres The German Democratic Forum (Formul Democrat Germanilor) (☎ 142 443, fax 152 272) is at Str Bicazului 2. The Alliance Française (☎/fax 411 626) is at Blvd Eroilor 25.

Medical Services The pharmacy opposite the market at the northern end of Str Nicolae Bălcescu is open 7 am to 8 pm weekdays, and 8 am to 3 pm Saturday. The very modern EuroFarmacie, Str Republicii 7, is open 7.30 am to midnight daily.

The Walled City

Piaţa Sfatului is the heart of medieval Braşov. On the square's western side stands the small **Mureşenilor House Memorial Museum** (Muzeul Memorial Casa Mureşenilor; ☎ 143 685), which honours the family of Jacob Mureşan, the first editor of the *Gazeta Transylvania*, a political newspaper first published in the 19th century. The touching display of letters, photographs and memorabilia traces the lives of the talented family; open 9 am to 3 pm weekdays ($0.20).

In the square's centre stands the **council house** (Casa Sfatului; 1420) in which the town councillors, known as centurions, would meet. The 'keeper of the fairs' lived in the **Trumpeter's Tower** on top of the council house. The council house today houses the **Braşov Historical Museum** (Muzeul Judeţean de Istorie; ☎ 472 363) in which the history of the Saxon guilds is recounted. The museum is open 10 am to 6 pm Tuesday to Sunday in summer (9 am to 5 pm in winter); $0.50.

Opposite is the Renaissance **Hirscher House** (built 1539–45), also known as the 'Merchants' House'. It was built by Apollonia Hirscher, the widow of Braşov mayor Lucas Hirscher. Her daughter was buried here adorned in the family's finest jewels. But she returned to life when a grave digger broke into the coffin. Overjoyed, the widow built Hirscher House and donated it to the city. Today it shelters the Cerbul Carpaţin restaurant.

Braşov's famed **Black Church** (Biserica Neagră), the largest Gothic church between Vienna and Istanbul and still used by German Lutherans today, looms just south of the square. The church was built between 1383 and 1477, and its name comes from its appearance after a fire in 1689. The original statues on the exterior of the apse are now inside and Turkish rugs hang from every balcony. Worshippers drop coins through the wooden grates in the floor. According to signs, written in Romanian and German, on the church's facade, it's forbidden to walk

Contents – Text

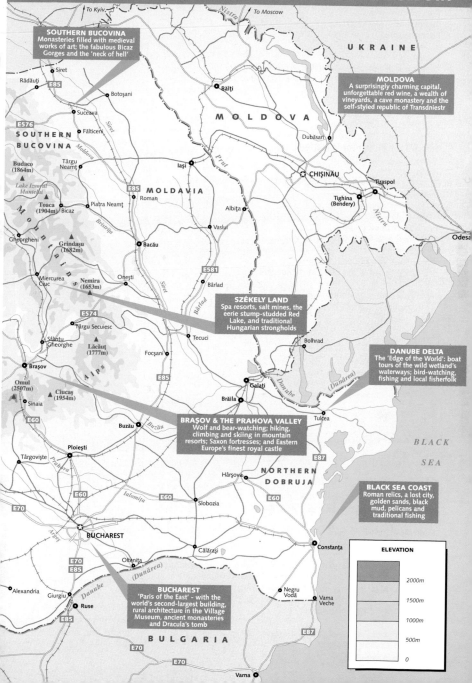

ROMANIA & MOLDOVA

To Kyiv
To Moscow

UKRAINE

SOUTHERN BUCOVINA
Monasteries filled with medieval works of art; the fabulous Bicaz Gorges and the 'neck of hell'

MOLDOVA
A surprisingly charming capital, unforgettable red wine, a wealth of vineyards, a cave monastery and the self-styled republic of Transdniestr

Rădăuţi
Siret
E85
Botoşani

Suceava

Bălţi

MOLDOVA

Dubăsari

E576

SOUTHERN
BUCOVINA

Fălticeni

Budaco
(1864m)
Lake Izvorul
Muntelui

Târgu
Neamţ

Toaca
(1904m)
Bicaz

Gheorgheni

Grindaşu
(1682m)

Piatra Neamţ

Iaşi

CHIŞINĂU

Tiraspol

Tighina
(Bendery)

Roman

E85

MOLDAVIA

Albiţa

Vaslui

Odesa

Miercurea
Ciuc

Nemira
(1653m)

Oneşti

E581

Bârlad

E574

Târgu Secuiesc

SZÉKELY LAND
Spa resorts, salt mines, the eerie stump-studded Red Lake, and traditional Hungarian strongholds

DANUBE DELTA
The 'Edge of the World': boat tours of the wild wetland's waterways; bird-watching, fishing and local fisherfolk

Sfântu
Gheorghe

Lăcăuţ
(1777m)

Tecuci

Bolhrad

Braşov

Focşani

Galaţi

Omul
(2507m)

Ciucaş
(1954m)

Sinaia

Brăila

Tulcea

BLACK
SEA

Buzău

BRAŞOV & THE PRAHOVA VALLEY
Wolf and bear-watching; hiking, climbing and skiing in mountain resorts; Saxon fortresses; and Eastern Europe's finest royal castle

E60

Târgovişte

Ploieşti

E60

Hârşova

NORTHERN
DOBRUJA

E87

BLACK SEA COAST
Roman relics, a lost city, golden sands, black mud, pelicans and traditional fishing

E60

Ialomiţa

E60

Slobozia

E60

E70

BUCHAREST

Călăraşi

Constanţa

Oltenita

ELEVATION

Alexandria

Giurgiu

Ruse

BUCHAREST
'Paris of the East' - with the world's second-largest building, rural architecture in the Village Museum, ancient monasteries and Dracula's tomb

Negru
Vodă

Vama
Veche

2000m

1500m

1000m

500m

0

E85

BULGARIA

E70

Varna

E87

Nistru
Prut
Siret
Moldova
Bistriţa
Siret
Bârlad
Danube (Dunărea)
Prahova
Buzău
Argeş
Dunărea
Danube

Mountains
Alps

Romania & Moldova
2nd edition – May 2001
First published – May 1998

Published by
Lonely Planet Publications Pty Ltd ABN 36 005 607 983
90 Maribyrnong St, Footscray, Victoria 3011, Australia

Lonely Planet Offices
Australia Locked Bag 1, Footscray, Victoria 3011
USA 150 Linden St, Oakland, CA 94607
UK 10a Spring Place, London NW5 3BH
France 1 rue du Dahomey, 75011 Paris

Photographs
All of the images in this guide are available for licensing from
Lonely Planet Images.
email: lpi@lonelyplanet.com.au

Front cover photograph
Road signs near Bucharest (Nicola Williams)

Romanian title page photograph
Old Clock Tower, Sighişoara (Dave Greedy)

Moldovan title page photograph
Soviet monument, Piaţa Libertăţii, Chişinău (Dan Herrick)

ISBN 1 86450 058 1

text & maps © Lonely Planet 2001
photos © photographers as indicated 2001

Printed by Craft Print International Ltd, Singapore

Although the authors
and Lonely Planet try
to make the informa-
tion as accurate as
possible, we accept
no responsibility for
any loss, injury or
inconvenience sus-
tained by anyone
using this book.

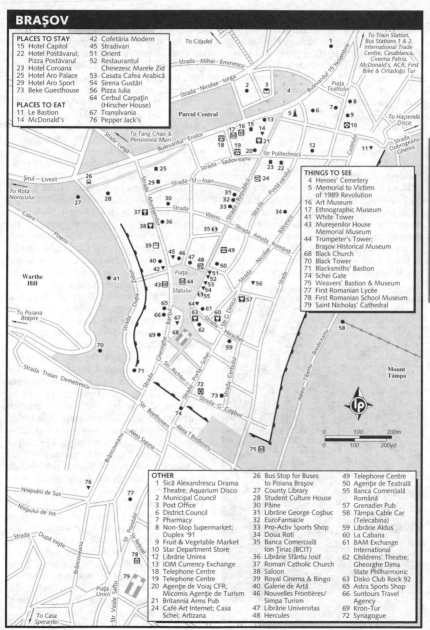

BRAŞOV

PLACES TO STAY
15 Hotel Capitol
22 Hotel Postăvarul;
    Pizza Postăvarul
23 Hotel Coroana
25 Hotel Aro Palace
29 Hotel Aro Sport
73 Beke Guesthouse

PLACES TO EAT
11 Le Bastion
14 McDonald's

42 Cofetăria Modern
45 Stradivari
51 Orient
52 Restaurantul
    Chinezesc Marele Zid
53 Casata Cafea Arabică
54 Sirena Gustări
56 Pizza Iulia
64 Cerbul Carpaţin
    (Hirscher House)
67 Transilvania
76 Pepper Jack's

THINGS TO SEE
4 Heroes' Cemetery
5 Memorial to Victims
   of 1989 Revolution
16 Art Museum
17 Ethnographic Museum
41 White Tower
43 Mureşenilor House
   Memorial Museum
44 Trumpeter's Tower;
   Braşov Historical Museum
68 Black Church
70 Black Tower
71 Blacksmiths' Bastion
74 Schei Gate
75 Weavers' Bastion & Museum
77 First Romanian Lycée
78 First Romanian School Museum
79 Saint Nicholas' Cathedral

OTHER
1 Sică Alexandrescu Drama
   Theatre; Aquarium Disco
2 Municipal Council
3 Post Office
6 District Council
7 Pharmacy
8 Non-Stop Supermarket;
   Duplex '91
9 Fruit & Vegetable Market
10 Star Department Store
12 Librărie Unirea
13 IDM Currency Exchange
18 Telephone Centre
19 Telephone Centre
20 Agenţie de Voiaj CFR;
   Micomis Agenţie de Turism
21 Britannia Arms Pub
24 Café Art Internet; Casa
   Schei; Artizana

26 Bus Stop for Buses
   to Poiana Braşov
27 County Library
28 Student Culture House
30 Pâine
31 Librărie George Coşbuc
32 EuroFarmacie
33 Pro-Activ Sports Shop
34 Doua Roti
35 Banca Comercială
   Ion Ţiriac (BCIT)
36 Librărie Sfântu Iosif
37 Roman Catholic Church
38 Saloon
39 Royal Cinema & Bingo
40 Galerie de Artă
46 Nouvelles Frontières/
   Simpa Turism
47 Librărie Universitas
48 Hercules

49 Telephone Centre
50 Agenţie de Teatrală
55 Banca Comercială
   Română
57 Grenadier Pub
58 Tâmpa Cable Car
   (Telecabina)
59 Librărie Aldus
60 La Cabana
61 BAM Exchange
   International
62 Childrens' Theatre;
   Gheorghe Dima
   State Philharmonic
63 Disko Club Rock 92
65 Astra Sports Shop
66 Suntours Travel
   Agency
69 Kron-Tur
72 Synagogue

TRANSYLVANIA

too close to the exterior walls due to the danger of falling stones and debris.

The church's organ, built by Buchholz of Berlin in 1839, has 4000 pipes and is believed to be the only Buchholz preserved in its original form. Since 1891, organ recitals have been held in the church during July and August, at 6 pm Tuesday, Thursday and Saturday ($2). Equally impressive is the church's bell. It weighs seven tonnes and is the largest in Romania.

The church is open 10 am to 3.30 pm daily except Sunday ($0.40 adults, $0.20 children, students and pensioners).

Head north-east into the new town along Str Republicii, the main pedestrianised street. At its northern end is a **wooden cross** to commemorate victims of the December 1989 revolution. In the **Heroes' Cemetery** opposite, a memorial slab lists those who died.

Head west to Blvd Eroilor 21 where the **Art Museum** (Muzeul de Artă; ☎ 144 384)

and the **Ethnographic Museum** (Muzeul de Etnografie; ☎ 152 252) adjoin each other. The former has a permanent pottery and decorative arts exhibition; a national art gallery of Romanian paintings from the 18th century to contemporary times; and temporary exhibitions ($0.40/0.20).

Silver crafted in Braşov during the 16th century, fur and sheepskin coats, Saxon cloth costumes and Romanian girdles are among the exhibits in the ethnographic museum ($0.40/0.20).

Both museums are open 10 am to 6 pm Tuesday to Sunday.

Continue west to the end of Blvd Eroilor then south along Str După Ziduri, following the western **defensive wall**, built in the 15th century as protection against the Turks. The wall was 12m high and 3km long. Seven bastions were also raised around the city at the most exposed points, each one defended by a guild whose members, pending danger, tolled their bastion bell. The **Blacksmiths' Bastion** (Bastionul Fierarilor) is at the southern end of Str Dupa Ziduri. To the west lie the **Black Tower** (Turnul Neagru) and **White Tower** (Turnul Alba).

Continue to follow the city wall southwest, past **Catherine's Gate** (Poarta Ecaterinei; 1559) to the 16th-century **Weavers' Bastion** (Bastionul Ţesătorilor) on Str Castelui. Visit the **Weavers' Bastion Museum** (Muzeul Bastionul Ţesătorilor; ☎ 472 368) with a fascinating scale model of 17th-century Braşov created in 1896; open 10 am to 4 pm Tuesday to Sunday ($0.20).

Above the Weavers' Bastion is a pleasant promenade through the forest overlooking Braşov. Halfway along is the **Tâmpa cable car** (Telecabina Tâmpa; ☎ 143 732) offering stunning views from the top of Mount Tâmpa; open 10 am to 6 pm weekdays, and 10 am to 7 pm weekends ($1 return).

Braşov's original defensive fortress was built on this mount but, when Vlad Ţepeş attacked Braşov (1458–60), the citadel was dismantled, and 40 merchants were impaled on top of Mount Tâmpa. You can hike to

MARTIN MOOS

Braşov's monumental Black Church

Continued on page 153

TRANSYLVANIA

Exploring the Carpathian Mountains

THE CARPATHIAN MOUNTAINS

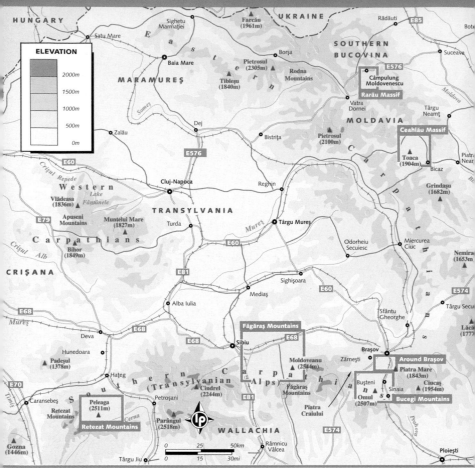

ELEVATION

2000m
1500m
1000m
500m
0m

HUNGARY

UKRAINE

Satu Mare

Sighetu Marmaţiei

Farcău (1961m)

Rădăuti

E85

Borşa

SOUTHERN BUCOVINA

Suceava

Baia Mare

Pietrosul (2305m)

Rodna Mountains

E576

Câmpulung Moldovenescu

MARAMUREŞ

Tibleşu (1840m)

Rarău Massif

Moldova

Vatra Dornei

Târgu Neamţ

Someş

Zalău

Dej

Bistriţa

MOLDAVIA

Ceahlău Massif

E576

Pietrosul (2100m)

Toaca (1904m)

Piatra Near

E60

Bicaz

Crişul Repede

Cluj-Napoca

Reghin

W e s t e r n

Lake Fântânele

Vlădeasa (1836m)

Grindaşu (1682m)

E79

Apuseni Mountains

Muntélui Mare (1827m)

TRANSYLVANIA

Turda

Mureş

Târgu Mureş

C a r p a t h i a n s

Crişul Alb

Bihor (1849m)

E60

Odorheiu Secuiesc

Miercurea Ciuc

Nemira (1653m)

CRIŞANA

E81

Sighişoara

Mediaş

E60

E574

Târgu Secu

Mureş

E68

Alba Iulia

Sfântu Gheorghe

Lăca 1777

Deva

Hunedoara

E68

E68

Sibiu

Făgăraş Mountains

E68

Braşov

Around Braşov

Padeşul (1378m)

Haţeg

S o u t h e r n

Zărneşti

Piatra Mare (1843m)

Caransebeş

Retezat Mountains

C a r p (Transylvanian

Moldoveanu (2544m)

Buşteni

Ciucaş (1954m)

Peleaga (2511m)

Cindrel (2244m)

A l p s)

Făgăraş Mountains

Sinaia

Timiş

Cerno

Petroşani

E81

C a r p a t h i a

Omul (2507m)

Bucegi Mountains

Gozna (1446m)

Retezat Mountains

Parângul (2518m)

Piatra Craiului

n s

Ploieşti

WALLACHIA

E574

Pohorta

Târgu Jiu

0   25   50km
0   15   30mi

Râmnicu Vâlcea

COLIN SHAW

Walking in the Southern Carpathians

The Carpathian Mountains, dubbed the 'backbone' of Romania, dominate the country's landscape, as any traveller to Romania will undoubtedly discover. Their many glaciers, canyons, caves and lakes offer a wealth of natural beauty, history and adventure matched only by the region's rich cultural heritage.

Home to Europe's cheapest ski slopes, the mountains offer limitless opportunities for exploration. There are activities to suit all tastes and budgets, from such vigorous pursuits as mountain climbing and hiking, to tranquil railway journeys.

The Carpathians' key mountain passes – the Trans-Făgărașan Highway, Prislop Pass and Tihuta Pass – all offer stunning panoramic views as they twist and turn from one range to the next.

GEOGRAPHY

The Carpathian Mountains curve down from Slovakia and southern Poland through western Ukraine and into Romania, where they account for about a third of Romania's area. The Romanian Carpathians are traditionally divided into the Eastern Carpathians (Carpații Orientali), the Southern Carpathians (Carpații Meridionali) also known as the 'Transylvanian Alps', and the Western Carpathians (Carpații Occidentali). The highest point in the Romanian Carpathians is Mount Moldoveanu (2543m), part of the Făgăraș Mountains south-east of Sibiu.

The Eastern Carpathian arc extends some 350km from the Maramureș Mountains in the north, to Piatra Mare and the Postăvarul Massif in the south. The Rarău Massif in southern Bucovina and the Ceahlău Massif in Moldavia occupy the central expanse of the Eastern Carpathians.

The great divide separating the Eastern and Southern Carpathians is known as the Prahova Valley. The Southern Carpathians stretch some 250km across Transylvania from this valley west to the Danube Strait. Forming this chain are the Bucegi, Piatra Craiului, Făgăraș, Cindrel (Cibin) and Retezat Mountains.

The Western Carpathians, essentially the Apuseni Mountains, are a cluster of massifs straddling Transylvania and Banat in the country's north-west.

NATIONAL PARKS & NATURE RESERVES

Title page: Entrance to Scărișoara Ice Cave, Apuseni Mountains (photograph by Colin Shaw)

Romania's first nature reserve was established in 1932. Today the country has 586 protected areas including 13 national parks, 18 protected landscapes and 46 scientific reserves, most of which are harboured within the Carpathian Mountains.

While Romania's national parks aren't exactly the best managed in the world, recent initiatives have paved the way for the protection of the Carpathians' natural wonders for future generations. In June 1999

Major Parks & Reserves

Of the Carpathian Mountains' numerous national parks and reserves, some highlights are listed here.

Bucegi Nature Reserve

The Bucegi Nature Reserve protects the entire 300 sq km of the Bucegi mountain range. The reserve contains a variety of forests and abundant botanic species including edelweiss. It is also home to the woodpecker. To find out more about the wonders of this reserve, visit the Bucegi Nature Reserve Museum in Sinaia (see the Transylvania chapter).

Retezat National Park

The Retezat Mountains encompass Romania's first national park, established in 1935 on 13,000 hectares. Today it has been declared a Unesco Biosphere Reserve and expanded to 54,400 hectares. It has some 300 plant species and its wilds are roamed by black mountain goats, bears, foxes and stags. Come migration season, the monk eagle is known to pass by.

Piatra Craiului

The Piatra Craiului range, 25km in length, stretches from Zărneşti in the north to Podu Dâmboviţei in the south. Since 1939 the area has been protected but it was only declared a national park in 1990. Since 1999 it has been administered under guidance from the European Ecological Network (Eeconet). Its treasures include mountain cocks, black goats, wolves, stags and unusual hazel-coloured bears.

Ceahlău Massif

The 5200-hectare area of the Ceahlău Massif has been protected since 1941, as the Ceahlău Massif National Park (Parcul Naţionale Muntele Ceahlău). Among its many treasures are countless flower species and rare fauna such as the cliff butterfly (a bird also found in the Bicaz

the World Bank provided Romania with much-needed funding ($5.5 million) to support biodiversity projects within the Romanian Carpathian chain. The funding is being used to develop Piatra Craiului as a national park and to implement park regulations and facilities in the Retezat and Bucegi Mountains.

Additional funding has been received from the EU Life Nature Program for the conservation and regeneration of both the Bucegi and Piatra Craiului Mountains' natural habitats. The program also aims to establish Bucegi as a national park.

FLORA

The Carpathian Mountains are among the least-spoilt mountains in Europe, with alpine pastures above and thick beech, fir, spruce and oak

Major Parks & Reserves

Gorges) and mountain cock. You can also spy deer, black mountain goats and bears.

Apuseni Mountains

The Apuseni Mountains were recognised as a geological reserve in 1938. At their centre is a karst plateau with an extensive cave system lying beneath. Wild boars, deer, stags and bears continue to inhabit the region's pine forests, but their future survival is jeopardised by un-controlled hunting in these parts. The Apuseni Mountains have been earmarked for the creation of a future national park.

Slătioara Forest Reservation

Many of the 320 plant species, including the 'lady's shoe' orchid *(cypri-pedium calceolus)* and the edelweiss *(floare de colț;* literally 'flower of stone'), that grow in the Rarău Mountains can be found in the Slătioara Forest Reservation (Codrul Secular de la Slătioara; 790m to 1350m) on the eastern side of the mountain range. The reservation, established in 1913, covers an area of 408 hectares containing virgin woods more than 100 years old. Much of it is out of bounds and only a small part can be freely explored.

Todirescu Flower Reservation

The crowning glory of the Rarău Massif is the glorious Todirescu Flower Reservation (Fânețele Montane de la Plaiul Todirescu; 1933), which sprawls for 44 hectares across Todirescu Mountain on the southern edge of the Slătioara Reservation. In July its meadows are ablaze with colour. Tulips, bluebells, daffodils, daisies, chrysanthemums and the poisonous omagul *(aconitum anthora)* are just some of the many floral delights found here.

The reservation is easily accessed from Slătioara village (see Eastern Carpathians in the Hiking & Climbing section later in this chapter).

---

forests below. About 1350 floral species have been recorded in the Carpathians. Typical alpine species include yellow poppy, Transylvanian columbine, saxifrage and, in the southern Carpathians, the protected edelweiss.

Beech trees cover the northern foothills of the Southern Carpathians and fir and common spruce trees dress the slopes above 1000m. Alpine forests rich in sycamore, maple, poplar and birch can be found at altitudes between 1200m and 1500m.

Juniper tree, little willow and bilberry bush are dominant in the subalpine forests above 1700m. Less fertile zones in this region are home to common spruce forests.

Right: Edelweiss, a Carpathian native

LPP

Carnivorous Carpathians

The Carpathian Large Carnivore Project (CLCP) is the biggest project of its type in Europe. Through its extensive pioneering research and field studies, coupled with its innovative ecotourism program, it works towards the future survival of Romania's large wolf, brown bear and lynx populations.

Set up in 1993, the project is based in the Bucegi Nature Reserve in the Southern Carpathians, with its headquarters in Prejmer, near Braşov. Its field cabin in Zărneşti is home to two wolves called Crai and Poiana, rescued as cubs by project workers, from a fur farm in central Romania. Crai and Poiana were then hand-raised at the field cabin, today happily mingling with tour groups and serving as vital educational tools for the CLCP.

Tracking radio-tagged wolves, bears and lynx, by 4WDs, snow-mobiles, ultralight deltaplane, on skis and on foot, is an integral part of the project wardens' work. Since 1994 more than a dozen wolves have been briefly caught, tranquilised, fitted with radio-tagged collars, then set free to roam wild once more. Wardens can then follow the feeding and behaviour patterns of the pack at large.

The radio tags also enable project wardens to discern the extent of human persecution of wolves. Of the dozen wolves that have been tagged so far, two have been shot by hunters, one by a shepherd, and another was poached.

Sheep provide a rich food supply for both wolves and bears in summer. The CLCP conducted a study of the cost of

LISA BORG

FAUNA

Most Carpathian wildlife dwells in the lower mountain forests. Beech forests shield over 100 bird species, including the green woodpecker, ring dove, grey owl and jay. The mountain cock, hazel hen, black woodpecker and golden pheasant are among the species living in the common spruce forests.

The highest concentration of large carnivores anywhere in Europe is found in the Romanian Carpathians. Some 5400 brown bears (half of Europe's bear population) and 3500 wolves (over a third of Europe's wolves), along with 2000 lynx (35% of Europe's lynx), roam these

Carnivorous Carpathians

livestock lost to large carnivores from 17 shepherd camps in a 1000-sq-km area between May and July 1999. The study found that, on average, 9.23 sheep from each camp were taken, costing each shepherd $277.

TRUDI CANAVAN

The CLCP's research of Romania's impressive brown bear population has highlighted the need for greater public awareness and government action. Due to earlier overpopulation of bears, the animals have become dependent on feeding from garbage bins in Racadav, a Braşov suburb. Alarmingly, this is on the increase; during the 1999 summer 25 bears, including 11 cubs, were counted feeding around the suburb. While no lethal attacks have occurred to date, the potential for danger is increasing as the human population becomes less fearful and more careless. The CLCP has been lobbying the government to mount a public awareness campaign to highlight the potential dangers.

As part of the its education program, the CLCP is building a new glassed bear hide. The hide, holding up to eight people, allows optimum viewing of the carnivores in their habitat without endangering either side. The bear hide will be operational by mid-2001.

The CLCP is a joint venture between the Munich Wildlife Society (☎ 8822-921 20, fax 921 12, ⓔ wgm.ev@t-online.de), Linderhof 2, D-82488 Ettal; and the Wildlife Research Department, Şoseaua Ştefaneşti 128 sect 2, Bucharest RO-72904. The CLCP's Web site is at www.clcp.ro.

forests, and their numbers are growing. It is not uncommon for tamer wolves and bears to prowl around the suburbs of Braşov and Poiana Braşov at night rummaging for food. While they pose little threat to tourists, the phenomenon is increasing.

The pioneering Carpathian Large Carnivore Project runs a comprehensive conservation program for these large carnivores and their habitat (see the boxed text 'Carnivorous Carpathians' for details of the project).

Other animals found throughout the Carpathian forests include the stag, wild boar, badger, deer and fox, while Romania's thriving chamois population inhabits the rocky kingdom above the forests.

Gateways to the Carpathians

Southern Carpathians

The city of Braşov is the best accommodation and orientation point for travel in this region. The easiest access to Piatra Craiului is from Zărneşti, 15km north-west of Bran, both to the south-west of Braşov. Both Bran and Zărneşti provide good accommodation possibilities.

The Bucegi Mountains are best approached from the resorts of Buşteni and Sinaia, both accessible by rail from Braşov.

The Făgăraş Mountains are harder to access. The train stations along the Braşov-Sibiu line are about 8km to 15km north, poorly serviced by bus and difficult to hitch from. The main access points are the villages of Victoria and the Sâmbăta complex.

The Cindrel Mountains can best be tackled from Păltiniş, 32km west of Sibiu. Approach the Retezat Mountains from the east at Petroşani or from the north at Ulpia Traiana-Sarmizegetusa or Nucşoara. Petroşani has a couple of downmarket hotels.

Western Carpathians

The major access hub is Cluj-Napoca, which has plenty of accommodation and amenities.

Eastern Carpathians

In Moldavia, Durău and Bicaz provide the best jumping-off points to start treks into the Ceahlău Massif, while Câmpulung Moldovenesc makes a good base for the Rarău Massif.

The main entrance into the Ronda Mountains is from the Complex Turistic Borşa, 10km east of Borşa town in the country's far north.

Opportunities for bear- and wolf-watching are offered by Enzian Travel (☎ 01704-823 442, fax 822 915, ℮ travel@enzia.com), 67 Highsands Avenue, Rufford, Lancashire, L40 1TE, UK, which organises six-day group tours from £359 (US$530). In Romania contact Carpathian Nature Tours (☎ 095-512 096, ℮ hkkurmes@verena.net), Str Vlad Ţepeş 9, Mediaş 3125, or Antrec in Bran (☎/fax 068-236 884), Str Lucian Bologa 10, Bran.

SKIING & SNOWBOARDING

Romania's most famous ski resorts are Sinaia, Predeal and Poiana Braşov, all in the Carpathian Mountains between Bucharest and Braşov. They are fully developed resorts, with cable cars, chairlifts and modern resort hotels.

The ski season runs from December to mid-March. You can hire gear from all the major hotels in the resorts. For general information on the resorts' facilities, accommodation and transport, see the relevant sections in the Transylvania chapter. Travel agencies specialising in ski holidays are listed under Organised Tours in the Getting Around chapter. Ski passes for the three major resorts are sold on a point system (see the accompanying table). The prices quoted in the table are from the 1999–2000 ski season.

Before setting out on your skiing trip purchase a copy of the excellent *Travel Guidebook Ghid Turistic*, available from most bookshops in Braşov. It has piste maps of Poiana Braşov and Predeal. For information on maps for Sinaia and Buşteni see those sections in the Transylvania chapter.

Also worth contacting for information about ski routes is the Salvamont mountain rescue organisation; see the 'Mountain Rescue' boxed aside later in this chapter.

POIANA BRAŞOV

Poiana Braşov, off the main railway line, has few black slopes but guarantees good skiing from December to mid-March. This resort is popular with snowboarders, and has the best-developed ski school.

A gondola, stationed near Hotel Teleferic, takes you up to Cristianul Mare (1802m). Cable cars – one departing from next to the gondola station and the other from near Hotel Bradul – drop you off near Cabana Cristianul Mare (1690m, $2.60 return, six minutes).

Sign up for ski school at any of the hotels or through the tourist centre (☎ 068-262 310). A six-day ski school, consisting of four hours' group tuition a day, costs $60/45 for adults/children (four-day course $30/22, five-day course $50/38). Private lessons are $15/25 for one/two adults an hour, and $10/18 for children. A three-day snowboarding course costs $30. Ski instructors speak English, German and French. Skis, poles and boots can be hired through the ski school inside the tourist centre or through its hotel representatives, for $9/7 for

Comparison of Ski Resorts

	Poiana Braşov	Predeal	Sinaia
ski runs	10	6	12
cable cars	2		2
chairlifts	1	2	2
drag lifts	6	2	5
point tariff per lift			
cable car	8 points		7 points
chairlift	6 points	5 points	3 points
drag lift	2 points	3 points	1 point
ticket prices			
6-point ticket		$1.50	$1.80
10-point ticket	$2.90	$2.60	$3.10
20-point ticket	$5.50	$5.15	
30-point ticket	$7.90		
60-point ticket	$14.70		$12.30

adults/children per day. Cross-country skis will cost you $6 a day and snowboards are $10 a day.

PREDEAL

Predeal, the smallest of these main resorts, attracts fewer skiers. Its central ski school is the Fulg de Nea (☎ 068-456 089) at Str Teleferi-icului 1. A six-day ski school comprising two/four hours per day group tuition costs $20/35. A day's rental of skis, poles and boots is $6. Most of the hotels also arrange ski school and hire; however, they simply go through the ski school and add their own commission.

Predeal's chair *(telescaun)* and drag *(teleski)* lifts, run by the Clăbucet Zona de Agrement (☎ 068-456 451), depart from the eastern end of Str Telefericului.

At the time of writing, plans to link Predeal with Azuga, a small ski resort in the Prahova Valley south of Predeal, by cable car had been put on hold, and it now seems unlikely that the project will get off the ground within the next couple of years.

SINAIA

Sinaia offers wild skiing around Mount Furnica, and its slopes are considered Romania's most challenging. Its exposed position often sees cable cars grinding to a halt as the wind blows up. Skiing is, on average, guaranteed four days out of seven.

A map showing the various skiing routes and ski lifts (closed Monday) is inside the Montana cable-car station (☎ 044-311 674), behind Hotel Montana.

Most hotels arrange ski school and hire, but it's cheaper to go direct to the central ski school, Snow (☎/fax 044-311 198), behind Hotel Montana at Str Cuza Vodă 2a. Private lessons cost $10 an hour; group tuition is $7 per person an hour. The hire of boots, poles and skis costs $10 a day.

Located on top of the Bucegi plateau above the Sinaia resort is an 8km cross-country route, as well as a 13-bend bobsled track where the Ski-Biathlon Club (☎ 044-374 815, 01-211 5550) hosts a biathlon each year.

BUŞTENI, PĂLTINIŞ & FUNDATA

Beyond Romania's three main resorts there are other opportunities to ski. Buşteni, 10km south of Predeal, has one cable car ($2, open 9 am to 4.30 am, closed Monday), at the western end of Str Telecabinei.

In Păltiniş, 32km south-west of Sibiu, skis and sleds can be rented from Club Sportiv at the south-eastern end of the resort or Cabana Păltiniş. The cabana is next to the teleferic station where you can get a chairlift up the mountain ($1.20 return).

The most popular spot for **cross-country skiing** is at Fundata, 25km south of Bran, along one of three marked courses, ranging from 1km to 3km long. Costs are $1 a day for adults and $0.50 for children (☎ 094-298 024).

HIKING & CLIMBING

Romania's Carpathian Mountains offer endless opportunities for hikers, the most popular areas being the Bucegi and Făgăraş ranges, south and west of Braşov. Other Carpathian hiking zones include the Retezat National Park, north-west of Târgu Jiu; the Apuseni Mountains, south-west of Cluj-Napoca; and the Ceahlău Massif, between Braşov and Suceava. Buşteni, near the Bucegi Mountains, is considered the premier mountaineering centre.

Marked trails traverse most of Romania's mountain ranges and lower-lying foothills.

MAPS

Detailed hiking maps are hard to find – check at tourist offices (or the Internet). It's easiest to buy maps in Braşov, Cluj-Napoca and Sibiu before you head out.

The most up-to-date map of the Bucegi Mountains is *Munţii Bucegi Hartă Turistică* (Amco Press, 1999, $1.10). For the Făgăraş Mountains look out for the *Munţii Făgăraşului Pliant Turistic* (EMCO, $1.20).

For the Retezat the prerevolution *Trasee Turstice în Masivul Retezat* (Publiturism, 1983) is still widely available and easier to use than the *Hartă Turistică Montană Munţii Retezat* (Cartografica, 1997, $1.20).

The Transylvania Ecological Club in Cluj-Napoca (see the Transylvania chapter) publishes a map of the region and the handy *Padiş* guide ($1.20), which lists the hiking trails in the plateau.

The *Mount Postăvarul – Mountain Routes for Tourists* (Artfilco, 1999, $1) clearly shows all routes around Braşov.

The hiking map of the Ceahlău Massif, the *Masivul Ceahlău Hartă Turistică* (Publiturism, 1990), is difficult to find.

See also the Maps section in the Facts for the Visitor chapter.

SOUTHERN CARPATHIANS
Postăvaru Massif

The Postăvaru Massif nestles between the Cheii Valley, Timişului Valley and Poiana Braşov resort, just south of Braşov. Strictly speaking, the

---

Warning

Romania's network of marked hiking trails is undergoing major changes. At the time of writing, a review action by county councils was under way, with each county devising and implementing new paths and changing marked signs. Unfortunately, as with most things in Romania, this process will take some time, and it means that existing maps and guides may no longer be accurate. We strongly advise that you check routes with local tourist offices or organisations such as Salvamont or the Mountain Guide Association of Romania (see later in this chapter) before setting out on any hiking expedition.

Hiking Dos & Don'ts

• Before setting foot in the mountains buy a good-quality hiking map and check the length and difficulty of your planned route.
• Never go hiking alone. Always hike with a group of three or more.
• Inform the voluntary mountain rescue team Salvamont (see later in this chapter) of your plans, including an outline of the route you intend to follow.
• Make certain you are wearing the correct clothing and have adequate supplies of food and water (the spring water in the mountains is not reliably drinkable).
• Always carry a first-aid kit in your pack.
• Check the weather forecast before you set out.
• Do not light fires in wild areas and do not leave campfires unattended.
• Do not litter. Leave only your footprints behind.
• Do not pick the wild flowers.
• Never take unsignposted routes without the guidance of an expert. See the main text for guide contacts.

massif is part of the Eastern Carpathians, but for convenience it has been included here in the Southern Carpathians.

From **Poiana Braşov** you can hike to **Cristianul Mare** (1802m, three hours, marked with red crosses), the massif's highest peak. From the top the trail leads down to the road which links Timişu de Jos (on the Sinaia-Braşov rail line) with Timişu de Sus (2½ hours, red triangles). Turn left for Jos, right for Sus.

You can also hike directly down to **Timişu de Jos** from Cabana Cristianul Mare in three to four hours. The trail is marked from the cabana with blue stripes, then blue crosses. Instead of following the blue-cross trail where the path diverges, you can continue following the blue-stripe trail which eventually takes you over the top of Tâmpa Mountain to **Braşov**. This trail (1½ hours) actually follows the old Braşov road.

From Poiana Braşov you can also easily hike to **Râşnov** (two to three hours, blue stripes) or tackle the more strenuous hike to Predeal (five to seven hours, yellow stripes).

For information on the cabana see the Poiana Braşov section in the Transylvania chapter.

Piatra Craiului

Local climbers rave about the twin-peaked 'Stone of the Prince' – Piatra Mică (1816m), marked by a large stone cross, and Piatra Mare (2238m) – which offers climbers one of Romania's greatest challenges.

In May/June and September, Piatra Craiului receives heavy rainfall. Summer storms are frequent and in winter much of the mountain cannot be accessed. Avalanches are common.

If you're hiking from Bran, the quickest route is along the dirt road to Predulut, through the village of Tohaniţa to **Zărneşti**. From Zărneşti,

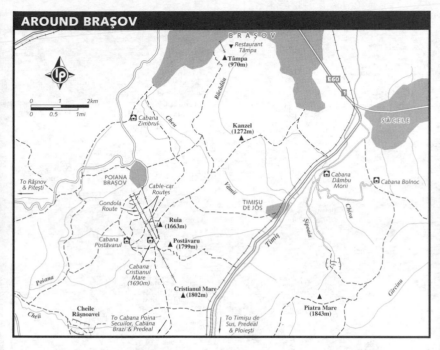

AROUND BRAŞOV

follow the road signposted 'spre Cabana Plaiu Foii 12km'. Some 2km along this road, a diverging trail takes you to the **Colţii Chiliilor** peak (two hours, marked with blue stripes).

From **Peştera**, you can hike along the dirt track to Măgura and again head north to Zărneşti.

From **Cabana Plaiu Foii**, which is the main access point into Piatra Craiului, a trail leads through Fantăna lui Botorog to **Cabana Curmătura** (three hours, 6km, yellow triangles). A map with all the trails marked is inside the Salvamont office, opposite Cabana Plaiu Foii.

The most challenging route from Cabana Plaiu Foii is through the Cheile Zărneştiului to the Regugiul Grind and up to **Vârful Omu** (2502m, three to four hours, red circles). This route is not possible in winter and is only recommended for experienced climbers; ropes are needed in places.

For details on the cabanas see the Around Bran section in the Transylvania chapter.

Bucegi Mountains

The Bucegi Mountains are Romania's best-kept secret, rivalling Slovakia's Tatra Mountains and even the Alps when it comes to trekking. Getting lost is difficult, thanks to a network of marked trails, while most cabanas are open year-round to shelter hikers and cross-country skiers.

EXPLORING THE CARPATHIAN MOUNTAINS

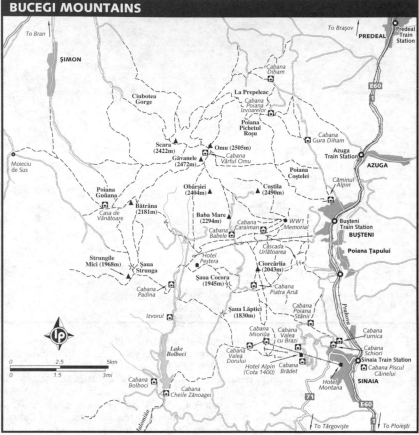

BUCEGI MOUNTAINS

The only danger is the weather: winter is severe and summer thunderstorms are common.

From **Buşteni** take the cable car up to **Cabana Babele** (2206m). From Babele a trail leads to the giant WWI memorial cross at 2284m (one hour, marked with red crosses). From here, an unmarked footpath heads north to the red-and-white TV transmitter, looking like a rocket about to take off, atop the **Coştila peak**. Alternatively a trail (three to four hours, blue crosses) leads from the lower cable-car station to **Cabana Caraiman** (2025m) where you can pick up the trail to the WWI cross (one hour, red circles).

From Babele you can hike south following a yellow-stripe trail to **Cabana Piatra Arsă** (1950m). From here you can pick up a blue trail that descends to **Sinaia** via Poiana Stănii (five hours). The beginning

Climbing & Mountaineering Clubs

Braşov is the main centre for Transylvania's numerous climbing and mountaineering clubs. If you intend heading south to the Bucegi Mountains or west to the Făgăraş range, consider contacting a local club beforehand. Leading clubs in Braşov include:

Nature Protection Society (Asociaţia Pentru Protecţia Naturii; ☎ 068-419 210) Str Maior 44
Amicii Salvamont Tourism Club (☎ 068-142 289) Str Hirschner 8
Dinamo Braşov (☎ 068-419 751) Str Nicopole 34
Mountain Guide Association of Romania (Associaţia Ghizilor Montani Din România; ☎ 068-185 631, ⓔ agmr@go.ro) Str Toamanei 2

of this trail is poorly marked – make sure you study the map on the cabana's wall carefully.

A more ambitious expedition involves taking the cable car from Buşteni and hiking north-west across the mountains to **Bran Castle**, where there are buses to Braşov. You can do this in one strenuous day if you get an early start from Babele, but it's preferable to take two days and camp freelance or spend a night at **Cabana Vârful Omu** (2505m). As you look north from Babele, you'll see a red-and-white TV transmitter on a hill. To the left is a trail leading to Cabana Vârful Omu (two hours, yellow-marked) on the summit. North of Babele the scenery becomes dramatic, with dizzying drops into valleys on either side. From Omu to Bran Castle is tough but spectacular – a 2000m drop, through the tree line into thick forest, then onto a logging road leading to the castle (six hours, yellow triangles). Don't even think of climbing up from Bran to Omu.

For details on the cabanas see the Buşteni and Sinaia sections of the Transylvania chapter.

Făgăraş Mountains

In summer a steady stream of backpackers descends on the Făgăraş Mountains in central Romania – the most spectacular hiking area in the country. To hike the Făgăraş you must be in good physical shape. The trails are well marked, but keep the altitude in mind and be prepared for cold and rain at any time. From November to early May these mountains are snow-covered; August and September are the best months to visit.

The easiest access is from Sibiu. Local trains on the Făgăraş line to Braşov pass many starting points.

One of the best stations to get off is Ucea (59km from Sibiu), from where you can catch one of seven daily buses to **Victoria**. From Victoria you can hike to **Cabana Turnuri** (1520m) in about six hours. The scenery is stunning once you start the ascent. The next morning head for **Cabana Podragu** (2136m), four hours south.

FĂGĂRAŞ MOUNTAINS

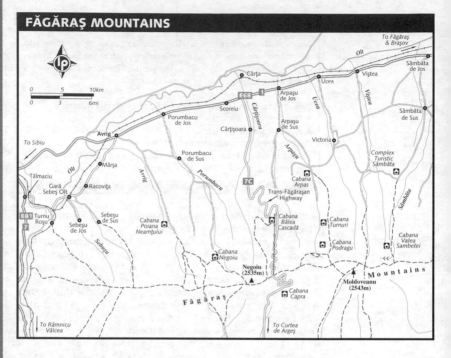

Cabana Podragu makes a good base if you want to climb **Mount Moldoveanu** (2543m), Romania's highest peak. It's a tough uphill climb, but the views from the summit are unbeatable. Otherwise, hike eight hours east, passing by Mt Moldoveanu, to **Cabana Valea Sambetei** (1407m). From Cabana Valea Sambetei you can descend to the railway in Ucea, via Victoria, in a day.

For details of the cabanas see Făgăraş Mountains in the Transylvania chapter.

Cindrel Mountains

The Cindrel (or Cibin) Mountains' highest peaks – Mount Cindrel (2244m) and Mount Frumoasa (2170m) – shelter two large glacial lakes.

From **Păltiniş**, 32km south-west of Sibiu, hiking trails are well marked. Starting at Club Sportiv is a 4km walk to **Şanta** where there is a small refuge for campers to spend the night.

The most popular route (3.5km, red circles) descends to the **Cibin Gorges** (Cheile Cibinului). From here the trail continues north-east, past **Lake Cibin** to **Cabana Fântânele**. The next day continue in the same direction to **Sibiel** village (three to 3½ hours, blue crosses). Alternatively, follow another blue-cross trail to the neighbouring village of **Fântânele**.

Sleeping in the Mountains

In most mountain areas there's a network of cabins or chalets (cabana) with restaurants and dormitories. Prices are much lower than those of hotels and no reservations are required, but arrive early if the cabana is in a popular location – eg, next to a cable-car terminus. Expect to find good companionship rather than cleanliness or comfort. Many are open year-round and cater for skiers in winter.

You'll also come across unattended, empty wooden huts (refuges) in the mountains. These are intended as shelter for hikers and anyone can use them.

Cabanas invariably close for renovations at some time or other and it is always wise to check with the local tourist office before heading off.

It is possible to camp freelance in the mountains and most cabanas allow camping on their grounds, but it's best to check with local tourist offices on camping regulations.

Heading back south from Cabana Fântânele, a trail (red crosses and blue circles) cuts down the valley to **Şaua Şerbănei** where you pick a separate trail leading to the **Cînaia** refuge (7½ to eight hours whole trip, blue circle).

More adventurous alpinists should follow the trail from **Cabana Păltiniş** south, past the Cînaia refuge (5½ to 6½ hours, red stripe) to the summit of **Mount Cindrel**. Heading northwards, red stripes also indicate the way to **Răşinari** village (six to seven hours), with its Cabana Mai.

Retezat Mountains

The Retezat Mountains lie in the south-west corner of Transylvania. The mountains, comprising two peaks, gain their name (meaning 'cut off') from the flat-topped pyramid shape of these peaks. The main access point is **Ulpia Traiana-Sarmizegetusa**, north-west of the mountains, from where a trail (6½ hours, 19.5km, red crosses) leads to **Cabana Gura Zlata**. This trail follows a dirt track which, in dry weather, is suitable for vehicles too. Continuing 12km south you come to **Lacu Gura Apei**.

Another northerly access point is **Nucşoara**. Hikers can catch a local train from Simeria (36km), Petroşani (44km) or Târgu Jiu (94km) to the Ohaba de Sub Patria halt, then follow the trail south, through Nucşoara, to **Cabana Peitrele** (six to seven hours, blue stripes). This and the Gura Zlata are the two most popular cabanas in the Retezat Mountains, with numerous hiking trails marked from each.

From Ohaba de Sub Patria (9km) take a local train to **Pui** train station, from where you can hike 3km south along a paved road to Hobiţa. From Hobiţa a trail leads to **Cabana Baleia** (4½ hours, blue triangles).

The main starting point from the east is **Petroşani**, at the northern end of the Jiu Valley. Daily buses run to **Câmpu lui Neag**, 28km west.

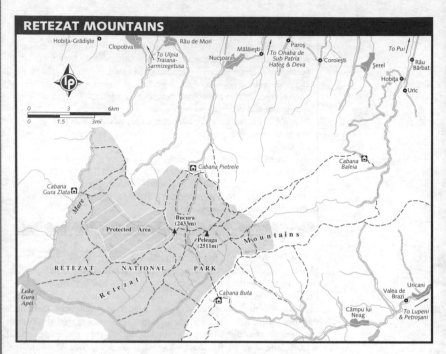

RETEZAT MOUNTAINS

There is a cabana in Câmpu lui Neag where you can take a breather before picking up one of a number of mountain trails. From here a 3½- to four-hour trail leads to **Cabana Buta** in the south-eastern Retezats.

WESTERN CARPATHIANS
Apuseni Mountains
South-west of Cluj-Napoca, the Western Carpathians harbour the Apuseni Mountains. The central part is dominated by the peaks of Bihor (1849m) and Vlădeasa (1836m). Most travellers head straight for the **Padiş Plateau**, where numerous caves and subterranean rivers hide beneath the earth's surface. An officially protected area, the plateau's highest peaks are Mount Măgura Vânătă (1642m) and Mount Cârligatele (1694m).

Hikers should beware of drinking what appears to be natural spring water. Many of the karst plateau's small springs originate from polluted rivers.

You can access Padiş by road from the east in **Poiana Horea** or from the west in **Pietroasa**. Both roads are difficult to navigate in bad weather but eventually lead to **Cabana Padiş** (1280m, 45 beds) from where numerous hiking trails begin. Bookings for the cabana can be made through the Tourism Agency Romanta (☎/fax 064-255 064) in Bologa (see Huedin & Around in the Transylvania chapter).

Mountain Rescue

Emergency rescue is provided by Salvamont (Asociaţia Naţionale a Salvatorilor Montani dîn România), a voluntary mountain rescue organisation with 26 stations countrywide. Its members are skilled climbers, skiers and medics.

Contact Salvamont via the local hospital, mayor's office *(primăria)* or through its headquarters in Braşov. However, in an emergency dial ☎ 961.

Salvamont's major contact points are as follows:

Braşov (☎/fax 068-471 517) County Council Service, Str Varga 23
Buşteni (☎ 044-320 048, 322 005) Primărie, Blvd Libertăţii 91
Poiana Braşov (☎ 068-186 176) Cabana Cristianul Mare (1690m)
Sinaia (☎ 044-313 131) Primărie, Blvd Carol I; also a station at Cota 2000 at top of chairlift
Zărneşti (☎ 092-737 911/916, 092-734 867) opposite Cabana Plaiu Foii

Bear in mind this is a voluntary organisation which relies on limited funding from local authorities. Equipment is minimal and outdated, and mountain rescue by helicopter is financially impossible.

From **Gârda de Sus**, 10km west of Albac, a trail leads to Cabana Padiş (five to six hours, blue stripes). Few hikers access Padiş from **Stâna de Vale** in the north-west although it is possible (5½ to six hours, red stripes).

From Cabana Padiş the most popular circuit leads south-west along the polluted Ponorului River to the fantastic **Ponor Citadela** (Cetăţile Ponorului; six hours, blue circles). The citadel is one of the plateau's greatest natural wonders, leading underground to a damp chamber in which the Ponorului River sinks its way through the chamber's numerous holes; some are as deep as 150m.

Another trail, marked first by red stripes then red circles, leads from the cabana north along a track to **Poiana Vărăşoaia**. From here, red circles bear east to the **Rădesei Citadel** (Cetăţile Rădesei), another underground chamber with impressive rock formations. The route then circles **Someşul Cald**, a natural storage lake, before heading back south to the cabana. If you continue to follow the red stripes north through the Stâna de Vale ski resort you'll arrive at **Cârligatele Peak** (1694m).

For information on caving, see Caving later in this chapter. The Apuseni region's caves, including the Bear Cave, Scărişoara Ice Cave and Meziad Cave, are discussed in the Crişana & Banat chapter.

Turda Gorge

You can hike the length of the stunning Turda Gorge (Cheile Turzii) in under an hour, but plan on camping in order to explore the network of marked trails – see the map outside Cabana Cheile Turzii or ask the cabana staff for a free photocopied map of the *Cheile Turzii şi Împrejurimi Trasee Turistice*.

Most people access the gorge from **Cabana Cheile Turzii** (450m), at the southern foot of Turda Gorge. To reach the cabana from **Turda** village, a trail (three to four hours, 13km, blue crosses) leads hikers through Mihai Viteazul village to the cabana. There is also a cross-country route from Turda (two hours, red crosses). By vehicle, the turn-off marked Cheile Turzii is 2km west of Mihai Viteazul on the main Turda-Abrud road.

A good two-hour trek is the red-cross trail through the gorge, followed by the red-circle trail up and over the peak before returning to Cabana Cheile Turzii.

It is also possible to approach the gorge at its more dramatic northern end, from **Petreştii de Jos**. Upon entering the village, bear left at the first fork; from here, a trail is marked with red crosses.

CEAHLĂU MASSIF

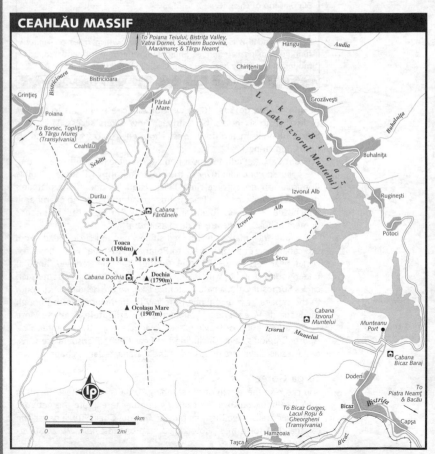

Mountain Myths

Throughout the centuries many myths have arisen explaining the unique formations of the Carpathians. The power of these rocky mountains is reflected in the drama of the stories surrounding them. These two legends come from varying times but are typical of the tales you will hear.

The mighty **Ceahlău Massif** is where the supreme god of the ancient Dacians, Zamolxe, made his home.

Dochia, the beautiful daughter of the Dacian leader Decebal, being pressured to marry Traian, the leader of the conquering Roman army, escaped to the Ceahlău Mountains. But Traian caught up with her as she tended her sheep. Dochia then called upon the god Zamolxe to change her to stone. He granted her wish and she and her sheep became rocks – thereby creating the imposing Dochia Peak.

The **Rarău Massif** takes its name from the Romanian word *rău*, meaning 'evil', 'harm' or 'a fated place'. Therefore it is not surprising that a gruesome tale is associated with the naming of its most prominent formation, the Lady's Stones (or the Princess' Rocks).

Legend has it that it was on top of these rocks that Moldavian prince Petru Rareş (r. 1527–38) commanded his family to hide after he was driven from the throne by the Ottomans in 1538 and imprisoned in Transylvania. His terrified wife, fearing an attack by the Turks, climbed to the top of the highest stone. Desperate to deny the invaders the prize of the royal jewels or another royal hostage, she concealed the precious gems on the peak then flung herself to her death.

It's possible to go from Turda Gorge to Cluj-Napoca, via Deleni and Camping Făget (10 to 12 hours, 29km, red stripe). For details of the cabana see Turda in the Transylvania chapter.

EASTERN CARPATHIANS
Ceahlău Massif

The awe-inspiring Moldovan Olympus (Olimpul Moldovei) range encompasses the Ceahlău Massif. Protected under the Ceahlău Massif National Park, the massif's highest peak is Ocolaşu Mare (1907m).

Hiking trails into the massif lead from Durău, Ceahlău village, Bicaz, Bicazul Ardelean (10km west of Bicaz towards the Bicaz Gorges) and Neagră (5km west from Bicaz Ardelean). Most trails culminate at the **Cabana Dochia**, topping Dochia Peak (1790m). The mountain-rescue team Salvamont has rescue points at Cabana Dochia and **Cabana Izvorul Muntelui**.

Popular marked hiking trails are best tackled in summer.

Rarău Mountains

The Rarău Mountains are a popular hiking spot despite their sinister reputation (see the boxed text 'Mountain Myths').

From May to October you can access these mountains and **Cabana Rarău** (1400m) from **Câmpulung Moldovenesc** by car. As you enter

RARĂU MASSIF

Câmpulung Moldovenesc from the east, a road is signposted on the left 'Cabana Rarău 14km' (hiking: three to four hours, red circles). Do not attempt to drive in bad weather unless you have a 4WD, as the road is narrow and extremely pot-holed and rocky in places.

A second mountain road – slightly less pot-holed – leads up to the cabana (hiking: four to five hours, yellow crosses) from the village of **Pojorâta**, 3km west of Câmpulung Moldovenesc. This road is not marked on maps. Turn left at the fork after the village post office, cross the railway tracks, then turn immediately left along the dirt road. Note the large stones of **Adam and Eve** as you enter the village.

Cabana Rarău can also be accessed from the south in the village of **Chiril**, 24km east of Vatra Dornei on the main Vatra Dornei–Durău road. This is the best of the three road options for those determined to drive (hiking: three to four hours, blue circles).

From Cabana Rarău a trail (30 minutes) leads from to the foot of Rarău's most prized rocks, the **Lady's Stones** or Princess' Rocks (Pietrele Doamnei). A clutter of crosses crowns the highest (1678m) in memory of the climbers it has claimed. The view from the top is superb.

A trail marked by red stripes and red triangles (five hours) leads from the cabana to the **Slătioara Forest Reservation**. From here another trail (red triangles) leads to the **Todirescu Flower Reservation** (see the boxed text 'Major Parks & Reserves', earlier in this chapter).

For details on Cabana Rarău, as well as Cabana Zugreni, which is closer to Chiril, see Rarău Mountains in the Moldavia chapter.

Rodna Mountains
The Rodna's peaks, Pietrosu (2305m) and Ineu (2279m), are the loftiest in the Eastern Carpathians. For details on hiking trails check with the staff at Hotel Cerbal (☎ 062-344 199). See the Borşa section in the Maramureş chapter.

CAVING

Some 12,000 caves *(peştera)* in Romania have been documented but only four are protected: the **Peştera Ghetarul de la Scărişoara**, an ice cave in the Apuseni Mountains ranked as the world's second-largest subterranean glacier (see the Crişana & Banat chapter); the **Peştera Cetătile Ponosului** between Cluj-Napoca and Oradea which has 100m-high passages; and the 3566m-long **Peştera Muierii** (Women's Cave) and the **Peştera Closani**, both in western Wallachia. All four are gated, but only the Scărişoara Ice Cave and the Peştera Muierii are open to tourists.

One of Romania's best caves, also open to tourists, is the impressive **Peştera Urşilor** (Bear Cave), north-west of Oradea. The cave gained its name after bear skeletons were found in its first gallery. For details see the Crişana & Banat chapter.

The southern Banat, Dobruja and the Apuseni Mountains are considered the most rewarding caving terrain.

The Emil Racoviţa Institute of Speleology, listed here, can arrange an expedition to Romania's largest cave, the Peştera Humpleu in the Padiş Plateau. This river cave is 30km long and large enough to house six full football stadiums.

Serious cavers can contact local caving clubs to get permission to enter caves not open to the public. Cavers have to provide their own equipment. Make contact with the following associations *well* in advance if you hope to organise an expedition through them:

Emil Racoviţa Institute of Speleology (☎/fax 064-195 954), Str Clinicilor 5, RO-3400 Cluj-Napoca.
Romanian Speleological Federation (☎/fax 064-187 657, e speo@ mail.soroscj.ro) Piaţa 14 Iulie 4, RO-3400 Cluj-Napoca; or Str Frumoaşa 31, RO-78114 Bucharest

The Web site www.uib.no/people/nglbn has general information about Romanian speleology and these associations.

MOUNTAIN BIKING

Given Romania's ideal mountain-biking terrain, it is not surprising that the sport has taken off in a big way in recent years. The most active biking clubs are in Cluj-Napoca, Sibiu, Oradea and Târgu Mureş.

At the time of writing, the Napoca Cyclotourism Club (NCC)'s elaborate plan for eight mountain-bike routes and eight cycle routes was awaiting approval by the Minister of Tourism. The planned mountain-bike routes will be concentrated in the Carpathian Mountains, with routes taking in some of the Carpathians' most spectacular passes and mountain roads. The cycle routes will link all Romania's major cities including Bucharest, Braşov, Cluj-Napoca, Timişoara, Arad, Iaşi, Galaţi and Constanţa, and will provide connections to cycle routes in all neighbouring countries.

The following can help you organise mountain-bike rental, guides and/or tours:

Buşteni – Hotel Silva (☎ 044-312 412), next to cable-car station on Str Telecabinei: bike rental ($1.50/5 an hour/day)
Cluj-Napoca – Napoca Cyclotourism Club (☎/fax 064-142 953, ⓔ office@ccn.ro), Str Septimiu Albini 133, Apt 18; rental, guides and expeditions. Web site: www.dntcj.ro/NGOs/napoca
Oradea – Bike Sport Club (☎ 059-121 745), Str Nufărului 39; rental and tours
Poiana Braşov – Hotel Caraiman (☎/fax 068-262 061) and Hotel Sport (☎ 068-262 313); bike rental ($2/8 an hour/day)
Sibiu – Boua Bikes Club (☎ 069-218 310), Str Avram Iancu 25; rental and tours
Sinaia – Snow ski centre (see Skiing earlier in this chapter); bike rental ($2/8 an hour/day). At the time of writing, Surmont Sport (☎ 044-311 810), Str Cuza Vodă 2, was planning a bike-hire and guide service.
Târgu Mureş – Robike Mountain Bike Service (☎ 065-160 385), Str Bolyai 24; bike hire ($10.50 a day) and tours

HORSE RIDING

Romania is a country steeped in horse tradition. For centuries horses have been used to plough, pull logs, cart crops and provide transport. Rarely used for leisure, horses remain vital to the daily lives of villagers. It is not uncommon to spy a dusty horse-drawn wagon rattling along Romania's major roadways.

Throughout the Carpathians a network of trails leading to some of the country's most beautiful and remote areas can be explored on horseback. However, the true potential for such adventures is yet to be realised. The best on offer is the Ştefan cel Mare Equestrian Centre (☎ 063-388 470, ⓔ jcross@elcom.ro) located in the Eastern Carpathians in the small village of Lunca Ilvei. The centre offers trail-riding excursions by the hour/half-day/full day for $10/25/50, with longer circuit rides also available.

In Poiana Braşov the Centrul de Echitaţie (☎ 068-262 161), 300m down the road to Braşov, has horse riding for $7 per hour. In winter, horse-drawn sleigh rides are $4 an hour.

MOUNTAIN RAILWAYS

Romania is a paradise for rail enthusiasts. Pre-WWI steam locomotives using narrow-gauge lines have been lovingly restored, enabling travellers to train through some of Romania's most remote regions. A commercially used narrow-gauge steam train still trundles along forestry lines in the mountains from Vişeu de Sus in the Maramureş

The Decline of the Incline

For many generations Romania's oldest forestry railway snaked its way up the western flanks of Mount Vrancrei (1777m), east of Braşov, from the spa town of Covasna to Comandău village (1012m). What was so unique in its appeal was its inclined plane.

The forestry railway, completed in 1890, was the first of its kind in the country to use iron rails and steam locomotives. Its purpose was to transport wood down the valley from Comandău, a primitive logging settlement.

Every weekday two steam trains transporting trimmed wood lumbered up the valley to Siclău (1236m). Here the wood was loaded onto open wagons to make the final part of its journey down the inclined plane to Covasna. Horses were used to manoeuvre the loaded wagons into position then, with the careful use of brakes, the wood was slowly lowered down the mountain. Its weight was counterbalanced against empty wagons at the bottom of the line.

Sadly, this spectacle can no longer be viewed. In October 1999 operations came to a grinding halt. Due to financial strains, the railway line and sawmill, despite having been restored after a fire swept through the region in 1997, closed. Most of the steam locomotives that once trundled its lines have been removed and scrapped. Those that remain have been placed in storage.

This has left the Comandău community, at the top of the line, without income – the sawmill and railway were their lifeline. Government plans to regenerate the community and preserve the railway as a working museum had not eventuated at the time of writing, and the villagers are left in limbo.

With the closure of this line, the forest railway of Vişeu de Sus, in the Vaser Valley in Maramureş, remains the last commercially used steam narrow-gauge railway in Romania. However, today most of the lumber from the forest is hauled by diesel locomotives. It's possible for the public to take special steam-train journeys along this line, as part of organised tours (see Vişeu & Vaser Valleys in the Maramureş chapter).

region (see that chapter for details). Romania's only specialist steam train adventure company is Ronedo Tourist Agency (☎ 040-231 870, fax 231 306, e ronedo@decebal.ro), Blvd Decebal 59, Piatra Neamţ, in Moldavia. Unfortunately steam tours cost – expect to pay from $1079 per person in a group of 15 or more. For details on tours, check the agency's Web site at www.decebal.ro/ronedo.

Hans Hufnagel's *Wälder & Dampf* (Forest & Steam) coffee-table book includes photographs and parallel German and English texts to trace the history of Romania's forestry railways. It can be obtained through the author at: Ing. Hans Hufnagel, Ackerweg 94, 2483 Ebreichsdorf, Austria (e hufi@mycity.at or hufi@ntmail.mycity.at).

ORGANISED TOURS

A variety of operators run tours into the Carpathians, offering hiking, climbing, caving, kayaking, cycling and mountain-biking expeditions as well as culture- or nature-focused tours and photo safaris.

The organisations Roving Romania, Over the Wall and Green Mountain Holidays have good selections. See the Organised Tours section at the end of the Getting There & Away chapter for details of tour operators outside Romania, and the corresponding section in the Getting Around chapter for those within Romania. See also the 'Carnivorous Carpathians' boxed text earlier in this chapter for wolf- and bear-watching tours.

Continued from page 129

the top following zigzag trails (one hour, red triangles) from the cable-car station or yellow triangles from Aleea Brediceanu opposite Le Bastion cafe. It's worth the effort.

In 1580 a new **citadel** was built in Braşov, on top of Citadel Hill (Dealul Cetăţii). Today it houses two good beer patios, a so-so disco and an expensive restaurant. Steps lead up to it from Str Nicolae Iorga, on the north side of Heroes' Cemetery.

Schei District
In Saxon Braşov, Romanians were not allowed to enter the walled city but were banished to the Schei quarter in the south-west. Entry to this quarter from the walled city was marked by the **Schei Gate** (Poarta Schei).

Through the Schei Gate at the southern end of Str Poarta Schei the sober rows of Teutonic houses change to the small, simpler houses of the Romanian settlement. Almost immediately on the left you come to **Str Storii**, the narrowest street in Braşov. Farther south along Str Prundului, is the first **Romanian lycee** which opened in Braşov in 1850 and where the first Romanian opera *Crai Nou* (New Moon), written by Ciprian Porumbescu (1853–83), was performed in 1882. Today it houses the Andrei Saguna National College.

Continue south to Piaţa Unirii to the black-spired Orthodox Church of **St Nicolae din Scheii**, first built in wood in 1392 and replaced by the stone church in 1495 by the Wallachian prince Neagoe Basarab (r. 1512–21) who supported the Romanian community in Saxon-dominated Transylvania. In 1739 the church was enlarged and its interior heavily embellished; open 6 am to 9 pm daily. Beside the church is the **First Romanian School Museum** (Muzeul Primei Şcoli Româneşti; 1495) on the site of a Romanian school. Wallachian Orthodox priests came in 1556 and opened a printing press; open 9 am to 5 pm Tuesday to Sunday ($0.50).

The School Museum has a small **ethnographic section** in which the history of the century-old Schei **Juni Pageant** (Sărbătoarea

junilor) colourfully unfolds. This traditional folk festival takes place on the first Sunday in May. Single men – Juni – don traditional Schei armour and sword in hand they ride from Piaţa Unirii, through the Schei Gate, to Piaţa Sfatului, followed by the married men – the Old Juni. During Saxon domination, this was the one day of the year Romanians were allowed to enter the walled city.

Activities
Hire a helicopter for an aerial twirl of Braşov. Call Brex Trans (☎ 143 666, fax 151 248). The downside? It's $417 an hour.

Braşov is a good base for hiking and climbing in the Carpathians. See the Exploring the Carpathian Mountains special section for a list of Braşov's hiking and climbing clubs, and details on skiing at nearby Poiana Braşov.

Special Events
Beyond the fantastic Juni Pageant (see Schei District, earlier) in mid-May, Braşov hosts other annual festivals well worth attending

The International Chamber Music Festival is usually held the first week in July in various venues around town, with a final concert at Bran Castle.

In August an International Photographic Art Exhibition is hosted at the art museum, and in September/October, Piaţa Sfatului hosts a one-week International Beer Festival – another goodie.

December welcomes the beautiful De la Colind la Stea (From the Carol to the Star) music festival. Choirs and theatre groups from various countries perform traditional Christmas carols and nativities. The four-day festival is usually held in the Sică Alexandrescu Drama Theatre.

Places to Stay
Camping The closest camping ground, *Camping Darste (☎ 259 080, 339 967, fax 339 462, Calea Bucureşti 285)*, 10km southeast of the centre, has wooden huts for $6 a night and tent space for $3. The only other convenient camping ground near Braşov is at Râşnov (see the Râşnov section, later).

Private Rooms & Guesthouses It's hard to miss *Maria and Grig Bolea* (☎ 311 962) at the train station, as they meet almost every train. Some travellers have said they found the couple to be on the pushy side and they can be a bit alarmist about the dangers of Braşov (ignore their advice: the same rules apply as in any other city in the world). Their rooms are good value, though, at $10 per person. Warning: be wary of fake 'Marias' lurking around the train station.

A less aggressive option is the peaceful *Beke Guesthouse (Str Cerbului 32)*, run by the friendly Hungarian-speaking Beke family. Clean, inviting singles/doubles with shared bath are $10/8–10 per person. The only downside is there is no phone number to book ahead.

Also worthwhile is the *Centrul de Studii Hospice – Casa Sperantei (☎/fax 151 501, Str Piatra Mare 101)*, a short walk south of Piaţa Unirii in the old town. Although officially reserved for visiting British doctors, rooms are available for travellers. A bed for the night in one of its double/triple/quad rooms costs $7.50 per person. For bookings contact the office at Str Poarta Schei 16 (☎ 419 780, fax 152 475, [e] medipal@deu roconsult.ro).

The modern *Pensionea Muri (☎ 418 740, fax 422 564, Str de Mijloc 62)*, 1.5km north of the centre, offers clean singles/ doubles for $28/38 including breakfast. The pension also has a laundry service, sauna and a restaurant.

Hotels The cheapest is the rather miserable *Hotel Aro Sport (☎ 142 840, Str Sf Ioan 3)*, behind the Aro Palace Hotel. Single/double rooms with shared bath are $11/14. Call ahead as rooms often get booked out.

The one-star *Hotel Postăvarul (☎ 144 330, fax 141 505, Str Politehnicii 2)*, in the middle of the old town, has singles/doubles/triples with shared bath for $14/21/32. Next door, the overpriced *Hotel Coroana (☎ 144 330, fax 154 427, Str Republicii 62)*, dating from 1910, charges $50/64 for singles/doubles with a private bath; breakfast is included.

The three-star high-rise *Hotel Capitol (☎ 118 920, fax 115 834, Blvd Eroilor 19)*, a relic from the 1960s, charges $51/84 for above-average rooms, including breakfast.

The four-star *Hotel Aro Palace (☎ 142 840, fax 150 427, [e] arobv@deuroconsu lt.ro)*, on Blvd Eroilor, has an Art Deco facade which faces Parcul Central. Plush rooms with cable TV, phone and fridge are nice if you can spare $94/110; credit cards are accepted. The in-house *Pergola restaurant* specialises in Italian cuisine.

Places to Eat

Restaurants A local favourite for pizza and pasta is *Pizza Iulia*, on Str Nicolae Bălcescu, with good food, low prices and friendly staff. Home delivery is also available.

The reasonably priced *Sirena Gustări (Piaţa Sfatului 14)* is a good place to try Romanian specialities such as *sarmale* (stuffed vine leaves) and *mămăligă* (Romanian polenta), and has an English menu.

Another excellent spot for traditional Romanian dishes is *Rota Norocului (☎ 412 324, Str Crişan 6)*, a short walk west from Aro Palace. Expect to pay around $3 for a full meal.

Braşov's most famous restaurant is *Cerbul Carpaţin (☎ 143 981, Piaţa Sfatului 12)* in the Saxon-built Hirscher House (1545). The wine cellar opens in summer from 7 pm to midnight, and a large restaurant upstairs serves meals until 10 pm year-round. Some nights there's live folk music.

Stradivari (☎ 151 165, Piaţa Sfatului 1), on the north-eastern side of the square, serves small but authentic portions of spaghetti and lasagna for around $1.50. Service is on the slow side but the food is worth waiting for. The downstairs pizzeria opens from noon daily.

The overly opulent *Restaurantul Chinezesc Marele Zid (☎ 144 089, Piaţa Sfatului 10)* serves average Chinese food at staggering prices – $14 for an eight-course set meal. Credit cards are accepted.

For the city's most authentic Chinese, head straight to *Tang-Chao (Str Lungă 119)*, situated 1km north of the centre. This cosy restaurant serves up delicious main meals from $2 – you pay an extra $0.25 to use chopsticks.

Less spot-on is **Pepper Jack's** (☎ 417 614, Str Brâncoveanu 38), a rather expensive Mexican restaurant just south of the centre. A main meal here averages around $4.50. For something a little cheaper and tastier try the Transylvanian section in the restaurant's cellar.

For a bird's-eye view of Braşov, hike up Citadel Hill to the superb **Cetate Braşov** (☎ 417 614, Dealul Cetăţii) terrace restaurant, housed within the walls of the old fortress. Chamber-music recitals and folk dances are regularly held in the medieval saloon restaurant.

Cafes On Aleea Tiberiu Brediceanu, **Le Bastion** serves light snacks and delicious cappuccinos on its pleasant outside terrace. Inside, the conservatory-style cafe is warm and cosy on rainy days.

Top-notch for ice-cream floats, cakes and coffee is **Casata Cafea Arabică** (Piaţa Sfatului 12). The outside terrace is always full so get there early.

Coffee lingerers will love **Orient** (Str Republicii 2), a dimly lit cafe with outside seating overlooking the main square. Eight types of coffee are served including the traditional Turkish-style sand coffee for $0.40.

Another popular spot is **Café Art** (☎ 472 535, Str Republicii 48), on the top floor of the Casa Schei building. This warm and friendly cafe serves a wide variety of coffees, most mixed with liberal dashes of alcohol.

Fast Food The **Transilvania** complex, on Str Gheorghe Bariţiu off the southern end of Piaţa Sfatului, slaps out fast food to the tinkle of one-armed bandits; open 10 am to midnight Monday to Saturday, and noon to midnight Sunday.

Cofetăria Modern (Str Mureşenilor 1), while not as modern as the name would suggest, sells everything from cakes and pastries to potato chips and chocolate bars.

North of the city centre is **Casablanca**, on Blvd 15 Novembrie next to Cinema Patria. Sporting bright red-and-white awnings and a large terrace, this is the perfect place to sit and relax after a movie. It serves a good range of kebabs, burgers and pizzas for around $1 and has a handy self-service salad bar.

McDonald's has two outlets in the city, one at the northern end of Str Republicii and a second east of the centre at Calea Bucureşti 106.

Self-Catering Braşov's **fruit & vegetable market** is at the northern end of Str Nicolae Bălcescu, next to **Star**, the central department store. Nearby in Duplex '91, a shopping complex alongside the market, is the spotlessly clean **Non-Stop Supermarket**.

The small but good **pâine** on Str Weiss, just off Str Republicii, sells delicious freshly baked bread.

Entertainment

Cinemas Braşov has six cinemas, all of which show films in their original language with subtitles in Romanian. The most central are the **Royal** (☎ 419 965, Str Mureşenilor 7) and the **Astra** (☎ 419 621, Str Lungă 1).

Bars & Discos The top pub in town, with traditional smoke-filled atmosphere, is the **Britannia Arms Pub**, tucked in an alley beside McDonald's on Str Republicii. Despite its name, it has absolutely no connection with anything British.

Second in line for a quick pint is the **Grenadier** (Str Grigoraş Dina 2), opposite Pizza Iulia. The beer is more expensive and the crowd more elite.

The mobile-phone-carrying set can be found at **Saloon** (☎ 141 611, Str Mureşenilor 11–13) knocking back a few drinks after work. **La Cabana** (Str Hirscher 1), opposite the Children's Theatre, is owned by the same proprietors.

Taste various Romanian wines at the **Cetate Braşov** wine cellar on Citadel Hill.

Lounge back in a comfy couch with your favourite drink or dance the night away at **Disko Club Rock 92** (Str Hirscher 1). Also on the scene is **Haçienda** (Str Carpaţilor 17), a large disco in an old factory east of the centre. Entry into the three-level club varies from $1 (discos) to $2 (live bands).

Another hot spot is the **Aquarium** disco in the Sică Alexandrescu Drama Theatre (see

TRANSYLVANIA

the following section). On summer weekends an open-air disco is held in the *Grădina de Vară*, up on the hill in the citadel.

The *Student Culture House* (*Casa de Cultură Studenteasca; Blvd Eroilor 29*), next to the Transylvania University, hosts everything from discos to drama. Performances by the Student English Theatre Club (Clubul de Teatru în Engleză) are held here occasionally.

Theatre & Classical Music The *Sică Alexandrescu Drama Theatre* (*Teatrul Dramatic Sică Alexandrescu;* ☎ *418 850, Piaţa Teatrului 1*) has plays, recitals, and opera year-round. The *Gheorghe Dima State Philharmonic* (*Str Apollania Hirscher 10*) is housed in the same building as the *Children's Theatre* (*Teatrul Pentru Copii;* ☎ *142 289*). Ask for details about the Drama Theatre and Philharmonic at the Agenţie de Teatrală at Str Republicii 4, just off Piaţa Sfatului. There is also a *Puppet Theatre* (*Teatrul de Păpuşi Arlechino;* ☎ *142 873*) on Str Ciucaş.

Shopping

Unusual ceramics can be picked up at the Galerie de Artă at Str Mureşenlior 3. Artizana at Str Republicii 48 sells traditional folk costumes, rugs and sculptures.

For water bottles, whistles, boots and anything else you might need for hiking (except maps) go to the superb Astra Sports on the western side of Piaţa Sfatului; it accepts credit cards. The smaller Pro-Activ sports shop at Str Republicii 17 has a good selection of sportswear and shoes.

Getting There & Away

Train Advance tickets are sold at the Agenţie de Voiaj CFR office (☎ 142 912), Str Republicii 53, open 8 am to 6 pm weekdays, and 9 am to 1 pm Saturday. International tickets can also be purchased in advance from Wasteels (☎ 424 313), in the train station hall. Discounts are available for students and business travellers.

Braşov is well connected to Sighişoara, Cluj-Napoca and Oradea by fast trains. Local trains to/from Sinaia run frequently. Local Braşov-Sibiu trains drop off hikers headed for the Făgăraş Mountains. To Budapest, the

international trains *Dacia* (10 hours, 7.29 pm), *Traianus* (9½ hours, 8.52 am) and *Ister* (9½ hours, 9.52 pm) go daily. The *Pannonia Expres* (9.58 am) runs to Budapest (10 hours), Bratislava (14 hours) and Prague (19¾ hours). The *Carpati* (22¼ hours, 11.11 pm) goes to Warsaw via Kraków.

The left-luggage office (open 24 hours) is located in the underpass that leads out from the tracks.

Bus Major daily bus services from Autogară 1, next to the train station, include one to Iaşi (326km), Gheorgheni (150km), Miercurea Ciuc (101km), Piatra Neamţ (238km), Târgu Neamţ (280km), Târgu Mureş (172km) and Sfântu Gheorghe ($0.60, 32km); and two to Târgovişte (90km) and Bacău (179km).

Autogară 2, west of the train station at Str Avram Iancu 114, has buses to Râşnov, Bran and Moieciu, marked 'Moieciu-Bran', every half-hour ($0.50, pay the driver). Other major daily buses include one daily to Făgăraş (65km), Câmpulung (84km) and Curtea de Argeş (184km); two to Piteşti (143km); and fourteen to Zărneşti (19km).

The main bus stop in town is the 'Livada Poştei' at the western end of Blvd Eroilor in front of the County Library (Biblioteca Judeţeană). From here catch bus No 20 to Poiana Braşov ($0.50, 13km, every 30 minutes). Buy your ticket from the kiosk opposite the Student Culture House before boarding. Bus No 25 leaves every half-hour for Cristian (5km).

Hungary & Turkey International buses arrive/depart from Autogară 1. Every Thursday there's a 7 am bus to Budapest ($15, 17 hours). A private bus to Istanbul ($33, 16 hours) leaves Thursday and Sunday at 8 am. Buy these tickets from the Ortadoğu Tur office, Blvd Garii 24a.

Germany Daily private buses depart from Braşov to Germany. Ticketing agencies include Double T (☎ 410 466), Str Republicii 9; Kron-Tur (☎ 151 070, 471 473, ⓔ krontour@deltanet.roknet.ro), Str Gheorghe Bariţiu 12; and Touring (☎ 150 402), Piaţa Sfatului 25.

Getting Around

Bus Bus No 4 runs from the train station and Autogară 1 into town, stopping at Piaţa Unirii in the centre. From Autogară 2, take bus No 12 or 22 from the 'Stadion Tineretului' stop on Str Stadionului into the centre. Turn right out of the bus station, walk to the end of Str Avram Iancu, then right onto Str Stadionului. The bus stop is in front of the stadium.

Car Avis (☎ 413 775) has an office inside Hotel Aro Palace. The Hertz (☎ 471 485) office is next to Cinema Patria at Blvd 15 Noiembrie 56.

Taxi To avoid being ripped off by unscrupulous taxi drivers, call one of Braşov's most reputable companies, Martax (☎ 313 040) or CCB (☎ 414 141).

Bicycle For bike repairs and parts, try Doua Roti (☎ 470 207) at Str Nicolae Bălcescu 55, open 8 am to 4.30 pm weekdays, or First Bike at Calea Bucureşti 66, open 9 am to 8 pm weekdays, and 10 am to 4 pm Saturday.

AROUND BRAŞOV

There are plenty of things to see and do around Braşov. As well as the Saxon fortresses of Prejmer, Hărman and Râşnov, you can easily visit the mountain resort of Poiana Braşov or the acclaimed Bran Castle (you may be disappointed) in a day.

Prejmer & Hărman

Prejmer (Tartlau) is an unspoiled Saxon town, first settled in 1240, with a picturesque 15th-century **citadel** surrounding the 13th-century **Gothic Evangelical church** in its centre. The fortress was the most powerful peasant fortress in Transylvania. Its 272 small cells on four levels lining the inner citadel wall were intended to house the local population during sieges. Its outer defensive wall – 4.5m thick – were the thickest of all the remaining Saxon churches. The Unesco World Heritage-listed fortress is open 10 am to 3 pm Tuesday to Friday and 11 am to 3 pm weekends.

Hărman (Honigburg – literally 'honey castle'), 7km from Prejmer, is a small Saxon village, also with a 16th-century peasant **citadel** at its centre. Inside the thick walls is a weathered **clock tower** and a 15th-century **church**; open 9 am to noon and 1 to 5 pm Tuesday to Sunday. Ask for the key from the *Burghüter* (warden). The colourful houses facing the main square are typical of the Saxon era, with large rounded doors and few windows. Like Prejmer, rural Hărman hasn't changed much since the 19th century.

Getting There & Away From Braşov, trains leave for Ilieni (the station closest to Prejmer Citadel) at 6.13 and 8.18 am, and 12.30, 1.15, 4.34 and 8.33 pm (20 minutes). As you arrive at Ilieni look for the tall tower of the citadel church, to the right (south) of the railway line. Walk south on Str Nouă for about 500m, then left on Str Alexandru Ioan Cuza, which you follow to the end. Turn left to reach Str Şcolii on the right. The citadel is straight ahead.

From Ilieni trains leave for Hărman and Braşov at 5.31, 7.23 and 9.24 am, and 1.24, 4.21, 6.27 and 9.49 pm. If you decide to visit Hărman – seven minutes by train from Ilieni – walk 200m north-east from its station, turn right, cross the highway and continue straight for 2km to the centre of town.

Râşnov

Everyone who makes the trip to Râşnov (formerly spelt Rîşnov) agrees that the ruins of its 13th-century hilltop **fortress** (Cetatea Râşnov; ☎ 068-230 255) are more dramatic and less touristy than the castle at Bran. As with Hărman and Prejmer, the fortress was built by the local population as protection against Tartar, and later Turkish, invasions. Indeed, almost immediately after its completion, the fortress suffered its first Tartar attack in 1335. The fortress remained functional until 1850 when it was abandoned and fell into ruin. Visitors who make their way here can wander around the grounds, the church, chapel, weapons tower and jail and peer down the 154m-deep well. The fortress is open 6 am to 5 pm Tuesday to Sunday ($0.50).

Places to Stay & Eat In Râşnov, *Camping Valea Cetăţii* and *Hotel Cetate* (☎ 068-230 266) adjoin each other directly below the castle on the road to Poiana Braşov, about 2km from the bus stop to/from Braşov. The camping ground, open from June to August, has cabins for $5 per person, tents $2.50. The hotel, open year-round, offers doubles/triples with private bath for $15/19 and has a restaurant.

Getting There & Away Buses marked 'Bran-Moieciu' leave every half-hour from Braşov's Autogară 2 for both Râşnov (40 minutes) and Bran (one hour). It's best to visit Bran first (see the Bran section later) and then stop at Râşnov on the way back.

From the bus stop in Râşnov, walk 100m east towards the mountains, turn right at Piaţa Unirii and watch for the hillside stairs in the courtyard of the unmarked Casa de Cultură (on your left). The castle is a 15-minute walk uphill. A second entry route leads from a road between the camping ground and Hotel Cetate (see Places to Stay & Eat).

POIANA BRAŞOV
☎ 068
Poiana Braşov (1030m), on the slopes of Postăvarul Massif in the southern Carpathians, is Romania's premier ski resort. Unlike its sister resort of Sinaia, 'Braşov's Clearing' offers few challenges for advanced skiers. But the beauty of this intermediate resort lies in its sheltered, forested location which guarantees good skiing between early December and mid-March. Some years, you can ski here as late as May. In summer take the cable car to the top of Mount Postăvarul (1802m) for a panoramic view of Braşov and the surrounding Carpathians (for details see the special section Exploring the Carpathian Mountains).

Orientation
Streets aren't named but a large map of the resort in the car park (next to the central bus stop) indicates exactly where the hotels and cable cars are. Good references are the Amco Press *Braşov* map which has an excellent map of Poiana Braşov and the *Travel Guidebook-Ghid Turistic* which

includes piste maps of Poiana Braşov (see the earlier Braşov section).

The cheapest hotels are around the Complex Favorit at the eastern end of the resort. The information centre, post office and pharmacy are also here.

Information
Tourist Offices The tourist office (☎ 262 310/325/271, fax 150 504) is inside the Complex Favorit. From the main bus stop turn left along the main road and then immediately right; the office is 50m along this road on the left.

The tourist centre acts as the coordinating body for Hotels Piatra Mare and Ciucaş. It has information on all types of accommodation vacancies. Staff can also arrange folklore evenings and day trips to Bran-Moieciu ($23.50), Sinaia ($16.50), Sighişoara ($19.50) and Sibiu ($21); open 8 am to 8 pm daily. Tours can also be booked through one of the centre's representatives in each of the hotels.

Ski lessons and hire can be arranged through the resort's central ski school, based in the tourist office, or through one of its reps.

For tour operators with ski packages to Poiana Braşov, see Organised Tours in the Getting Around chapter.

Money There is a 24-hour shop and currency exchange, which cashes travellers cheques, at the foot of Hotel Alpin, open 10 am to 5.30 pm daily.

Telephone To make international telephone calls, the cable-car (telecabina) station next to Hotel Bradul has a cardphone.

Medical Services The resort clinic *(dispensar medical)*, next to Complex Favorit, opens 9 am to 5 pm daily. It operates a 24-hour emergency service (☎ 262 121).

Activities
For information on hiking, skiing, snowboarding, mountain biking and horse riding, see the Exploring the Carpathian Mountains special section.

Places to Stay

Most travel agencies in Braşov take bookings for hotels in Poiana Braşov. Except for a couple of weeks over Christmas and New Year, you can always find a room at the resort. Nightly rates in all the hotels include breakfast.

Cabanas At 1690m, *Cabana Cristianul Mare*, a large wooden chalet with an attached restaurant overlooking the slopes, is open throughout the year except for a few weeks in November. Fifteen minutes downhill from Cristianul Mare is the calmer *Cabana Postăvarul* (☎ *312 448*), at 1585m. It has a better atmosphere with fewer cablecar tourists, but it's sometimes closed. Both offer beds in shared rooms for $5.20 per person.

Hotels En route to Poiana Braşov from Braşov you pass *Hotel Restaurant Valea Cetăţii* (☎ *230 266*), a pretty chalet, beautifully furnished (for the price), with bargain rooms at around $7 per person. It's not in the resort centre but it's cheap.

Cheapest options in the resort include the slightly shabby *Poiana Ursului* (☎ *262 216*), next to the tourist village in the 'cheap end' of the resort. It has double/triple rooms with shared bathroom for $22/26. Farther south of Poiana Ursului is the two-star *Hotel Ruia* (☎ *262 202, fax 262 902*) with comfortable doubles for $24.

The 66-room *Hotel Caraiman* (☎/*fax 262 061*), behind the Cristal Fitness Centre, has single/double rooms with private bathroom for $18/22. It also rents out mountain bikes.

Close to Hotel Caraiman is the two-star *Hotel Şoimul* (☎ *262 111, fax 262 154*), with 107 doubles costing $23. Opposite, the more inviting *Hotel Ciucaş* (☎/*fax 262 181*), also two-star, offers a more friendly – and expensive – service. Modern rooms cost $43/55.

Among the nicest places to stay in Poiana Braşov is *Casa Viorel* (☎ *262 431, fax 262 148*, e *coliba@brasovia.ro*), hidden amid forest at the southern end of the resort. Run by the same enterprising couple who run the thriving Outlaws' Hut (see Places to Eat), it

has six doubles costing $40, two luxury doubles for $50 and two suites for $60.

Next door to Hotel Caraiman, the two-star *Hotel Piatra Mare* (☎ *262 226*) charges $32/55. The hotel has a tourist office and a currency exchange.

The Sport, Bradul and Poiana Hotels at the southern end of the resort are owned by the Hotel Ana group (☎ 262 313, fax 262 252) – the *Poiana* has rooms for $38/50. The *Bradul*, hidden among trees, has singles/doubles/triples for $32/42/53. *Hotel Sport*, wedged between the Poiana and Bradul, is the most exclusive of the three, with singles/doubles for $42/59.

Poiana Braşov's other top hotels include the three-star *Hotel Alpin* (☎ *262 343, fax 252 211*, e *poianacibela@ronline.ro*) which you pass as you enter the resort from Braşov. It has 133 rooms, most with a balcony and all with a mini bar and cable TV, for $46/60. Luxury apartments are $132.

The new three-star *Hotel Tirol* (☎ *262 460/455, fax 262 439*) offers comfortable singles/doubles for $72/96.

Places to Eat

The famed *Coliba Haiducilor* (☎ *262 137*, e *coliba@brasovia.ro*), or 'Outlaws' Hut' as it is generally known, is unbeatable. It is beautifully decorated in traditional rustic style with dried corn cobs strung from the ceiling and sheepskins lining the walls. A fire burns in the hearth in winter and live folk bands play. In autumn, jars of pickles adorn the small 'museum' outbuilding in which traditional weaving looms are displayed. The restaurant, at the southern end of the resort, is open year-round.

Animal lovers may want to avoid the *Sura Dacilor* (*Dacians' Grange;* ☎ *262 327*), next to the Cristal Fitness Centre, which has even more sheepskins on the walls than the Outlaws' Hut, plus a couple of wild boar skins. Enough to put you off eating. The food is excellent, however (yes, they do serve bear steaks!).

A bit of a trek north, but worth it, is *Stâna* (☎ *475 948, mobile 094-330 929*), a rustic restaurant housed on a sheep farm 1.3km along a dirt track off the main road leading to Poiana Braşov (signposted 200m before entering Poiana Braşov). Homemade cheese and other delectable products are served here.

Getting There & Away

From Braşov, bus No 20 runs from the Livada Poştei bus stop opposite the County Library (Biblioteca Judeţeană) at the western end of Blvd Eroilor to Poiana Braşov ($0.50, 13km, every 30 minutes).

BRAN

☎ 068

For many travellers, Bran, 30km south of Braşov, is their first (or only) glimpse of rural Romania. And indeed, for most, the experience lives up to expectation. This was the first part of Romania to be developed as a tourist hub in the 1960s. Many properties were never nationalised and cash was poured into the little village to make it the gold mine it is today.

Travellers who set foot farther afield in other rural areas will quickly realise that Bran, with its luxury villas and private cottages kitted out with hot water and indoor bathrooms, is not representative of Romania.

The town is nestled in a mountain pass between the Bucegi and Piatra Craiului ranges and during the 15th and 16th centuries was an important frontier town on the main road leading from Transylvania into Wallachia.

Orientation & Information

The centre of Bran lies either side of the main Braşov-Piteşti road (Str Principală) which cuts through the village from north to south. The entrance to Bran Castle, signposted 'Muzeul Bran', is on the left as you enter the town from Braşov. The main cluster of shops and cafes and the currency exchange are centred on this junction.

The bus stop is farther south on Str Principală, next to the park. From the bus stop, turn right along Str Principală and then right onto Str Aurel Stoian to get to the Bran Imex tourist office. The central post and telephone office is south of Bran centre, past the Vama Bran museum on the road to Moieciu.

Bran Castle

Despite popular myth, Bran Castle, commonly known as 'Dracula's castle', was *not* built by Vlad Ţepeş, the 15th-century Wallachian prince upon whom the novelist Bram Stoker is (incorrectly) supposed to have based his bloodthirsty vampire, Count Dracula. The castle, perched atop a 60m peak in the centre of Bran village, was in fact built by the people of Braşov in 1382 to defend the Bran mountain pass against Turks.

From 1920 the castle was inhabited by Queen Marie. Bran Castle remained a summer royal residence until the forced abdication of King Michael in 1947.

Bran Castle, with its fairytale turrets and Mediterranean whitewashed walls, is far from menacing. Much of the original furniture imported from Western Europe by Queen Marie is still inside the castle's thick stone walls. A fountain in the courtyard conceals a labyrinth of secret underground passages. Tour guides will tell you that Vlad Ţepeş might have sought refuge for a few days in Bran on his flight from the Turks in 1462 following their attack on the Poienari fortress in the Argeş Valley (see Poienari & Arefu in the Wallachia chapter).

Free guided tours of Bran Castle are available in English, French, Romanian and Italian. Your ticket for the castle ($2.60, $1.80 with a student card) includes entrance to the open-air **ethnographic museum** at the foot of the castle and the **Vama Bran Museum** (see the following section). The complex is open 9 am to 4 pm Tuesday to Sunday.

Around Bran Castle

From the castle, walk south along Str Principală past the centre of the village to the **Vama Bran Museum** (Muzeul Vama Bran), housed in the former customs house. Various archaeological treasures as well as many photographs of the castle are displayed.

Opposite the former customs house are some remains of the old **defensive wall** which divided Transylvania from Wallachia (best viewed from the soldiers' **watchtower** in the castle). On the southern side of the wall is a small stone **chapel**, built in 1940 in memory of Queen Marie. The church, now abandoned and boarded up, is a copy of a church in the queen's palace grounds in Balcic, Bulgaria (formerly southern Dobruja). A **memorial tomb** to the queen has been carved in the mountain, on the north side of the wall.

Special Events
September is the month of the Sâmbra Oilor, a pastoral festival celebrated with great gusto in Bran and its surrounding villages.

Places to Stay
Cabanas A rustic chalet on the hillside 600m from the castle, *Cabana Bran Castel* (☎ 236 404) provides accommodation for $4 per person in a dorm room with shared bath. Meals are served and it is open year-round. From the bus stop, turn right along Str Principală then right along Str Aurel Stoian (or cut across the park instead); continue for 50m and then turn left onto a narrow path by the side of the yellow-painted hospital. Cross the bridge over the stream and bear left up to the cabana.

Private Rooms Antrec (☎/fax 236 884, Str Lucian Bologa 10) arranges inexpensive accommodation in private homes in and around Bran; open 8 am to 9 pm daily June to August (shorter hours the rest of the year). If you call in advance, staff will meet you out of office hours. The agency can also arrange long- and short-term rentals for an entire property.

For a whirlwind of luxury and decadence, go for the *Vila Alba*. The villa is owned by a rich Romanian emigre; but the house is run by a friendly, down-to-earth couple. A night's stay, including breakfast, is $60 a double. Book through Antrec.

Hotels The one-star *Han Bran* (☎ 236 556), two blocks from the castle on the right as you enter Bran from the north along Str Principală, charges $10/15 for singles/doubles with private shower and toilet. Hot water flows from 7.30 pm to 11 pm. The front terrace is a good place for a meal.

Vila Bran (☎ 236 866, Str Principală 238), superbly positioned in a picturesque orchard, has rooms for $15/24 including break-fast. This two-building complex also has a billiard room, fitness room and tennis court.

The *Bran Benzin* (☎ 238 088) petrol station at the northern end of Bran has six rooms above the station. Doubles with shared/private bath are $13.50/16.

Places to Eat
All hotels have restaurants. However, nothing can beat the homemade cheese, jam, țuică and other culinary delights you will be treated to if you stay in a private home. *Bella Italia Pizzeria* (☎ 236 488), opposite the Vama Bran Museum on the road south out of the village, serves good pizza for around $1.10. For other provisions visit the *Dracula Market*, on the corner of Str Principală and the turn-off to the castle; or at the *alimentară* close by on Str Principală.

Entertainment
At weekends, Bran youths flock to the Cabana Bran Castel to boogie the night away in its terrace disco; open 9 pm to 5 am Friday and Saturday, and 6 pm to midnight Sunday.

Getting There & Away
Buses marked 'Bran-Moeciu' ($0.50, one hour) depart every half-hour from Braşov's Autogară 2. From the bus stop in Bran the castle is easy to spot. Return buses to Braşov leave Bran every half-hour between 5.30 am and 7.30 pm; on weekends buses run between 6.40 am and 5.40 pm. All buses to Braşov stop at Râşnov and Cristian.

From Bran there are also buses daily to Zărneşti (40 minutes, departing at 6.10, 8.30, 9.10 and 11.10 am, and 2, 2.10 and 6.10 pm; reduced services on weekends); and to Moieciu (15 minutes, hourly between 7 am and 7 pm).

AROUND BRAN
Bran's surrounding villages are spectacular in their rural attractions. Modern luxury villas abound but the wild landscape remains untouched. Traditional occupations such as sheep farming, wool weaving and cheese making are vital to the villagers' daily survival. Agro-tourism is well developed and finding a bed for the night is no problem.

TRANSYLVANIA

Some 3km south-east along a dirt track from Bran is the village of **Şimon**, from where hiking trails lead into the Bucegi Mountains. **Moieciu**, 4km south of Bran on the road to Câmpulung, is known for its pine-aroma cheese, still religiously made by many families in the village. From Moieciu, a dirt track leads north-west to **Peştera**, named after the village's 160m-long cave said to be full of bats. From Peştera, it's an easy 6km ride north through Măgura to **Zărneşti**, an access point for walks in the **Piatra Craiului** range. This 25km-long range stretching from Zărneşti down to Podu Dâmboviţei offers excellent climbing and hiking.

A few kilometres south-east of Moieciu is **Cheia**, home to one of the region's few intact 19th-century painted churches. Wool has been manufactured in this village since the Middle Ages. Continuing south along the upper course of the Moieciu River, you reach **Moieciu de Sus** with another pretty village church. Hiking trails into the **Bucegi Mountains** are marked from here.

Staggering views of the mountains unfold along the road signposted to Câmpulung, proffering a breathtaking panorama at 1290m before reaching **Fundata**, 25km south of Bran, where you can **cross-country ski**, or hire a **mountain bike** ($0.75 per day).

Continuing south along the same road, you come to **Podu Dâmboviţei**, home to the Peştera Dâmbovicioarei. This 870m-deep cave is not particularly noteworthy but the drive to it is. Sheer rock faces line either side of the road, as do villagers who stand on the roadside selling their homemade cheese (caşcaval de casă), sausages, smoked and dried meats, and milk fresh from the cow. Don't miss coajă, a unique cheese wrapped in bark.

Antrec (see Private Rooms in the Bran section) provides English- and French-speaking guides and arranges hikes, fishing trips, bear-watching and cheese-tasting tours in the area.

For details on hiking, climbing, skiing and mountain biking in this region, see the earlier Exploring the Carpathian Mountains special section.

Places to Stay

Antrec (see Private Rooms in the Bran section) arranges *homestay* accommodation in most villages around Bran.

Crăiasa Munţilor (☎ 068-476 763), in the centre of Moieciu de Sus at No 20, has several doubles with pottery stoves and wooden furnishings for $13 a night. Bathrooms are shared.

Casa Orleanu (mobile ☎ 098-605 867, 098-590 385, e cemmoeciu@yahoo.com), at No 125, has six rooms for two or four people, decked out in rustic style and costing $20 per person a night including breakfast and evening meal. The enterprising Mihai and Nathalie who run the place also run the adjoining Centrul de Ecologie Montană, a mountain and ecology centre which organises guided hikes and botanical/nature trails and hires out mountain bikes. To get here from the end of the village opposite the trout basin, bear left where the road forks.

Several other private homes along the same dirt track have less interesting rooms to let.

The *Hotel-Restaurant* (☎ 068-236 471), on the Câmpulung road just before Fundata, has eight terraced rooms offering stunning mountain views for $7 a double.

Cabana Plaiu Foii, nestled at 849m at the foot of Piatra Craiului, attracts climbers and walkers. When it reopens in 2001 after extensive renovations, it will charge about $2.50 per night for a dorm bed. You can also pitch your tent for free. From the western end of Str Mitropolit Meţianu in the centre of Zărneşti village, follow the unpaved road signposted 'Plaiu Foii', bearing left at both forks in the road. En route (almost immediately after the first fork), you pass the field cabin of the Carpathian Large Carnivore Project (see the Exploring the Carpathian Mountains special section).

PREDEAL
☎ 068

It might well be Romania's highest (1033m) but it's definitely not Romania's hottest skiing spot. Unlike its sister resorts, Predeal has just a couple of slopes, which generally attract hordes of local kids on school camps.

Orientation

The shops and main facilities in the resort are around the train station at the western end of town. Shops selling hiking gear and a currency exchange are inside the Complex Commercial; turn right out of the train station and walk 50m along Blvd Mihai Săulescu. The best map is the Amco Press *Brașov* map which includes an excellent map of Predeal (see Brașov earlier).

Information

Tourist Offices The Agenție de Turism Ingrid (☎ 456 972, fax 456 376), inside the train station building, sells a good selection of hiking maps of the Bucegi and Făgăraș Mountains and arranges accommodation in the resort; open 10 am to 4 pm Monday to Saturday. The staff do not speak English.

Staff at the Tourist Information Centre (☎ 455 330), in its new modern building in the front of the train station, at Str Intrarea Gării 1, are better informed and are willing to phone around to see where there are vacancies; open 10 am to 6 pm daily. There is a third tourist office, Predeal SA (☎ 455 330, e arp@deltanet.ro) at Blvd Mihai Bălescu 17. Visit its Web site at www.predeal.ro.

Money You can change money in the Bachide Exchange (☎ 455 524) inside the Complex Cioplex on Blvd Mihai Săulescu 28; open 10 am to 9 pm daily. Hotel Orizont also has an exchange office.

Post & Telephone The central post office, opposite the Complex Commercial on Blvd Mihai Săulescu is open 8 am to 7 pm weekdays. The telephone office, in the same building, is open daily the same hours.

Emergency The emergency clinic (*dispensar policlinic;* ☎ 456 313) is opposite Hotel Bulevard on Blvd Mihai Săulescu.

Activities

The Fulg de Nea (literally 'Snow Flake'; ☎ 456 089) centre, close to the ski lift at Str Teleferciului 1, has Predeal's central ski school, a ski club with fitness centre and sauna and an **ice skating** rink in winter ($2.60 including skate hire). A horse-drawn **sledge ride** is $2 per person a day. Outside there are three **tennis** courts, costing $1.55 an hour for the court, and $1 for a racquet and ball.

For details on skiing see the Exploring the Carpathian Mountains special section.

Places to Stay

Camping A *camping ground* 15km north of Predeal on the main road to Brașov with ten cabins and ample tent sites will be opening late 2000. Prices were unavailable at the time of writing. From the train station catch the main bus to Brasov and ask the driver to drop you off at the camping ground.

Cabanas At the foot of the ski lift *(telescaun)*, *Cabana Sosire* (☎ 455 431) has doubles/triples for $16/24 a night. The cabana also has a disco. Bookings are made through Hotel Premier (see Hotels later).

Doubles with shared bath and no breakfast at *Chalet Vânătorul* (☎ 455 285), some 3km west of the resort on the road to Trei Brazi, cost $20. Hiking trails lead from Trei Brazi to Poiana Brașov (see the Exploring the Carpathian Mountains special section).

Private Rooms Providing you arrive in Predeal at a reasonable time of day, you will be surrounded by a swarm of babushkas the minute you step off the train offering you a room *(cazare)* for the night. Buy a map of the resort from the tourist office inside the train station building (see Tourist Offices earlier) and clarify exactly where the room you are being offered is before you agree to even see it. Bargain too! The going rate in mid-2000 was around $10 a night.

Hotels The one-star *Hotel Rozmarin* (☎ 456 422, Str Mihai Săulescu 159), tucked away at the north-eastern end of the resort, has cheap, clean doubles/triples with shared shower for $11/13, including breakfast.

East of the railway tracks is *Hotel Carpați* (☎ 456 273, fax 455 411, Str Nicolae Bălcescu 1). It offers doubles with private bath for $12. Budget-conscious backpackers should ask for a room in the hotel's *Villa*

TRANSYLVANIA

Bălcescu, on the same street. Doubles with private bath cost a bargain $9.

Hotel Cirus (☎ *456 035, Str Avram Iancu*), in front of Hotel Orizont, charges $13 for doubles with private bath, excluding breakfast. The entrance is off Str Trei Brazi.

The cheerful *Hotel Carmen-Ana* (☎ *456 656, 456 517, Str Mihai Săulescu 121*), close to the train station, has reasonably priced singles/doubles with private bath for $12/19.

The one-star *Hotel Robinson* (☎/fax *456 753, Str Muncii 6*) has rather shabby double/triple rooms for $11/13. More inviting is the ageing *Hotel Predeal* (☎ *456 705, fax 455 433*) opposite. Singles with private bath are $14 and doubles with/without balcony are $24/20, including breakfast.

Predeal's top hotel is the modern three-star *Hotel Orizont* (☎ *455 150, Str Trei Brazi 6,* e *orizont@com.pcnet.ro*). It has all the mod cons including a health club, swimming pool, tennis court, sauna, and massage parlour. The hotel's Romanian restaurant and flashy cocktail bar overlook the swimming pool. Singles/doubles with cable TV and private bath cost $20/24.

One of the resort's more expensive hotels is *Hotel Premier* (☎ *457 140, fax 455 413,* e *hotelpremier@xnet.ro*) on Str Teleferic next to Cabana Sosire. Doubles cost $40 including breakfast. The hotel also has a fitness centre, billiard room and sauna. It takes bookings and is the reception for Cabana Sosire.

Villas Predeal boasts villas galore, many very luxurious and privately owned. A handful of these upmarket properties – including one which belonged to Ceauşescu (see Places to Eat) – are owned by the government but can be rented out by the Predeal Protocol Service (☎ 455 222, fax 455 435), Str Nicolae Bălcescu 39. They cost between $58 and $154 a night for the entire villa. Bookings can made through Hotel Robinson (☎/fax 456 753).

The *Fulg de Nea* ski school (see Activities) operates a 16-bed villa behind the ski centre. A bed in a double room with private bath is $6. Book in advance as it is often filled with groups of school children. The centre also has rooms on the 2nd floor of

the ski centre for $6 per person. Breakfast isn't included.

Places to Eat
Most hotels have a restaurant of sorts. The *Restaurant Vulturul*, on Str Panduri below the town council building, serves wholesome meals at a reasonable price. Junk-food addicts will find a clean, modern *fast-food* outlet opposite Hotel Carmen, close to the train station, on Blvd Mihai Săulescu.

The restaurant inside the *Fulg de Nea* ski centre serves hearty portions averaging around $4 in a warm and cosy atmosphere; it sometimes has live folk bands and a bonfire outside in summer.

Highly recommended is *Casa Ţărănească* (*Str Libertăţii 63*), housed inside what was Ceauşescu's private holiday villa. The luxury villa, with its large, lamp-lit terrace surrounded by fir trees, is now a folklore restaurant. It serves traditional Romanian dishes to the sound of serenading violinists. A meal costs around $6 including alcohol.

Getting There & Away
The Agenţie de Voiaj CFR (☎ 456 203) is inside the train station building at Str Intrarea Gării 1.

Predeal is on the main Cluj-Napoca–Braşov–Bucharest line with most local and express trains which serve this route stopping at Predeal. Between here and Braşov (35 to 45 minutes) there are some 35 trains daily. Most trains that arrive/depart from Braşov call at Predeal too.

The *Dacia* and *Pannonia Expres* trains to Budapest both call at Predeal exactly five minutes before/after calling at Braşov. The *Muntenia*, *Ister*, and *Traianus* – all of which go to Budapest – also stop in Predeal (see Braşov's Getting There & Away section). In addition, the Bucharest-Warsaw train stops at Predeal, departing Predeal daily at 10.38 pm and arriving in Warsaw 25 hours later at 11.04 pm.

BUCEGI MOUNTAINS
West of the Prahova River rise the Bucegi Mountains, a spectacular range offering a multitude of well-marked walks, short and

long, as well as downhill and cross-country skiing, and climbing. The towns of Buşteni and Sinaia (see the following sections) provide the easiest access, with cable cars taking hikers up to the trails and pistes. For details, see the Exploring the Carpathian Mountains special section.

BUŞTENI
☎ 044

Ten kilometres south of Predeal, along the main road running through the Prahova Valley between Braşov and Sinaia, is Buşteni (885m), a pleasant market town tucked below the mighty Caraiman (2284m) and Coştila (2490m) peaks to the west and Mount Zamora (1519m) to the east. Between the Caraiman and Coştila peaks lie the highest conglomerate cliffs in Europe.

Buşteni, coupled with Sinaia, is the main starting point for hikes into the Bucegi Mountains (see the Exploring the Carpathian Mountains special section). Rock climbers consider Buşteni to be Romania's premier climbing centre.

Orientation
The train station backs onto the main street, Blvd Libertăţii, and is easily identifiable by the large WWI memorial in front of it. The cable car, Hotel Caraiman, post office and commercial complex are at the southern end of town. Turn left out of the train station and walk straight down Blvd Libertăţii. The *primărie* (town hall), post office and Hotel Caraiman are clustered together 20m from the station on the left. To get to the cable car, continue along Blvd Libertăţii for 200m then turn right along Str Telecabinei.

The tourist office is 50m north of the train station; from the station turn right along Blvd Libertăţii.

Maps There is a large-scale map of Buşteni on Blvd Libertăţii in front of the post office on which all the hotels, cable-car station and walking trails are marked.

Information
Tourist Offices The Carpatours tourist office (☎ 320 027, fax 320 120), Blvd Lib-

ertăţii 202, is open 9 am to 7 pm Monday to Saturday, and 9 am to noon Sunday. More helpful is the Asociaţia de Turism Ecologia şi Sociala (☎/fax 320 772) at Str Caraiman 7. The English- and French-speaking staff will happily assist lost travellers and can organise bookings for the region's cabanas. There is a second office at the train station at Blvd Libertăţii 190, open 9 am to 5 pm weekdays.

Money Change money at the Exchange House, 20m past Hotel Caraiman on the right at Blvd Libertăţii 142; open 9 am to 6 pm Monday to Saturday, and 9 am to 2 pm Sunday. The Banca Română pentru Dezvoltare, near Hotel Caraiman on Blvd Libertăţii, has an ATM. The bank is open 8.30 am to 12.20 pm Monday to Thursday, and 8.30 am to 11.30 pm Friday.

Post & Telephone The post and telephone office is 20m south of the train station; open 7 am to 9 pm weekdays.

Email & Internet Access Ilcofon (☎ 321 780, ⓔ clucian@transdata.ro), at Blvd Libertăţii 93, charges $0.95 per hour for Internet access; open 10 am to 10 pm daily.

Medical Services Spital Mobil de Urgentă şi Descarerare (SMURD; Emergency Mobile Hospital and Rescue; ☎ 320 006, ⓔ faamed@fx.ro) has a base at Str Libertăţii 69.

Cezar Petrescu Memorial Museum
Between the wars, Buşteni was home to Romanian novelist Cezar Petrescu (1892–1961), whose realist works attempted to reflect a 'psychology of failure' in modern Romanian life. His house at the northern end of the town on Str Tudor Vladimirescu is now a memorial museum, open 9 am to 5 pm Tuesday to Sunday ($0.25). Turn right out of the train station along Blvd Libertăţii; Str Tudor Vladimirescu is the fourth street on the left.

Activities
The Bucegi Mountains offer numerous hiking trails, accessible from the top of

Buşteni's cable car. From Buşteni, you can also hike 8km south to Sinaia or 10km north to Predeal. Mountain-bike hire is available as well. See the Exploring the Carpathian Mountains special section for details.

Places to Stay

Cabanas At *Cabana Gura Diham (☎ 321 108)*, 3km north of Buşteni along a dirt road, doubles cost $13, including breakfast. Bathrooms are shared. It also has a camping ground where you can pitch a tent. During summer, minibuses depart from outside the train station every hour for Cabana Guru Diham (see Getting There & Away). To hike, turn right out of the train station along Blvd Libertăţii and take the third left along Str Horea; the chalet is at the northern end.

Cabana Babele (☎ 315 304), at 2206m, has provided refuge to hikers since 1937. Today it offers beds in double rooms and mattresses on dorm floors, costing between $3 and $6 depending on the season and level of comfort you want. *Cabana Caraiman* (2025m) has 40 places in shared rooms. Prices start at $3. Both are open year-round.

Cabana Vârful Omu has 35 mattresses in dormitories for $2 per person. Meals are served only occasionally. It is dependably open from May to September.

See the Sinaia section for other cabanas in the Bucegi Mountains.

Private Rooms & Guesthouses Carpatours (see Tourist Offices) arranges accommodation in hotels, villas and cabanas in Buşteni, charging a 5% commission.

The homely two-star *Oti-Dor* pension *(☎ 321 820, Str Caraiman 20)* has clean, simple doubles/triples with shared bath for $5/4 per person, breakfast not included. Its 60-seat restaurant opens from 8 am daily.

Hotels The most central hotel, the dreary *Hotel Caraiman (☎ 320 156, fax 320 121, Blvd Libertăţii 89)*, charges $10 for a double with private shower. Breakfast is not included. The hotel has a restaurant, cafe and disco.

Cheaper and more cheerful is *Hotel BTT (☎ 320 138, fax 320 056, Blvd Libertăţii*

153). Doubles start at $8 per person, including breakfast. Other facilities include a basketball court and disco.

Nestled beneath the cable-car station, the large *Hotel Silva (☎ 321 412, fax 320 950)* on Str Telecabinei offers doubles with TV, telephone and private bath for $24, including breakfast.

Places to Eat

You can stock up on supplies in the commercial complex at the southern end of Blvd Libertăţii or at the cluster of shops at the foot of the cable-car station. The *Vinuri la Litru*, housed in a small caravan on the right on Blvd Libertăţii, en route to the cable car, sells homemade wine for $0.50 a litre, or the more potent Rachiu Tescovină (39.4% proof) for $1 a litre; open 9 am to 12.30 pm daily.

Getting There & Away

Train Buşteni has no Agenţie de Voiaj CFR. Buy tickets at the train station on Blvd Libertăţii. As with Predeal, Buşteni is on the main Bucharest–Cluj-Napoca line with all local trains between Braşov and Bucharest stopping at Buşteni.

Bus From Buşteni, buses to Azuga and Sinaia depart every 45 minutes between 6 am and 10 pm from the main bus stop on Blvd Libertăţii. A number of privately run minibuses also travel to Azuga and Sinaia. The buses depart when they are full ($0.25, pay the driver).

During the summer, minibuses marked *Gura Diham* depart for Cabana Guru Diham. They leave on the hour, between 7 am and 10 pm from outside the train station. Return buses leave Gura Diham hourly between 7.30 am and 10.30 pm.

SINAIA
☎ 044

This well-known ski resort snuggles at an altitude of 800m to 930m in the narrow Prahova Valley, at the foot of the fir-clad Bucegi Mountains. Cable cars whisk skiers and hikers up to 1400m at the foot of Mount Furnica (2103m) and farther up still to 2000m. Sinaia is a convenient day trip from Braşov.

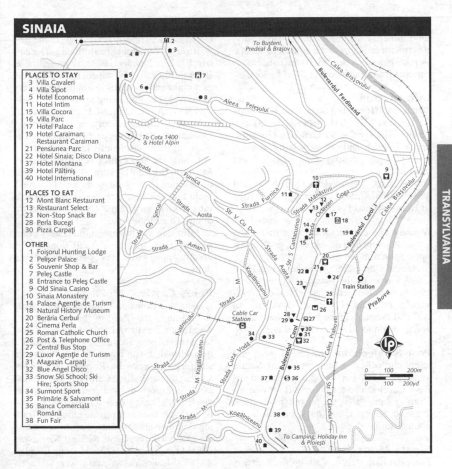

SINAIA

PLACES TO STAY
3 Villa Cavaleri
4 Villa Șipot
5 Hotel Economat
11 Hotel Intim
15 Villa Cocora
16 Villa Parc
17 Hotel Palace
19 Hotel Caraiman;
   Restaurant Caraiman
21 Pensiunea Parc
22 Hotel Sinaia; Disco Diana
37 Hotel Montana
39 Hotel Păltiniș
40 Hotel International

PLACES TO EAT
12 Mont Blanc Restaurant
13 Restaurant Select
23 Non-Stop Snack Bar
28 Perla Bucegi
30 Pizza Carpați

OTHER
1 Foișorul Hunting Lodge
2 Pelișor Palace
6 Souvenir Shop & Bar
7 Peleș Castle
8 Entrance to Peleș Castle
9 Old Sinaia Casino
10 Sinaia Monastery
14 Palace Agenție de Turism
18 Natural History Museum
20 Berăria Cerbul
24 Cinema Perla
25 Roman Catholic Church
26 Post & Telephone Office
27 Central Bus Stop
29 Luxor Agenție de Turism
31 Magazin Carpați
32 Blue Angel Disco
33 Snow Ski School; Ski
   Hire; Sports Shop
34 Surmont Sport
35 Primărie & Salvamont
36 Banca Comercială
   Română
38 Fun Fair

TRANSYLVANIA

The resort is alleged to have gained its name from Romanian nobleman Mihai Cantacuzino who, following a pilgrimage he made to the biblical Mount Sinai in Israel in 1695, founded the Sinaia Monastery.

Sinaia later developed into a major resort dubbed the 'Pearl of the Carpathians' after King Carol I selected Sinaia for his summer residence in 1870. His palace, open to visitors today, is considered the most beautiful in Romania.

Until 1920, the Hungarian-Romanian border ran along Predeal Pass, just north of Sinaia.

For reader convenience, this area has been included in Transylvania in this book, even though is is strictly part of Wallachia.

Orientation
The train station is directly below the centre of town. From the station climb up the stairway across the street to busy Blvd Carol I. Hotel Montana and the cable car are to the left; the monastery and palace are uphill to the right.

Maps The *Sinaia Ghid Turistic*, published in 1997 by Bel Alpin Tour, includes a good town map as well as a small hiking map of the southern Bucegi Mountains. Ironically, it is practically impossible to find in Sinaia. Purchase a copy for $1.10 in Buşteni or Predeal from tourist offices and kiosks.

Information

Tourist Offices Staff at the Palace Agenţie de Turism (☎ 312 051, ☎/fax 310 625), opposite Villa Parc at Str Octavian Goga 11, speak English and are very helpful; open 8 am to 9 pm weekdays, and 9 am to 2 pm weekends.

The Luxor Agenţie de Turism (☎/fax 314 124) at Blvd Carol I 22 arranges day trips to Bran ($4) and Poiana Braşov ($6.50).

Money The currency exchange inside the Luxor Agenţie de Turism offers good rates; open 8 am to 8 pm daily.

Banca Comercială Română, on Blvd Carol I next to the *primărie* (town hall), cashes travellers cheques, gives cash advances on Visa/MasterCard and has an ATM. It is open 8 am to 5.30 pm weekdays, and 8.30 am to 12.30 pm Saturday.

Post & Telephone The central post and telephone office is between Hotel Sinaia and Hotel Montana on the opposite side of Blvd Carol I. The telephone office is open 7 am to 8 pm daily; the post office is open 7 am to 5.30 pm weekdays, and 8 am to noon Saturday.

Sinaia Monastery

From the train station, walk up the stairway to town, turn left and then make a quick right onto Str Octavian Goga, which passes Villa Parc before curving left at Mont Blanc Restaurant. There's a stairway here, at the top of which is Sinaia Monastery (Mănăstirea Sinaia). Some 20 monks live here today. The large Orthodox church (Biserica Mare) dates from 1846, and the smaller, older church (Biserica Veche) from 1695. Monks retreated into the Bucegi Mountains from the 14th century but it was not until the late 17th century that they built a monastery.

Tache Ionescu (1859–1918), a leading liberal statesman who led the Romanian

delegation at the Paris Peace Conference (1918–20) and briefly headed one of the first postwar governments in Romania (December 1921 to January 1922), is buried here. Born in Ploieşti, Ionescu contracted cholera as a child and was sent to Sinaia Monastery to convalesce. Following his death, his second wife, Adina Olmazu, built a vast mausoleum at the monastery in his memory. Quotations from his speeches are carved in stone on the mausoleum's interior walls.

Beside the new church is a small **History Museum** (Muzeul de Istorie) in which some of the monastery's treasures are displayed, including the first translation of the Bible into Romanian (in the Cyrillic alphabet) dating from 1668.

Admission to the entire monastery complex is free, though a small donation is greatly appreciated; it is open 8 am to 9 pm daily.

Peleş Castle

It is apt that Romania's most exquisite castle should lie in the 'Pearl of the Carpathians'. The magnificent royal palace with its fairytale turrets, rising above acres of green meadows sprinkled with haystacks, was built as a summer residence by Romania's longest-serving monarch, King Carol I. It was the first castle in Europe to have central heating and electricity. During Ceauşescu's era, its 160 rooms were used as a private retreat for leading communists and statesmen from around the globe. US presidents Richard Nixon and Gerald Ford, Libyan leader Moamar Gaddafi and PLO leader Yasser Arafat were all entertained by the Romanian dictator in Peleş' fanciful rooms, each furnished to reflect a different European country.

Construction started on the 3500 sq metre edifice, built in a predominantly German-Renaissance style, in 1875. More than 400 craftsmen laboured on the palace, which was finally completed 39 years later, just months before the king died in 1914.

Rembrandt reproductions line the walls of the king's office while a row of books in the library conceals a secret escape passage leading to the 2nd floor of the castle. There is a gallery of mirrors and the dining room has a leather-clad ceiling. Scenes from age-old Romanian fairytales adorn the stained-glass windows in the poetry room.

In the Florence hall, Michelangelo reproductions hang below a ceiling carved from gilded linden wood. The Venetian room is equally impressive.

Peleş Castle was closed from 1947 to 1975 when it was briefly opened as a museum. After extensive renovation work it reopened in 1990. Guided tours ($3, 45 minutes) of the castle are compulsory; guides speak English, French and Spanish. Tickets are sold at the booth at the foot of the castle drive.

The castle is open 9.15 am to 3.15 pm Wednesday to Sunday. To ensure you get a tour in a language other than Romanian, do not enter the castle through the main entrance but walk under the arches in the centre of the building to the entrance signposted 'foreign tourists'. The castle itself is signposted 'Muzeul Peleş' from the top of the steps leading down to the train station.

Pelişor Palace & Foişorul Hunting Lodge

Marie, wife of King Carol's nephew Ferdinand (1865–1927), did not get on with her uncle-in-law and could not stand Peleş Castle. So, in fine royal fashion, King Carol built Ferdinand and Marie a castle of their own in Sinaia, just a few hundred metres uphill from Peleş.

Exactly 10 years after the young couple moved to Romania following their marriage in 1892, Pelişor Palace was completed. Built in a mock German-medieval style, the castle was furnished according to Marie's own designs – pretty pastel decorations in a simple Art-Nouveau style. Most of the furniture was imported from Vienna. Marie had four apartments while Ferdinand had just one.

The bed in which Romania's second king died at the age of 62 from cancer can still be seen today. Marie died nine years later in the golden room, the walls of which are entirely covered in heavy gold leaves.

The Warrior Queen

'There is only one man in Romania and that is the Queen.' That is how a French diplomat described Queen Marie of Romania whose diplomatic coup at the Paris Peace Conference in 1919 bolstered Romania's flagging image abroad and assured her legendary status.

Queen Marie (1875–1938), the granddaughter of Britain's Queen Victoria, married Ferdinand I (1865–1927), heir to the Romanian throne, in 1892 when she was 17. Despite widespread horror in Britain at her mismatch to a prince of a 'semibarbaric' country, Marie developed a strong kinship with Romania, declaring, 'My love for my country [Romania] is my religion'.

Following an alleged love affair with American aristocrat Waldorf Astor, she knuckled down to twisting her tongue around the Romanian language and acquainting herself with Romanian politics.

During the second Balkan War (1913) the princess ran a cholera hospital for Romanian soldiers on the Bulgarian side of the Danube. In 1914 Ferdinand I was crowned king and Marie became queen.

Despite proving herself to be a 'viable political force', Queen Marie remained the 'people's princess' throughout her reign. At the outbreak of WWI she wrote her first book, *My Country*, to raise funds for the British Red Cross in Romania.

Prior to her evacuation to Iaşi in 1916, she worked in hospitals in Bucharest, distributing food and cigarettes to wounded soldiers. In Iaşi she set about reorganising the appallingly makeshift hospitals and became famed for her courageous refusal to wear rubber gloves in the typhus wards.

After she represented Romania at the peace conference in Paris, the French press dubbed her the 'business queen'. A mother of six, she wrote over 100 diaries from 1914 until her death in 1938. During her lifetime 15 of her books were published. Her autobiography, *The Story of my Life*, appeared in two volumes in 1934–35.

Queen Marie is buried in Curtea de Argeş. Her heart, originally encased in a gold casket and buried in Balcic, southern Dobruja (Bulgaria), is safeguarded in Bucharest's National History Museum.

Pelişor Palace is open 9.15 am to 3.15 pm Wednesday to Sunday ($2). Thirty-minute tours of 20 of the castle's 70 rooms (in English or French) are compulsory.

At the western end of the Peleş estate is the Swiss-chalet-style Foişorul Hunting Lodge, built as a temporary residence by King Carol I before Peleş Castle was completed. Here Marie and Ferdinand spent their first summer together in Romania. Here also their son, later to become King Carol II, briefly lived with his mistress Elena Lupescu. During the communist era, Ceauşescu used it as his private hunting lodge. The building is in state hands and is closed to visitors.

Bucegi Nature Reserve Museum
Behind Hotel Palace in the central park, this small natural history museum (Muzeul Rezervaţiei Bucegi; ☎ 311 750) features some of the natural wonders of the Bucegi Nature Reserve, which encompasses the 300 sq km Bucegi mountain range. Through funding supplied by the EU Life-Nature Program, the Bucegi Nature Reserve is being made into a national park. Two rooms in the cellar exhibit various stuffed animals, flowers and birds, including the edelweiss, which is abundant in the Bucegi Mountains. Temporary art exhibitions are displayed on the ground floor. In summer the museum is open 9 am to 7 pm daily (to 5 pm Monday). In winter it is open 9 am to 5 pm daily ($0.50).

Activities
Sinaia offers plenty of hiking and skiing options, with cable cars taking you up into the Bucegi Mountains. For details on skiing, hiking and mountain biking, see the Exploring the Carpathian Mountains special section.

Places to Stay
Camping There's a *camping ground* at Izvorul Rece, 4km south of central Sinaia, but only three buses a day go there from a stop on Blvd Carol I, just past Hotel Montana.

Cabanas A prime spot for beer-thirsty skiers is *Hotel Alpin* (☎ 312 351, ☎/fax 312 353) at Cota 1400 – at 1400m no less – next to the cable-car station. A room for the night costs $14/20/28 for a single/double/triple. Breakfast can be provided for an extra $4 per person.

Just below it at 1300m is *Cabana Brădet* (☎ 311 551), with beds in shared rooms for $6 a night year-round. There are similar prices for shared rooms at *Cabana Valea cu Brazi* (☎ 313 635), above the cable car at 1500m; a path leads up from Hotel Alpin.

Cabana Piatra Arsă (☎ 311 911), a large, modern chalet, charges between $3 to $9 for a bed. It also serves inexpensive meals and is open year-round.

For details of other cabanas within hiking reach of Sinaia, see the preceding Buşteni section.

Private Rooms Hang around the train station for a few minutes and you'll probably be offered a private room. The going rate is $8 to $10 per person.

Hotels Among the cheapest places to stay is the small *Pensiunea Parc* (☎ 314 821, fax 311 018) on Blvd Carol I, next to the Berăria Cerbul. Doubles with shared bath are $10, breakfast not included. Also good value is the tiny *Villa Parc* (☎ 313 856, Str Octavian Goga 2), which has doubles with/without private bath for $15/12.

West of Str Octavian Goga is the one-star *Hotel Intim* (☎ 315 496/111, Str Furnica 1). Double rooms with private bath start from $14.

Hotel Furnica (☎ 311 850, fax 311 150, Str Furnica 50) offers well-priced double/triple/quad rooms for $20/40/48. All rooms have private bath and include breakfast.

The attractive, two-star *Hotel Păltiniş* (☎ 314 623/624, fax 111 033, Blvd Carol I 65–67), at the southern end of the resort, has singles/doubles with private shower for $20/27, including breakfast.

Opposite, the luxurious three-star *Hotel International* (☎ 313 851, 314 855, fax 313 855, Str Avram Iancu 1) charges $23/30/43 for singles/doubles/triples including breakfast. Other facilities include an unfriendly tourist agency and a telephone and fax centre.

In the centre of the resort are the high-rise **Hotel Sinaia** (☎ 311 551, fax 310 625, Blvd Carol I 8) and **Hotel Montana** (☎ 312 751, fax 314 051, Blvd Carol I 24). At the time of writing, the Sinaia was undergoing major renovations. Old singles/doubles cost $22/37 and renovated rooms cost $35/60. Rooms with private bath, telephone and cable TV are good value at the Montana at $24/37, including breakfast.

Northwards up Str Octavian Goga is Sinaia's most elegant hotel, **Hotel Palace** (☎ 310 625, fax 312 051, Str Octavian Goga 4). Dating from 1911, it has all facilities including a hairdresser, night bar, restaurant and nightclub. Rooms are $33/46; admission to the nightclub (10 pm to 5 am) is $1. Opposite, the more intimate **Villa Cocora** (Str Octavian Goga 5) offers luxury apartments for $58; bookings can be made through Hotel Palace. Behind the Palace is **Hotel Caraiman** (☎ 313 551, fax 310 625), overlooking the park with its entrance on Blvd Carol I, with rooms for $22/37. The hotel has a good Romanian restaurant.

Rivalling Hotel Palace in location and luxury is **Hotel Economat** (☎ 311 151, fax 311 150, Aleea Peleşului 2), housed in a wonderful 19th-century manor house inside the Peleş Castle complex. Rooms here costs $21/43. The hotel also takes bookings for the four-star **Villa Cavaleri**, directly opposite Pelişor Palace, and the eight-room **Villa Şipot** close by. Both villas are often inhabited by state guests but it is possible to stay here if you book in advance. It costs around $535 a night for an entire villa.

Three kilometres south of central Sinaia is the flashy **Holiday Inn** (☎ 310 440, fax 310 551, Str Toporşilor 1). Rooms with all the mod cons start from a staggering $110/140. A luxury apartment is $240. The hotel also has a pool, restaurant, disco and bar.

Places to Eat

Restaurant Select, on Str Octavian Goga close to Hotel Palace, is a large establishment with slow service and below-average food. The terrace is a popular hangout, though, as is the disco bar.

For a touch of France, try **Mont Blanc** (☎ 310 105), a French restaurant on Str Octavian Goga opposite Hotel Palace. Dishes, starting at around $4, include filet de boeuf au poivre (peppered beef steak), salade de foie de volailles (chicken liver salad) and a typical salade Lyonaise (salad with croutons and a fried egg).

Pizza fans can dine at **Pizza Carpaţi**, on Blvd Carol I next to Magazin Carpati, or the more popular **pizzeria** (Blvd Carol I 18) inside the Perla Bucegi complex opposite.

The **Non-Stop Snack Bar** (Blvd Carol I 12), near Hotel Sinaia, offers a variety of fast-food options from pizza to local specialities as well as beer, all served 24 hours. It isn't hard to miss; just listen for the blaring music!

Entertainment

Films are shown in English with Romanian subtitles at **Cinema Perla**, on Blvd Carol I opposite Hotel Sinaia. During summer, there is a **fun fair** for kids outside Hotel Păltiniş at the southern end of Blvd Carol I.

The **Berăria Cerbul**, on Blvd Carol I at Str Octavian Goga, is a traditional bar serving Romanian beer and barbecued şaşlik, hot dogs and grilled meats in its summer garden. It is generally packed.

There are discos practically everywhere you turn in Sinaia. The **Blue Angel Disco** next to the Magazin Carpati is open 9 pm to 3 am weekdays, and 9 pm to 4 am Saturday. Alternatively, try the crowded **Disco Diana** inside Hotel Sinaia; open 9 pm to 3 am ($1.50).

Getting There & Away

Train Sinaia is on the Bucharest-Braşov rail line – 126km from the former and 45km from the latter. All express trains stop here, and local trains to Buşteni (8km), Predeal (19km) and Braşov are quite frequent. Approaching Sinaia from the south, don't get off at the 'Halta Sinaia Sud' – a small stop 2km south of Sinaia centre.

There are two trains to Constanţa daily except Sunday (four hours).

The left-luggage office, open 24 hours, is on platform No 1 ($0.45/0.90 for a small/large bag).

Bus Buses run every 45 minutes between 6.20 am and 10.45 pm from the central bus stop on Blvd Carol I to Azuga and Buşteni.

FĂGĂRAŞ MOUNTAINS

The dramatic peaks of the Făgăraş Mountains form a serrated line south of the main Braşov-Sibiu road and shelter dozens of glacial lakes. The famed Trans-Făgăraşan Highway, open for only part of the year, cuts through the range from north to south. For details on hikes in the region, see the Exploring the Carpathian Mountains special section.

Făgăraş & Victoria

Despite its name, Făgăraş town is not the prime access point to the Făgăraş Massif. Most hikers pass straight through en route to neighbouring Victoria, the main access point to hike south into the mountains. Făgăraş' only attraction is its 13th-century fortress which houses the **Făgăraş County Museum** (Muzeul Ţării Făgăraş), open 9 am to 3.30 pm Tuesday to Friday, and 9 am to 2.30 pm weekends.

Places to Stay Mircdia Tur (☎/fax 068-210 455), Str Tăbăcari, Bl 4, arranges accommodation in and around Făgăraş. Staff speak English and French. While you're there ask to see the manager's amazing collection of postcards, dating from 1896, of the Făgăraş region.

In Victoria the dreary *Hotel Victoria* (☎ 068-241 916, 242 091) on Piaţa Libertăţii, the main square, has doubles with/without private bath for $6/$4.

More inviting is the *Palermo Hotel* (☎ 068-242 973), on Str 1 December 1918 next to the post office. Clean doubles cost $13, not including breakfast. The hotel's exchange office cashes travellers cheques; open 8 am to 12.30 pm weekdays.

Cabanas in the Făgăraş Mountains include *Cabana Turnuri* (1520m, 20 beds), a six-hour hike from Victoria, and four hours to the south, *Cabana Podragu* (2136m, 68 beds).

Getting There & Away

Făgăraş' bus and trains stations are next to each other on Str Negoiu. The bus station is all but completely closed. Daily services still running include one to Braşov (65km), Mediaş (weekdays only) and Sighişoara. Trains from Făgăraş to Braşov and Sibiu stop at Ucea.

The bus station in Victoria, on Str Tineretului, is serviced by buses from Făgăraş. The nearest train halt is 7km north of Victoria at Ucea. All local trains from Braşov, Făgăraş and Sibiu stop here. Buses depart daily from outside Ucea station to Victoria (8.25 am and 12.15, 2, 4, 4.50, 7.35 and 9 pm). Buses from Victoria to Ucea depart at 4.30, 6.15, 7.40 and 11.45 am, and 1.10, 3.10, 3.45, 6.50, 7.30 and 11 pm.

Sâmbăta

Ten kilometres south of Victoria lies the Sâmbăta complex, home to one of Romania's wealthiest monasteries and a key access point to the Făgăraş Mountains. Nicolae Ceauşescu rightly deemed the place sufficiently idyllic to build a private luxury villa for himself and Elena in the grounds of the monastery.

The **Brâncoveanu Monastery** (Mănăstirea Brâncoveanu; 1696) derives its name from its original founder, Wallachian prince Constantin Brâncoveanu (r. 1688–1714), who built the Orthodox monastery on the family estate. The Brâncoveanu Monastery, seen by the Habsburgs as the last bastion of Orthodoxy in the Făgăraş region, was practically destroyed.

In 1926, restoration work started on Sâmbăta's ruins and was completed in 1946. Despite not being an original, the monastery remains a fitting testament to the great art renaissance inspired by the 17th-century Wallachian prince. Its fame today is derived from its workshops of glass icons, run by the monastery's monks, residents since the early 1990s. There is a **glass icon museum** (☎ 068-241 239/237) in the complex ($0.25). The monastery is open 10 am to 5 pm Tuesday to Sunday; admission is free.

Places to Stay The *Complex Turistic Sâmbăta*, close to the main entrance of the monastery, has wooden huts for $5 a night. Bathrooms (toilet and sink only) are shared and there is a small bar and restaurant. The complex is also planning to build a 20-room hotel which should be operational by summer 2001.

Campers should head straight to *Cabana Sâmbăta Popas* (810m), signposted 1km north from the monastery complex. A bed in a wooden hut starts at $2 per person and you can pitch your tent for free.

From the cabana, a trail (three hours, red triangles) leads to *Cabana Valea Sambetei* (1407m, 100 beds). From here, further trails go to the Moldoveanu and Negoiu peaks. For more information on hiking routes, see the Exploring the Carpathian Mountains special section.

SIBIU
☎ 069 • postcode 2400 • pop 170,000
Sibiu is just far enough off the beaten track to be spared the tourist tide that occasionally engulfs Braşov. Founded in the 12th century on the site of the former Roman village of Cibinium, Sibiu (Hermannstadt to the Saxons, Nagyszében to Hungarians) has always been one of the leading cities of Transylvania. During the peak of Saxon influence, Sibiu had some 19 guilds, each representing a different craft, within the sturdy city walls protected by 39 towers and four bastions.

Under the Habsburgs from 1703 to 1791 and again from 1849 to 1867, Sibiu served as the seat of the Austrian governors of Transylvania. Much remains from this colourful history, especially in the old town, one of the largest and best preserved in all Romania.

Sibiu's few remaining Saxons continue to follow in their ancestors' footsteps, playing a leading role in the town's cultural life. Sibiu's remaining German-speaking Saxon community celebrates the traditional Maifest on 1 May when they flock to Dumbrava forest. The town also hosts an International Astra Film Festival in May and an International Theatre Festival in June.

In local elections in June 2000 Johanis Klaus of the German Democratic Forum won, gaining 70% of the votes, leaving Sibiu with an ethnic German mayor.

Orientation
The adjacent bus and train stations are not far east of the centre of town. From the station, walk straight up Str General Magheru four blocks to Piaţa Mare, the historic centre.

Maps Hotel Bulevard sells a rather cumbersome, poster-size city map (1997) for $1.10.

The Agenţie de Turism inside Hotel Continental offers a free, handier city map, published in the mid-1990s with all the tourist sights clearly marked.

Topnotch is the multilingual *Sibiu... de la A la Z* (2000) with text in English, German and Romanian. It includes maps, hotel and restaurant listings, historic sights etc and is sold for $1.50 in most bookshops.

Information
Tourist Offices Sibiu lacks an efficient tourist office. The official Agenţie de Turism (☎ 218 100, fax 210 125) inside Hotel Continental is useless (except for its free map).

Hotel Împăratul Romanilor has a better tourist office (☎ 210 7420) whose staff speak English, French and German and are willing to help.

The ACR (☎ 447 359), Str General Vasile Milea 13, is two blocks east of Hotel Continental.

If you plan to head out to Păltiniş, contact the Agenţie de Turism Păltiniş (☎ 218 319); open 8 am to 4 pm weekdays.

Money There are IDM exchanges giving cash advances on Visa/MasterCard at Piaţa Mică 9, Str Papiu Ilarian 12, and Parcul Tineretului 20; all are open from 8 am to 8 pm weekdays, and 9 am to 2 pm Saturday. There are also currency exchanges inside the Bulevard and Împăratul Romanilor Hotels.

Banca Comercială Română, Str Nicolae Bălcescu 11, changes travellers cheques, gives cash advances and has an outside ATM; open 8 am to noon weekdays. The BCIT, behind Hotel Continental on Str Someşului, offers the same services; open 9 am to 3.30 pm weekdays.

Post & Telephone The central post office, on Str Mitropoliei, is open 7 am to 8 pm weekdays. Sibiu's telephone centre, Str Nicolae Bălcescu 13, is open 6.30 am to 10 pm weekdays, 7 am to 10 pm weekends.

DHL Worldwide Express (☎ 211 567) has an office out of the centre of town at Str Teclu 43; open 9 am to 5 pm weekdays.

Email & Internet Access Verena Internet Service (☎ 212 567, fax 424 554, ⓔ office@verena.net), Str Calea Cisnadiei 50, has online access at $0.50 per hour; open 9 am to 6 pm daily, except Monday, Friday and Sunday when it is open 10 am to 1 pm.

Bookshops Sibiu has a number of quality bookshops which sell English- and German-language books as well as city guides, dictionaries and postcards; the Librărie Dacia Traian at Piața Mare 6 has the best stock of guides and books. It also sells a hiking map for the Retezat Mountains, as does the Librăria Mihai Eminescu at Str Nicolae Bălcescu 31. Neither sells maps of the Făgăraș range.

The English-language bookshop, Librăria Thausib at Piața Mică 3, has the largest selection of English-language novels. The Librărie Humanitas Academic bookshop opposite Kodak Express on Str Nicolae Bălcescu sells mainly textbooks and reference books.

Libraries & Cultural Centres The British Council Centre & Library (☎/fax 211 056) is housed in the main building of the Lucian Blaga University at Blvd Victoriei 10. An annual subscription to the library is $1.20. The American Library of Romania is next door to the British library in the same building.

The American Centre & Library (☎ 216 062, extension 121) and the German Cultural Centre & Library (☎ 216 062, extension 123) are also housed in the university; just to confuse things, however, they are inside the block on the opposite side of the street. Both buildings have the same street address – Blvd Victoriei 10.

The French Cultural Centre (☎ 218 287) is inside the Student Culture House (Casa de Cultură Studențească) at Str Mitropoliei 3.

Medical Services The best-stocked pharmacy is the Farmacie Nippur-Pharm at Str Nicolae Bălcescu 5; open 9 am to 7 pm weekdays, and 9 am to 2 pm Saturday. The Farmasib pharmacy, Str Nicolae Bălcescu 53, is open 7 am to 10 pm weekdays, and 8 am to 9 pm weekends.

Historic Centre
There's no better place to begin your visit than at the top of the former **Council Tower** (Turnul Sfatului; 1588) which links Piața Mare with its smaller sister square, Piața Mică. Built as a defensive tower and later used as a cereal storehouse, it now houses a small **History Museum** (Muzeul de Istorie); closed Monday ($0.85). The view of the Făgăraș Mountains beckoning to the south is superb.

Walk along Piața Mare to the baroque **Roman Catholic Cathedral** (Biserica Romano Catolică), built between 1726 and 1733 by a Jesuit order. The monument inside the church marks the resting place of general commander Otto Ferdinand, Count of Abensberg (1677–1747), who served as military commander of Transylvania between 1744 and 1747. In front of the cathedral on the square you will find a large **memorial statue** to the people who fought in the 1848 peasant uprisings.

Close by at Piața Mare 4–5 is the **Brukenthal Museum** (Muzeul Brukenthal; ☎ 217 691), the oldest and finest art gallery in Romania. Founded in 1817, the museum is in the baroque palace (1785) of Baron Samuel Brukenthal (1721–1803), former Austrian governor. Apart from the paintings, there are excellent archaeological, folk art and butterfly collections. Brukenthal's library is also still intact. The museum is open 9 am to 5 pm in summer, and 10 am to 4 pm in winter, Tuesday to Sunday ($1.15).

At Piața Mare 10 is the 15th-century Gothic **Haller's House** (Casa Haller), which belonged to the family of Mayor Petrus Haller for 350 years. Next door is the house in which linguist **Andreo Cseh** (1895–1978) first expounded his modernist theories on the teaching of Esperanto in 1920.

Just west along Str Samuel Brukenthal, at Str Mitropoliei 2, is the **Primăria Municipiului** (1470), now the **City History**

Museum (Muzeul de Istorie; ☎ 218 143) which contains further exhibits from Brukenthal's palace; open 9 am to 5 pm in summer, and 10 am to 4 pm in winter, Tuesday to Sunday.

Nearby, on Piaţa Huet, is the Gothic **Evangelical Church** (Biserica Evanghelică; 1300–1520), its great five-pointed tower visible from afar. Note the four magnificent baroque funerary monuments on the upper nave, and the 1772 organ with 6002 pipes. The tomb of Mihnea Vodă cel Rău (Prince Mihnea the Bad), son of Vlad Ţepeş, is in the closed-off section behind the organ. This prince, who ruled Wallachia from 1507 to 1510, was murdered on the square in front of the church after attending a service in March 1510. Don't miss the fresco of the Crucifixion (1445) up in the sanctuary. The church is open 11 am to 3 pm weekdays, and organ concerts are held every Sunday in winter at 7 pm (summer schedule not known at time of writing – check the schedule outside for dates). Opposite is the **Brukenthal School** (Liceul Brukenthal).

To reach the lower town from here, walk down the 13th-century **staircase passage**, on the opposite side of the church from where you enter, or go down the stairs beneath the 18th-century **Staircase Tower** (Turnul Scărilor). Otherwise, cross the photogenic **Iron Bridge** (1859) on nearby Piaţa Mică. The bridge's nickname is 'Liar's Bridge' after the tricky merchants who met here to trade and the young lovers who declared their undying love. It is meant to collapse if anyone tells a lie while standing on it. It didn't when Ceauşescu crossed it.

Piaţa Mică is small and quaint, its buildings a muted rainbow of pretty pastel colours. The wonky stairway leading to Piaţa Aurarilor at its eastern end leads down to a maze of narrow cobblestone streets. At Piaţa Mică 26 is the **Pharmaceutical Museum** (Muzeul de Istoria Farmaciei; ☎ 218 191), with a small collection of antique drug jars and medical tools; open 10 am to 6 pm Tuesday to Sunday ($0.80).

A couple of doors down on the same side of the square is the **Artists' House** (Casa Artiştilor), an exhibition hall which hosts various temporary exhibitions.

The **Franz Binder Museum of World Ethnology** (Muzeul de Etnografie Universală Franz Binder; ☎ 218 195), Piaţa Mică 11, has a permanent display called 'Culture and Art of the Peoples of the World' which includes an Egyptian mummy. The museum is open 10 am to 6 pm in summer, and 9 am to 5 pm in winter, Tuesday to Sunday ($0.80).

Heading north-east from Piaţa Mică along Str Avram Iancu, you come to the **Ursuline Church**. Founded by Dominican monks in the 15th century, it was later transformed into a school, then turned over to the Ursulines in 1728.

South of the Historic Centre

Go back to Piaţa Mică, then walk south-west along Str Mitropoliei to the **Orthodox Cathedral** (1906), a miniature copy of the Hagia Sofia in Istanbul.

Cobblestone lane leading to the artisans' quarter in Sibiu

TRANSYLVANIA

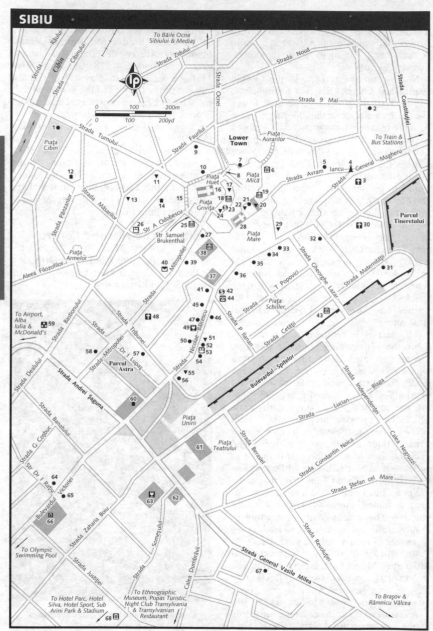

SIBIU

TRANSYLVANIA

To Băile Ocna
Sibiului & Mediaş

Strada Zidului

Strada Nouă

Strada Ocnei

Strada 9 Mai

Strada Constituţiei

To Train &
Bus Stations

Strada Faurului

Lower
Town

Piaţa
Aurarilor

Strada Turnului

Piaţa
Cibin

Strada Râului

Strada Cibinului

Strada Mălsarilor

Strada Pânzarilor

Strada Avram Iancu

General Magheru

Piaţa
Huet

Piaţa
Mică

Parcul
Tineretului

Str A Odobescu

Piaţa
Griviţa

Piaţa
Mare

Str Samuel
Brukenthal

Piaţa
Armelor

Aleea Filozofilor

Mitropoliei

Strada Gheorghe Lazăr

Strada Maternităţii

T Popovici

Piaţa
Schiller

Strada

Strada P Ilarian

Strada Cetăţii

Strada Tribunei

Strada Bastionului

Strada Banatului

Strada Dr I Lupaş

Strada Mitropoliei

Parcul
Astra

Strada Nicolae Bălcescu

To Airport,
Alba
Iulia &
McDonald's

Strada Dealului

Bulevardul Spitelor

Strada Independenţei

Strada Blaga

Strada Lucian

Calea Negruzzi

Strada Andrei Şaguna

Piaţa
Unirii

Strada Berastei

Piaţa
Teatrului

Strada Constantin Noica

Strada G Coşbuc

Str Dr I Raţiu

Bulevardul Victoriei

Strada Zaharia Boiu

Strada Ştefan cel Mare

Str Justiţiei

Strada Someşului

Calea Dumbrăvii

Strada Revoluţiei

To Olympic
Swimming Pool

Strada General Vasile Milea

To Braşov &
Râmnicu Vâlcea

To Ethnographic
Museum, Popas Turistic,
Night Club Transylvania
& Transylvanian
Restaurant

To Hotel Parc, Hotel
Silva, Hotel Sport, Sub
Arini Park & Stadium

0   100   200m
0   100   200yd

SIBIU

PLACES TO STAY
12 Hotel Halemadero
14 Hotel Leu
37 Hotel Împăratul Romanilor
60 Hotel Bulevard
62 Hotel Continental

PLACES TO EAT
11 Restaurant Timiş
13 Restaurant Select
17 Domar Cofetărie & Patiserie
20 La Turn
22 Dori's
24 Restaurant Union
29 Pupa Alimentar & Fast Food
51 Restaurant Mara
55 Restaurant Bumita

THINGS TO SEE
3 Ursuline Church
4 Statue of Nicolaus Olahus
6 Pharmaceutical Museum
7 Artists' House
8 Iron Bridge
10 Staircase Tower
15 Staircase Passage
16 Evangelical Church
18 Franz Binder Museum of
    World Ethnology

19 Council Tower; History
    Museum
25 City History Museum
28 Cathedral
30 Franciscan Church
31 Haller Bastion
33 Andreo Cseh's House
34 Haller's House
38 Brunkenthal Museum
39 House where Avram
    Iancu stayed
43 Natural History Museum
48 Orthodox Cathedral
59 Soldisch Bastion
68 Museum of Hunting Arms &
    Trophies

OTHER
1 Market
2 Mihu Reisen Travel Agency
5 Surmont Sports; Boua Bikes
    Club
9 Sibiu's First Hospital
21 Librăria Thausib
23 IDM Currency Exchange
26 Puppet Theatre; Cinema
    Tineretului; Disco-Bar
    Meridian
27 Casa Food Shop

32 Philharmonic & Art Café
35 Librărie Dacia Traian
36 Farmacie Nippur-Pharm
40 Post Office
41 Agenţie de Voiaj CFR
42 Banca Comercială Română
44 Telephone Centre
45 Tarom
46 Agenţie de Teatrală
47 Librărie Humanitas
49 Café Bar Liliacul
50 Trans-Europa Travel Agency
52 Prima
53 Cinema Pacea
54 Librăria Mihai Eminescu
56 Farmasib
57 Agenţie de Turism Păltiniş
58 French Library; Student
    Culture House
61 Radu Stancu State Theatre
63 Disco Bar Mega Vox; Culture
    House
64 University, German &
    American Libraries
65 University, British &
    Romanian-American Libraries
66 Palace of Justice
67 Automobil Clubul Roman
    (ACR)

TRANSYLVANIA

Str Mitropoliei is lined with memorial plaques on almost every house wall. Avram Iancu, the Romanian leader of the 1848 revolution, stayed for a few days at Str Mitropoliei 7 in 1848 on his way to the Apuseni Mountains. Poet Mihai Eminescu rested at Str Mitropoliei 22 between 18 and 30 June 1868.

The influential **Transylvanian Association for Romanian Literature & Culture**, known as Astra, was founded in 1861 at Str Mitropoliei 20, in protest at the intense Magyarisation of Transylvania in the mid-19th century. Astra's nationalist calls for Romanians to stand up for their liberty and identity were voiced in *Tribuna*, Transylvania's first Romanian newspaper, written and printed in Sibiu from 1884.

The house at Str Mitropoliei 19 bears a **memorial plaque** to Transylvania's Memorandumists of 1892, the leaders of the Romanian National Party who addressed a memorandum to the emperor Franz Joseph in Vienna in 1892 in which they called for an end to discrimination against Romanians in Romania. The emperor forwarded it to the Hungarian government who sent it back without opening it, and 29 members of the National Party were convicted of agitating against the state and imprisoned.

At the southern end of Str Mitropoliei, turn left onto Str Tribunei, then right along Str Cetăţii, the start of a pleasant walk north-east along a section of the old **city walls**, constructed during the 16th century. As in Braşov, different guilds protected each of the 39 towers – there's the Linenmakers' Tower, the Potters' Tower and the Barbers' Tower. Walk north up Str Cetăţii, past the **Thick Tower**, also built in the 16th century and later used to house Sibiu's first theatre. Close by at Str Cetăţii 1 is the **Natural History Museum** (Muzeul de Istorie Naturală; ☎ 218 191), dating from 1849.

The **Haller Bastion** stands at the northernmost end of Str Cetăţii. The bastion is

Battle for the Roma Crown

Unlike other ethnic minorities, Romania's Roma (Gypsies) do not seek their own nation-state. Rather, their aspirations lie in the rival leadership of Roma king Florin Cioabă and Roma emperor Iulian Rădulescu – two self-proclaimed chieftains who battle for Roma rights in Romania in between battling each other. Their flamboyant lifestyles represent the glittering uppercrust of Romania's largely impoverished Roma community.

Florin Cioabă was crowned king of 'all Roma everywhere' in Sibiu in February 1997, at the age of 41. The Pentecostal minister inherited the 24-carat gold coin crown from his late father, Ioan Cioabă.

Ioan Cioabă crowned himself Roma king in 1992. A survivor of a WWII Transdniestran concentration camp, he served as president of the Nomadic Metal-Working Gypsy trade union during the Ceauşescu era. As king he fought for Roma children to be accepted into state schools and, being illiterate himself, established the first adult education centres for fellow Roma.

Self-styled emperor Iulian Rădulescu – a cousin of the late Cioabă – holds court at his palace on the same upmarket street in Sibiu as his rival king. Rădulescu's 20-room villa is painted pink, blue, grey and green, and is guarded by a wizened old fortune teller and two stone elephants.

He crowned himself emperor of all Roma in 1993, marking the occasion by marrying his common-law wife with whom he had lived for 35 years. The couple – the first of the coppersmith clan (*căldărari*) to wed in church – were paired off by their parents during childhood (traditionally Roma are forbidden from marrying *gaujes* – non-Roma). The emperor's crown, comprising 40 gold coins studded with diamonds and rubies, was valued at $87 million. His bride wore a blue dress symbolising the nomadic clan's traditional roof – the sky – and bore a chain made up of nine 14g gold coins minted in Austria in 1915. Throughout the ceremony she refrained from touching her groom. Under Roma law, a wife is subordinate to her husband and is therefore expected to demonstrate her subservience in public.

More recently, Rădulescu gained his Baccalaureate qualification in 1999, at the age of 61, from an agricultural college in Aiud, north of Sibiu.

In anticipation of his death, emperor Rădulescu plans to build a $30 million marble mausoleum for himself near Sibiu as a 'symbol of Roma pride'.

named after the 16th-century city mayor Petrus Haller, who had the red-brick tower built with double walls in 1551. When Sibiu was hit by the plague, holes were drilled through the walls to enable corpses to be evacuated more quickly from the city. The bastion was consequently dubbed the 'gate of the corpses'.

South of the centre, close to the university, is a **Museum of Hunting Arms & Trophies** (Muzeul de Arme şi Trofee de Vânătoare; ☎ 217 873) at Str Şcoala de Înot 4. At the south of this street is the city stadium, backing into the 21-hectare **Sub Arini Park** (Parcul Sub Arini) filled with tree-lined avenues and beautifully laid-out flower beds. The **Complex Nataţie Olimpia** is also here, complete with swimming pool, canoeing and rowing facilities, and tennis courts.

If you have an extra afternoon, it's worth taking in the **Museum of Traditional Folk Civilization** (Muzeul Civilizaţiei Populare Tradiţionale Astra; ☎ 242 599), farther south in Dumbrava Park (take trolleybus No T1 from the train station). It's open 10 am and 6 pm in summer, and 9 am to 4 pm in winter, Tuesday to Sunday ($1). A great many authentic rural buildings and houses have been reassembled in the park to create an open-air ethnographic museum. Ask about guided tours of the site in English. At the adjacent **zoo** you can hire a boat and row yourself around the lake. The **city cemetery** is also here.

Activities

The Boua Bikes Club (☎ 218 310), Str Avram Iancu 25, arranges mountain-bike activities and hire.

Places to Stay

Camping The closest camping ground is **Popas Turistic** (☎ *214 022*), beside the Hanul Dumbrava Restaurant 4km southwest of the town centre (take trolleybus No T1 from the train station direct to the site). Worn-out cabins cost $12 for a single or double; tent sites cost $5. It's open reliably from June to September.

There is also a *camping ground* 14km north of Sibiu in Băile Ocna Sibiului (see Around Sibiu, later).

Private Rooms If you hang out at the bus or train station long enough, you're bound to get an offer of a private room. Alternatively, try Antrec (☎/fax *220 179*), 10km from Sibiu in the village of Rusciori at house No 114. It arranges rooms in private houses in villages surrounding Sibiu for around $10 a night, including breakfast.

Hotels – City Centre Below Piaţa Huet, just off Str Turnului, is *Hotel Leu* (☎ *218 392, Str Moşion Roată 6)*, with simple rooms for $5 per person. The proprietors speak German. Better value is the three-room *Hotel Halemadero* (☎ *212 509, Str Măsarilor 10)*, farther west, which overlooks a pleasant garden and patio and charges $18 for double rooms with private bath. The adjacent bar is a friendly hangout.

Hotel Bulevard (☎ *210 15, Piaţa Unirii 10)* is an appealing place, dating from 1876. It was here, in what was then the 'Haberman Café', that 19th-century poet George Coşbuc came to brainstorm. The hotel today is a worthwhile splurge at $18/28 for spacious singles/doubles with private bath.

Sibiu's most colourful hotel is the central three-star *Hotel Împăratul Romanilor* (Roman Emperor; ☎ *216 500, fax 213 278, Str Nicolae Bălcescu 4)*. It was founded in 1555 as a restaurant called 'La Sultanul Turcilor' (To The Turks' Sultan). The hotel has 96 rooms, split into three categories: 'A' rooms, with a street view, cost $29/44 for a single/double; 'B' rooms face the back yard and cost $27/40; 'C' rooms, for $25/38, are 'very small'. All rooms have a

private bath and TV; rooms with a s are $1 cheaper. Breakfast is included.

The nearby 15-storey *Hotel Continental* (☎ *218 100, fax 210 902,* e hc@starne .ro, Calea Dumbrăvii 2–4) was renovated with business travellers in mind. Every room now has a colour TV and porters carry in your bags. The cost is $55/83, including breakfast.

Hotels – South of the Centre There is a cluster of hotels next to the municipal stadium (a taxi from the train station costs $1.50). The old two-storey *Hotel Sport* (☎ *422 472, Str Octavian Goga 2)*, on the eastern side of Hotel Parc, has rooms for $6 per person, but it's often fully booked by sporting groups.

Larger and more expensive is the grim, eight-storey *Hotel Parc* (☎ *424 455, Str Şcoala de Înot 3)*, overpriced at $11/17 for less-than-average rooms with private bath, TV and telephone. Prices include a breakfast of stale bread and instant coffee.

A better choice is the chalet-style *Hotel Silva* (☎ *442 141, fax 216 304, Aleea Eminescu 1)*, overlooking the tennis courts in the tranquil, tree-filled Sub Arini Park, 30m to the east of Hotel Parc. Rooms with private bath and TV cost $21/25 and an apartment is $36. Breakfast is included.

Places to Eat

The restaurant in *Hotel Împăratul Romanilor* (see Places to Stay) is rather stuffy; it is generally full of rich tourists speaking loudly and gaping in amazement at the elaborate, sliding glass ceiling. *Restaurant Bumita*, farther south along Str Nicolae Bălescu, is cheaper, more local, and has nice wooden tables with red tablecloths on the street. *Restaurant Mara* (Str Nicolae Bălcescu 21) is a small, quiet bistro with an English-language menu.

La Turn, on Piaţa Mare next to the old council tower, has a large terrace overlooking the square and serves traditional Romanian cuisine; its downside is its proximity to the permanent jam of impatient, horn-honking motorists queuing to drive beneath the council tower onto Str Avram Iancu.

...'s (Piaţa Mică 14) is the top place in ... for a cheap – and delicious – fill. The patisserie serves freshly baked sesame- ...ed bread and yoghurt. It's generally ...acked. Opposite, the ageing **Restaurant Union** (Piaţa Mică 7) fails to attract the same sort of crowds.

On the western side of the square is the upmarket **Domar Cofetărie & Patiserie**. It has a great selection of naughty-but-nice cakes and pastries and serves excellent fresh coffee. Again, it's always packed.

Another fun cafe is the bohemian **Art Café** on Str Filarmonicii, inside the state philharmonic building. The cafe is through a red-and-gold-painted door which leads to the cellar; its walls are covered with graffiti and adorned with musical instruments.

Restaurant Select (Str Târgu Peştelui 2), just west of the centre, is an upmarket restaurant serving traditional Romanian food at slightly above-average prices; it is good for a splurge.

If you want to eat dirt-cheap food with the locals, go to **Restaurant Timiş** on Str Turnului not far from the market.

On the eastern side of Piaţa Mare is the **Pupa** alimentar and fast-food outlet; hot dogs, hot sandwiches and vegetarian pizza slices for less than $1 are served through a small window facing the street. Sit on the chairs outside and watch the world go by.

For those who absolutely crave a Big Mac there is a **McDonald's** attached to the Shell petrol station, west of the centre on Str Alba Iulia.

Self-Catering Stock up on vegetables and fruits at the **market** on Piaţa Cibin, north-east of Str Măsarilor near Hotel Halemadero. **Capa** (Str Mitropoliei 1), opposite the History Museum, is a small, clean food shop selling a good variety of products; open 8 am to 6 pm Monday to Saturday. For foreign imports go to **Prima** (Str Nicolae Bălcescu 2); open 7.30 am to 9 pm weekdays, 7.30 am to 7 pm Saturday, and 9 am to 3 pm Sunday.

Entertainment
Cinemas Sibiu has three cinemas: **Cinema Pacea** (Str Nicolae Bălcescu 29) is a conventional cinema. **Cinema Tineretului** (☎ 211 420), on Str Alexandru Odobescu adjoining the hip Bar Meridan, is quite a treat. The auditorium-cum-disco is filled with sofas and coffee tables, inviting you to sit back in comfort and relax over a beer while watching your favourite Hollywood hero in action.

Studionul Astra (☎ 218 195, extension 26, Piaţa Mică 11) screens alternative art films; it also hosts the annual International Astra Film Festival in May.

Clubs & Bars The **Disco-Bar Meridan** (☎ 212 166) inside the Cinema Tineretului complex is an alternative cellar club with tribal art-style paintings on the wall, dim lighting and fascinating relics. Its mellow blues and funky jazz attracts a bohemian crowd. The bar is open 24 hours. The **Disco Bar Mega Vox**, downstairs in the Culture House (Casa de Cultură), in front of Hotel Continental, is popular on summer week- ends (entry from the rear of the building).

Café Bar Liliacul (Str Nicolae Bălcescu 21) in the centre is a great place to unwind over a drink or two; open 8 am to 10 pm Monday to Saturday, and 10 am to 8 pm Sunday.

South of the centre is the rather tacky **Night Club Transylvania** (Str Gorăslău 1) attached to the Transylvanian Restaurant. Its mirrored walls and fake spider webs speak for themselves! The club is open 11 pm to 4 am daily.

Theatre & Classical Music Performances at the **Philharmonic**, on the corner of Str General Magheru and Str Filharmonicii, and the **Radu Stancu State Theatre** (Teat- rul de Stat Radu Stancu; ☎ 413 114, Blvd Spitelor 2–4), just off Piaţa Unirii, are well worth attending. Plays at the theatre are usually in Romanian, but there is a German- language section within the theatre. Tickets for both venues are sold at the Agenţie de Teatrală (☎ 217 575), Str Nicolae Bălcescu 17; open 8 am to 8 pm weekdays, and 9 am to 3 pm Saturday. The Radu Stancu State Theatre hosts the International Theatre Festival in June.

The **Puppet Theatre** *(Teatrul de Păpuşi;* ☎ *211 420),* on Str Alexandru Odobescu in the same building as Cinema Tineretului, is only open between October and July. Ask at the cinema for details of shows.

Getting There & Away

Air Tarom operates an afternoon flight to Bucharest on Monday, Wednesday, Friday and Saturday. Tickets ($40/80 single/ return) are sold at Tarom (☎ 211 157), Str Nicolae Bălcescu 10; open 8 am to noon, and 1 to 6 pm weekdays.

Train The Agenţie de Voiaj CFR office (☎ 216 441), next to Hotel Împăratul Romanilor at Str Nicolae Bălcescu 6, is open 7.30 am to 7.30 pm weekdays.

The train station is at the eastern end of Str General Magheru, on Piaţa 1 Decembrie. For Sighişoara (95km) you may have to change at Copşa Mică or Mediaş. For Alba Iulia (92km) you may have to change at Vinţu de Jos.

The left-luggage office is clearly marked at the western end of the main platform (open 24 hours).

Bus The bus station is opposite the train station at the eastern end of Str Nicolae Teclu Major, on Piaţa 1 Decembrie. Daily bus services include one to Cluj-Napoca (230km) in summer only, Târgu Mureş (125km) and Piteşti (260km); and two daily to Sighişoara (92km).

Buses for Păltiniş depart from the bus stop at the eastern end of Str 9 Mai at 7, 9 and 11 am and 3 pm ($1.13, 1½ hours, 32km); pay the driver. Return buses depart from the central bus stop in Păltiniş.

Mihu Reisen (☎ 211 744, 214 979), Str 9 Mai 52, operates buses to Germany. Its office is open 8 am to 7 pm weekdays. A bus departs from outside its office on Saturday at 5 am. It stops at various cities in Hungary and Austria en route to Germany. The return bus leaves Aschaffenburg in Germany on Wednesday. Atlassib (☎ 229 224), Str Tractorului 14, offers identical services.

TransEuropa (☎ 211 296, ☎/fax 210 364, e rezervari@transeuropa.ro), Str Nicolae Bălcescu 41, sells tickets for buse. ern Europe too. Reisebüro Kessler 118), Str Beiltz 22, has a daily bus c ing from Sibiu to Germany at 6 am.

Getting Around

To/From the Airport Sibiu airport (☎ 229 235) is 5km west of the centre. Tarom runs a shuttle bus, departing from its city-centre office one hour before flights depart.

Bus & Trolleybus Tickets for public transport cost $0.20 for a double-journey ticket and are sold from kiosks next to most bus stops. Trolleybus Nos 1 and 2 connect the train station with the centre.

Taxi To call a taxi dial ☎ 444 444, 222 222 or 212 121.

AROUND SIBIU
Băile Ocna Sibiului

The bubbling spa resort of Băile Ocna Sibiului, 18km north of Sibiu on the railway line to Copşa Mică, is packed during summer weekends. Known as Salzburg to the Saxons, the many natural pools and geological curiosities around Ocna Sibiului make it a popular bathing resort. Some of the bubbling lakes are formed in abandoned salt mines. There is a large **camping ground** in the forest next to the train halt; get off at Băile Ocna Sibiului, *not* Ocna Sibiului, 2km north.

From Sibiu there are eight local trains leaving daily to Băile Ocna Sibiului (15 minutes, 12km).

Cisnădie, Răşinari & Păltiniş

Eight kilometres south of Sibiu, on the road to Păltiniş, is the Saxon fortified church of Cisnădie (Heltau in German, Nagydisznód in Hungarian). Work started on defensive walls around the church in 1430 but they were destroyed by a Turkish attack on the town in 1493. In 1601, the Habsburg general George Basta murdered three villagers on the church porch.

Ask in the village for the key to the bell tower which offers fantastic views of this red-roofed town. Three main streets run

...isnădie; the church is south of the ...treet.

...shepherd village of Rășinari, famed ...s local carpentry and sheep farming, is ...n south of Cisnădie. Ethnographic ex-...ibits – including the long wooden ladels (*tâlv*) used for sampling the plum brandy (*țuică*) stored in large wooden kegs – are displayed in the Rășinari village museum. The village is also the birthplace of Romanian poet and politician Octavian Goga (1881–1939) who served as prime minister for 44 days in 1937.

From Rășinari you can hike to Păltiniș, 32km south-west of Sibiu, nestled at an altitude of 1442m at the foot of the Cindrel Mountains (also known as the Cibin Mountains). Păltiniș in the 1920s was a fashionable resort, the last remnants of its golden past being wiped out in 1992 when its wooden nine-pin bowling (*popice*) alley was moved from Păltiniș to the open-air museum in Sibiu. Well-marked hiking trails from Păltiniș take you into the **Cindrel Mountains** (see the Exploring the Carpathian Mountains special section). From Păltiniș it is an easy day's hike to most of the villages in Mărginimea Sibiului (see the following section).

Places to Stay Antrec (see Sibiu's Places to Stay section) arranges rooms in *private homes* in the surrounding villages from $10 per person a night, including breakfast.

In Rășinari village there is the popular *Cabana Mai* (☎ 069-557 269) on the main road from Sibiu to Păltiniș. A comfortable double costs $25 a night, breakfast included. Directly behind the cabana is a stream where you can enjoy an afternoon fishing and staff will even cook your catch for you.

Bookings for Păltiniș' *Villa Sinaia* can be made in advance through the Păltiniș tourist agency (☎/fax 069-218 319), Str Tribunei 3, Sibiu. Comfortable double rooms with private bath cost $14, including breakfast. The somewhat ghastly 39-room *Hotel Cindrelul* (☎ 069-213 237), the mainstay hotel in the resort, has doubles/triples starting at $18/19.

Getting There & Away Local buses run from Sibiu bus station to Cisnădie (30 minutes, 8km) every half-hour between 5 am and 8 pm.

To get to Rășinari, take trolleybus No T1 from Sibiu train station to the Palace Hotel, opposite Dumbrava Park. Then take the tram (same side of road as Dumbrava Park) to Rășinari.

From Sibiu, buses for Păltiniș depart from the bus stop at the eastern end of Str 9 Mai at 7, 9 and 11 am and 3 pm ($1.13, 1½ hours, 32km); pay the driver. Return buses depart from the central bus stop in Păltiniș.

Mărginimea Sibiului

Mărginimea Sibiului ('borders of Sibiu') embraces the region west of Sibiu, which runs along the county border towards Sebeș. Traditional occupations such as shepherding, weaving and carpentry are still very much alive in its pretty little villages, where painting icons on glass and colouring eggs outweigh any 20th-century invention.

Lying 15km west of Sibiu is the delightful **Cristian** (Grossau in German, Kereszténysziget in Hungarian). The village, settled by Saxons since the 14th century, is a picture postcard of red-roofed houses and vibrant washed walls, overshadowed by a grandiose fortified church in the centre of the village. Visitors can climb the tower of the church for an aerial view. Ask for the key at the green-painted house, down the road behind the eastern fortress wall.

The history of the church is told in the small village museum (Muzeul Sătesc), next to the local prefecture in the centre of the village. It is theoretically open noon to 5 pm Tuesday to Sunday; if it is closed during these hours ask for the key at the prefecture.

From Cristian, it is worth making a short detour through **Orlat**, home to one of the largest village orphanages in Romania, to **Sibiel**. Sibiel's **Glass Icon Museum** (Muzeul de Ioane pe Sticlă), one of Romania's best, is well worth visiting. The museum, in a blue-painted building next to the village church (1765), houses a collection of more than 600 icons richly painted on glass.

From Sibiel, head back north to **Sălişte**, another quaint village rich in local folklore. In **Galeş**, 2km west of Sălişte, is a small ethnographic and art museum (Muzeul de Etnografie şi Artă Populară). It is at the southern end of the village, across the bridge opposite a salami factory. If you get lost ask in the village for the salami factory (Fabrica de Salamuri). A dirt track leads from Galeş to **Poiana Sibiului**, famed for its fantastic coloured eggs decorated with brightly coloured geometric motifs.

Places to Stay & Eat In Cristian, you can stay at *Hotel Spack* (☎ 069-579 262, Str II 9). Staying here is comparable to a cosy night at home. The small, family-run *pensione* has beds in doubles/triples for $13 per person, including breakfast. The hotel does not provide evening meals so bring your own supplies.

For *private home* accommodation, Sibiel's agro-tourism scheme involves some 20 families who open their homes to tourists, feeding you with fresh eggs and milk for breakfast and laying on a small feast of home-grown produce at dinnertime. This successful scheme is run by Dorina Petra (☎ 069-554 198) who can generally be found at the museum (☎ 069-553 818). A night's accommodation including all meals costs $20 per person.

Getting There & Away Local trains from Sibiu to Sebeş stop at Cristian (15 minutes, 15km), Sibiel (25 minutes, 23km), Sălişte (35 minutes, 30km) and Miercurea Sibiului (1¼ hours, 58km). There are five trains daily between Sibiu and Sebeş.

MEDIAŞ
☎ 069

Mediaş is a small but thriving industrial town, 55km north of Sibiu, on the banks of the Târnava Mare River. It was in Mediaş (Mediasch in German, Medgyes in Hungarian) that Saxon church leaders met in 1544 to mark the first Lutheran synod in Transylvania. Today it's a predominantly Ro-

manian town, with the Saxon influence ing on in the painted houses.

The black pit of **Copşa Mică**, 11km so of Mediaş, is a major junction for connecting trains between Sibiu and Sighişoara. During the communist era, the town was home to the Carbosin carbon-black processing plant which belched out thousands of tons of soot annually, leaving *everything* black and killing off all vegetation within a 6km radius. Should you have the misfortune to change trains in Copşa Mică, you can view the abandoned plant, shut since 1993, from the train platform.

Orientation
Mediaş train station is at Str Unirii 3. The bus station is a couple of blocks farther north on Str Unirii. Hotel Central is a three-minute walk from the train station: turn left along Str Unirii and then right onto Str Stephan Ludwig Roth. Cross the roundabout and cut through a small alleyway on the other side of the street towards the red-and-white building with the satellite dish on top. To get to the centre, turn right at the roundabout and continue along Str Stephan Ludwig Roth until you reach Piaţa Regele Ferdinand I. Walk up Str George Enescu, at the northern end of the square, to reach the church.

Information
The tourist office (☎ 841 885), inside Hotel Central, sells tickets for buses to Germany and maps of the Sibiu district; only open 7 am to 3.30 pm Monday.

Change money and get cash advances on Visa/MasterCard at the Banca Agricolă, next to Hotel Central on Piata Corneliu Coposu 2. It also has an ATM accepting Visa and is open 8 am to 1 pm weekdays.

The telephone office is a couple of blocks farther north, towards the fresh fruit and veg market *(piaţa agrolimentară)* on Str Mihai Eminescu. The post office is next to the train station on Str Unirii.

Things to See
The fortified **Evangelical Church of St Margaret** dominates the old town. A church was built on the site in the 13th century but

...not until 1447 that the present edifice ...constructed. A 74m-tall tower (struck ...ightning four times) was added in 1482, ...hile the church's altar, dating from 1485, ...s considered one of Transylvania's most precious pieces of medieval Saxon art.

Close to the church is the Mediaş **school** (Liceul Teoretic) in which a small exhibition on the life and works of teacher, writer and activist Stephan Ludwig Roth (1796–1849) is housed. Born into a middle-class Saxon family in Transylvania, Ludwig Roth studied in Germany and Switzerland but returned to Mediaş where he worked as a professor at the school. He actively opposed Habsburg efforts to introduce Hungarian as the official teaching language. In 1848, Habsburg forces arrested him and on 11 May 1849 he was executed in Cluj-Napoca. A statue of him stands in the small park in front of the school.

There is a small local **history museum** (☎ 841 299), next to the Hungarian Reformed church on Str Viitorului; open 9 am to 5 pm Tuesday to Sunday.

Places to Stay & Eat

Despite being the only hotel in town, the 128-room *Hotel Central* (☎ 841 787, Piata Corneliu Coposu 2) does not charge astronomical prices. Basic singles/doubles with private bathroom start at $9/18 a night, including a good breakfast. All the staff speak excellent English.

The popular *Pizzeria Criss (Str 1 Septembrie 21)* has excellent, good-value pizzas at around $1.30. The only downside is that it is often packed and spare tables are hard to find. The *Ana Café*, on Str George Enescu opposite the theatre school, is a pleasant local hangout with a terrace overlooking the fortified church.

Getting There & Away

Train The Agenţie de Voiaj CFR (☎ 841 351) is on the central square at Piaţa Regele Ferdinand I, 5. Mediaş is on the main Cluj-Napoca–Bucharest line. To get to Sighişoara from Sibiu you have to change trains at Copşa Mică or Mediaş. All international trains between Bucharest and Budapest stop

at Mediaş (see Sighişoara's Getting There & Away section).

Left-luggage facilities (open 24 hours) are in the main ticket hall.

Bus There are eight daily buses to Târgu Mureş (71km) but few others. Tickets for private buses to Western Europe are sold at the travel agency inside Hotel Central; buses depart from outside the hotel. A bus departs from Mediaş to Germany at 5 am Tuesday.

SIGHIŞOARA
☎ 065 • postcode 3050

Sighişoara (Schässburg in German, Segesvár in Hungarian) is a perfectly preserved medieval town in beautiful hilly countryside. Nine towers remain along Sighişoara's intact city walls, which encircle sloping cobbled streets lined with 16th-century burgher houses and untouched churches.

Settled by the Romans, the town was first documented as Castrum Sex in 1280. Saxon colonists settled here from the 12th century onwards. These Saxons were nicknamed *saşi* by the local population. Prior to 1989 there were some 3000 Saxons living in Sighişoara. Since 1990, however, the Saxon community has plummeted to less than 500.

Today the town continues to burst with life, particularly on Wednesday and Saturday when Roma and villagers from outlying regions come into town on their horse-drawn wagons to sell their wares at the market. In summer, Sighişoara is packed every day with tourists.

Sighişoara was also the birthplace of Vlad Ţepeş and therefore attracts hordes of Dracula tourists.

All trains between Bucharest and Budapest (via Oradea) pass through here, so look out for it from the window if you're foolish enough not to get off.

Orientation

Follow Str Gării south from the train station to the Soviet war memorial, where you turn left to the large Orthodox church. Cross the Târnava Mare River on the footbridge here and take Str Morii to the left, then keep

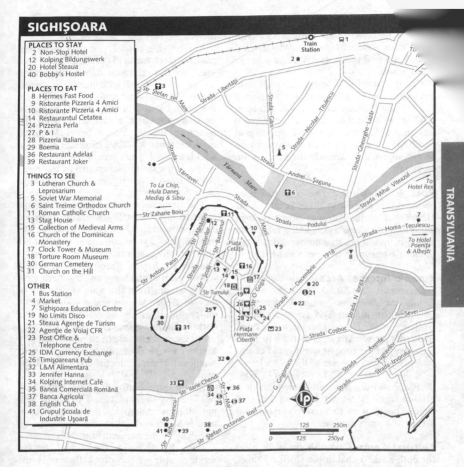

SIGHIŞOARA

PLACES TO STAY
2 Non-Stop Hotel
12 Kolping Bildungswerk
20 Hotel Steaua
40 Bobby's Hostel

PLACES TO EAT
8 Hermes Fast Food
9 Ristorante Pizzeria 4 Amici
10 Ristorante Pizzeria 4 Amici
14 Restaurantul Cetatea
24 Pizzeria Perla
27 P & I
28 Pizzeria Italiana
29 Boema
36 Restaurant Adelas
39 Restaurant Joker

THINGS TO SEE
3 Lutheran Church &
   Leprosarium
5 Soviet War Memorial
6 Saint Treime Orthodox Church
11 Roman Catholic Church
13 Stag House
15 Collection of Medieval Arms
16 Church of the Dominican
   Monastery
17 Clock Tower & Museum
18 Torture Room Museum
30 German Cemetery
31 Church on the Hill

OTHER
1 Bus Station
4 Market
7 Sighişoara Education Centre
19 No Limits Disco
21 Steaua Agenţie de Turism
22 Agenţie de Voiaj CFR
23 Post Office &
   Telephone Centre
25 IDM Currency Exchange
26 Timişoareana Pub
32 L&M Alimentara
33 Jennifer Hanna
34 Kolping Internet Café
35 Banca Comercială Română
37 Banca Agricola
38 English Club
41 Grupul Şcoala de
   Industrie Uşoară

going all the way up to Piaţa Hermann Oberth and the old town. Many of the facilities you'll want are found along a short stretch of Str 1 Decembrie 1918.

Maps The best available map of the city, and the fortified old town, is the *Sighişoara Touristic Map* ($0.50), published by FRH Impex in 1997 with brief historical explanations in English, German and Romanian.

The A5-sized *Sighişoara Tourist Guide* ($0.80) includes a detailed history of the old town in English, French, German and Romanian, and a centrefold city map. Both

are sold at the reception of Hotel Steaua and at the Librărie Hyperion bookshop at Str 1 Decembrie 1918 11.

Information
Tourist Offices The Steaua Agenţie de Turism (☎ 771 072, fax 771 932), next to the Hotel Steaua at Str 1 Decembrie 1918 12, sells city guides, maps and tickets for buses to Hungary and Germany, arranges private accommodation (see Places to Stay later) and has an exchange office. It is open 9 am to 5 pm weekdays, and 9 am to 1 pm Saturday.

The IDM Exchange, next door to ...a Perla on Piaţa Hermann Oberth, ...s cash advances on Visa/MasterCard ...m 8 am to 8 pm weekdays, and 8 am to ...pm Saturday.

Change travellers cheques and get cash advances on Visa/MasterCard at Banca Comercială Română at Str 1 Mai 12, open 8.30 am to noon weekdays. The bank also has an ATM. Banca Agricolă, opposite at Str 1 Mai 7, also gives cash advances on Visa/MasterCard; open 8 am to noon on weekdays.

Post & Telephone The post and telephone centre is close to Hotel Steaua on Str Hermann Oberth. The post office is open 7 am to 8 pm weekdays, and the telephone centre is open 7 am to 9 pm weekdays, and 8 am to 1 pm and 5 to 8 pm Saturday.

Email & Internet Access You can access the Internet for $0.50 per hour at the Sighişoara Education Centre (e edcenter@ enc.elsig.ro), funded by Eastern Nazarene College, at Str Horea Teculescu 37; open noon to 9 pm weekdays, and 10 am to 2 pm Saturday. At the time of writing, the centre was planning to relocate to the citadel.

Kolping Internet Café (☎/fax 777 664, e Bjacint@usa.net) at Str Ilarie Chendi 3 also charges $0.50 per hour for Internet access; open 10 am to 8 pm weekdays, and 10 am to 4 pm Saturday.

Cultural Centres English speakers meet for coffee and a chat at the Coffee House, held every Tuesday at 7 pm at the English Club, Str Ştefan Octavian Iosif 20. The charitable organisation is funded by the Eastern Nazarene College in the US, which runs a very successful program aimed at helping Sighişoara's street children.

Things to See

All Sighişoara's sights are in the old town – the medieval **citadel** – perched on a hillock and fortified with a 14th-century wall. A century later the 14 towers and five artillery bastions were added. Today the citadel, which is on the Unesco World Heritage list, retains just nine of its original towers and two of its bastions.

Entering the citadel, you pass under the massive **clock tower** (Turnul cu Ceas). Formerly the main entrance to the fortified city, the tower is 64m tall with sturdy base walls measuring an impenetrable 2.35m. Inside the 1648 clock is a pageant of figurines, each representing a character from the Saxon pantheon: Peace bears an olive branch, Justice has a set of scales and Law wields a sword. The executioner is also present and the drum-player strikes the hour. Above stand seven figures, each representing a day of the week.

The figurines can be inspected through glass from the **History Museum** (Muzeul de Istorie), in the 14th-century tower. The museum has a good collection of WWI-era photographs, a bust of the museum's founder Dr Joseph Bacon (1857–1941), a scale model of the town and a superb view of Sighişoara from the walkway on top of the 7th floor. As you make your way up, under the clock tower on the left is the **Torture Room Museum**.

On the western side of the clock tower is a small house containing a **collection of medieval arms** (Colecţia de Arme Medievale).

All three museums are open 9 am to 5.30 pm Tuesday to Sunday, and 10 am to 5.30 pm Monday. Admission to all three museums is $1.25 and tickets can be purchased from any of the museum entrances.

Immediately inside the citadel, on the western side of the clock tower, is the 15th-century **Church of the Dominican Monastery** (Biserica Mănăstirii). The Gothic church became the Saxons' main Lutheran church in 1556. In theory the church is open 9 am to 7 pm Monday to Saturday, and 10 am to 2 pm Sunday, though unfortunately it is generally closed. Classical, folk and baroque concerts are often held here.

Continuing west towards Piaţa Cetăţii, you come to the house in which Vlad Ţepeş was born in 1431 and reputedly lived until the age of four. The **Dracul house**, complete with its original river-stone floor, is now a beer bar and restaurant, Restaurantul Cetatea (see Places to Eat).

Piaţa Cetăţii is the heart of old Sighişoara. It was here that markets, craft fairs, public executions and witch trials were held. In 1603 a nobleman was tried in the square in front of 12 judges for high treason. He was found guilty and had his right hand chopped off before being impaled. The 17th-century **Stag House**, overlooking the square on the corner of Str Şcolli Bastionul, is considered the most representative example of the citadel's architecture. It is currently under restoration (until 2001).

From the square, turn left up Str Şcolii Bastionul to the 172 steps of the **covered stairway** (*scara acoperită*), which has tunnelled its way up the hill since 1642, to the Gothic **Church on the Hill** (Biserica din Deal). This Gothic Bergkirche (1345) – also Lutheran – is currently undergoing restoration. A path leads from in front of the church to the adjacent **German cemetery**. The gates are open 8 am to 8 pm between May and October, and 9 am to 4 pm from November to April.

Behind the church are the remains of the **Goldsmiths' Tower**. The goldsmiths, tailors, carpenters and tinsmiths, the only craftsmen to have their guilds and workshops inside the citadel, built eight fountains (34m deep) within the city walls to ensure a continuous water supply during times of siege. Guilds existed until 1875.

From the church, head back down the hill, cross Piaţa Cetăţii, then head down Str Bastionul. At its northern end is a **Roman Catholic church** (1894).

Apart from their two churches in the citadel, Sighişoara's Saxon community had a third **Lutheran church**, deliberately sited well outside the city walls. The church, just west of the train station off Str Libertăţii, was used in the 17th century as an isolation compound for victims of the plague and later of leprosy. Many, however, were taken to the **leprosarium** (Siechhof) adjoining the small Lutheran church. Church records show that as many as 38 people died every day. To get to the church, turn right out of the train station along Str Libertăţii, then right along Str Ştefan Mare. The tin-spired church is on the rig

Out of Town Four kilometres north-east of Sighişoara in **Albeşti** (Fehéregyháza in Hungarian) village is the **Sándor Petőfi Museum** (Muzeul Petőfi Sándor). The Hungarian poet Sándor Petőfi (1823–49) led the 1848 revolution with Lajos Kossuth against the Habsburgs and died here during the battle.

The only downside of the museum is that the entire exhibition is explained in Hungarian. It is open 9 am to 3.30 pm Tuesday to Sunday ($0.50).

To get to Albeşti, take any of the northbound buses which leave every 10 minutes from the main bus stop at the southern end of Str Podului. In Albeşti, get off at the bus stop in the centre of the village and turn right along Str Muzeului, a gravel road. At the fork, bear left and continue along the road, past the village cemetery until you reach a church; the museum is opposite.

Special Events

During the last three days of July, Sighişoara hosts its Medieval Days (Festivalul de Artă Medievală Sighişoara), during which people dress in traditional costume and stage music and theatrical performances. For information, contact the Fundaţia de Artă Medievală Sighişoara (mobile ☎ 092-311 622), Str Griviţei 4. Alternatively contact the Agenţia de Impresariat ISIS (☎/fax 774 662, @ isis@sighi soara.com), Str Andrei Şaguna 8.

A music festival takes place every year in mid-July.

Places to Stay

Camping You can camp on a hill above the town – a half-hour hike up from the train station. Walk east along the train tracks to a bridge, then cross the tracks and turn left to a road which leads up. At the end of this road is the **Dealul Gării Restaurant** (☎ 771 046), where you can camp for $3 or rent a bungalow for $10 a double.

There's a better camping ground at **Hula Daneş** (☎ 771 052), but it's 4km out of town on the road to Mediaş; three buses a

The Dracula Myth

Fifteenth-century Wallachian prince Vlad Ţepeş is all too often credited with being Dracula, the vampire-count featured in the classic Gothic horror story *Dracula* (1897) written by Anglo-Irish novelist Bram Stoker.

This madcap association of these two diabolical figures – one historical, the other fictitious – is nothing more than a product of the popular imagination. But while Romanians increasingly reap the tourist reward of this confusion, many are concerned that the identity of a significant figure in their history has been overshadowed by that of an immortal literary vampire.

The 'real' Dracula, Vlad Ţepeş, was born in 1431 in Sighişoara, and ruled Wallachia in 1448, 1456–1462 and 1476. He was outrageously bloodthirsty, but he was not a vampire. His princely father, Vlad III, was called Vlad Dracul (from the Latin 'draco', meaning 'dragon') after the chivalric Order of the Dragon accredited to him by Sigismund of Luxembourg in 1431. The Romanian name Drăculea – literally 'son of Dracul' – was bestowed on Vlad Ţepeş by his father, and was used as a term of honour. Another meaning of 'draco', however, was 'devil' and this was the meaning that Stoker's novel popularised.

While Vlad Ţepeş was undoubtedly a strong ruler and is seen by some Romanians as a national hero and brave defender of his principality, his practices were ruthless and cruel. Notorious for his brutal punishment methods, ranging from decapitation to boiling and burying alive, he gained the name 'Ţepeş' ('impaler') after his favourite form of punishing his enemies – impaling. A wooden stake was carefully driven through the victim's backbone without touching any vital nerve, ensuring at least 48 hours of suffering before death.

MARTIN HARRIS

Vlad Ţepeş, prince of Wallachia

Ţepeş rarely ate without a Turk writhing on a stake in front of him. Contrary to popular belief, this torture was not unusual at the time among rulers in Europe. Ţepeş' first cousin, Ştefan cel Mare, is said to have 'impaled by the navel, diagonally, one on top of each other' 2300 Turkish prisoners in 1473.

By contrast, Bram Stoker's literary Dracula was a blood-sucking vampire – an undead corpse reliant on the blood of the living to sustain his own immortality. Until 1824 in Stoker's adopted England a wooden stake was commonly driven through the heart of suicide victims to ensure the ill-fated corpse did not turn in its grave into a vampire. In Romania,

---

day marked 'Cris' leave from the bus station, beside the train station. Bungalows here cost $5 a double. The camping ground operates between 1 May and 1 September.

Hostels Open between 20 June and 16 September, *Bobby's Hostel* (☎ 772 232, *Str Tache Ionescu 18*), based in the technical school dormitory, has beds in double/dormitory rooms for $6/5. Hot water runs between 9 am and 1 pm and 7 and 11 pm in the shared bathrooms. It's a 25-minute walk

from the train station, but Bobby will arrange to have backpackers met at the station. The reception is in the building behind the Grupul Şcoala de Industrie Uşoară. Bobby's also hires out mountain bikes for $4 per day.

Private Rooms The Steaua Agenţie de Turism (see Tourist Offices, earlier) can arrange rooms in private homes in the centre of Sighişoara starting at $7.50 per person. Contact the office in advance as it

The Dracula M

vampires form an integral part of traditional folklore. The seventh-born child is particularly susce[...]ible to this evil affliction, identifiable by a hoof as a foot or a tail at the end of its spine.

Stoker set *Dracula* in Transylvania, a region the novelist never set foot in. The novel, originally set in Austria, was first entitled *The Undead*. But following critics' comments that it was too close a pastiche of Sheridan le Fanu's *Camilla* (1820) – a vampire novel set in southern France – Stoker switched titles and geographical settings. Count Dracula's fictitious castle on the Borga pass was inspired by Cruden Bay castle in Aberdeenshire where Stoker drafted much of the novel. The historical facts were uncovered at the British Museum in London.

While Vlad Ţepeş died in 1476, Count Dracula lives on, sustaining an extraordinary subculture of fiction and film. The novel itself has never been out of print (it was first translated into Romanian in 1990), while movie-makers have remade the film countless times, kicking off with Murnau's silent *Nosferatu* in 1922, followed by Universal Pictures' *Dracula* in 1931.

Dracula fan clubs have been set up around the globe. The New York club alone attracts over 5000 hungry members, many of whom meet up with fellow fans at the annual Dracula World Congress. Worthy members of the Transylvanian Dracula Society meanwhile can lay claim to a noble title within the House of Dracula or to a knighthood of the Count Dracula Order. Ironically the society, set up in 1971, only came out of the closet in 1990; Ceauşescu, known as everything from the 'genius of the Carpathians' to the 'anti-Christ', was too closely compared to both Vlad Ţepeş and Dracula for society members to pursue their vampirish activities without being persecuted·

Vlad tucking into his 'stake' dinner

cannot always organise a room on the spot. **Kolping Bildungswerk** (☎ 774 909, Str Mănăstiri 10) provides accommodation, in the heart of the citadel, at $5 per person in two/four/six-bed rooms; meals are extra.

Hotels The best deal is the small, clean **Non-Stop Hotel** (☎ 775 901, Str Libertăţii 44), directly opposite the train station, with doubles with shared bath for $10.

The dreary two-star **Hotel Steaua** (☎ 771 594, fax 771 932, Str 1 Decembrie 1918 12)

charges $14/18 for musty single/double rooms with bath ($10/14 without), breakfast included.

More upmarket is the luxurious **Hotel Poeniţa** (☎ 772 739, Str Dimitrie Cantemir 24), a 20-minute walk from the centre through a charming rural neighbourhood. A double in this large villa costs $20, including breakfast and free use of the miniature swimming pool in the front garden.

Hotel Rex (☎ 777 615, fax 771 932, Str Dumbravei 18), 1km north-east of the centre,

TRANSYLVANIA

...efully furnished doubles for $22, in-
...g breakfast. The hotel *restaurant* is
...nest in town. If you don't fancy the 15-
...ute walk along a busy road, take any bus
... Albeşti for one stop from the bus stop at
...he southern end of Str Podului.

Five kilometres from Sighişoara on the main Sighişoara-Mediaş road is the new Dracula-themed *Hotel Dracula* (☎ 772 211, 742 211, mobile 094-707 799). The three-star hotel has excellent doubles for $16; breakfast is an extra $3 per person.

Places to Eat

Dracula freaks can indulge their ghoulish hunger by dining at *Restaurantul Cetatea*, in Vlad Ţepeş' former house in the citadel. There is a restaurant upstairs and a *berărie* (beer bar) downstairs. The food here is above average and reasonably priced.

Beyond that, the popular place to hang out – for tourists at least – is the brilliantly located *P & I (Piaţa Hermann Oberth 7)*, a large terrace cafe and patisserie above the park. It only serves sweet snacks but is a pleasant place to lounge in the sun. For a plate of spaghetti ($1.60), go to the small *Pizzeria Italiana (Piaţa Hermann Oberth 1)* across from P & I.

Pizzeria Perla, on Piaţa Hermann Oberth, has a good selection of pizzas and pastas, as well as traditional soups and cutlets. Try the Dracul pizza for a spicy treat or, if you're desperate to take a break from your daily diet of pork and fries, go for the *pelmeni* topped with cheese and ham (it's good). The restaurant is open until 11 pm daily (until 9 pm in winter).

The Italian-inspired *Ristorante Pizzeria 4 Amici* has two outlets: one at Str Morii 7 and the other across the park at Str Octavian Goga 12. Both have tables outside and compete with the P & I to be the busiest hangout in town.

Good, traditional Romanian dishes are served at the small, seldom-frequented *Restaurant Adelas*, on Str Cooperatorilor, just off the main street; the day's menu is on a blackboard outside.

More expensive is the modern *Restaurant Joker (Str Tache Ionescu 19)*, opposite

the entrance to Bobby's Hostel. Soups start from $0.75 and main meals are around $2.

The unexciting *Boema (Str Muzeului 6)*, in a courtyard off Str Şcolii, has a monopoly on outdoor dining in the citadel.

Hermes Fast Food (Str 1 Decembrie 1918 54) doles out burgers between 8 am and 8 pm weekdays, and 7 am to 3 am Saturday.

The daily *market* off Str Târnavei has a good selection of fruits, vegetables and cheese. The *L&M Alimentar* on Str Ilarie Chendi is well stocked.

Entertainment

One of the most colourful bars in town is the small and cosy *Jennifer Hanna*, not far from Bobby's Hostel on Str Ilarie Chendi. Run by a Roma, it attracts a completely local crowd and serves Bere Ciuc brewed in Miercurea Ciuc as its house beer.

A popular spot with local students and expats alike is the *Timişoareana Pub (Piaţa Hermann Oberth 4)*, tucked away in an alley between P & I and Pizzeria Italiana; open 10 am to late daily.

The place to be seen, however, is the up-market *No Limits* disco (☎ 518 961), on Str Turnului to the right of the arched entry to the citadel; open 10 pm to 4 am. Reservations are advised.

Getting There & Away

Train The Agenţie de Voiaj CFR (☎ 771 820), Str 1 Decembrie 1918 2, is open 7.30 am to 7.30 pm weekdays. International tickets can only be bought here.

All trains between Bucharest and Budapest stop at Sighişoara. The daily *Pannonia Expres* and *Dacia* pass through at 11.57 am and 9.20 pm, arriving in Budapest 8½ hours later; from Budapest the *Pannonia Expres* continues on to Prague. The daily *Ister* and *Traianus* trains to Budapest also stop in Sighişoara.

For trains to Sibiu you have to change at Copşa Mică or Mediaş. All trains between Bucharest (via Braşov) and Cluj-Napoca stop at Sighişoara.

The left-luggage office (open 24 hours) is on the main platform.

Bus The bus station (☎ 771 260) is next to the train station on Str Libertăţii. Daily bus services include two to Sibiu (92km), one to Bistriţa ($1.95, 146km) and Făgăraş (92km), eight to Târgu Mureş (54km), three to Criş (17km) and five to Apold (15km).

A private bus to Germany departs at 7 am Friday from outside Hotel Steaua. Tickets and schedules are available from the Steaua Agenţie de Turism (see Tourist Offices earlier) and from most travel agencies.

Getting Around
Taxis are not allowed in the citadel, which is restricted to residents' cars only. To call a taxi dial ☎ 771 484 (24 hours).

SAXON FORTIFIED CHURCHES
The Târnave plateau, which stretches for some 120km between Braşov and Sighişoara, is traditionally known as Burzen Land (Ţara Bârsei in Romanian). It was to this region that Saxons – mainly from the Franken region in western Germany – were invited by the Hungarian king Geza II in 1123. In the 15th and 16th centuries, following the increased threat of Turkish attacks on their towns, the settlements were strengthened with bulky city walls and fortified churches. Defensive towers in the churches served as observation posts and entrances were guarded with a portcullis that could be quickly lowered as the enemy advanced.

Since 1989, following the mass exodus of Saxons to Germany, Saxon communities and culture have faced extinction. German president Roman Herzog warned Romania's Saxons during a state visit: 'You can't pack your homeland in a bag and take it with you to Germany.'

Particularly fine examples of the Saxon churches are the numerous fortified churches which dominate settlements immediately west of Sighişoara and around. These tiny villages are poorly served by public transport but within easy hiking distance of one another.

Around Mediaş
Bazna (Baassen in German), a small village first settled in 1302, is 15km north-west of Mediaş. Its late-Gothic St Nicholas' Cr was built at the start of the 16th century the ruins of a 14th-century original. highlight is the three pre-Reformation bell (1404) in the church tower. The 6m-tall wall that surrounded the church was partly dismantled in 1870 because the villagers needed bricks to build a wall around the village school.

From 1842 onwards the village developed as a small spa resort following the discovery of natural springs which released natural gases. Wooden huts were built over the springs to contain these sulphurous gases. Sufferers from rheumatic pains would then take a 'smelly bath' in these huts. To get to Bazna from Mediaş head north towards Târnăveni (formerly spelt Tîrnăveni) for 10km then turn left to Bazna.

Băgaciu (Bogeschdorf) is 12km north of Mediaş. Follow the main northbound road, then turn right along a minor road signposted 'Delenii'. The pre-Reformation, late-Gothic altar in its church, restored in Vienna in 1896, is considered to be the best-preserved Saxon church altar.

Heading 4km south along the dirt track from here, you come to **Curciu** (Kirtsch). The decorative stone frieze above the western door, featuring apes and other animals, is unique to this 14th-century village church.

Towards Sibiu
There are a number of fine churches southwest of Mediaş along the road to Sibiu via Copşa Mică. In Copşa Mică, make a small detour by heading south along a dirt track to **Valea Viilor** (Wurmloch). The village, dating from 1263, has a quaint fortified church which was raised at the end of the 15th century and surrounded by 1.5m-thick walls. It is on Unesco's list of World Heritage sites.

From Copşa Mică, continue south-west along the main Sibiu road. After just a couple of kilometres, you pass through the village of **Axente Sever** (Frauendorf) with a Saxon church dating from 1322–23.

Şeica Mică (Kleinschelken), first settled in 1316, is 5km farther south. The village was engulfed by fire several times during

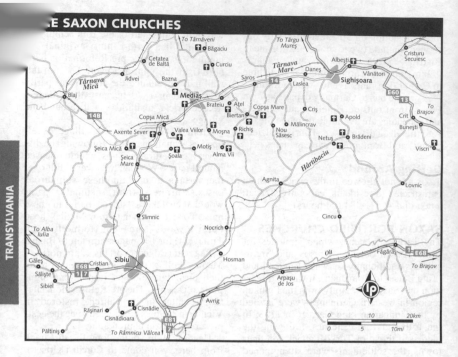

SAXON CHURCHES

the 16th century but remarkably its local church, built in 1414, survived. Its beautiful baptismal font is late-Gothic (1447) and cast from iron. In the church courtyard stands an old well, surrounded by 15m-tall walls.

There are also small fortified Saxon churches in **Şoala**, 4km east along a dirt track, and in **Şeica Mare**, 13km south of its sister village.

From Mediaş you can also head south towards Agnita. Ten kilometres south along this minor road is **Moşna** (Meschen). Its village church, dating from the 14th century, was completely rebuilt in 1485 in a late-Gothic style. Its centrepiece is the tall bell tower, eight storeys high.

Alma Vii (Alemen) is just a few kilometres south of Moşna. The four-towered church was built at the start of the 14th century and fortified in the early 16th century.

See also Around Sibiu, earlier, for details of other fortified churches in the region.

Towards Sighişoara

The eastward journey from Mediaş to Sighişoara is delightful. Some 5km east on the main road is the village of Brateiu. From Brateiu, continue east along the main road for a further 5km then turn right at the turn-off for **Aţel** (Hetzeldorf). The church, dating from the 14th century, was heavily fortified in 1471. In 1959 the northern tower was levelled to uncover a secret tunnel leading to a neighbouring farmstead.

Heading back along the main road, you come to a turn-off on the right leading to a fantastic example of the Saxon heritage. The fortified church of **Biertan** (Birthälm), 9km south of the main road, is listed as a Unesco World Heritage site. The present church was built by the Saxons in the late 15th century. Its altar (1483–1550), modelled on a Viennese altar, has 28 panels. The magnificent 15th-century walls which fortify the church stand 12m tall. Biertan's Saxon priest, who cared for six other parishes after their priests left for Germany, abandoned his 400-strong congregation in 1995. He too moved to Germany.

Six kilometres south of Biertan is the small village of **Richiş**, likewise dominated by a fantastic stone church.

From Biertan you can also head east for 2km along a dirt track to **Copşa Mare** (Grosskopisch). The church dates from the early 14th century and was fortified to fend off Turkish and Tartar invasions in the 16th century but failed to fend off Székely troops, who attacked the village in 1605 and destroyed the church.

Continuing east along the main Mediaş-Sighişoara road, you arrive at **Laslea**, less than 1km off the road just before **Daneş** village. Nine kilometres south of Daneş is **Criş**. From Laslea, energetic hikers can trek for some 10km south to **Nou Săsesc**; bear right where the road forks or, alternatively, bear left to get to **Mălincrav**.

From Sighişoara there are a number of churches you can easily hike to. Fifteen kilometres south is **Apold** and 6km farther south is **Brădeni**. Four kilometres farther south-west is **Netuş**. The Saxon church trail is endless!

Viscri is some 45km south-east of Sighişoara. Follow the road towards Braşov and turn right in Buneşti. From here, a dirt track leads to the remote village. First mentioned in 1400, the village was heavily destroyed by fire in 1638. Its one-room church was built in the 12th century by Székelys and taken over by Saxon colonists in 1185. It is now recognised as a Unesco World Heritage site.

Székely Land

The eastern realms of the Carpathians, known as Székely Land (Ţara Secuilor in Romanian, Székelyföld in Hungarian), are home to the Székelys, an ethnic group whose people have their own national anthem, language (a dialect of Hungarian) and culture.

The origins of the Székely (pronounced 'say-kay') people are disputed. Debates rage as to whether they are descendants of

Attila the Hun, who arrived in Transylvania in the 5th century, or the Magyars, who migrated from Russia in the early Middle Ages. The simplest explanation is that the Székelys are direct descendants of Hungarians who arrived from the 9th century onwards. Three 'nations' were recognised in medieval Transylvania: the Székelys, the Saxons and the nobles.

During the 18th century the Székelys suffered at the hands of the Habsburgs, who attempted to convert this devout Protestant ethnic group to Catholicism. Thousands of young Székely men were conscripted into the Austrian army. Local resistance throughout Székely Land led to the massacre of Madéfalva in 1764, following which thousands of Székelys fled across the border into Romanian Moldavia.

Following the union of Transylvania with Romania in 1918, some 200,000 Hungarians – a quarter of whom were Székelys – fled to Hungary. It was during this period that the Székelys composed their own national anthem.

Maps

The *Ţara Secuilor, Székelyföld, Székely Land* map (Cartographia) includes a detailed map of the region complete with lengthy historical explanations in Hungarian; $4 in bookshops and travel agencies.

TÂRGU MUREŞ
☎ 065 • postcode 4300 • pop 167,000
Târgu Mureş (formerly spelt Tîrgu Mureş) is traditionally a Hungarian stronghold. Called Marosvásárhely in Hungarian, Neumarkt in German, it was first documented under the name 'Novum Forum Sicolorum' in 1322. The town, overlooking the Mureş River, developed as a leading garrison town and later as an important cultural and academic centre. In 1658 it was attacked by Turks who captured 3000 inhabitants and transported them back to Istanbul as slave labour.

During the Ceauşescu regime, Târgu Mureş was a 'closed city' with all ethnic groups other than Romanians forbidden to settle here. Large numbers of ethnic Romanians from other parts of Romania were

...oved into Târgu Mureş to further dilute ...e Hungarian community. Not surprisingly, the town's Hungarian population gradually dwindled.

In 1990, Târgu Mureş gained notoriety as the pressure cooker of major interethnic tension, following bloody clashes between Hungarian students, demonstrating for a Hungarian language faculty in their university, and Romanians who raided the local Hungarian political party offices. The mob attempted to gouge out the eyes of Transylvanian playwright András Sütő who remains blind in one eye. The violence was apparently stirred up by the nationalist political group Vatra, which paid Romanian peasants from outlying villages to travel to Târgu Mureş, and armed them with pitchforks and axes.

Today Târgu Mureş is quiet and tranquil. Despite the many Transylvanian Hungarians who have fled to Hungary since 1990, the town's population is evenly divided between Romanians and Hungarians who both demonstrate a sense of shame over the events of 1990.

However, with the defeat of the city's ethnic Hungarian mayor, Imre Fodor (mayor since 1992), in the June 2000 local elections by Dorin Florea of the extreme-right Convenţia Democratic din România (CDR), a dark cloud has again been cast over the city, threatening the uneasy peace.

Orientation

The train and bus stations are south of the centre. From the train station – a 15-minute walk into town – turn right along Str Mihai Sadoveanu, bearing right where the road forks. Continue north, across the river, until you reach Piaţa Unirii. From here, continue north onto Piaţa Trandafirilor – the main pedestrianised street where most hotels and travel agencies are. The citadel is at the northern end of Piaţa Trandafirilor.

From the bus station, turn right along Str Gheorghe Doja and follow the street north to Piaţa Unirii.

Maps The handy *Hartă Judeţul Mureş* city map (Editura Grai, 1999) also includes maps of Sighişoara and Reghin and costs $1.25 in bookshops.

Information

Tourist Offices Târgu Mureş has no official tourist agency but the enthusiastic staff at Corbet Transair (☎/fax 168 463, e transa ir@netsoft.ro), Piaţa Trandafirilor 43, compensate. The dynamic young team book airline tickets, arrange accommodation and organise car rental and cycling tours.

Less spot-on are the staff at Inter Tours (☎ 164 011, fax 166 489, e office@interto urs.ro), Str Bartok Bela 1–3. The agency can organise English-, French- and German-speaking guides for $16 a day, arranges trips to Sovata and sells tickets for private buses to Germany and Hungary (see the Getting There & Away section); open 8 am to 4 pm weekdays, and 9 am to noon Saturday.

Turism Grand, an agent for Antrec, (☎ 160 287, ☎/fax 160 675), Piaţa Trandafirilor 21, arranges accommodation and sells bus tickets for Germany; open 9 am to 6 pm weekdays.

The ACR (☎ 161 515), next to the Agenţie de Voiaj CFR at Piaţa Teatrului 1, is open 8 am to 4 pm Monday to Wednesday and Friday, 8 am to 5.30 pm Thursday, and 8 am to 1 pm Saturday.

Money There are currency exchanges in most hotels. The IDM Exchange on the corner of Piaţa Trandafirilor and Str Horea gives cash advances on Visa/MasterCard and changes Eurocheques; open 8 am to 8 pm weekdays, and 9 am to 1 pm Saturday. You can cash travellers cheques and get cash advances on Visa/MasterCard at the Banca Comercială Română on the corner of Str Gheorghe Doja and Blvd 1 Decembrie 1918; open 8 am to 6 pm weekdays. It has an ATM outside.

Post & Telephone The central post office is next to Librăria Mihai Eminescu on Piaţa Teatrului; open 7 am to 8 pm weekdays. The telephone centre is close to Hotel Grand on the corner of Piaţa Victoriei and Blvd 1 Decembrie 1918; it's open 7 am to 9 pm daily.

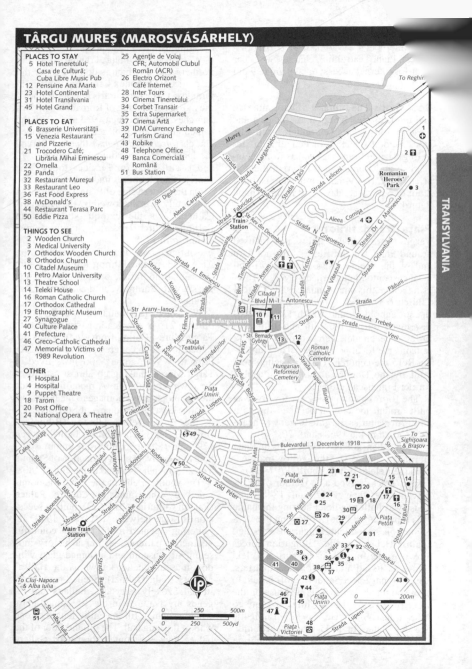

& Internet Access Electro Orizont .nternet (☎ 219 793, ℮ electro@orizo :t), Piaţa Teatrului 2, charges $0.75 per .ır for Internet access; open 9 am to 9 pm .aily.

Bookshops The Librăria Mihai Eminescu and the Librărie Hyperion, on the east and western side of Piaţa Teatrului respectively, stock a good selection of Penguin classics in English and French as well as Romanian-English and Romanian-Hungarian dictionaries. Librăria Mihai Eminescu is open 8 am to 6 pm weekdays, and 8 am to noon Saturday.

Piaţa Trandafirilor

Târgu Mureş' main sights are focused around Piaţa Trandafirilor. At the northern end of the square cross Piaţa Petöfi and head east onto Piaţa Bernády György. Towering above this small square is the **Citadel Church & Fortress**, founded on the site of the stronghold around which Târgu Mureş developed during the 13th and 14th centuries. The citadel, perched on a hillock, remains the focal point today. The Hungarian Reformed church (1316) it shelters was built by the Dominicans on the site of a former Franciscan monastery.

The fortress, comprising six towers, was built around the church between the 15th and 17th centuries. Its **gate tower** was heavily restored in the 1960s and '70s.

Nestled beneath the citadel walls on Piaţa Bernády György is the yellow-painted, baroque **Teleki House** (built 1797–1803). Joseph Teleki served as governor of Transylvania between 1842 and 1848. The house was built as a hotel bearing the name 'Kis Pipa' (Small Pipe). Following the 1848 revolution, in which Hungarians rebelled against Habsburg rule, Hungarian forces took over the fortress, using part of Teleki House as its administration headquarters. Revolutionary poet Sándor Petöfi is said to have sought shelter in Teleki House on the night of 29 July 1849 while en route to Albeşti, near Sibiu. He was killed in battle two days later. In 1935 the Teleki family donated the building to the Hungarian

Reformed Church which today uses it as the administrative headquarters.

Walk back to Piaţa Trandafirilor, the northern end of which is dominated by the magnificent **Orthodox Cathedral** (Catedrăla Ortodoxă). The cathedral's interior is one of the most breathtaking of Romania's modern churches. Built between 1933 and 1938, the cathedral partially replaced the tiny wooden church (*biserica de lemn*) that had served the local Orthodox community since 1773 and is still used for services today. The church is north of the citadel at Str Doiceşti.

On the eastern side of Piaţa Trandafirilor, completely overshadowed by the Orthodox Cathedral, is the baroque-style **Roman Catholic church** (Biserica Sfântul Jonos) dating from 1728.

Continue south down Piaţa Trandafirilor. At No 11 is the **Ethnographic Museum** (Muzeul Etnografic), open 9 am to 4 pm Tuesday to Saturday, and 9 am to 2 pm Sunday.

West of Piaţa Trandafirilor, at Str Aurel Filmon 21, is the leading **synagogue** in Târgu Mureş. Dating from 1900, it was designed to seat a congregation of over 500. Prior to WWII, some 5500 Jews lived in Târgu Mureş, making up almost a third of the town's population. A memorial outside the synagogue pays homage to the holocaust victims. East of the square, at Str Bolyai 17, is the **Bolyai-Teleki Library** (Biblioteca Bolyai-Teleki). The library, built between 1799 and 1805 in an imposing empire style, houses the private book collection of Samule Teleki, which he donated to the city in 1802.

The southern end of the square is dominated by the fantastic **Culture Palace** (Palatul Culturii; ☎ 167 629), built in secessionist style between 1911 and 1913. Its glittering steepled roofs, tiled in colourful geometric patterns, shelter a history museum, art museum and a stained-glass window museum, better known as the **Hall of Mirrors** (Sala Oglinzi). Scenes from traditional Székely fairytales, ballads and legends are featured in the 12 stained-glass windows which fill the entire length of one wall of the long hall. The ground floor of the palace houses a contemporary **Art Gallery**

(Galeria de Artă) featuring some unusual ceramics, paintings and sculptures. The Culture Palace is open 10 am to 4 pm Tuesday to Friday, and 9 am to 1 pm weekends.

The **Prefecture**, with a tiled roof and bright green spires, is next door to the Culture Palace. A plaque on its facing facade pays tribute to those from Târgu Mureş who died during WWI. In the small park in front is a statue of **Lupoaica Romei** (the wolf of Rome), identical to that in Bucharest. The statue of Romulus and Remus being suckled by the wolf was given to Târgu Mureş by the city of Rome in 1924. Close by, at the most southern end of the pedestrianised street, on Piaţa Unirii, is the town's **Greco-Catholic Cathedral**, a Romanian Orthodox church until its congregation opted to accept the authority of the Vatican.

Behind the church is a **memorial** to the victims of the 1989 revolution.

University & Around

Târgu Mureş enjoys a strong academic tradition and its medical and drama schools are considered the most distinguished in the country. Eminent scholars include mathematicians Farkas Bólyai (1775–1856) and his son János Bólyai (1802–60) who revolutionised Euclidean geometry.

The university area lies north-east of the citadel. From Piaţa Bernády György walk east along Str Bernády György onto Str Mihai Viteazul. Immediately behind the citadel walls is the private **Petru Maior University** (Universitatea Petru Maior). It is named after a leading 19th-century intellectual and staunch defender of the rights of Romanians living in Transylvania, who published *The History of the Origin of the Romanians in Dacia* in 1812.

Immediately opposite is Târgu Mureş' **Theatre School**. Founded primarily as a Hungarian school before the war, it quickly became renowned as the top drama school in Transylvania. However, during the ethnic purges on all non-Romanians during Ceauşescu's regime, the school's flawless reputation suffered serious damage; Romanian students were given preferential treatment over Hungarian students and

today 40% of the school's population Hungarian.

Continue north-east along Str Miha Viteazul, then turn right onto Str Nicolae Grigorescu. Immediately after the students' Culture House (Casa de Cultură), turn left along Str Dr Gheorghe Marinescu. The **Medical University** (Universitatea de Medicină şi Farmacie) is a magnificent 1950s building beyond the hospital.

Directly opposite the university is the **Romanian Heroes' Park** (Parcul Eroilor Români), dominated by a large memorial to those who died during WWII.

Activities

Mountain-bike rental and tours are offered by the Robike Mountain Bike Service – see Getting Around, later.

Special Events

Carnival comes to Târgu Mureş on the last weekend in June when the city hosts its Târgu Mureş Days. At the end of May, a two day Art-Fest takes place. In the village of Voivodeni, 25km north of Târgu Mureş, a week-long folk festival is celebrated most years in June or July.

Places to Stay

The cheapest bet is *Hotel Sport* (☎ *131 913, Str Griviţa Roşie 33*) a five-minute walk from the train station. It is popular with locals passing through town for the night. Single/double/triple rooms cost $4/7.50/11. Two rooms share one bathroom. A two-room apartment with private bath is $12.

East of the centre near the Theatre School is the upmarket *Pensiune Ana Maria* (☎ *164 401, Str A L Papui Ilarian 17*). This small, privately run hotel has eight beautifully furnished rooms complete with 'real' double beds and crisp, white linen sheets for $18/26/33.50, including the best breakfast in town.

Hotel Tineretului (☎ *217 441, 216 774, Str Nicolae Grigorescu 17–19*), inside the university students' Culture House, has 44 double rooms with shared bath for $28 a night including breakfast. Romanians pay just $18.

the centre, the cheapest is *Hotel Tran-vania* (☎ *165 616, fax 166 028, Piaţa Trandafirilor 46)*, with pleasant singles/doubles for $16/30 and a four-person apartment for $60, including breakfast. Staff speak English and do their best to help, though seldom smile.

The unexciting *Hotel Grand* (☎ *160 711, fax 130 289, Piaţa Victoriei 28–30)* has clean, old-fashioned rooms, most of which are usually guestless. Rooms with private shower are $17/30 a night, including a coffeeless breakfast (coffee is an extra $0.40).

Drab from the outside but bright inside is the expensive *Hotel Continental* (☎/fax *160 999, fax 216 247, ⓔ contims@netsoft.ro, Piaţa Teatrului 6)*. Plush singles/doubles/triples with private bath cost $50/64/75, including breakfast.

Places to Eat

Restaurants & Cafes One of the most modern – and pricey – places in town is *Ornella*, on Piaţa Teatrului behind Hotel Continental. It serves good espresso, cappuccino, and amazing chocolate-filled crepes on its terrace. The terrace of the cheaper *Trocodero*, on Piaţa Teatrului beneath the Librăria Mihai Eminescu bookshop, is a popular lunch spot; light snacks only.

Restaurant Mureşul was traditionally the top restaurant in town, though it's now looking a little tired. It has a pleasant terrace overlooking Piaţa Trandafirilor and the beefsteak served on a wooden platter and topped with a fried egg ($2.60) is quite a treat.

Next door, the modern *Restaurant Leo* serves pizzas, steak and chips in a fast-food atmosphere. You can dine outside on the busy street or inside at one of its many bench tables.

For excellent Hungarian goulash ($0.80) you can't beat *Restaurant Terasa Parc*, just off the southern end of Piaţa Trandafirilor. It has a wonderfully pleasant outdoor courtyard; open 8 am to midnight daily.

Excellent pizzas and pasta are served at *Venezia Restaurant and Pizzerie*, opposite the Roman Catholic church. Try the *rustica* pizza ($1.85), a delicious mix of ricotta cheese, pork and Italian spices.

The *Brasserie Universităţii*, on Str Mihai Viteazul, is a small shopping and cafe complex serving the student fraternity.

Fast Food Next to Cinema Artă, *Fast Food Express* slaps out kebabs and hamburgers for $0.60; open 24 hours. The small, modern *Panda* (Piaţa Trandafirilor 15) serves microwaved pizza and an excellent choice of 'pick and mix' salads costing around $1.20/1.80 for a small/large tub; open 24 hours.

McDonald's, at the southern end of Piaţa Trandafirilor, has outdoor seating and is open 8 am to 11 pm daily (to midnight Friday to Sunday).

Eddie Pizza, on Str Gheorghe Doja, south of the centre on the way to the bus station, serves pizzas for $1.15, ham and *sniţel* burgers for $0.30 and omelettes; open 24 hours.

Self-Catering Stock up on groceries at the *Extra* supermarket at Piaţa Trandafirilor 36–41; open 6.30 am to 9 pm daily.

Entertainment

Cinemas Films in English are screened at *Cinema Tineretului* (Piaţa Trandafirilor 14), at $0.62/0.42 for adults/students, and *Cinema Artă* ($0.80/0.52) on the opposite side of the square.

Discos The disco at the *Cuba Libre Music Pub* (Str Nicolae Grigorescu 17–19), inside the university's Culture House (☎ 216 066), rocks from 10 pm to 4 am Thursday to Sunday.

Opera & Theatre The main focus of Piaţa Teatrului is the *National Opera & Theatre* (☎ 212 335, 214 240) which hosts a colourful array of plays and operettas in Romanian. Tickets can be bought in advance from the ticket office (☎ 212 522) inside the main theatre building; open 10 am to 1 pm and 5 to 7 pm Tuesday to Friday, and 10 am to 1 pm weekends. The theatre breaks for summer in July and August.

Târgu Mureş also has a small *puppet theatre* just north of Piaţa Petőfi on Blvd Timişoarei.

Getting There & Away

Air Tarom operates five weekly flights between Bucharest and Târgu Mureş ($43/70 single/return). The Tarom office (☎ 136 200) at Piaţa Trandafirilor 6–8 is open 8 am to 6 pm weekdays, and 8 am to noon Saturday.

Train The Agenţie de Voiaj CFR (☎ 166 203) at Piaţa Teatrului 1 is open 7.30 am to 7.30 pm weekdays. Its staff speak English and are of the rare species who smile.

From Târgu Mureş there is one train daily to Budapest: the *Claudiopolis* departs at 1.03 pm, arriving in Budapest (783km) at 10.22 pm. The return train leaves Budapest at 12.05 pm and arrives in Târgu Mureş at 11.22 pm.

Târgu Mureş is at the end of a branch line off the main Cluj-Napoca–Bucharest line. To get to Alba Iulia from Târgu Mureş, you often have to change trains at Războieni or Teiuş.

The left-luggage room (open 24 hours) is next to the information office, as you enter from the platform.

Bus The bus station (☎ 121 458, 137 774) is a five-minute walk south of the train station on Str Gheorghe Doja. Daily bus services include one to Braşov (172km), Sibiu (125km), Bistriţa (92km), Cluj-Napoca (108km), Făgăraş (146km), Mediaş (71km) and Miercurea Ciuc (140km); two to Corneşti (20km) and Găleşti (25km); three to Odorheiu Secuiesc (115km) and Sovata (67km); and four to Sighişoara (54km). On weekends some services are reduced.

Hungary A public bus departs from Târgu Mureş for Budapest at 8 am Friday, arriving at Budapest Népstadion at 6.45 pm. The return bus leaves Budapest on Sunday at 2 pm, arriving in Târgu Mureş at 1.45 am the following morning. Tickets ($6.50/10.50 single/return) are sold in advance at the bus station in Târgu Mureş.

More expensive private buses also depart daily from Târgu Mureş for Budapest. Inter Tours (see Tourist Offices, earlier) operates a daily bus to Budapest ($12.50/19 single/return), departing from the central bus station at 4 pm Monday, Wednesday, Thursday and Saturday, 6 pm T̶ 3 pm Friday and 7 am Sunday.

Western Europe TransEuropa (☎ 164 0r̶ Piaţa Trandafirilor 22, operates a bus se̶ vice from Târgu Mureş to Germany departing from outside the office at 7 am on Tuesday, Thursday and Saturday.

The German bus companies König Reisen and Mihu Reisen also operate buses to/from Târgu Mureş. Buses leave from outside the offices of Turism Grand (see Tourist Offices, earlier) at 8 am Friday and Saturday. A Kessler bus departs from the same place at 5.30 am daily. Tickets have to be bought in advance from the Turism Grand travel agency.

Getting Around

To/From the Airport Târgu Mureş airport (☎ 132 738) is 10km south of the city in the Ungheni district. Tarom operates a shuttle bus for its clients; it meets incoming flights and leaves 1½ hours before outgoing flights.

Bus Târgu Mureş is small enough to cover by foot. Bus Nos 2, 16 and 17 go to the bus station. Bus Nos 11, 18, 20 and 23 run from the centre along Str Mihai Eminescu to the hospitals and university area.

Taxi To call a taxi dial ☎ 941 or 943.

Bicycle Bicycle is a popular form of local transport in Târgu Mureş. The young team at Robike Mountain Bike Service (☎ 160 385), Str Bolyai 24, are able to help you with all your biking needs – though they don't have maps. They even hire bikes for $10.50 a day. The shop works in conjunction with Corbet Transair (see Tourist Offices) organising biking tours around Transylvania. See also Mountain Biking in the special section Exploring the Carpathian Mountains.

AROUND TÂRGU MUREŞ

Sovata spa resort, Praid salt mines and Corund, famed for its traditional black pottery, can all be visited in a day trip from Târgu Mureş.

a Băi & Praid

a Băi (Szováta in Hungarian) is 67km of Târgu Mureş. The spa developed as ashionable resort in the early 19th entury and retains much of its former elegance. Five lakes dominate the resort, bearing such colourful names as Red Lake (Lacu Roşu), Hazelnut Lake (Lacu Aluniş) and Black Lake (Lacu Negru). Each is renowned for its curative waters although it was the largest lake – aptly named Bear Lake (Lacu Ursu) – which most bathers flocked to during the 19th century. It allegedly cured sterility. The Hazelnut and Black Lakes were popular for their sapropelic mud. Sovata's salted lakes continue to draw crowds today.

The salt mines and lakes of Praid (Parajd in Hungarian) are an easy 7km south from Sovata. Asthma sufferers and folk with bronchial disorders are treated in the underground sanatorium sheltered in part of the giant salt mines, still operational today. Guided tours are available.

Trans-Tur (☎ 066-240 272, ☎/fax 570 484), Str Principală 211, Praid, is an agent for Antrec and arranges rooms in rural homes in Praid and its surrounding towns and villages. Some 31 families are involved in this flourishing agro-tourism scheme. A bed for the night starts at $15 and meals cost an additional $2.

Getting There & Away Sovata Băi is 3km east of Sovata village. From Târgu Mureş, buses depart daily for Sovata Băi (1½ hours) at 6.15 am, noon and 1, 2.30, 3.30 and 6 pm. There are no buses from Târgu Mureş to Praid. From Miercurea Ciuc there are buses daily to Sovata Băi via Praid, departing at 6.45 am and 2.30 pm.

All Târgu Mureş' hotels arrange excursions to Praid. From the train halt (a scheduled stop) in Sovata village, there are local trains daily to Praid (15 minutes, 7km) at 10.22 am and 6.22 pm. From Praid, trains leave for Sovata at 3.30 and 11.30 am.

Corund

Continuing for 12km south from Praid towards Odorheiu Secuiesc you pass through the small village of Corund (Korond), where the age-old craft of pottery remains the mainstay of the village today. Coachloads of tourists descend on the place in summer en route to/from Sovata and Praid.

Local potters sell their wares from openair stalls set up in the centre of the village. Many simply lay out their colourful crafts on the grass.

The history of this potters' village is briefly outlined in the small **History Museum** (Muzeul de Istorie), housed in a small white cottage down a mud road, just off the main road, in the village centre. If it's locked, continue along the mud road to house No 461 and ask for the key. As you enter the village from the north, this road is on the left immediately before the main cluster of craft stalls.

Trans-Tur in Praid (see Sovata & Praid previously) can arrange accommodation in private houses in Corund for $15 a night.

ODORHEIU SECUIESC
☎ 066

Odorheiu Secuiesc (Székelyudvarhely in Hungarian) lies 48km west of Miercurea Ciuc on the road to Sighişoara. Settled on an ancient Roman military camp, Odorheiu Secuiesc developed as a small craft town during the reigns of the Hungarian Árpád kings between the 11th and 13th centuries. In 1485 King Matthias Corvinus (r. 1458–90) granted Odorheiu Secuiesc 'free royal town' status, enabling its many different craft guilds to host commercial fairs. Trade boomed until the 1600s when, following a series of damaging attacks by the Turks, the town fell into decline.

With a 98% ethnic Hungarian population, Odorheiu Secuiesc is the most Hungarian town in Romania.

Orientation

The train station at Str Bethlen Gábor 63 is a 10-minute walk from the centre. Exit the station and turn left (south) down Str Bethlen Gábor until you come to Piaţa Harghitei. From here bear right to get to Piaţa Libertăţii.

The bus station is 100m south of the train station at Str Târgului 10. Exit the bus

ODORHEIU SECUIESC (SZÉKELYUDVARHELY)

PLACES TO STAY & EAT
6 Hotel Târnava; ATM
8 Bohem Bar & Fast Food
12 Restaurant Fényes

OTHER
1 Greco-Catholic Church
2 Citadel
3 Gössel Beer Bar
4 Franciscan Church
  & Monastery
5 Telephone Office
7 Korona Bar
9 Hungarian Reformed
  Church
10 Corvina Bookshop
11 Roman Catholic Church
13 Haáz Rezsó Museum
14 Post Office; ACR
15 Orthodox Church
16 Banc Post

To Train & Bus Stations,
Agenție de Voiaj CFR,
Chapel of Jesus & Miercurea Ci

TRANSYLVANIA

0   150   300m
0   150   300yd

station and turn right on to Str Bethlen Gábor then head south into town.

Many of the sights are around Piața Libertății. To get to the citadel, walk north-east from the square along Str Cetății. Str Kossuth Lajos runs south off Piața Libertății.

Maps Buy a copy of the excellent city map *Odorheiu Secuiesc Map of the Town* (Top-Gráf, 1998) for $1.20 from the Corvina bookshop at Piața Libertății 23; open 9 am to 6 pm weekdays, and 9 am to 1 pm Saturday.

Information

The staff at the reception of Hotel Târnava are helpful and speak some English; the hotel also has an ATM. Get cash advances on Visa/MasterCard at the Banc Post on Str Kossuth Lajos, opposite the Orthodox church; it's open 8 am to 1 pm, and 2 to 5.30 pm weekdays, and has an outside ATM.

The post office at Str Kossuth Lajos 33 is open 7 am to 8 pm weekdays. The tele-phone office, on Piața Libertății near Hotel Târnava, is open 7 am to 9 pm weekdays. The ACR (☎ 212 046, 211 804) has an office in the same building as the post office; the entrance is around the back down an alley off the main street.

Things to See

Odorheiu Secuiesc's medieval **citadel** (vár), built between 1492 and 1516, is almost fully intact today, and houses an agricultural college. Visitors can freely stroll in the grounds around its inner walls.

Odorheiu Secuiesc has no fewer than two Greco-Catholic, two Orthodox, three Hungarian Reformed, and four Roman Catholic churches. From the citadel, walk south down Str Cetății towards the main square, Piața Libertății. At the western end of the square stands the **Franciscan Monastery & Church** (Szent Ferencrendi Templom és Kolostor; built 1712–79). Walk east past the impressive **city hall** (1895–96) to the 18th-century

...ue **Hungarian Reformed Church** (Re-
...nátus Templom). Bearing right onto
...ţa Márton you come to one of the town's
...rst **Roman Catholic churches** (Római Ka-
tolikus Plébániatemplom; built 1787–91).

Unfortunately, the town's best church
lies 2km north of the centre on Str Bethlen
Gábor. The **Chapel of Jesus** (Jézus kápolna)
is among the oldest architectural monuments in Transylvania, built during the
early 13th century. The chapel gained its
name from the war cries of Székely warriors who, during a Tartar invasion in 1241,
cried to Jesus for help. They won and built
a chapel to commemorate their victory.

Odorheiu Secuiesc's colourful history is
explained – in Hungarian – in the **Haáz
Rezsó Museum** at Str Kossuth Lajos 29.
The museum was founded from a collection
of folk objects belonging to local art teacher
Haáz Rezsó from 1900 onwards. It is open
9 am to 5 pm Tuesday to Sunday.

Places to Stay & Eat

At the two-star *Hotel Târnava* (*Târnava
Szálló;* ☎ *213 963, fax 218 371, Piaţa Libertăţii 16*), in the centre of town, mediocre
singles/doubles start from $9.50/12 a night,
including breakfast. Another alternative is a
room in the *motel* above the petrol station
on your left as you enter Odorheiu Secuiesc
on the main road from the south.

Restaurant Fényes (*Str Kossuth Lajos
19*) is your typical large, empty, age-old
restaurant. For fast food, look no further
than *Bohem*, on Piaţa Harghitei, a simple
bar and fast-food joint.

Korona Bar overlooking Piaţa Libertăţii,
and *Gössel* beer bar opposite the citadel ruins
on the corner of Str Cetăţii and Str Tompa
Lázló, are two pleasant drinking holes.

Getting There & Away

Train The Agenţie de Voiaj CFR, for booking advance train tickets, is at the train station (☎ 213 653) at Str Bethlen Gábor 63.
Odorheiu Secuiesc is on a branch line off the
main Braşov–Cluj-Napoca railroad.

From Odorheiu Secuiesc there are local
trains to Sighişoara from where you can
take a train to Cluj-Napoca, Copşa Mică,

Braşov, Mediaş, Oradea, Predeal and Târgu
Mureş. Local trains from Odorheiu Secuiesc to Sighişoara (1¼ hours) depart at 6.17
am, and 2.21 and 9.15 pm. Return trains
depart from Sighişoara at 4.20 and 11.41
am, and 8.30 pm.

Bus The bus station (☎ 217 979) is located
north-east of the centre at Str Târgului 10.
From Odorheiu Secuiesc there is one bus
daily to Gheorgheni (102km) except weekends, five buses a day to Târgu Mureş
(115km), and seven buses a day to Miercurea Ciuc (48km).

GHEORGHENI & AROUND
Gheorgheni

Approximately 90% of the population of
Gheorgheni ('gore-gen'; Gyergyószentmik-
lós in Hungarian) – nestled between the
Gurghiu Mountains and the Eastern
Carpathians – is Hungarian. Dubbed the
'cold pole', due to its long winters, it has
little to see but makes a good base for exploring the surrounding region

The **Tarisznyás Márton County Museum**
(Városi Múzeum Tarisznyás Márton),
named after its Székely founder, is in an
18th-century building on Piaţa Petőfi
Sándor and worth a visit.

Places to Stay There's a camping ground
at *Motel 4* (☎ *066-165 062*), on Blvd Lacu
Roşu, 4km east of the centre. Camping
costs $2.50 per person. In Gheorgheni, the
Szilágyi Hotel (*Szilágyi Szálló;* ☎ *066-164
591*), on Piaţa Libertăţii, has double/triple
rooms with private bath for $11/15.50.

Doubles with shared bath cost $5 at
Hotel Sport (*Sport Szálló;* ☎ *066-161 270,
Str Stadionului 11*). *Hotel Mureş* (*Maros
Szálló;* ☎ *066-161 904*), on Blvd Frăţiei
opposite the Culture House, was closed for
renovation at the time of writing and was
due to open again early 2001.

Getting There & Away The bus and train
stations are 1.5km west of the centre on Str
Gării.

There are three daily buses to Cluj-
Napoca (168km) and daily buses to Braşov

(150km), Lăzarea (6km), Odorheiu Secuiesc (102km), Miercurea Ciuc (57km), Piatra Neamţ (82km) and Târgu Neamţ (160km).

Buses to Budapest leave from Piaţa Libertăţii ($14, 6 am, noon and 4 pm daily except Saturday). Tour Inform (☎/fax 066-164 568), Piaţa Libertăţii 17, sells tickets for private buses to Hungary.

Lăzarea & Ditrău

Just 6km north of Gheorgheni on the road to Topliţa is the tiny village of Lăzarea (Gyergyószárhegy). Dating from 1235, the predominantly Hungarian village is dominated by its 16th-century castle. It was to Lăzarea Castle that Gábor Bethlen, later to become prince of Transylvania (r. 1613–29), came to seek solace following the death of his son in 1590. The castle is open to visitors 9 am to 5 pm Tuesday to Sunday.

Below the castle is a 17th-century Franciscan monastery. Signposts from the centre of the village also direct tourists to the village water mill and water-powered sawmill.

Ditrău (Ditró), 8km north of Lăzarea, was the site of a bloody battle (1658) between Turkish-Tartar forces and local villagers. The Székely army, which included many women, forced the Turks to retreat. An obelisk in memory of those who died stands on the hilltop, known as 'Tartar Hill'.

Places to Stay Lăzarea has a thriving agro-tourism scheme, thanks to the Belgian charity Opération Villages Roumains. A bed for the night in a *private home* is $13 per person, including breakfast. Full board costs $17. It is also possible to hire a local guide to show you around for $10 a day. The agrotourism office (☎/fax 066-164 191), signposted 'Birou OVR', is in the centre of the village next to the post office at Str Principală 1082. If it is closed, ask for the house of Emma Pap, who lives at house No 1285.

Lacu Roşu

From Gheorgheni the road heads east 26km across the Bucin mountain pass to reveal Lacu Roşu (Red Lake in English, Gyilkos tó in Hungarian). The lake is strangely filled with dead tree stumps which jut out of its murky waters at 45° angles a᷍ sidered one of Romania's weirdes. wonders. Legend has it that the 'red l. 'killer lake' was formed from the fl᷍ blood of a group of picnickers who had misfortune to be sitting beneath the mou. tain side when it collapsed, crushing then. to death. In fact, a landslide did occur in 1838, eventually flooding the valley and damming the Bicaz River.

The thriving alpine resort which sprang up around Lacu Roşu in the 1970s is today, unfortunately, as dead as the tree stumps in the lake. From Lacu Roşu, the road continues east to the magnificent Bicaz Gorges in Moldavia. This road is among the most dramatic in the country and should not be missed (see the Bicaz & the Bicaz Gorges section in the Moldavia chapter).

Places to Stay Wild camping is permitted, every other house displays a *cazare* (room) sign and there are plenty of hotels and villas to choose from.

Top-notch is *Vila Borş (mobile ☎ 094-129 791 or 092-760 159)*, a little white palace overlooking the southern end of the lake. Once Ceauşescu's hunting lodge, its palace is open to all; visitors can even sleep in the dictator's former bedroom. Regular doubles with/without private bath cost $22/17. The villa is signposted on the left almost immediately after you enter Lacu Roşu from the south.

In the centre of the resort overlooking the lake is the recently renovated *Vila Andrei (mobile ☎ 095-611 720)*. Doubles/triples with private bath are $15/20. The villa also has a handful of cheaper three/four-bed rooms with shared bath for $4 per person.

Getting There & Away There is a daily bus from Gheorgheni to Lacu Roşu, (26km, 8.30 am). From Miercurea Ciuc there is a bus daily to Piatra Neamţ via Lacu Roşu (10.20 am).

MIERCUREA CIUC

☎ 066 • postcode 4100 • pop 47,000

Miercurea Ciuc (Csíkszereda in Hungarian), 85km east of Sighişoara, is the capital of Székely Land. It is also renowned for the

TRANSYLVANIA

...r (pronounced 'chook') that is ...here.

...city was founded during the reign of ...arian king Ladislaus I (r. 1077–95) ...and a castle which the king built for ...mself. Craft fairs were held every Wednesday around the citadel walls and Miercurea Ciuc quickly developed into a prosperous commercial centre and the hub of Székely cultural activities.

Miercurea Ciuc is the stronghold of Székely culture. Most signs in the town are written in Hungarian. Given its location in the Ciuc depression, Miercurea Ciuc is one of the coldest towns in Romania. Its annual average temperature is 5.9°C.

A rash of traditional Székely villages – **Leliceni** (4km south-east), **Misentea** and **Ciucsângeorgiu** (another 2km and 4km south), and **Armaseni** (2km north of the latter along a dirt track) – lie within easy reach of Miercurea Ciuc.

Orientation

The train and bus stations are a 10-minute walk west of the centre on Str Braşovului. Exit the train station and bear right along Str Mihail Sadoveanu towards Piaţa Majláth

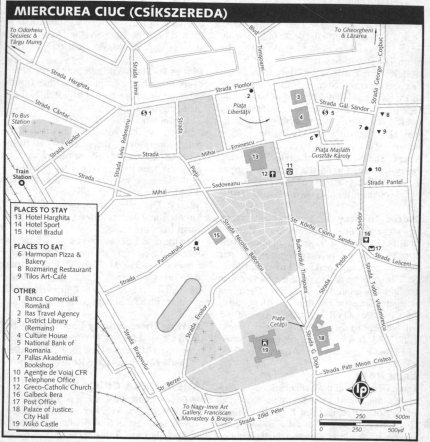

MIERCUREA CIUC (CSÍKSZEREDA)

To Odorheiu Secuiesc & Târgu Mureş

To Gheorgheni & Lăzarea

To Bus Station

Train Station

Piaţa Libertăţii

Piaţa Majláth Gusztáv Károly

Piaţa Cetăţii

To Nagy-Imre Art Gallery, Franciscan Monastery & Braşov

PLACES TO STAY
13 Hotel Harghita
14 Hotel Sport
15 Hotel Bradul

PLACES TO EAT
6 Harmopan Pizza & Bakery
8 Rozmaring Restaurant
9 Tilos Art-Café

OTHER
1 Banca Comercială Română
2 Itas Travel Agency
3 District Library (Remains)
4 Culture House
5 National Bank of Romania
7 Pallas Akadémia Bookshop
10 Agenţie de Voiaj CFR
11 Telephone Office
12 Greco-Catholic Church
16 Galbeck Bera
17 Post Office
18 Palace of Justice; City Hall
19 Mikó Castle

Strada Harghita · Strada Cântar · Strada Florilor · Strada Inimii · Blvd Timişoarei · Strada George Coşbuc · Strada Florilor · Strada Gál Sándor · Strada Liviu Rebreanu · Strada · Strada · Mihai Eminescu · Sadoveanu · Strada Pantel · Strada Nicolae Bălcescu · Str Kőrösi Csörna Sandor · Bulevardul Timişoara · Sándor · Petőfi · Strada Leliceni · Strada Tudor Vladimirescu · Strada Patinoarului · Strada · Strada Erolor · Strada Braşovului · Strada Berzei · Strada G Doja · Strada Patr Miron Cristea · Strada Zöld Péter

0   250   500m
0   250   500yd

Gusztáv Károly. At the crossroads, turn left along Blvd Timişoara to get to Piaţa Libertăţii – the other main square. The bus station is 50m north of the train station.

Maps Buy a copy of the quality *Miercurea Ciuc Map* when you arrive. It is published by Topo Service in English, Romanian and Hungarian, and costs $1.20 in bookshops.

Information

The staff at Hotel Bradul (see Places to Stay) at Str Nicolae Bălcescu 11 are helpful and speak English.

The Itas travel agency (☎ 122 202, fax 111 555), Str Florilor 26, sells tickets for buses to Hungary and arranges excursions to places of interest in the region.

Change money and get cash advances on Visa/MasterCard at the Banca Comercială Română (Kereskedelmi Bank), Str Florilor 19. The bank is open 8.30 am to 5 pm weekdays and 8.30 am to noon Saturday.

The post office is on Str Leliceni, not far from the Galbeck Berărie; open 7 am to 1.30 pm and 2 to 8 pm weekdays, and 8.30 am to 1 pm Saturday. The central telephone office is at the western end of Piaţa Majláth Gusztáv Károly on the corner of Blvd Timişoara; open 7 am to 8 pm weekdays, 8 am to 3 pm Saturday, and 2 pm to 8 pm Sunday.

City Centre

Miercurea Ciuc's centrepiece is its **Mikó Castle** which today houses the impressive **Székely Museum of Csík** (Csíki Székely Múzeum; ☎ 111 727). The castle (built 1611–21) was built as a residence for the Hungarian commander-in-chief of the Székely districts, Ference Mikó. Dubbed the 'Golden Bastion' for its sheer luxury and Renaissance finery, the castle was burnt to the ground by Tartars in 1661. The castle was then rebuilt in 1716.

The history of the town is told in the museum, and a library of some 8000 books survives from Miercurea Ciuc's 17th-century Franciscan monastery. There are also many archaeological exhibits and an ethnographic section featuring the traditional, brightly coloured woven fabrics;

open 9 am to 5 pm Tuesday to S $($0.50)$. Statues of the 1848 revolutio Nicolae Bălcescu (1819–1852) and F garian poet Sándor Petőfi (1823–49) sta in front of the entrance.

Miercurea Ciuc's **Palace of Justice** (1904) and **city hall** (1884–98), both built in an eclectic style, face Bălcescu and Petőfi on the opposite side of Piaţa Cetăţii.

From Piaţa Cetăţii walk back north up Blvd Timişoara into the modern centre. At the northern end of Piaţa Libertăţii turn right onto Str Florilor, then take the first right. This leads you to the heart of the city's **Civic Centre**, created in the late 1980s as part of Ceauşescu's systemisation plans. While most of the older buildings in this area were bulldozed to make way for concrete blocks, a canary-yellow, regal building which housed the **National Bank of Romania** (1903) managed to survive – just. In 1984 the entire building was uprooted from its foundations and moved 128m east on rollers to make way for the **district library**, which has since been demolished.

Miercurea Ciuc was also the birthplace of the revered Székely painter Nagy Imre (1893–1976). The **Nagy-Imre Art Gallery** (Nagy-Imre Galéria; ☎ 113 963), south of the centre at Str Nagy Imre 175, displays various works by the artist whose body rests in the walls of the whitewashed church. The gallery is open 9 am to 5 pm Tuesday to Sunday ($0.30).

Franciscan Monastery

Two kilometres south of the centre in the Şumuleu district (Csíksomlyó in Hungarian) is a fine Franciscan monastery, built in 1442 by Iancu de Hunedoara (János Hunyadi), governor of Hungary in 1446–52, to commemorate his great victory against the Turks at Marosszentimre.

The monastery today is a major pilgrimage site for Székelys who flock here on Whit Sunday to celebrate their brotherhood. The pilgrimage dates from 1567 when, in an attempt to convert the Székely peoples to Catholicism, Hungarian troops attacked the monastery. On Whit Sunday a bloody battle was fought on a field close to the

…ery, from which the Székely side
…ged triumphant.

…aces to Stay

…otel Sport (Sport Szálló; ☎ 116 161), on
Str Patinoarului, is Miercurea Ciuc's bargain-
basement hotel. Surprisingly user-friendly,
it is close to the stadium, and has double
rooms with shared bath for $10 a night. It
also has four rooms with private bath for
$14. The hotel reception is in room No 19
on the 2nd floor.

Around the corner is **Hotel Bradul**
(Fenyö Szálló; ☎ 111 493, fax 171 176, Str
Nicolae Bălcescu 11), next to the town's
hockey club. This 198-room tower block
has singles/doubles with private bath for
$15/22.50, including breakfast.

Hotel Harghita (Hargita Szálló; ☎ 171
543, fax 113 181), overlooking the central
Piaţa Libertăţii on the corner of Str Mihai
Eminescu and Blvd Timişoara, considers itself the classy joint in town. Rooms with private bath are $17/28, including breakfast.

Places to Eat

The extremely stylish **Tilos Art-Café** (Cafe-
neaus Tilos; ☎ 116 814) on Str Gál Sándor
is decked out like an old-fashioned bookshop inside and has tables on the street
outside in summer. The town's young
bohemians hang out here.

Harmopan Pizza slaps out microwaved
pizza doused with ketchup for about $1 a
slice. It also has a **bakery** inside which sells
great fresh bread and cakes. From the southern end of Piaţa Libertăţii turn left onto Str
Mihai Eminescu.

Rozmaring Restaurant (☎ 115 841), on
Str Gál Sándor, is a traditional Hungarian
restaurant serving more substantial meals.

Entertainment

Off-beat art films are screened weekly at the
Kriterion Art-Video Film Klub on Str
George Coşbuc, inside Kriterion House (Ház
Kriterion) above the Pallas Akadémia Book-
shop. Look for posters inside Tilos Art-Café.

The **AMI Club** disco is held in the Culture
House (Városi Művelődési) from 10 pm to
2 am Friday and 10 pm to 3 am weekends.

For a good old pint of British bitter look
no further than **Galbeck Berărie** (Galbeck
Söröző) on the corner of Str Petőfi Sándor
and Str Leliceni.

Getting There & Away

Train The Agenţie de Voiaj CFR (☎ 111
924), at the eastern end of Piaţa Majláth
Gusztáv Károly at Str Petőfi Sándor 23, is
open 7.30 am to 6 pm weekdays.

From Miercurea Ciuc there are five local
trains and six express trains daily to Braşov
(2¼ to 3¼ hours, 95km) and two express
trains daily to Bucharest (five hours, 234km).

Bus The bus station (☎ 124 334) is 50m
north of the train station on Str Braşovului.
Miercurea Ciuc is well served by buses to
other destinations in Romania. Daily ser-
vices include two buses to Sovata Băi via
Praid (92km); Piatra Neamţ (139km) via
Gheorgheni (57km); Târgu Mureş (140km)
and Târgu Neamţ (217km); six daily to
Odorheiu Secuiesc (48km); and four to
Băile Tuşnad (29km).

Buses to Budapest leave Miercurea Ciuc
bus station at 7 am Wednesday and 3.30 pm
Friday. Tickets for buses to Budapest
($14/22 single/return) must be purchased in
advance and are sold at the station.

Tickets for the more expensive private
buses to Budapest can be purchased from
Itas travel agency (see Information).

SFÂNTU GHEORGHE

☎ 067 • postcode 4000 • pop 67,000
Sfântu Gheorghe (Sepsiszentgyörgy), on
the banks of the Olt River, is a truly Hungarian stronghold with more than two-thirds
of its population laying claim to Székely
origin. The town has its own Hungarian
daily newspaper, Háromszék, and one of
Romania's two Hungarian State Theatres,
while most street signs and shop boards
bear just one language – Magyar.

First documented in 1332, Sfântu Gheorghe developed as a cultural centre for the
Székelys from the 15th century onwards
when it became a free town, bearing the
right to host commercial fairs. The town
was left devastated by Turkish attacks

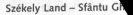

SFÂNTU GHEORGHE (SEPSISZENTGYÖRGY)

PLACES TO STAY
1 Hotel Consic
8 Hotel Bodoc
16 Hotel Parc

PLACES TO EAT
11 Restaurant Sugás
   Vendéglő
12 Tribel F
17 Restaurant Parc

OTHER
2 Memorial House of
   Gyárfás Jenö
3 Automobil Clubul
   Român (ACR)
4 Culture House
5 Statue of Mihai Viteazul
6 Prefecture

7 Képtár Art Gallery
9 Agenţie de Turism
   Treff; Currency
   Exchange
10 Post & Telephone Office
13 Hungarian State Theatre
14 County Library
15 Hungarian Democratic
   Alliance
18 Alimentar
19 House of Archways
20 Orthodox Cathedral
21 Agenţie de Voiaj CFR
22 Banca Comercială
   Română
23 International Tourism
   & Trade (IT&T)
24 Székely National
   Museum

TRANSYLVANIA

between 1658 and 1671, its population dwindling further after the plague swept through the city in 1717.

Orientation

The bus station and train stations are on Str Avanţului, 10 minutes' walk from the centre. Top-Gráf produces the superb *Sfântu Gheorghe Map of the Town* (1997) with a city map, Romanian-Hungarian street register, and a short historical explanation of the town in English, Romanian and Hungarian. It is sold for $1.25 in most bookshops and travel agencies.

Information

Tourist Offices International Tourism & Trade (IT&T; ☎ 316 375, fax 351 551, ⓔ it&t@honoris.ro), Str Jozef Bem 2, is the top travel agency-cum-tourist office in town. Its English-speaking staff arrange car rental, guided tours, plus accommodation at Ceauşescu's former hunting lodge. The

office is open 9 am to 5 pm weekdays. Also top-notch are the staff at the Agenţie de Turism Treff (☎/fax 351 591, ⓔ treff@ planet.ro) at Str Petőfi Sándor 5. The agency has local guides and translators for hire, sells maps and has a currency exchange; open 9 am to 4 pm weekdays.

Money The currency exchange inside the Agenţie de Turism Treff is open 9 am to 3.30 pm weekdays. You can get cash advances on Visa/MasterCard and cash travellers cheques at Banca Comercială Română, opposite IT&T on Str Jozef Bem, open 7.30 am to 11 am weekdays. There is also an ATM outside.

Post & Telephone The central post and telephone office is on the corner of Str Oltului and Str Petőfi Sándor. The post office is open 7 am to 8 pm weekdays, and 9 am to noon Saturday. The telephone office is open 7.30 am to 9 pm daily.

⌐l Centres The Democratic Alli-
⌐⌐ Hungarians in Romania (Romániai
⌐⌐ar Demokrata Szövetség; ☎ 316 152,
⌐⌐314 839) has its office at Str Gábor
⌐⌐on 14. It has a small library with mater-
⌐al in English as well as Hungarian.

Things to See

It was inside the building at Str Gábor Áron
14 (today housing the Democratic Alliance
of Hungarians in Romania) that revolutionary Áron Gábor announced to his comrades
on 23 November 1848 that the town should
'Bring in the cannons!' in their fight against
Habsburg rule. The cannons he was refer-
ring to were cast in his small village work-
shop just outside of Sfântu Gheorghe (see
the Around Sfântu Gheorghe section).

From Str Gábor Áron walk south to the
end of the park then turn left along Str Spi-
tatului Gábor. At the junction turn right along
Str Kós Károly until you reach the **Székely
National Museum** (Székely Nemzeti Múzeum; ☎ 312 442). The building itself is a
masterpiece, designed by leading Hungarian
architect Kós Károly (1883–1977) between
1911 and 1913. The museum, founded in
1879, provides the most comprehensive display of Székely culture today.

The museum has a large open-air section
exhibiting Székely porches, gates and
wooden houses. The main building has a
large exhibit on the 1848 revolution. It's open
9 am to 5 pm Tuesday to Sunday ($0.25).

From the museum, walk north up Str Kós
Károly, past the modern **Greco-Catholic
Church** (Unitárius Templom) built in 1991
on the right, until you come to the **Orthodox Cathedral** (Román Ortodox Kate-
drális), set slightly back off the road. Dating
from the 16th century, the church was only
designated a cathedral in the early 1990s
following the establishment of a bishopric
for Covasna and Harghita counties.

Continue north along Piaţa Libertăţii,
past the Hungarian State Theatre and adjoining art and crafts shop, then head west
towards Piaţa Gábor Áron. At the northern
end of the park you pass the **Képtár Art
Gallery**, which hosts a fine range of contemporary international art exhibitions.

Places to Stay

The cheapest is *Hotel Consic* (☎ 326 984,
Str Grigore Bălan 31), with doubles/triples
with private bath for $7.50/11.50 and four-
bed rooms with shared shower for $11;
breakfast isn't included.

The friendliest is *Hotel Parc* (☎ 311 058,
fax 311 826, Str Gábron Áron 14), hidden
amid wooded grounds. Singles/doubles/
triples with private bath and cable TV are
$16/20/27, including breakfast.

The dreariest is *Hotel Bodoc* (☎ 31 292,
fax 153 787), on Str Petöfi Sándor, your old-
style state hotel which has 40 singles/doubles
on offer for $23/26, including breakfast.

Arcus Castle (1870), built by Baron
Szentkereszti, was extensively renovated
under the orders of Ceauşescu. He poured
huge amounts of cash into it and stayed
there only twice. Travellers can stay in the
castle for $80 for a luxury apartment. Meals
can also be provided for an extra $4 per per-
son. Book through IT&T (see Tourist Offices), which can also provide transport to
the castle, 3km south of town.

Places to Eat

Sfântu Gheorghe offers few eating options.
The hot spot in town is the cheap and cheerful *Tribel F* (☎ 352 353), on Piaţa Libertăţii. The restaurant is divided into two
distinct sections: one side is an old-
fashioned self-service canteen, the other a
more hip pizzeria and bar. Its outside terrace
overlooks the main street.

Marginally more upmarket is the dreary
Restaurant Sugás Vendéglő, on Piaţa Libertăţii, which has all the characteristics of an
old Soviet-type ghetto. Much nicer is
Restaurant Parc (☎ 312 052), on Str Gábron
Áron next to Hotel Parc, overlooking the
wooded grounds. The restaurant specialises
in traditional Hungarian and Romanian
cuisine. A full meal costs around $2.

Stock up on supplies at the *Alimentar*
opposite the central park on the corner of
Str Şcolli and Piaţa Libertăţii.

Getting There & Away

Train The Agenţie de Voiaj CFR (☎ 311
680) at Str Şcolli 3 is open 9 am to 4 pm

weekdays. From Sfântu Gheorghe five trains daily go to Covasna (28km), four to Târgu Secuiesc (44km) and 14 to Braşov (32km).

Bus The bus station is 50m north of the train station on Str Avanţului. Daily bus services include nine to Arcus (3km); two to Covasna (28km); one bus a day to Băile Tuşnad (32km), Miercurea Ciuc (78km), Piatra Neamţ (214km), Târgu Neamţ (315km) and Braşov (32km); and three daily to Bodoc (11km). Services are reduced on weekends.

AROUND SFÂNTU GHEORGHE

The Fairy Queen Valley, an inclined-plane railway (until recently the last of its kind still in use in Europe) and the birthplace of the compiler of the first English-Tibetan dictionary are all here.

Covasna

The spa town of Covasna (Kovászna in Hungarian), 28km east of Sfântu Gheorghe in the 'Fairy Queen Valley' (Valea Zânelor), has long been dubbed the 'valley of a thousand springs' for its popular curative mineral water. The black mud that bubbles from the resort's 'Devil's Pond' (Baia Dracului) is more menacing.

The main appeal of this typical Romanian spa resort (560m) is its unique **inclined plane**, the starting point of Romania's oldest narrow-gauge forestry railway which snakes 10km up the western flanks of Mount Vrancei (1777m) to **Comandău** village. Unfortunately it's no longer in operation, but you can view the inclined plane from the bottom of the line in Covasna. A dirt road leads south-west from the centre of Covasna. See the Exploring the Carpathian Mountains special section for more information on the railway.

Places to Stay Covasna resort is centred on Valea Zânelor (formerly spelt Valea Zînelor) at the south-eastern end of Covasna village proper. *Hotel Covasna* (☎ 067-340 401, fax 342 222), on Str 1 Decembrie 1918, has doubles for $40 in high season, breakfast included. A minimum of seven

days stay is required. The more upm... *Hotel Căprioara* (☎ 067-340 401, fax . 222), a large concrete block next door, h... singles/doubles for $29/$46.

Getting There & Away From Sfântu Gheorghe there are two buses daily to Covasna (28km, 11 am and 3.30 pm).

Covasna is on a small branch railway line between Sfântu Gheorghe and Breţcu. Daily train services from Covasna include six trains daily to Sfântu Gheorghe (40 minutes), and four daily to Târgu Secuiesc (30 minutes) and Breţcu (two hours).

Târgu Secuiesc & Around

Târgu Secuiesc (Kézdivásárhely; literally 'market town'), 24km north of Covasna, is a quiet market town famed for the role a local ironsmith played in the 1848 uprising against Habsburg rule of Hungary.

The 1848 revolution in Székely Land was primarily led by Hungarian Liberation Front leader Lajos Kossuth and poet Sándor Petőfi. From October 1848 until June 1849 the revolutionaries were supplied with cannons cast by Székely ironsmith Áron Gábor who ran a small foundry in Târgu Secuiesc. Gábor cast the cannons from melted-down church bells donated by surrounding Székely villages happy to lose their church bell for the 'cause'. The cannons consequently became known as 'cannons of brass', while Áron Gábor was immortalised in a folk song praising his warfare creations. One of the cannons and tools used by the ironsmith are displayed in Târgu Secuiesc's **Áron Gábor Museum**. A statue of Áron Gábor stands in the central square.

Gábor was born 16km east of Târgu Secuiesc, in the village of **Breţcu** (Bereck). On 2 July 1849, following the intervention of Russian troops on behalf of the Habsburgs, he was shot in battle at **Chichis** (Kökös), 10km south of Sfântu Gheorghe. Revolutionaries attempted to carry their wounded leader to his home village for burial but in **Moacşa** (Maksa), 20km short of Târgu Secuiesc, he died. Fearing the approach of Russian troops, they buried Gábor in Moacşa. A large memorial tombstone rests

e his grave in the centre of the village
y.

etting There & Away Local trains from
Sfântu Gheorghe to Târgu Secuiesc via Covasna leave Sfântu Gheorghe daily at 5.08
am, and 1.07, 5.52 and 9.30 pm. Return
trains from Târgu Secuiesc depart at 7.12
am, and 3.25, 7.25 and 11.30 pm.

Băile Bálványos & Băile Tuşnad

From Târgu Secuiesc, it is a straight 26km
drive north to the unusual spa resorts of
Băile Bálványos and Băile Tuşnad, which
nestle in the eastern and western shores of
Lake St Anne (Lacu Sfânta Ana; Szt Anna
tó). Approaching from Sfântu Gheorghe,
you cross the spectacular Tuşnad Pass.

Lake St Anne, inside a volcanic crater on
Mount Ciumatu (950m), is steeped in legend. It is also the site of a Székely pilgrimage each year on 26 July. Since the
12th century pilgrims have flocked here to
pay homage to St Anne, the traditional protector of young women. Székely women
unable to conceive would also come here to
pray for a child. A wooden chapel was built
during the 12th century, which by the 17th
century had been replaced by a larger stone
building to serve the 30,000 to 40,000 pilgrims who visited the lake each year. It
remains a popular pilgrim site today.

Băile Bálványos is a small spa overlooking the lake to the east. It is the hot springs
in Băile Tuşnad (Tusnádfürdó), on the
lake's western shores, however, that attract
most travellers.

Places to Stay In Băile Bálványos, you
can stay at *Hotel Carpaţi* (☎/fax 067-360
700, ☎ 067-361 449, 01-312 9240). It has
singles/doubles for a pricey $40/60 a night.
The hotel offers numerous hot bath and
therapy treatments.

In Băile Tuşnad, you can camp at *Camping Univers* (☎ 066-116 319, Str Voinţa
18). There are also plenty of small villas
and private houses displaying *cazare*
(rooms) signs outside. The leading hotel for
self-pampering is *Hotel Tuşnad* (☎ 068-
151 258, fax 066-115 074, Str Olt 45). It

offers a mind-boggling choice of health
treatments including mud wraps, medical
gymnastics and cures for nervous-system
disorders. In summer a night in one of its
108 doubles is $25, including three meals a
day. The hotel is popular with group tours.

Getting There & Away There are buses to
Băile Tuşnad from Miercurea Ciuc (29km,
four daily) and Sfântu Gheorghe (32km,
one daily, 8.30 am).

Băile Tuşnad is also served by local trains
from Braşov (1½ hours), Sfântu Gheorghe
(45 minutes), Miercurea Ciuc (45 minutes)
and Gheorgheni (two hours). Six trains daily
follow this route. Don't alight at Tuşnad station, 6km north of Băile Tuşnad, by mistake.

Northern Transylvania

During WWII, northern Transylvania fell
under pro-Nazi Hungarian rule. Under the
Diktat of Vienna of 30 August 1940, the
Axis powers, Germany and Italy, forced
Romania to cede 43,493 sq km and a population of 2.6 million to Hungary. During the
four years of occupation, thousands of
Romanians were imprisoned and tortured
while entire villages were massacred.
Northern Transylvania was not recovered
until 25 October 1944 when, following the
liberation of Satu Mare, the territory fell
back into Romanian hands.

CLUJ-NAPOCA

☎ 064 • postcode 3400 • pop 332,000
Cut in two by the Someşul Mic River, Cluj-
Napoca is as Hungarian as it is Romanian.
Its location has long made its a crossroads,
which explains its present role as an educa-
tional and industrial centre. Known as
Klausenburg to the Germans and Kolozsvár
to the Hungarians, Cluj has added the old
Roman name of Napoca to its official title
to emphasise its Daco-Roman origin.

The history of Cluj-Napoca goes back to
Dacian times. In AD 124, during the reign
of Emperor Hadrian, Napoca attained

municipal status and Emperor Marcus Aurelius elevated it to a colony between AD 161 and 180. Documented references to the medieval town, known as 'Castrum Clus', date back to 1183. German merchants arrived in the 12th century and, after the Tartar invasion of 1241, the medieval earthen walls of *castrenses de Clus* were rebuilt in stone. From 1791 to 1848 and after the union with Hungary in 1867, Cluj-Napoca served as the capital of Transylvania.

Though less picturesque than either Sighişoara or Braşov, it has several good museums and a relaxed, inviting atmosphere. You could see all the sights in a busy afternoon, but cheap accommodation makes it easy to spend a few days. Nearby Turda Gorge (Cheile Turzii) is also worth a look.

Orientation

The train station is 1.5km north of the centre. To get to the centre, walk left out of the station, buy a ticket at the red L&M kiosk across the street and catch tram No 101 or a trolleybus south down Str Horea. Get off the trolleybus immediately after crossing the river; on tram No 101 you go two stops and then continue walking south until you cross the river.

All major bus services arrive/depart from bus station No 2 (Autogară 2) across the bridge from the train station, north of town. Bus station No 1 (Autogară 1), on Str Aurel Vlaicu, on the eastern side of town, no longer operates.

Maps The quality *Cluj-Napoca, Kolozsvár, Klausenburg* map (1999) includes a city map, detailed city-centre map and lists the major sights in Romanian and Hungarian. It is $3 in most bookshops.

Information

Tourist Offices Ave Tour (☎ 198 915), previously the state-run tourist office, at Calea Moţilor 1, has still not broken free of its bleak past. For practical help and information approach one of the private agencies (see Travel Agencies, later). Ave Tour is open 8 am to 8 pm weekdays and 10 am to 2 pm weekends.

The Transylvania Ecological (Clubul Ecologic Transilvania; ☎/fax 626, e cetcluj@mail.dntcj.ro), run ma▪ by university students at Str Sindicatelor Apt 6, open from 11 am to 5 pm weekdays arranges tours and activities in rural areas of Transylvania.

The Web site www.cjnet.ro has general information on the city.

Youth Hostels România (YHR; ☎ 198 067, fax 186 616, e yhr@mail.dntcj.ro) has its head office at Piaţa Ştefan cel Mare 5; open 9 am to 4 am weekdays. The office makes bookings for youth hostels throughout Romania. For details visit the YHR Web site at www.dntcj.ro/yhr.

The ACR (☎ 432 111) is at Blvd 21 Decembrie 1989 131.

Money Black-market moneychangers lurk in front of the Agenţie de Turism KM0 on Piaţa Unirii, outside Hotel Continental and around the taxi rank in front of St Michael's Church. Hence this area of the city centre is duly known by locals as 'Wall Street'. Most change forints for lei and vice versa, but be extremely careful (scams are common).

Change money officially at the Prima Exchange office at Str Bolyai 2–4. It gives cash advances on Visa/MasterCard; open 24 hours.

Change travellers cheques and get Visa/MasterCard cash advances at Banca Comercială Română, Str Gheorghe Bariţiu 10–12; open 8 am to 12.30 pm weekdays, it has two outside ATMs. Banca Română pentru Dezvoltare, Piaţa Unirii 7, also gives cash advances on Visa and has an ATM; open 8.30 am to 1 pm and 2 to 4 pm weekdays.

Post & Telephone The telephone centre is behind the main post office, Str Regele Ferdinand 33, and is open 7.30 am to 8 pm weekdays, and 8 am to 1 pm Saturday. The post office is open 7 am to 8 pm weekdays, and 7 am to 1 pm Saturday. Queues are shorter at the post office opposite the student culture house on the corner of Piaţa Lucian Blaga and Str Petru Maior; open 6 am to 4.45 pm weekdays. A smaller telephone office at Piaţa Unirii 5 is open 7 am to 10 pm daily.

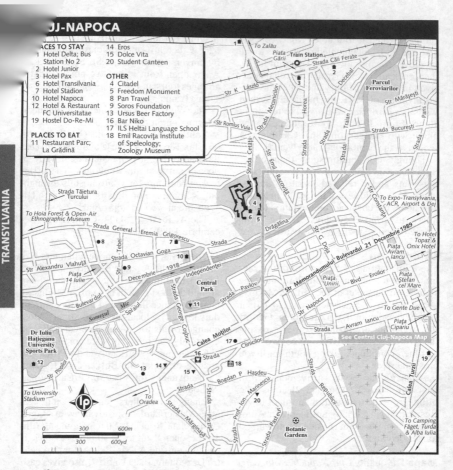

J-NAPOCA

ACES TO STAY
1 Hotel Delta; Bus Station No 2
2 Hotel Junior
3 Hotel Pax
6 Hotel Transilvania
7 Hotel Stadion
10 Hotel Napoca
12 Hotel & Restaurant FC Universitatae
19 Hostel Do-Re-Mi

PLACES TO EAT
11 Restaurant Parc; La Grădină

14 Eros
15 Dolce Vita
20 Student Canteen

OTHER
4 Citadel
5 Freedom Monument
8 Pan Travel
9 Soros Foundation
13 Ursus Beer Factory
16 Bar Niko
17 ILS Heltai Language School
18 Emil Racoviţa Institute of Speleology; Zoology Museum

Email & Internet Access Supernet (☎ 430 425, ⓔ setsala@supernet.dntcj.ro) at Str Iuliu Maniu 1 charges $0.80 per hour for Internet access; open 24 hours.

Travel Agencies The Continental Agenţie de Turism (☎ 195 405, 191 441, fax 193 977, ⓔ conticj@codec.ro) inside Hotel Continental at Str Napoca 1 arranges tours, makes hotel bookings and rents cars. It is open 9 am to 5 pm weekdays.

Consus Travel (☎ 192 928, ☎/fax 193 044, ⓔ consus@cjx.logicnet.ro) at Str Gheorghe Şincai 15 can book you into most hotels at a slightly better rate than if you approach the hotel direct. It also rents cars and arranges weekend trips to the Apuseni Mountains, Maramureş, and Poiana Braşov for around $220. It is open 9 am to 5 pm weekdays. For prices on tour packages visit its Web site at www.dntcj.ro/consus.

Top-notch for travellers' advice and service, Pan Travel (☎/fax 420 516, ⓔ mail@ pantravel.ro), west of the centre at Str Grozavescu 13, is worth tracking down. The agency arranges private accommodation, has a variety of regional tours, rents cars and can even organise mobile-phone rental. Visit Pan Travel's Web site at www.pantravel.ro.

Bookshops The University Bookshop (Li brărie Universităţii), Piaţa Unirii 9, stocks English-language novels; open 8 am to 7 pm weekdays, and 9 am to 2 pm Saturday.

Libraries & Cultural Centres The Soros Foundation for an Open Society (Fundaţia Soros pentru o Societate Deschisă România; ☎ 420 480, fax 420 470, Ⓔ office@soroscj .ro) at Str Tebei 21 runs a small English-language library which stocks the latest is-sues of *Time*, *Newsweek* and *The Economist* as well as some British dailies. It is open between October and mid-July from noon to 7.30 pm Monday, 11 am to 7.30 pm Tues-day to Thursday, and 10 am to 2 pm Satur-day. Web site: www.soroscj.ro.

The German Cultural Centre (Deutsches Kulturzentrum; ☎ 194 492), Str Universită-ţii 7–9, hosts cultural events, film evenings etc. Its library is open 10 am to 2 pm Mon-day, Wednesday and Friday, and 2 to 4 pm Tuesday and Thursday. The German De-mocratic Forum (Demokratisches Forum der Deutschen; ☎ 196 748) is represented at Str Memorandumului 8.

There is a British Council library (☎/fax 194 408) at Str Avram Iancu 11, with an excellent stock of books, magazines and videos; open 2 to 5 pm Monday and Wed-nesday, and 9 am to 2 pm Tuesday, Thurs-day and Friday. You have to be a member ($1.20 a year) to borrow books.

The French Cultural Centre (Centre Cul-turel Français; ☎ 198 551, 197 595, fax 193 536, Ⓔ ccfc@mail.soroscj.ro), inside a branch of the art museum at Str Ion Brătianu 22, arranges contemporary art exhibitions, modern music festivals, jazz nights and other cultural events. Its library is open 2 to 5 pm Monday, 10 am to 7 pm Tuesday to Friday, and 9 am to 1 pm Saturday.

The American Cultural Center & Library (☎ 194 315, extension 134), Str Ion Brătianu 22, is open 8 am to 2 pm weekdays.

Medical Services The Spernat Napoca pharmacy on the corner of Piaţa Avram Iancu and Str Iuliu Maniu is open 8 am 8 pm weekdays, and 8 am to 2 pm Saturda On Sunday the central pharmacy at Piaţ Unirii 11 is open 8 am to 8 pm daily.

Piaţa Unirii
The vast 14th-century **St Michael's Church** dominates Piaţa Unirii. The neo-Gothic tower (1859) topping the Gothic hall church creates a great landmark. The church is con-sidered to be one of the finest examples of Gothic architecture in Romania and was built in four stages. The three naves and vestry were the last to be completed at the end of the 16th century. The choir vaults, built in the 14th century, were rebuilt in the 18th century following a fire. Daily services are held in Hungarian and Romanian and organ concerts often take place in the evening.

Flanking the church to the south is a huge **equestrian statue of Matthias Corvinus** (Mátyás Corvinus) – the famous Hungarian king, the son of Iancu de Hunedoara (János Hunyadi) and ruler of Hungary between 1458 and 1490 – erected in 1902.

Since the early 1990s, this statue has been at the centre of controversy, largely due to the efforts of the notoriously anti-Hungarian mayor of Cluj-Napoca, Gheor-ghe Funar. Having erased the *Hungariae* of the original *Hungariae Matthias Rex* in-scription on the statue, Funar later gave the go-ahead for an archaeological dig to take place in front of the statue. In 1997 the Na-tional History Museum director called a halt to the excavation works, making it clear that the statue would not be removed or destroyed, and wanted to cover the dig site, preserving it pending restoration. The mayor of Cluj has withheld permission for this, stalling a resolution of the issue. No real archaeological work is proceeding and the ugly pit continues to scar Piaţa Unirii.

On the eastern side of the square is the excellent **National Art Museum** (Muzeul de Artă; ☎ 196 952), housed inside the baroque Banffy Palace, built in 1791. Its 22 rooms are filled with priceless paintings and arte-facts, including a 16th-century church altar. It is open 10 am to 4.30 pm Wednesday to Sunday ($0.40). The art museum runs a

TRANSYLVANIA

Nutty Nationalism

Among his other anti-Hungarian antics, Cluj-Napoca's extreme-right mayor is also responsible for the current name of Hotel Transilvania, on Citadel Hill. The hotel was, in fact, once called Hotel Belvedere. But when mayor Funar discovered that the treaty giving northern Transylvania to Hungary in 1940 was signed in Belvedere Palace he ordered that the hotel change its name. In more recent times Funar decreed that the Hungarian Consulate and the Hungarian State Theatre were the only two places in the city allowed to display signs in Hungarian.

The mayor also installed a memorial plaque to pro-Nazi Ion Antonescu in the regional council building in March 2000, only for the Cluj Prefet to order its immediate removal.

Against all odds, mayor Funar was re-elected in June 2000.

smaller gallery close to the university at Str Ion Brătianu 22.

A **Pharmaceutical Museum** (Muzeul Farmaciei) is diagonally across the street at Str Regele Ferdinand 1, on the site of Cluj-Napoca's first apothecary (1573); open 10 am to 4 pm weekdays usually, but at the time of writing, it was closed for renovations and due to reopen in June 2001.

If you want to see locally produced contemporary arts and crafts – which are also for sale – cross the square to the stylish **art gallery** (Galeria de Artă) on the western side of Piața Unirii; open 9 am to 5 pm weekdays.

On the south-western corner of the square, at the western end of Blvd Eroilor, stands a **Memorandumist monument**, an obelisk topped with a bronze bell, in honour of Transylvania's Memorandumists of 1892. The monument was erected in 1994 following an archaeological dig unearthing remains of what is believed to have been the largest brooch factory in the Roman empire. A treasure trove of 40 different brooches and 8000 moulds was found, some of which are now displayed in Cluj-Napoca's history museum.

An **Ethnographic Museum** (Muzeul Etnografic al Transilvaniei) with Transylvanian folk costumes, household items and farm implements is just west off the square at Str Memorandumului 21. It is open 9 am to 5 pm Tuesday to Sunday ($1). This is only the indoor section, however, and true ethnographic fiends should head to the **open-air section** (*secția în aer liber*) north-west of the centre in the Hoia forest ($1.25). Traditional sawmills, wells, wine and oil presses, roadside crosses, fruit dryers, potters' workshops, sheepfolds and much more are all here in this marvellous outdoor display of folk architecture.

Piața Muzeului & Around

Str Matei Corvin leads north from the north-western corner of Piața Unirii to the **birthplace of Matthias Corvinus** (of the controversial statue fame). The house, No 6, is closed to the public. At the northern end of Str Matei Corvin, Str Roosevelt leads into Piața Muzeului. On the eastern side of the square is a beautifully decorated **Franciscan church** (Biserica Franciscanilor).

At the western end of the square, inside the archaeology and art history institute at Str Constantin Daicoviciu 1, you'll find the **National History Museum of Transylvania** (Muzeul Național de Istorie a Transilvaniei; ☎ 195 677), open since 1859. All the captions are in Romanian but the museum can usually provide you with an English- or French-speaking guide. This museum presents one of the most comprehensive accounts of Transylvanian history; open 10 am to 4 pm Tuesday to Sunday ($0.25).

On the southern side of the square, behind the **statue of Constantin Daicoviciu** (1898–1973), are the remains of an archaeological dig. The remains of two original Roman walls uncovered on the north-eastern corner of the square, opposite the music school housed in a former monastery on Str Victor Deleu, will be preserved as an **archaeological park** (*parc arheologic*). Excavations started in 1991 after construction workers uncovered parts of walls while laying the foundations for a block of flats. A wooden trunk filled with bronze statuettes

CENTRAL CLUJ-NAPOCA

PLACES TO STAY
1 Vila Casă Albă
3 Hotel Piccola Italia
12 Hotel Vlădeasa
32 Hotel Victoria
40 Hotel Central-Melody
48 Vila Continental
65 Continental Hotel;
Continental Agenţie
de Turism

PLACES TO EAT
11 Restaurant
Privighetoarea
14 Fast Food
16 Pizza Pazza
20 Fast Food Junior
29 Hubertus
36 Boema Grădină de Vară
50 Hungry Bunny
61 Pizza Y
70 Colours Café
71 Napoca 15

THINGS TO SEE
2 Synagogue of Deportees
16 Franciscan Church
21 Emil Isac Memorial House
22 National History
Museum of Transylvania
23 Statue of Constantin
Daicoviciu
24 Archaeological Park
25 Birthplace of Matthias
Corvinus
26 Pharmaceutical Museum
28 Hungarian Reform Church
34 Orthodox Cathedral
39 National Art Museum
44 Art Gallery
49 Ethnographic Museum
53 Archaeological Dig;
Memorandumists' Monument
54 Statue of Matthias Corvinus
73 Babeş-Bolyai University
75 Hungarian Reformed Church

76 Tailors' Bastion
79 House at Strada
Avram Iancu 20

OTHER
4 Music Pub
5 Cinema Favorit
6 Cinema Republicii
7 Tarom
8 Agenţie de Voiaj CFR
9 Complex Comercial
Mihai Viteazul; McDonald's
10 Market
13 Central(c) Department
Store & Cafe
17 Central Post Office;
Telephone Centre
18 Banca Comercială Română
19 Hungarian State Theatre
& Opera
27 24-Hour Supermarket;
Shopping Mall
30 House at Str Iuliu Maniu 17

31 House at Str Iuliu Maniu 21
33 Spernat Napoca Pharmacy
35 Cinema Victoria
37 Prima Exchange Office
38 Supernet
42 Diesel Club
43 Harley Davidson Club
45 Flash Bar
46 Transylvanian
Ecological Club
47 Ave Tour
51 Pharmacy
52 Agenţie de Turism KMO
56 Puck Puppet Theatre
57 Agenţie de Teatrală
57 National Theatre &
Opera House
58 Art Club
59 Youth Hostels România
60 French Cultural Centre;
American Cultural Center &
Library; Small Art Museum
62 Telephone Office
63 Bancă Romăna Pentru
Dezvoltare
64 University Bookshop
66 Consus Travel & Rent a Car
67 Post Office
68 Lucian Blaga University
Library
69 Student Culture House
72 Cinema de Artă
74 State Philharmonic
77 German Cultural Centre;
US Embassy Information
Bureau
78 British Council Library

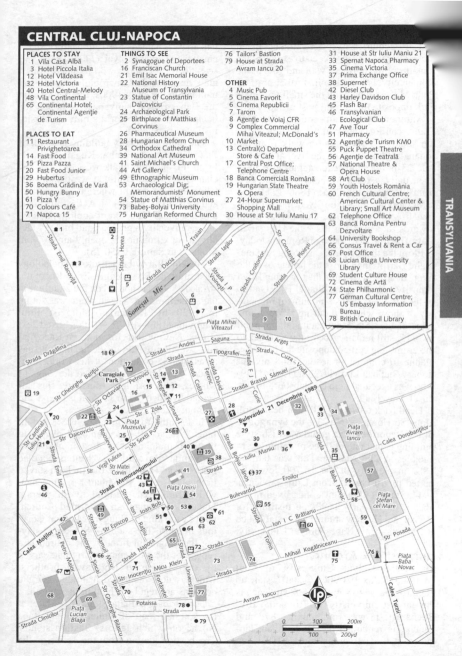

1268 silver coins dating from the 1st and 3rd centuries were later found. Local archaeologists are also keen to excavate the remains of the northern wall and gate of the Roman city, believed to lie farther north of Piaţa Muzeului beneath the small **Caragiale Park** opposite the central post office.

Another **Franciscan church** (Biserica Franciscanilor) stands at the western end of the square. A five-minute walk from the square heading towards the river at Str Emil Isac 23 is the **Emil Isac Memorial House**, open daily, except Monday and Tuesday, from 1 to 5 pm. Emil Isac (1886–1954) was a Memorandumist who lived much of his free life in this house. Continuing north towards the river you'll see the **Hungarian State Theatre**, one of two in Romania today.

From the theatre walk east along Str Gheorghe Bariţiu then cross the bridge over the river. Bear west towards the towering Hotel Transilvania on top of **Citadel Hill**. On top of the hill is an obelisk monument in memory of those who died during WWI. Some ruins of the 15th-century citadel, enlarged in 1715, still remain. Above the entrance to the crumbling edifice opposite the hotel is a plaque to commemorate the 1848 revolutionary Stephan Ludwig Roth (1796–1849) who was executed here by Habsburg troops on 11 May 1849.

Head back down the hill then bear north along Str Horea. At No 23 is the **Synagogue of the Deportees**. The grand Moorish-style building is just one of three remaining synagogues in Cluj-Napoca. This was built in 1887 in memory of the 16,700 Jews deported to Auschwitz from Cluj-Napoca in 1944. Some 18,000 Jews once lived in the ghetto. In the early 1990s an institute for Jewish and Hebrew studies was established at Cluj-Napoca's Babeş-Bolyai University.

University & Around

The Babeş-Bolyai University of Cluj (☎ 194 315, fax 191 906, ⓔ staff@staff.ubbcluj.ro), home to some 17,500 students, is the largest university in Romania after Bucharest. It was founded in 1872 and Hungarian remained the predominant language at the university until 1918 when

Transylvania became part of Romania. The university is named after 19th-century mathematician Farkas Bólyai (1775–1856) and scientist Victor Babeş who founded Romania's first school of microbiology and morphology in the early 1900s. Internationally, the Babeş-Bolyai University is famed for being home to the world's only university institute of speleology.

The main university building is south of Piaţa Unirii at Str Mihai Kogălniceanu 1. From this building walk west to Piaţa Lucian Blaga, then continue west along Str Clinicilor. Bear right where the road forks and walk up the small hill. At the top, on the left, is a small **Museum of Zoology**, housed in the university's geology and biology faculty at Str Clinicilor 5; open 9 am to 3 pm Monday to Saturday ($0.75).

The **Emil Racoviţă Institute of Speleology** (Institutul de Speleologie Emil Racoviţă, ☎/fax 195 954) is housed on the 2nd floor in the same building. The institute was set up in 1920 by Romanian biologist Emil Racoviţă (1868–1947; see the boxed text 'Brave New World' for more on Racoviţă) and a small **museum** inside the institute has a fascinating collection of his work. It includes extraordinarily detailed drawings of whales, plus original transparencies invented by Racoviţă in 1905. It is open 9 am to 5 pm weekdays.

Just south of the university is Str Avram Iancu. At No 20 is a memorial plaque to those Romanians who died in the 1848 revolution. Revolutionary leaders Nicolae Bălcescu and Gheorghe Bariţiu both stayed in this house. On Str Mihail Kogălniceanu, which runs east, parallel to Str Avram Iancu, is a **Hungarian Reformed Church**, built by the king of Hungary Matthias Corvinus in 1486. The statue of St George slaying the dragon in front of the church is a replica of the 14th-century original, carved by the Hungarian Kolozsvári brothers, which is now displayed in Prague. Organ concerts are regularly held in the church.

Farther east is Piaţa Ştefan cel Mare, at the southern end of which is Piaţa Baba Novac on which **Tailors' Bastion** stands. The bastion, dating from the 1550s, is the

Brave New World

Emil Racoviţă (1868–1947) was Romania's most heroic scientist. He created a new branch of science through which the great mysteries of the underground world came to be unravelled.

The son of an Iaşi nobleman and a Sorbonne graduate, Emil Racoviţă's first pioneering move was in 1897 aboard the *Belgica* for a polar expedition led by Norwegian explorer Roald Amundsen (the first man to reach the South Pole, in 1911).

In March 1898 the *Belgica*, a wooden whaler, became trapped in Antarctic ice. It remained grounded until March 1899 when the intrepid explorers succeeded in cutting a 75m-long channel through the 6m-thick icepack. Ice drifts had shifted the ship 3500km during the 12 months it was stuck. Not surprisingly, the 19-strong crew was given up for dead. The expedition provided the first meteorological data recorded hourly over a one-year period, as well as a collection of 1600 botanical and zoological specimens.

Emil Racoviţă's adventures whirled him around the globe. In 1904 he discovered a new species of cave crustacean in Majorca. In 1905 he pioneered the use of photographic slides. And in 1907 he published a paper on the problems of biospeleology (*Essai sur les problèmes biospéléologiques*), marking the birth of biospeleology as an independent science. During his lifetime he explored some 1200 caves in Europe (many of which were in Romania) and Africa.

In 1919 Emil Racoviţă was offered the post of zoology professor at Cluj-Napoca's university. He refused, explaining he could only come to Cluj-Napoca if a speleology institute were established. In 1920 the world's first institute of speleology, headed by Romania's greatest biologist, opened.

Emil Racoviţă remained in Cluj-Napoca until 1940 when, following the Hungarian occupation of northern Transylvania, his institute sought refuge in Timişoara. He returned to Cluj-Napoca in 1944, only to be struck down by pneumonia. Even on his deathbed, Emil Racoviţă remained loyal to his homeland: while famine raged through the country, the heroic professor gracefully declined a dish of chicken and sour cream offered to him, explaining he would eat the same as his famine-struck countrymen – dry *mămăligă*.

only one that remains from the medieval fortified city. The square on which it stands is named after one of Mihai Viteazul's generals who was executed by Hungarian nobles here in the 17th century.

Cluj-Napoca's fragrant **Botanic Gardens** (1930) lie just south of the university at Str Republicii 42. Covering 15 hectares, the green lawns embrace greenhouses, a Japanese garden and a rose garden with some 600 different varieties. In summer allow several hours to explore it. The gardens are open 9 am to 8 pm daily ($0.25).

West of the Centre

Heading west from Piaţa Muzeului, if you continue along Str Gheorghe Bariţiu past the Hungarian State Theatre, then left along Str Independenţei, you'll reach **Central Park** (Parcul Central), where you can hire boats to row on the small lake. West of the park

is the Ursus Beer Factory where Ursus beer has been brewed since 1878.

The **university stadium**, farther west, is home to FC Universitatea who have matches here regularly. The stadium is close to the Olympic-sized swimming pool (☎ 188 777) at the southern end of **Dr Iuliu Haţieganu University Sports Park** (Parcul Sportiv Universitar Dr Iuliu Haţieganu). Here you will find outside tennis courts, a fitness club, running tracks, an athletes pavilion and the FC Universitatea's clubhouse. The park is open 9 am to 9 pm daily ($0.20).

Activities

Cluj-Napoca is a major centre for mountain biking and caving enthusiasts, with the Apuseni Mountains to the south-west offering a wealth of caves and trails. For details, see the Exploring the Carpathian Mountains special section.

Places to Stay

Camping Up in the hills 7km south of Cluj-Napoca is *Camping Făget (☎ 196 234)*. Open from mid-May to mid-October, the 143 bungalows go for $6/8 a double/triple. It's $2/3/5 (single/double/triple) to pitch a tent. The summer-only restaurant here closes at 8 pm. To reach the camping ground take bus No 35 from Piaţa Mihai Viteazul south down Calea Turzii to the end of the line. From here it is a marked 2km hike to the site.

Private Rooms Rural tourism experts Antrec (☎ 198 135, 424 536), at Piaţa Avram Iancu 15, can arrange rooms in private houses around Cluj-Napoca from $5 a night. Meals cost extra.

The Transylvania Ecological Club (see Tourist Offices, earlier) publishes a glossy brochure with photographs of all the private homes you can stay at in the Apuseni Mountains and north-western Transylvania. A bed for the night costs between $10 and $15, including breakfast. Contact the office for a copy of the brochure and to book accommodation.

Pan Travel (see Travel Agencies) can arrange rural accommodation in villages throughout the Cluj district and Transylvania from $12 a night, including breakfast.

Hostels Between 1 July and 1 September, *Hostel Do-Re-Mi (☎/fax 186 616, Str Braşov 2–4)* offers a bed in a dormitory for $7. From the train station take trolleybus No 3 three stops to Piaţa Cipariu, walk south along Str Andrei Mureşanu, then take the first right along Str Zrínyi Miklóos. At the end of the street turn left onto Str Braşov and go 50m to the right.

Hotels – Budget & Mid-Range The five-storey *Hotel Delta (☎ 132 507)*, at bus station No 2 across the bridge from the train station, is convenient and cheap at $5 for a bed in a shared room. There is no hot water and no shower; rooms only have a sink.

Opposite the train station is the basic *Hotel Pax (☎ 136 101, Piaţa Gării 1–3)*. It is noisy but clean and in summer you'll have to battle with hordes of other back-packers for a room. Singles/doubles/triples with shared bath are $12/17/23. Some 150m east of the train station is *Hotel Junior (☎ 432 028)*, on Str Căii Ferate, with simple, modern singles/doubles for $15 per person including breakfast.

Farther afield, *Hotel Stadion (☎ 182 826, fax 420 770, Str General Grigorescu 5–7)*, behind Hotel Napoca, has singles/doubles/triples with private shower for $15/18/25.

The quietest of the cheaper hotels, due to its location on a small, tree-lined avenue, is the three-room *Hotel Piccola Italia (☎ 136 110, Str Emil Racoviţă 20)* next door to the four-star Vila Casa Albă. Doubles with TV and private bath cost $20, breakfast included. The hotel is run by an elderly couple and has no bar or restaurant.

The renovated *Hotel Central-Melody (☎ 197 465, Piaţa Unirii 29)* overlooks the square and charges $23 for a double with private bath.

East of the centre is the pleasant *Hotel Topaz (☎ 414 021, Str Septimiu Albini 10)*. Comfortable two-star singles/doubles are $25/27 and three-star are $32/39. All include breakfast. Next door is the marginally cheaper *Onix Hotel (☎ 414 076, fax 414 047, Str Septimiu Albini 12)*. It charges $20/22 for two-star rooms and $26/29 for three-star rooms; breakfast included.

A cheap option in the city centre is *Hotel Vlădeasa (☎ 194 429, Str Regele Ferdinand 20)*; it's good value at $19/34 for singles/triples without bath, $35/40 for doubles/triples with bath. The reception is through an archway adjacent to Restaurant Vlădeasa.

Expensive for the ageing rooms it offers is the towering *Hotel Napoca (☎ 180 715, fax 185 627, Str Octavian Goga 1–3)*, close to Central Park. Singles/doubles with private shower cost $22/35, including breakfast. A double with private bath is $49 and luxury apartments start at $60. The hotel accepts credit cards.

The stately *Continental Hotel (☎ 191 441, fax 195 175, @ conticj@codec.ro, Str Napo-ca 1)* is on the square. It has singles/doubles for $28/36 with shared bath, $50/62 with private bath. The hotel is a member of Youth

Hostels Romania and has 40 'hostel' doubles – basic rooms with shared bath – for $9 per person including breakfast. Bookings must be made in advance through Continental Agenţie de Turism (see Tourist Offices).

Hotels – Top End A fair bet is the modern *Hotel Victoria* (☎ 197 963, fax 197 573, Blvd 21 Decembrie 1989 52–54). Its 18 single/double rooms have cable TV and cost $49/60 and apartments are $89. The hotel has a pleasant terrace cafe.

Well located in the centre is the elegant, four-star *Vila Continental* (☎ 195 582, fax 1933 977, Str Gheorghe Şincai 6). Luxurious rooms cost $64/80 and apartments are $100.

Attractive from a distance but ugly close up is the three-star *Hotel Transilvania* (☎ 432 071, fax 432 076), overlooking the city on Citadel Hill. It remains an old favourite with business travellers. Luxury singles/doubles with satellite TV and telephone are $65/88 and apartments are $115, including breakfast.

A good splurge is the four-star *Vila Casa Albă* (☎/fax 432 277, Str Emil Racoviţă 22). It's surrounded by gardens near the base of Citadel Hill and costs $105 for a double with bath, including breakfast. The hotel has one of the best restaurants and terrace cafes in town.

Places to Eat

Restaurants Any student will be the first to tell you that the food slapped out in the *student canteen* on the Str Professor Ion Marinescu campus is pretty disgusting. The canteen cuisine on the Str Observatorului campus is considered no better. But if you want a full meal for less than $1, these are the places to go. Both are open during term (September to July) 9 am to 6 pm daily.

Among the top places to eat in town is the trendy *Napoca 15* (☎ 190 655, Str Napoca 15) street-terrace cafe and restaurant. Its oozing hot breaded cheese, for $1.20, just melts in your mouth. Have a Napoca house salad with it and you'll be coming back for more.

The small *Pizza Y* (Piaţa Unirii 1) is in a courtyard just off the southern end of the square. It serves an amazing 34 types of pizza, from $1.20 to $2.40, as well as plenty of pastas and fresh salads.

Much larger is *Gente Due* (☎ 197 006, Piaţa Cipariu 9), a popular pizzeria and restaurant south-east of the centre. It serves pizza, pasta and antipasto as well as vegetarian meals and even home delivers.

For hearty portions of meat, potatoes and more traditional soups, spicy meatballs and hot breaded cheese, *Restaurant Privighetoarea* (☎ 193 480, Str Regele Ferdinand 16), close to Hotel Vlădeasa, is the place to go. This small restaurant tends to attract a lot of older people thanks to the $1.20 'pensioners' special'. The attached fast-food outlet to the left serves a variety of pizzas, salads and light snacks.

If you want game (quail on good nights), head for *Hubertus* (☎ 196 743, Blvd 21 Decembrie 1989 22). It has a small courtyard decorated in hunting motifs. Cognac is the traditional start to a meal here.

Popular for its lakeside location rather than its cuisine is *Restaurant Parc* and adjoining *La Grădină* terrace cafe on the south-western edge of Central Park. Live bands play here most weekends and you can hire paddle boats for $0.50 per person per half-hour.

Diners who are into football should look no further than the upmarket *FC Universitatea* restaurant in Dr Iuliu Haţieganu University Sports Park. The entrance from the road is on Str Plopilor.

Cafes In a courtyard off the main street is *Boema Grădină de Vară* (Str Iuliu Maniu 34), a pleasant terrace cafe. It has live music some evenings.

If you want to mingle with a younger crowd try the *Student Club*, run by university students in a garden directly behind the Student Culture House. You can enter from the street at Piaţa Lucian Blaga 1–3 or from the official entrance inside the house.

Nearby at the funky *Colours Café*, on the corner of Str Inocenţiu Micu Klein and Str Potaissa, the beer flows until well into the early hours of the morning. The outside beer garden, located across the street on the opposite corner, is generally packed with rowdy students.

Bar Niko and *Dolce Vita*, behind the student campus on Str Piezişă, are two other busy student haunts worth a drink or two. Close by is the low-budget *Eros* cafe *(Str Moţilor 102)*. On the wall outside is a memorial plaque to eight people who died here on 21 December 1989.

The *Continental Café (Str Napoca 1)*, adjoining Hotel Continental, serves calorie-laden chocolate cakes and other sweet delights.

Fast Food The *Fast Food* joint beside the central department store on Str Regele Ferdinand is cheap and convenient. Pizzas start at $0.65 and a plate of vegetables, spaghetti, meat stew, cutlet and fries etc is around $1.

Almost directly opposite on the same street is the Italian-inspired *Pizza Pazza* which, with its bizarre concoction of toppings, certainly lives up to its 'nutty' name.

The *Hungry Bunny (Piaţa Unirii 12)* serves up Western-style doughnuts for $0.50 and burgers, including the 'Bunny Chicken' for $0.95, from 10 am daily.

Fast Food Junior, opposite the Hungarian State Theatre & Opera, on the corner of Str Emil Isac and Str Pavlov, is a clean, modern outlet. Its cheap eats include pizza slices from $0.05, hamburgers and kebabs.

McDonald's, in front of the central market on Piaţa Mihai Viteazul, is open 7.30 am to midnight Sunday to Thursday, and 7.30 am to 1 am Friday and Saturday.

Self-Catering For fresh produce, stroll through the packed *central market*, behind McDonald's on Piaţa Mihai Viteazul. For tinned and dry products, the central department store *Centrală* on Str Gheorghe Doja is open 8 am to 9 pm weekdays, 9 am to 3 pm Saturday. The small *supermarket & shopping mall* on the corner of Str Memorandumului and Str Dávid Ferenc is open 24 hours.

Entertainment

Posters advertising what's on where are displayed on billboards outside the Student Culture House on Piaţa Lucian Blaga.

Cinemas Cluj-Napoca has four cinemas: *Cinema de Artă* on the corner of Str Universităţii and Str Ion Brătianu, *Cinema Republicii* on Piaţa Mihai Viteazul, *Cinema Victoriei* on Blvd Eroilor and *Cinema Favorit (Str Horea 6)*. They all show films in their original languages with subtitles in Romanian. Tickets cost between $0.50 and $1 for adults and $0.35 to $0.75 for students.

Bars & Clubs A favourite haunt among students, expats and diplomats alike is the alternative and very funky *Music Pub* (☎ 432 517, *Str Horea 5*), not far from the train station. The beer flows until 3 am inside this trendy cellar bar which hosts live folk, jazz and rock bands most weekends. Ursus Premium Pils costs $0.35 a pint.

On the western side of Piaţa Unirii is a trio of popular clubs. *Diesel Bar* (☎ 198 441, *Piaţa Unirii 17)* and *Flash Bar* (☎ 199 020, *Piaţa Unirii 10)* attract a more stylish, young crowd. Less stylish is the *Harley Davidson Club* (*Piaţa Unirii 15*), a couple of doors down from Diesel Bar. It does have billiard tables, however.

The *Art Club (Piaţa Ştefan cel Mare 14)*, next door to the Agenţie de Teatrală, is a hip cafe so laidback you're compelled to sit and chat for hours on end. Plastered on the wall are posters advertising rock concerts and jazz festivals. It has one pool table and is open 9 am to midnight weekdays, and noon to midnight weekends.

Theatre & Classical Music The neo-baroque *National Theatre & Opera House* (1906) on Piaţa Ştefan cel Mare was designed by the famous Viennese architects Fellner and Hellmer and a performance here is well attended. Tickets can be bought in advance from the Agenţie de Teatrală (☎ 195 363) at Piaţa Ştefan cel Mare 14; open 11 am to 5 pm Tuesday to Friday. Tickets for classical concerts hosted by the *State Philharmonic (Filarmonica de Stat;* ☎ 430 063), on Str Mihail Kogălniceanu, are also sold here. Look out for performances at the *Puck Puppet Theatre (Teatrul de Păpuşi Puck; Blvd Eroilor 8)* in a courtyard.

Plays and operas in Hungarian are performed at the *Hungarian State Theatre & Opera* (☎ 193 468, Str Emil Isac 26–28) close to the river. Tickets are sold in advance at the box office inside the theatre.

Organ recitals are held two or three times a week in St Michael's Church (see Piaţa Unirii, earlier). The Sală de Expoziţii inside the Lucian Blaga university library (Biblioteca Lucian Blaga) on Piaţa Lucian Blaga occasionally hosts classical music and organ concerts. Ask for information at the library office, open 8 am to 1.45 pm and 2.30 to 9 pm weekdays.

Getting There & Away

Air Tarom has daily flights, except Sunday, to/from Bucharest via Oradea ($57/97 single/return). Tickets can be bought at the airport one hour before departure or from the Tarom city office (☎ 432 524) at Piaţa Mihai Viteazul 11. It is open 7 am to 1 pm and 2 to 7 pm weekdays, and 9 am to 2 pm Saturday. Air Transilvania (☎/fax 193 245), Piaţa Ştefan cel Mare 14, and Aerotravel (☎/fax 433 124, 136 926, e aerotravel@mail.dntcj.ro), Str Horea 1, are both agents for Tarom.

Train The Agenţie de Voiaj CFR (☎ 432 001), Piaţa Mihai Viteazul 20, is open 7 am to 7 pm weekdays. Tickets for international trains have to be bought in advance from this office.

The speedy *Ady Endre* train to Budapest leaves Cluj-Napoca daily at 7.50 am (4¼ hours). Slower daily Braşov-Budapest trains which stop at Cluj-Napoca include the *Corona* and the *Claudiopolis* (6½ hours).

Cluj-Napoca is well served by national trains. For Sibiu you sometimes have to change trains at Copşa Mică. For Alba Iulia, you often have to change at Teiuş.

The left-luggage office (open 24 hours) is near the restaurant.

Bus Buses to southern and central Transylvania depart from Autogară 2. Daily bus services include one daily to Abrud (127km), Alba Iulia ($2, 99km), Brad ($2.50, 165km) and Sibiu (230km); two to Baia Mare ($2.50); four daily to Câmpeni

(116km); 13 to Turda ($1, 27km) and five to Zalău (86km).

Buses to Budapest ($6.50/13 single/return, 399km) depart at 7 am Monday and Friday from Autogară 2. Tickets are sold at the station.

There are also more expensive private buses to Hungary and Western Europe. The Agenţie de Turism KM0 (☎ 191 114, fax 196 557), Piaţa Unirii 10, sells tickets for these.

Getting Around

To/From the Airport Cluj-Napoca airport (☎ 416 702) is 8km east of the town centre in the Someşeni district. Bus No 8 runs from Piaţa Mihai Viteazul to the airport.

Tram, Trolleybus & Bus Tram No 101 runs from the train station into town. Bus No 27 takes you within a 10-minute walk of the open-air ethnographic museum northwest of the centre in Horea forest.

Car One of the cheapest rental deals in town is offered by Consus Rent a Car (see Travel Agencies) at Str Gheorghe Şincai 15, with Opels/Daewoos for $40/55 a day. A chauffeur-driven car costs $100 a day.

Jet Tour (☎/fax 194 498), Str Regele Ferdinand 7, rents out sturdy white Dacias for $41 a day, including 300 free kilometres a day. Avis (☎ 439 403) has its office in the lobby of Hotel Victoria at Blvd 21 Decembrie 1989 52–54; open 9 am to 5 pm weekdays.

Taxi To call a cab dial ☎ 166 666 or 166 866.

Bicycle Ask about rental at the Napoca Cycloturism Club (Clubul de Cicloturism; ☎ 142 953); see the Exploring the Carpathian Mountains special section. The Hobby Bike shop on Str Emil Petrovici 2 sells spare parts and fixes broken bicycles; open 10 am to 6 pm weekdays.

TURDA

☎ 064 • postcode 3350 • pop 62,000

Turda, 27km south-east of Cluj-Napoca, was an important salt-mining town in the 13th century. In the mid-16th century it was the seat of the Transylvanian Diet and

TRANSYLVANIA

hence one of the richest towns in the region. Today this small market town preserves a number of stately baroque and Magyar facades. Your reason for coming here will, however, be strictly practical – to hike or catch a bus to Turda Gorge (Cheile Turzii), located 9km west.

Turda hit the national headlines in 1997 when hundreds of crows attacked the town, Hitchcock-style.

Orientation & Information

Turda's handful of shops is centred on the main street, Str Republicii. The central post and telephone office is at Str Republicii 31; open 7 am to 8 pm daily.

You can change money at the Banca Post at Str Republicii 24, open 8.30 am to 12.30 pm weekdays. The bank also has an ATM. The Prima Currency Exchange at Str Republicii 33 is open 9 am to 4.30 pm weekdays, and 9 am to 12.30 pm Saturday.

Salt Mines

Salt was first mined at the Turda salt mines at Str Salinelor 54 in 1271. Following their closure in 1932, the abandoned 45-sq-km mines were used as a cheese deposit for the region. Today, part of the site serves as a day centre for sufferers of lung and bronchial diseases, as the centre remains at a constant 10°C.

Most of the deeper mines, including Ghezala (80m), which is partially filled with a lake, are no longer safe. But visitors can take a one-hour guided tour around the Rudolph mine and along a 400m stretch of the 900m-long main tunnel. It is open 9 am to 1 pm daily ($1.50).

To get to the mine, turn left at the first fork in the village (approaching from the north) onto Str Basarabiei. Go straight across the crossroads to the end of Str Tunel, then turn left onto Str Salinelor.

Turda Gorge

Turda Gorge (Cheile Turzii) is a short but stunning break in the mountains south-west of Turda. You can hike the gorge's length in under an hour, so plan on camping a night or two in order to explore the surrounding network of marked trails. For details see the Exploring the Carpathian Mountains special section.

Băile Turda

Only 2km east of Turda lies the small spa resort of Băile Turda, allegedly built on the site of an old Roman salt mine. The resort's outdoor swimming pool gets packed in summer. There are a couple of tennis courts and a small zoo *(parcul zoologic)*, open 10 am to 6 pm Tuesday to Sunday.

Places to Stay & Eat

In Turda, *Potaissa Hotel* (☎ *311 625*), on Piaţa Republicii, charges $23/18 for rooms with/without bath for both single and double. More fun is the over-the-top, Dracula-inspired *Castelul Prinţul Vânător* (☎ *316 850, Str Suluţiu 4–6*). A night's fantasy costs $15 a double. In the hotel's restaurant you can sink your teeth into a bear steak for the same price as the room.

In Băile Turda, *Hotel Bradul* (☎ *315 029, Str Ceanului 1*) has singles/doubles in what is no more than a private house for $7.50 per person. The bathroom is shared and hot water is not guaranteed. Close by, on Str Ceanului next to the bus stop, is the busier *Hotel Arieşul* (☎ *316 844, fax 314 569*) which offers medicinal baths, saunas and massages as well as single/double rooms for $14/19, including breakfast.

At Turda Gorge's northern end, you can freelance camp in the grassy valley. Otherwise, try the noisy *Cabana Cheile Turzii*, at the southern foot of the gorge. It's $1 per tent or $8/9/12 for single/double/triple rooms in the main building. An on-site *restaurant* serves simple meals. To get there, buses to Corneşti or Câmpeni stop 2km west of Mihai Viteazul village, next to the signposted turn-off for Cheile Turzii (the gorge). From here it is a 5km hike along a gravel road to the cabana. If you are driving, do not attempt this steep road after heavy rains.

Getting There & Away

From Cluj-Napoca's Autogară 2 there are 13 buses between 4.30 am and 8 pm for Turda village ($1, 27km). The last bus back from Turda to Cluj-Napoca is at about 5 pm.

From Turda there are buses to Corneşti and less frequent ones to Câmpeni, going via the Turda Gorge turn-off. Both depart from Piaţa Republicii in the centre of the town.

From the centre of Turda, bus No 15 runs from Str Republicii to Băile Turda ($0.25, every 15 minutes except Saturday) and bus No 20 runs to Câmpia Turzii ($0.25, every 10 minutes, weekdays only).

ZALĂU
☎ 060

Zalău, 86km north-west of Cluj-Napoca, is an uninspiring provincial town in the foothills of the Meşes Mountains. The first town to be chronicled in Transylvania, it was here that the Roman-Dacians built what is today believed to have been the most important military and cultural stronghold in the Roman-Dacian empire.

Orientation & Information

The bus station is 1km north of the centre at Str Mihai Viteazul 54. Bus No 1 runs from the centre to the train station, which is 6km north of the centre in the village of Crişeni.

You can change money, cash travellers cheques and get cash advances on Visa/MasterCard at the Banca Comercială Română at Piaţa Iuliu Maniu 2; open 8.15 am to 1 pm weekdays. It has an outside ATM also.

Roman Porolissum

The Roman settlement of Porolissum in AD 106 stood on the ultimate northern boundary of Roman Dacia. The settlement was rapidly fortified, following which it developed as a leading administrative, economic and civilian centre. By the end of the 2nd century, it had been granted the status of a municipality.

The 'Municipium Septimium Porolissensis', which some historians believe could even have briefly served as the capital of Dacia, was built within the walls of a giant castle. The 20,000 inhabitants who lived behind the walls were defended by some 7000 soldiers.

Many of the walls have today been rebuilt on the original site of the Porolissum above Zalău town. The main entrance to the castle, the stadium and the amphitheatre, have all been partially reconstructed enabling visitors to appreciate the magnitude of an original Roman stronghold; open officially 9 am to 6 pm daily. A lone shepherd, who tends the site, guides visitors around for $0.20 per person. If he is not at the main entrance to the complex, try the house marked 'casă' on the small dirt track leading up to the castle.

To get to the Porolissum, take bus No 8 from the central bus stop on Str Mihai Viteazul to the village of Moigrad. From here it is a good 20-minute hike uphill to the fortress.

The history of the Roman fortress is explained in the **Zalău History Museum** (Muzeul de Istorie; ☎ 612 223), in Zalău town centre at Str Unirii 9. Various Roman-Dacian statues unearthed in the Porolissum are displayed here. A small **Art Museum** (Muzeul de Artă; ☎ 633 137) is close by at Str Gheorghe Doja 6. Both are open 10 am to 6 pm Tuesday to Friday, and on alternate weekends ($0.30 each).

Places to Stay

Hotel Porolissum (☎ 613 301), on Str Unirii, has OK singles/doubles/triples with private bath for $14.50/18.50/22.50.

Next door is the marginally more modern *Hotel Mereş* (☎ 661 050, 613 093, Str Unirii 5). Rooms with private bathroom and hot water all day are $25/27.50/33, including a breakfast of fresh bread, jam, eggs and decent coffee. It accepts Visa/MasterCard.

Some 10km south of town on the main Zalău–Cluj-Napoca road is the large *Popasul Romanilor* (☎ 661 094), with comfortable doubles with private bathroom for $18, breakfast included.

Getting There & Away

Train The Agenţie de Voiaj CFR (☎ 612 885) is at Str Tudor Vladimirescu 2. Zalău is on a small branch line between Carel and Jibou. To get to Dej, Braşov, Székely Land, Baia Mare and Bucharest, change trains at

Jibou. From Zalău there is one direct train daily to Satu Mare (two hours), and 12 trains daily to Jibou (45 minutes).

Bus The bus station is 1km north of the centre at Str Mihai Viteazul 54. Daily bus services from Zalău include one to Târgu Lapuş (76km) and Ciucea (31km), two to Baia Mare (100km) and Huedin (58km), three to Bucium (15km) and Oradea (176km), and five to Cluj-Napoca (86km).

TREZNEA & IP

Following the annexation of 43,493 sq km of northern Transylvania to pro-Nazi Hungary in August 1940, police plundered the village of Treznea, massacring 86 villagers. They then continued north-west to Ip, 16km west of Şimleu Silvaniei, where they murdered a further 158 villagers. Both villages have been known ever since as 'villages of the Romanian Martyrs' (Localităţi Martire ale Neamului Românesc).

In the old cemetery in Treznea is a **memorial grave** to the victims. The oldest killed was 86, the youngest three years old.

To get to Treznea, follow the Zalău–Cluj-Napoca road for 10km, then turn left at the signpost for the 'Localităţi Martire ale Neamului Românesc'. One bus daily departs at 4.15 pm for Treznea from Zalău bus station. Ip is only accessible by private transport. Head 4km north from Zalău then turn left to Şimleu Silvaniei. Ip is located 42km west along this road.

CLUJ-NAPOCA TO BISTRIŢA

There are a few places worth stopping at on the main road north-east from Cluj-Napoca to Bistriţa, some of which are pleasant, while one is chilling.

Gherla

A predominantly Armenian settlement called Armenopolis in the 17th century, the small market town of Gherla (population 24,572) is 45km north of Cluj-Napoca. It has a pretty Renaissance-style castle and a baroque Armenian church (1784–1804).

But the town is best known for its prison. **Gherla prison**, still functioning today, gained notoriety in the 1950s for its so-called 'student re-education program'. Under this scheme, hundreds of dissident students were psychiatrically manipulated so that they became torturers of fellow inmates. In 1951 the re-education program was halted but conditions inside the prison remained harsh. In 1970, during floods, 600 prisoners drowned in their cells after the prison director ordered the inmates to be locked in before fleeing the building himself.

In the cemetery close to the prison is a **memorial** to those who died at Gherla, erected in 1993.

The prison, at Str Andrei Mureşan 2, is on the left as you enter Gherla at its southern end. As you face the prison from the main road, the cemetery is to the right on Str Dejului.

Gherla has a small **History Museum** (Muzeul de Istorie), just off the main square at Str Mihai Viteazul 6, which conveniently fails to mention the existence of any prison; open 8 am to 3 pm weekdays.

Places to Stay There is a cheap one-star *hotel* on the main square, Piaţa Libertăţii. Just 1km south of the town is *Băile Băiţe* (☎ 060-241 576), a large complex with an outside swimming pool, tennis courts, terrace restaurant and bar. Its 24 double rooms cost $20 a night.

Nicula

The small village of Nicula, 9km east of Gherla, is famed for its 16th-century monastery and exquisite icons painted on glass.

The age-old folk art of painting on glass was practised in Nicula as early as the 11th and 12th centuries. Icons of the saints were painted and put in peasants' houses to keep evil spirits at bay. Nicula only became famed for its glass icons in the 18th century when, according to legend, an icon of the Virgin Mary in the wooden church of the village monastery miraculously started shedding tears. Henceforth, icons painted on glass in Nicula became much sought-after items as it is believed that an icon of the Virgin Mary contains healing powers. Peasants wash the icon with water from the

View towards the Apuseni Mountains, where the Scărişoara Ice Cave is sheltered

Autumn colours in the eastern Carpathians

Făgăraş Mountains with Vidraru reservoir

Statue of Matthias Corvinus, Cluj-Napoca

Harman's 15th-century Saxon church

Orthodox church, Băile Tuşnaud

Lake at Băile Tuşnaud spa resort

City centre, Cluj-Napoca

epiphany then give this water to people consumed by an evil spirit.

Năsăud & Around

Năsăud is actually 24km north of Bistriţa. At Beclean, 26km east from Dej on the Cluj-Napoca–Bistriţa road, you can continue south-west to Bistriţa or bear left to make a detour via Năsăud.

This region is best known for its strong folk traditions and for the many writers who have sought inspiration in these parts. In **Salva**, 2km west of Năsăud, men still don their traditional straw or felt hats topped with peacock feather while women adorn their hair with dozens of tiny braids.

Nine kilometres north of Năsăud is **Coşbuc**, a small village overlooking the Salva River and named after the poet George Coşbuc (1866–1918) who was born and spent his childhood years in the village. The life and works of the man known as the 'poet of peasantry' are recounted in the small memorial **museum** – a white cottage in the centre of the village.

The novelist **Liviu Rebreanu** (1885–1944) was born in the village of the same name, 3km south of Năsăud on the road to Bistriţa. Rebreanu left his village at the age of 23 to serve a year in the Habsburg army before moving to Bucharest to establish himself as a writer. The **Liviu Rebreanu Memorial House** (Casa Memorială Liviu Rebreanu) is immediately on the right as you enter the village from the north.

Both museums are open 9 am to 5 pm Tuesday to Sunday ($0.20).

Places to Stay Năsăud's lone hotel, the two-star *Sălăuţa* (☎ *063-372 601*), on Str Ioan Prodan, is an age-old establishment with grim but dirt-cheap singles/doubles for $2.50/5 a night. A supposedly 'luxury' apartment is $10. Rooms have private bathrooms but there is no hot running water. Breakfast is not included.

BISTRIŢA

☎ 063 • postcode 4400

Bistriţa lies at the south-western end of the Bârgău Valley and Tihuţa mountain pass

which leads from Transylvania into Moldavia. This small market town is at the heart of 'Dracula land'. It was here that Bram Stoker made his leading character, Jonathan Harker, stay the night on the eve of St George's day before continuing his journey east to Dracula's castle.

First chronicled in 1264, Bistriţa (Bistritz in German) was one of the seven towns founded by the Saxons whose presence still lives on in the old town's quaint 15th- and 16th-century merchants houses. Witch trials were common events in Bistriţa during medieval times.

Orientation

The bus and train stations are next to each other at the western end of town on Str Rodnei. Exit the station and walk to the eastern end of Str Rodnei then turn right along Str Gării. At the crossroads, turn left along Str Gheorghe Şincai to get to the central square, Piaţa Centrală.

The hotels are clustered north-east of the central square around Piaţa Petru Rareş. The Bistriţa River cuts across the south of the town.

Maps The accurate *Hartă Stradală a Municipiului Bistriţa*, published by Mediaprint, is sold for $0.50 in bookshops and newsagents.

Information

Tourist Offices The Tourist Information Centre (☎/fax 219 919, e cit@elcom.ro), inside the House of Culture at Str Albert Berger 10, offers the best advice and can help arrange accommodation; open 9 am to 6 pm weekdays.

The Coroana Tourist Company (☎ 231 803, fax 232 260), Piaţa Petru Rareş 7a, sells tickets for private buses to Germany, arranges day trips to Dracula's castle on the Tihuţa pass, and is an agent for Tarom and rural tourism specialist Antrec.

Adjoining its office is the Transylvanian Society of Dracula (☎ 231 803, fax 232 260). Both offices are open 8 am to 6 pm weekdays.

The ACR has an office at Str Dornei 45.

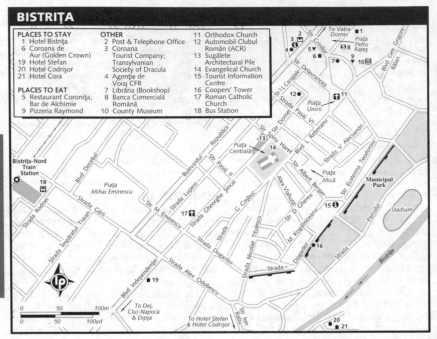

BISTRIŢA

PLACES TO STAY
1 Hotel Bistriţa
6 Coroana de
  Aur (Golden Crown)
19 Hotel Stefan
20 Hotel Codrişor
21 Hotel Cora

PLACES TO EAT
5 Restaurant Coroniţa;
  Bar de Alchimie
9 Pizzeria Raymond

OTHER
2 Post & Telephone Office
3 Coroana
  Tourist Company;
  Transylvanian
  Society of Dracula
4 Agenţie de
  Voiaj CFR
7 Librăria (Bookshop)
8 Banca Comercială
  Română
10 County Museum

11 Orthodox Church
12 Automobil Clubul
   Român (ACR)
13 Sugălete
   Architectural Pile
14 Evangelical Church
15 Tourist Information
   Centre
16 Coopers' Tower
17 Roman Catholic
   Church
18 Bus Station

Money You can change money, cash travellers cheques and get cash advances on Visa/MasterCard at the Banca Comercială Română next to Hotel Bistriţa on Piaţa Petru Rareş. The bank is open 8 am to 6 pm weekdays, and 8 am to 12.30 pm Saturday. It has an ATM outside.

Post & Telephone The post office is adjacent to the telephone office on Piaţa Petru Rareş. Both are open 7.30 am to 8 pm weekdays, and 8 am to 1 pm Saturday.

Bookshops Books and city maps are sold in the large bookshop at Str Petru Rareş 2–3; open 8 am to 7 pm weekdays, and 10 am to 2 pm Saturday.

Things to See
The large **evangelical church** (Biserica Evanghelică) dominates Piaţa Centrală. Built by the Saxons in the 14th century, the Gothic-style church with its magnificent

76.5m-tall steeple still serves the small Saxon community remaining in Bistriţa today. At the time of writing, the church was being renovated.

Facing the church on the north side of the square is the **Sugălete** pile, the domain of Bistriţa's Saxon merchants. Built between 1480 and 1550, the 13 houses were bound together with stone arches. In the 16th century, a portico was added to the length of the terraced buildings.

Walk east along Blvd Liviu Rebreanu to Piaţa Unirii, where an **Orthodox church** (Biserica Ortodoxă; built 1270–80) is the centrepiece. A **statue** of Romanian novelist Liviu Rebreanu stands on the square.

The **Bistriţa County Museum** (Muzeul Bistriţa) is just north-east off Piaţa Unirii at the western end of Blvd General Grigore Bălan; open 10 am to 6 pm Tuesday to Sunday ($0.25).

What remains of the city's 13th-century walls lie south of the town along the municipal park's north-west side. Bistriţa suffered numerous attacks by the Turks and Tartars during the 16th and 17th centuries and the citadel and most of the bastions intersecting the city wall were destroyed. In 1530, Petru Rareş (r. 1541–46), prince of Wallachia, besieged Bistriţa, forcing its Saxon inhabitants to finally surrender. The **Coopers' Tower** remains at the east of the park, close to the bridge across the Bistriţa River.

Out of Town The small village of **Dipşa**, known as Dürrbach to the Saxons, is 7km south of Bistriţa. On top of the southern wall of the Gothic Lutheran church (1489) is a unique stone sculpture of an open-mouthed pig. Legend has it that a swineherd was tending his snouting pigs when one suddenly disclosed a gold coin. The rest of the pigs then excitedly uncovered an entire treasure trove of gold pieces. The villagers were so elated by their good fortune that they built a church in thanks to the pigs.

Places to Stay
Private Rooms Antrec (☎ 231 803, fax 232 260), the specialist in agro-tourism, arranges rooms in private homes for $9 to $15 a night, including breakfast. It also has a local tour guide service. Its office is inside the Coroana Tourist Company (see Tourist Offices).

Hotels Bram Stoker's character Jonathan Harker stayed at the *Coroana de Aur* (☎ 232 470, fax 232 667, Piaţa Petru Rareş 4) on 3 May 1893. So do most foreign tourists. The two-star 'Golden Crown' exploits its fictitious links and charges $20 for a double room with private bath, including breakfast.

The privately-run *Hotel Ştefan* (☎ 221 594, Blvd Independenţei 11) has 12 simple doubles with private bath costing $15 a night, including breakfast.

Across the river, just south of the centre, is one of Bistriţa's nicest hotels. *Hotel Codrişor* (☎ 227 352, 233 214, fax 236 476, Str Codrişor 29), straddling the old city walls, overlooks the park. It has an outside

---

Devilish Diversions

The Transylvanian Society of Dracula (see Tourist Offices) arranges **Dracula tours** which take in the kitsch castle on the Tihuţa Pass.

It also arranges mock 18th-century **witch trials** in Bistriţa. Women suspected of witch-craft had their feet and hands bound before being immersed in the river. If they sank, it meant they were innocent. Survival was the ultimate proof of a pact with the devil, and the woman was then taken to the central square and burnt at the stake.

The Dracula Society re-enacts these grue-some events, down to a 'witch', judge and jury and a thronging crowd. Fortunately, trad-ition says that if a man from the onlooking crowd asks the judge for the woman's hand in marriage, she is saved. The show is only put on for groups. To book, contact the society well in advance.

---

swimming pool (packed in summer) and a pleasant terrace restaurant. Luxury double rooms with cable TV cost $20 and larger apartments are $30. The pool fee for non-guests is $0.30. Behind the Codrişor is the more modest *Hotel Cora* (☎/fax 221 231, Str Codrişor 23). Its 24 singles/doubles – all with private bath and TV – cost $11/15. At the time of writing, another seven rooms were being added.

Hotel Bistriţa (☎ 231 154/205, fax 231 826, Piaţa Petru Rareş 2) has rooms with private bath for $15/23 including breakfast.

Places to Eat
Breaded brains and Golden Mediaş wine, officially endorsed by the Transylvanian Dracula Society, are served in *Restaurant Coroniţa* adjoining the Coroana de Aur hotel. The expensive, ghoulish restaurant is open 10 am to 11 pm daily. At the time of writing, the society was busily making preparations for the opening of the medi-eval *Bar de Alchimie*, in the restaurant's cellar. Its cocktails include 'Black Magic' and 'Moon & Sun'.

A popular local hangout is the small *Pizzeria Raymond* on Piaţa Petru Rareş.

Getting There & Away

Train The Agenţie de Voiaj CFR is next door to the Coroana Tourist Company on Piaţa Petru Rareş. It is open 10 am to 5 pm weekdays. Bistriţa is at the end of a branch line from Ludus. You have to change trains at Sărăţel to get to Braşov, Baia Mare and Satu Mare, and the Székely Land. There are 15 local trains daily from Bistriţa to Sărăţel (15 minutes).

Bus From Bistriţa bus station there are two daily buses to Târgu Mureş ($2, 92km) and Vatra Dornei ($1.75, 83km), and one to Sighişoara ($1.95, 146km).

BÂRGĂU VALLEY

From Bistriţa the road runs east up the Bârgău Valley and across the Tihuţa mountain pass, to Vatra Dornei in Moldavia. From here, the painted monasteries of southern Bucovina can be easily accessed (see the Moldavia chapter).

June is a fine time to travel this stretch. Tiny wild strawberries the size of redcurrants are abundant. Villages along this road are dotted with peasants and children selling the sweet berries.

The village of **Livezile**, 8km east of Bistriţa along the valley road, is home to a small folk museum. And 2km south of the main road a little farther up the valley, in **Bistriţa Bârgăului**, is *Popasul Montana* where you can camp.

From **Mureşeni** the road starts to climb steeply on its approach to the **Tihuţa Pass**, which peaks at 1200m. A trail (marked with red circles) leads from here to **Piatra Fântânele** at the top of the pass.

The main reason most people break their journey at Piatra Fântânele is not so much for the fine hiking that it offers but rather for the grand **Hotel Castel Dracula**, a complete commercial con that somehow manages to persuade guests otherwise, despite its blatant tackiness. The castle-hotel, better known as Dracula's castle, towers 1116m high on the spot where Stoker sited his fictitious Dracula's castle. The architect who designed the jagged-edged building clearly studied the *Dracula* movies. Rooms are kitted out thematically, the highlight being 'Dracula's vault' where visitors are given a short, candlelit tour of the life and loves of Dracula. A coffin said to contain Dracula's bones rests in one corner.

During its construction in the 1980s, members of the Dracula Society in London wrote a stiff letter of complaint about such a kitsch castle being built so close to southern Bucovina's great medieval painted monasteries.

In the small village of **Lunca Ilvei**, 20km north of Piatra Fântânele, is the Ştefan cel Mare Equestrian Centre (☎ 063-388 470). The centre offers the unique opportunity to explore the surrounding mountains and valleys by horseback (see the Exploring the Carpathian Mountains special section).

Places to Stay

Cabana Valea Străjii in Mureşeni has a handful of wooden bungalows which it rents out in summer. On the opposite side of the main road is the *Popasul Turistic* restaurant; open 8 to 1 am daily.

Hotel Castel Dracula (☎ 063-266 841, fax 266 119) has singles/doubles/triples

---

The Order of Transylvanian Knights

To become a knight in the Order of Transylvanian Knights, intrepid travellers to the realm of the undead have to pass six tests of chivalry – answer a riddle, show strength of arm, archery, walk a straight beam, dance a minuet and jump over a flaming fire.

Once accepted, knights can mingle with other knights (of which there are 10 in Romania and 50 elsewhere) and aspire to become a baron. Portraits of the six barons worldwide of the Order of Transylvanian Knights are displayed in Hotel Castel Dracula, high up on the Bârgău mountain pass (better known as the Borgo pass to Dracula fans).

with private bath for $35/43/52, including breakfast. Luxury apartments are $57. The hotel accepts credit cards and has a sauna, restaurant and bar. Nonguests can visit Dracula's vault for $0.15.

Farther east, **Vila din Carpaţi** (☎ 030-374 312), 6km south of Poiana Stampei and 26km west of Vatra Dornei, has five modern double rooms with a bath shared between two rooms for $15 per person. It also has wooden cabanas to rent.

In Lunca Ilvei is the friendly **Vila Lunca Ilvei** (Str Principală 33). A bed in one of its single/triple/five-bed rooms is $6 per person, including breakfast. A member of Youth Hostels Românía, the villa offers discounts to hostel members. Bookings can be made through Pan Travel (☎ 064-420 516) in Cluj-Napoca.

Getting There & Away
Buses run between Bistriţa and Vatra Dornei twice daily ($1.75, 83km).

West & South-West Transylvania

Traces of ancient civilisation are more evident in this region south of Cluj-Napoca than anywhere else in Romania. The cradle of the early Dacian kingdom was in the south-western realms of these parts. The kingdom managed to withstand attacks by its powerful Roman neighbour until AD 106 when the Dacian stronghold was finally conquered. The Roman emperor Trajan created a new capital north of the Retezat Mountains. Remains of the great gold, copper and salt mines are still evident.

The union of Transylvania with Romania in 1600 and again on 1 December 1918 was proclaimed in Alba Iulia, the largest city in this region. Every 1 December hundreds of people descend upon the city to celebrate Romania's national day.

During the 18th and 19th centuries this region served as a stronghold of resistance against Habsburg domination, giving birth to the first great uprising by Romanian peasants in 1784 and remaining the only region not be conquered by Habsburg forces during the 1848–49 revolution.

APUSENI MOUNTAINS
The northern tip of west Transylvania is dominated by the Apuseni Mountains. In the heart of these mountains lies the Padiş plateau, a heavily karstic area offering hikers numerous trails to the treasure trove of fantastic caves and grottos that lie west on the Banat-Transylvania border. See the Exploring the Carpathian Mountains special section for details on hiking and caving in the region.

At the southern foot of the Apuseni Mountains is the Arieş Valley, running west from Turda towards Abrud.

Abrud
Abrud is a dull and dusty town, appealing only as a base to explore the Roşia Montană gold mine. Ten kilometres east of Abrud are the staggering basaltic twin peaks of the **Detunatele** (1169m). The main access point for these magnificent peaks – known as Detunata Goală (Hollow) and Detunata Flocoasă (Flocky) – is in **Bucium** village. From Abrud, head east along the main Abrud– Alba Iulia road for 1km. Turn left at the turning signposted for Mogoş and continue for 9km until you reach Bucium. The trail leading to the top of the Detunatele (red stripes) begins at the bottom of a narrow dirt track beside the white church in the village centre. From the Detunatele a trail (2½ hours, blue circles and red triangles) leads to Roşia Montană.

Places to Stay *Hotel Abrud* (☎ 058-780 466, Str Republicii 12) at the southern end of the town has 44 doubles with private bathroom ranging from $15 to $30.

Getting There & Away From Abrud bus station there are 10 daily buses to Câmpeni (10km), two to Deva (68km), three to Cluj-Napoca (127km) and four to Alba Iulia (150km) and Brad (32km). There is also one bus on to Avram Iancu (30km, weekends only).

Roşia Montană

Roşia Montană is 7km north-east of Abrud. From the Abrud-Câmpeni road, turn east 4km north of Abrud at the signpost for Roşia Montană (literally 'Red Mountain').

Gold has been mined in this village since Dacian times. The Romans exploited this gold mine, which enjoyed its most lucrative period during their rule. Enough gold was allegedly mined to build a road of gold from Roşia Montană to Rome. Between WWI and WWII, Romania was ranked second in Europe in gold extraction, mainly due to Roşia Montană's lucrative gold mine.

From 1854, open-casting mines were used to extract the gold ore. The primary gold reserves exploited by the Romans were believed to have long dried up. But in April 2000 a Canadian mining company, Gabriel Resources, uncovered a gold deposit believed to be the largest in Europe. According to news reports the company is planning to invest $250 million in the mine in a bid to extract 90% of the 250 tons of gold and 1370 tons of silver believed to lie in the deposit.

A 400m-long stretch of the **old Roman galleries** is open to visitors. More than 150 dark steps lead down to the galleries, believed to be over 2000 years old and snaking 2km underground. A larger chamber, where the miners would camp for weeks at a time, is still intact, as are the tracks along which small children or ponies would lug up the carts of ore to the surface.

Outside the mine entrance is a **mining museum** with reproductions of water-powered wooden stamps used to crush the ore in the 18th century. During the 19th century there were 700 such stamps positioned on the shores of Roşia Montană's surrounding lakes. Each winter, when the lakes froze, work at the mine would grind to a halt.

An important feast day for the village of Roşia Montană occurs on 6 October. The holiday celebrates Varvara, the patron saint of the mine.

The gold mine (☎ 058-780 088/979) is opposite the police station at the western end of the main street of Str Principală. The museum is open 7 am to 3 pm daily. There is also a **gold museum** in Brad, 32km south-west of Abrud; open 9 am to 2 pm weekdays ($0.50). For groups of five or more the museum will open out of hours. Tours can be booked through the secretary of the Mining Enterprises (☎ 054-655 800) and must be arranged a day in advance.

Getting There & Away Roşia Montană is virtually impossible to visit without private transport. At the time of writing, the bus service from Abrud had been cancelled.

From Roşia Montană you can hike to Bucium (see Abrud, earlier). From Cluj-Napoca there is one bus daily to Brad (165km).

Avram Iancu & Mount Găina

From Câmpeni, head west for 6km then turn left along the dirt track, through the village of Vidra, to Avram Iancu. This logging village was known as Vidra de Sus until it was renamed after the revolutionary leader Avram Iancu (1824–72) who was born here. A memorial and small museum honour the village's greatest hero. Legend has it that he went insane, spending the last years of his life wandering in the mountains playing a flute.

About 9km west of Avram Iancu, on the hill top of Mount Găina (1486m), a **Girls' Fair** (Târgul de Fete) is held every year on a Sunday around 20 July. The 'market' is the biggest event of the year for the surrounding villages whose people flock to the mountain top every year to sing, dance and light bonfires. The fair originated as a crude matchmaking venue. Today it's just an excuse for a big party.

Horea

Head 20km west along the main road from Câmpeni to Albac. Turn right here and follow the dirt track to Horea village, named after the peasant revolutionary. Horea (1730–85), who was born here as Vasile Nicola-Ursu, led the great peasant rebellion of 1784 following which the Habsburg emperor Joseph II abolished serfdom.

Horea, Cloşca and Crişan were arrested by Habsburg forces, and put to a ghastly death in Alba Iulia.

Gârda de Sus, the entryway to the awe-inspiring **Scărişoara Ice Cave**, is 10km west of Albac. See the Scărişoara Ice Cave section in the Crişana & Banat chapter.

There are three buses daily from Câmpeni to Horea (28km).

Places to Stay In Albac 7km south of Horea, *Hamul Giorgioma* (☎ 058-777 052) has comfortable four/six-bed rooms with private bathroom for $8/13 a night. The family-run hotel also has a small restaurant.

Opération Villages Roumains (☎/fax 058-777 057) arranges rural accommodation in *private homes* in the region. Its office is in Albac inside the *primărie* in the centre of the village. It charges $10 to $12 a night including breakfast, and also offers half/full-board starting at $15/16. Out of hours, ask in the village for local representative Marta Maghiar (mobile ☎ 094-274 219) who lives at house No 13.

HUEDIN & AROUND

Huedin (Bánffyhunyad in Hungarian) is 52km west of Cluj, and lies at the heart of a predominantly Hungarian enclave known as Kalotaszeg by the ethnic Hungarians. Kalotaszeg is seen as the stronghold of Magyar culture in Transylvania today.

A small, unexciting place, Huedin serves merely as a stepping-stone from Transylvania to the Banat. Its village church, famed for its painted wood-panel ceiling is worth a look.

The Tourism Agency Romanta (see Places to Stay) arranges hiking trips in the Padiş area, folk evenings, cycling and fishing trips. The office can be contacted 9 am to 9 pm daily. Accommodation and trips should be booked in advance.

Mănăstireni

Mănăstireni (Magyargyerömonostor in Hungarian) is 16km south-east of Huedin. A minor road from the main Cluj-Napoca–Huedin road leads south through Bedeciu to the village, noted for its 13th-century **church**. It was built by the Gyeröffy family, with a Gothic apse added in the 15th century. Many original wood carvings are visible inside the church which also boasts a fine wood-panelled ceiling. During the 1848 revolution, 200 Hungarians died at the

battle of Mănăstireni; they were buried in a mass grave which today rests beneath lake waters in the village.

Heading back to Huedin you pass Izvorul Crisului, known as Körösfő to Hungarians. Towering on a hill top above the village is a small church (1764) considered to be among the most representative of the Protestant churches in this region.

Poieni, Bologa & Săcuieu

Twelve kilometres west of Huedin is the small village of Poieni, 2.8km from Bologa. The ruins of a 13th-century **medieval fortress** tower above it. Some 81m of the original wall remains, as do remnants of the citadel's bastions. You can hike up the hill to the ruins from the centre of the village.

Equally interesting is the old **watermill** *(moară de apă)*, still in use today. Clothes continue to be washed in the whirlpool close to the mill. The entrance to the mill is 3km from the main road on the left in the centre of the village. The citadel can clearly be seen opposite.

In Săcuieu, 10km south of Bologa, on top of Dealul Domnului (950m, literally 'God's Hill') is one of Romania's few sequoia trees, of which the predominantly Hungarian residents are extremely proud.

Ciucea

Ciucea village, farther west, is a place of pilgrimage for Romanians and Hungarians alike, having been home to Romanian poet and politician Octavian Goga (1881–1939) and to Hungary's most controversial 20th-century poet, Endre Ady (1877–1919).

The house in which Goga lived, at the eastern end of the village next to the silver-spired church, is today a memorial **museum** (Muzeul Octavian Goga). Goga was born in a small village close to Sibiu but lived in a mansion in Ciucea between 1915 and 1917, prior to his move into politics which led to his disastrous 44-day reign as prime minister in 1937.

Goga, who campaigned fervently for the rights of Romanians in the face of Hungarian domination, bought this country mansion from the afore-mentioned Endre Ady. The

TRANSYLVANIA

poet, who slammed Hungary as a cultural backwater, spent several years living in Ciucea towards the end of his life.

Also on the complex is a **wooden church**, dating from 1575 and transported to Ciucea from the Cluj region at the end of the 16th century. It is today cared for by a group of nuns. The church and museum are open 9 am to 5 pm Tuesday to Sunday. Taking photographs of any of the buildings is forbidden.

Places to Stay
Pension Romanta (☎/fax 064-255 064), next to the Bologa turn-off on the main Huedin-Poieni road, has three doubles for $11 a night.

The pension also runs the efficient Tourism Agency Romanta (☎/fax 064-255 064), which arranges rural accommodation in *private homes* in this region. A bed for the night, including breakfast, starts at $6.

In Sâcraiu village, 6.5km from Huedin, is a small agro-tourism scheme run locally by Vince István (☎ 064-257 580) at No 291. Follow the main road that leads to the reform church on the hill, and the house is on the right. Accommodation can be arranged in 30 houses in the area starting from $7 a night per person. You can even try sleeping in a hay barn for $2 a person. Vince, who speaks German and English, also produces wood carvings and will happily teach interested travellers the art.

The two-star *Hotel Montana (☎ 064-253 090)*, 2km from the centre of Huedin on the main road to Cluj-Napoca, has doubles/triples for $15/23. There is also a 24-hour restaurant with a large outdoor dining area.

AIUD & AROUND
Heading south from Cluj-Napoca and Turda towards Alba Iulia, you pass through Aiud, where wine has been produced since 1293. One of urban Transylvania's oldest fortresses, dating from the 14th century, stands in the town, while the former 17th-century Bethlen college now houses a local **history museum**.

More ominously, Aiud is known as the former home of a communist prison in the

1950s where some 3500 political prisoners were interned.

Blaj, 26km north-east of Alba Iulia, is best known as once the hotbed of Romanian nationalism. Three mass rallies took place on the 'field of liberty' *(câmpul libertăţii)* here between April and September 1848 sparking off a countrywide revolution. Blaj is on the main Bucharest–Braşov–Cluj-Napoca line and plenty of daily express and local trains stop here.

ALBA IULIA
☎ 058 • postcode 2500 • pop 72,400
The imposing fortifications of Alba Iulia (known as Karlsburg and Weissenburg to Germans, Gyula Fehérvar to Hungarians), near the Mureş River between Cluj-Napoca and Deva, dominate the south-western flank of Transylvania.

Alba Iulia was known by the Dacians as Apulum, serving both as the capital of Upper Dacia and later, during Roman times, as the largest centre in the Dacian province of the Roman empire. During the 9th and 10th centuries, Apulum was known as Bălgrad-Cetatea Albă.

From 1542 to 1690 Alba Iulia was the capital of the principality of Transylvania and it was here in 1600 and again on 1 December 1918 that the union of Transylvania with Romania was proclaimed. Romania's national day (1 December) is still a time of major celebrations in Alba Iulia today.

Modern Alba Iulia is the seat of Alba County and the source of some of Romania's best champagne (three million bottles a year are produced here). Alba Iulia's 18th-century citadel is justly famous, but there's not much else to see or do.

Orientation
The city is divided into three parts. The citadel – the pedestrianised 'upper town' – houses all the historic sights, museums and university buildings. The new town is west of the citadel, while the lower town area resembles a building site – most of the town's older buildings were bulldozed under Ceauşescu to make way for a civic centre that never happened.

The adjacent bus and train stations are 2km south of the citadel. From the stations, take any bus marked *centru* ($0.20, pay on board) to the second stop, on Blvd 1 Decembrie 1918 close to the culture house.

Maps The *Judeţul Alba* map (1998) has a comprehensive city map and a map of the Alba district. It is sold for $1.25 from most hotels and travel agencies. At the time of writing, street names were changing. While the map provided in this guide uses the new names, any maps you purchase which were produced before 2000 will have incorrect street names.

Information

Tourist Offices The Transylvania Turism office (☎ 813 206) adjoining Hotel Transilvania at Str Iuliu Maniu 22 sells comprehensible city maps; open weekdays 9 am to 5 pm. The Cetate Apuseni tourist office (☎ 815 152, fax 831 501, ℮ cetate@cristal .dntcj.ro), inside the Complex Hotelier Cetate, Str Nicolae Iorga 3, offers similar services; open 8 am to 4 pm weekdays.

The ACR (☎ 812 485) has an office and service centre close to the bus and train stations at Blvd Ferdinand 64.

Money Change money at the Platinum Exchange Office adjoining the Magazin Universal Unirea department store, on the corner of Blvd Regele Carol I and Calea Moţilor in the lower town; open 8.30 am to 5.30 pm weekdays. The Romania Exchange, close by at Calea Moţilor 3, is open 9 am to 5 pm weekdays, and 9 am to noon Saturday. There are also currency exchanges inside Hotel Parc and Hotel Cetate.

The Banca Comercială Română, Blvd Regele Carol I 35, cashes travellers cheques, gives cash advances on Visa/MasterCard and has an ATM; open 8.30 am to 2 pm weekdays. Banc Post, on Calea Moţilor, offers the same services 8 am to 1 pm weekdays.

Post & Telephone The central telephone centre and post office are next to each other on Piaţa Natiunii in the lower town. The telephone office is open 7 am to 8 pm daily;

the post office is open the same hours weekdays only.

Email & Internet Access You can access the Internet for $0.50 an hour at Club 76 (☎ 819 540), Str Avram Iancu 3.

Medical Services The pharmacy on Blvd Horea in the new town is open 7.30 am to 8 pm weekdays, 8 am to 8 pm Saturday and 8 am to 7 pm Sunday.

Alba Carolina Citadel

The imposing Alba Carolina Citadel, richly carved with sculptures and reliefs in a baroque style, dominates the city of Alba Iulia. It was originally constructed in a Vauban style in the 13th century, although the fortress you see today was built between 1714 and 1738 to a design of Italian architect Giovanni Morandi Visconti.

Str Mihai Viteazul runs up from the lower town to the **first gate** of the fortress, adorned with sculptures inspired by Greek mythology. From here, a stone road leads to the **third gate** of the fortress, dominated by an equestrian statue of Carol VI of Austria. Above the gate is **Horea's death cell** (Celula lui Horia), now housing a small museum to commemorate the leader of the great 1784 peasant uprising.

A footpath leads from the gate to an **Orthodox church** (Biserica Memorială Sfânta Treime), outside the south-eastern corner of the inner fortress walls. The wooden church, brought to Alba Iulia in 1990 from Maramureş, stands on the site of a former Metropolitan cathedral built by Mihai Viteazul in 1597 and destroyed by the Habsburgs in 1713. The remains of the cathedral were later used to build a new church in the south of the city, close to the train and bus stations.

Today the Romanian army occupies the **Princely Court**, former residence of the princes of Transylvania, which was built in several stages from the 16th century onwards. In front of it, on Str Mihai Viteazul, stands a large **equestrian statue** of Mihai Viteazul (Michael the Brave), ruler of Romania from 1593 to 1601. On 1 November

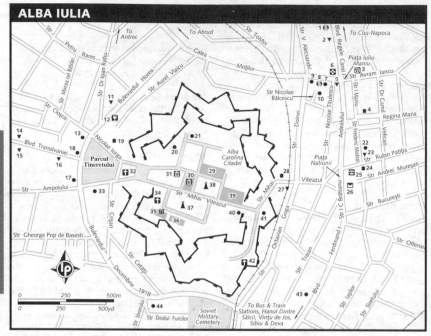

ALBA IULIA

1599 he visited Alba Iulia to celebrate the unification of Wallachia, Moldavia and Transylvania – a union that crumbled after his assassination a year later.

The statue faces **Unification Hall** (Sala Unirii; built 1898–1900), built as a military casino. In this hall the act of unification between Romania and Transylvania was signed during the Great Assembly of 1 December 1918. It is open 9 am to 4.30 pm Tuesday to Sunday ($0.25).

In the park on the eastern side of Unification Hall is a **Costozza monument**, to commemorate the soldiers and officers of the 50th infantry regiment of Alba Iulia who were killed while fighting in the Habsburg army against Italy in the battle of Costozza in 1866.

Inside the former Babylon building (1851) just west of Unification Hall is the impressive **Unification Museum** (Muzeul Unirii). The museum vividly recounts the history of Romania from the Paleolithic and Neolithic periods through to 1944 and is considered one of the top museums in the country on the history of Transylvania. Of particular interest is the Apulum exhibit which includes statuettes and ceramic pots discovered during excavations around the citadel on the site of the old Roman town.

One corner of the Unification Museum is devoted to the peasant revolutionaries Cloşca, Crişan and Horea. The highlight is a replica of the wheel used to crush Cloşca and Horea to death in 1785 (Crişan sensibly killed himself in prison before he could be tortured to death). A plaque on the wall recounts the orders issued by the judge who determined their ghastly death:

...they are to be taken to the torture place and there killed by being tied to a wheel and squashed – first Cloşca, then Horea. After being killed their bodies are to be cut into four parts and the head and body impaled on the edge of different roads for everyone to see them. The internal organs – their hearts and intestines – will be buried in the place of torture...

ALBA IULIA

PLACES TO STAY	THINGS TO SEE	OTHER
4 Hotel Transilvania; Transylvania Turism	20 Former Military Hospital	1 Banca Comercială Română
19 Hotel Cetate; Cetate Apuseni Tourist Office	21 Batthyaneum Library	3 Club 76
24 Hotel Parc	30 Unification Hall	6 Magazin Universal Unirea; Platinum Exchange Office
28 Pensiunea Flamingo	31 Unification Museum	7 Agentie de Voiaj CFR
	32 Orthodox Cathedral	8 Romania Exchange
	34 Catholic Cathedral	9 Banc Post
PLACES TO EAT	35 Catholic Episcopal Palace	10 Central Market
2 Ristorante Roberta	36 Former Princely Court	12 Ursus Grădină de Vară
5 Central Pensuine	(Military Base)	13 Pharmacy
11 Club Casa Alba	37 Equestrian Statue of	17 Dacia Supermarket
14 Eis Kaffe Paradis	Mihai Viteazul	18 B&B Magazin Alimentar
15 Adakaleli Tuna Patiserie	38 Costozza Monument	22 Albena Tours
16 Terasa Dakota	39 Military Base	25 Telephone Centre
23 Prometeu	40 Entrance to Horea's Cell	26 Post Office
27 P & H Terrace Cafe	41 1784 Uprising Memorial	29 University
	42 Orthodox Church	33 Casa de Cultură
	44 Fork's Hill	43 Automobil Clubul Român (ACR)

The museum is open 10 am to 4.30 pm Tuesday to Sunday ($0.25). All information is presented in Romanian.

Just beyond the statue is the 18th-century **Catholic Cathedral**, built on the site of a Romanesque church destroyed during the Tartar invasion of 1241. Many famous Transylvanian princes are buried here.

The nearby **Orthodox Cathedral** (originally known as the 'Church of the Coronation') was built on the old site of the citadel guardhouse in 1921–22 for the coronation of King Ferdinand I and Queen Marie on 15 October 1922. Their frescoed portraits remain intact on the rear wall of the church. Designed in the shape of a Greek circumscribed cross by architect Gheorghe Ştefănescu, the cathedral is surrounded by a wall of decorative colonnades which form a rectangular enclosure. A 58m-tall bell tower marks the main entrance to the complex. Marble inscriptions within the church pay homage to the most important events in Alba Iulia's history, including the first printing, in 1648, of the New Testament in Romanian by Metropolitan Simeon Ştefan. During the communist era, many of the cathedral's original frescoes were plastered over. Many have since been repainted.

The **Batthyaneum Library**, founded at the end of the 18th century in a former church, is situated in the north-eastern area of the citadel, as are the former **military hospital** and the late-Renaissance **Abor Palace**.

Fork's Hill

Just south of the citadel is Fork's Hill (Dealul Furcilor), the spot where peasant revolutionaries Horea and Cloşca died. It is marked with a small **obelisk monument**. A year after their grisly deaths, on 22 August 1785, Emperor Joseph II abolished serfdom among Romanian peasants in Transylvania.

Places to Stay

Camping On Highway DN1 3km south of town, *Hanul Dintre Sălcii* (☎ 812 137) camping ground has tired double/triple/ quad rooms in the main building for $3/4/5. The bath is shared and hot water is a hit-or-miss affair. There is also tent space available here.

Private Rooms Albena Tours (☎ 812 140, fax 810 385), Str Fredric Mistral 2, arranges rooms in private houses in surrounding villages for $10 to $13 a night.

Hotels The cheapest hotel is *Pensiunea Flamingo* (☎ 816 354, Str Mihai Viteazul 6), next to the eastern entrance to the citadel. It charges $5 per person for a bed in one of its two/three/four/five-bed rooms. The bath is shared and breakfast is an extra $1.50.

TRANSYLVANIA

Next in line for the budget-conscious is the 1960s *Hotel Transilvania* (☎ *812 547, Str Iuliu Maniu 22)*, which charges $20 for double rooms with private bath and TV; a single person in a double pays $14, including breakfast on the terrace.

More expensive is two-star, 12-storey *Hotel Cetate* (☎ *811 780, fax 815 812, Str Nicolae Iorga 3)*, in the new town, overlooking the citadel. Singles/doubles with private bath cost $20/31, including breakfast. Apartments are $35 and you have to pay $1/5 extra if you want a room with a black-and-white/colour TV.

Hotel Parc (☎ *811 723, fax 812 130, Str Rubin Patiţia 4)* has expensive singles/doubles for $29/36, including breakfast. It accepts credit cards.

Out of Town In Vinţu de Jos, 10km south of Alba Iulia, *Motel Lutsch 2000 Plus* (☎*/fax 743 851)* charges a reasonable $8/6 for double rooms with/without private bath. Breakfast costs an extra $1.

Places to Eat

Restaurants Alba Iulia has few private restaurants, making it difficult to avoid the hotel restaurants. The Italian-inspired *Ristorante Roberta* (☎ *819 980)*, on Blvd Regele Carol I, is a slick Western-style restaurant serving pizzas for around $1 and large bowls of spaghetti from $1.50.

In the new town is the flash *Club Casa Alba* (☎ *834 158)*, on Blvd Horea close to Hotel Cetate. It has an upmarket restaurant specialising in Transylvanian cuisine, an outside terrace and a 24-hour bar-cum-disco – all of which are great as long as you can stand the deafening music. Equally loud is *Ursus Grădină de Vară* directly opposite, open 10 am to midnight daily from 1 May to 1 October.

Central Pensuine, on Str Ardealului in the old town, is a typical, age-old establishment offering few thrills or frills. The restaurant offers a three-course set menu for a mere $1.50.

Cafes If you are only seeking a light snack, there are plenty of terrace cafes to choose from. *Prometeu (Str Rubin Patiţia 4)* is a modern, clean cafe touting a fast-food-type menu. The *P & H* terrace cafe *(Str Mihai Viteazul 7)* is under the trees next to the eastern entrance to the fortress walls. It sells Ursus beer for $0.40.

Beyond that, most cafes are in the new town. *Terasa Dakota*, on Str Transilvaniei, is a lively terrace cafe with a small menu of pizzas and burgers. Close by is the excellent *Eis Kaffe Paradis (Blvd Transilvaniei 14)*. It serves the most scrumptious ice-cream sundaes you're likely to encounter in the whole of Romania. Expect to pay around $0.50 for a bowl of chocolate, vanilla, peach melba and fruit ice cream topped with fresh fruit, chocolate sauce and lots of cream.

Self-Catering There is a small *market* selling fresh fruit and vegetables as well as dried and tinned products behind the Agenţie de Voiaj CFR office off Calea Moţilor on Str Nicolae Bălcescu. It can be reached from Calea Moţilor. *Adakaleli Tuna Patiserie*, on Blvd Transilvaniei opposite Eis Kaffe Paradis, sells delicious freshly baked bread and scrumptious pastries; open 6 am to 8 pm daily.

B&B Magazin Alimentar (Blvd Transilvaniei 2) in the new town is open 6.30 am to 9 pm weekdays, 8 am to 8 pm Saturday, and 8 am to 2 pm Sunday. The *Dacia* supermarket on the corner of Str Ampoiului and Blvd 1 Decembrie 1918 is open 6 am to 9 pm weekdays, and 6.30 am to 9 pm Saturday.

Getting There & Away

Train The Agenţie de Voiaj CFR (☎ 813 689) at Str Moţilor 1 is open 7 am to 7 pm weekdays. International train tickets for the four daily Budapest trains that stop at Alba Iulia (6¼ hours) can only be bought in advance from this office.

To get to Alba Iulia from Sibiu, you have to change trains at Vinţu de Jos. From Târgu Mureş you often have to change at Războieni or Teiuş.

Bus Direct services from Alba Iulia's bus station include two daily to Cluj-Napoca (99km) and Sibiu (71km), one to Oradea

(251km), and five to Abrud (150km), Aiud (16km) and Câmpeni (75km).

DEVA
☎ 054 • postcode 2700 • pop 77,000

Deva, south-west from Alba Iulia, is a small mining town with its own citadel. The citadel was blown to smithereens in 1849 after its gunpowder deposits exploded, but is a popular haunt with visitors nonetheless.

Deva is home to Romania's top gymnastics club, Cetate Liceul de Educaţie Fizica şi Sport Deva, the training ground for the country's elite Olympic gymnastics team.

Orientation
The train and bus stations are five minutes' walk north of the centre at Piaţa Garii. From the train station, walk straight up Str Libertăţii until it meets Blvd 1 Decembrie. From the crossroads, Blvd 1 Decembrie leads into Piaţa Victoriei and Blvd 22 Decembrie to the east. The main hotels, telephone office, and Cinema Patria are centred on Piaţa Victoriei and Blvd 1 Decembrie. Citadel Hill is at the western end of Blvd 1 Decembrie. At the time of writing, some of Deva's streets were about to be renamed.

Information
Tourist Offices The official Agenţie de Turism (☎/fax 213 173) is inside Hotel Sarmis at Piaţa Victoriei 3. It is open 8 am to 5 pm Monday to Thursday, and 8 am to 1 pm Friday.

Mondo Turism (☎ 212 162), Blvd 1 Decembrie 11, is open 9 am to 4 pm weekdays; it sells city maps for $0.25.

The ACR (☎ 212 822, fax 219 419) office is behind Hotel Sarmis at Str G Coşbuc 22.

Money There are currency exchange offices inside Hotel Sarmis and Hotel Deva. Change travellers cheques and get cash advances on Visa/MasterCard at the Banca Comercială Română behind Hotel Sarmis on Str G Coşbuc; open 8.30 am to 1.30 pm weekdays. It has an ATM outside.

Post & Telephone The post office on Blvd Decebal is open 7 am to 7 pm week-

days. The telephone centre is on the corner of Str Libertăţii and Blvd 1 Decembrie; open 24 hours. A post office also adjoins the main train station building.

Email & Internet Access You can access the Internet for $0.60 per hour at Club 4U, Str Gheorghe Bariţiu; open 10 am to 4 pm daily.

Citadel
Standing on top of a hill (300m), the 14th-century Cetatea crowns the small mining town below. Work started on the stone fortress in 1385 under the Habsburg Ardeal kings. Legend says that the wife of the mason was buried alive in the fortress walls to ensure its safe-keeping.

Religious activist Dávid Ferenc (1510–79), advocator of the Greco-Catholic faith, was imprisoned in Deva's citadel, where he died. In 1784, during the peasant uprising led by Horea, Crişan and Cloşca, the fortress served as a refuge for terrified nobles fearful of being killed by the militant peasants. In 1849, Hungarian nationalists attacked Austrian generals sheltering in the fortress. The four-week siege ended with the mighty explosion of the castle's gunpowder deposits which left the castle in ruins.

A brief history of Deva and its sister citadels, as well as extensive archaeological findings from the various sights amid the Orăştie Mountains, are exhibited in the small but excellent **Hunedoara-Deva County Museum** (Muzeul Judeţean Hunedoara-Deva), housed in the former Magna Curia Palace. This palace was built by Prince Gábor Bethlen in 1621. It is at the foot of Citadel Hill adjoining a small park.

Housed in a separate building next to the palace is the **Natural History Museum** (Muzeul Stiinţe ale Naturi). Both museums are open 9 am to 5 pm Tuesday to Sunday.

Places to Stay
Private Rooms Contact the excellent Opération Villages Roumains (☎ 216 499), Str George Enescu, Block 2, Scara A, Apt 5, which arranges rooms in rural homes in Deva and its surroundings from $12 per person a night, including breakfast. It also

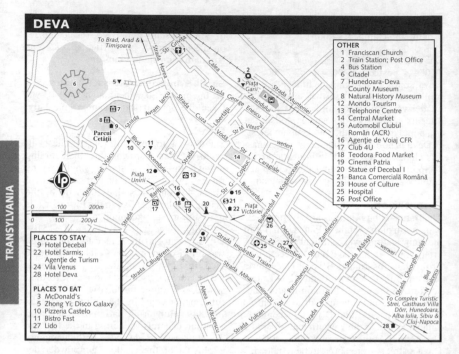

DEVA

OTHER
1 Franciscan Church
2 Train Station; Post Office
4 Bus Station
6 Citadel
7 Hunedoara-Deva County Museum
8 Natural History Museum
12 Mondo Tourism
13 Telephone Centre
14 Central Market
15 Automobil Clubul Român (ACR)
16 Agenţie de Voiaj CFR
17 Club 4U
18 Teodora Food Market
19 Cinema Patria
20 Statue of Decebal I
21 Banca Comercială Romănă
23 House of Culture
25 Hospital
26 Post Office

PLACES TO STAY
9 Hotel Decebal
22 Hotel Sarmis; Agenţie de Turism
24 Vila Venus
28 Hotel Deva

PLACES TO EAT
3 McDonald's
5 Zhong Yi; Disco Galaxy
10 Pizzeria Castelo
11 Bistro Fast
27 Lido

has a representative in Lesnic village (house No 184), 10km west of Deva.

Hotels The cheapest hotels in town are **Hotel Sarmis** (☎ 214 730/731, fax 215 873, Piaţa Victoriei 3) and **Hotel Deva** (☎ 211 290, fax 615 873, Blvd 22 Decembrie 110), run by the same company. Both are cold, two-star concrete blocks with large restaurants. Singles/doubles with private bath are $20/35, breakfast included. The Deva has a few triples for $45.

The overrated **Hotel Decebal** (☎ 212 413, fax 219 245), on Blvd 1 Decembrie close to the foot of Citadel Hill, charges an over-the-top $35/45/50 for single/double/triple two-star rooms. Three-star singles/doubles are an even pricier $50/55.

Enjoyable but not cheap is the luxurious **Vila Venus** (☎ 212 243, fax 230 028, Str Mihai Eminescu 16), behind the culture house. Double rooms start at $50, including breakfast.

Out of Town The closest camping ground is the well-maintained **Complex Turistic Strei** (☎/fax 260 581), 17km east of Deva on the road to Sibiu. It has clean two-bed cabins for $8 and plenty of space for tents. Every Thursday, Friday and Saturday from early June to late August, the site rocks to the pulsing sounds of its giant, all-night, open-air disco.

Nine kilometres east of Deva, in Simeria village, is **Gasthaus Villa Dörr** (☎ 261 316, ☎/fax 261 906, Str Biscaria 90, ✉ doerr@smart.ro). The hotel, run by a young German- and Romanian-speaking couple, has good, clean singles/doubles/triples with private bath for $13/25/38.

Places to Eat
For pizza try the 24-hour **Bistro Fast** (☎ 219 320, Str 1 Decembrie 18), or **Pizzeria Castelo** on the corner of Blvd 1 Decembrie and Str 1 Avram Iancu. Both serve pizzas from around $1.

At the foot of Citadel Hill is *Zhong Yi* (☎ *209 135)*, a large Chinese restaurant. Meals are on the expensive side at around $6 per person.

Beer-seekers can try the excellent *Lido* (☎ *227 536)* terrace cafe and bar close to Hotel Deva on the corner of Blvd 22 Decembrie and Blvd Decebal. Its menu lists a variety of Thai, Chinese and French dishes from $2.50. *McDonald's (Calea Zarandului 21)* is conveniently located close to both the train and bus stations.

You can stock up on supplies at the *central market*, just off Str G Coşbuc, or the *Teodora Food Market* close to Cinema Patria on Blvd 1 Decembrie.

Entertainment
In summer the large *Disco Galaxy* is held behind the park at the foot of Citadel Hill, adjacent to the Zhong Yi restaurant; open 9 pm to 3 am weekends from early May to late August ($1).

Shopping
Sporthaus Brenner (☎ 234 460, ℮ Brenner@ deva.iiruc.ro), Str Libertăţii 2, is run by an enthusiastic bunch of young climbers and mountaineers who can give local advice about hiking in the Retezat Mountains. The shop sells water bottles, rucksacks, tents and clothing (but not maps) and is open 10 am to 6 pm weekdays.

Getting There & Away
Train The Agenţie de Voiaj CFR (☎ 218 887) at Blvd 1 Decembrie, Block A, is open 8 am to 8 pm weekdays. Buy tickets in advance here for the four daily trains from Deva to Budapest (4½ hours, 403km).

There are no direct trains to Hunedoara but plenty of buses.

Bus The bus station is next to the train station at Piaţa Garii. There are six local buses that leave for Hunedoara (22km) between 6 am and 4.30 pm.

Other services include one bus daily to Oradea (190km) and Timişoara (159km), and two daily to Câmpeni (83km) and Abrud (68km).

HUNEDOARA
Hunedoara, south of Deva, is famous for two things – its grim steel mills and an intact 14th-century Gothic castle considered to be one of Transylvania's greatest architectural gems. But Ceauşescu wished to tarnish this symbol of Hungarian rule (both János Hunyadi and his son Matthias Corvinus, two famous Hungarian kings, made notable improvements to Hunedoara Castle).

Still, the **castle** itself, believed to be built on old Roman fortifications, is evocative, with three pointed towers, a drawbridge and high battlements. Five marble columns with delicate ribbed vaults support two halls (1453), the Diet Hall above and Knight's Hall below. The castle wall was hewn out of 30m of solid rock by Turkish prisoners.

The fortress was extensively restored by Iancu de Hunedoara (János Hunyadi in Hungarian) from 1452 onwards. The castle, restored in 1952, today houses a **feudal art museum**.

To get to the castle from the adjacent bus and train stations, head south along Blvd Republicii, then turn right onto Blvd Libertăţii. The castle, signposted from the bridge, is open 10 am to 5 pm Tuesday to Sunday ($0.50).

Places to Stay
You can pitch a tent for free at *Camping Orient* (☎ *054-206 609)*, 7km south of Hunedoara on the shores of Lake Cinciş. Otherwise, pay $1.50 per person for a bed in one of its two/three/four-bed bungalows. The site is open from early May to late September.

Hunedoara has one hotel, *Hotel Rusca* (☎/fax *054-712 002, Blvd Dacia 25)*, a five-minute walk from the train station. OK singles/doubles with private bath are $14/16 including breakfast.

Getting There & Away
The bus and train stations are at Blvd Republicii 3. There are six daily buses from Deva to Hunedoara (22km).

From Bucharest, Braşov, Sibiu and Arad take a train to Simeria then change onto a local train to Hunedoara. Alternatively, take a train as far as Deva then get a bus.

From Hunedoara there are 12 trains to Simeria (30 minutes).

THE DACIAN & ROMAN CITADELS

The area immediately south of Hunedoara is an archaeologist's delight, being home to the capital of Dacia (Sarmizegetusa), a church built from a Roman soldiers' mausoleum (Densuş), as well as the capital of Roman-conquered Dacia (Ulpia Traiana-Sarmizegetusa). The fortresses are recognised as Unesco World Heritage sites.

Archaeologists at the National History Museum of Transylvania (☎ 064-191 718, 195 677) in Cluj-Napoca arrange frequent digs and summer camps. Contact the museum in advance to arrange some volunteer work on site.

Sarmizegetusa

Dacians settled in what is today Romania from the 3rd century BC onwards. The Dacians built up a magnificent kingdom, centred in Sarmizegetusa (the capital) and surrounded by a defensive circle of fortifications in the Orăştie Mountains.

Sarmizegetusa remained unconquered by the Romans until AD 106 when Roman forces led by Trajan forced the Dacians to retreat north. The Dacian city was divided into three parts – two civilian areas and the middle sacred zone which contains the places of worship. Visitors are allowed to walk around the ruins.

Dacian Sarmizegetusa is a good 30km south of Orăştie along a dirt road, past the villages of Orăştioara de Jos, Bucium and Orăştioara de Sus. The ruins are actually 8km from the village of Grădiştea de Munte, at the end of the dirt track.

Costeşti

Sarmizegetusa was defended in the northwest by a fortress at Costeşti on the banks of the Oraşului River, the ruins of which remain. From Sarmizegetusa follow the road back north towards Orăştie and bear right at the turn-off for Costeşti.

The fortress at Costeşti, conquered by the Romans in AD 102, was 45m by 45m

square and was defended by several surrounding walls. The entire northern stretch from here along the banks of the Orăşului to Orăştie was protected by lookout towers and bastions. Remains of a Roman camp once fortified with ramparts and ditches still remain between the villages of Bucium and Orăştioara de Jos.

Densuş

The church in Densuş is on Romania's top-10 list of fabulous historic treasures. The stone church, built between the 11th and 12th centuries, stands on the ancient site of an edifice dating from the 4th century which archaeologists believe to have been the mausoleum of a Roman soldier. The church was constructed from stones taken from the Roman city of Ulpia Traiana-Sarmizegetusa.

Archaeologists conclude that the church, believed to have been built as a court chapel, was built by a Romanian noble family, only falling under Hungarian rule from the 14th century onwards. There are fragments of a 15th-century fresco inside the church.

Densuş is east of Sarmizegetusa. From Orăştie bear 18km west to Simeria then continue south for 33km to Haţeg. From here, follow the Caransebeş road 7km south-west to Toteştii. In Toteştii, turn left. Densuş is at the end of this dirt track.

Ulpia Traiana-Sarmizegetusa

Following the Romans' defeat of Decebal's forces in AD 106, they built up a spectacular array of towns for themselves, setting their capital of conquered Dacia in Ulpia Traiana, some 15km south of Densuş on the main Caransebeş road. Just to confuse things, the name of the former Dacian capital was added to the Roman city's name. It was now known as Ulpia Traiana-Sarmizegetusa.

Archaeologists have unearthed only a fraction of the great city, which was believed to have covered an area of 60 hectares. During the early 14th century, the stones of the Sarmizegetusa ruins were used by local villagers to build churches and it was not until the 1800s that the dismantled ruins fell under the protection of the Deva Archaeological Society and later of the National Museum of Transylvania. Remains of the Roman Forum, complete with 10m-tall marble columns, have already been uncovered, as have numerous temples devoted to the Roman deities, the amphitheatre, the palace of Augustales, a mausoleum and two suburban villas on the northern side of the town. Many tools, ceramics, ivory combs and other Roman treasures yielded from Sarmizegetusa are exhibited in the Deva history museum.

Every summer, between 21 July and the end of August, archaeologists from Cluj-Napoca descend upon Ulpia Traiana-Sarmizegetusa to continue their long task. There is a permanent archaeological base (*baza arheologica*; ☎ 054-762 170) close to the site which welcomes visitors year-round.

Places to Stay

Opération Villages Roumains (054-646 194), Str Principală 63a in Beriu, 8km south of Orăştie on the road to Dacian Sarmizegetusa, arranges accommodation in *private homes* throughout the region from $12 a night, including breakfast. It can also supply tourists with an English- or French-speaking guide for $10/20 for a half/full day.

There is a small *camping ground* next to the archaeological site in Sarmizegetusa. There are a handful of bungalows which cost $5 a night, and camping is free. The site is open from 1 May to 1 October. Staff at the archaeological base can also help with accommodation and can often point you in the direction of rooms in private homes.

In Haţeg, try *Hotel Belvedere* (☎ 054-777 604), 2km from the centre on the road to Petroşani. The hotel has ordinary singles/doubles for $5/10. There is also a swimming pool and in summer an open-air disco.

Three kilometres south-east of Haţeg at Sântămaria Orlea is the overpriced *Hanul Sântămaria Orlea* (☎ 054-777 768). Doubles/triples cost around $25/38.

RETEZAT MOUNTAINS

The Retezat Mountains lie immediately south of Ulpia Traiana-Sarmizegetusa. They boast Romania's first national park, now declared a Biosphere Reservation, and shelter a multitude of glacial lakes. See the earlier Exploring the Carpathian Mountains special section for details on hiking in the region.

East of the Retezat Mountains lies the **Jiu Valley**, Romania's largest mining region, centred on the towns of Petroşani, Petrila and Câmpii lui Neag in the northern end of the valley. Petroşani makes a useful base for hiking expeditions into the Retezat Mountains.

From Petroşani you can head 57km south down the Jiu Valley to Târgu Jiu (see the Wallachia chapter). The southbound road running parallel to this road to the east is said to be the highest road in Romania, peaking at 2142m. It is only possible to cross the mountains along this road by 4WD vehicles.

From Târgu Jiu there are seven trains daily to Petroşani (1¼ to 1¾ hours). To get to Petroşani from Hunedoara and Deva, take a local train to Simeria from where there are eight trains daily to Petroşani.

Wallachia

Wallachia is a flat, tranquil region of farms and small-scale industrial complexes stretching across the Danube plain north to the crest of the Carpathian Mountains. The Danube River flows along the southern edge of Wallachia and is best seen between Moldova Veche and Drobeta-Turnu Severin in the west, where it breaks through the Carpathians at the legendary Iron Gates, a gorge on the Romanian and Yugoslav border.

Towns such as Calafat, Giurgiu and Călăraşi are industrial river ports with little to offer – most travellers quickly pass through on the way to/from Bulgaria. Other towns, including Târgu Jiu, home of the famous Romanian sculptor Constantin Brâncuşi, and Curtea de Argeş, are jumping-off points for the southern Carpathians. From here the spectacular Trans-Făgărăşan highway – said to be one of the highest roads in Europe – cuts dramatically across the Făgărăş Mountains, passing en route what is considered to be Romania's most authentic 'Dracula's castle'.

History

Before the formation of Romania in the 19th century, the Romanians were known as *Vlachs*, hence *Wallachia*. Today these names are seldom used in Romania since both are considered derogatory – they originated in the 3rd century with the Goth word for 'foreigner'. Romanians call Wallachia 'Ţara Românească' (land of the Romanians).

Founded by Radu Negru in 1290, this principality was subject to Hungarian rule until 1330 when Basarab I (ruled 1310–52) defeated the Hungarian king Charles I and declared Wallachia independent, the first of the Romanian lands to achieve independence. The Wallachian princes *(voievozi)* built their first capital cities – Câmpulung Muscel, Curtea de Argeş and Târgovişte – close to the protective mountains, but in the 15th century Bucharest gained ascendancy.

After the fall of Bulgaria to the Turks in 1396 Wallachia faced a new threat, and in

Highlights

- Learn what systemisation meant in Scorniceşti, Ceauşescu's home village
- Hike up 1480 steps to the 'real' Dracula's castle at Poienari
- Take a train trip along the Danube River from Drobeta-Turnu Severin to Băile Herculane
- Peek into Bulgaria from Ostrov then head east to the Derveni Monastery
- Enjoy the 'Brâncuşi sculpture tour' in Târgu Jiu

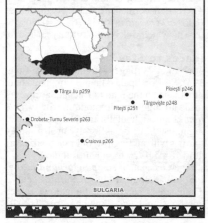

1415 Mircea cel Bătrân (Mircea the Old; r. 1386–1418) was forced to acknowledge Turkish suzerainty. Other Wallachian princes such as Vlad Ţepeş (r. 1448, 1456–62, 1476) and Mihai Viteazul (r. 1593–1601) became national heroes by defying the Turks and refusing to pay tribute. In 1859 Wallachia was united with Moldavia, paving the way for the modern Romanian state.

PLOIEŞTI

☎ 044 • postcode 2000 • pop 254,000

Ploieşti (pronounced ploy-esht), the main city in Prahova County, lures few tourists except those passing through on the way to the resorts of the Carpathian Mountains.

Oil has been refined in Ploieşti since 1857, accounting for Romania's ranking as first in Europe and sixth in the world in oil production between WWI and WWII. In 1936 Romania produced 8.7 million tons of oil. Sadly, since the mid-1970s Ploieşti's oilfields have rapidly declined. Today the town is heavily industrial with frighteningly bad pollution.

Orientation

Ploieşti has four train stations although most travellers will only use the southern (Gara Sud) and western (Gara Vest) ones. If you are arriving from Moldavia you'll alight at Gara Sud, a 15-minute walk from the centre. Exit the station and head north up Blvd Independenţei to Piaţa Victoriei. All the hotels, museums and restaurants are centred on this square.

If you arrive in town from Transylvania you will probably arrive at Gara Vest. From here, take bus No 1 or 2 to Piaţa Victoriei in the centre.

If you are coming from Bucharest or Târgovişte you could arrive at either station; get off at the southern station, as it's closer to the centre.

Information

The best tourist office is the Agenţia de Turism Passion (☎ 114 507, ☎/fax 115 118, e passion@starnets.ro) at Piaţa Victoriei 3 (entrance from Str Mihail Kogălniceanu).

The exchange office inside Hotel Prahova on Str Dobrogeanu Gherea is open 8 am to 8 pm weekdays, and 8.30 am to 1 pm Saturday. The Banca Agricolă, on the corner of Str Cerceluş and Blvd Independenţei, cashes travellers cheques, gives Visa/MasterCard cash advances and has an ATM; it's open 8.30 am to 2 pm weekdays. The BCIT next to the post office on Blvd Independenţei offers the same services; open 9 am to 3 pm weekdays.

The central post and telephone office is south of Piaţa Victoriei on Blvd Republicii; open 7 am to 8 pm weekdays, and 8 am to noon Saturday.

Intranet (☎ 141 823, e intranet@iuterpl us.ro), next to McDonald's on Piaţa Victoriei, offers Internet access for $1.50 per hour; open 10 am to 7 pm Monday to Saturday.

Things to See

Ploieşti is noted for its **Clock Museum** (Muzeul Ceasului), housed in a 19th-century building on Str Nicolae Simachei. Numerous types of clocks, including an 18th-century rococo Austrian clock that belonged to the Wallachian prince Alexandru Ioan Cuza are displayed; open 9 am to 5 pm Tuesday to Sunday ($0.25).

Close by at Str Dr Bagdasar 8 is Europe's only **Museum of Oil** (Muzeul Naţional al Petrolului; ☎ 123 564). Captions are in Romanian; open 9 am to 5 pm Tuesday to Sunday ($0.10).

Travellers interested in war history or coins shouldn't miss the **History & Archaeology Museum** (Muzeul de Istorie şi Arheologie; 1865), housed in a former girls' school at Str Toma Caragiu 10; open 9 am to 5 pm Tuesday to Sunday ($0.25). The museum has a memorial room to the Romanian novelist Ion Bassarabescu (1870–1952), famed for his 1927 novel *Priza*. The house in which he lived from 1940 until his death still stands on Str Ştefan cel Mare.

In the central park on Piaţa Victoriei, there is a **memorial** to the victims of the 1989 revolution. The **Culture Palace** (Palatul Culturii), at the northern end of the square, houses a dull **Biology Museum** (Muzeul de Biologie Umană) and an **Art Museum** (Muzeul de Artă Populară). The museums are open 9 am to 5 pm weekdays and 9 am to 1 pm weekends ($1). The main **Art Museum** (Muzeul de Artă) is housed in a large white building at Blvd Independenţei 1; open 9 am to 4.30 pm weekdays.

Opposite the **Culture Palace** (Casa de Cultură) lies the impressive **St John's Cathedral**, dating from 1810. To its east lies the **Central Market**, partly housed in two large, domed buildings.

Places to Stay

Agenţia de Turism Danalex (☎/fax 193 372), Piaţa Victoriei, Block west, Apt 30, is

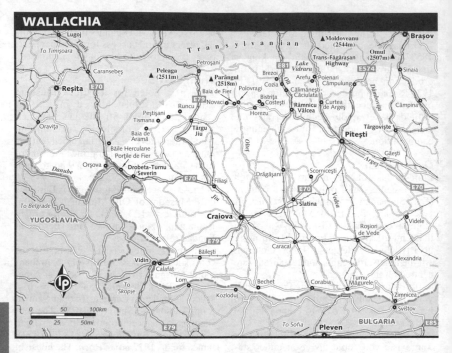

WALLACHIA

---

an agent for Antrec and arranges rooms in *private homes* from $10 a night, including breakfast.

Ploieşti has three hotels: the cheapest and gloomiest is the two-star *Hotel Prahova* (☎ 126 850, Str Dobrogeanu Gherea 11). Single/double rooms with private bathroom cost $14/20, including breakfast. A room with a TV costs an extra $0.50 per person per night.

Undergoing a major face-lift is the two-star *Hotel Central* (☎ 126 641, fax 122 243, Blvd Republicii 9) overlooking Piaţa Victoriei. Unrenovated single/double/triple rooms – with private bathroom, breakfast and a TV – are $17/26/32. Renovated rooms are $30/40/46, and apartments are $89.

The modern, three-star *Hotel Turist* (☎/fax 190 441, Str Tache Ionescu 6), with pleasant balconies overlooking the street, charges $31 for doubles, regardless of whether there is one or two of you; breakfast included.

Places to Eat

Eating options are limited. The *Braserie*, on Piaţa Victoriei above Cinema Patria, offers prime views of the city and serves a variety of uninspiring light snacks. Equally unappealing but favoured for its views of the cathedral is *Restaurant Ciocârlia* (Blvd Republicii 65). Much nicer is *Boulevard*, near the Clock Museum, which has the best summer garden in town. Across from Boulevard is the Italian-inspired *Club Mediteraneo*. Pizzas start from $1.75; closed Thursday.

For fast food you can't beat *McDonald's* on Piaţa Victoriei.

Vast amounts of vegetables, dry products, alcohol and fresh fish are housed in the two monster-sized halls of the *Central Market* (Halele Centrale), close to the cathedral on Blvd Unirii.

Getting There & Away

Train Trains to/from Târgovişte and Moldavia use the Gara Sud station, closest to

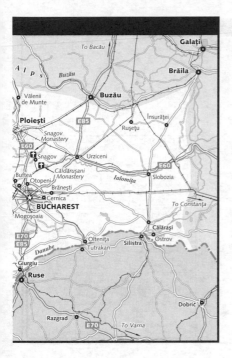

the town centre, at Piaţa 1 Decembrie 1918. Trains to/from Bucharest and Transylvania use Gara Vest. Advance tickets are sold at the Agenţie de Voiaj CFR (☎ 142 080) at Blvd Republicii 17; open 7 am to 8 pm weekdays (entrance from the pedestrianised street next to the Omnia department store).

From Gara Sud there is a daily train to Chişinău in Moldova (13¾ hours, 10.37 pm). The *Bulgaria Expres* stops at Gara Sud at 6.13 pm, arriving in Sofia at 7.15 am. Northbound, the train departs from Ploieşti at 9.04 am, arriving in Chernivtsi (Cernăuţi) at 8.10 pm.

Trains to Budapest from Bucharest stop at Ploieşti Vest (12 hours, daily at 1.09 and 8.08 am, and 5.41 and 8.06 pm) as does the daily Warsaw train (13½ hours, 9.24 pm).

Bus There are two stations: long-distance buses arrive at/depart from the northern bus station (Autogară Nord) at Str Griviţei 25. Buses to nearby villages use the southern

bus station (Autogară Sud), a two-minute walk from the southern train station on Str Depoului.

Daily services to/from the southern bus station include one to Bucharest (59km), eight to Câmpina (32km) and two to Târgovişte (52km).

Getting Around
Bus, tram and trolleybus tickets are sold at the public transport office (☎ 126 941) marked 'Coreco' on your left when you exit from Gara Sud. Bus Nos 1 and 2 go from Gara Sud to Piaţa Victoriei in the centre and then on to Gara Vest. From Gara Vest, bus No 2 continues to the university.

AROUND PLOIEŞTI
Câmpina
Heading north into the Prahova Valley you come to Câmpina (formerly spelt Cîmpina). Approaching this small town, 32km north of Ploieşti, you pass a memorial to pioneering pilot Aurel Vlaicu, who met his death in 1913 after his plane crashed as he attempted to cross the Carpathians.

Câmpina's main attraction is its **Nicolae Grigorescu Museum** (Muzeul Nicolae Grigorescu), Blvd Carol I 166, dedicated to the life and works of one of Romania's most exciting painters. Nicolae Grigorescu (1838–1907) started his career painting icons to support his family. He studied in Paris, doing a short stint at the studio of Sebastion Cornu where he studied with Pierre Auguste Renoir. His works attracted the attention of the Barbizon group and of Napoleon III, who bought two of his paintings in 1867. During the Romanian War of Independence (1877–78), Grigorescu worked as a frontline correspondent as an artist.

Farther north along Blvd Carol I is **Haşdeu Castle** (1888), considered one of the most bizarre castles in Romania. It was built by history professor Bogdan Petriceicu Haşdeu in memory of his academically brilliant daughter, Iulia, who died of tuberculosis at the age of 19. Although Iulia was buried in the Belu cemetery in Bucharest it was here that her father held seances to communicate with her.

WALLACHIA

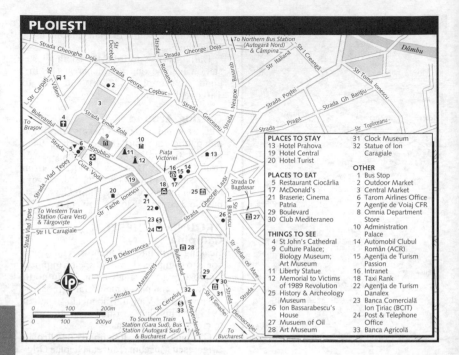

PLOIEŞTI

PLACES TO STAY
13 Hotel Prahova
19 Hotel Central
20 Hotel Turist

PLACES TO EAT
5 Restaurant Ciocârlia
17 McDonald's
21 Braserie; Cinema Patria
29 Boulevard
30 Club Mediteraneo

THINGS TO SEE
4 St John's Cathedral
9 Culture Palace; Biology Museum; Art Museum
11 Liberty Statue
12 Memorial to Victims of 1989 Revolution
25 History & Archeology Museum
26 Ion Bassarabescu's House
27 Musuem of Oil
28 Art Museum

31 Clock Museum
32 Statue of Ion Caragiale

OTHER
1 Bus Stop
2 Outdoor Market
3 Central Market
6 Tarom Airlines Office
7 Agenţie de Voiaj CFR
8 Omnia Department Store
10 Administration Palace
14 Automobil Clubul Român (ACR)
15 Agenţia de Turism Passion
16 Intranet
18 Taxi Rank
22 Agenţia de Turism Danalex
23 Banca Comercială Ion Ţiriac (BCIT)
24 Post & Telephone Office
33 Banca Agricolă

The two-star ***Hotel Muntenia*** (☎ 044-333 090, fax 333 092, Blvd Carol I 61) has reasonably priced single/double rooms for $24/32.

From Ploieşti's southern bus station there are eight buses daily to Câmpina (32km). There are also five daily trains from Ploieşti Vest to Câmpina.

TÂRGOVIŞTE
☎ 045 • postcode 0200 • pop 99,000

All eyes were on Târgovişte, 49km north-west of Bucharest, following the dramatic arrest here of communist president Nicolae Ceauşescu and his wife Elena on 22 December 1989. Four days later, the first bloody images of the hastily arranged court session and execution inside Târgovişte's military garrison flashed across the world's TV screens to prove that the two were in reality dead.

The Ceauşescus hijacked a car in Titu, 44km north-west of Târgovişte, where they were spotted by two soldiers who finally caught up with them in Târgovişte. They were tried in secret on Christmas Day then shot by a firing squad three hours later.

Târgovişte (formerly spelt Tîrgovişte) is a charming market town dating from 1396. It served as the capital of Wallachia from 1418 until 1659, after when the capital was moved to Bucharest. During the 15th century, Vlad Ţepeş, the notorious impaler with whom the fictitious Dracula is associated, held princely court here.

Orientation

The train station is a good 20-minute walk west from the centre. Exit the station and head east, past the military barracks (see Things to See later) up Blvd Castanilor, then turn right into Blvd Mircea cel Bătrân (previously Str Victoriei). All eastbound buses along this street stop in the centre. The bus station and central market are 3km north-west of town; turn right as you leave the station, then cross the large roundabout and take any eastbound bus down Calea Câmpulung.

Târgovişte's centre is divided into two parts, both within close proximity of each other. The main shops, banks and hotels are in the modern centre clustered around Central Park (Parcul Central), which is straddled by Blvd Libertăţii to the north and Blvd Mircea cel Bătrân to the south. The Princely Court and key museums are in the older part of town, along Calea Domnească, which cuts across the town from north to south.

Information

Tourist Offices Staff at the tourist office (☎ 634 491), adjoining Hotel Valahia on Blvd Libertăţii, speak some English and are generally helpful. Your best bet is to head straight for the Princely Court where you can buy tourist brochures in English or French covering all the main sights.

Money The Quantum exchange office, on the corner of Blvds Independenţiei and Mircea cel Bătrân, is open 9 am to 6 pm weekdays and 9 am to 2 pm Saturday. You can cash travellers cheques, get cash advances on Visa/MasterCard or use the ATM at the Banca Comercială Română on Blvd Mircea cel Bătrân; open 8 am to 12.30 pm weekdays.

Post & Telephone The central post office (dating from 1906) on Str Dr Marinoiu is open 7.30 am to 8 pm weekdays and 8 am to 1 pm Saturday. The telephone office on Str Ion Rădulescu is open 7 am to 8.30 pm daily.

Email & Internet Access Via Est Computers (☎/fax 213 235, e office@viaromwest.ro), Calea Domnească, Block X2, has Internet access for $0.50 per hour; open 9 am to midnight daily.

Things to See

The **military barracks**, where the Ceauşescus were executed, are immediately on the right as you leave the train station. At the hasty trial the pair faced joint charges of being accomplices to the murder of some 60,000

people, of genocide, and of attempting to flee Romania with state money, totalling $1 billion, stashed away in foreign bank accounts. None of the charges was proven. It's forbidden to enter or to take photographs of the garrison at the western end of Blvd Castanilor.

The bloodthirsty prince Vlad Ţepeş resided at the **Princely Court** (Curtea Domnească). The court was built in the 14th century for Mircea cel Bătrân (Mircea the Old) and remained a residence for Wallachia's princes until the reign of Constantin Brâncoveanu (r. 1688–1714). Mircea cel Bătrân fortified his court with defensive towers. From the 27m **Sunset Tower** (Turnul Chindiei), guards would announce the closing of the city gates as the sun went down. The tower today houses an exhibition recounting the happenings and horrors of Vlad Ţepeş' life. All the captions are in Romanian.

Immediately south of the entrance to the court is a small **Art Museum** (Muzeul de Artă). The local **History Museum** (Muzeul de Istorie Dâmboviţa) is not far away on the corner of Calea Domnească and Str Justiţei. The new **Museum of Romanian Police** (Muzeul Poliţiei Române), behind both the Art and History Museums, is open 9 am to 5 pm Tuesday to Sunday ($1).

A fascinating **Museum of Printing & Old Romanian Books** (Muzeul Tiparului şi al Cărţii Româneşti Vechi; ☎ 612 877) is housed in a 17th-century palace built by Constantin Brâncoveanu for his daughter Safta at Str Justiţei 3–5. Its prize exhibit is a manuscript dating from 1521, believed to be among the earliest texts written in Romanian (in the Cyrillic alphabet) to be preserved. A small **Writers' Museum** (Muzeul Scriitorilor Dâmboviţeni) adjoins the book museum.

Opposite is the **University Church** (Biserica Universităţii), dating from the 19th century. In front of it are busts of local academic Ienăchiţă Văcărescu (1740–97) and Radu de la Afumaţi, ruler of Wallachia from 1522 to 1529.

Heading south-west along Str Stelea, you pass the **Stelea Church** complex (Complexul Biserica Stelea), founded as a monastery by Moldavian prince Vasile Lupu (r. 1634–53)

WALLACHIA

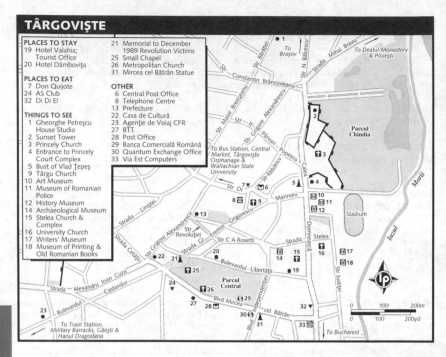

TÂRGOVIŞTE

PLACES TO STAY
19 Hotel Valahia;
   Tourist Office
20 Hotel Dâmboviţa

PLACES TO EAT
7 Don Quijote
24 AS Club
32 Di Di El

THINGS TO SEE
1 Gheorghe Petreşcu
   House Studio
2 Sunset Tower
3 Princely Church
4 Entrance to Princely
   Court Complex
5 Bust of Vlad Ţepeş
9 Târgu Church
10 Art Museum
11 Museum of Romanian
   Police
12 History Museum
14 Archaeological Museum
15 Stelea Church &
   Complex
16 University Church
17 Writers' Museum
18 Museum of Printing &
   Old Romanian Books

21 Memorial to December
   1989 Revolution Victims
25 Small Chapel
26 Metropolitan Church
31 Mircea cel Bătrân Statue

OTHER
6 Central Post Office
8 Telephone Centre
13 Prefecture
22 Casa de Cultură
23 Agenţie de Voiaj CFR
27 BTT
28 Post Office
29 Banca Comercială Română
30 Quantum Exchange Office
33 Via Est Computers

in 1645 as a peace offering to Wallachian ruler Matei Basarab. Few archaeological relics of interest are displayed at the small **Archaeological Museum** (Muzeul de Arheologie) at Str Stelea 4.

The Princely Court and all Târgovişte's museums are open 9 am to 7 pm Tuesday to Sunday ($0.50 each).

Continue west along Str Stelea, then left along Str Raudiţie onto Blvd Libertăţii. In **Central Park** a marble cross stands outside a **small chapel** dedicated to the victims of the December 1989 revolution. The 18th-century **Metropolitan Church** (Biserica Mitropoliei) is in the park. At its monks' quarters, the 16th-century **Dealu Monastery** on a hill 3km north-east of the centre, the head of the great Wallachian prince Mihai Viteazul (Michael the Brave) is buried. Beheaded on the orders of the Habsburg general George Basta on 3 August 1601, Viteazul is still hailed as the crusader of Romanian nationalism. It was at this monastery

that he had sworn his allegiance to the Hungarian emperor Rudolph II in 1598.

A few blocks north is the partially frescoed **Târgu Church** (Biserica Târgului), on Str Ion Rădulescu. The 1654 church was painted during the 17th and 18th centuries but destroyed during an earthquake in 1940. Extensive renovations followed in 1941 and again in the 1970s. Inside is a memorial plaque to local priest and teacher Professor Georgescu, who was among the thousands to die while toiling under communist forced labour to build the Danube–Black Sea Canal in Dobruja.

Testament to Romania's thousands of abandoned children is Marin Răducu's mural painting entitled **Wall of Childhood** (Zidul Copilăriei în Imagini). The mural decorates the concrete wall surrounding Târgovişte's largest orphanage. The painter, who spent his own childhood in an orphanage in Siliştea Gumeşti in the south of Dâmboviţa County, embarked on the project in the early 1990s in a bid to brighten up the lives of those who lived inside the grey compound. Many of the 105 children in the orphanage helped Răducu paint the wall. The orphanage (Casa de Copii; ☎ 612 327) is in a run-down housing area in the western suburbs at Str Moldovei 5, close to the Wallachian State University. Visitors are welcome to visit the orphanage.

Heading out of town north along Str Maior Brezişeanu, you pass the small **Gheorghe Petreşcu House Studio** (Casa Atelier Gheorghe Petreşcu). The Romanian still-life, landscape and portrait painter (1872–1949) spent the last 20 years of his life in Târgovişte, where he captured most of the town's major sights on canvas.

Places to Stay

Providing you speak basic Romanian or are an expert at wild gesticulations, you should be able to secure yourself a bed for the night in a *private home* with BTT (☎ 634 224, 213 776), Blvd Mircea cel Bătrân, Block H1. A private room should cost around $10.

Overlooking the central square is *Hotel Valahia* (☎ 634 491, Blvd Libertăţii 7). Spacious single/double rooms with private bath cost $17/20, including breakfast.

The three-star *Hotel Dâmboviţa* (☎ 213 370, fax 613 961, Blvd Libertăţii 1) has some rooms with balconies overlooking the park for $21/29, while other rooms without the view but just as pleasant are $19/26. All include breakfast.

Some 22km south of Târgovişte on the main road to Piteşti (Şoseaua Târgovişte-Găeşti), is *Hanul Dragodana* (☎ 711 109), a large inn offering double rooms with private bath for $10. The inn's large 24-hour restaurant is popular with truckers.

Places to Eat

Di Di El (☎ 211 952, Calea Domenască, Block A), a five-minute walk from Hotel Valahia, serves huge, well-topped pizzas and great spaghetti for no more than $5 including a bottle of wine. It has an outside terrace and takeaway service.

The *AS Club* (☎ 613 208, Str Arsenalului 13) is a small, cheap restaurant frequented by locals. The outside terrace is a good spot for coffee and light snacks.

Highly recommended for its Romanian cuisine is the popular *Don Quijote (Str Dr Marinoiu 9)*, opposite the main post office. The restaurant's cosy interior, complete with a stone fireplace, is inviting.

Getting There & Away

Train Advance tickets are sold at the Agenţie de Voiaj CFR (☎ 611 554), just north of the train station at Blvd Castanilor 2; open 7 am to 7 pm weekdays.

From Târgovişte there are five local trains daily to Ploieşti Sud (1¾ hours). To get to Târgovişte from other cities, you have to change trains at Ploieşti Sud.

Bus Major daily services from Târgovişte include 13 to Bucharest (78km), four to Câmpulung (73km), two to Ploieşti (52km) and Braşov (90km), and one to Râmnicu Vâlcea (267km).

PITEŞTI

☎ 048 • postcode 0300 • pop 186,000

Piteşti is a large, industrial, heavily polluted town that most Romanians will tell you to avoid. They're right. Nevertheless, the city is one of Romania's great commercial centres with one of the country's few stretches of motorway *(autostrada)* bringing motorists the 114km west from Bucharest. Since 1966, Dacia cars – modelled on the old Renault 12 and the butt of endless jokes – have been produced here. In mid-1999, French car manufacturer Renault paid $50 million for a majority stake in Dacia and intends to invest a further $220 million over the next five years.

Orientation

Confusingly, Piteşti has two bus stations and two train stations but most travellers only use the stations in the south. Buses to/from Bucharest and other major cities in Romania all arrive/depart from the southern bus station (Autogară Sud), off the southern end of Blvd Brătianu on Str Abatorului Târgul din Vale. All Bucharest and Curtea de Argeş trains stop at the southern

WALLACHIA

train station (officially Piteşti Sud but known as Piteşti) on Blvd Republicii. Bus Nos 2, 4 and 8 run between the train station and town.

Blvd Republicii leads west from the train station to the town centre. The main pedestrianised street, Str Victoriei, is where all the hotels, restaurants and tourist offices are. It runs parallel to Blvd Republicii.

Maps The outdated *Municipiul Piteşti* map (1997) includes a detailed city map and a map of Argeş County. It is sold for $1 at the tourist office and at the reception of Hotel Argeş on Piaţa Muntenia.

Information
Tourist Offices The tourist office (☎ 625 450) adjoining Hotel Muntenia (separate entrance on Str Victoriei) arranges excursions to Curtea de Argeş, sells maps and organises car rental; open 8 am to 6 pm Monday to Thursday and 8 am to 4 pm Friday.

Money There is a currency exchange inside Hotel Muntenia. The Banca Comercială Română, Blvd Republicii 83, cashes travellers cheques, gives cash advances on Visa/MasterCard and has an ATM; open 8 am to 12.30 pm weekdays.

Post & Telephone The central post office is opposite the church at the southern end of Str Victoriei; open 8 am to 8 pm weekdays, and 8 am to noon Saturday. The telephone office at Blvd Victoriei 8 is open 7 am to 9 pm daily.

Things to See
After WWII, **Piteşti prison**, just north of the centre on Str Negru Vodă, was selected by the communist government as the site for its 'Student Re-education Centre' because of its high security and its isolation. Operational since 1900, it was not until 1949, following the arrest of some anticommunist students in 1948 on charges of belonging to the National Peasant Party, the Iron Guard, or the Zionist movement, that psychiatric abuse became a major feature of the already harsh prison regime. The experiment was part of a crackdown during which an estimated 180,000 people were rounded up and sent to labour camps and prisons. More than 30 prisoners died and hundreds were tortured during the four years of the experiment. See the boxed text 'From Victim to Torturer'.

Today a tall, mosaic-tiled **column** in memory of those who died marks the spot where the prison stood. It stands between the first two of three apartment blocks built on the site. A **military hospital** (Spitalul Militar; 1881) still stands opposite.

The existence of the prison and the atrocities committed are completely ignored in the county **History Museum** (Muzeul Judeţean de Istorie) overlooking the small central park at Str Armand Călinescu 4; open 10 am to 6 pm daily except Monday ($0.20). Crossing the park towards Blvd Republicii you pass the **monument** in memorial to those who died in the 1907 peasant uprising.

On Str Victoriei, the unusual St George's Church (Biserica Sfântul Gheorghe), also known as the **Princely Church** (Biserica Domnească), was built by Prince Constantin Şerban and his wife Princess Bălasa between 1654 and 1658. The church housed a school in the 18th century.

West of the centre in the Trivale district is a large **forest and park** (Parcul Pădurea Trivale). Approaching the park along Str Trivale from the centre, you pass **Heroes' Gate** (Poarta Eroilor), erected in 1916–18 in memory of those who died during WWI. Farther into the forest is a **zoo**; open 10 am to 7 pm Wednesday to Sunday ($0.20). From June to August, a bus runs from Autogară Sud to the zoo hourly between 8.30 am and 7.30 pm.

Places to Stay
Piteşti's central hotels are within spitting distance of one another. The one-star *Hotel Argeş* (☎ 625 450), on Piaţa Muntenia opposite the Muntenia, is the cheapest, charging $10 for doubles with shared bath.

The smallest and friendliest is the two-star *Hotel Carmen* (☎ 222 699, *Blvd Republicii 84*). Doubles with private bath cost $17. Oddly enough breakfast is only included for one person; the extra breakfast costs $1.75.

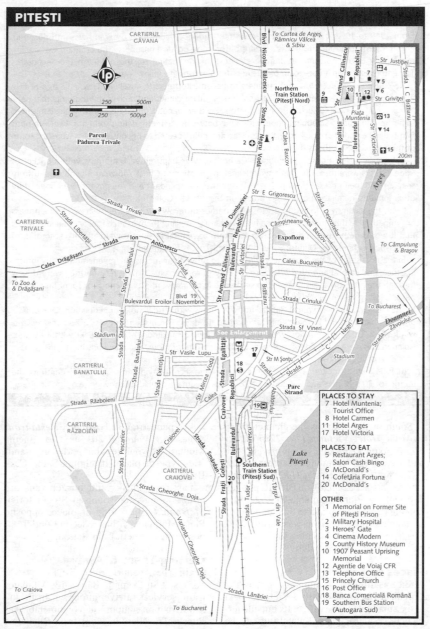

PITEŞTI

PLACES TO STAY
7 Hotel Muntenia;
  Tourist Office
8 Hotel Carmen
11 Hotel Arges
17 Hotel Victoria

PLACES TO EAT
5 Restaurant Arges;
  Salon Cash Bingo
6 McDonald's
14 Cofeţăria Fortuna
20 McDonald's

OTHER
1 Memorial on Former Site
  of Piteşti Prison
2 Military Hospital
3 Heroes' Gate
4 Cinema Modern
9 County History Museum
10 1907 Peasant Uprising
   Memorial
12 Agentie de Voiaj CFR
13 Telephone Office
15 Princely Church
16 Post Office
18 Banca Comercială Română
19 Southern Bus Station
   (Autogara Sud)

WALLACHIA

From Victim to Torturer

From 1949 to 1952 a unique and experimental 'student re-education program' was introduced in Piteşti, Gherla and Aiud prisons as a means of torturing political prisoners. The program was implemented by Eugen Ţurcanu, an inmate at Piteşti prison, acting on the orders of the Securitate. Ţurcanu rounded up a core team of torturers from among his fellow inmates.

Re-education induced tortured prisoners to become torturers themselves. The first stage of this grotesque process involved the prisoner confessing all his crimes and 'anti-state' thoughts that he'd failed to earlier reveal to Securitate interrogators. He then signed a declaration in which he consented to his 're-education'. Scrubbing floors with a rag between the teeth, eating soup hog-like with both hands tied behind the back, licking toilets clean and being beaten to unconsciousness were just some of the persuasive methods used.

Religiously inclined prisoners, dubbed 'Catholics', were baptised each morning with a bucket of urine. Others were forced to don a white sheet in imitation of Christ and wear a penis carved from soap around their necks. Fellow prisoners kissed the soap pendant and the prisoner was flogged by other inmates in imitation of Christ's ordeal on the road to Golgotha.

Next, the victim was forced to disclose the names of fellow inmates who'd shown him kindness or sympathy. He then had to renounce his own family, 'reviling them in such foul and hideous terms that it would be next to impossible ever to return to natural feelings towards them', according to former political prisoner Dimitru Bacu in his novel The Anti-Humans.

In the final stage of the program, victims had to prove their successful 'regeneration' – by inflicting the same mental and physical abuse on new prison recruits. If they refused they were driven through the program again. Those who slackened in their new role as re-educator spent time in the prison's incarceration cell, black room, or isolation cell.

The incarceration cells were 1.8m-tall upright coffins with a small hole for ventilation. One or two prisoners had to stand in these cells for eight to 15 days. The black room was 2.7 sq metres and windowless. Up to 30 prisoners were detained here for a maximum of three weeks without water. Isolation cells were reserved for sentences of three months or more, and many prisoners kept in these cells died of tuberculosis.

In 1954 Eugen Ţurcanu and 21 other prisoners were secretly tried and sentenced to death for the murder of 30 prisoners and the abuse of 780. The Securitate denied all knowledge of the program.

South of the centre is the characterless, two-star **Hotel Victoria** (☎ 622 566, Str Maior Şonţu 2). Doubles with private bath and TV are $19 including breakfast.

The towering, three-star **Hotel Muntenia** (☎ 625 450, fax 214 556), on Blvd Republicii overlooking Piaţa Muntenia, has doubles ranging in price from $15 to $28, depending on how recently the room was refurbished. The hotel's facilities include a billiard room, bar, restaurant and nightclub.

Places to Eat

Choice is limited. A popular spot is the **Cofetâria Fortuna**, on Blvd Victoriei next to the small telephone office. Its outside terrace is good for people-watching on the busy pedestrianised street. **Restaurant Argeş** (Str Victoriei 20), next to Cinema Modern, is your regular pork cutlet-and-fries type of place. It adjoins Salon Cash Bingo.

Fast-food kiosks and burger vans are dotted along pedestrianised Str Victoriei. **McDonald's** has pride of place, opposite Piaţa Muntenia. It has a second outlet opposite the southern train station.

Getting There & Away

Train The Agenţie de Voiaj CFR (☎ 630 565) is at Str Domniţa Bălaşa 13. All major train services arrive at/depart from the southern train station, listed on timetables as Piteşti. Travellers heading from Bucharest to Curtea de Argeş have to change trains at Piteşti.

Bus

All major services use Autogară Sud. Daily services include two to Alexandria (272km) and Râmnicu Vâlcea (75km), three to Braşov (136km), five to Bucharest (108km), and one to Craiova (142km) and Târgu Jiu (174km).

Two buses depart daily from Autogară Sud to Istanbul. Tickets are sold by the Öz Murat travel agency (☎ 221 151) at the bus station.

SCORNICEŞTI

Some 38km south-west of Piteşti, off the main E70 highway to Craiova, lies Scorniceşti, one of the most publicised villages in Romania, not least because it was the birthplace of Nicolae Ceauşescu. The communist dictator actually only spent the first 11 years of his life in the small rural village. The village first made national headlines in 1976 when the remains of Europe's first *Homo sapiens* were allegedly found here.

In 1988 Scorniceşti gained further notoriety when, as part of the president's systemisation scheme (see the boxed text 'Systemisation'), the centre of the village was bulldozed and rebuilt with characterless apartment blocks. A gigantic football stadium was consequently added to the concrete montage – a present from Ceauşescu to his home town. Scorniceşti was among the first villages to be razed under the scheme, although the ornate street lamps and grandiose flowerbeds which run the length of the central street somehow failed to make their way into other systemised villages.

Ceauşescu's childhood home was spared. Prior to 1989, the small cottage housed a museum dedicated to the dictator. Following the December revolution the museum was closed. The house is tended by Ceauşescu's sister who lives in a small house opposite. A photograph of Ceauşescu at his mother's funeral in 1977 and another of him and Elena admiring corn in a field are displayed on the chimney breast in the hallway. In the bedroom there is a painting of his parents and, above the bed, a tapestry portrait of Ceauşescu.

The house is not officially open to visitors, but if you are willing to face Ceauşescu's formidable sister she may let you in.

Ceauşescu's mother Alexandra (1889–1977) and father Andruţa (1890–1972) are buried in the family grave in the village cemetery farther north along the main road; continue past the Ceauşescu house and turn left at the junction.

Scorniceşti is signposted west off the main Piteşti-Craiova road. The house is at the northernmost end of the village. Drive through the centre and continue along the main road until you cross a small bridge. The house is the first on the left, immediately after the bridge.

CURTEA DE ARGEŞ

☎ 048 • postcode 0450

Curtea de Argeş, a princely seat in the 14th century after the capital of Wallachia was moved here from Câmpulung Muscel, is a welcoming place for visitors. The church is considered to be the oldest monument preserved in its original form in Wallachia, while the monastery (or episcopal cathedral), made from polished, sculpted stone on the fringe of the town, is unique for its chocolate-box architecture and the host of royal tombs it hides.

Orientation

The train station, a 19th-century architectural monument, is 100m north of the bus station on Str Albeşti. To get to the centre – a 10-minute walk – turn left along Str Albeşti, then bear right at the fork up the cobbled Str Castanilor. Cross the small square and turn left along Str Negru Vodă. At the crossroads continue straight until you reach a statue of Basarab I, where the road forks in three directions. All the major sights, camping ground and hotels (signposted) are a short walk from here. Continue walking straight ahead, past the princely court on the left, for Blvd Basarabilor.

Information

The tourist office inside Hotel Posada, at the northern end of Blvd Basarabilor, is open 8 am to 4 pm weekdays. The hotel also

Systemisation

Ceaușescu's systemisation plan, approved in 1974 but not implemented until 1988, condemned thousands of villages to being bulldozed off the map in a bid to curb private farming and create more state agricultural land. Displaced villagers were to be uprooted to purpose-built communal apartment blocks where – according to propaganda – a new life utilising the 'experience of the peasant with the efficiency of the Marxist worker' awaited them.

Of Romania's 13,123 villages, all but 5000 were destined to be destroyed by the year 2000. Some three million people would have to abandon their homes, cattle and traditional rural lifestyle in the process.

Ceaușescu ignored the fact that it was these small farmsteads that produced 20% of the country's milk, 25% of its fruit and 14% of its meat. Instead he greedily focused on the additional 4.5% of agricultural land the state would acquire by squeezing the rural population into a smaller geographical area.

The first villages to be systemised in August 1988 were Buda, Demieni, Odoleanu and Vlădiceasca in the Ilfov district north of Bucharest, and Scornicești (Ceaușescu's home village). Villagers were given just a few days' notice to evacuate their homes which were flattened to make way for new 'agro-industrial complexes'. Few accommodation blocks had running water, while kitchens were shared by up to 10 families. Despite being assured otherwise, there was no opportunity for villagers to grow their own fruit and vegetables or keep livestock, leaving many in dire financial straits.

Widespread hostility from the West forced Ceaușescu to abandon systemisation in 1989. Pressure was also exerted on the Romanian government by Hungary, who perceived the scheme as a tool for destroying the last remaining strongholds of Hungarian culture in Transylvania. For the thousands sentenced to a life of misery confined within four grey walls devoid of their ancestors' warming spirits, the damage had already been done.

has a currency exchange. The post office at Blvd Basarabilor 121 is open 7 am to 8 pm weekdays. The telephone office, in the same building, is open the same hours plus 8 am to 2 pm Saturday.

You can change money, cash travellers cheques or use the ATM at the Banca Comercială Română, farther north along Blvd Basarabilor; open 8 am to 2 pm weekdays.

Things to See

The ruins of Curtea de Argeș' **Princely Court** (Curtea Domnească), an ensemble originally comprising a church and palace, are in the centre. The church was built in the 14th century by Basarab I, whose statue stands in the square outside the entrance to the court. Basarab died in Târgoviște in 1352. His burial place near the altar in the princely church at Curtea de Argeș was discovered in 1939. The princely court was rebuilt by Basarab's son, Nicolae Alexandru Basarab (r. 1352–68) and completed by Vlaicu Vodă

(r. 1361–77). While little remains of the palace today, the 14th-century church (built on the ruins of a 13th-century church) is almost perfectly intact. The church is lovingly tended by a dedicated, French-speaking caretaker who guides visitors around; open 9 am to 5 pm daily ($0.75).

Opposite the entrance to the court is the **County Museum** (Muzeul Orășenesc; ☎ 711 446) at Str Negru Vodă 2, open 9 am to 4 pm Tuesday to Sunday. Rising on a hill behind the park opposite are the ruins of the 14th-century **Sân Nicoară Church** (Biserica Sân Nicoară). Also signposted from here is the tiny, 17th-century **Olari Church** (Biserica Olari), at the end of a dirt track.

Back in the centre, walk past the Princely Court and head north along Str Basarabilor for 1km until you reach **Curtea de Argeș Monastery** (Mănăstirea Curtea de Argeș). The fantastic episcopal cathedral was built between 1514 and 1526 by Neagoe Basarab (r. 1512–21) with marble and mosaic tiles from Constantinople. Legend has it that the wife of the master stonemason, Manole, is embedded in the stone walls of the church, in accordance with a local custom which obliged the mason to bury a loved one alive within the church to ensure the success of his work. Manole could not bear to continue life without his wife and killed himself.

The current edifice dates from 1875 when French architect André Lecomte du Nouy was brought in to save the monastery, which was in near ruins, from demolition.

The white marble tombstones of Carol I (1839–1914) and his poet wife Elizabeth (1853–1916) lie on the right in the monastery's *pronaos* (entrance hall). On the left of the entrance are the tombstones of King Ferdinand I (1865–1927) and British-born Queen Marie (1875–1938) whose heart, upon her request, was put in a gold casket and buried in her favourite palace in Balcic in southern Dobruja. Following the ceding of southern Dobruja to Bulgaria in 1940, however, her heart was moved to a marble tomb in Bran. Today, it rests in Bucharest's National History Museum. Neagoe Basarab and his wife Stâna are also buried in the pronaos.

In the park opposite lies the legendary **Manole's well** (fântâna lui Manole), a natural spring. The story goes that the doomed Manole fell to the ground from the roof of the monastery when, during the building process, his master, Neagoe, removed the scaffolding. With the aid of miraculous wings made from roofing tiles, he made it as far as the park before coming down to earth with an almighty bump. The natural spring marks his landing pad.

Places to Stay

The friendly *Camping Sân Nicoarâ (☎ 722 126, Str Plopis 34)*, behind Sân Nicoarâ church, has wooden chalets with double beds for $7 and six-bed apartments for $21. The communal showers are clean but there is no running hot water. Turn right at the Basarab I statue along Str Sân Nicoarâ. The site is 100m up the hill on the right.

Hotel Posada (☎ 711 800, fax 711 802, Blvd Basarabilor 27–29, e posada@starne ts.ro) has decent doubles with private

shower/bath for $17/21 and doubles with cable TV and bath for $28.

Six kilometres north of Curtea de Argeş, in Albeşti de Argeş, is the large **Hanul Albeşti** inn; open from June to August only.

Places to Eat

The *Black & White Café (Blvd Basarabilor 123)* is a popular, air-conditioned cafe which serves light snacks during the day and is transformed into a busy bar at night. Farther north, *Montana Restaurant & Pizzerie*, on Blvd Basarabilor, serves up plenty of fresh pizzas and beer. Most nights there is live music.

Traditional dishes are served at *Restaurant Capra Neagrâ*, on Str Alexandru Lahovary just off the southern end of Blvd Basarabilor. It has a great terrace.

After hours, *Disco Club Cristal (Str Episcop Ghenadie 12)*, a smoky bar with two billiard tables, is *the* place to hang out. Otherwise, *Disco Tiamo*, on Blvd Basarabilor inside Cinema Unirea, rocks 10 pm to 5 am Thursday to Sunday ($0.50).

Getting There & Away

Major daily bus services include two to Bucharest (4½ hours), Braşov (four hours) and Câmpulung Muscel (1½ hours); four to Râmnicu Vâlcea (50 minutes); and nine to Poienari (40 minutes, services are reduced on weekends).

There are five trains daily to Piteşti (one hour) and four to Bucharest (3½ hours).

POIENARI & AREFU

From Curtea de Argeş, most Dracula fiends head north up the Argeş Valley to **Poienari citadel** (Cetatea Poienari). In 1459, Turks captured by Vlad Ţepeş, in revenge for killing his father and brother, marched along this route. At the end of the march, the Turks built the defensive fortress for the bloodthirsty prince. The result – a castle strategically positioned to guard the entrance from Transylvania into the Argeş Valley – is considered by Dracula buffs to be Romania's 'real' Dracula's castle.

Some 1480 steps lead up from the side of a hydroelectric power plant to the castle ruins. A substantial amount of the castle, which towers on a crag above the village, fell down the side of the mountain in 1888. Tickets to the castle are sold by the castle-keeper at the top of the steps ($0.50).

Six kilometres south of Poienari citadel is **Arefu**, a tiny village inhabited solely by descendants of the minions who served Vlad Ţepeş – or at least that is the line upon which Arefu markets itself! Tourists following the Dracula trail come here in their droves to sit around camp fires, sing folk songs and listen to tales told by villagers whose forebears mingled with the notorious impaler.

Legend has it that in 1462, when the Turks besieged Poienari citadel, the Arefians helped Vlad Ţepeş to escape into the mountains. His wife, convinced they would not escape alive from the surrounded castle, had already flung herself from the turret. As an expression of gratitude, Ţepeş gave the Arefians their pasture lands. A document signed by Mircea Ciobanul (1545–52) in 1540 attests to the people of Arefu having earlier been granted 16 mountains and 14 sheepfolds by Ţepeş.

Just 1km north of the fortress lies the artificial **Lake Vidraru**, which was dammed between 1961 and 1966 to feed the hydro-electric power plant. From here the **Trans-Făgărăşan highway**, a mountain pass which peaks at 2034m, crosses the Carpathians into Transylvania. The tunnel cutting between the Negoiu and Moldoveanu peaks is 845m long. The pass, allegedly built by the army as a training exercise, is only open for some three months of the year. A sign at the side of the road south of Poienari citadel tells you whether it is open or closed.

Places to Stay

Villagers in Arefu are accustomed to having tourists stay in their homes. Ask for a room in the shop in the centre of the village or go to the school director who coordinates the local *agro-tourism* set-up. The director's house is the large one on the right as you enter the village. Accommodation can also be arranged in advance through the Transylvania Society of Dracula (☎/fax 01-679 5742, ☎/fax 231 4022), Blvd Primăverii 47,

Bucharest, which arranges guided tours to Poienari with overnight stays in Arefu.

Two kilometres south of Poienari in Căpăţânenii is *Popasul Drumeţul* (☎ 048-730 389), which has basic double wooden huts for $4 a night. The camping ground is just off the main Curtea de Argeş–Poienari road, on the side road to Arefu.

The large, chalet-style *Cabana Cumpăna*, on the western side of Lake Vidraru, runs a small camping ground and has two/three/five-bed rooms in its main building for $18/23/33 a night, including breakfast. It costs $1.50 per person to pitch a tent. Advance bookings can be made through Hotel Posada in Curtea de Argeş.

On the eastern side of the lake is the small *Casa Argeşeana* (☎ 048-730 309), which has a handful of double rooms for $5 a night. Continue north towards Lake Bâlea and Sibiu to find the popular *Hotel Bâlea Cascadă*.

WEST TO TÂRGU JIU

Poienari village proper lies 5km south of the main road which leads west from Curtea de Argeş to the industrialised town of **Râmnicu Vâlcea** (formerly spelt Rîmnicu Vîlcea). Antrec (☎ 050-749 706) has an office here, and there is a camping ground 2km north of the town run by the same company that manages *Hotel Alutus* (☎ 050-736 601, fax 737 760, Str General Praporgescu 10), which is in the town centre. Single/double rooms in the hotel vary from $21/28 to $28/37 depending on the storey of the room.

From Râmnicu Vâlcea you can head north up the Olt Valley to **Călimăneşti-Căciulata**, a jaded twin-spa resort which has lost much of its appeal since the days when it was among Europe's most fashionable resorts. It was a favourite haunt of Napoleon III and was awarded a gold medal for its mineral waters at Vienna in 1873. The old Roman town comes to life during the first week of August, when it hosts a large folk music and crafts festival.

Accommodation can be arranged through Călimăneşti-Căciulata SR (☎/fax 050-750 270, 750 990), Calea lui Traian 413.

Medieval Sibiu's Piaţa Griviţa

Villagers in traditional Székely costumes

Street scene in the Saxon town of Mediaş

Târgovişte's 14th-century Princely Court complex, where Vlad Ţepeş resided

MARK DAFFEY

Bran Castle, known as 'Dracula's Castle', sits in a mountain pass south of Braşov.

MATTHIAS LÜFKENS

The superb royal Peleş Castle in Sinaia

NICOLA WILLIAMS

Elizabeth, king Carol I's wife, Peleş Castle, Sinaia

Just a couple of kilometres north lie the **Cozia & Turnul Monasteries**. The monastery at Cozia was built by Mircea cel Bătrân in the late 14th century and today shelters the Wallachian prince's tomb. The original fountain dates from 1517, to which another was added by Constantin Brâncoveanu in 1711. A museum is also sheltered in the complex.

Costeşti

Fifty-one weeks of the year, the mountain village of Costeşti in the southern Carpathians, 2km north along a dirt track signposted off the main Râmnicu Vâlcea–Târgu Jiu road, is a sleepy village. During the first week of September, it buzzes with flamboyant dancing and music-making, horse-trading and copper-pot-selling, as Romania's Roma (Gypsy) community flocks to Costeşti by horse and cart (or expensive Mercedes as the case may be!) to celebrate Romania's largest **Roma festival**.

Thousands of Roma attend the Costeşti fair during which lucrative business deals are struck and marriages arranged. The festival is also attended by the two rival figureheads of the Roma community – the self-proclaimed emperor of Roma worldwide, Iulian Rădulescu, and the Romanian Roma king, Florin Cioabă (see the boxed text 'Battle for the Roma Crown' under Sibiu in the Transylvania chapter).

The village of Costeşti is 82km east of **Cem Romengo**, a symbolic 'Roma State' declared in an outlying district of Târgu Jiu by emperor Iulian Rădulescu in March 1997. The Cem Romengo, which has no official frontiers, was proclaimed after 40 Roma were arrested for building houses on state-owned agricultural land.

Bistriţa & Arnota Monasteries

Bistriţa Monastery (Mănăstirea Bistriţa), one of Romania's most impressive monasteries, is 6km north of Costeşti. The current Brâncoveanu-style building (1856) was built on the site of a former 15th-century monastery. The first book printed in Wallachia (1508) is preserved in the monastery. Until 1982 the monastery sheltered one of the country's largest schools for handicapped

children, now housed in a separate building at the entrance to the monastery estate. Some 800m from the main monastery building is the **Peştera Sfântul Gheorghe**, a hillside chapel hidden in the 'St George' cave in the hillface and previously used to keep the monastery's treasures safe.

From Bistriţa Monastery a forest road leads 4km north to the smaller **Arnota Monastery** (Mănăstirea Arnota). Ancient crosses are carved in the sheer rock face lining the southern end of this road. Wallachian prince Matei Basarab, who had the monastery begun in 1636 (it was completed in 1706), is buried here.

Horezu Monastery

Equally splendid in riches and magnitude is the fortified Horezu monasterial complex, a Unesco World Heritage site 7km farther west along the Târgu Jiu road. Built during the reign of Constantin Brâncoveanu, it is considered one of Romania's most remarkable examples of the unique synthesis of Western and Oriental architectural styles for which he became famed. The church has an unusually large pronaos and open porch supported by ornate stone-carved columns. During the 17th and 18th centuries Horezu housed the country's most prestigious fresco-painting school.

Three kilometres south of the turn-off for Horezu Monastery is the village of **Măldăreşti**, home to an ethnographic museum housed in a traditional *cula* dating from 1688. Culas – small, square, two-floored houses with an outside porch supported by two pillars – were built in Romania until the end of the 18th century.

Places to Stay Horezu Monastery is signposted off the main road 1km east of Horezu village. There is a small *Popas Turistic* with simple wooden huts at the western end of the village.

Antrec, which has an agent in Târgu Jiu (see the Târgu Jiu section later), arranges rooms in *private homes* for $5 to $10 a night; alternatively you can contact the families involved in the agro-tourism scheme direct. In Horezu village contact the Figura family (☎ 050-860 113), the Bălasa family (☎ 050-860 375) or the Dăscălete family (☎ 050-860 094).

Polovragi & the Women's Cave

From Horezu a dirt road heads west to the 18th-century **Polovragi Monastery** (Mănăstirea Polovragi), founded by Radu the Handsome (r. 1474–75) in 1470. Every year in June the monastery hosts a folk craft fair. Close to the monastery is a small cave.

The **Women's Cave** (Peştera Muierilor), at the gateway to the Galbenul Gorges, 3km from Baia de Fier, was named following the discovery of bones on the cave's upper floor. Archaeologists believe these bones to be those of women who used to retreat into the cave for safety during invasions in the Middle Ages. The cave is one of the few in Romania to be properly lit and equipped with guides, who show tourists around.

TÂRGU JIU

☎ 053 • postcode 1400 • pop 98,000

Târgu Jiu is home to the internationally famed modernist sculptures of Constantin Brâncuşi (1876–1957). It also lies in the heart of the Jiu Valley mining region. Frequent strikes in this region from the 1980s onwards paralysed industrial activity, forcing the communists to give in to the miners' militant demands. The miners' mass descent upon Bucharest in 1990 ended in bloodshed and their 1991 rampage led to the fall of Petre Roman's first postrevolution government.

As part of its grand plan to close the country's unprofitable pits, the government offered lucrative redundancy pay-offs to miners. A mass exodus of miners and their families from the Jiu Valley's industrial towns followed.

In early 1999, 10,000 striking miners smashed their way through police barricades as they marched towards Bucharest in protest against layoffs and low wages. After a 17-day strike, a deal was struck with the government for pay rises and the reopening of pits closed in 1998. But when the government reneged on the deal six days later, more violent protests and riots were sparked.

Protest leader Miron Cozma was eventually sentenced to 18 years in prison over the deadly 1991 protests. This harsh sentence was intended to show the IMF that the government was determined to forge ahead with plans to close hundreds of coal mines and loss-making factories, and pay off Romania's staggering $3 billion foreign debt.

During WWII, Târgu Jiu prison was home to communist leader Gheorghe Gheorghiu-Dej; Nicolae Ceauşescu, the then secretary-general of the Union of Communist Youth; and Ion Iliescu, who replaced Ceauşescu as president in 1990.

Orientation

Târgu Jiu centre, east of the Jiu River, is a 15-minute walk from the bus and train stations. Exit the station and turn right along Str Nicolae Titulescu, which becomes Blvd Republicii, until you reach Str Unirii, the main thoroughfare, which cuts across town from east to west. Head 500m west along Str Unirii then turn right onto Calea Victoriei. The main hotels, shops and restaurants are dotted along the pedestrianised section of this street.

Information

Tourist Offices The official tourist office, OJT Gorj (☎/fax 214 010), adjoining Hotel Gorj on Calea Eroilor, is actually quite helpful and some staff speak English. It is an agent for Antrec and can arrange rooms in private homes in surrounding villages, provide a guide for the day for $15 and arrange picnics in the countryside for $15.

The Automobil Clubul Român (ACR; ☎ 214 563, fax 212 593) has an office on Calea Victoriei.

Money There is a currency exchange inside the ACR office, open 9 am to 4 pm weekdays. The Banca Română Pentru Dezvoltare, in the centre on Calea Victoriei, cashes travellers cheques, gives cash advances on Visa/MasterCard and has an ATM; open 8 am to 2 pm weekdays.

Post & Telephone The post office at the southern end of Str Vasile Alecsandri is

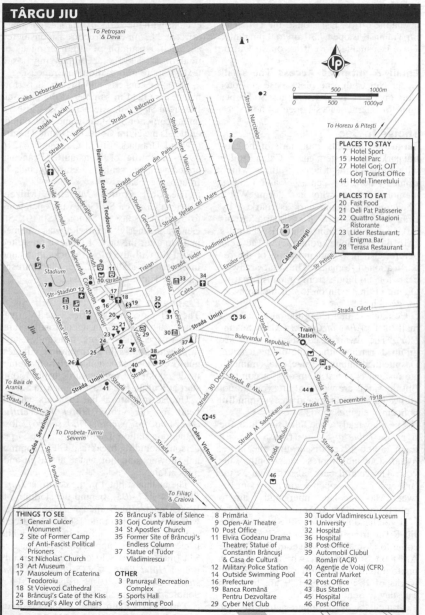

TÂRGU JIU

To Petroşani & Deva

To Horezu & Piteşti

To Baia de Arania

To Drobeta-Turnu Severin

To Filiaşi & Craiova

0   500   1000m
0   500   1000yd

WALLACHIA

PLACES TO STAY
7 Hotel Sport
15 Hotel Parc
27 Hotel Gorj; OJT Gorj Tourist Office
44 Hotel Tineretului

PLACES TO EAT
20 Fast Food
21 Deli Pat Patisserie
22 Quattro Stagioni Ristorante
23 Lider Restaurant; Enigma Bar
28 Terasa Restaurant

THINGS TO SEE
1 General Culcer Monument
2 Site of Former Camp of Anti-Fascist Political Prisoners
4 St Nicholas' Church
13 Art Museum
17 Mausoleum of Ecaterina Teodoroiu
18 St Voievozi Cathedral
24 Brâncuşi's Gate of the Kiss
25 Brâncuşi's Alley of Chairs
26 Brâncuşi's Table of Silence
33 Gorj County Museum
34 St Apostles' Church
35 Former Site of Brâncuşi's Endless Column
37 Statue of Tudor Vladimirescu

OTHER
3 Panuraşul Recreation Complex
5 Sports Hall
6 Swimming Pool
8 Primăria
9 Open-Air Theatre
10 Post Office
11 Elvira Godeanu Drama Theatre; Statue of Constantin Brâncuşi & Casa de Cultură
12 Military Police Station
14 Outside Swimming Pool
16 Prefecture
19 Banca Română Pentru Dezvoltare
29 Cyber Net Club
30 Tudor Vladimirescu Lyceum
31 University
32 Hospital
36 Hospital
38 Post Office
39 Automobil Clubul Român (ACR)
40 Agenţie de Voiaj (CFR)
41 Central Market
42 Post Office
43 Bus Station
45 Hospital
46 Post Office

open 7 am to 8 pm weekdays. The central telephone office, just around the corner at Str Traian 1, is open 7.30 am to 9 pm daily. There is a smaller post office on Str Unirii.

Email & Internet Access The small Cyber Net Club, one block east of Hotel Gorj on Calea Eroilor, charges $0.50 per hour for Internet access; open 24 hours.

Things to See
Târgu Jiu's **Brâncuşi tour** starts in the central park at the western end of Calea Eroilor with three of the four sculptures which Brâncuşi built between 1937 and 1938 in memory of those who died during WWI. The entrance to the park is marked by Brâncuşi's *Gate of the Kiss* (Poarta Sărutului), an archway reminiscent of Bucharest's 'Arc de Triomphe' constructed the year before, also in commemoration of the re-unification of Romania. The stone archway bears folk art motifs from Brâncuşi's native Oltenia. Flip a coin on top of the archway for good luck!

Continue farther along the park's central mall to the *Alley of Chairs* (Aleea Scaunelor). The dwarf-sized stone stools are grouped in trios either side of the avenue. Despite their minuscule size, one's immediate instinct is to test them out for comfort. But the stools are works of art; you are not allowed to sit on them and an ever-mindful policeman ensures tourists don't.

The alley leads to the third sculpture, the riverside *Table of Silence* (Masa Tăcerii). Each of the 12 stools around the large, round, stone table represents a month of the year. The central park, also known as the Brâncuşi park, is open 6 am to 10 pm between May and December, and 7 am to 8 pm from January to April.

If you head north along the banks of the Jiu River from the *Table of Silence*, you come to a small **Art Museum** (Muzeul de Artă) on Str Stadion, which includes a photographic exhibition on the life and works of Brâncuşi; open 9 am to 5 pm Tuesday to Sunday ($0.25).

Brâncuşi's most famed sculpture, the *Endless Column* (Coloana Fără Sfârşit), lies at the eastern end of Calea Eroilor on a direct axis with the *Table of Silence*. The magnificent 29.35m-tall structure is considered as much a triumph of engineering as of modern art. See the accompanying boxed text for more information on Brâncuşi.

Open-air concerts and theatrical performances are held in summer at the **open-air theatre** at Str Vasile Alecsandri 53. Close by, on the corner of Str Stadion and Str Confederaţiei, is the **Elvira Godeanu Drama Theatre** (Teatrul Dramatic Elvira Godeanu; ☎ 216 494). A **statue** of Constantin Brâncuşi, armed with his sculpting chisel, stands in front of the theatre.

The **Gorj County Museum** (Muzeul Judeţean Gorj) on Str Geneva is open 9 am to 5 pm Tuesday to Sunday ($0.10). Str Geneva, formerly Str Griviţa, was renamed in 1996 after the city of Geneva presented Târgu Jiu with the **trio of clocks** that stand in front of the **statue of Tudor Vladimirescu** on Piaţa Tudor Vladimirescu.

Places to Stay
The OJT Gorj tourist office (see Information earlier) acts as an agent for the rural tourism specialist Antrec. It arranges stays in *private homes* in surrounding villages; guests can also experience delicious homemade cooking. Single/double/triple rooms start at $5/8/9. Breakfast is an extra $2.

Undiscriminating backpackers should head for the grotty *Hotel Tineretului* (☎ 244 682, Str Nicolae Titulescu 26), close to the train station. Double rooms are $7 per person, including breakfast. Clean communal showers and hot water are a hit-and-miss affair.

The cheapest hotel in the centre is *Hotel Sport* (☎ 214 402), behind the stadium off Blvd Constantin Brâncuşi. Double rooms with private bath on the 1st and 2nd floors are $13 a night including breakfast while triples on the less-appealing 3rd floor cost $11 (meals extra). Close by, the reasonably priced *Hotel Parc* (☎ 215 981, Blvd Constantin Brâncuşi 10) charges $18/24 for doubles/triples, including breakfast.

Târgu Jiu's main hotel is the 12-storey *Hotel Gorj* (☎ 214 814 fax 214 010, Calea

Constantin Brâncuşi

One of the 20th century's greatest sculptors was Constantin Brâncuşi (1876–1957), who endowed his native Târgu Jiu with the *Endless Column* in 1937. Taking pride of place in Târgu Jiu's central park, the 29.35m-tall sculpture, threaded with 15 steel 'beads', ranks among the world's 100 most important monuments according to the New York-based World Monuments Fund.

Brâncuşi was orphaned at the age of 10 and taught himself to read, write and sculpt. In 1904 he won a scholarship to Paris' School of Fine Arts, making most of the journey from Romania to the French capital on foot. During the communist crackdowns of the 1950s, Brâncuşi, still based in Paris, was declared *persona non grata* and the Endless Column's engineer was imprisoned for 'anti-state activities'.

After years of neglect had led to the deterioration of the *Endless Column*, a US$3.7 million project to restore the column was announced in 1999. Funding for its restoration – and also for the *Table of Silence* and the *Gate of the Kiss* – would be provided by Romania, the World Monuments Fund, the World Bank and AmEx. In a mammoth operation the impressive column was dismantled and taken away for intensive restoration. In mid-December 2000, the *Endless Column* was returned to its pride of place in the central park.

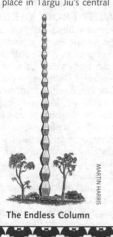

MARTIN HARRIS

The Endless Column

Eroilor 6). Double/triples are cheapest on the top eight floors – $19/24 including breakfast – where the water pressure is at its worst (on bad days expect no more than a dribble). Hot water is available from 6 to 8 am, and 7 to 11 pm).

Places to Eat
Most eating places are clustered around Hotel Gorj and along the pedestrianised end of Calea Victoriei. Immediately opposite the hotel is the cheap and cheerful *Lider Restaurant*, on Calea Eroilor, which serves mainly pizza. After you've eaten, stop for a quick drink at the modern *Enigma* bar downstairs.

Next door is the more upmarket *Quattro Stagioni Ristorante*, a funky Italian restaurant which is also packed. Third in line is the *Deli Pat Patisserie*, handy for a quick cup of coffee and a creamy cake.

Great *mititei* (spicy meatballs) are cooked while you wait at *Terasa Restaurant*, behind Hotel Gorj on Calea Victoriei. Wash them down with local beer served on tap. The terrace is open pretty much non-stop in summer.

There's a clean, modern *Fast Food* just off Calea Victoriei. Hamburgers and hot dogs are $0.45; sandwiches are a mere $0.30.

Stock up on fresh fruit and vegetables at the *central market*, south of the stadium park on Str Unirii.

Getting There & Away
Train The Agenţie de Voiaj CFR (☎ 121 924), next to the central market at Str Unirii, Block 2, is open 7 am to 7.30 pm weekdays.

Târgu Jiu is served by a branch line from Filiaşi, which is on the main Bucharest-Timişoara line. Major daily train services include six local trains to Filiaşi (three hours), five to Craiova (2¾ hours), and an express train to Bucharest (4¾ hours). Northbound, there are five trains to Simeria (three hours), and six trains to Petroşani (1¼ to 1¾ hours).

In summer there is one train daily to Constanţa (seven hours).

Bus The bus station is 100m south of the train station off Str Nicolae Titulescu. Major daily services include one to Bucharest (257km) via Piteşti (174km), Petroşani (57km), Sibiu and Timişoara (280km); and

WALLACHIA

two to Craiova (102km) and Drobeta-Turnu Severin (82km). Buses run four times a week to Deva (150km) and Hunedoara (137km).

WEST FROM TÂRGU JIU

Runcu village, 16km west of Târgu Jiu, is the site of the large folk art and crafts fair (Simpozion Satul Românesc Traditional) held every year during the last weekend in August. Continuing west, turn left 1km before Peştişani and follow the dirt track for a couple of kilometres until you reach **Hobiţa**, the birthplace of Constantin Brâncuşi. The sculptor lived in the village until the age of 10 when he moved to Craiova. The tiny cottage in which he spent his childhood years now houses a small museum dedicated to the artist.

Some 20km farther west is **Tismana Monastery** (Mănăstirea Tismana; 1375), one of Romania's oldest monasteries and an important centre of Slavonic writing. The original monastery was founded by monk and calligrapher Nicodim in a small stone church, later to be grandly rebuilt in 1508 by Wallachian prince Radu cel Mare. The region west beyond Tismana is a major karst area in the south-western Carpathians, providing intrepid explorers with countless caves. In **Padeş**, there is a stone pyramid monument constructed in 1921 to mark the spot where Craiovan-born revolutionary Tudor Vladimirescu (1780–1821) issued his 'Proclamation of Padeş' on 4 February 1821. In his proclamation, Vladimirescu, who later died at the hands of the Turks, called for the 'evil ones' ruining the country to be disposed of, leading to a series of uprisings against Ottoman rule in 1821.

Some 10km south-west of Padeş is the **Ponoăre Nature Reservation**, a protected lilac forest stretching for some eight hectares. Each spring, a folk festival is held to mark the blossoming of the trees.

DROBETA-TURNU SEVERIN

☎ 052 • postcode 1500 • pop 118,000

Drobeta-Turnu Severin is on the bank of the Danube (Dunărea) River bordering Yugoslavia. Though of ancient origin, the present town was laid out in the 19th century when its port was built. A three-hour stop is enough to see the best of Drobeta-Turnu Severin.

Orientation

From the train station, walk up the steps opposite the main station building to Blvd Republicii (Blvd Carol I). Follow this road east for 600m or so to Hotel Continental Parc, at the intersection of Str Bibiescu. The town centre lies one block north of here. The bus station is out of town at the eastern end of Str Brâncoveanu.

The Hala Radu-Negru indoor market is at the northern end of Str Coştescu; open 6.30 am to 8 pm weekdays, 7 am to 2.30 pm Saturday, 7.30 am to noon Sunday. The Decebal department store is a block farther north.

Information

Change money, cash travellers cheques or get cash on Visa/MasterCard at the Banca Comercială Română, on the corner of Str Coştescu and Str Aurelian; open 8.30 to 11.30 am and 1.30 to 6.30 pm weekdays and 10 am to noon Saturday.

The post office, open 8 am to 8 pm weekdays and 8 am to 1 pm Saturday, is adjacent to the telephone office, at Str Decebal 41. The telephone office is open 8 am to 8 pm weekdays, and 8 am to 2 pm Saturday.

Things to See

At the eastern end of Blvd Republicii is the excellent **Iron Gates Museum** (Muzeul Porţilor de Fier; ☎ 325 922), open 9 am to 5 pm daily except Tuesday ($0.40). Housed in the former Trajan school for girls, dating from 1922, the museum was opened the day before the 1972 unveiling of the mammoth Porţile de Fier hydroelectric power station, 10km west. It contains a fine exhibition on the natural history of the Danube.

Other sections of the museum cover history, ethnography, popular art, astrology, the evolution of man, and archaeology. Particularly impressive is the scale model of the Roman bridge constructed across the Danube in AD 103 by the Syrian architect Apollodor of Damascus, on the orders of the Roman emperor Trajan. The **Trajan**

DROBETA-TURNU SEVERIN

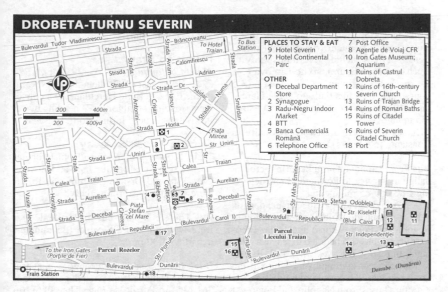

PLACES TO STAY & EAT	7	Post Office
9 Hotel Severin	8	Agenţie de Voiaj CFR
17 Hotel Continental	10	Iron Gates Museum;
Parc		Aquarium
	11	Ruins of Castrul
OTHER		Dobreta
1 Decebal Department	12	Ruins of 16th-century
Store		Severin Church
2 Synagogue	13	Ruins of Trajan Bridge
3 Radu-Negru Indoor	14	Ruins of Roman Baths
Market	15	Ruins of Citadel
4 BTT		Tower
5 Banca Comercială	16	Ruins of Severin
Română		Citadel Church
6 Telephone Office	18	Port

bridge stood just below the site of the present museum, and the ruins (ruinele podului lui Traian) of two of its pillars can still be seen towering beside the Danube. Northeast of the bridge ruins lie the remnants of **Castrul Drobeta**, a 2nd- to 6th-century Roman fort built to protect the bridge.

West of the castle ruins, also in the museum grounds, are the ruins of the 16th-century medieval **Severin Church** (Biserica Mitropoliei Severinului), including the remains of the crypt which lie protected beneath glass today.

In the Iron Gates Museum basement there is an **aquarium** displaying various fish species prevalent in the Danube, including the giant Somnul fish as well as various types of carp (which amusingly translates as 'crap' in Romanian!).

Eleven kilometres north of Drobeta is **Topolniţa Cave** (Peştera Topolniţa), which ranks among the largest caves in the world (more than 10,000m long on four levels).

Places to Stay & Eat
BTT (☎/fax 315 131), Str Bibiescu 4, sometimes arranges *private rooms* ($10 per person); open 9 am to 6 pm weekdays.

The cheapest hotel is the friendly *Hotel Severin* (☎ 312 074, Str Mihai Eminescu 1), a pleasant 15-minute walk from the train station. Good-value singles/doubles cost $20/ 27, including a clean, private bathroom (with hot water) and breakfast. Its restaurant is a couple of doors down Str Mihai Eminescu.

Hotel Traian (☎ 311 796, fax 310 290, Blvd Tudor Vladimirescu 74) has rooms with private bathroom for $24/33, not including breakfast. The hotel has a restaurant, tacky summer garden and 24-hour billiard bar.

The most expensive and luxurious hotel is the three-star *Hotel Continental Parc* (☎ 312 851/852, fax 316 968, Blvd Republicii 2), boasting clean, comfortable rooms with private bathroom and breakfast for $44/59 and apartments for $88. Its restaurant, considered to be the best in town, has a delightful outside terrace in the park.

Getting There & Away
Train The Agenţie de Voiaj CFR (☎ 313 117) at Str Decebal 43 is open 7.30 am to 7.30 pm weekdays. There is one daily train to Belgrade (8½ hours).

WALLACHIA

All express trains between Bucharest and Timişoara stop here. Local trains make slower, more frequent trips in both directions. Services include five trains daily to Bucharest (five hours), six to Craiova (1½ to 2½ hours), seven to Timişoara (3½ hours), and 10 trains daily to Băile Herculane (40 minutes to 1¼ hours) and Orşova (25 minutes).

In summer there are two trains daily to Constanţa (5¾ hours).

Bus From Drobeta-Turnu Severin there is a daily bus service to Porţile de Fier (departing 1.30 pm, 25 minutes).

A private bus ($7; pay the driver) departs daily from outside Drobeta's train station to Negotin and Pojarevat in Yugoslavia. Theoretically the bus is scheduled to leave at midnight. In reality, it leaves when full. Expect to wait between two and four hours at the Porţile de Fier–Kladova border crossing.

Return buses from Negotin and Pojarevat likewise depart for Drobeta-Turnu Severin when they are full.

PORŢILE DE FIER, ORŞOVA & THE CAZAN GORGES

Ten kilometres west of Drobeta-Turnu Severin are the famous **Iron Gates** (Porţile de Fier) at Gura Văii, a monstrous, concrete hydroelectric power station. On top of the dam wall runs the road linking Romania to Yugoslavia.

Construction first started on the power station – a Romanian-Yugoslav joint venture – in 1960 but took 12 years to complete. For details on the Iron Gates Museum, see the preceding Drobeta-Turnu Severin section.

The Iron Gates at Gura Văii stand on the site of **Old Orşova** (Orşova Veche), one of 13 settlements to be swallowed up by the artificial lake, created to curb this treacherous stretch of the Danube. Before 1918, it marked the border of Hungarian-controlled Banat.

New Orşova (Orşova Nouă) lies 15km upstream of Gura Văii. Between Gura Văii and **Comarnic**, a village 2km north of New Orşova, the railway is said to cross 56 viaducts and bridges and go through nine tunnels. A farther 15km upstream are the spectacular **Cazan Gorges** (Cazanele Mici and Cazanele Mari).

Places to Stay

Motel Continental (☎ 052-329 235, fax 326 778), 12km east of Drobeta-Turnu Severin on the E752 to Băile Herculane, is a convenient stopping point for those heading by car into Yugoslavia or farther north to Banat.

Getting There & Away

Train Most major trains to/from Drobeta-Turnu Severin stop at Orşova. Between Gura Văii and Orşova (30 minutes, 15km) there are four local trains daily.

Bus There is a daily bus to Porţile de Fier from Drobeta-Turnu Severin (25 minutes, departing 1.30 pm).

Boat It is possible to arrange a boat trip along the Danube from Orşova port (☎ 052-361 415) to Porţile de Fier. The 20km trip has to be arranged well in advance and will only be taken seriously by the harbour master if it involves a group of at least 10 people. Those lucky enough to get a trip off the ground can expect to pay about $50 an hour for the privilege.

CRAIOVA

☎ 051 • postcode 1100 • pop 311,000

The university town of Craiova, founded on the site of the Dacian stronghold of Pelendava, midway between Drobeta-Turnu Severin and Piteşti, prides itself on its strong academic tradition and the wealth of prominent characters who have passed through on their journey to stardom: Wallachian prince Mihai Viteazul was born here and the world-famous sculptor Constantin Brâncuşi carved his first sculptures from scrap wooden crates here. The first cartridge fountain pen was invented by Craiovan-born Petrache Poenaru (1799–1875).

Today Craiova is better known as the source of Craiova beer, the producer of diesel locomotives, and the home of the Rodac car factory which produced the Oltcit (the Romanian version of the Citroën Axel) and the sporty Cielo car.

CRAIOVA

PLACES TO STAY & EAT
1 Hotel Jiul
16 Student House
25 Braseria Minerva
28 Restaurant Militar
30 Restaurant Perinița
31 Il Girasole Caffetteria

THINGS TO SEE
6 Art Museum
9 Natural History Museum
12 Holy Trinity Church
13 Statue of Mihai Viteazul
14 Prefecture
15 Statue of Alexandra Cuza
23 History Museum
24 St Hramul's Church
29 Ethnographic Museum

OTHER
2 Agenție de Voiaj CFR
3 Tarom Airlines Office
4 Post Office
5 National Theatre; Librăria Thalia
7 Banca Comercială Română
8 Art Gallery
10 Opera & Operetta Theatre
11 Alliance Française Cultural Centre
17 TTC Currency Exchange
18 Mapamond Agenție de Turism
19 Oltenia Philharmonic
20 Mercur Department Store
21 Automobil Clubul Român (ACR)
22 Voodoo Games
26 New York Café
27 Crama Haiducilor
32 Bingo Victoria
33 Art
34 Telephone Centre
35 Central Post Office

Prior to the war in Yugoslavia, IAR93 subsonic jet fighter-bombers were manufactured in Craiova for the Romanian and Yugoslav airforces. Production ground to a halt in 1992, however, after the UN imposed trade sanctions against Yugoslavia. Workers at the plant blocked the Craiova-Pitești highway with a military plane in mid-1997 in a desperate bid to get their jobs guaranteed.

Following the outbreak of the conflict in Kosovo in 1999, UN sanctions against Yugoslavia were widened. With the conflict's end and the change of Yugoslav government, trade sanctions were finally lifted in late 2000.

Orientation

The northern bus station (Autogară Nord), from which buses to/from most other towns arrive/depart, is next to the train station, 1km north-east of the centre on Blvd Carol I (Blvd Republicii). Bus No 1 runs from the train station to the centre and Autogară Nord. There are no buses to the southern bus station (Autogară Sud); a taxi from the centre should cost no more than $1.

Information

Tourist Offices The Mapamond Agenție de Turism (☎ 415 071, fax 415 173, e map amond@cisnet.ro), the local agent for Antrec, overlooks the central square on the corner of Str Olteț and Calea Unirii. Staff speak English and happily assist lost tourists; open 9 am to 7 pm weekdays and 9 am to 12.30 pm Saturday.

The ACR office (☎ 416 166), Str Ion Marinescu, Block 2–4, takes bookings for its motel (see Places to Stay); open 8.30 am to 4 pm Monday, Wednesday and Friday, 8.30 am to 7 pm Tuesday and Thursday, and 8.30 am to 1 pm Saturday.

Money The TTC currency exchange at Str Olteț, Block 1, offers competitive rates;

WALLACHIA

open 9 am to 8 pm Monday to Saturday. The Banca Comercială Română, on the corner of Calea Unirii and Str Alexandru Ioan Cuza, cashes travellers cheques, gives cash advances and has an ATM; open 8 am to 1 pm and 2 to 6 pm weekdays.

Post & Telephone The central post office, on the corner of Blvd Stirbei Vodă and Calea Unirii, is open 7 am to 8 pm weekdays and 8 am to 1 pm Saturday. The central telephone office, nearby at Calea Unirii 69, is open 7.30 am to 8 pm weekdays.

Email & Internet Access At Voodoo Games (☎ 413 916), Str Madona Dudu, Block 10, online access costs $0.30/0.50 for 30 minutes/one hour; open 24 hours.

Bookshops Librăria Thalia, inside the National Theatre on Calea Bucureşti, sells a decent range of English- and French-language novels; open 10 am to 7 pm weekdays and 10 am to 5.30 pm Saturday.

Cultural Centres The best information source for French-speakers is the Alliance Française (☎/fax 412 345) at Str Ion Marinescu 10. The centre arranges exhibitions,

Craiova-born Mihai Viteazul
(Michael the Brave)

plays, and film nights every month; open 11 am to 6 pm weekdays and 10 am to 1 pm Saturday.

Things to See

Overlooking Calea Unirii, in the central square, is a **statue of Mihai Viteazul** who was born in Craiova. To its eastern side is the **prefecture**, bearing a memorial plaque to Craiova's victims of the 1989 revolution.

Close by at Str Popa Şapcă 4 is a small **Natural History Museum** (☎ 419 435); open 9 am to 5 pm daily except Monday ($0.35). In the park opposite is the red-brick **Holy Trinity Church** (Biserica Sfânta Treime). Behind the church on Str Ion Marinescu is the city's **Opera & Operetta Theatre**, a former school which was a revolutionary hide-out during June 1848.

North from the square up Calea Unirii is Craiova's **Art Museum** (Muzeul de Artă; ☎ 412 342), considered by most to be a highlight of a visit to the town; open 9 am to 5 pm daily except Monday ($0.35). The museum is housed in the Dinu Mihail Palace, built in 1900–07 by the wealthy Romanian nobleman Constantin Dinu Mihail. It was home to former Polish president Ignacy Moscicki in 1939 and later to Ceauşescu. Its numerous rooms take you through the history of art in Romania and the rest of Europe. The exhibition crescendos with the Constantin Brâncuşi cabinet in which some early works of the sculptor are displayed, including the magnificent *Kiss*, the *Thigh* and *Miss Pogany*. The orphaned Brâncuşi lived in a house at Str CA Rosetti 14 until 1895 when he began boarding at the Craiova Trade School.

Craiova's old town lies east of Calea Unirii around Piaţa Veche (Old Square). An excellent **Ethnographic Museum** (Muzeul Olteniei Secţia de Etnografie; 1699), housed in a former governor's house, stands on Str Dimitru at the end of Str Hala. In its rose-bedded grounds is **St Dimitru Church** (1652). Farther north, at Str Madona Dudu 44, is a **History Museum** (Secţia de Istorie a Muzeului Olteniei; ☎ 418 631), in an ivy-clad 19th-century building. Displayed inside **St Hramul's Church** (1928) opposite is the Madona Dudu icon said to perform miracles for those who pray in front of it.

Places to Stay

Mapamond (see Tourist Offices earlier), an agent for Antrec, arranges rooms in *private homes* in surrounding villages for $10 a night; breakfast is an extra $3.

It is worth asking if there are any rooms going in the *student dorms* at the main university building, on the corner of Blvd Republicii and Calea Bucureşti. Or try the student house (Casa Studenţilor), south of the main building on Blvd Universităţii.

The cheapest rooms in town can be found at *Motel ACR* (☎ 190 000, Str Nicolae Titulescu 175) north of the centre. OK doubles including breakfast cost $19. The motel's few apartments are $38. Hot water is limited to only a few hours in the morning and evening.

The most expensive hotel in town is the two-star *Hotel Jiul* (☎ 414 166, 565 541, fax 412 462, Calea Bucureşti 1–2). This large concrete block has singles/doubles for $51/65, including breakfast. A 'matrimonial room' (ie, with genuine double bed as opposed to two singles pushed together) is $65.

At the time of writing, the grand old *Hotel Minerva* on Str Mihail Kogălniceanu, protected as an architectural monument, had closed indefinitely.

Places to Eat

Eating options are limited in Craiova and tracking down a full meal can be tough. If you don't have an aversion to uniforms, a good place to go is the *Restaurant Militar*, on Str Dumitru, adjoining the hotel reserved for the military. Traditional *caşcaval* (pressed, breaded cheese) and pork cutlets are served in the beer garden outside, which specialises in the golden beer brewed in the town.

Braseria Minerva, on Str Mihail Kogălniceanu, has pride of place in what was the glorious Hotel Minerva. Main meals are around $2.50 and the menu is available in English, German and French. *Restaurant Periniţa* at the southern end of Calea Unirii serves Craiova beer for $0.30 a bottle and cooks up *şaşlik* on a barbecue when there are enough customers.

Constantin Brâncuşi's early sculpture *Kiss* can be seen in Craiova's Art Museum.

Step back in time at *Il Girasole Caffetteria*, on Calea Unirii, a true 1950s-style cafeteria complete with staff dressed in uniforms reminiscent of the time. *McDonald's* is east of the centre on Calea Bucureşti; open 8 am to midnight daily.

Entertainment

It's well worth seeking a glimpse of Craiova's cultural scene. Highly recommended are performances at the impressive *National Theatre* (Teatrul Naţional), on Calea Bucureşti, and the *Opera & Operetta Theatre* (Teatrul de operă şi operată; Str Ion Marinescu 12). Tickets for both are sold at the Agenţia Teatrală (☎ 413 755), adjoining the main National Theatre building; open 10 am to 12.30 pm and 4 to 6.30 pm daily.

Classical concerts are performed by the *Oltenia Philharmonic* (Filarmonica Oltenia), on Calea Unirii. The ticket office (☎ 411 284), open 10 am to 1 pm and 4 to 7 pm daily, is inside the main Philharmonic building ($0.75/0.35 for adults/students).

Bars At the trendy *New York Café*, on Calea Unirii opposite Bingo Victoria, sink back in one of the many comfortable black lounges and enjoy your favourite drink. Not far away is the popular *Art* cellar bar, on Calea Unirii. Adorning its walls are contemporary works from local artists. Also worth a look is *Crama Haiducilor*, on Str Dumitru.

Getting There & Away

Train Advance train tickets are sold at the Agenţie de Voiaj CFR (☎ 411 634), opposite Hotel Jiul in the Complex Comercial Unirea; open 7 am to 7.30 pm weekdays.

All express trains between Bucharest and Timişoara stop here. Services include 13 trains daily to Bucharest (three hours, 209km), seven to Timişoara (five hours), six to Drobeta-Turnu Severin (1½ to 2½ hours) and five local trains to Calafat (2½ hours).

Bus Craiova has two bus stations: the northern bus station (Autogară Nord), from which buses to/from most other towns arrive/depart, is next to the train station on Blvd Carol I (Blvd Republicii). Major daily bus services include one to Piteşti (142km) and two to Horezu (111km), Râmnicu Vâlcea (180km) and Târgu Jiu (102km).

The Öz Murat travel agency (☎ 418 780), outside Autogară Nord, runs a bus to Istanbul via Bucharest. It departs at 10.30 am daily except Saturday ($26/51 single/return).

The southern bus station (Autogară Sud), 5km south of the centre, serves pinprick-sized villages south of Craiova.

CALAFAT

The small town of Calafat, on the Danube opposite Vidin in Bulgaria, makes a convenient entry/exit point to/from Bulgaria. Car ferries cross the river hourly and there are frequent local trains to/from Craiova, from where you can catch an express train on to Bucharest or Timişoara. Apart from the **Muzeul de Artă** on Str 22 Decembrie and a monument to the 1877–78 War of Independence against the Turks, there isn't much to see or do in Calafat.

The ferry landing is in the centre of Calafat, about four blocks from the train station. Exiting the ferry you'll see several exchange kiosks near customs. The Banca Agricolă, opposite the post office on the way from the ferry to the train station, changes cash at the official rate.

There are five local trains daily to/from Craiova (2½ hours). If you're continuing on to Bucharest or elsewhere, buy a ticket for your final destination and, as soon as you reach Craiova, go into the train station and purchase a compulsory seat reservation for your onward express train.

The car ferry to Bulgaria crosses the Danube hourly year-round ($12.50 plus an additional $2 per person in cash only). Cars can spend several hours waiting to cross but pedestrians can avoid the queues and walk on in both directions.

In March 2000, after almost a decade of negotiations, the Romanian and Bulgarian governments agreed on the construction of a new bridge here over the Danube River (although Romania wanted the bridge to be built farther east). The $155 million bridge, funded by the Bulgarian government and the EU, will connect Calafat with the Bulgarian city of Vidin. Its construction, expected to last three years, will provide employment for over 2000 of the Jiu Valley's unemployed miners.

GIURGIU
☎ 046 • postcode 8375

The main route from Bucharest to Bulgaria is via the border town of Giurgiu, on the northern shores of the Danube River. The *Bulgaria Expres* and *Bosfor* trains both rumble across Giurgiu's 4km-long bridge across the Danube on their journeys south.

For motorists and foot passengers there are three ways of crossing from Giurgiu into Ruse, Bulgaria – the small *bac* (ferry), the larger ferry, *Ro-Ro*, or the road bridge (see Getting There & Away). You cannot cross the bridge on foot; a line of taxis waits at its northern end to motor individual travellers the 4km south for $30.

Giurgiu town itself is ugly, with nothing to see or do.

Orientation & Information

Giurgiu's train and bus stations are five minutes' walk from the centre. Exit the station and walk up Str Gării to the main street. Giurgiu's northern train station (Giurgiu Nord) is 5km out of town; local trains run between the two train stations. Most trains heading for Bulgaria depart from Giurgiu Nord.

The post office and central market are on Str Constantin Brâncoveanu. Turn right at the bridge crossing, then right onto Str Constantin Brâncoveanu. To get to the centre from here, turn left onto the main street.

Places to Stay

A five-minute walk from the train and bus stations is the shabby *Hotel Victoria* (☎ *212 569, Str Gării 1*). Singles/doubles are $6/8. To get to the hotel from Str Gării, walk under the arches next to the lotto shop and cross the small play area; the hotel is just around the corner.

Motel Prietenia (☎ *221 971*), or Motel Vamă (literally 'Customs Motel') as it is known locally, is no more than 100m from the road bridge into Bulgaria. Well-priced doubles with private bath are $16. A good restaurant serving home-made dishes adjoins it. If the queue at the bridge is long, pop in here for a strong coffee.

The large three-star *Hotel Steaua Dunării* (☎ *217 270, Str Mihai Viteazul 1*), next to the main ferry terminal, is large and generally half-empty. Singles/doubles with private bath are $30/38. The hotel's huge restaurant has a limited menu.

Five kilometres from the centre on the northbound Şoseaua Bucureşti road to Bucharest is the small and friendly *Mini-Motel* (☎ *210 150*). Clean single/double/triple rooms with private bath are $8/10/15.

Getting There & Away

Train Most Giurgiu-Ruse trains depart from Giurgiu Nord train station (☎ 215 106). There are daily local trains to Ruse from Giurgiu Nord (15 minutes, 4km) at 8.31 am and 6.21 pm.

The daily *Bosfor* train to Istanbul from Bucharest passes through Giurgiu Nord at 4 pm (16 hours). On its return journey it leaves Istanbul at 9.50 pm, arriving in Giurgiu at 1.39 pm. The daily *Bulgaria*

Expres from Bucharest stops at Giurgiu at 10.22 pm.

Car & Motorcycle The main E70 highway from Bucharest to Giurgiu leads directly to the bridge crossing, signposted 'Punctul de frontieră Giurgiu'. Toll tickets are sold from the row of kiosks marked 'casa' on the left as you approach the customs control zone ($10/3 per car/motorcycle, plus an additional $6 *service taxe ecological* levied by the Bulgarian authorities).

Ferry The main ferry terminal where the *Ro-Ro* boat arrives/departs is next to Hotel Steaua Dunării ($25/5 per car/foot passenger, plus $6 ecological tax). The crossing from Giurgiu to Ruse takes 20 minutes; boats leave every three hours and the ferry operates 24 hours a day.

Approaching Giurgiu from Bucharest, turn left at the bridge crossing (see under Car & Motorcycle). It is also signposted from the main street in town. The return ferry from Ruse to Giurgiu follows the same schedule. Large vehicles generally favour this crossing.

Cheaper and quicker, with smaller queues, is the *bac* (ferry) which departs from the main port; follow the signs to the port from the centre of town ($10 for a car, plus an additional $1 for every passenger, and $1 for foot passengers, plus $6 ecological tax). The crossing takes 10 minutes and the ferry operates 24 hours, departing when full.

CĂLĂRAŞI, OSTROV & AROUND

The surreal entry by road from the northwest into **Călăraşi** (population 77,856), beneath an ungainly 'bridge' of rusting conveyor belts forming an intricate maze to the city's steel works, says it all about this city. Largely industrial, the town offers absolutely no reason to come here except to catch the next ferry out – across the Danube to Ostrov from where you can cross into Silistra in Bulgaria.

For travellers without private transport, it is much simpler to cross the Danube into Bulgaria at Giurgiu (see the Giurgiu section earlier). The Călăraşi crossing is not served by public transport and is only suitable for motorists. From the centre of Călăraşi, you have to go 8km south to the port from where you catch a makeshift ferry across the Danube to **Ostrov** (still in Romania).

The ferry takes cars, trucks and foot passengers ($2/0.25 per car/foot passenger; tickets sold on board). The crossing takes 20 minutes and the ferry operates 24 hours, departing when full.

Once in Ostrov you can continue east to the Black Sea coast, or cross the border into Silistra, Bulgaria. As you come off the ferry a one-way street leads you directly to the customs control point. Continuing past the border control, the eastbound road to Dobruja follows a barbed-wire fence which marks the Romanian/Bulgarian border for a farther 200m.

Ostrov village proper is 5km east of the ferry terminal and border crossing. From here, for some 15km the eastbound road follows the twists and turns of the magnificent Danube River, making it one of the most scenic drives in Romania. This majestic riverside stretch peaks at the **Derveni Monastery** (Mănăstirea Derveni) which overlooks Lake Bugeaculi, south of the Danube. The road continues east into Northern Dobruja.

Northern Dobruja

Northern Dobruja (Dobrogea) is the land between the Danube River (Râul Dunărea) and the Black Sea (Marea Neagră). Its 245km stretch of Black Sea coast *(litoral)* is Romania's hottest tourist spot; in midsummer it resembles a massive outdoor party, with beachfront barbecues and plenty of beer.

There are nine main resorts, most of them named after mythical gods: Mamaia, Eforie Nord, Eforie Sud, Costineşti, Neptun-Olimp, Jupiter-Aurora, Venus, Saturn and Mangalia. Mamaia, north of Constanţa, and the ancient Greek coastal town of Mangalia (Callatis), offer wide, sandy beaches and attract an older crowd. Eforie Nord is famous for its curative black mud while in Neptun-Olimp, a former Communist Party playground, days merge with nights in an orgy of blasting beach music and flashy nightclubs. Costineşti is one gigantic students' playground. Eforie Sud, Jupiter-Aurora, Venus and Saturn – concrete jungles from the late 1960s – are dilapidated, dying resorts.

At the south end of the coast are the charming fishing villages of Doi Mai and Vama Veche.

The high season runs from mid-May to mid-September. From October to late April, the beaches are quiet, few hotels are open, and the weather is cold.

Cheap accommodation is scarce; expect to pay $30 and up for a comfortable hotel room. Advance reservations are advised from mid-June to August. Private rooms are only widely available in Costineşti, Doi Mai and Vama Veche.

In summer private minibuses shuttle beach-hoppers along the coast, stopping at all the resorts between Constanţa and Mangalia. Maps are widely available although most of the resorts do not have street names.

History

Northern Dobruja became part of Romania in 1878 when a combined Russo-Romanian army defeated the Turks in Bulgaria. Southern Dobruja was ceded to Bulgaria.

Highlights

- Discover Roman Tomis in Constanţa's archaeological museum and adjoining mosaic museum
- Bathe in black mud at Eforie Nord
- Be a beach bum on Mamaia's golden sands
- Explore the ancient Greek and Roman cities of Histria
- Study pelicans on Lake Furtana
- Tour the Danube Delta's narrow waterways by boat with a local fisherman

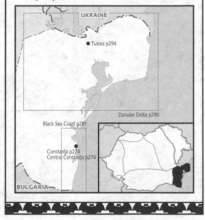

In antiquity the Dobruja region was colonised first by the Greeks then by the Romans, both of whom left behind much for visitors to admire. Histria, 70km north of Constanţa, is the oldest Greek settlement in Romania, founded in 657 BC. From AD 46, Dobruja was the Roman province of Moesia Inferior. At Adamclisi (Tropaeum Traiani) the Romans scored a decisive victory over the Geto-Dacian tribes, making possible their expansion into regions north of the Danube.

Dobruja later fell under Byzantine control, and in 1418 was conquered by the Turks.

NORTHERN DOBRUJA

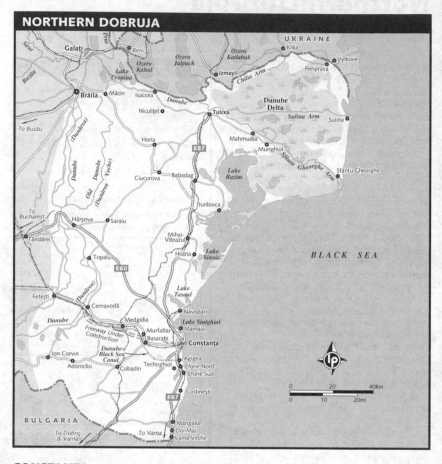

CONSTANŢA
☎ 041 • postcode 8700 • pop 347,000

Constanţa is Romania's largest port and second-largest city. In ancient times Constanţa was the Greek-controlled town of Tomis, which the Romans later renamed after emperor Constantine (ruled AD 306–37) who fortified and developed the city. By the 8th century the city had been destroyed by invading Slavs and Avars.

After Constanţa was taken by Romania in 1877, the town grew in importance, with a railway line being built to it from Bucharest. By the early 1900s it was a fashionable seaside resort frequented by European royalty.

Despite the dirty, crowded beaches, the picturesque old town has a peaceful Mediterranean air. Its few excellent museums can easily be seen in an afternoon. The city is the main transport hub on the Black Sea coast and the gateway to other resorts.

Constanţa hosts an annual folk music festival during the last weekend in August.

Orientation
Constanţa's train station and main southern bus station (Autogară Sud) are 2km west of

the old town. The northern bus station (Autogară Nord) is 3km north of the centre on Str Soveja.

Most facilities are on the pedestrianised Str Ştefan cel Mare, at the south-western end of which is the Tomis department store. Most travel agencies are on Blvd Tomis, which runs from the new town in the north to the old town and port in the south.

Maps The best city map, *Constanţa* (Amco Press, 1999), includes a map of the city centre, the port and Mamaia, and shows public transport routes. It costs $1.20 in major hotels and travel agencies.

Information

Tourist Offices Staff at the Info Litoral Tourist Information Centre (☎ 555 000, fax 555 111, ℮ info@infolitoral.ro), Str Traian 36, Scara C, Apt 31, are friendly and well informed. Visit the Info Litoral Web site at www.infolitoral.ro.

The Agenţie de Turism Intern (☎/fax 615 777, ℮ atict@fx.ro), Blvd Tomis 46, sells maps and can arrange accommodation in private rooms in Mamaia. It's open 9 am to 9 pm weekdays, and 9 am to 4 pm Saturday, from 1 May to 1 October. In winter, hours are reduced. There is a second office at Blvd Tomis 69 (☎ 617 181, fax 617 127), open the same hours.

Money Most hotels and travel agencies have exchange outlets. The Danubius Exchange at Blvd Ferdinand 44 offers good rates.

Banca Comercială Română, Str Traian 1, changes travellers cheques, gives cash advances on Visa/MasterCard and has an ATM. There is a second branch at Str Traian 68. Both are open 8.30 am to 2 pm weekdays. Banca Română pentru Dezvoltare, near the Mahmudiye Mosque at Str Arhiepiscopiei 9, offers identical services; open 9 am to 2 pm. The BCIT, Str Ştefan cel Mare 32–34, is open 9 am to 2.30 pm weekdays.

Post & Telephone The central telephone and post office is at Blvd Tomis 79 on the corner of Str Ştefan cel Mare. The telephone section is open 7 am to 10 pm daily,

while the post office is open 7 am to 8 pm weekdays, and 8 am to 1 pm Saturday. There is a smaller post office in the old town at the south end of Str Revoluţiei.

Email & Internet Access Net Games Internet, Str Cuza Vodă 48, charges $0.60 per hour to send emails; open 10 am to 6 pm weekdays, 11 am to 6 pm Saturday.

Travel Agencies The Danubius travel agency's English-speaking staff arrange day trips to the Danube Delta ($63), Murfatlar ($23) and other resorts on the coast. It has an office at Piaţa Ovidiu 11 (☎ 619 039, fax 619 041) and another at Blvd Ferdinand 36 (615 836, fax 618 010, ℮ danubis@gmb.ro). Both are open 9 am to 7 pm weekdays, and 9 am to 2 pm Saturday.

For advance hotel bookings try Contur Agenţie de Turism (☎ 613 192, ℮ contur@impromex.ro) at Piaţa Ovidiu 14. Rooms are usually cheaper through here than through the hotels direct.

Romar travel agency (☎/fax 614 800) at Blvd Tomis 66 sells Tarom air tickets. Nouvelles Frontières/Simpa Turism (☎ 660 468, fax 664 403, ℮ office@simpaturism.ro) at Str Răscoalei 1907, 9, organises accommodation and is an agent for Hertz.

Bookshops The best bookshop in town for English- and French-language novels is the Librăria Sophia bookshop at Str Dragoş Vodă at Str Ecaterina Varga; open 9.30 am to 6 pm weekdays, and 10 am to 2 pm Saturday.

Libraries & Cultural Centres The British Council (☎/fax 618 365) runs a small library on the 2nd floor of Constanţa district library (Biblioteca Judeţeană Constanţa) at Blvd Ferdinand 7; open 4 to 8 pm Monday, Wednesday and Friday, and 9 am to 3 pm Tuesday and Thursday.

The French Institute (Institut Français de Constanţa; ☎/fax 619 438), Blvd Ferdinand 78, hosts music, theatre and film festivals.

Medical Services The Farmacie Ovidus is just off Str Remus Opreanu on Blvd

Revoluţiei; open 8 am to 7.30 pm weekdays, and 8 am to 1 pm Saturday. The pharmacy next to the Agenţie de Turism Intern on Blvd Tomis is open 7 am to 8 pm weekdays, 9 am to 5 pm Saturday, and 9 am to 2 pm Sunday.

Dangers & Annoyances Constanţa is a notorious haunt for street hustlers and thieves. Don't change money on the streets and beware of boys who crowd around you acting friendly – they'll pick your pockets and steal your pack.

Unfortunately, travellers are now the target of a new scam involving local public transport.

The basic scam goes something like this: a foreign traveller boards the bus or tram and enters their ticket in the ticket machine which stamps three holes in it. The ticket official, who has been travelling incognito, pulls out their badge and asks to inspect the traveller's ticket. When the unsuspecting traveller obligingly hands it over, the ticket official swiftly replaces the ticket with one they have concealed in their hand which has been stamped twice.

The ticket official then points to the regulations that are posted in the bus or tram (in Romanian only!), stating that tickets should only have three holes. They argue that the traveller must have stamped the ticket twice as the machine can't possibly stamp four holes. To prove their point they even offer the traveller a blank ticket so they can try for themselves. As the traveller has no proof of stamping their ticket only once, they're issued with an on-the-spot fine of $8 (150,000 lei).

The best way to avoid this scam is to hold your ticket up and make the ticket official count the holes before passing it over, or buy and stamp two tickets so if you're caught out you can simply pull out the second one which only has three holes.

Walking Tour

Constanţa's most renowned attraction is the **History & Archaeological Museum** (Muzeul Naţională de Istorie şi Arheologie; ☎ 618 763) at Piaţa Ovidiu 12. Its exhibits include 24 2nd-century Roman statues

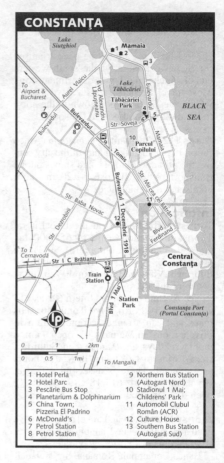

CONSTANŢA

1 Hotel Perla
2 Hotel Parc
3 Pescărie Bus Stop
4 Planetarium & Dolphinarium
5 China Town; Pizzeria El Padrino
6 McDonald's
7 Petrol Station
8 Petrol Station
9 Northern Bus Station (Autogară Nord)
10 Stadionul 1 Mai; Childrens' Park
11 Automobil Clubul Român (ACR)
12 Culture House
13 Southern Bus Station (Autogară Sud)

discovered under the old train station in 1962. Don't miss the statue of the serpent Glykon which is carved from a single block of marble. The museum is open 9 am to 8 pm daily in summer, and 10 am to 6 pm Tuesday to Sunday in winter ($0.75). Pick up a copy of the excellent English-language guide to the museum for $1.20.

Roman archaeological fragments spill over onto the surrounding square. Facing these is another museum, which shelters a gigantic 3rd-century **Roman mosaic** (Edificiul Roman cu Mozaic) discovered in 1959. A staircase led from the museum's lower terrace to the Roman public thermal baths, at the southern end of the cliff. Parts of these remain today. The museum is open 9 am to 8 pm daily in summer, and 10 am to 6 pm Tuesday to Sunday in winter ($1). The English-language guide *The Roman Paved Mosaic from Tomis*, sold at the ticket office for $1.20, is worth every cent.

The **statue of Ovid** (1887) commemorates the outlaw-poet who was exiled to Constanţa in the 8th century. His grave is believed to lie below the statue.

South of the square, on Str Arhiepiscopiei, is the **Mahmudiye mosque** (1910), which has a 140-step minaret which you can climb when the gate is unlocked. Two blocks farther south is the **Orthodox cathedral** (1885). A small **archaeological site** lies south of it, displaying walls of houses dating from the 4th to 6th centuries. Constanţa's **Roman Catholic church** (Biserica Romano-Catolica Sfântul Anton) is one street west of the Orthodox cathedral at Str Nicolae Titulescu 11.

Continue south to the small **Ion Jalea museum** (Muzeul Ion Jalea; ☎ 618 602) in a Moorish-style house (closed Monday); $0.25. One block west of the museum is the **Saligny monument**. The Romanian engineer Anghel Saligny (1854–1923) designed the Cernavodă bridge (1895) over the Danube and constructed Constanţa's modern port (1899–1910).

From the monument, a peaceful promenade meanders along the waterfront, offering sweeping views of the Black Sea. On summer evenings this is a popular hangout for kids, entwined couples and old men playing chess. Have a beer or coffee on the terrace of Constanţa's French-style Art-Nouveau **cazino** (1910). Opposite is a dismal **aquarium** (☎ 611 277), open 9 am to 8 pm daily from June to mid-September (hours are reduced in winter); $0.50. Farther along the promenade is the **Genoese lighthouse** (1860) and the **pier**, with a fine view of old Constanţa. Behind the lighthouse, a tragically poised **statue of Mihai Eminescu** (1934) looks out to the sea.

Return to Piaţa Ovidiu and follow Blvd Tomis north-west to the Grand Supermarket.

Glykon was one of several Roman statues discovered beneath Constanţa's train station

Halfway up Blvd Tomis you pass the **Geamia Hunchiar mosque** (1868), built with stones from the gate of the former Ottoman fortress destroyed in 1828.

Farther along Blvd Tomis is the worthwhile **Folk Art museum** (Muzeul de Artă Populară; ☎ 616 133).

When you reach the supermarket, turn left and explore Victoria Park, which has remains of the 3rd-century **Roman city wall** and the 6th-century Butchers' tower, pieces of Roman sculpture and the modern **Victory monument** (1968).

If you continue north-west along Blvd Tomis you come to the **art museum** (Muzeul de Artă; ☎ 617 012). Contemporary art exhibitions are held in the adjoining **small art gallery**. Both open 9 am to 8 pm daily ($0.50/0.25 adults/students, closed Monday in winter).

The **Naval History Museum** (Muzeul Marinei Române; ☎ 619 035) is housed in the old Navy high school at Str Traian 53. The captions are all in Romanian. It's open 9 am to 6 pm Tuesday to Sunday ($0.50).

NORTHERN DOBRUJA

CENTRAL CONSTANŢA

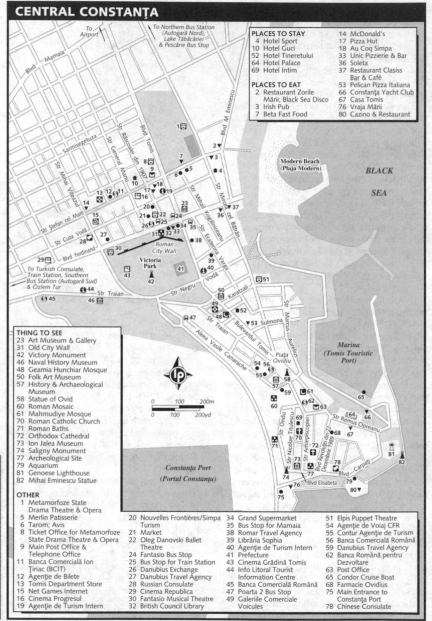

PLACES TO STAY
4 Hotel Sport
10 Hotel Guci
52 Hotel Tineretului
64 Hotel Palace
69 Hotel Intim

PLACES TO EAT
2 Restaurant Zorile
  Mării; Black Sea Disco
3 Irish Pub
7 Beta Fast Food

14 McDonald's
17 Pizza Hut
18 Au Coq Simpa
33 Unic Pizzierie & Bar
36 Soleta
37 Restaurant Clasiss
  Bar & Café
53 Pelican Pizza Italiana
66 Constanţa Yacht Club
67 Casa Tomis
76 Vraja Mării
80 Cazino & Restaurant

THING TO SEE
23 Art Museum & Gallery
31 Old City Wall
42 Victory Monument
46 Naval History Museum
48 Geamia Hunchiar Mosque
50 Folk Art Museum
57 History & Archaeological
  Museum
58 Statue of Ovid
60 Roman Mosaic
61 Mahmudiye Mosque
70 Roman Catholic Church
71 Roman Baths
72 Orthodox Cathedral
73 Ion Jalea Museum
74 Saligny Monument
77 Archeological Site
79 Aquarium
81 Genoese Lighthouse
82 Mihai Eminescu Statue

OTHER
1 Metamorfoze State
  Drama Theatre & Opera
5 Merlin Patisserie
6 Tarom; Avis
8 Ticket Office for Metamorfoze
  State Drama Theatre & Opera
9 Main Post Office &
  Telephone Office
11 Banca Comercială Ion
  Ţiriac (BCIT)
12 Agenţie de Bilete
13 Tomis Department Store
15 Net Games Internet
16 Cinema Progresul
19 Agenţie de Turism Intern

20 Nouvelles Frontières/Simpa
  Turism
21 Market
22 Oleg Danovski Ballet
  Theatre
24 Fantasio Bus Stop
25 Bus Stop for Train Station
26 Danubius Exchange
27 Danubius Travel Agency
28 Russian Consulate
29 Cinema Republica
30 Fantasio Musical Theatre
32 British Council Library

34 Grand Supermarket
35 Bus Stop for Mamaia
38 Romar Travel Agency
39 Librăria Sophia
40 Agenţie de Turism Intern
41 Prefecture
43 Cinema Grădină Tomis
44 Info Litoral Tourist
  Information Centre
45 Banca Comercială Română
47 Poarta 2 Bus Stop
49 Galeriile Comerciale
  Voicules

51 Elpis Puppet Theatre
54 Agenţie de Voiaj CFR
55 Contur Agenţie de Turism
56 Banca Comercială Română
59 Danubius Travel Agency
62 Banca Română pentru
  Dezvoltare
63 Post Office
65 Condor Cruise Boat
68 Farmacie Ovidius
75 Main Entrance to
  Constanţa Port
78 Chinese Consulate

Heading north towards Mamaia, you pass Constanţa's **Planetarium & Dolphinarium** (Planetarium şi Delfinariu), on the south-eastern shores of Lake Tăbăcăriei; open 8 am to 9 pm daily from June to mid-September, and 8 am to 4 pm during winter. Tickets for both cost $0.50 and are sold 30 minutes before the show starts. Trolleybus No 40 stops directly outside the Dolphinarium.

Activities
You can sail aboard the *Condor* (mobile ☎ 094-689 228), moored at the marina, known as the Tomis Turist Port (Portul Turistic Tomis), at the east end of Str Remus Opreanu opposite the Yacht Club ($3 per person an hour for a group of 14). The boat sails from 9.30 am from May to September.

Rent paddle and rowing boats from the beach attendants on the *plaja modern* (modern beach), north of the marina. Steps lead down to the beach from Str Negru Vodă and Str Ştefan cel Mare.

Places to Stay
Camping The nearest *camping ground* is in Mamaia, 6km north of Constanţa, but an easy 20-minute trolleybus or minibus ride will take you there (see the Mamaia section later).

Hotels Sport enthusiasts should opt for the modern *Hotel Sport* (☎ 617 558, fax 611 009, Str Cuza Vodă 2). Single/double/triple rooms with private bath are $19/25/35, including breakfast. The hotel has a gym and small sports complex, but is usually full with athletic groups.

The five-storey two-star *Hotel Tineretu-lui* (☎ 613 590, fax 611 290, Blvd Tomis 24) has neat, clean singles/doubles with private bath for $26/33, including breakfast.

In 1882 Romanian poet Mihai Eminescu briefly stayed at *Hotel Intim* (☎/fax 618 285, Str Nicolae Titulescu 9). Two-star rooms cost $26/33 and three-star rooms cost $38/45, including breakfast. The hotel has an elegant dining room and terrace.

Equally fine is the 1914 *Hotel Palace* (☎ 614 696, fax 617 532, Str Remus Oprea-nu 7), overlooking the marina. Two-star rooms cost $20/28 and three-star rooms are a pricey $59/79, including breakfast.

Constanţa's top hotel is the three-star *Hotel Guci* (☎/fax 638 426, Str Răscoalei 1907, 23) behind the central post office. Luxurious rooms are $95/102 and $127 for a suite. Other facilities include an expensive restaurant, jacuzzi, sauna and gym.

Other accommodation is available in Mamaia, just to the north (see that section, later).

Places to Eat
Restaurants & Cafes For Italian-inspired delights try *Pelican Pizza Italiana* (☎ 615 976, Str Sulmona 9). It has a fine terrace garden and serves cocktails. For those who prefer the flavours of France visit *Au Coq Simpa* (☎ 614 797, Str Ştefan cel Mare 19). Both restaurants have erotic night shows, so if you don't want to be subjected to half-naked women prancing around eat early!

Unic Pizzerie & Bar (☎ 616 369, Blvd Ferdinand 7) is a hot choice for pizza lovers. Pizzas come in small ($1) and large ($2) sizes.

Worth the splurge is the *Cazino Restaurant* (☎ 617 416, Blvd Elisabeta 2), if only for the large outdoor terrace overlooking the Black Sea. In summer there's live music on the terrace.

The flashy *Restaurant Clasiss Bar & Café*, on Str Mircea cel Bătrân, is housed in a circular concrete tower overlooking the beach. Opposite is *Soleta* (☎ 614 511), an inexpensive and authentic Lebanese restaurant. Its extensive menu is in French, Romanian and Lebanese.

Close by is the friendly *Irish Pub* (☎/fax 550 400, Str Ştefan cel Mare 1), with a pleasant terrace overlooking the beach. It serves an expensive range of grilled meats and fish dishes – the Irish Mixed Grill is $3.75 – and has a vast drinks list. Opposite is *Restaurant Zorile Mării* (Str Ştefan cel Mare 2), a popular lunch spot for restless sunbathers.

China Town (☎ 540 590, Str Zorelelor 67), almost opposite the Dolphinarium, is good. The fried rice is of the Romanian variety but the meat and fish dishes are tasty. It's usually crammed with expats. Next door is the equally popular *Pizzeria El Padrino*.

Light snacks and copious amounts of beer are served in the **Constanţa Yacht Club**, on Str Remus Opreanu, a cafe specialising in seafood dishes, overlooking the marina. Heading back into town from the marina, you pass the cheap and cheerful **Casa Tomis** *(Str Remus Opreanu 8)*.

Last-minute and late-night snacks can be grabbed at **Vraja Mării**, on Blvd Elisabeta adjacent to the main port entrance.

Fast Food Fast-food outlets serving kebabs, burgers and hot dogs are dotted all over town. There are some inside the modern **Galeriile Comerciale Voicules**, off Blvd Tomis. **Beta Fast Food** in the central park on Str Ştefan cel Mare has a terrace where you can drink beer and munch on traditional Romanian *mititei* (spicy meat balls) with mustard.

McDonald's has an outlet adjoining the Tomis department store on Str Ştefan cel Mare and another next to the Dolphinarium on Blvd Mamaia. **Pizza Hut** *(☎ 518 413)* on Str Răscoalei 1907 home delivers.

Self-Catering Stock up on fruit, cheese and vegetables at the **central market** between the train station and southern bus station. There is another market, just behind the bus stop for the train station, off Str Răscoalei 1907.

The **Grand Supermarket** *(Blvd Tomis 57)*, on the corner of Blvd Ferdinand, has an excellent choice of cakes and biscuits. Freshly baked breads and pastries are sold at the **Merlin Patisserie**, on Str Ştefan cel Mare opposite Beta Fast Food.

Entertainment

Foreign films are presented in the original languages at **Cinema Progresul** *(☎ 664 411, Str Ştefan cel Mare 33)* and **Cinema Republica** *(☎ 616 287, Blvd Ferdinand 58)*. In summer, films are also screened at **Cinema Grădină Tomis**, an outside cinema in Victoria Park. Tickets are sold one hour before the film starts (usually around 9.30 pm).

Colourful cabarets, pantomimes and musicals are performed at the **Fantasio Musical Theatre** *(Teatrul de Revista Fantasio; ☎ 615 416, Blvd Ferdinand 11)* behind

Cinema Grădină Tomis. The **Elpis Puppet Theatre** *(Teatrul de Păpuşi Elpis; ☎ 618 992, Str Karatzali 16)* is fun too.

The more literary should head to the **Metamorfoze State Drama Theatre & Opera** *(Teatrul Dramatic Metamorfoze şi Opera; ☎ 619 440, Str Mircea cel Bătrân 97)* in the central park. Tickets are sold at the ticket office at Blvd Tomis 97; open 9 am to 3 pm and 4 to 6 pm weekdays, 9 am to noon Saturday, and 5 to 6.50 pm Sunday. Performances start at 7 pm. The theatre is also home to the **Black Sea Philharmonic** *(Filarmonica Marea Neagră)*.

Ballets are performed at the **Oleg Danovski Ballet Theatre** *(☎ Teatrul de Balet Oleg Danovski; ☎ 660 346, Str Răscoalei 1907, 5)*. Tickets for all performances are sold at the Agenţie de Bilete *(☎ 664 076)* at Str Ştefan cel Mare 34, open 10 am to 5 pm daily.

The **Black Sea Disco** *(Str Ştefan cel Mare 2)*, adjoining Restaurant Zorile Mării, is an excellent place to unwind after a day of sightseeing and sunbathing; open 10 pm to 6 am daily except Monday.

Spectator Sports

FC Farul Constanţa, the city's cherished football team, has its home ground at Stadionul 1 Mai *(☎ 616 142, fax 644 827)* in Parcul Copilului (literally 'children's park'), in the northern suburbs at Str Primăverii 2.

Getting There & Away

Air In summer there are international flights to/from Constanţa's Mihail Kogălniceanu airport *(☎ 258 378)*, 25km from the centre. See the Getting There & Away chapter for details.

Between May and September Tarom *(☎ 662 632)*, Str Ştefan cel Mare 15, runs daily flights on Wednesday, Friday, Saturday and Sunday from Constanţa to Bucharest; ($50/100 for a single/return). Its office is open 8 am to 6 pm weekdays, and 8.30 am to 12.30 pm Saturday.

Train Constanţa's train station is near the bus station at the west end of Blvd Ferdinand. The left-luggage office (open 24

hours) is downstairs inside the passageway from the main hall to the tracks.

The Agenţie de Voiaj CFR (☎ 617 930), Aleea Vasile Canarache 4, is open 7.30 am to 7 pm weekdays, and 7.30 am to 1 pm Saturday.

From Constanţa the *Basarabia* train runs daily to Chişinău in Moldova (13¾ hours, 6.02 pm). The *Ovidius* train to Budapest also runs overnight (17 hours, 5.45 pm) via Bucharest and Arad.

In winter there are reduced services to other cities in Romania. Services to most major towns in Transylvania and Banat only run in summer. All trains to Mangalia stop at Eforie Nord, Eforie Sud, Costineşti and Neptun.

Bus Constanţa has two bus stations: private buses to Istanbul ($25/50 a single/return, 17½ hours, 2 and 3 pm) depart daily from the southern bus station (Autogară Sud), next to the train station on Blvd Ferdinand. Tickets are sold in advance from Özlem Tur (☎ 514 053, 672 144) just outside the bus station.

From Constanţa's northern bus station (Autogară Nord) daily services include one to Brăila (277km) and Măcin (218km); two to Histria (52km) and Hârşova (84km); and five to Tulcea ($2.30, 125km).

If you're travelling south along the Black Sea coast, buses are infinitely more convenient than the trains. Exit Constanţa's train station, turn right and walk 50m to the long queue of private minibuses. One leaves every 30 minutes for Mangalia ($1, pay the driver), stopping at Eforie Nord, Eforie Sud, Neptun-Olimp, Venus and Saturn.

Getting Around
To/From the Airport Mihail Kogălniceanu airport (☎ 258 378) is 25km northwest of the centre on the road to Hârşova. Tarom runs a shuttle bus from its office at Str Ştefan cel Mare 15, 1½ hours before flight departures. All public buses to Hârşova stop at the airport. Allow yourself a good hour for the journey.

Bus & Trolleybus Public transport runs daily from 5 am to 11.30 pm. A ticket valid for two journeys costs $0.20. Trolleybus No

100 links the train station and Autogară Sud with Autogară Nord. Trolleybus Nos 40, 41 and 43 go from Autogară Sud to the old town. No 43 continues to the stadium south of Lake Tăbăcăriei, and No 41 goes to Mamaia. No 40 goes to the Pescărie bus stop at the southern edge of Mamaia, from where you can catch trolleybus No 41 or 47 to the centre of Mamaia.

Bus No 42 departs from the Fantasio bus stop on Blvd Ferdinand to Autogară Nord.

Car & Motorcycle Avis (☎/fax 616 733) shares an office with Tarom at Str Ştefan cel Mare 15; open 9 am to 5 pm weekdays, and 9 am to 1 pm Saturday. Nouvelles Frontières/Simpa Turism (see Travel Agencies earlier) is an agent for Hertz.

The Automobil Clubul Român (ACR; ☎ 611 849, fax 691 220) has an out-of-town office at Blvd Tomis 141, building T-1, between Constanţa and Mamaia.

MAMAIA
☎ 041
Mamaia, an 8km strip of beach between the freshwater Lake Mamaia (or Siutghiol) and the Black Sea, just north of Constanţa, is Romania's most popular resort. Mamaia is an above-average example of the Black Sea's resorts, with golden sands, abundant greenery and a festival atmosphere. According to legend, the resort gained its name from the desperate cries of a fair maiden, who, during the time of the Ottoman Empire, was kidnapped by a Turk and taken out to sea in a boat. As the wind howled, her frantic cries for her mother – 'Mamaia! Mamaia!' – could be heard for miles around.

Orientation
The resort lines both sides of the Constanţa-Năvodari road which runs along the coast. Some hotels and restaurants are on the promenade which is parallel to this road. The Pescărie bus stop is at the southern end of Mamaia.

Information
The Agenţia de Turism (☎ 831 168, fax 831 052, @ mamaia@gmb.ro), on the highway

side of Hotel Riviera, arranges car rental and accommodation; open 7 am to 4 pm Monday to Thursday, and 7 am to 1 pm Friday.

Every hotel has a currency exchange, but to change travellers cheques and get cash advances on Visa/MasterCard you have to go to Constanţa. Most of the large hotels accept credit cards.

The telephone and post office is 200m south of the Cazino complex on the promenade; open 8 am to 8 pm weekdays from June to September.

Salvamar operates medical huts on the beach between 15 June and 15 September.

Things to See & Do

Mamaia's number-one attraction is its wide, golden **beach** which stretches the entire length of the resort. From the Cazino complex a concrete **pier** (1935) leads out to sea.

In summer, boats ferry tourists across the Lake Mamaia to **Ovidiu Island** (Insula Ovidiu), departing every hour, on the hour, between 10 am and midnight from the wharf opposite the Staţia Cazino bus stop ($3 return). The wharf is signposted 'Debarcaderul Cazino: Mamaia – Insula Ovidiu'.

Some 50m north of Hotel Bucureşti is a **water-sports** school, offering waterskiing, yachting, windsurfing and rowing on Lake Mamaia. The **tennis** courts at Grădina Boema, on the highway between the Doina and Victoria Hotels, cost $7 per hour including equipment rental.

Places to Stay

Staff at the Centrul de Cazare Cazino (☎ 831 209), on the 1st floor of the Cazino complex, have lists of available accommodation; open 10 am to 9 pm daily from 10 June to 10 September.

Camping The small *Popas Tabăra Turist* (☎ 831 357), at the northern end of Mamaia's 8km strip, is always full in summer. It costs $2 per person for a tent and $4 for a bed in a wooden hut. Take bus No 23 from Mamaia's Pescărie bus stop to the Staţia Tabăra Turist bus stop.

Adjoining the site is the *Enigma Party Zone* disco.

Two kilometres farther north, the larger *Popas Mamaia* (☎ 831 357) charges $2 for a tent, and $6 for a bed in a hut. Rates drop between September and April. Bus No 23 stops outside the site.

Popas Hanul Piraţilor (☎/fax 831 704), 1km farther north, has double wooden huts for $10 and two-room villas for $20. Again, take bus No 23.

Beach Chalets Both *Cazino Delta Pensiune* (☎ 831 665), inside the Cazino complex on the southern side, and the *Mini-Hotel* (☎ 831 878), on the northern side of the Cazino, offer whitewashed, terraced chalets overlooking the beach. They have double chalets (basic rooms with mattresses) with shared bathroom and cold water for $7.

Hotels Some 500m north of the Cazino, *Hotel Victoria* (☎ 831 028, fax 831 024) has clean singles/doubles with private bath for $12/24.

The next best option is the friendly *Hotel Flora* (☎ 831 059, fax 831 889), nestled between Hotel Ovidiu and Hotel Sulina. Pleasant rooms with private bath are $20/26. The hotel has a swimming pool for guests' use only.

Hotel Perla (☎ 831 670) and *Hotel Parc* (☎ 831 670) are high-rises at the most southern end of Mamaia, near the Pescărie bus stop. Both have standard rooms and mid-range prices: $18/24/30 for a single/double/triple.

The two-star *Hotel Condor* (☎ 831 142, fax 831 906), just left of the Staţia Cazino bus stop, has doubles with private bath for $45. It also has a large restaurant, currency exchange and snack bar. Next door is the three-star *Hotel Albatros* (☎ 831 381, fax 831 346), with rooms with bath for $40/50.

Mamaia's most exclusive beachfront hotel is the four-star *Hotel Rex* (☎ 831 595, fax 831 690), a large, pre-WWII white building some 200m north of Hotel Bucureşti. It has a picture-postcard swimming pool – for guests' use only – on a terrace above the beach. Luxurious rooms cost $90/110 and an apartment is $150.

Places to Eat

Almost every hotel has an adjoining restaurant and numerous *fast-food stands* line the busy pedestrianised street.

The Cazino's *Delta Restaurant* serves traditional Romanian dishes on wooden platters. Be sure to try the pastrami with *mămăligă* (corn mush) at least once during your stay; swill it down with a bottle of Murfatlar wine for no more than $5 a head. Folk bands play most evenings in summer.

Opposite the southern end of the Cazino complex is the new *Fish Garden* where you can taste the best of the Black Sea.

In the northern part of the resort, the touristy *Hanul Piraţilor Restaurant*, across the road from the Popas Hanul Piraţilor hotel, is the place to enjoy a good mixed grill and plenty of wine. Ovidiu Island's thatched-roof *Rustic Restaurant* is famous for seafood and worth a visit.

Getting There & Away

Train Tickets for trains departing from Constanţa (see the earlier Constanţa section) can be bought in advance at the Agenţie de Voiaj CFR (☎ 617 930) adjoining the post and telephone office on the promenade.

Bus The simplest and quickest way to travel between Constanţa and Mamaia is by minibus. Minibus No 304 departs from Constanţa's train station every 10 minutes and drives north along Mamaia's 8km strip, stopping at major hotels. Trolleybus No 41 or 47 also takes you from Constanţa to Mamaia's Staţia Cazino bus stop.

Alternatively, catch trolleybus No 40 from Constanţa to the Pescărie bus stop near Hotel Parc then change to trolleybus No 47 to the centre of Mamaia (or you might opt for a 20-minute stroll along the beach to the centre).

In summer a shuttle runs up and down Mamaia's 5km boardwalk.

To get to Constanţa's northern bus station, take the southbound bus No 23 from the Staţia Cazino stop in Mamaia to the bus stop on the south-western shore of Lake Tăbăcăriei.

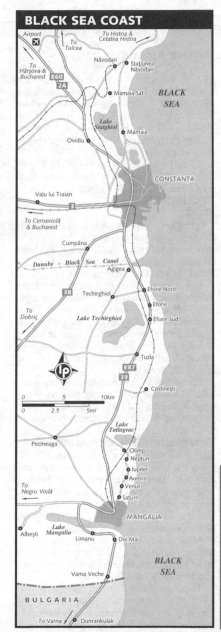

BLACK SEA COAST

The northbound bus No 23 goes to the neighbouring resort of Năvodari.

Getting Around

Trolleybus tickets valid for two journeys ($0.20) are sold at the kiosk next to the Staţia Cazino bus stop. In low season the kiosk shuts, so stock up on tickets before you leave Constanţa or buy them at the Pescărie bus stop. Buy tickets for the shuttle bus to Constanţa from the driver ($0.20 for a single journey).

To call a taxi dial ☎ 953 or 690 000.

EFORIE NORD & LAKE TECHIRGHIOL

☎ 041

Eforie Nord, 17km south of Constanţa, is the first large resort south of the city. The beach is below 20m cliffs. Tiny **Lake Belona**, behind the southern end of the beach, is a popular bathing spot.

South-west of Eforie Nord lies **Lake Techirghiol**, famous for its black sapropel mud, effective against rheumatism. Mud-covered sun-worshippers strutting along the beach are not an uncommon sight in Eforie Nord. Lake Techirghiol's waters are four times as salty as the sea; the lake is 2m below sea level.

Eforie Nord's hotels accommodate some 19,000 sun- or mud-loving tourists every year. Avoid the town if you have an aversion to crowded beaches and blaring pop music.

Orientation & Information

The train station is a few minutes' walk from the centre. Exit the train station and turn left. Turn left after Hotel Belvedere and then right onto Blvd Republicii, the main street. City maps are posted at the station and around town. Buses from Mangalia and Constanţa stop on Blvd Republicii.

Most hotels and restaurants are on Str Tudor Vladimirescu which runs parallel to Blvd Republicii along the beach. The beach is a 10m drop from the road.

The Agenţia de Turism Intern (☎ 741 188), Blvd Republicii 6, 50m north of the bus stop, arranges private rooms from $10 per person; open 8 am to 4 pm Monday to Saturday from June to September. There is a currency exchange in practically every hotel. The telephone office inside the central post office at Blvd Republicii 11 is open 7 am to 10 pm daily; the post office is open 9 am to 6 pm weekdays.

Mud Baths

Wallow in black mud! Popas Şincai (see Places to Stay) offers the cheapest bath in town. Its mud baths (baia de nămol), on the northern shores of Lake Techirghiol, are open 8 am to 8 pm daily from mid-June until the beginning of September ($0.60, pay reception staff). There are separate beaches for men and women.

Most of the major hotels offer mud baths at more extortionate prices. There are public thermal baths (băi termale) at the northern end of Blvd Republicii. Most tour groups seeking extensive pampering head straight for the băza de tratament adjoining the Delfinul, Meduza and Steaua de Mare Hotels.

Places to Stay

Camping The low-budget traveller's first stop should be **Popas Şincai** (☎ 741 401), a few hundred metres west of Eforie Nord's train station. Walk west to the far end of the railway platform, cross the tracks and follow a path to a breach in the wall. Tent sites are $4 per tent and two-room huts are $5 per person.

Camping Meduza (☎/fax 742 385), behind the Minerva and Prahova Hotels at the northern end of the beach, has better facilities. Walk north along Str Tudor Vladimirescu and turn immediately left after Club Maxim. This site is closer to the beach but farther from the train station. Tent spaces are $2 per person and clean two-bed bungalows are $5.

Hotels The resort's most upmarket address, **Europa Hotel** (☎ 742 990, Blvd Republicii 19), was closed at the time of writing.

The two-star **Hotel Delfinul**, **Hotel Meduza** and **Hotel Steaua de Mare** (☎ 704 125, fax 704 124, Str Tudor Vladimirescu 39–43) are a trio of concrete high-rises at the northern end of the resort. The hotels, owned by the same company, specialise in natural cures and mud baths. Single/double rooms in all three start from $20/35.

Places to Eat

Cofetăria Pescăruş, opposite the post office, has great pastries. *Restaurant Berbec*, on Str 1 Mai at the northern end of the beach, is famous for its folk-dancing shows. It charges around $10 for a meal and music.

Nunta Zamfirei is a Romanian restaurant famed for its folk song-and-dance shows. Walk north along Blvd Republicii and turn left onto the small track opposite the public thermal baths.

Marginally more tranquil is the *Vraja Mării* restaurant, nestled between the shores of Lake Belona and the Black Sea.

Getting There & Away

The Agenţie de Voiaj CFR (☎ 617 930) is inside the post office building at Blvd Republicii 11.

All trains between Bucharest and Mangalia stop at Eforie Nord, but you're better off on a private bus (see Getting There & Away under Constanţa).

COSTINEŞTI

☎ 041

Costineşti, 9km south of Eforie Sud, is a small fishing village. Until 1989 the village-resort, which hosted a pioneer youth camp in 1949 and the first international student camp in 1956, was only open to young people. Today anyone can stay here.

Costineşti buzzes in July and August when the holiday radio station Radio Vacanţa broadcasts from the beach, blasting music across loudspeakers. A national film festival, a young actors' festival and a jazz festival are all key events in July and August.

For the rest of the year Costineşti reverts to being a simple, sleepy village.

Orientation & Information

Costineşti is 4km east of the Constanţa-Mangalia highway. The post office and Agenţie de Voiaj CFR (☎ 617 930) are

north-west of the beach, just off the main road into the resort.

Places to Stay & Eat

There is a large *camping ground* off the main road to the beach; a two-bed hut costs $5 a night. More upmarket are the canary-yellow bungalows at the *Complex Turistic Stefania* (☎ 734 070, fax 734 602), immediately on the left as you enter Costineşti from the north. Double bungalows with a sink and toilet are $11; doubles in the main building are $30. The complex is only open from June to the end of August.

Most houses have a sign outside advertising *cazare* (rooms). *Vila Claudia* (☎ 734 341) charges $10 per person a night (cheaper during winter). Home-cooked meals are extra. Follow the signs from the centre of the village.

The *Complex Iunona* (☎ 734 454, fax 734 315, Str Principală 82) has wooden chalets to let and can arrange accommodation in private homes. So can BTT (☎ 734 000, ☎/fax 734 077) inside *Hotel Forum*, overlooking the southern end of the beach.

Getting There & Away

From mid-June to mid-September there are 18 trains daily between Constanţa and Costineşti Tabără (40 minutes), 2km south of Costineşti train station proper. Get off at Costineşti Tabără for the beach and resort.

From Costineşti Tabără, trains continue south to Neptun (10 minutes) and Mangalia (20 minutes).

NEPTUN-OLIMP

☎ 041

Before the 1989 revolution, Neptun-Olimp, 6km south of Costineşti, was the exclusive resort of Romania's Communist Party. Ceauşescu had his own luxury villa, fit for a king, built here. Today, the 'party' is well and truly alive here.

Orientation

Olimp, by rights a separate resort from Neptun, lies on the northern fringe of Neptun, overlooking Lake Tatlageac. To its south, handsome villas and luxury hotels, bathed in the shade of the Comorova forest, overlook the artificial lakes of Neptun I and Neptun II which separate the resort from the sea. Together the two resorts form a vast expanse of hotels and discos.

Information

The Dispecerat Cazare (room dispatcher; ☎ 701 300) can give you information on hotels and take bookings. The office is inside the Levent Market on the main street; open 24 hours a day between June and September.

Most hotels have tourist desks with English-speaking staff who will help you with organised tours along the coast.

Cash travellers cheques at the Banca Comercială Română, on the main street of Neptun in the resort's centre, 8.30 to 11.30 am weekdays. The exchange office attached to the Levent Market is open 9 am to 5 pm weekdays from June to September.

The post office and telephone centre is just north of Hotel Clăbucet on Neptun's main street.

Activities

If you get bored with sunbathing on the beach, there are numerous activities to chose from: you can ride through town in a traditional **horse-drawn cart** ($2.50 for 15 minutes); play **mini-golf** at the course opposite Hotel Miorița on the main street in Neptun or close to Hotel Arad heading towards Olimp; play **tennis** at the court next to the Miorița mini-golf course; or hire a side-by-side **tandem** from the kiosk opposite Disco Why Not? on the main street.

Jet skis can be hired from the northern end of Neptun's beach or from the jetty in Neptun. There is also a **yacht club** (☎ 752 395) on the beach in Neptun. Both resorts have a **bowling** alley: **Bowling Neptun** is immediately on the right as you enter Neptun from the south. **Bowling Olimp** is behind the beachfront Hotel Amfiteatru.

Places to Stay

Camping At the southern end of Lake Neptun II, *Holiday Village Neptun* (☎ 701 224, fax 731 447) is open year-round. In July and August, a double brick cottage is $9 per person, a double hut with running water is $6 per person and camping is $2 per person. *Camping Olimp* (☎ 731 314, fax 731 447) at the northern end of Olimp's tourist strip charges similar prices. Both camping grounds are packed in summer.

Hotels Neptun-Olimp's hotels are not for budget travellers. Its 34 one-, two- and three-star hotels charge from $22 to $36 for a double, without breakfast. Without reservations you'll pay more.

Neptun's hotels are along the main street. Those at its southern end overlook the two Neptun lakes. Lined up along Lake Neptun I you'll find *Hotel Midia* (☎ 731 915, fax 731 447), *Hotel Tomis* (☎ 731 121, fax 731 447), *Hotel Istria* (☎ 731 819, fax 731 447), and *Hotel Callatis* (☎ 731 619, fax 731 447), all of which are two-stars; and the one-star *Hotel Traian* (☎ 731 122, fax 731 447). Another cluster of hotels – including *Hotel Apollo* where the Agenţie de Voiaj CFR is based – lies north-west of Lake Neptun II; none of them have a lake view.

Most of the hotels in Olimp look out to sea. The main hotels are *Hotel Panoramic* (☎ 701 033, fax 701 133), *Hotel Amfiteatru* (☎ 701 032, fax 701 132) and *Hotel Belvedere* (☎ 701 034, fax 701 134), all three-star hotels with steps to the beach.

North of this lie the sky-rise *Hotel Transilvania* (☎ 701 030), *Hotel Moldova* and *Hotel Muntenia* (☎ 731 916, fax 731 447), *Hotel Oltenia* (☎ 731 021, fax 731 447) and *Hotel Banat* (☎ 731 618, fax 731 447), named after regions in Romania.

Places to Eat

In this heaving resort crammed with fast-food joints, one of the most beautiful places to eat is the tranquil *Restaurant Insula* (☎ 731 722), which comprises a series of floating wooden rafts moored on Lake Neptun I. Traditional Romanian dishes are served here.

Also known for its local cuisine and colourful folklore shows is *Calul Bălan* (☎ 731 524), on the left as you enter Neptun's main street from the south.

Getting There & Away

Train Advance train tickets can be purchased from the Agenţie de Voiaj CFR (☎ 617 930) inside Neptun's Hotel Apollo (see Places to Stay). Halta Neptun station is within walking distance of the Neptun-Olimp hotels, midway between the two resorts.

All trains travelling between Bucharest, Constanţa and Mangalia, local and express, stop at Halta Neptun.

Bus Private buses from Constanţa and Mangalia will drop you on the main highway, 2.5km from Neptun-Olimp's hotels (see Getting There & Away under Constanţa).

JUPITER-AURORA, VENUS & SATURN

☎ 041

The uninspiring resorts of Jupiter-Aurora, Venus and Saturn run along the 10km stretch of coast between Neptun-Olimp and Mangalia. Unlike their larger neighbours, these purpose-built resorts hold little appeal. Rusty carousels and water slides decay on the beach while flagging discos desperately try to pull in crowds with tacky wet T-shirt and beach-beauty competitions. The upside is that hotel accommodation is cheaper.

Information

There are post offices in Venus and Saturn; the Venus post office also houses an Agenţie de Voiaj CFR (☎ 617 930) where you can buy train tickets in advance. None of the resorts has a train station.

Activities

The **Mangalia Stud Farm** (Herghelia Mangalia; ☎ 753 215) is at the southern end of Venus, 3km from Mangalia. It has a small racecourse and experienced riders can ride for $7 an hour.

Across the street from Hotel Adriana, there is a **thermal bath** (signposted 'Băi Mezotermale'), with hot, sulphurous water and medicinal mud. It's open daily from mid-May to September, with separate entrances for women and men ($3).

Places to Stay

Camping Saturn (☎ 751 380, fax 755 559), at the northern end of the Saturn resort behind the Minerva restaurant, has double wooden huts for $2.50 a night. A four-person tent costs $1 a night to pitch. The site has communal showers but no hot water. It has tennis courts too (bring your own racquet and balls).

There are some 55 *hotels* spread between the four resorts; a double room with private bath costs no more than $10.

Getting There & Away

Private buses shuttle beach-hoppers along the coast from Mangalia, through Saturn, Venus and Jupiter-Aurora, to Neptun-Olimp and Eforie Nord. The small minibuses stop in the centre of Saturn, Venus and Jupiter-Aurora (see Constanţa's Getting There & Away section).

MANGALIA

☎ 041 • postcode 8727 • pop 44,000

Ancient Greek Callatis (now Mangalia) contains several minor archaeological sites. It is a quiet town and attracts many elderly European tour groups. Mangalia is the second most important harbour of Romania, although mainly for military purposes.

Orientation

Mangalia's train station is 1km north of the centre. Turn right as you exit the station and follow Şoseaua Constanţei (the main road) south. At the roundabout, turn left for Hotel Mangalia and the beach or continue straight for the pedestrianised section of Şoseaua Constanţei where most facilities are located.

Buses between resorts stop in front of the train station and at Staţia Stadion, the central bus stop just south of the roundabout on Şoseaua Constanţei.

Information

Tourist Offices Your best bet for information is the reception of Hotel President. Staff speak English, French and German. There are also information boards in Hotel Mangalia which are updated regularly. The hotel's tourist office organises day trips to the Danube Delta ($63) and Murfatlar vineyards ($23).

Money Most hotels have currency exchanges. The OK Exchange at Şoseaua Constanţei, opposite the Patisserie Peach Pitt, is open 8 am to 8 pm Monday to Saturday, and 8 am to 1 pm Sunday. Cash travellers cheques, get cash advances on Visa/MasterCard or use the ATM at the Banca Comercială Română, Şoseaua Constanţei 25 (open 8 am to noon weekdays); or at Banca Agricolă on the beachfront at Str Teilor 7 (open 8 to 11.30 am weekdays).

Post & Telephone The telephone and post office is at Str Ştefan cel Mare 16. The post office is open 7 am to 8 pm weekdays; the telephone section is open 7 am to 10 pm daily.

Email & Internet Access The Graphity Internet Café Club (☎ 758 284) at Ştefan cel Mare 5 is open 9 am to 9 pm daily. Emailing costs $0.50 per hour.

Things to See
Mangalia's sights can be seen in two to three hours. At the south side of Hotel Mangalia (see Orientation), along Str Izvor, are the ruins of a 6th-century **Palaeo-Christian basilica** and a fountain (Izvorul Hercules) dispensing sulphurous mineral water. Some 50m north of Hotel Mangalia, is a small white building which houses the **Mangalia laboratory** (1994). Studies have been made here on the 32 new species found in Movile cave in Limanu, 9km south of Mangalia (see Limanu, Doi Mai & Vama Veche, following). The laboratory is open upon request.

Return to the roundabout and continue south along Şoseaua Constanţei to the **Callatis Archaeological Museum** (Muzeul de Arheologie Callatis; ☎ 753 580). It has a good collection of Roman sculptures and is open 9 am to 8 pm daily from June to August. Adjacent to the museum is the **Farul outdoor cinema** (Grădină de Vară Farul). Just past the high-rise building next to the museum are some remnants of a 4th-century **Roman-Byzantine necropolis**.

Continue south another 500m on Şoseaua Constanţei to the centre of town. Cultural events take place in the **Casă de Cultură**, which has a large mural on the facade; the **Disco Galaxy** adjoins it. At the end of Şoseaua Constanţei turn right onto Str Oituz where you pass the Turkish **Sultan Esmahan Mosque** (Moscheea Esmahan Sultan; 1460).

From here, head east down Str Oituz to the beachfront where, in the basement of Hotel President, remains of the walls of the ancient Greek Callatis citadel dating from the 2nd to 7th centuries are exhibited in the **Callatiana Archaeological Reservation** (Muzeul Poarta Callatiana); open 24 hours.

Places to Stay
Camping The nearest *camping grounds* are in Jupiter-Aurora and Saturn. To get to Camping Saturn from Mangalia, follow Şoseaua Constanţei 1km north from Mangalia's train station to the Art-Deco Saturn sculpture, turn right, walk 50m then turn left.

Private Rooms Antrec (☎ 759 473, fax 757 400), Str George Murnu 13, Block D, Apt 21, arranges rooms in private homes in Mangalia and other costal resorts from $15 a night.

Hotels The popular choice is *Hotel Mangalia (☎ 752 052, fax 753 510, Str Rozelor 35)*. Single/double rooms cost $42/45 in high season. It is one of the few hotels on the coast with full wheelchair access; there are ramps onto the beach.

Surprisingly pleasant are the three two-star hotels on the promenade: *Hotel Zenit (☎ 751 645, fax 632 650, Str Teilor 7)*, *Hotel Astra (☎ 751 673, fax 632 650, Str Teilor 9)* and *Hotel Orion (☎ 751 156, fax 632 650, Str Teilor 11)* all have doubles with private bath for $25.

Mangalia's luxury, four-star *Hotel President (☎/fax 755 861/862, @ hotelpresident@impromex.ro, St Treilor 6)* is the top place to stay on the coast. Rooms vary in price from $41/60 to $66/86 depending on which floor the room is on and whether it has a view. Luxury apartments are $162.

Places to Eat

Get fresh pastries and superb coffee at *Patiserie Peach-Pitt*, on Şoseaua Constanţei close to the archaeological museum. For fast food, salads and soups try the self-service *Fast Food* outlet, beneath the *Terasa President* on the beach in front of Hotel President.

For a splurge try *Café Jolly* inside Hotel President's business centre; it has five-course set menus for around $10. For a stiff pint of beer with the locals go to *Restaurant Casino*, immediately north of Hotel President.

Stock up on packed-lunch delights at the *food market* (Piaţa Agroalimentară) behind Hotel Zenit on Str Vasile Alecsandri.

Getting There & Away

Train The Agenţie de Voiaj CFR (☎ 752 818) adjoins the central post office at Str Ştefan cel Mare 16; open 9 am to 5 pm weekdays.

Mangalia is at the end of the line from Constanţa. From Constanţa there are 18 trains daily in summer to Mangalia (43km, one to 1½ hours). In winter the service is greatly reduced. Many of these trains are direct to/from Bucharest's Gara de Nord (269km, 4½ hours). In summer there are also express trains to/from Iaşi, Sibiu, Suceava and Timişoara.

Bus Private minibuses from Constanţa stop at Mangalia's train station and near the roundabout at the central Staţia Stadion bus stop (see Getting There & Away under Constanţa).

LIMANU, DOI MAI & VAMA VECHE

While Limanu, 9km south of Mangalia, gained international fame following the 1986 discovery of its Movile Cave (see the boxed text 'Cave Dwellers'), the cave is a research area and is closed to the public.

The Lipovani fishing village of Doi Mai (literally '2 May'), 5km south of Limanu, attracts Romania's most bohemian sunseekers and remains relatively untouched by the rest of the coast's tourist mania. In the 18th century a handful of Lipovani – descendants of

Cave Dwellers

In 1986 the Romanian speleologist Cristian Lascu made the fantastic discovery of the **Movile Cave** (Peştera Movile). The cave, 3.5km from Limanu, contained 32 new species of flora and fauna and two new genuses dating from the Upper Miocene period five million years ago. These creatures energise themselves via chemosynthesis, feeding on a thick layer of sulphur-consuming bacteria formed on top of the water in the vacuumed cave. Other than at Movile, this unique phenomenon is only known to exist some 5000m below sea level.

the Old Believers, a schismatic sect of the Russian Orthodox church – settled in Doi Mai. Their descendants today are characterised by a hardy nature and heavy vodka-drinking habits.

Equally tranquil is the border village of Vama Veche (literally 'old custom point'), 4km south of Doi Mai. The beach here is wide with fine golden sands. Some people bathe nude.

Camping is permitted on the beach in both Vama Veche and Doi Mai. Neither village has a hotel. Antrec (see Places to Stay, Mangalia) can arrange accommodation in Doi Mai. In Vama Veche ask at the local snack bar. Note that sanitary facilities in the village are poor; many houses have no running water.

Getting There & Away

Bus The private minibuses serving the coast stop short of Doi Mai and Vama Veche.

Bulgaria From the south end of Vama Veche you can walk or drive across the border into Bulgaria. The crossing is open 24 hours. If you cross on foot, be prepared for a 6km hike to Durankulak, the first settlement inside Bulgaria. Alternatively, hitch a ride, although few cars pass.

Motorists can also cross into Bulgaria at Negru Vodă, 15km west of Mangalia on the main Constanţa-Dobrič highway (No 38).

Kardam, the first village inside Bulgaria, is 5km from the border crossing.

THE DANUBE–BLACK SEA CANAL

The Danube Canal runs for 64km from Cernavodă in the west to Agigea on the eastern coast. The canal, which opened in 1984, shortens the sea trip from Constanţa to Cernavodă by 400km.

Cernavodă

The train from Bucharest crosses the Danube at Cernavodă on a great **iron bridge** designed by Romanian engineer Anghel Saligny (1854–1923) and erected in 1895. The railway follows the canal for most of its journey from Cernavodă to the coast.

Cernavodă has the dubious distinction of housing Romania's only **nuclear power plant**, inaugurated in April 1996. It's on the eastern side of town.

The Candu reactor, a Canadian design, was the first to be built in Europe and the first Western-designed reactor to be built in eastern Europe. Cernavodă's nuclear power plant is constructed in a recognised earthquake zone; three quakes have occurred in this region since 1979.

Construction work started on the plant in 1978. Speedy workmanship was allegedly so shoddy that, following the Canadian partners' direct intervention, the plant was closed until international safety standards were met. Guided tours of the plant have to be arranged well in advance with the plant's public relations unit (☎ 041-238 339, ext 1312/1202).

Murfatlar

As they approach Constanţa, the canal and railway pass through the Murfatlar area, where Romania's best dessert wines are produced. The profitable Murfatlar vineyards are west of the small town of Basarabi, some 14km west of Constanţa. Wine-tasting and guided tours of the factory are possible – but only for groups of 20 or more. It is open 8 am to 3 pm daily. Most travel agencies arrange group wine-tasting tours to Murfatlar.

The Death Canal

The Danube–Black Sea canal took 30,000 people nine years to construct. Some 300 million cubic metres of land were manually excavated and 4.2 million cubic metres of reinforced concrete shifted by workers. This canal was only part of a centuries-old dream to build an inland waterway linking the North and Black Seas, which was finally realised in 1992 when a 171km canal between the Main and Danube Rivers in Germany was opened.

Thousands of lives were lost during the communists' first attempt at building the canal – or 'death canal' *(canalul morţii)* as it was known – between 1949 and 1953. During the communist purges of this period some 180,000 political prisoners were interned in forced-labour camps in Romania; 40,000 of them were worked to death on the project. Ironically, the project was abandoned in 1953 and not resumed again until 1975 when a more suitable and properly researched route was followed.

Together with the House of the People in Bucharest, the canal has gone down in history as one of the communists' most costly follies – and not just financially.

ADAMCLISI

In the south-western part of Adamclisi, 45km south-west of Basarabi, archaeologists have uncovered remains of the Roman city of Tropaeum Traiani. The city was destroyed during Goth attacks in the 3rd century and not rebuilt until the reign of Constantine I (r. AD 306–37). Following the domination of Dobruja by the Turks in 1418, the settlement was renamed Adamclisi ('man's church').

There is also a giant triumphal Roman monument. The original **Tropaeum Traiani monument** was built (AD 106–9) to honour the Traian victory over the Dacians in Adamclisi. It contains the mausoleum of one of Traian's high-ranking officers who was killed in the battle. Today's monument is a replica of the original. The sides of the base are decorated with pictorial scenes, depicting the Roman battles.

Pillars, friezes and other fragments of the original monument are displayed in the **Tropaeum Traiani Museum** (Muzeul Tropaeum Traiani). To get to the museum head west from the monument into Adamclisi. Turn right at the 'Muzeul Adamclisi' signpost in the centre of the village, then turn left. The museum is at the end of this road. The remains of the fortress and the Tropaeum Traiani are visible from the lookout point here. To get the best view, however, continue west out of Adamclisi for a couple of kilometres until the hillside complex rises magnificently into view in the north. The museum and monument are open 9 am to 5 pm Tuesday to Sunday.

Getting There & Away
Adamclisi is difficult to reach by public transport. Buses departing daily from Constanţa's northern bus station (Autogară Nord) to Daeni via Ostrov pass through Adamclisi, so ask the driver to drop you off.

From Constanţa's southern bus station (Autogară Sud), the one daily bus to Băneasa stops at Adamclisi.

HISTRIA
Heading into the Danube Delta, you can make a small detour to Histria (formerly spelt Istria), 70km north of Constanţa. It was founded by Greek merchants in the 7th century BC. Approaching Histria along the coastal road from the south you pass through the seaside resort of **Năvodari**, an industrial town designated as a youth resort in 1959 and home to the state-run **Petromidia oil refinery**, Romania's most modern refinery (built in the 1980s).

Histria was settled in 657 BC by Greek traders and rapidly became a key commercial port, superseding Constanţa. But subsequent Goth attacks coupled with the gradual sandlocking of the harbour led to its equally rapid decline. By the 7th century AD the town was abandoned.

Citadel
If you've seen the lost city of Pompeii, Histria Citadel (Cetatea Istria) may disappoint. If you haven't, you will find the walls, baths and paved roads left at the **Histria Archaeological Complex** (Complexul Arheologic Histria) quite superb. Visitors are free to walk around the original streets of the ancient fortified city.

Archaeological relics uncovered at the site are displayed in the **Muzeul Histria** (Histria Museum) at the entrance to the site. From the entrance, paths lead visitors through the ancient city's remains, and pass by the big tower *(turnul mare)* into the western sector where most of the public buildings, thermal baths *(băilor romane)* and the civil basilica *(basilica civilă)* were. Many of the original foundations remain and some of the original mosaic floor is visible in the baths. Close by is the Christian basilica *(basilica creştină)*, built with stones from the old theatre in the 6th century AD.

On the cliffs in the eastern sector is the 'sacred zone' *(zona sacră)* where archaeologists have removed the Roman remains to uncover remains of a **Greek temple** *(temple grecesc)*. Archaeologists believe the temple was built at the end of the 6th century BC.

The ruins of Histria Citadel fall under the protection of the Danube Delta Biosphere Reserve Authority (see the following Danube Delta section). If you have your own transport the citadel is a good trip from Mamaia or Constanţa.

The complex, 4km south of Histria village, is open 9 am to 8 pm daily ($1). From Constanţa, turn east off the main road at the signpost for 'Cetatea Histria'. The complex is a further 7km along this road.

Places to Stay
There are no hotels or camping grounds in Histria but you can get a bed for the night if you ask people in the village.

Camping in Năvodari is only for the downright crazy or desperate. *Camping Năvodari*, adjoining the petrol station on wasteland to the right as you enter the resort, was closed at the time of writing.

Your only other option is the new *Max Hotel* (☎ 041-762 263), farther north along the coast road, where doubles are an overpriced $50; breakfast not included.

NORTHERN DOBRUJA

Getting There & Away

Getting to Histria is tough without private transport. Buses depart daily at 6.30 am and 5.30 pm for Histria from Constanţa's northern bus station.

Danube Delta

At the end of its long journey across Europe the mighty Danube River empties into the Black Sea just south of the Ukrainian border. Here the Danube splits into three channels – the Chilia, Sulina and Sfântu Gheorghe arms, creating a 5800-sq-km wetland which provides sanctuary for 300 species of birds and 160 species of fish. Reed marshes cover 156,300 hectares, constituting one of the largest single expanses of reed beds in the world.

The Danube Delta (Delta Dunarii) is protected under the Danube Delta Biosphere Reserve Authority (DDBRA), set up

in response to the ecological disaster that befell the delta during Ceauşescu's attempt to transform it into an agricultural region. Now 18 protected areas – 50,000 hectares including a 500-year-old forest and Europe's largest pelican colony – are off-limits to tourist and anglers. The delta is also included in Unesco's World Heritage list.

Ceauşescu's meddling in the natural water flow of the area – involving draining and reclaiming land, ploughing up reed beds and engineering water channels – affected the entire ecological balance of the delta, and DDBRA scientists acknowledge that the original ecosystem of this region can never be fully restored. However, through education and the promotion of a disciplined approach to tourism, the DDBRA is making great strides towards the revival of this wonderful wetland.

You need time and patience to explore the Danube Delta. All three main channels are easily accessible. However, commercial

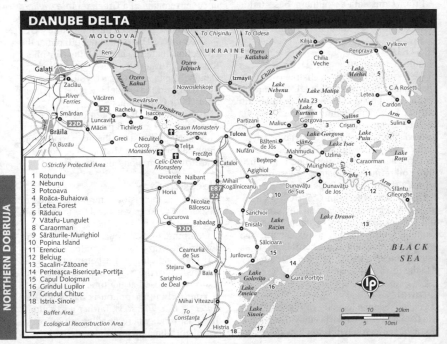

DANUBE DELTA

○ Strictly Protected Area

1 Rotundu
2 Nebunu
3 Potcoava
4 Roảca-Buhaiova
5 Letea Forest
6 Răducu
7 Vătafu-Lungulet
8 Caraorman
9 Sărăturile-Murighiol
10 Popina Island
11 Erenciuc
12 Belciug
13 Sacalin-Zătoane
14 Periteaşca-Bisericuţa-Portiţa
15 Capul Doloşman
16 Grindul Lupilor
17 Grindul Chituc
18 Istria-Sinoie

Buffer Area

Ecological Reconstruction Area

traffic has driven birds deeper into the wetland. So if it's exotic wildlife you're seeking, your best bet is to explore the smaller waterways in a kayak, rowing boat or motorboat with a local fisherman.

Wherever you intend to go in the delta, stock up on supplies and mosquito repellent.

Finally, no trip to the delta is complete without sampling some local Danubian cuisine. Pickled and fresh fish, fish kebabs or fishermen's borsch are on the menu of the day, every day.

Warning: do not drink Danube water!

History
In 1940 Romania was forced to relinquish the 340-sq-km delta area north of the Danube to the Soviet Union (now part of Ukraine).

The delta's population incorporates large Ukrainian (24%) and Lipovan (13%) communities. Lipovans are descendants of the Old Believers sect who fled Russia and sought refuge in the delta. They are scattered in Mila 23, Sfântu Gheorghe, Jurilovca and Periprava. The delta population is mainly elderly; young people leave the remote wetland for large cities as soon as they can.

Climate
The Danube Delta is the most humid region in Romania, particularly during summer (maximum 22.2°C). In spring around 70% of the region is flooded. Winters are mild (minimum: -1.2°C) and it is extremely rare for the main channels to ice over. Even the smaller waterways rarely freeze.

Bird-Watching
Halfway between the North Pole and the equator, the Danube Delta is a major migration hub for thousands of birds. Prime times are mid-April to mid-May and late October when half the world's population of red-breasted geese winter here. Long-tailed ducks, whooper swans, black-throated divers and clouds of white storks are equally abundant at this time.

Some 280 bird species have been recorded in the delta. Europe's largest white pelican and Dalmatian pelican colonies are

---

Delta Permits

All visitors need a permit to travel in the delta. As a tourist, you're fined $200 if you enter a protected zone without a permit. They cost $1 and are sold in Tulcea at travel agencies and at hotel receptions in Crişan, Sulina and Murighiol. Permits are automatically included in tours organised by travel agencies. You also need a permit to fish or camp.

---

also here. Protected species typical of the delta include the roller, white-tailed eagle, great white egret, mute and whooper swans, falcon and bee-eater.

Protected zones shield the largest bird colonies. Large green signs in most villages, most in Romanian, show visitors where these zones are and what birds can be found there. There are 65 observation towers dotted throughout the delta. Bird-watchers usually congregate around Lake Furtuna, Murighiol, the brackish areas around Lake Razim and Lake Babadag, and Histria.

Ibis Tours (see Organised Tours later in this section) in Tulcea arranges bird-watching trips, as do specialist travel agencies abroad (see the Getting There & Away chapter).

Fishing
Sport fishing is allowed in designated areas year-round, except during the spawning period from 1 April to 1 June. You must have a permit from the Fishing & Hunting Association (Asociaţia Judeţeană a Vânătorilor) in Tulcea (see Information under Tulcea). There are some 75 fish species in the delta's waters including pike, Danubian herring and Black Sea sturgeon. The most common catch is carp.

Getting Around
Most hotels and travel agencies in Tulcea arrange day trips in the delta on small motorboats (see Travel Agencies under Tulcea). If your time is limited approach the boatmen direct and negotiate a private trip.

In the delta proper it's easy to hire rowing boats from fishermen. This is the only way

NORTHERN DOBRUJA

MARTIN HARRIS

The red breasted goose, a regular visitor to the Danube Delta

to penetrate the delta's exotic backwaters. Allow yourself at least three or four days.

Navrom Ferries Passenger ferries to towns and villages in the delta are operated by the government-subsidised Navrom. Delta residents get an 80% discount. The ferries serve all three channels year-round.

A Sulina ferry departs from Tulcea at 1.30 pm Wednesday and Friday. The return ferry departs from Sulina at 7 am Thursday and Sunday ($5.75/4.50 for 1st/2nd class). It stops at Partizanui, Maliuc, Gorgova and Crişan. To get to Mila 23 and Caraorman disembark at Crişan and catch a local boat onwards.

The Sfântu Gheorghe ferry departs from Tulcea at 1.30 pm Wednesday and Friday ($6.25/4.50, five hours). The return ferry leaves at 6 am Thursday and Sunday. These boats stop at Bălteni de Jos, Mahmudia and Murighiol.

Ferries to Periprava from Tulcea depart at 1.30 pm Wednesday and Friday ($8.50/6.25, four hours), stopping also at Chilia Veche. Return ferries leave Periprava at 5 am on Thursday and Sunday.

Ferry tickets are sold at Tulcea's Navrom terminal from 11.30 am to 1.30 pm. In summer the queues are long, so get in the correct line early (each window sells tickets to a different destination).

Hydrofoils There are hydrofoils daily from Tulcea to Maliuc ($2.50), Crişan ($5) and Sulina ($5.50, 1½ hours). The hydrofoil to Sulina departs from the AFDJ Galaţia terminal, next to the floating ambulance, at 2 pm daily. Return hydrofoils depart from Sulina at 7 am daily. Purchase tickets when boarding the hydrofoil.

Organised Tours Tulcea's hotels and travel agencies offer day trips between mid-May and September (see Travel Agencies under Tulcea)

Ibis Tours in Tulcea (☎/fax 040-511 261, e ibis@tix.ssiti.ro), Str Griviţei 1, Block C1, Apt 9, arranges wildlife tours in the delta and Dobruja led by professional ornithologists for $25 a day. For more information visit Ibis Tours' Web site at www.ibistours.net.

TULCEA
☎ 040 • postcode 8800 • pop 97,000
Tulcea ('tool-cha'), a modern industrial city, is an important port and gateway to the Danube Delta paradise. It was settled by Dacians and Romans from the 7th to 1st centuries BC. The city has a broad riverfront promenade but offers few other attractions, so tourists usually arrange to catch the first ferry into the delta.

Tulcea hosts the annual International Folk Festival of Danubian Countries in August.

Orientation
The Tulcea arm (braţul Tulcea) of the Danube loops through Tulcea, cutting off the northern part of town from the main part of Tulcea where all the facilities are. The northern part of Tulcea is known as Tudor Vladimirescu.

The bus and train stations and ferry terminal are on Str Portului, overlooking the river at the western end of town. Lake Ciuperca lies west of the stations.

Central Tulcea focuses on the promenade which stretches along the southern banks of the river; private boats for hire are moored here. A block south of the promenade is Piaţa Unirii. The Diana department store is here.

Maps An adequate city map is included in the *Tulcea* guide, sold for $1.20 in all the museums. The best map of the Danube Delta is the *Delta Dunării*, sold for $1.50 at Hotel Delta.

Information

Tourist Offices The DDBRA's (☎ 518 924, fax 518 975, @ deltainfo@tim.ro) new tourist information centre is behind the Culture House at Str Portului 34a; open 8 am to 4 pm weekdays. It sells maps of the delta and travel permits.

Fishing and hunting permits are sold at the Fishing & Hunting Association (Asociaţia Judeţeană a Vânătorilor; ☎ 511 404) at Str Isaccea 10; open 7 am to 2 pm Monday to Friday, also 5 to 8 pm on Wednesday and Friday, and 7 am to 1 pm Saturday. A map in the window highlights the areas where tourists are allowed to fish and hunt.

The Danube Delta Research Institute (☎ 524 550, 531 520, fax 533 547, @ office indd@tim.ro), 1km south of the centre at Str Babadag 165, has a small information centre; open 7.30 am to 4 pm Monday to Thursday, and 7.30 am to 1 pm Friday.

The ACR (☎ 515 151) office on the river front organises boat trips and books rooms on its expensive floating hotel.

Money All the hotels have currency exchanges. The Banca Comercială Română, on Str Toamnei near the Delta Research Institute, cashes travellers cheques, gives cash advances on Visa/MasterCard and has an outside ATM; open 8 to 11 am weekdays. Banca Agricolă is next to the ethnographic museum on Str 9 Mai.

Post & Telephone The post office and telephone centre are at Str Păcii 6. The former is open 7 am to 8 pm weekdays, and 8 am to noon Saturday; the latter is open 7 am to 8 pm daily.

Travel Agencies Danubius Travel Agency (☎/fax 516 649) on Str Păcii, inside Hotel

Europolis, arranges boat day trips to Crişan each Sunday depending on numbers for $19 per person, including lunch. It's open 8.30 am to 6.30 pm weekdays, and 9 am to 1 pm Saturday.

Nouvelles Frontières/Simpa Turism (☎/fax 515 753, @ office@simpaturism.ro), inside Hotel Delta, arranges day trips along the Sulina arm to Crişan and back along the Old Danube via Mila 23 for $25 per person.

The Navitur Agenţie de Turism (☎ 518 894, fax 518 953) inside the Navitur House Boat, opposite Hotel Delta, arranges day trips along the Sulina arm for $15 per person. The boat departs at 10 am. Staff speak no English. Turn up an hour before departure and pray sufficient people have signed up for that day's trip.

Private motorboats cost $10 an hour for up to 10 people. Ustinescu Boat Hire (☎ 526 042) has a boat moored opposite the ACR. It is one of many boats in the harbour that do day trips.

Emergency A floating ambulance station (*staţia de ambulanţă*) is moored in front of the Culture House on the river front. The station is staffed 24 hours and some of its crew speak English. In an emergency dial ☎ 961.

Things to See

As you stroll along the river note the **Independence Monument** (1904) on Citadel Hill, at the far eastern end of town. You can reach the monument by following Str Gloriei from behind Hotel Egreta to its end. Some ruins of the citadel can be seen in the **archaeological site** next to the **History & Archaeology Museum** (Muzeul de Istorie şi Arheologie; ☎ 513 676).

On Str Independenţei to the east, you'll see the Turkish minaret of the **Azizie Mosque** (1863).

At the southern end of Str Gloriei, turn left onto Str 9 Mai; the **Ethnographic Museum** (Muzeul de Etnografie) has traditional costumes, fishing nets, rugs and carpets among its exhibits.

The **Natural History Museum & Aquarium**, Str Progresului 32, has a good collection of Danube fish and detailed exhibits on

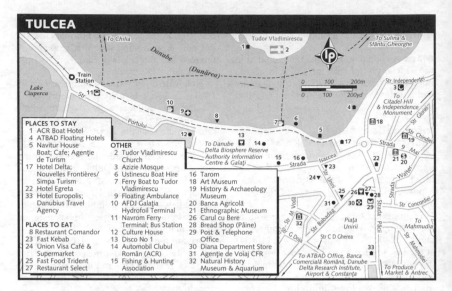

TULCEA

PLACES TO STAY
1 ACR Boat Hotel
4 ATBAD Floating Hotels
5 Navitur House
  Boat; Cafe; Agenţie
  de Turism
17 Hotel Delta;
  Nouvelles Frontières/
  Simpa Turism
22 Hotel Egreta
33 Hotel Europolis;
  Danubius Travel
  Agency

PLACES TO EAT
8 Restaurant Comandor
23 Fast Kebab
24 Union Visa Café &
  Supermarket
25 Fast Food Trident
27 Restaurant Select

OTHER
2 Tudor Vladimirescu
  Church
3 Azizie Mosque
6 Ustinescu Boat Hire
7 Ferry Boat to Tudor
  Vladimirescu
9 Floating Ambulance
10 AFDJ Galaţia
  Hydrofoil Terminal
11 Navrom Ferry
  Terminal; Bus Station
12 Culture House
13 Disco No 1
14 Automobil Clubul
  Român (ACR)
15 Fishing & Hunting
  Association
16 Tarom
18 Art Museum
19 History & Archaeology
  Museum
20 Banca Agricolă
21 Ethnographic Museum
26 Carul cu Bere
28 Bread Shop (Pâine)
29 Post & Telephone
  Office
30 Diana Department Store
31 Agenţie de Voiaj CFR
32 Natural History
  Museum & Aquarium

delta wildlife. In front of the Greco-Orthodox church, opposite the museum, is a **memorial** to local victims of the 1989 revolution.

Tulcea's museums are open 8 am to 4 pm daily, except Monday ($0.40).

Places to Stay

A no-camping regulation within Tulcea's city limits is strictly enforced by police. Seek local advice from BTT (☎ 512 496) at Str Babadag 1. BTT operates a camping ground at Lake Roşu, south of Sulina in the delta.

Antrec (☎/fax 510 463), Str Păcii 121 Block 128, Scara C, Apt 1, arranges accommodation in *private homes* from $7 a night, including breakfast. It also arranges local guides and boat hire.

Rooms in Tulcea are expensive, with little choice. The cheapest is *Hotel Egreta* (☎ 517 103, Str Păcii 1) at $15/23 for a single/double, including breakfast.

Hotel Europolis (☎ 512 443, Str Păcii 20) has rooms with private bath and cable TV for $17/23, including breakfast.

Rooms at the high-rise *Hotel Delta* (☎ 514 721, Str Isaccea 2) are an overpriced $43/54, including breakfast.

Boatels Moored opposite Hotel Delta is the *Navitur House Boat* (☎ 518 894, fax 518 953). The boat is not the cleanest and staff speak little English, but double cabins with shared bath (no hot water) are $10 a night. There is a small bar-cafe aboard.

Nouvelles Frontières/Simpa Turism takes bookings for rooms aboard the *Cormoran Floating Hotel*, moored close to Murighiol (Sfântu Gheorghe arm) at Uzlina. Singles/doubles are $28/34 with shared bathroom. There is a restaurant, bar, disco and sun-bathing terrace on board. For an extra charge, guests can waterski, windsurf, and hire small rowing boats or motorboats to explore the delta. The agency also arranges accommodation in the more expensive *Cormoran Boarding House* where rooms costs $33/42.

Top of the range are the three-star *Delta 3* and the four-star *Delta 2* run by ATBAD (☎ 514 114, ℮ atbad@tlx.ssitl.ro), St Babadag 11. Nightly rates start at $120 per person for a group of six, dropping to $68 for a group of 16. Rates include full board and transfers.

The *ACR* also operates a floating hotel; see Tourist Offices.

Places to Eat

Top-notch for the choice it offers is *Restaurant Select* (*Str Păcii 6*). It serves great fish, frog legs, pizza and the local speciality, *tochitura Dobrogeana* ($2), which is chopped meat swamped in a spicy sauce and served with *mămăligă* (corn mush), salty sheep's cheese and a fried egg. The menu is in six languages.

For fresh fish afloat try the large air-conditioned *Restaurant Comandor*, moored halfway between Hotel Delta and the train station.

An excellent spot for cheesy pizzas and pasta is *Fast Food Trident*, on Str Babadag, opposite the Diana Department Store.

Fast Kebab, on Str Unirii, the only genuine fast-food outlet in Tulcea, slaps out cold, bland kebabs ($0.60) and felafels ($0.90) from 8 am daily.

The *Union Visa Café*, on Str Unirii is not bad for a drink and quick snack; its adjoining grocery has all the basics.

Stock up on picnic supplies at the *produce market* at the end of Str Păcii. Fresh bread is sold at the *Pâine* counter next to the post office on Str Păcii.

Entertainment

The outside terrace of *Carul cu Bere*, next to Restaurant Select, is a fun place to enjoy a beer and people-watch. There are beer gardens along the river-front promenade, too. The funky *Disco No 1*, just past the ACR office on the promenade, rocks from 8 pm to 2 am Monday to Saturday ($0.50).

Shopping

There is a fishing tackle shop which carries a good stock of sleeping bags, jackets, maps, gas stoves and other survival gear next to the Fishing & Hunting Association office on Str Isaccea; open 10 am to 6 pm weekdays, and 7 am to 1 pm Saturday.

Getting There & Away

Train The Agenţie de Voiaj CFR (☎ 511 360) at Str Babadag 4 is open 9 am to 4 pm weekdays. From the train station on Str Portului there are three trains daily to/from Constanţa via Medgidia (four hours). The daily express train from Bucharest takes five hours. The overnight local train to/from Bucharest is bearable if you go 1st class; arrive early to get a seat.

Bus The bus station adjoins the Navrom ferry terminal on Str Portului. There are three daily buses from Tulcea to Bucharest (263km); six to Zaclău (110km); and five to Măcin via Isaccea (93km); from Măcin you can then hitch to Smârdan where you can catch a ferry across the Danube to Brăila in Moldavia.

Private minibuses run daily from the bus station to Constanţa ($2.25, 123km, hourly between 6 am and 7 pm) and to Murighiol, via Mahmudia.

Getting Around

A small motorboat departs every half-hour for Tudor Vladimirescu ($0.08), leaving from the riverfront. Look for the sign 'Dunărea Tulcea–Tudor Vladimirescu'.

TULCEA TO PERIPRAVA

The 120km Chilia channel (braţul Chilia), the longest and largest channel, snakes along Romania's border with Ukraine before fanning out into some 40 tiny rivers forming a mini-delta of its own.

Navrom ferries only call at **Chilia-Veche** and **Periprava**. Between these two settlements the river passes between two islands, **Babina** (Ostrovul Babina) and **Cernovca** (Ostrovul Cernovca). These islands were diked by Ceauşescu in the late 1980s as part of his drive to turn the delta region into agricultural land.

Babina and Cernovca had been one of the delta's most important feeding spots for migratory birds and sheltered numerous bird breeding and nesting places, before this diking cut them off from the delta's natural flooding regime. In 1994 the DDBRA began a major ecological reconstruction program which has included the reflooding of the two islands. With the reconstruction completed in 1996, the DDBRA has now set up a permanent monitoring process of the area.

South-east of Babina and Cernovca islands, close to Periprava, lies the impressive

Letea forest (Pădurea Letea) covering 2825 hectares. A national park since 1938, it is today protected by the DDBRA. Tourists can visit Letea village nearby and spend a few days touring the surrounding waterways. Expect to pay local fishermen $45 to $60 a day.

Getting There & Away

For information on ferries to/from Chilia-Veche and Periprava, see Getting Around at the beginning of this Danube Delta section.

TULCEA TO SULINA

The Sulina arm, the shortest channel of the Danube, stretches 63.7km from Tulcea to Sulina, the delta's largest village. The ferry's first stop is at **Partizani**, a small fishing village with accommodation at the *Ilgani de Sus Cabana*. Next stop is **Maliuc**, a popular stop for tour groups that lunch at *Hotel Salcia* (☎ operator 991). Single/double rooms cost $10/15 with breakfast. Ask at reception about camping behind the hotel. From Maliuc you can hire fishing boats for tours of smaller waterways to the north for $10 to $15 per hour. North of Maliuc is **Lake Furtuna**, a snare for bird-watchers.

The ferry's next stop is the junction with Old Danube, 1km upstream from **Crişan**. At the junction's tip is the rustic *Hotel Lebăda* (☎ 041-543 347), which at the time of writing was being renovated to a three-star hotel. The hotel is expected to reopen in early 2001. Next door is the DDBRA's **Crişan Centre for Ecological Information & Education**, featuring wildlife displays, a library and a video room; open 8 am to 4 pm Tuesday to Sunday. At the main Crişan ferry dock, ask about side trips to **Mila 23** or **Caraorman** (you'll need a permit). Be sure to take food and water on any expedition into the delta.

SULINA

☎ 040

Sulina is a romantic spot on the eastern edge of Europe. Its river-front promenade is lovely at sunset. Just over 50% of the delta's population lives in here. Sulina is not connected to the European road network so there are only a few vehicles in town (boats are the preferred mode of transport).

A canal dug between 1880 and 1902 shortened the length of the Tulcea-Sulina channel from 83.3km to 62.6km, ensuring Sulina's future as the Danube Delta's main commercial port. After WWI Sulina was declared a 'free port' and trade boomed. Greek merchants dominated business here until their expulsion in 1951. The Sulina channel has been extended 8km out into the Black Sea by two lateral dikes.

While not the best base for seeing delta wildlife, Sulina is a pleasant village with a beach, a 19th-century lighthouse and an old cemetery. If you get a cheap room you may want to stay for a while.

Orientation & Information

Sulina is easily navigated. The ferry dock is in the centre of town, with a few shops and bars to the west, and Hotel Sulina and the Black Sea to the east. There are no banks. The DDBRA office at No 1 is open 10 am to 6 pm Tuesday to Sunday.

Things to See

Sulina's sparse attractions include a few old **churches**, a defunct **lighthouse** (1870) and an overgrown 19th-century **British cemetery** which you pass on the way to the beach.

The beach, 2km from town, has an accumulation of Danube silt. This has required the creation of a channel out into the Black Sea. You'll also see a long line of Romanian radar installations among the dunes, pointed out to sea.

Places to Stay

You can *camp* in the cow pasture opposite Hotel Sulina or on the beach. BTT operates a camp site at Lake Roşu, to the south.

As you get off the ferry, watch for people offering *private rooms*. The going rate is around $6 per person.

A few hundred metres west along the river front from the Sulina Cinema is a small sign pointing to *Hotel Astir* (☎ 543 379), previously Hotel Ochiş, which you enter from the rear. Rooms are $5 per person.

The privately run *Hotel Jean Bart* (☎ 543 123) is a quick 10-minute walk from the ferry landing; turn right as you exit the harbour. A bed in a two/three/four-bed room costs $8 per person.

Getting There & Away
For information on ferries and hydrofoils see Getting Around at the start of this Danube Delta section.

TULCEA TO SFÂNTU GHEORGHE
The Sfântu Gheorghe arm (braţul Sfântu Gheorghe) stretches 109km south-east from Tulcea to the fishing commune of Sfântu Gheorghe. A road runs along more than half of the Sfântu Gheorghe arm, making it more accessible to travellers.

From Tulcea, a potholed road leads 13km south-east to **Nufăru**, a village boasting archaeological finds from the 12th and 13th centuries. The ferry's first stop is at **Bălteni de Jos**, 3km south-east of **Victoria** which is accessible by road.

The ferry's second stop is at **Mahmudia**, 28km from Tulcea, developed on the site of the ancient Roman walled city of Salsovia (meaning 'sun city'). There are no hotels in Mahmudia.

Ferries stop at **Murighiol**, 45km from Tulcea; also accessible by road. Murighiol ('violet lake'), a Roman military camp in the 2nd century BC, was renamed 'Independenţa' under the communist era but has since reverted to its Turkish name.

Murighiol is centred on a large purpose-built hotel, camping ground and boat-rental complex – *Camping & Hotel Pelican*, adjacent to the Navrom ferry port. A bed in a hotel room/wooden hut is $9/4 a night and a tent site is $3. See also Boatels under Tulcea.

Local fishermen waiting to take tourists out on the water hang out in the hotel bar. Expect to pay around $17 an hour. The most popular day trip is east to **Uzlina** (1½ hours by motorboat), once reserved as an exclusive hunting ground for Ceauşescu.

Today his hunting lodge here houses a DDBRA **Information & Education Ecological Centre** (Complex pentru Instruire Informare Ecologica Crişan), open 8 am to 4.30 pm weekdays.

The protected zones of **Lake Uzlina** and **Lake Isac** north-east of the village are home to large pelican colonies. Protected **Lake Sărăturii** (87 hectares), immediately west of Murighiol, is another bird-watcher's paradise. From Murighiol, the road continues 5km south to **Dunavăţu de Sus**.

The ferry continues downstream from Murighiol, past Ivancea – one of the delta's largest geese nesting areas – to the ancient fishing village of **Sfântu Gheorghe** ('sfantu gore-gay'). This is one of the best villages in the delta to sample traditional cooking; but the black caviar for which Sfântu Gheorghe is famed is a delicacy reserved strictly for religious feasts. Sfântu Gheorghe is the only village in the delta where Black Sea sturgeon are caught but most caviar is exported.

There is no hotel in Sfântu Gheorghe but you can stay in private homes. Gicu Constantin in Niculiţel (see Upriver from Tulcea, later) also arranges private accommodation in Sfântu Gheorghe.

Getting There & Away
For details on buses and ferries to/from Murighiol, Mahmudia and Bălteni de Jos, see Getting Around at the start of the Danube Delta section, and Tulcea's Getting There & Away section.

AROUND LAKE RAZIM
Lake Razim, which flows into Lake Goloviţa at its southern end, is the largest permanent water expanse in the delta. Between 1969 and 1978 the western shores of both these lakes were empoldered (reclaimed) for fish farming.

On Lake Razim's eastern shores, the **Holbina** polder's natural vegetation remains preserved, including pockets of oak forest.

From Tulcea a dirt road leads south to **Agighiol** on the north-western tip of Lake Razim. Houses in all the villages along this route are crowned with thatched-reed roofs, typical to the delta. Reeds are cut by hand in winter and used to weave baskets, thatch roofs and insulate walls. They were cut and

NORTHERN DOBRUJA

harvested in vast amounts under communism. The DDBRA discourages commercial cutting as reed beds act as a natural filter for the water passing through the delta. Since 1990 reed cutting has been reduced by 90%.

Continuing south from Agighiol you pass through **Sarichioi**, a small village overlooking the protected **Popina Island** (Insula Popina). This 98-hectare island is the most important nesting area in the delta for shelduck, but is still recovering from overgrazing during the 1980s.

In the centre of **Enisala**, 8km south, is a **peasant museum** (Muzeul Gospodăria Tărănească) inside a 19th-century cottage; open 10 am to 6 pm Wednesday to Sunday. On a hill above the village the remains of a 13th-century **citadel** command staggering views. The marshes between the Babadag and Razim Lakes lure many bird-watchers.

Babadag is on the south-western edge of Lake Babadag. The **Mosque Ali Gazi Pasha**, built at the start of the 17th century, is Romania's oldest existing Muslim monument. It houses a small oriental art exhibition. It is opposite the bus station on Str Mihai Viteazul. From here head north to **Hotel Dumbrava** (☎ 047-561 302), on Str Republicii, which has doubles for $8.

From Enisala the road continues to run parallel with Lake Razim's shores, passing through **Sălcioara**. The stretch of road from Enisala to Sălcioara is occasionally closed for use as a target range for the Romanian army. Adjoining **Lake Goloviţa** is a fish farm. From here you can hire a boat to take you across to **Gura Portiţei** (1½ hours), on the eastern shores of Lake Goloviţa. Camping is forbidden.

Getting There & Away
Few buses from Tulcea head this far south, making this part of the delta almost impossible to explore without private transport.

Hitching is tough; few motorised or horse-powered vehicles pass.

UPRIVER FROM TULCEA
The road journey from Tulcea to Galaţi is interesting. Be sure to check out Niculiţel's

paleo-Christian basilica. This region is also home to Europe's only known leper colony (see the boxed text).

Celic-Dere & Cocoş Monasteries
From Tulcea, head west along the main Tulcea-Smârdan road for 29km, then turn left for the Celic-Dere Monastery (Mănăstirea Celic-Dere; 1838) and its **religious ethnographic museum**.

Cocoş Monastery (Mănăstirea Cocoş; 1838), 38km west of Tulcea, houses a **medieval book and icon museum**, open 10 am to 4 pm Tuesday to Sunday. To get to the monastery from Celic-Dere, go back onto the Tulcea-Smârdan road and continue west for 7km. Turn left at the signpost for Niculiţel and continue, past the village, for another 7km.

Niculiţel
The ruins of a 4th-century **paleo-Christian basilica** (Basilica Martirică Niculiţel) are in Niculiţel, 31km west of Tulcea. It was only uncovered in 1971 following heavy storms which exposed part of the martyrs' crypt, which contained bones of four martyrs.

A modern building shields the remains where archaeologists work today. Parts of the church walls have been reconstructed, and the centre of the church is still to be excavated; open 10 am to 2 pm, and 3 to 7 pm daily.

North of Niculiţel, **swamps** stretch for some 10km to the Danube. Bargain with a local fisherman to take you exploring in a kayak.

Places to Stay & Eat Local French and English teacher **Gicu Constantin** (☎ 040-516 166) runs a small B&B scheme for $8 per person a night from his home in Niculiţel at Str Gurgoaia 746. An excellent local guide ($10 a day), he arranges bird-watching tours, swamp rides and boat trips on the Delta.

Isaccea to Măcin
Isaccea is 8km north-west of the Niculiţel turn-off on the main Tulcea-Smârdan highway. The settlement was fortified by the

Europe's Only Leper Colony

In January 2000 a 54-year-old Romanian woman from eastern Moldavia was admitted to hospital suffering severe facial disfigurement caused by leprosy, the first case to be diagnosed in decades. Ashamed of her appearance, she avoided medical attention despite 20 years of pain.

Romania is home to Europe's only known remaining leper colony, based in the village of Tichileşti. The leprosarium, home to 29 patients, is conveniently isolated in Romania's backwaters in the Danube Delta. Its existence was wholly denied during the Ceauşescu regime and even today few delta residents know of, or admit to, its chilling presence.

The colony was founded in 1929 when 180 lepers were banished from northern Bucovina (present-day Ukraine). Orthodox monks from Tichileşti Monastery gave the lepers shelter and in 1931 a hospital was established in the small village. Queen Marie, known for her work with cholera sufferers in the Balkan wars, financed the building of two pavilions at Tichileşti.

Between 1952 and 1957 there were over 280 leprous exiles in Tichileşti, the only specialist sanatorium in Romania which provided leprosy victims with medical care and moral support. Traditionally lepers were shunned and reviled by society, being forced to wear distinctive clothing and rattle a wooden clapper to warn others of their 'filthy' approach.

Following auctions of Ceauşescu's personal belongings in 1998 and 1999, some clothes were donated to the leper colony – ironic that they are now wearing the dictator's clothes considering it was he who forced them to retreat into the closed village.

The leprosarium is funded by the state. The patients today, the longest-living being 93 years old, require continual treatment and lead a semi-independent life in small cottages in the 'leper village'.

Tichileşti is a closed village. Only friends and relatives are allowed to enter it.

Romans who named it Noviodunum. The Ottomans then gained control of Isaccea along with the Danubian fortress downstream at Chilia in 1484.

Just a few kilometres west of Isaccea, between the tiny villages of Revărsăre and Rachelu, is a small dirt-track road leading to **Tichileşti**, home of Europe's last remaining hospital for leprosy sufferers (see the boxed text 'Europe's Only Leper Colony').

The ruins of a Roman wall built around the ancient city of Arrubium can be seen in **Măcin**, 40km west of Isaccea on the Dobruja-Moldavia border. For a superb aerial view, hike 11km south to **Greci** and climb Ţuţuiatul peak (467m).

You can cross the Danube into Brăila at **Smârdan**, 13km west of Măcin. The small ferry makes the 10-minute crossing every half-hour ($2/0.75 car/foot passenger).

NORTHERN DOBRUJA

Crişana & Banat

The plains of Crişana (north of the Mureş River) and Banat (to the south) merge imperceptibly into Yugoslavia's Vojvodina and Hungary's Great Plain. Until 1918 all three regions were governed jointly, and although Subotica (Yugoslavia), Szeged (Hungary) and Timişoara now belong to three different countries, all three cities bear the unmistakable imprint of the Habsburg Empire.

Oradea, Arad and Timişoara, which were once large military fortresses intended to defend Austria-Hungary's south-eastern flank, were handed to Romania following WWI, despite their predominantly Hungarian populations. The Hungarian element is still strong throughout the region, especially in architecture. In Banat you'll also see the Slavic influence of the Serbs.

It's logical then that the 1989 revolution should have begun in the west, where the ethnically mixed population had always been at the margin of communist economic development. Drained of food and resources to finance Ceauşescu's great projects around Bucharest, facing increasing marginalisation of national minorities and better informed through Hungarian and Yugoslav TV coverage of the political changes in East Germany, Czechoslovakia etc, the western part of the country exploded in December 1989. Visitors making a pilgrimage along the 'freedom trail' will want to visit the Hungarian church in Timişoara where it all began.

Crişana and Banat are the door to Romania from the west. All trains from Hungary and Yugoslavia pass through one of its gateway cities: Timişoara or Oradea.

History

Historical Banat is today divided between western Romania, eastern Hungary and northern Yugoslavia. First settled in the 6th century BC, by AD 106 the region was incorporated into the Roman province of Dacia. From the end of the 9th century until the Ottoman conquest of Banat in 1552, the region was under Hungarian rule.

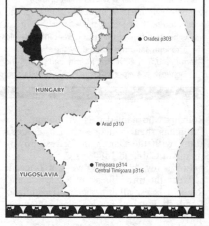

In 1699 the Turks relinquished Hungary to Austria but held Banat until their defeat by Habsburg prince Eugene of Savoy in 1716. In 1718 Banat became part of the Austro-Hungarian empire, after which time Swabians from south-west Germany arrived to colonise the region.

The Treaty of Trianon in 1920 split the territory among Romania, Hungary and Yugoslavia, setting Banat's current borders. At the outbreak of WWII there were 130,000 Germans in this region. Both WWII and the collapse of communism in 1989 saw a mass exodus of Germans from this region.

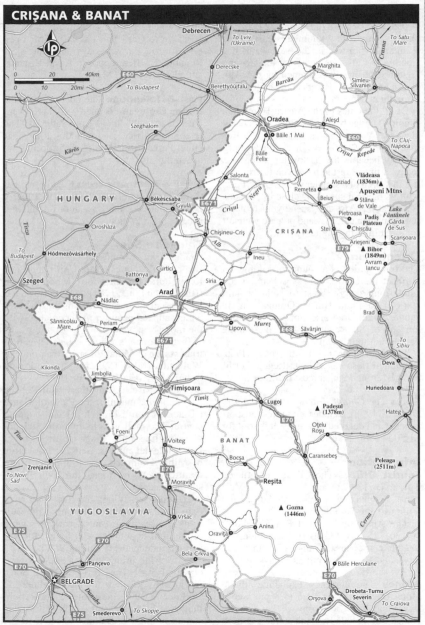

ORADEA

☎ 059 • postcode 3700 • pop 224,000

Oradea, only a few kilometres east of the Hungarian border, is the seat of Bihor County. It's also the centre of the Crişana region, a fertile plain drained by the Alb, Negru and Repede Rivers at the edge of the Carpathian Mountains.

Of all the cities of the Austro-Hungarian Empire, Oradea best retains its 19th-century elegance. When Oradea was ceded to Romania in 1920, this example of Habsburg majesty became the backwater it remains today, a time capsule preserved for romantics in search of a simpler world. Băile Felix with its thermal springs is close by. Oradea is a great place to stop, spend your remaining Romanian currency and prepare yourself for a return to the ruthless West.

Orientation

The train station is a couple of kilometres north of the centre; tram Nos 1 and 4 run south from Piaţa Bucureşti (outside the train station) to Piaţa Unirii, Oradea's main square. Tram No 4 also stops at the northern end of Str Republicii – a five-minute walk south to the centre.

The main square north of the river is Piaţa Republicii (also called Piaţa Regele Ferdinand I), around which most facilities lie.

Maps The *Ghidul Practic Al Municipului Oradea* (1998) includes a public-transport scheme and detailed city maps. It is sold for $1.50 in some bookshops.

Information

Tourist Offices The Cibela Agenţie de Turism (☎ 130 737, fax 134 089), Str Vulcan 1, is open 8 am to 6 pm weekdays, and 9 am to 5 pm Saturday.

The Automobil Clubul Român (ACR; ☎ 130 725, fax 135 415), Piaţa Independenţei 31, is open 8.30 am to 4.30 pm weekdays, and 10 am to 1 pm Saturdays.

Money The currency exchange inside Hotel Dacia is open 7 am to 8 pm weekdays, and 9 am to 1 pm weekends. The Banca Comercială Română, at the southern end of Piaţa Independenţei, cashes travellers cheques, gives cash advances on Visa/MasterCard and has an ATM; open 8.30 am to 1 pm weekdays. The bank's Str Republicii office, opposite Rasid Restaurant, also has an ATM.

Post & Telephone The post office at Str Roman Ciorogariu is open 7 am to 8.30 pm weekdays, and 8 am to 1 pm Saturday. The telephone office is down the alley near Hotel Parc, at Str Republicii 5; open 7 am to 9 pm daily.

Email & Internet Access Liberty Internet Café, Str Republicii 35, next to Liberty Bingo, charges $0.50 per hour for Internet access; open 24 hours.

Things to See

Oradea's most imposing sights are on its two central squares, Piaţa Unirii and Piaţa Republicii. The Orthodox **Moon Church** (Biserica cu Lună; 1784) on Piaţa Unirii has an unusual lunar mechanism on its tower which adjusts position in accordance with the moon's movement.

In the square's centre stands an equestrian **statue of Mihai Viteazul**, the prince of Wallachia (ruled 1593–1601), who is said to have rested in Oradea in 1600. West of the statue, overlooking the Crişul Repede River, is the magnificent **Vulturul Negru** ('Black Vulture'; 1908) hotel and shopping centre. The mall with its fantastic stained-glass ceiling links Piaţa Unirii with Str Independenţei and Str Alecsandri. A **statue of Mihai Eminescu**, the 19th-century Romantic poet, overlooks the river on its southern banks.

Heading west along the river, turn right onto Piaţa Decembrie. In front of the **Cultural House** in the central park is a large **monument** to soldiers who fought for Romanian independence during WWI.

Across the bridge the magnificent neoclassical **State Theatre** (Teatrul de Stat), designed by Viennese architects Fellner and Hellmer in 1900, dominates Piaţa Republicii. Nearby, in the centre of Parcul Traian, stands a small **museum** dedicated to the

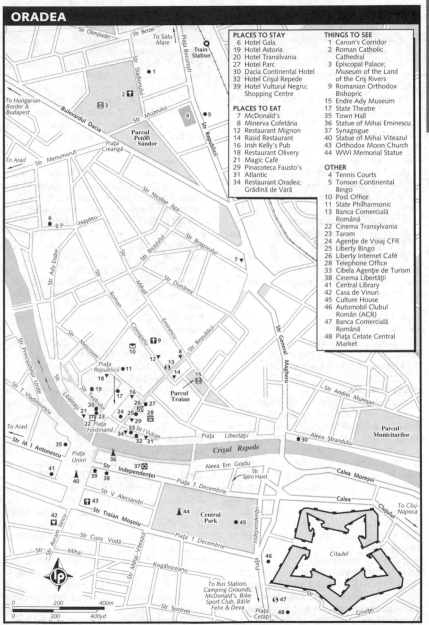

ORADEA

PLACES TO STAY
6 Hotel Gala
19 Hotel Astoria
20 Hotel Transilvania
27 Hotel Parc
30 Dacia Continental Hotel
32 Hotel Crişul Repede
39 Hotel Vulturul Negru;
   Shopping Centre

PLACES TO EAT
7 McDonald's
8 Minerva Cofetăria
12 Restaurant Mignon
14 Rasid Restaurant
16 Irish Kelly's Pub
18 Restaurant Olivery
21 Magic Café
29 Pinacoteca Fausto's
31 Atlantic
34 Restaurant Oradea;
   Grădină de Vară

THINGS TO SEE
1 Canon's Corridor
2 Roman Catholic
   Cathedral
3 Episcopal Palace;
   Museum of the Land
   of the Criş Rivers
9 Romanian Orthodox
   Bishopric
15 Endre Ady Museum
35 State Theatre
36 Statue of Mihai Eminescu
37 Synagogue
40 Statue of Mihai Viteazul
43 Orthodox Moon Church
44 WWI Memorial Statue

OTHER
4 Tennis Courts
5 Tonson Continental
   Bingo
10 Post Office
11 State Philharmonic
13 Banca Comercială
   Română
22 Cinema Transylvania
23 Tarom
24 Agenţie de Voiaj CFR
25 Liberty Bingo
26 Liberty Internet Café
28 Telephone Office
33 Cibela Agenţie de Turism
38 Cinema Libertăţii
41 Central Library
42 Casa de Vinuri
45 Culture House
46 Automobil Clubul
   Român (ACR)
47 Banca Comercială
   Română
48 Piaţa Cetate Central
   Market

Hungarian poet Endre Ady (1877–1919) who lived for four years in Oradea prior to his undignified death from syphilis.

The **Roman Catholic cathedral** (built 1752–80) on Str Stadionului is the largest in Romania. Organ concerts are occasionally held here.

The adjacent **Episcopal Palace** (Episcopia Ortodoxă Română; 1770) boasts 100 fresco-adorned rooms and 365 windows, and houses the **Museum of the Land of the Criş Rivers** (Muzeul Ţării Crişului), with history and art exhibits relevant to the region; closed Monday. Immediately outside the museum entrance, busts of Romania's leading statesmen and kings stand on parade. To the right are busts of Wallachia's princes.

Note **Canon's Corridor** nearby, a series of archways along Str Stadionului that dates back to the 18th century.

The **citadel**, south of the river, was built in the 13th century. Unfortunately it's not worth visiting, as it's been converted into government offices.

Activities

Mountain biking and cycling activities and information are available from the Bike Sport Club – see the Exploring the Carpathian Mountains special section for details.

Places to Stay

Camping From May to mid-September you can camp at *Băile 1 Mai*, 9km southeast of Oradea. Cabins/tent sites are $5/1.50 per person. *Camping Venus* (☎ *318 266*), 500m farther down the road, charges $2.70 per person for two/three-bed bungalows. Take a southbound tram No 4 (black number) from the train station or an eastbound tram No 4 (red number) from Piaţa Unirii to the end of the line, then bus No 15 to the last stop. There's a large thermal swimming pool nearby and Băile Felix is a mere 30-minute walk.

Private Rooms Attimond Traveling Agency (☎ *137 744*), Str Ady Endre 41a, an agent for Antrec, arranges accommodation in surrounding villages for $12 a night including breakfast.

Hotels The best bet for budget-conscious backpackers is *Hotel Parc* (☎*/fax 418 410, Str Republicii 5–7*). Spacious and spotlessly clean singles/doubles with shared bathroom are $8/13 and doubles with private bath are $18. Breakfast is an extra $2.

South of the river stands the 1908 Art-Nouveau *Hotel Vulturul Negru* ('Black Vulture'; ☎ *135 417, Str Independenţei 1*), a hotspot with students and backpackers. Rooms are musty and worn but otherwise OK. It charges $7/14 without bath and $17 for doubles with private bath.

Some rooms at *Hotel Crişul Repede* (☎ *132 509, Str Libertăţii 8*) overlook the river. Rooms with private bath are $10/18 including breakfast. Marginally more up-market is the two-star *Hotel Astoria* (☎ *131 663, Str Teatrului 1*). It has a handful of cramped singles without baths for $8; the rest are doubles with shower/bath for $22/26. All include breakfast.

The privately run *Hotel Gala* (☎*/fax 467 177, Str BP Haşdeu 20*) has clean, comfortable singles/doubles for $40/60 including breakfast. The hotel has a good restaurant and arranges free transfers for guests.

The modern nine-storey *Dacia Continental Hotel* (☎ *418 655, fax 411 280,* ⓔ *dacia@rdsor.ro, Aleea Ştrandului 1*) caters for business travellers, charging $70/107 for luxurious rooms with all the mod cons, breakfast included. The hotel has a night bar and swimming pool.

Places to Eat

Restaurants & Cafes Worth tracking down is *Restaurant Oradea & Grădină de Vară* (*Piaţa Republicii 5–7*). The tender grilled beefsteak topped with a fried egg is delicious, as are its many other grilled meats, all for no more than $2. Live bands often play in the summer garden.

A couple of doors down is *Pinacoteca Fausto's* (*Str Republicii 3*), a cross between a cafe and restaurant. Its terrace on the main street is packed from morning to night. It serves up a small selection of Romanian dishes and lots of beer. Another cafe/restaurant is *Minerva Cofetăria*, on Str Republicii next to Galeria de Arta. It serves delicious pastries and coffee and its terrace is great for people-watching.

Restaurant Mignon, (☎ *419 518, Str Roman Ciorogariu 1)* is the city's most elegant – and expensive – choice, serving quality continental cuisine. A full meal including wine is about $7 a head.

The lively *Restaurant Olivery (☎ 432 959, Str Moscovei 12)* is an unpretentious cellar restaurant with quality food at reasonable prices. Expect to pay around $3 for a full meal.

Irish Kelly's Pub, on Str Republicii opposite Hotel Parc, has a large terrace and is a popular spot to enjoy a beer and a bowl of Romanian-style Irish stew.

Towards the river bank, the *Atlantic* on Str I Vulcan has various fish dishes – not tested, but not raved about locally either! West of Piaţa Republicii on the river bank is the *Magic Café* where you can sip on locally produced Frutti-Fresh fizzy drink and watch fishermen catch their dinner.

Fast Food & Self-Catering On Str Republicii (corner of Parcul Traian) is *Rasid Restaurant*, a modern fast-food outlet serving kebabs, burgers and fries for around $1. *McDonald's* has an outlet at Blvd Republicii 30 and another, south of the centre, on the corner of Str Nufărului and Str Ciheiului.

The slick *Tonson Continental Bingo* complex, close to the train station at the north end of Str Republicii, has a few snacks on offer to munch while you play bingo or wait for your train; open 24 hours.

For fresh produce your best bet is the central market *Piaţa Cetate*, next to the citadel on Piaţa Independenţei.

Entertainment

Cinemas The highly atmospheric *Cinema Libertăţii (☎ 134 097, Str Independenţei 1)*, in the Vulturul Negru building, shows films in their original language with Romanian subtitles, as does *Cinema Transylvania (☎ 131 171)*, on Piaţa Republicii. Tickets cost $0.60.

Bars Most of Oradea's terrace cafes and restaurants double as bars by night; the

Grădină de Vară at Restaurant Oradea has the largest terrace. At the traditional *Casa de Vinuri* ('wine shop') on Str Avram Iancu, you can get your empty water bottle, beer bottle or mug filled with quality local wine at a bargain price! It's open 8 am to 8 pm Monday to Saturday, and 9 am to 1 pm Sunday.

Theatre & Classical Music Tickets for performances at the *State Philharmonic (Filarmonica de Stat; ☎ 130 853, Str Moscovei 5)* can be purchased from the ticket office inside the Philharmonic from 10 am to 6 pm weekdays. The ticket office inside the *State Theatre (Teatrul de Stat; ☎ 130 835 Str Madach Imre 3–5)* is open 10 to 11 am and 5 to 7 pm daily. Tickets cost between $3 and $10.

Kids big and little will enjoy the shows at Oradea's *Puppet Theatre (Teatrul de Păpuşi; ☎ 133 398, Str Vasile Alecsandri 8)*.

Getting There & Away

Air Tarom operates two daily flights Monday to Thursday and one daily on Friday and Saturday from Oradea to Bucharest ($60/$100 single/return, one hour). Tickets are sold at the Tarom office (☎/fax 131 918) at Piaţa Republicii 2; open 6.30 am to 8 pm weekdays, and 11 am to 2 pm Saturday.

Train The Agenţie de Voiaj CFR (☎ 130 578), Str Republicii 2, is open 7 am to 7 pm weekdays. International tickets must be purchased at the CFR office in advance, not at the train station.

The left-luggage office (open 24 hours) at the station is beside the restaurant on the main platform.

Express trains run north to Satu Mare, south to Arad and east to Cluj-Napoca.

Four trains run each day from Oradea to Budapest's Nyugati station ($16, four hours): the *Corona* (4.12 am), *Ady Endre* (8.02 am) and *Claudiopolis* (6.32 pm) express trains, and one local train, the *Partium* (3.34 pm). If you don't already have a ticket, take bus No 11 from Oradea's train station or take a local train to the border at Episcopia Bihor (eight minutes), where you can easily buy a train ticket to Hungary with lei.

Bus From Oradea bus station, south of the centre at Str Râzboieni 81, there are three daily services to Beiuş (63km), and one to Deva (190km) and Satu Mare (133km).

Most of the travel agencies arrange bus excursions to Budapest in Hungary at competitive rates. A daily public bus to Budapest ($5/9 single/return, 10 hours, departs 7.30 am) leaves from outside the train station. Purchase your ticket from the driver before departure.

A daily bus also departs from Oradea bus station for Debrecen in Hungary ($4/7.50 single/return, 5 am).

Car & Motorcycle The border crossing into Hungary for motorists at Borş, 16km west of Oradea, is open 24 hours.

Getting Around

Oradea airport (☎ 413 985/951) is 6km west of the centre on the Oradea-Arad road. Tarom runs a shuttle bus to/from the airport, which leaves from its office one hour before flights are scheduled to arrive or depart.

BĂILE FELIX
☎ 059

Băile Felix, 8km south-east of Oradea, is a famous year-round health spa where city dwellers flock to splash in thermal pools and nap in the sun. In summer the atmosphere is rowdy in the best sense. There's a large open-air thermal swimming pool here and several smaller pools covered by the rare *Nymphea lotus thermalis*, a giant white water lily.

The most popular public pools are Strand Apollo and Strand Felix, by the Staţia Băile Felix bus stop. Both are open 7 am to 6 pm daily (closed from November to April); $1. Bring your own bathing suit and towel.

Places to Stay

The nearest official *camping grounds* are 3km away at Băile 1 Mai (see Oradea's Places to Stay section).

Some of the cheapest rooms can be had at *Hotel Lotus* (☎ 318 248) in the centre of the resort, and *Hotel Someş* (☎ 318 214) in the north-western corner. Singles/doubles in both cost $42/55.

Hotel Termal (☎ 318 214), near the train station, has an on-site swimming pool. *Hotel International* (☎ 318 445), on the eastern side of the resort, has a good restaurant and bar. Rooms in both cost $48/61.

If you find Băile Felix's concrete highrises cold and uninviting head to the friendly *Pensiunea Diana* (☎ 318 517), on the right as you exit the resort on the main road to Deva. The family-run pension has clean doubles – most with 'matrimonial' beds, some with private bath – for $24, breakfast not included. There is also a kitchen and laundry available for guests.

Getting There & Away

Three local trains a day run from Oradea to Băile Felix (11km, 20 minutes), but it's easier to take tram No 4 (red number) east from Piaţa Unirii, or tram No 4 (black number) south from Oradea's train station to the end of the line at Cartierul Nufărul. From here bus No 14 runs directly to the spa ($0.40, pay the driver), stopping first at Staţia Băile Felix before circling past the major hotels. Returning, it's quickest to board at Staţia Strand Apollo, 50m south of Staţia Băile Felix.

MEZIAD CAVE

Sixty-three kilometres south of Oradea, approaching the western fringe of Transylvania's vast Apuseni Mountains, is the small market town of **Beiuş** from where the Meziad Cave (Peştera Meziad) can be reached. The cave, discovered in 1859, is not the most spectacular but it is one of the few freely accessible, with guides to show visitors around.

To reach the cave from Beiuş, follow the signpost for Peştera Meziad from the town centre (11km). When you get to the village of Remetea, bear right at the fork next to the Cămin Cultural building and continue for 9km until you reach Meziad. Turn left at the first fork, then cross the small white bridge to a gravel road. The main office for the cave is 4km along this road. The entrance to the cave is a further 1.5km.

Officially the cave administration is open 9 to 11 am and 2 to 4 pm Tuesday to Sunday ($1). If you intend to explore the cave alone, bring a torch.

Places to Stay

Cabana Meziad, opposite the administration office, has dorm-beds for $3 per person. The cabana is open year-round, but if no-one is around inquire at No 117 in Meziad village. Wild camping is permitted around the cave and in the cabana grounds.

One kilometre from Beiuş is *Motel Desira* (☎ 059-320 940), adjoining a petrol station north-west of the town on the Beiuş-Oradea road. Clean doubles are $15 including breakfast.

Getting There & Away

The train and bus stations adjoin each other on the southern edge of town. Travellers will find little use for Beiuş's train services, which include only a few trains daily to Holod, 20km north, and Vaşcău.

Buses are marginally more useful. Services include one daily to Meziad (24km), Chişcău (21km), Pietroasa (20km) and Deva (127km); four to Oradea (63km); and five to Ştei (21km). Services are greatly reduced on weekends.

STÂNA DE VALE

Stâna de Vale is a small alpine resort (1300m) in the Pădurea Craiului Mountains in the Bihor Massif. It lies at the end of a forest road 27km east of Beiuş. Between December and February it is transformed into a bustling ski centre. In summer it is a pitifully quiet hiking resort.

The ski lift is next to the camping ground. It is possible to hire skis and have lessons. A couple of hiking trails lead into the Apuseni Mountains. A trail (5½ to six hours, marked with red stripes) takes you to **Cabana Padiş** in the heavily karstic Padiş zone (see the Exploring the Carpathian Mountains special section). Another more challenging trail (six hours, blue triangles) leads to **Cabana Meziad**. Don't attempt it in bad weather or in winter.

Places to Stay & Eat

In summer, your best bet is to bring your own tent and pitch it in the *camping ground* at the western end of the resort. The resort's main hotel is *Hotel Iadolina* (☎ 059-130

508). Doubles/triples cost $17/25 and apartments are $34. *Cerbul Vila & Restaurant*, opposite the Iadolina, is only open in winter.

Getting There & Away

There are no public buses or trains to/from Stâna de Vale. From Beiuş you can catch a privately run minibus to Stâna de Vale from outside the Justice Court in the town's centre. There is no set schedule and the minibuses are not marked, so ask around. Otherwise, hitch or hike.

BEAR CAVE

Although it's not easy to reach, the Bear Cave (Peştera Urşilor) – named after skeletons of the extinct cave bear *(Ursus spelaeus)* were found by quarry workers in 1975 – is one of Romania's finest caves and well worth a day trip from Oradea, 82km north-west.

The magnificent galleries of Peştera Urşilor (482m) extend over 1000m on two levels. Stupendous stalactites and stalagmites loom from every angle, creating uncanny shapes in the half-darkness. The stalactites, many of which are believed to be 22,000 to 55,000 years old, grow 1cm every 20 years.

Compulsory guided tours allow you to spend an hour or so exploring the cold (a constant 10°C) stalactite-filled chambers. The site is dependably open 10 am to 5 pm Tuesday to Sunday from May to September ($1.50/0.75 for adults/students; $3.50 for cameras).

Various ethnographic exhibits are displayed in the small **Ethnographic Museum** (Muzeul de Etnografic), opposite Camping Fluturi; open 24 hours. If no-one is around ask at the camping ground bar.

Places to Stay

In the centre of Chişcău, 1km from Peştera Urşilor, *Camping Fluturi* has a dozen wooden cabins with bedding and shared bathrooms for $6 a night, but no running hot water.

Getting There & Away

Oradea's Cibela Agenţia de Turism will arrange day trips to the site on special request. The trip, costing $12.50 per person for a minimum of eight people, must be booked well in advance.

Otherwise there is one daily bus from Beiuş to Chişcău (3.30 pm). By private transport, head south from Oradea, through Beiuş. Follow the road for a further 10km along the Crişul Negru River, then turn right at the turn-off for Pietroasa and Peştera Urşilor. Continue along this road; the cave is signposted on the right.

SCĂRIŞOARA ICE CAVE

Cave buffs should head straight to this fantastic ice cave (Peştera Ghetarul de la Scărişoara), commonly known as the Scărişoara Ice Cave.

The cave was first documented in 1863 by Austrian geographer Arnold Schmidt, who wrote up his findings, accompanied by detailed maps of its numerous chambers. His early documentation enabled the Romanian scientist and speleologist Emil Racoviţa (1868–1947) to pursue further explorations between 1921 and 1923. Believed to be one of only 10 of this kind in Europe, the cave is filled with 7500 cubic metres of ice. The ice, at an altitude of 1150m, dates to the ice age when the Apuseni Mountains were shrouded in glaciers.

The maximum temperature inside the cave in summer is 1°C; in winter it drops to -7°C. Safety precautions inside the cave are not up to Western standards and lighting is nonexistent. Bring your own torch or ask the keeper for an oil/carbon lamp (lampă cu carbid).

Officially the cave is open 10 am to 4 pm Tuesday to Sunday, although opening hours tend to be haphazard ($1.20). You must visit in groups of two or more.

Getting There & Away

From Beiuş, head south to Ştei. Two kilometres farther south, turn left, following the signs for Arieşeni, a village renowned for its traditional folk customs and wooden church, and for Gârda de Sus. From Gârda de Sus, a dirt track leads to the ice cave, 18km farther east in the Arieş Valley. It is impossible to access the cave from Scărişoara village.

GÂRDA DE SUS & AROUND

The village of Gârda de Sus lies in the Arieş River valley in the Apuseni Mountains. Until 1932 it was classified as part of Scărişoara village. Traditional folk costumes, resembling those worn by early Dacian tribes, are still worn in the village for festivals.

Two kilometres west of Arieşeni on the border of Bihor and Alba Counties is a small **ski slope** (753m long), signposted 'Teleschi Vârtop'; open 9 am to 6 pm daily between December and May.

Some 20km south of Gârda de Sus is the village of **Avram Iancu**, formerly known as Vidra de Sus, a good access point for the colourful Girls' Fair held each year on top of Mount Găina.

Places to Stay

Camping *Popas Turistic Gârda*, at the western end of Gârda de Sus, has small wooden bungalows for rent in the summer for $3 per person. It also has a small restaurant and bar.

Private Rooms The Belgian charity Opération Villages Roumains has helped local people in Gârda de Sus establish their own agro-tourism scheme whereby tourists can

Funeral Festivities

Three days of festivities follow a death in Gârda de Sus in accordance with the village *mioriţa* (folkloric song). As the legend goes, two shepherds, Muntenia and Moldavia, plotted to kill fellow shepherd Transylvania whose flock was greater than theirs. Informed by his sheep of the sinister plan the wise shepherd told his flock, 'If I die, lay three flutes by my head, one made from bone, another from birch and the third from a different type of wood'. He also asked them to tell his mother, 'I am not dead but I married nature and am rejoicing with my wife through the mountains and forest, singing as wind with my flutes'. Transylvania was murdered soon after. Ever since, for three days and three nights, the villagers of Gârda join the bereaved in their celebration of the *mioriţa* whereby death is but a pipe song.

stay in their homes. The local representative in Gârda de Sus is Ioan Stefanuţ (mobile ☎ 094-700 871) at house No 31. In Arieşeni, 8km west, ask for Marta Maghiar (mobile ☎ 094-278 219) at house No 13.

Hotels The modern *Complex Turistic Arieşeni* is 8km west of Gârda de Sus. A bed in a comfortable wooden cabin with a shared bathroom is $3.50/2.50 in summer/winter. It also has a number of double rooms in heated villas equipped with a kitchen, dining room and TV. A bed in a villa starts at $4/3 per person in summer/winter. The restaurant and bar are open 24 hours. Advance bookings can be made through the Complex Hotelier Cetate (☎ 058-811 780, fax 815 812, 831 501), Str Unirii 3, Alba Iulia.

Getting There & Away
From Gârda de Sus, hikers can head north to the Padiş Plateau. A trail marked by blue stripes (five to six hours) leads from the village to Cabana Padiş (see the Exploring the Carpathian Mountains special section).

ARAD
☎ 057 • postcode 2900 • pop 185,000
Arad, 57km north of Timişoara, sits in winemaking country on the banks of the Mureş River, which loops around Arad's 18th-century citadel then flows west to Szeged in Hungary. Arad developed as a major trading centre during Turkish occupation of the city between 1551 and 1687. There's not much to see here except elegant late-19th-century architecture, commissioned while the town was part of the Austro-Hungarian empire.

Arad is the main gateway into Hungary. Consider stopping, if only to spend your remaining lei before crossing the border.

Orientation
The train station is a few kilometres north of the centre, with the bus station two blocks west on Blvd Revoluţiei. Take tram No 1, 2 or 3 south down Blvd Revoluţiei (known simply as 'the boulevard') into town.

Maps Detailed city maps are included in the *Hartă Turistică a Judeţului Arad* (1999)

city guide and the excellent *Arad Ghidul Municipiului* (2000) in English and Romanian. Both are sold in most hotels and travel agencies for no more than $2.

Information
Tourist Offices Your best bet is the Agenţie de Turism Zărandul (☎ 257 279), opposite the town hall at Blvd Revoluţiei 76, which sells town maps and guides as well as tickets for buses to Germany; open 8 am to 5 pm weekdays. BTT (☎ 280 776, fax 281 556) has an office at Blvd Revoluţiei 16, off Piaţa Avram Iancu.

The ACR (☎/fax 281 445) is on Piaţa Independenţei; open 8 am to 3 pm weekdays, and 9 am to 1 pm Saturday.

Money There is a currency exchange inside the Tarom office at Str Unirii 1, open 7 am to 7.30 pm weekdays, and 9 am to 1.30 pm Saturday.

The Banca Comercială Română, Blvd Revoluţiei 72, gives cash advances on Visa/MasterCard and has an ATM; open 9 am to 6 pm weekdays, and 8 am to 12.30 pm Saturday. Banca Turco Română, on Piaţa Avram Iancu, offers identical services; open 9.30 am to 1.30 pm and 2.30 to 5 pm weekdays.

Post & Telephone The post office, adjoining the telephone office at Blvd Revoluţiei 44, is open 7 am to 8 pm weekdays, and 8 am to 1 pm Saturday. The telephone office is open 8 am to 10 pm daily.

Email & Internet Access Club Pro Net (☎ 270 533, ⓔ pronet@pro-net.ro), Blvd Revoluţiei 67, has Internet access for $0.50 per hour.

Things to See
Arad's large, star-shaped **citadel** was built under the orders of Habsburg Queen Maria Theresa between 1763 and 1783. Austrian architect and military general Filip Ferdinand Harsch was commissioned to design the Vauban-style, six-pointed star. It stands on the site of an old fortress built in 1551 by the Turks. The citadel houses a military base today and is closed to the public.

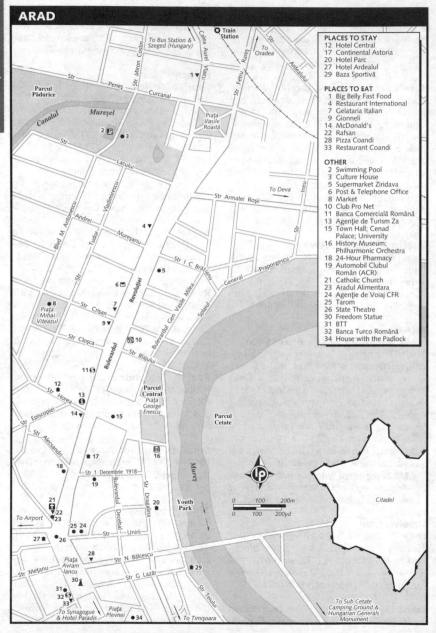

ARAD

PLACES TO STAY
12 Hotel Central
17 Continental Astoria
20 Hotel Parc
27 Hotel Ardealul
29 Baza Sportivă

PLACES TO EAT
1 Big Belly Fast Food
4 Restaurant International
7 Gelataria Italian
9 Gionneli
14 McDonald's
22 Rafsan
28 Pizza Coandi
33 Restaurant Coandi

OTHER
2 Swimming Pool
3 Culture House
5 Supermarket Ziridava
6 Post & Telephone Office
8 Market
10 Club Pro Net
11 Banca Comercială Română
13 Agenţie de Turism Za
15 Town Hall; Cenad
    Palace; University
16 History Museum;
    Philharmonic Orchestra
18 24-Hour Pharmacy
19 Automobil Clubul
    Român (ACR)
21 Catholic Church
23 Aradul Alimentara
24 Agenţie de Voiaj CFR
25 Tarom
26 State Theatre
30 Freedom Statue
31 BTT
32 Banca Turco Română
34 House with the Padlock

After crushing the liberal revolution of 1848, the Habsburgs hanged 13 Hungarian generals outside the citadel. A monument to these men stands in front of the Sub Cetate camping ground outside the southern walls of the citadel.

The U-shaped, neoclassical **town hall** on Blvd Revoluţiei is Arad's most impressive building. The clock ticking on the tower atop the 1876 building was purchased in Switzerland in 1878. Framing the town hall right and left is the steepled **Cenad Palace** (Palatul Cenad), constructed by the Arad Cenad railway company at the end of the 19th century; and the **Aurel Vlaicu University** building, decorated in Viennese rococo motifs and built in the same period to house the local administration's treasury.

Behind the town hall, on Piaţa George Enescu, is the local **History Museum** (Muzeul de Istorie), inside the Palace of Culture (built 1911–13), home to Arad's **philharmonic orchestra**. Busts outside pay homage to leading literary figures, including Romanian poet George Coşbuc (1866–1918), and post-Romantic historian Alexandru Xenopol (1847–1920).

To the east of the museum, along the Mureş River, lies the **Youth Park** (Parcul Copiilor). Close to the main entrance is a statue of 19th-century teacher Elena Ghiba Birta (1801–64).

At the southern end of Blvd Revoluţiei is the neoclassical **State Theatre** (Teatrul de Stat; 1874).

A **tree stump** into which apprentice blacksmiths used to hammer a nail to symbolise their acceptance into the guild once stood on a corner at Piaţa Plevnei, just south-west of the theatre. It was stolen in 1997. Although it has been recovered it has not been returned to its place. The house – known as the **House with the Padlock** (Casa cu Lacăt) after the padlocked metal bar which once kept the stump in place – was built in 1815 by local tradesman Joseph Winkler.

South of the theatre at Str Dobra 10 is the Jewish community's **synagogue**. It was built between 1827 and 1834 in typically Moorish style. Enter via Str Cozia.

Places to Stay

Camping The run-down *Sub Cetate* (☎ 285 256, 281 172, Str 13 Generali), 1.5km from the centre, has dirty cabins and tent sites for $2 per person. No public transport passes this way but it's a pleasant walk. There is a restaurant/bar and the site is open from March until early-October.

Private Rooms Antrec (☎ /fax 254 046), Str Vasile Milea 7, arranges rooms in private homes in and around Arad for about $12, including breakfast. Bookings can be made in advance through its Bucharest office.

Hotels Overlooking the Mureş River, *Bază Sportivă* (☎/fax 281 354, Str Teiului 1) has a few four-bed rooms above the sports club for $2.50 per person. You can also play tennis and hire canoes for $2.50 an hour each, or ride a jet ski for $10 for 15 minutes.

Not bad value is the neoclassic *Hotel Ardealul* (☎ 280 840, fax 281 845, Blvd Revoluţiei 98). The hotel, dating from 1841, has a music room where Brahms, Liszt and Strauss once gave concerts. Singles/doubles with private bathroom are $20/25 and a room with a 'matrimonial' bed is $30. Cheaper rooms with shared bath are $13/18.

The nine-storey *Hotel Parc* (☎ 280 820, fax 280 725, Blvd Dragalina 25), overlooking the river, has newly renovated singles/doubles for $27/28 and unrenovated singles/doubles/triples for $24/26/28. All include breakfast. The hotel can arrange a chauffeur taxi service for $0.20 per kilometre.

The quiet *Hotel Central* (☎ 256 636, fax 256 629, ✉ central@inext.ro, Str Horea 8), a modern five-storey building, is excellent value. Three-star doubles (matrimonial) with private bathroom are $40. Two-star singles/doubles are $25/33. All include breakfast. The hotel has a lovely terrace cafe overlooking its summer garden.

Arad's most expensive splurge, the *Continental Astoria* (☎ 281 700, fax 281 832, ✉ conti@inext.ro, Blvd Revoluţiei 79–81), charges $38/51 for comfortable rooms, including breakfast. Renovations that were planned should be under way by the time you read this.

The reasonable *Hotel Paradis (☎ 287 377, fax 600 525, Str Molidului 5)* is 5km south of the centre. Clean, simple doubles are $20; breakfast costs an extra $1.50.

Places to Eat

Restaurants & Cafes The glittering *Restaurantul Internaţional (☎ 257 145)*, on Blvd Revoluţiei, includes a brasserie and a restaurant serving English, Romanian, Greek, French and almost every kind of salad imaginable. Its lunch-time set menu is good value at only $2 per person.

For pizza and pasta the hot choice is *Pizza Coandi (☎ 281 514, Str Bălcescu 5)*. *Restaurant Coandi (☎ 284 688, Piaţa Avram Iancu 11)* is an unpretentious place for trying Romanian dishes. While you're eating, check out the amazing collection of international banknotes pinned to the walls – perhaps even add your own.

Gionneli, on Blvd Revoluţiei, is a slick cafe-restaurant, decked out Italian-style. Open 24 hours, it's best just for coffee. *Gelateria Italian*, on Blvd Revoluţiei a few doors farther north, serves the real McCoy, however, when it comes to Italian ice cream. It has 20 different flavours, including bubble-gum and cola, and is always packed.

Fast Food & Self-Catering The modern *Rafsan* fast-food outlet, on Blvd Revoluţiei, serves fresh sandwiches, salads and hamburgers 24 hours. Farther north is *McDonald's*. Great for its name if nothing else is *Big Belly Fast Food*, at the northern end of Blvd Revoluţiei.

Arad has two open-air *markets*, one on Piaţa Mihai Viteazul and another on Piaţa Catedralei, at the western end of Str Meţianu. The large Western-style *Supermarket Ziridava* on Blvd Revoluţiei is open 8 am to 9 pm Monday to Saturday. At the southern end of Blvd Revoluţiei is the well-stocked *Aradul Alimentara*, open 24 hours.

Entertainment

The *Philharmonic*, inside the Palace of Culture, holds concerts at 7 pm every Tuesday ($0.50). Tickets are sold at the box office (☎ 280 519) inside the culture palace two

hours before performances begin. Arad's Agenţia Teatrală, which sells tickets to local theatre performances, is at the back of the *State Theatre*, open 11 am to 1 pm Tuesday to Sunday.

Getting There & Away

Air Business Jet (☎/fax 284 010), inside Hotel Parc, operates international flights from Arad; open 9 am to 5 pm weekdays.

Tarom (☎/fax 280 777), Str Unirii 1, has daily flights to Bucharest, Tuesday to Saturday, ($60/100 single/return); open 7 am to 8 pm weekdays, and 9 am to 2 pm Saturday.

Train Tickets for trains to Hungary and Poland have to be bought in advance from the Agenţie de Voiaj CFR (☎ 280 977), which shares an office with Tarom at Str Unirii 1; open 8 am to 8 pm weekdays.

Arad is a major railway junction. Nine trains for Budapest (3¼ hours) depart from Arad daily. There is also one daily train to Warsaw (15½ hours, departing 5.38 am).

Or take a daily commuter train from Arad to Nădlac (1½ hours) then walk, hitch or take a taxi 6km to the border crossing and catch one of the seven daily trains from Nágylak, Hungary, to Szeged (1¼ hours).

To get to Hunedoara from Arad, you have to get a train to Deva and then take a bus from there to Hunedoara.

Arad is well served by trains to other destinations in Romania.

Bus A number of buses to Hungary depart from the bus station, two blocks west of the train station. Buses go daily to Szeged ($6), five times a week to Békéscsaba ($2.50) and once a week to Budapest ($10, seven hours). Tickets for Budapest and Békéscsaba are available at the ticket window but for Szeged you pay the driver directly. Don't go by the times posted at the station – ask.

Agencies along Blvd Revoluţiei sell expensive tickets on private buses to Hungary, so shop around. The Brisk Travel Agency (☎/fax 211 017), Str Mihai Eminescu 11, Apartment 12, sells tickets to Budapest and Germany. Armin Mayer Reisebüro (☎ 285 611, 456 175), Str Fântanele 44, and the

Agenţie de Turism Zărandul (see Tourist Offices) both sell tickets for the twice-weekly buses to Germany.

Car & Motorcycle The border crossing into Hungary is 52km west of Arad, in Nădlac. This is the major road crossing from Romania into Hungary and it can get congested. It is open 24 hours a day.

Getting Around
Tarom operates a free shuttle bus from its office to Arad airport (☎ 254 440). It departs one hour before flights are scheduled to take off.

TIMIŞOARA
☎ 056 • postcode 1900 • pop 332,000
Geographically out on a limb, Timişoara (pronounced 'ti-mi-shwa-ra'; known as Temesvár in Hungarian, Temeschburg in German) is often bypassed by travellers, yet for no good reason. Romania's fourth-largest city has a soothing Mediterranean air, with outdoor cafes and regal, Habsburg-era buildings fronting its two main squares. Opera and drama thrive here.

Unlike other cities in the country, few Romanians have a bad word to say about Timişoara, dubbed the 'city of flowers' after the ring of pretty parks which surrounds it. Locals view themselves as being residents of Romania's 'Primul Oraş Liber' (First Free Town), for it was here that protests in December 1989 ignited country-wide uprisings that eventually toppled Ceauşescu.

In part due to its proximity to Hungary, Timişoara is one of Romania's most developed cities. Timiş County, of which Timişoara is the administrative centre, is the richest agricultural area in Romania.

Orientation
The northern train station (Timişoara-Nord) is just west of the city centre. Walk east along Blvd Ferdinand to the Opera House and Piaţa Victoriei. A block farther north is the verdant Piaţa Libertăţii. Piaţa Unirii, the old town square, is two blocks farther north. Timişoara's bus station is beside the Idsefin

Market, three blocks from the train station. Take Str General Drăgălina south to the canal, cross the bridge and head west to the next bridge.

Confusingly, some street names have changed although locals still refer to them by their former names.

Maps The excellent *Hartă Timişoara* (GRAI, 1999) is sold in most bookshops and kiosks for $1.50. There is a tourist map in the bilingual city guide *What, When, Where Timişoara*, available free from most hotels.

Information
Tourist Offices The Cardinal (☎ 191 911, fax 191 027), Blvd Ferdinand 6, is Timişoara's unofficial tourist office; open 8 am to 6 pm weekdays, and 9 am to 1 pm on Saturday.

The Agenţie de Turism Banatul (☎ 198 862, fax 191 913) at Str 1 Mai 2, on the southern side of Hotel Timişoara, sells maps; open 9 am to 6 pm weekdays, and 9 am to 1 pm Saturday.

The ACR (☎ 133 333), Str Hector 1, is opposite the Berăria Bastion in the old city wall.

Money The Banca Comercială Română, Str 9 Mai just off Piaţa Libertăţii, cashes travellers cheques and gives cash advances on Visa/MasterCard; open 8.30 am to 12.30 pm weekdays. The same services are offered by the BCIT at Piaţa Unirii 3 (open 8.30 am

---

Timişoara Trivia

• Hollywood's original Tarzan was born in a Timişoara suburb.
• Frenchman Gustave Eiffel, who engineered Paris' Eiffel Tower, built a bridge over the city's Bega canal.
• Timişoara was the first European city to introduce horse-drawn trams (in 1869), and the first to sport electric street lighting (in 1889).
• The world record for drawing 'speed cartoons' is held by Timişoara artist Ştefan Popa (he can draw 131 cartoons in one minute).
• Every October Timişoara hosts Romania's week-long, national beer festival.

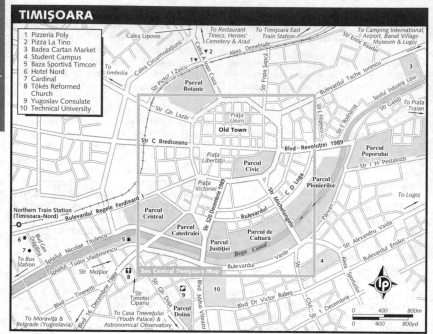

TIMIŞOARA

1 Pizzeria Poly
2 Pizza La Tino
3 Badea Cartan Market
4 Student Campus
5 Baza Sportivă Timcon
6 Hotel Nord
7 Cardinal
8 Tōkés Reformed Church
9 Yugoslav Consulate
10 Technical University

to 2.30 pm weekdays), and Banca Agricolă, close to Hotel International on Blvd CD Loga (open 9 am to noon weekdays). The currency exchange inside Hotel Continental also gives cash advances on major credit cards; open 8 am to 6 pm weekdays, 8 am to 3 pm Saturday, and 8 to 11 am Sunday.

Post & Telephone The central post office is two blocks east of Hotel Continental on Blvd Revoluţiei 2; open 7 am to 8 pm weekdays, and 8 am to noon Saturday. If there are huge queues, try the smaller post office near Hotel Banatul, open the same hours.

The central telephone office is just off Piaţa Victoriei on Blvd Mihai Eminescu; open 7 am to 9 pm daily. Faxes can also be sent and received here.

Email & Internet Access Internet Java, inside the Java Coffee House (see Places to Eat), charges $0.70 per hour for Internet access; open 24 hours.

Bookshops The Humanitas bookshop (☎ 133 180), Str Mercy 1, sells an outstanding range of English-language books about Romania, including a translation of the complete works of national poet Mihai Eminescu; open 10 am to 6 pm weekdays, and 10 am to 3 pm Saturday.

The Librăria Mihai Eminescu (☎ 194 123) on Piaţa Victoriei 2 stocks a less exhaustive range; open 9 am to 8 pm weekdays, and 9 am to 1 pm Saturday.

English-language novels and reference books are also sold at Librăria Noi; open 10 am to 6 pm weekdays, and 10 am to 2 pm Saturday.

Libraries & Cultural Centres The following centres may be useful to visitors.

British Council (☎/fax 197 678) Str Paris 1
Bulgarian Banat Unit (☎/fax 190 697) Piaţa Unirii 14
Democratic Union of Serbs (☎/fax 191 754) Blvd Victor Babeş 14

Euroregional Centre for Democracy (☎ 221 470, fax 221 469, e info–regionalnet.org) Str Semenic 10

French Cultural Centre (Centrul Cultural Francez; ☎ 190 544, 201 453, fax 190 543) Blvd CD Loga 46

German Democratic Forum (Demokratisches Forum der Deutschen; ☎/fax 199 222) Str Gheorghe Lazăr 10–12

Medical Services The Farmacie on the corner of Piaţa Libertăţii and Str Vasile Alecsandri is open 7.30 am to 8 pm weekdays, and 9 am to 2 pm Saturday. Vlad on Str Gheorghe Lazăr is open 24 hours. Opposite the central post office on Blvd Revoluţiei is Farmacie Remedia, open 7 am to 8 pm weekdays, and 8 am to 3 pm on Saturday.

Piaţa Unirii

Piaţa Unirii, in the heart of the old town, is Timişoara's most picturesque square. The eastern side of the square is dominated by the baroque 1754 **Roman Catholic Cathedral** (Catedrală Episcopală Romano-Catolică; ☎ 190 081). The main altar painting was completed by Michael Angelo Unterberger, director of the Fine Art Academy in Vienna. On the opposite side of the square is a **Serbian Orthodox Cathedral** (Biserica Ortodoxă Sârbă), built the same year as its Catholic counterpart; local Banat artist Constantin Daniel painted the interior.

The **Trinity Column**, in the centre of the square, was erected by the people of Timişoara at the end of the 18th century in thanks to God for allowing them to survive the plague that hit the town between 1738 and 1739. Overlooking the square is the baroque **Old Prefecture Palace** (Palatul Vechii Prefecturi; 1754), which houses an **Art Museum** (Muzeul de Artă); open 10 am to 4 pm Tuesday to Sunday ($0.50).

From Piaţa Unirii, take a small detour and walk east down Str Palanca to the **Banat Ethnographic Museum** (☎ 134 967), Str Popa Şapcă 1, housed in part of the city's remaining 18th-century **bastion**; open 10 am to 4.30 pm Tuesday to Sunday ($0.50). Trade fairs and exhibitions are hosted at the **Bastion Exhibition Centre** (Expo complex)

every month. In October a national beer festival is held here.

Two blocks west of the square at Str Mărăşeşti 6 is Timişoara's **Great Synagogue**, one of three still functioning in the town.

Piaţa Libertăţii to Piaţa Victoriei

Walk south past the **town hall** (1734), a baroque structure built on the site of 17th-century Turkish baths, to **Piaţa Libertăţii**. It was here that the leader of the 1514 peasant revolt, Gheorghe Doja, was tortured before being executed. Doja's peasant army, after an initial victory, was quickly quashed, captured and killed. Legend has it that upon Doja's public execution, his followers were forced to eat parts of his mutilated body as an appetiser before their own executions.

Continue along Str Lucian Blaga to the 14th-century Huniades Palace, which houses the **Banat History Museum** (Muzeul Banatului; ☎ 191 339). The captions are in Romanian, but it's still worth visiting. Sadly there is no formal exhibition on the 1989 revolution; open 10 am to 4.30 pm Tuesday to Sunday ($1.50).

The fortified **Huniades Palace**, built in 1307–15 by the Hungarian king Carol Robert, Prince of Anjou, was redesigned under the Habsburgs in the late 18th century.

From here head west to the marble 18th-century **National Theatre & Opera House**, which looks straight down **Piaţa Victoriei**, a colourful pedestrian mall. It was immediately in front of the Opera House on this square that thousands of demonstrators gathered on 16 December 1989, following the siege on László Tökés' house (see History in the Facts about Romania chapter). On 17 December tanks rolled into Opera Square and fired on the crowd. By 20 December the 100,000-strong crowd had taken over some tanks, and the army retreated. The bloodshed then spilled over to Bucharest. A memorial plaque on the front of the Opera House today reads: 'So you, who pass by this building, will dedicate a thought for free Romania'.

At the southern end of Piaţa Victoriei, there is a large wooden cross – a **memorial** to those who died. Behind the memorial cross towers the exotic Romanian Orthodox

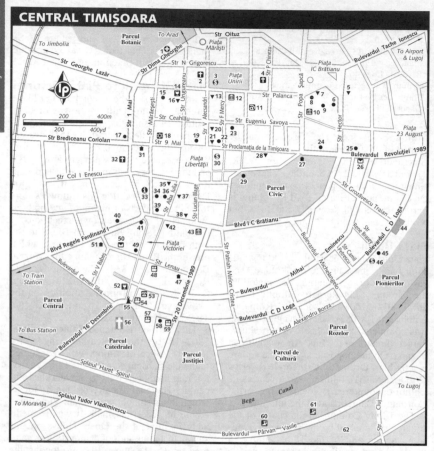

CENTRAL TIMIŞOARA

Metropolitan Cathedral, built between 1936 and 1946. Unique to the church are its electrical bells cast from iron imported from Indonesia. A collection of 16th- to 19th-century icons on wood and glass is displayed in the basement.

South of the Centre

The 1989 revolution began on 15 December 1989 at the **Tökés Reformed Church** (Biserica Reformată Tökés; ☎ 192 992), Str Timotei Cipariu 1, where Father László Tökés spoke out against the dictator. Following attempts by the Securitate to remove Tökés

and his wife from their home above the church, several thousand ethnic Hungarians and Romanians formed a human chain around the building. But Securitate troops broke through the human barrage and arrested the pair. The church upstairs on the 2nd floor is usually locked but someone in the office below may open it for you (leave a donation). The rest of the building is now apartments. Tökés' own small apartment is likewise privately inhabited.

Heading back into the centre, turn right at Blvd Vasile Pârvan along the south bank of the Bega canal. The **University of West**

CENTRAL TIMIŞOARA

PLACES TO STAY
27 Hotel Continental
31 Hotel Timişoara
44 Hotel International
47 Hotel Central
51 Hotel Banatul

PLACES TO EAT
5 Crama & Berăria Bastion
7 Horse Pizzeria
13 Hamburger Plus
16 Grizzly Restaurant & Pub
20 Marele Zid Chinezesc
21 Aroma Cafea
28 Springtime; Shopping Centre Bega
35 Restaurant N&Z
37 Universal Pizzerie & Fast Food
38 Brasserie Opera
42 McDonald's

THINGS TO SEE
2 Serbian Orthodox Cathedral
4 Roman Catholic Cathedral
9 Bastion Exhibition Centre

10 Banat Ethnographic Museum
12 Art Museum; Prefecture Palace
18 Great Synagogue
32 Greco-Catholic Church
43 Huniades Palace; Banat History Museum
55 Memorial to Victims of 1989 Revolution
56 Metropolitan Cathedral
62 University of West Timişoara

OTHER
1 Hospital
3 Banca Comercială Ion Ţiriac (BCIT)
6 Automobil Clubul Român (ACR)
8 Librăria Noi
11 Internet Java; Java Coffee House
14 Irish Pub
15 Stil Supermarket
17 Central Market
19 Farmacie
22 Humanitas Bookshop

23 Yugoslav Airlines (JAT)
24 Tarom
25 Farmacie Remedia
26 Central Post Office
29 Librărie Universitatea
30 Banca Comercială Română
33 Agenţie de Turism Banatul
34 Agenţia Teatrală
36 German State Theatre
39 National Theatre & Opera
40 Cardinal Tourist Agency
41 Agenţie de Voiaj CFR
45 French Cultural Centre
46 Banca Agricolă
48 Cinema Studio
49 Librăria Mihai Eminescu
50 Post Office
52 Violeta Bar
53 Telephone Office
54 Cinema Timiş
57 Outside Cinema (Cinema de Vară)
58 State Philharmonic Theatre
59 Cinema Capitol
60 Terasa Eminescu Complex
61 Strand Complex

Timişoara (UWT; ☎/fax 190 009) at Blvd Vasile Pârvan 4 is a vast modern complex, first established in 1944.

Two kilometres south of the centre, on Calea Martirilor, is Timişoara's **Astronomical Observatory** (Observatorul Astronomic), where hundreds gathered on 11 August 1999 to witness the total eclipse of the sun. To get to the observatory, take tram No 8 from the northern train station to Str Martirilor.

The **Banat Village Museum** (☎ 225 588), 6km north-east of the centre, exhibits some 20 monuments and more than 30 traditional peasant houses dating from the 19th century. The open-air display, created in 1917, is open noon to 8 pm Tuesday to Sunday from June to September (in winter 8 am to 4 pm). Take tram No 1 (black number) from the train station.

Activities

Luxury swimming pools with landscaped sunbathing terraces and beer gardens line the length of the dirty Bega canal, which flows through the town's south. Top of the range is the Strand complex (☎ 203 663), opposite the university at Blvd Pârvan Vasile 3; open 24 hours ($0.50).

The Terasa Eminescu (☎ 229 212) complex next door is a similar set-up which attracts a younger crowd; open 9 am to 7 pm daily ($1).

You can play tennis for $1.20 an hour and swim at the Baza Sportivă Timcon (☎ 193 089), adjoining the hotel at Splaiul Tudor Vladimirescu 15a. The centre has canoes too, officially only for club members, but competent canoeists should be able to persuade the staff otherwise.

Places to Stay

Camping The well-maintained *Camping International* (☎ 225 596, *Aleea Pădurea Verde 6*) is in the Green Wood forest on the opposite side of town from Timişoara-Nord train station (its main entrance is on Calea Dorobanţilor). From the station catch trolleybus No 11 to the end of the line. The bus stops less than 50m from the camping ground. A two/four-bed bungalow with central heating costs $15/30, and tent camping is $2 for two people. The small restaurant on the premises is open year-round.

Hotels – Budget Timişoara's cheaper options include *Casa Tineretului (Youth House; ☎ 162 419, Str Arieş 19)*, a modern building about 2km south of the centre. Rooms with shared bath are $10 per person. From the northern train station take tram No 8 to Str Martirilor.

Timişoara's best-value city-centre hotel is the surprisingly comfortable *Hotel Banatul (☎ 191 903, Blvd Ferdinand 5)*. Spotlessly clean first-class rooms with private bathroom are $12/17 for singles/doubles. Second-class rooms are also OK at $10 for a double.

Hotel Nord (☎ 197 504, Str General Drăgălina 47) around the corner from Timişoara-Nord train station has overpriced rooms with private bathroom for $20/28 a night. However heavy your pack is, don't be tempted to stay here; the trek into town is worth it!

The run-down *Baza Sportivă Timcon (☎ 193 089, Splaiul Tudor Vladimirescu 15a)*, south-west of the centre, has very basic rooms with shared bathrooms and cold water for $2 a night.

Hotels – Mid-Range & Top End The cheapest of the more expensive hotels is the small *Hotel Central (☎ 190 091, fax 190 096, Str Lenau 6)*, with doubles/apartments with private bath for $17/26.

The modern 11-storey *Hotel Timişoara (☎ 198 854, ☎/fax 199 450, Str 9 Mai 2)*, behind the Opera House, offers all the mod cons including a tourist office, currency exchange, hairdresser, top-class restaurant etc. Two-star single/double rooms are $38/50, including breakfast.

The three-star *Hotel Continental (☎ 134 144, fax 130 481, Blvd Revoluţiei 3)*, overlooking the Parcul Civic, is excellent value at $24/37. It has a disco, casino and a large terrace restaurant and cafe.

Set on a tree-lined avenue south of the centre is the four-star *Hotel International (☎ 199 339, 190 193, fax 190 194, 199 338, Blvd CD Loga 4)*. Originally built as a villa for Ceauşescu, it still attracts an elitist

crowd. Its luxury two/three-room apartments cost $70/80, followed by an extra $5 for each additional guest. The restaurant is highly recommended if you can afford to pay Western prices.

Places to Eat
Restaurants For typical Romanian dishes try *Restaurant N&Z (Str Alba Iulia 1)*, just off Piaţa Libertăţii. Its menu is displayed in pictures outside. Another excellent spot for Romanian cuisine is *Tinecz (☎ 123 963, Calea Aradului 51)*, north of the centre. A typical meal costs around $5.

Crowded with foreign tourists in summer is the *Crama Bastion*, with the bar *Berăria Bastion*, on Str Hector, in a section of the city's 18th-century fortifications. Its menu of meat and rice dishes is nothing special but the interior is a real blast from the past and the beer garden is idyllic in summer.

Grizzly Restaurant & Pub (Str Ungureanu 7), while not as impressive as its name suggests, serves good cheap meals. The *pui grizzly* (breaded chicken with carrot sauce) at less than $2 is a real treat.

Restaurants specialising in international cuisine are also starting to sprout: highly recommended is *Marele Zid Chinezesc (☎ 132 188, Str Alecsandri 2)*, just off Piaţa Libertăţii. The set menus are good value.

Leaning towards Italy in its choice of cuisine is *Horse Pizzeria*, on Str Popa Şapcă, tucked inside the bastion walls. Its 19 different types of pizza come in regular and mini sizes. The salami and *caşcaval* (cheese) pizza for $2 is excellent. Spaghetti and salad are also available.

North-west of the centre on Calea Lipovei is a cluster of pizza places. *Pizzeria La Tino (☎ 226 455, Calea Al Cuza)*, and the nearby *Pizzeria Poly (☎ 127 080)* next to the railway bridge, are both upmarket restaurants serving a huge variety of pizzas starting at $2. Pizzeria Poly has a number of vegetarian choices and home delivers.

Cafes There are plenty of terrace cafes to choose from in the centre. *Aroma Cafea*, on Piaţa Libertăţii, stocks a good range of pizzas, pastries and other light snacks.

Timişoara's Martyr Memorials

Numerous memorials for Timişoara's victims of the December 1989 revolution are encrusted in walls throughout town. Most are still honoured with fresh flowers.

A series of haunting sculptures has been built to create a memorial to the Timişoara martyrs. Outside Hotel Continental on Blvd Revoluţiei stands the modernist bronze sculpture **Evolution** (Evoluţie), symbolising an eternal knot.

Outside Timişoara's Greco-Catholic church, on the corner of Str Brediceanu Coriolan and Str 1 Mai, is the **Target Man** (Omul Ţintă), a life-size bronze sculpture of a skeleton writhing in pain.

Opposite the entrance to Hotel Central are the **Martyrs** (Martirii). A pile of faceless bodies lie stacked up, squashed to death. The larger-than-life corpses lie on a granite pedestal.

More conventional sculptures include the **Martyrs Fountain** (Fântâna Martirilor) behind Cinema Capitol on Blvd CD Loga; the **Young Heroes' Monument** (Monumentul Eroilor Tineri) in the small square off Piaţa Libertăţii; and the **Crying Church** (Biserica Plângătoare) on Piaţa Kütti.

East of the centre, on Piaţa Traian, is **Freedom's Bell** (Clopotul Libertăţii), a massive stone bell. Take trolleybus No 11 or bus No 26 to Piaţa Traian (formerly Piaţa Romanilor).

Painfully haunting is the **Winner** (Învingătorul), sculpted by Bucharest artist Constantin Popovici. The angular bronze statue features the skeleton of a man standing tall with his right arm raised to the sky in victory, while his left arm and leg have been amputated.

A sculptor from Munich carved the minimalist **Opening** (Deschidere), comprising a doorway of two large, upright steel plates on which two simple crosses are embedded. It stands in the grounds of the Youth Palace (Casa Tineretului), 2km south of the centre. Take tram No 8 from the northern train station.

Many of the victims of the 1989 revolution are buried in the **Heroes' Cemetery** (Cimitirul Eroilor), inside the main city cemetery north of the centre on Calea Lipovei. Opposite the main entrance to the cemetery stands a giant mausoleum sheltering an **eternal flame to the unknown soldier**; open 8 am to 8 pm weekdays, and 8 am to 5 pm weekends. Take trolleybus No 14 from Piaţa Mărăşti to the Cimitirul Eroilor stop on Calea Lipovei.

Brasserie Opera, on Blvd Republicii close to the Opera House, is an upmarket terrace cafe. Its small menu consists of mostly pizza and pastries.

The coffee-addicted will love the small *Java Coffee House (Str Pacha 6)*, which has wonderfully strong cappuccinos for $0.75. You can even sip your brew while surfing the Internet; open 24 hours.

If you want to get into the local student scene, try hanging out at the *university cafe*, next to the library in the main university building, south of the river at Blvd Pârvan Vasile 4.

Fast Food At *Hamburger Plus*, on Str Alecsandri, there's a variety of mushroom, Mexican, cheese and enchilada burgers, starting at $0.50. *Springtime*, on Str Proclamaţia de la Timişoara in the Shopping Centre Bega serves the usual hamburgers,

fries, cakes and ice cream from 9 am daily. *McDonald's* is on Piaţa Victoriei.

Universal Pizzerie & Fast Food (Str Alba Iulia 7) serves an inspired range of salads and sandwiches.

Self-Catering The 24-hour *Stil Supermarket (Str Mărăşeşti 10)* stocks an impressive array of imported and local products. It even has Western-style trolleys. Timişoara has a colourful produce *central market* on Str Brediceanu near the intersection of Str 1 Mai. The *Badea Cârţan market*, east of the centre on the corner of Piaţa Badea Cârţan and Blvd Tache Ionescu, sells domestic products and lots of fruit.

Entertainment

Cinemas Timişoara has five cinemas, all of which screen films in their original language with Romanian subtitles. Cinemas in

Tarzan of Timişoara

MGM's original Tarzan was born in Timişoara. Billed by the movie-makers as 'the only man in Hollywood who's natural in the flesh and can act without clothes', Johnny Weissmüller (1904–84) was a box-office hit in the 1932 *Tarzan the Ape Man*.

The Romanian-born actor went on to make 11 more Tarzan movies which featured the not-so-bionic Jane, and the yodelling jungle-cry (not really Weissmüller but a mix of recorded animal sounds). MGM allegedly paid Weissmüller's wife $10,000 to divorce him in a bid to appease lovestruck fans (Weissmüller married five times in all). In 1940 he was dropped by MGM and went on to shoot 16 *Jungle Jim* movies with Columbia before retiring in the 1950s.

Weissmüller was hot in the swimming stakes too. He was an Olympic gold medallist five times over in 1924 and 1928, and won 76 world and 52 national swimming titles for the USA during a five-year sporting career. He later modelled swimwear.

Throughout his life, Timişoara's Tarzan never declared himself Romanian. His family left Romania in 1907 for the US and he consequently claimed Pennsylvania as his birthplace to ensure his eligibility for the Olympics.

MARTIN HARRIS

the centre include *Cinema Studio* (☎ 190 759), on Str Lenau next to Hotel Central; *Cinema Timiş* (☎ 191 290), on Piaţa Victoriei; and the popular *Cinema Capitol* (☎ 190 759), on Blvd CD Loga next to the State Philharmonic Theatre.

The city sports an outside cinema too – *Cinema de Vară* – which is far more fun! It's on Blvd CD Loga ($1).

Bars & Discos Most people hang out at night in the terrace cafes on Piaţa Victoriei, downing bottles of the local Timişoreana Pils beer for around $0.50 a bottle. *Violeta Bar* at the southern end of the square is particularly popular. The *Irish Pub* (Str Ungureanu 9) has to be one of the coolest and most expensive bars in town. Only foreign beers are served; open 24 hours.

From October to May there's a disco in the *Casa de Cultură a Studenţilor* (Blvd Tinereţii 9). It's near the corner of Str General Drăgălina, three blocks south of the train station. Tram No 1 passes this way.

The ultraviolet *Park Place Disco* (Blvd Mihai Viteazul 1), south of the centre, pumps out funky tunes nightly 10 pm to 4 am (closed Monday).

Theatre & Classical Music Highly regarded throughout Romania is Timişoara's *National Theatre & Opera House* (Teatrul Naţional şi Opera Română), on Piaţa Victoriei. Tickets are sold at the Agenţia Teatrală (☎ 201 286) at Str Mărăşeşti 2; open 10 am to 1 pm, and 5 to 7 pm daily. Tickets start at $0.60.

Close by is the *German State Theatre* (Teatrul German de Stat; ☎ 201 291). The box office is inside the theatre on Str Alba Iulia, open 10 am to 7 pm daily, closed Monday.

Classical concerts are held most evenings at the *State Philharmonic Theatre* (Filharmonia de Stat Banatul; ☎ 195 012, Blvd CD Loga 2). Tickets can be bought at the box office inside the Philharmonic Theatre or from the Agenţia Teatrală on Str Mărăşeşti ($1/0.50 adults/students).

Some classical music concerts, folk dances and other traditional festivities are held on the *open-air stage* in the beautiful rose garden park, Parcul Rozelor. The main entrance is one block south of Blvd CD Loga.

Event details are generally advertised in the local press and on posters around town.

Getting There & Away

Air The Tarom office (☎/fax 190 150, 132 876) is opposite Hotel Continental at Blvd Revoluţiei 3–5; open 7 am to 1 pm and 3 to 7 pm weekdays, 7 am to 1 pm Saturday, and 8 to 11 am Sunday. Tarom has domestic flights from Timişoara to Bucharest ($100) daily except Sunday.

Train All major train services depart from the northern train station (Timişoara-Nord; ☎ 112 552, 193 806) at Str Gării 3. International tickets must be purchased in advance from the Agenţie de Voiaj CFR (☎ 191 889) at Piaţa Victoriei 2; open 8 am to 8 pm weekdays. The left-luggage office at the station is in the underground passageway to the tracks; open 24 hours.

One daily express train connects Timişoara with Belgrade. The *Bucureşti* leaves Timişoara-Nord at 7.58 am and arrives in Belgrade at 11.32 am (advance reservations are required).

It's also possible to reach Yugoslavia by taking a local train to the Romanian town of Jimbolia (one hour) and then a connecting train to Kikinda (19km, two daily).

Bus Twice-weekly buses connecting Timişoara to Békéscsaba and Szeged in Hungary depart from the bus station at the western end of Splaiul Tudor Vladimirescu. There is also a weekly service to Budapest ($8, eight hours). Purchase tickets from the driver.

Local daily services include two buses to Târgu Jiu, and one to Brad and to Câmpeni.

From Timişoara, there are two buses weekly to Germany. Tickets are sold at the Erna Mayer Reisebüro (☎ 191 903) inside Hotel Banatul.

Getting Around

To/From the Airport Timişoara airport (☎ 191 637) is 12.5km north-east from the centre on Calea Lugojului. Tarom runs a shuttle bus from its office on Blvd Revoluţiei. Bus No 26, which stops outside Hotel Continental, also goes to the airport.

Tram, Trolleybus & Bus Tickets ($0.15) are sold at kiosks next to tram and bus stops. All public transport runs between 4.45 am and 11.15 pm. Tram No 1 runs from the northern train station (Timişoara-Nord) to Piaţa Libertăţii, Hotel Continental and the eastern train station (Timişoara-Est). Tram No 4 runs from Hotel Continental to Piaţa Traian (Piaţa Romanilor). Trolleybus Nos 11 and 14 travel from the train station east down Blvd Ferdinand then turn north on Str 1 Mai.

Car Avis has an office at Timişoara airport (☎ 203 234). See the Getting Around chapter for details.

BĂILE HERCULANE
☎ 055 • postcode 1600

Legend has it that Hercules bathed in the curative natural springs still flowing today in the mountain spa resort of Băile Herculane. The first baths were built by Roman legions following their invasion of Dacia. Inspired by the incredible healing powers of the springs, they named the resort *Ad Aquas Herculi Sacras*, meaning the 'Holy Water of Hercules'.

During the early 19th century, Băile Herculane developed as a fashionable resort, attracting royal visits from Habsburg emperor Franz Joseph. Sadly, most of the grand hotels and baths stand empty and neglected.

Mount Domogled (1100m) towers over Băile Herculane to the west, dominating the Cerna Valley in which the resort lies. The extensive forest reservation, which has been protected since 1932, includes rare trees, turtles and butterflies.

Orientation

Băile Herculane lies either side of a road which follows the Cerna River. The train station is at the junction of the main Drobeta-Turnu Severin–Timişoara highway and the Băile Herculane turn-off.

The resort is split into three parts: the residential area is at the western end of the resort on Str Trandafirilor; the concrete blocks of the newer satellite resort are 2km east of the residential area, and the historic centre is at the resort's most eastern end (8km from the train station).

Information

The official Biroul de Turism (☎ 560 454) is opposite Hotel Apollo at Piaţa Hercules 5 but it's useless if you don't speak Romanian. Try the tourist office inside Hotel Roman or Hercules Hotel instead, where some of the staff speak English.

The currency exchange on the 3rd floor of Hotel Roman is open 10 am to 7 pm weekdays. You can cash travellers cheques at the Banca Comercială Română opposite Hotel Apollo, at Piaţa Hercules 4; open 8 am to noon weekdays, and 8.30 am to 1 pm Saturday. Banca Română Pentru Dezvoltare at Str Izvorului 5 has an ATM; open 8.30 am to noon weekdays.

The central post office is next to the CFR office on Piaţa Hercules; open 7 am to 8 pm weekdays. The telephone centre is near the Popas Flora camping ground on Str Castanilor; open 7 am to 8 pm daily.

Things to See

All the sights lie in the historic centre. Most of the Roman baths were destroyed during the Turkish and Austrian-Hungarian occupations. Some ancient Roman baths stand well preserved, however, in the **Roman Bath Museum** (Terma Română), inside Hotel Roman at Str Română 1. The 2000-year-old baths were served by a natural spring in the side of the mountain. Today, the flow of the natural spring is channelled into the hotel's 2nd-floor swimming pool. Hanging on the walls in one of the baths are replicas of engravings made by the Romans in praise to the Gods for curing their ills. An original carving of Hercules in the rock face of one of the walls is thought to have formed an **altar to Hercules**.

Natural springs from which drinking water flows – believed to be good for stomach problems – are dotted throughout the historic centre. To the side of the hotel flows the **Hercules II spring** (Izvorul Hercules).

At Str Cernei 14 stands the resort's **central pavilion**, built during the 1800s by the Habsburgs as a casino and restaurant. Today it houses a few small shops and a **History Museum** (Muzeul de Istorie), open 9 am to 4 pm Tuesday to Sunday. Beside the steps leading up to the museum entrance stands a 200-year-old **Wellingtoniă Gigantea tree**, famed for its enormous size. On the opposite side of the river stand the derelict **Austrian baths**.

Activities

Self-Pampering Wallowing in a thermal bath or being pummelled into oblivion by a masseur is all part and parcel of a stay in Băile Herculane. The crumbling old baths inside Hotel Apollo are officially only for those with a doctor's recommendation but it's worth asking anyway.

There is an outside pool and thermal spring 7km east from the centre, along Str Romană. In summer the pool is packed.

Hotel Roman and Hotel Afrodite both have thermal swimming pools which are open to nonguests ($1).

Hiking & Climbing Directly behind Hotel Roman stands the **Brigands' Cave** (Peştera Haiducilor). It is named after the thieves who would hide in the cave, waiting for their prey to roll by. A path leads up to the cave from the hotel. A second path (2.5km, marked with blue stripes) leads to the Grota cu Aburi cave. East of the cave lies the **Munk natural spring** (Izvorul Munk); from the centre a trail (3km, red stripes) starting at the Brasseria Central at Str Izvorului 1 leads to it.

South-east of the resort, the **White Cross** (Crucea Albă) is a popular hiking trail (marked with yellow stripes). It starts from Str 1 Mai next to Hotel Cerna.

The rock face behind Hotel Roman is popular with climbers in summer.

Places to Stay

Practically all the hotels in Băile Herculane have costly, short-stay rates (one to three days) and cheaper, long-stay rates (three to 21 days). All the prices listed below are short-stay rates. If you plan to stay longer, negotiate! The top hotels get full in July and August; then the resort dies from mid-September to mid-May.

Camping Located between the old and new resorts, the *Popas Flora* camping ground (☎ 560 929, Str Castanilor 25) has two- and four-bed bungalows overlooking the Cerna River. A bed costs $2.50 a night; there are communal showers (cold water only) and toilets. It's open May to October.

Hotels – Historic Centre Excellent value is the regal *Hotel Apollo* (☎ 560 688, 560 494, Piaţa Hercules 4), built in 1824 to serve the prosperous Apollo baths which date from 1821. Basic but clean single/double rooms with private bathroom and TV cost $5/8. Hot water flows from 7 to 9 am and from 7.30 to 9.30 pm Monday to Saturday.

Equally grand and slightly more upmarket is the two-star *Hotel Roman* (☎ 560 394/ 390, fax 561 411, Str Romană 1), built in the side of the mountain on the site of a natural spring (see Things to See). Rooms with cable TV, private bathroom and hot water from 7 am to midnight daily cost $15/23. Facilities include a bowling alley, pool tables, swimming pool ($1), sauna and gym.

Hotel Cerna (☎ 560 436, Str 1 Mai 1) has cheap rooms for $5/10. Bus No 1 from the train station stops outside. At the concrete-block *Hercules Hotel* (☎ 561 321, fax 560 910, Str Izvorului 7), rooms with private bathroom are $11/17.

Prior to 1989, Ceauşescu stayed at the elitist *Vila Belvedere* (☎ 561 429, fax 561 439, Str Nicolae Stoica Haţeg 46), close to the 19th-century Austrian baths. It has beautifully furnished doubles with private bathrooms for $20 and apartments for $30.

Hotels – Satellite Resort There is little difference between the three concrete monsters in the newer part of Băile Herculane. The 218-room *Hotel Afrodite* (☎ 560 730, Str Complexelor 2) offers rooms with private bathroom for $11/15. A colour TV is an extra $1 per night and hot water runs between 8 am and 8 pm.

Identical prices are charged at *Hotel Diana* (☎ 560 495, Str Complexelor 1) and also at the 210-room *Hotel Minerva* (☎/fax 561 770).

Out of Town The relaxing *Hotel Tierna* (☎/fax 560 632), 5km north of the centre, affords superb views from its position on the edge of Lacu Prisaca. Its 36 doubles cost $19 a night including breakfast. You can also play tennis or rent a rowing boat here for $0.75 per hour each.

Places to Eat

Băile Herculane has few restaurants beyond those inside its hotels. The in-house restaurants of Hotel Roman and Vila Belvedere serve the best food – $4 for a main meal without alcohol.

A popular spot for pizza is *Restaurant Dixi*, on Str Castanilor in the new centre. There is a 24-hour *mini-market* opposite Hotel Dacia in the new centre.

Entertainment

Next door to the mini-market is the popular *Bar Cezar*. The hottest nightspot in town is *Club 69*, on Str Izorului.

Young folk also hang out at the *discoteca*, in the basement of the old central pavilion at Str Cernei 10.

Getting There & Away

Train The train station is 5km south-west of the new resort. The Agenţie de Voiaj CFR (☎ 560 538) at Piaţa Hercules 5 is open 7 am to 6 pm weekdays.

The daily Bucharest-Belgrade train stops at Băile Herculane, which is on the main Timişoara-Bucharest line. Services from Băile Herculane include nine trains daily to Orşova (35 minutes), Drobeta-Turnu Severin (40 minutes to 1¼ hours) and Craiova (two to three hours); and seven daily to Timişoara (3¼ hours) and Bucharest (five to six hours).

Bus The small bus station (☎ 560 595) is between the old and new resorts on Str Castanilor. The only daily service is to Orşova, four times daily.

Getting Around

Bus No 1 runs every half-hour from the train station to the new resort, stopping outside the mini-market, to Hotel Cerna (Str Cernei) and Hotel Apollo (Piaţa Hercules), and to the historic centre ($0.20).

Maramureş

Maramureş, actually part of Transylvania, shares the same history as its southern neighbour, the major difference being that Dacian Maramureş was never conquered by the Romans, earning the region the title 'land of the free Dacians'. This, coupled with its mountainous terrain which was unsuitable for agriculture, meant it remained unscathed by collectivisation in the 1940s and by systemisation in the 1980s. This accounts for Maramureş' unique ethnographical standing today.

The region, cut off by a natural fortress of mountains, remains largely untouched by the 20th century. Social activities revolve around the village churches, dating from the 15th and 16th centuries. In Orthodox and Greco-Catholic churches alike, men still take their pews in front of the altar *(pronaos)*, while the wives take a back seat in the *naos*. Little boys sit on a balcony above the pronaos, and their sisters line up on benches in front of the men. As in all Orthodox churches in Romania, women are not allowed at the altar. Many villages in the region have abandoned their ancestors' traditional places of worship for ungainly new concrete churches.

Colourful traditional folk costumes, each bearing motifs typical to each village, are donned for special holidays. The rest of the year, men set off for the fields in their sober-coloured, wide-bottomed trousers decorated with 30cm-wide leather belts, while women do their chores in coarse navy-blue or black linen skirts, and cardigans.

Industrialisation has touched some parts of Maramureş, however, so travellers in search of days gone by may be disappointed. It is only farther afield, in the Mara and Izei Valleys, that medieval Maramureş truly comes alive.

Since 1999 eight wooden churches in Maramureş, in the villages of Bârsana, Budeşti, Deseşti, Ieud, Plopis, Poienile Izei, Rogoz and Surdeşti, have been included on Unesco's list of World Heritage sites.

Baia Mare and Satu Mare, the two main towns, offer few attractions and serve mainly

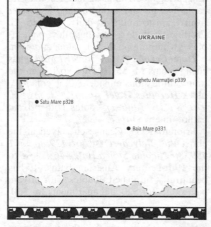

Highlights

- Drink *ţuică* (plum brandy) and eat strawberries at Ţurţ
- Tour the famed wooden churches: those in Surdeşti and Budeşti are among the best
- Visit the fascinating Merry Cemetery in Săpânta
- Ride on a steam train up the Vaser Valley, and stay overnight in a forest cabana
- Learn about the communist purges of the 1950s at Sighetu Marmaţiei's former communist prison

as stepping stones to the region's more remote spots. Maramureş is practically impossible to explore without private transport.

History

Maramureş, with Baia Mare as its capital, was first documented in 1199. Hungary gradually exerted its rule over the region from the 13th century onwards. Tartar invasions of the Hungarian-dominated region continued well into the 17th and 18th centuries, the last documented battle being on the Prislop Pass in 1717. Numerous churches sprang up in Maramureş around this time to mark the Tartars' final withdrawal from the region.

Maramureş was annexed by Transylvania in the mid-16th century, then ceded to the Austrian empire in 1699. It was not until 1918 that Maramureş was returned to Romania.

Between 1940 and 1944 the Maramureş region – along with northern Transylvania – fell under pro-Nazi Hungarian rule.

SATU MARE
☎ 061 • postcode 3900 • pop 130,000
Satu Mare, meaning 'big village', has a large ethnic Hungarian population. Many shop signs are written in both Hungarian and Romanian, and many people still refer to the town by its former Hungarian name, Szatmar.

Orientation
Satu Mare can easily be covered on foot. The train and bus stations are adjacent to each other at the north end of Str Griviţei, to the east of the centre. South of the centre, the Someş River crosses the town from east to west.

Maps The Accord Business & Travel agency (see the following paragraph) sells an excellent 1998 city map for a mere $0.15. Also worth picking up is the *Judeţul Satu Mare* (1993), which includes a brief lowdown of the town's historic and tourist sights.

Information
Tourist Offices The Accord Business & Travel agency (☎ 737 915, fax 717 069, 🖃 a-btt@p5net.ro) at Blvd Traian 7 is as good as any official tourist office. It sells maps, arranges tours and rents cars from $0.20 per kilometre. Accord is also the official agent for Antrec and arranges private accommodation in rural homes.

The Agenţia de Turism inside Hotel Dacia sells tickets for international buses from Bucharest and arranges tours of the region; open 9 am to 4 pm weekdays.

Money The Fortuna currency exchange at Piaţa Libertăţii 8 is open 8 am to 8 pm week-

days. There is also a currency exchange inside Hotel Aurora at Piaţa Libertăţii 11, open the same hours plus 8 am to 4 pm Saturday.

The Banca Română on Str 25 Octombrie cashes travellers cheques, gives cash advances on Visa/MasterCard and has an ATM; open 8.30 am to 1 pm weekdays. The Banca Comercială Română on Str 25 Octombrie offers the same services; open 8 am to 1 pm weekdays.

Post & Telephone The central post and telephone office, at the southern end of Str 25 Octombrie, is open 7 am to 8 pm weekdays. There is another post office on the corner of Str Mihai Viteazul and Str M Averescu; open 7 am to 8.30 pm weekdays, and 8 am to 1 pm Saturday. A second telephone office on Blvd Traian is open 7 am to 9 pm daily.

Email & Internet Access The Internet Café (☎ 770 023) at Blvd Traian 5 charges $0.75 per hour for Internet access; open 10 am to midnight daily.

Things to See
Satu Mare's sights are centred on Piaţa Libertăţii. There is a large **art museum** on the corner of Str Cuza Vodă and Piaţa Libertăţii; open 9 am to 5 pm Tuesday to Sunday; $0.20.

From Piaţa Libertăţii, walk through the alleyway next to Hotel Dacia, housed in the former **city hall and royal court** on the northern side of the square. Opposite the entrance to the **State Philharmonic** is the **Casa Memorială Erdós**, in which contemporary art and photographic exhibitions are hosted; open 9 am to 5 pm Tuesday to Sunday. Continuing north down the alley, you come to a small courtyard, in the centre of which stands a 45m-tall **fire tower** (Turnul Pompierilor; 1904).

A **Roman Catholic Cathedral** lies on the east side of Piaţa Libertăţii. Building began on the cathedral in 1786; its two towers were added in 1837. Badly damaged during WWII, it remained closed until 1961 when restoration was completed.

On Piaţa Păcii, immediately north, is the town's large **Hungarian Reformed Church**. In front of the church is a statue of Ferenc

MARAMUREŞ

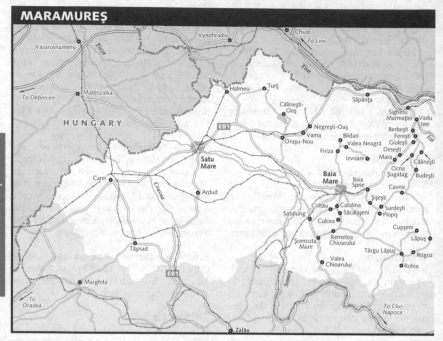

MARAMUREŞ

Kölcsey who founded the Hungarian school next door. Satu Mare's Orthodox community worships at the **Orthodox church** at the eastern end of Str 1 Decembrie 1918.

Prior to WWII, some 13,000 Jews lived in Satu Mare, which boasted eight synagogues and a school. Most Jews were deported to death camps in 1944 and their synagogues destroyed, although the **Great Synagogue** (1920) is still in use today.

In front of the Magazin Universal on Piaţa 25 Octombrie is a **statue of Corneliu Coposu**, former president of the National Peasant Democratic Party (PNŢCD), who spent 17 years as a political prisoner in communist prisons, including the one in Sighetu Marmaţiei. He died in 1995, one month after being awarded the Légion d'Honneur at the French embassy in Bucharest.

Satu Mare has a local **history museum** (☎ 737 526) at Blvd Vasile Lucaciu 21, open 9 am to 5 pm Tuesday to Sunday (to 2 pm Saturday); $1.

Places to Stay

Camping At *Steaua Nordului* (*'North Star';* ☎ *740 655, Str Botizului 30)*, 6km north of Satu Mare on the road to Vama, there are two-bed cabins for $5 a night. The restaurant and bar is open 24 hours. Bus No 32 runs here from Satu Mare centre.

Private Rooms Accord Business & Travel (see Tourist Offices) arranges accommodation in private rooms from $8 a night. Call in advance if you want a room.

Hotels The two-star *Hotel Sport* (☎ *712 959, Str Minelului 25)*, a five-minute walk from the centre, has the cheapest rooms in town. Double rooms with shared bathroom are $16 including breakfast (no singles). The hotel is often fully booked.

Hotel Dacia (☎ *714 276/277, fax 715 774, Piaţa Libertăţii 8)* is a stylish building with rooms to match. Comfortable singles/doubles cost $30/40, including breakfast.

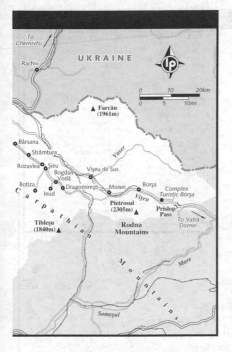

Its luxury apartments are $60. The hotel reception rents out board games for bored guests. Less prestigious and less luxurious is the three-star *Hotel Aurora* (☎ *714 199, fax 714 946, Piaţa Libertăţii 11*). Rooms are $27/40 and an apartment is $48.

Places to Eat

Satu Mare's hotel restaurants draw most diners. *Restaurant Corso*, on Piaţa Libertăţii next to the Philharmonic, offers the typical soup, pork cutlet and salad menu. It accepts credit cards. Also serving local cuisine but in a sunny, green environment is the outside *Mioriţa* terrace restaurant (*Str Mihai Viteazul 5*). Live bands play most nights.

If you want international cuisine go Italian at the not-very-Italian *Bella Italia Restaurant* (☎ *712 053, Str Ady Endre 10*); more authentic is *Shanghai* (☎ *770 056*), on Blvd Vasile Lucaciu, a small Chinese restaurant. Expect to pay around $4 for a meal at both.

Hello Margot (☎ *716 691, Str G Doja 1*) sells fast-food delights at staggeringly cheap prices; open 10 am to midnight daily. Very clean and offering a fine array of lush pastries and ice cream is *Fast Food Raphaelo*, on Str Cuza Vodă just off Piaţa Libertăţii.

Entertainment

Posters advertising what's on where in the city – including discos and rave parties – line the walls outside the State Philharmonic building.

A hip spot in town is the *Enigma* disco (☎ *711 224*), on Str Lăcrămioara. It rocks 9 pm to 5 am Friday to Sunday. *Club 99*, on Blvd Traian overlooking Piaţa Libertăţii, is another popular spot; it has a restaurant and an outside cafe on the square.

Theatre & Classical Music The *State Philharmonic* (☎ *712 666/616, Piaţa Libertăţii 8*) is tucked in an alleyway beside Hotel Dacia. Plays in Romanian are performed at the *Teatrul de Nord* (☎ *715 876, Str Horea 5*). Tickets for both are sold opposite at Agenţia Teatrală (☎ *712 106*), Str Horea 6; open 10 am to 4 pm weekdays.

Getting There & Away

Air Tarom (☎ *712 795*), Piaţa 25 Octombrie 9, operates Satu Mare–Bucharest flights daily except Sunday ($60/100 single/return); the office is open 8 am to 8 pm weekdays.

Train The Agenţie de Voiaj CFR (☎ *721 202*) at Piaţa 25 Octombrie, Block 9, is open 7 am to 7 pm weekdays.

There are daily trains to Budapest departing at 1.57 am and 11.04 am. There are frequent trains to other destinations including Arad, Baia Mare, Cluj-Napoca, Constanţa (summer only), and Oradea.

Bus The bus station (☎ *768 439*) is a 10-minute walk east of the centre.

A daily minibus to Budapest-Keleti departs from outside the train station ($10/20 single/return, 9.30 pm); pay the driver.

TransEuropa (☎ *711 466*), at Piaţa Libertăţii 23, sells tickets for buses from Bucharest to Western Europe.

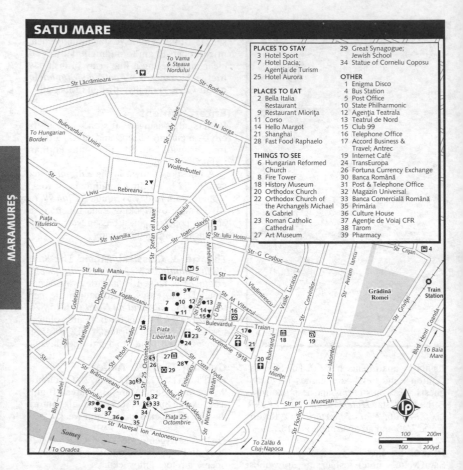

SATU MARE

PLACES TO STAY
3 Hotel Sport
7 Hotel Dacia;
  Agenţia de Turism
25 Hotel Aurora

PLACES TO EAT
2 Bella Italia
  Restaurant
9 Restaurant Mioriţa
11 Corso
14 Hello Margot
21 Shanghai
28 Fast Food Raphaelo

THINGS TO SEE
6 Hungarian Reformed
  Church
8 Fire Tower
18 History Museum
20 Orthodox Church
22 Orthodox Church of
  the Archangels Michael
  & Gabriel
23 Roman Catholic
  Cathedral
27 Art Museum

29 Great Synagogue;
  Jewish School
34 Statue of Corneliu Coposu

OTHER
1 Enigma Disco
4 Bus Station
5 Post Office
10 State Philharmonic
12 Agenţia Teatrala
13 Teatrul de Nord
15 Club 99
16 Telephone Office
17 Accord Business &
  Travel; Antrec
19 Internet Café
24 TransEuropa
26 Fortuna Currency Exchange
30 Banca Română
31 Post & Telephone Office
32 Magazin Universal
33 Banca Comercială Romană
35 Primăria
36 Culture House
37 Agenţie de Voiaj CFR
38 Tarom
39 Pharmacy

Local buses include 13 daily to Baia Mare (59km); one to Negreşti Oaş (50km), Oradea (133km) and Turţ (35km); and two to Sighetu Marmaţiei (122km).

Getting Around

Satu Mare airport (☎ 768 640) is situated 9km south of the city on the main Oradea–Satu Mare road.

Tarom runs a shuttle bus to/from the airport. It leaves town from the Str Mareşal Ion Antonescu bus stop, close to the Tarom office, one hour before flights are scheduled to depart.

ŢARA OAŞULUI
☎ 061

Ţara Oaşului, literally 'Land of Oaş', refers to the depression in the eastern part of Satu Mare district. The origin of the name is unclear although some say that Oaş is derived from the Hungarian word *vos* ('iron'), named after the supposed brutish, iron-like nature of the region's inhabitants.

Turţ

The northern village of Turţ, 27km northeast of Satu Mare, is home to Romania's finest **pălincă factory**. Since 1376, Fabrica

Capşun has produced *pălincă* – a fiery plum brandy almost identical to traditional Romanian *ţuică* except that it is distilled more than three times. It also produces *căpşunată*, a marginally milder strawberry liqueur. You can visit the factory and fill your empty bottle with *casă pălincă* – 52% proof – for about $1 per half-litre, at the grey house, 200m from the factory, behind the blue house. If you visit the village in mid-June you can join in the strawberry harvest.

The factory is opposite strawberry fields, at the southern end of the village.

To get to Turţ from Satu Mare, follow the northbound Budapest road to Turulung village. Turţ is signposted on the right just after the village.

Negreşti-Oaş & Around

Heading south-east from Turţ, through the lakeside **Călineşti-Oaş**, you come to Negreşti-Oaş. The main reason for stopping in this small village is to visit the **open-air museum** (Muzeul Satului Oşenesc), signposted down a small street; open 9 am to 5 pm Tuesday to Sunday (to 2 pm Saturday); $0.30. Its small collection includes a traditional farm and pig sty from Moişeni, a wine press from nearby Oraşu Nou, and a washing whirlpool and felting mill. Some people from the village use the water-powered whirlpool in the museum to wash their clothes.

There is also a small **Oaş History Museum** (Muzeul Ţării Oaşului) in the village, opposite Hotel Rebecca on Str Victoriei.

Four kilometres south of Negreşti-Oaş is **Vama**, traditionally a ceramics and pottery centre of which little evidence remains today. The village 'ceramika' store is now a 'magazin mixt' selling everything from second-hand coats to tins of vegetables. **Valea Măriei**, 2.5km west of Vama, is a small alpine resort offering accommodation.

Places to Stay & Eat

Oas Travel (☎ 851 266) at Str Victoriei 2, Apartment 3, in Negreşti-Oaş can arrange accommodation in *private homes* in some villages in the Satu Mare district.

The most idyllic accommodation is in Călineşti-Oaş. *Popas Turistic Lacu Albastru*, 1km south-west of Călineşti-Oaş opposite Lake Albastru, has small four-bed bungalows for $4 per person. It has communal showers and a small restaurant/cafe/bar.

More upmarket is the luxurious *Hotel Călineşti* (☎ 851 400), signposted on the right as you approach Lake Albastru from the south. It offers clean doubles for $14, breakfast not included.

Negreşti-Oaş' only hotel is the two-star *Hotel Oşanul* (☎ 851 162, Str Victoriei 89), with overpriced doubles/triples for $20/23, breakfast not included. It also has luxury apartments for $30.

Heading north from Negreşti-Oaş towards Săpânţa, you can pitch your tent at *Cabana Sâmbra Oilor*, just south of the Huta Pass.

In Valea Măriei is the modern *Cabana Pintar* (☎ 853 535). Double/triple rooms cost $11/16 and luxury apartments cost $18. The cabana has a restaurant and billiard bar. To reach the more attractive *Cabana Teilor* (☎ 851 329) and *Cabana Valea Măriei* (☎ 850 750), turn right along the forest track, immediately opposite Cabana Pintar. Cabana Teilor, at the end of the left fork, has a tennis court, excellent restaurant and singles/doubles for $10/18. Cabana Valea Măriei, at the end of the right fork, was closed for renovation at the time of writing. Accord Business & Travel in Satu Mare takes bookings for both cabanas.

Getting There & Away

There are buses daily except Sunday from Satu Mare to Negreşti Oas (1½ hours, 7 am and 3, 3.30 and 5.30 pm), from where they continue to Turţ. The return bus heads back to Satu Mare immediately.

BAIA MARE

☎ 062 • postcode 4800 • pop 149,000

Baia Mare ('big mine'), at the foot of the Gutâi Mountains, is the seat of Maramureş County. The town was first documented in 1329 and developed as a gold-mining town in the 14th and 15th centuries. In 1446 the town became the property of the Iancu de Hunedoara family. In 1469, under the rule of

Hungarian king Matthias Corvinus (Iancu de Hunedoara's son), the town was fortified.

Baia Mare gained notoriety during Ceauşescu's regime as home to the Romplumb and Phoenix metallurgic plants which released more than five billion cubic metres of residual gases into the atmosphere each year, smothering the town with a permanent sulphur-dioxide/metal powder smog. In the early 1990s, a new smoke stack was built in an attempt to alleviate air pollution.

The town was again thrown into the environmental hot seat, in early 2000, when a poisonous spill from the Aurul gold mine caused one of Europe's worst environmental disasters. On 30 January a tailings dam burst, causing cyanide-contaminated water to leak from the gold mine – part-owned by Australian Esmeralda Enterprises – contaminating the Someş and Tisa Rivers before spilling into the Danube and finally the Black Sea.

With six neighbouring countries affected, the water supply of 2.5 million people contaminated, fish stocks decimated and the rivers' ecosystems devastated, the full impact of the spill may not be known for another two decades. Drinking water remains unpotable and fish polluted. Despite protests from Greenpeace and ongoing compensation claims, the mine has since reopened.

Orientation

The train and bus stations, west of the centre on Str Gării, are a 15-minute walk from Piaţa Libertăţii, Baia Mare's central square. The Şasar River flows across the north of the town.

Maps The fold-up *Harta Municipiului Baia Mare* (1997) contains a detailed map of the city. It is sold for $0.90 at Hotel Mara. The *Baia Mare Ghid Turistic* (1997) map is larger and easier to follow. It costs $1.75 from Hotel Carpaţi.

Information

Tourist Offices Mara Holidays (☎ 226 656, ⓔ mara@sintec.ro), inside Hotel Mara at Blvd Unirii 11, arranges tours, sells maps, hires cars and is the local agent for Antrec; open 9 am to 5 pm weekdays.

BTT (☎ 432 635, fax 437 889) has an office at Blvd Traian 8; none of its staff speaks English.

Money You can change money at the Fortuna currency exchange opposite the Perla Centre on Str Progresului; open 8 am to 6 pm weekdays. The currency exchange inside the Tarom office at Blvd Bucureşti 5 is open 8 am to 5 pm Monday to Thursday, and 2 to 6 pm Friday.

The Banca Română Pentru Dezvoltare, next to the post office at Str Gheorghe Şincai, cashes travellers cheques, gives cash advances on Visa/MasterCard and has an ATM; open 8.30 am to 1 pm weekdays.

The Banca Agricolă, Blvd Unirii 16, and Banca Comercială Română, directly opposite at Blvd Unirii 15, offer the same services.

Post & Telephone The central post office and telephone office are on Gheorghe Şincai. The former is open 7 am to 8 pm weekdays and the latter is open the same hours daily.

Email & Internet Access Send emails or surf the net at the hip Java Web Internet Café, Blvd Unirii 6, open 24 hours. Prices per hour vary from $0.25 to $0.50 depending on what hour you're surfing.

Things to See

Despite the town's largely industrial suburbs, charming quarters in the old town have been retained. Transylvanian prince Iancu de Hunedoara (János Hunyadi in Hungarian), royal governor of Hungary between 1446 and 1453, lived in the now-crumbling, 15th-century house, **Casa Iancu de Hunedoara**, at Piaţa Libertăţii 18. In 1456 he successfully hammered the Turks on the banks of the Danube close to Belgrade. Hunedoara died of the plague in Belgrade that same year. His house today has temporary exhibitions arranged by the local history museum.

Hunedoara's life story and that of Baia Mare is told in the local **History Museum** (Muzeul de Istorie; ☎ 211 927), just off the north-eastern end of the square at Str

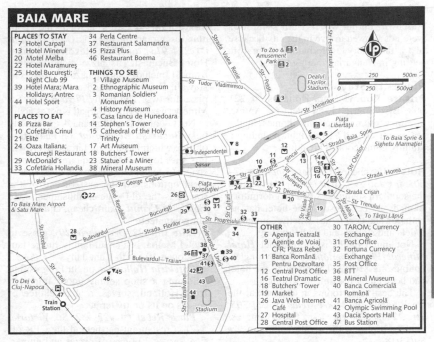

BAIA MARE

PLACES TO STAY
7 Hotel Carpaţi
13 Hotel Minerul
20 Motel Melba
22 Hotel Maramureş
25 Hotel Bucureşti;
   Night Club 99
39 Hotel Mara; Mara
   Holidays; Antrec
44 Hotel Sport

PLACES TO EAT
8 Pizza Bar
10 Cofetăria Crinul
21 Elite
24 Oaza Italiana;
   Bucureşti Restaurant
29 McDonald's
33 Cofetăria Hollandia

34 Perla Centre
37 Restaurant Salamandra
45 Pizza Plus
46 Restaurant Boema

THINGS TO SEE
1 Village Museum
2 Ethnographic Museum
3 Romanian Soldiers'
   Monument
4 History Museum
5 Casa Iancu de Hunedoara
14 Stephen's Tower
15 Cathedral of the Holy
   Trinity
17 Art Museum
18 Butchers' Tower
23 Statue of a Miner
38 Mineral Museum

OTHER
6 Agenţia Teatrală
9 Agenţie de Voiaj
   CFR; Plaza Rebel
11 Banca Română
   Pentru Dezvoltare
12 Central Post Office
16 Teatrul Dramatic
18 Butchers' Tower
19 Market
26 Java Web Internet
   Café
27 Hospital
28 Central Post Office

30 TAROM; Currency
   Exchange
31 Post Office
32 Fortuna Currency
   Exchange
35 Post Office
36 BTT
38 Mineral Museum
40 Banca Comercială
   Română
41 Banca Agricolă
42 Olympic Swimming Pool
43 Dacia Sports Hall
47 Bus Station

Monetăriei 1; open 9 am to 7 pm Tuesday to Friday and 10 am to 2 pm weekends.

Looming above the square is **Stephen's Tower** (Turnul Ştefan). The 14th-century Gothic-style tower was initially topped with a bell which was replaced by a mechanical clock in 1628. Behind the tower, on Str 1 Mai, is the **Cathedral of the Holy Trinity** (Catedrala Sfânta Treime), close to the local **Art Museum** (Muzeul de Artă; ☎ 213 964) at Str 1 Mai 8.

South from the museum on Str 22 Decembrie is the **central market**, around which lies the only remaining part of the 15th-century city walls – the **Butchers' Tower** where famous brigand Grigore Pintea Viteazul (see the later boxed text 'Romania's Robin Hood') was shot in 1703.

Heading north from Piaţa Libertăţii across the footbridge over the Şasar River, walk past the **Dealul Florilor Stadium** (Stadionul Dealul Florilor) where the Baia Mare football club plays. Open-air Masses are

often held on Sunday next to the WWI **Romanian Soldier's Monument** (Monumentul Ostaşilor Români) in the park.

North-west of the stadium is the **Ethnographic Museum** (Muzeul Etnografic; ☎ 212 845) in which all the traditional trades of the Maramureş region are represented.

An absolute must if you do not intend exploring Maramureş proper is the excellent **Village Museum** (Muzeul Satului), behind the Ethnographic Museum. Traditional wooden houses and churches, for which the region is famed, are exhibited; open 10 am to 5 pm daily, except Monday, between 15 May and 15 October ($0.30).

Baia Mare has a small **zoo** (☎ 276 998) adjoining an **amusement park** at Str Petőfi Sándor 28; open 10 am to 7 pm daily ($0.30).

The city's uninspiring **Mineral Museum** (Muzeul de Mineralogie; ☎ 437 651) is at Blvd Traian 8. Close by is the **Jewish Cemetery**. There is a monument here to the

Jews deported from Baia Mare to Auschwitz during WWII. Until 1848, Jews were not allowed to live in the city because of a 17th-century law forbidding them from settling in Hungarian mining towns.

Places to Stay
Private Rooms Mara Holidays (☎ 221 008) Blvd Unirii 11, an agent for Antrec, arranges rooms in private homes in the region for around $10 a night, including a yummy home-cooked breakfast.

Hotels The cheapest is *Hotel Sport* (☎ 224 001, fax 430 777, Blvd Unirii 14a), behind the southern stadium. A bed in a dormitory room is $3 per person. The hotel has no baths or showers – just smelly communal toilets and sinks – and no hot water.

Not much better is the derelict *Hotel Minerul (Piaţa Libertăţii 7)*. Shabby singles/doubles are $10/12. The phone to the hotel had been cut at the time of writing.

The best-value rooms in town are at the small family-run *Motel Melba* (☎ 211 705, Str 22 Decembrie 13). Clean singles/doubles/triples with private bathroom are $9/13/18.

Bang in the centre is *Hotel Bucureşti* (☎ 215 311, Str Culturii 4), overlooking Piaţa Revoluţiei. Singles with TV and a private bathroom are $16. Doubles – only available with shared bathrooms – without/with TV are $10/11. A luxury apartment with private bath and TV is $30. Adjoining the hotel is a noisy nightclub.

The most comfortable hotel in town is the three-star *Hotel Maramureş* (☎ 416 555, fax 416 555, Str Gheorghe Şincai 37). Singles/doubles with private bathroom, cable TV, hot water and balcony are $35/45. Larger and less atmospheric is *Hotel Mara* (☎ 226 660, fax 221 008, Blvd Unirii 11). Rooms with private bathrooms and TV are $40/49, including breakfast. The hotel has a restaurant, bar and conference hall.

Hotel Carpaţi (☎ 214 812, fax 215 461, Str Minerva 16) has pricey rooms at $55/70, including breakfast. A luxury apartment is $100.

Places to Eat
Restaurants & Cafes One of the most popular restaurants in town is *Oaza Italiana* (☎ 214 913), on Piaţa Revoluţiei behind Hotel Bucureşti. Its pizza menu, starting from $1, includes such amazing varieties as Hawaii, Deutschland and a 'you and me' pizza for two. The flashy *Pizza Bar* on Str Minerva next to Hotel Carpaţi is not as good.

Next door to Oaza Italiana is the equally busy *Bucureşti Restaurant*, on Piaţa Revoluţiei, which has a great terrace overlooking the fountains on square. It serves spaghetti, soups and salads as well as scanty meat options. At the eastern end of the square is the old state-establishment-style *Cofetăria Crinul* – dirt-cheap, and quality not guaranteed.

Elite (Str 22 Decembrie 20), close to Motel Melba, is a small family-run restaurant, open 10 am to 1 am daily.

Cofetăria Hollandia, on Str Progresului, adjoining a shop selling goods imported from Holland, serves a small choice of snacks on its pretty terrace.

Plaza Rebel (☎ 422 932, Str Victoriei 5–7), a restaurant-bar behind the CFR office, serves 30 types of pizzas and numerous hamburgers including the house special 'Hamburger Rebel' for $0.75, and has a vast cocktail list.

Towards the bus and train stations there are a couple of reasonable choices: *Restaurant Salamandra* (☎ 437 600), on Blvd Traian, is an excellent spot to try traditional dishes specific to the Maramureş region. Farther west is the similar *Restaurant Boema* (Blvd Traian 19), serving soups, salads and the like. Nearby is the popular *Pizza Plus* (☎ 434 385, Blvd Traian 13).

Fast Food The *Perla Centre*, on Str Progresului, sports a brightly lit, purple fast-food bar with 'point-and-order' service. Burgers and hot dogs cost around $1. Back on Blvd Unirii, on the corner of Blvd Bucureşti, is *McDonald's*.

Self-Catering The *central market* is beneath the Butchers' Tower on the corner of Str 22 Decembrie and Str Vasile Alecsandri.

Entertainment

Cinemas Baia Mare's two cinemas, the *Minerul (☎ 413 269, Piaţa Libertăţii 6)* and the *Dacia (☎ 414 265, Piaţa Revoluţiei 7)*, both screen films in their original languages with Romanian subtitles ($0.50).

Bars & Discos A popular place to hit the town is *Night Club '99 (Str Culturii 3)*, adjoining Hotel Bucureşti; open 6 pm to 4 am daily. Warning: some nights you'll be subjected to semi-naked women prancing around the stage.

Theatre Plays are performed in Romanian at the *Teatrul Dramatic (☎ 211 124, Str Crişan 4)*. Tickets can be bought in advance at the Agenţia Teatrală on the corner of Piaţa Libertăţii and Str Podul Viilor; open 9 am to noon and 4 to 6 pm daily, except Monday.

Getting There & Away

Air Tarom (☎ 216 465), Blvd Bucureşti 5, operates four flights weekly between Baia Mare and Bucharest; the office is open 8 am to 6 pm weekdays.

Train The train station (☎ 220 952) is 1km west of the centre at Str Gării 4. Advance tickets are sold at Agenţie de Voiaj CFR (☎ 421 613), Str Victoriei 5–7.

Trains from Baia Mare to Budapest (seven to eight hours) depart daily at 12.31 am and 9.39 pm.

Major train services include 10 trains daily to Satu Mare (one to 1¼ hours), two to Cluj-Napoca (5¼ hours), and one to Braşov (8½ hours) and Gheorgheni (5½ hours).

Bus The bus station (☎ 431 921) is next to the train station at Str Gării 2. The outlying villages are served by few buses from Baia Mare and your best bet is to head to Satu Mare or Sighetu Marmaţiei where buses are more frequent.

Daily bus services from Baia Mare include one daily to Satu Mare (59km), seven to Sighetu Marmaţiei (65km) stopping at Baia Sprie (10km), and two to Cluj-Napoca (152km) and Zalău (100km).

Getting Around

The airport (☎ 412 299, 433 394) is 9km west of the centre at Tăuţi Măgherăuş. Tarom runs a shuttle from its office, leaving town 1½ hours before flight departures. It also meets incoming flights.

AROUND BAIA MARE
Baia Sprie

Baia Sprie, 10km east of Baia Mare, is a small mining town first chronicled in 1329. The mine still operates today, mining approximately 156,000 tonnes of copper, lead and zinc ore annually.

A **roadside cross**, in memory of political prisoners who died in the mine during the communist purges of 1950–56, stands at the foot of the track which leads to the mine. During this period an estimated 180,000 people were interned in hard-labour camps such as those by the Danube–Black Sea canal, or in high-security prisons such as Piteşti, Gherla and Sighetu Marmaţiei. Between 1947 and 1964, some 200 to 300 political prisoners were committed to forced labour at the Baia Sprie mine, including Corneliu Coposu, secretary to National Peasant Party leader Iuliu Maniu who was himself imprisoned at Sighetu.

As you enter the centre of the village from the west, Baia Sprie mine is signposted 'Exploatarea Minieră' off Str Montana. The village church, bearing a traditional Maramureş tiled roof dating from 1793, is next to a monstrous new church in the centre. The church warden will happily unlock the new church for guests. A Chestnut Festival is held in the village each year.

Şurdeşti & Around

Approaching Şurdeşti from Baia Sprie, you pass through **Şişeşti** village, home to the Vasile Lucaciu Memorial Museum. Vasile Lucaciu (1835–1919), appointed parish priest in 1885, built a church for the village supposedly modelled on St Peter's in Rome. The church was ceremoniously named, and dedicated to, the Union of all Romanians (Unirii Tuturor Românilor).

The towering **church** at Şurdeşti, southwest of Baia Sprie, is one of the most magnificent in the Maramureş region and well worth the hike.

The tiny church's disproportionately giant church steeple is considered the tallest wooden structure in Europe – if not the world. The church was built in 1724 as a centre of worship for the Greco-Catholic faithful. It remains a Uniate church today. The entire interior of the church is original, down to the little boys' naughty etchings and names scratched in the church balcony especially reserved for them. The priest and his wife live in the house below the church; the priest's wife will gladly open the church for you. The church is signposted 'monument' from the centre of the village.

Two kilometres south of Şurdeşti is Plopiş is another fine church with a towering steeple. Ask for the key at the lone house nearby. Fourteen kilometres farther south is Lăschia. Its church dates from 1861 and has a bulbous steeple. Note the motifs carved on the outer walls, which are like those traditionally used in carpets.

The last wave of nomadic Tartar tribes from the Eurasian steppe settled in the mining town of Cavnic, 8km north of Şurdeşti, as late as 1717. A monument known as the Tartar stone stands in the centre of the small town, first documented in 1445. In 1952 and 1955, political prisoners were sent to the gold and silver mine here.

Heading north from Cavnic along the mountainous Neteda Pass (1040m) towards Sighetu Marmaţiei, you pass a small memorial plaque to those who died in the mines under the communist purges.

Baia Mare to Izvoare

North of Baia Mare a dirt road twists and turns through the remote villages of Firiza, Blidari and Valea Neagră, culminating 25km north of Baia Mare at Izvoare, where there are natural springs.

Viewing churches is not on the agenda here; wallowing in the mountainous rural countryside dotted with delightful wooden cottages and ramshackle farms is. Izvoare is dominated by pine forests and the rather ugly Statiunea Izvoare complex. The complex is closed between mid-June and mid-

September, when it is taken over by local schools as a summer holiday camp. The rest of the year it is open to travellers.

In winter a **ski lift** offers stunning aerial views of the fun **sculpture park** spread throughout the grounds of the Statiunea Izvoare complex.

This route is not served by public transport, and hitching is difficult as few vehicles pass by. A **hiking trail** (five to six hours, marked with red triangles) leads from Baia Mare to Izvoare; it starts some 3km north of Baia Mare along the Baia Mare–Izvoare road.

Places to Stay & Eat

Baia Sprie's only hotel, the upmarket *Giesswein Motel* (☎ 062-462 219) behind the Peco petrol station, charges $10/18 for comfortable singles/doubles.

Highly recommended is the *Mogoşa Chalet* (☎ 062-460 800, fax 462 771), which overlooks Lake Bodi at 731m. The chalet has single/double/triple/quad rooms with private bath and hot water costing $6.50 per person. Campers can pitch their tents by the lake. In summer you can hire boats and swim in the lake. In winter you can rent skis; the nearby chairlift and two ski lifts are open 9 am to 4 pm Tuesday to Sunday. Mogoşa Chalet is located 6km north-east of Baia Sprie. Follow the road to Sighetu Marmaţiei and turn right at the signpost for Mogoşa.

Less fancy is the *Complex Turistic Şuior* (☎ 062-460 842) about 1km farther along the same road from the Mogoşa Chalet. A bed in a basic two- or four-bed room with shared bathroom is $10. The complex has no running hot water, but it does have tennis courts, a ski lift, handball court, bar and restaurant.

From Cavnic, *Cabana Gutin Mina*, signposted 2.4km from the village, has seven rooms costing $7 per person a night.

In Firiza there is the clean and friendly *Motel Căprioara* (☎ 062-416 000, 437 676) which overlooks the lake. Doubles with shared bath are $9; its one triple room costs $10 and luxury apartments with private bath are $28.

ŢARA CHIOARULUI

The Ţara Chioarului region in the southwest part of Maramureş County takes in the area immediately south of Baia Mare. The numerous villages, most of which boast traditional wooden churches, form a convenient loop – ideal for a two-hour driving tour by private transport.

Things to See

Follow the main road south from Baia Mare to Cluj-Napoca for 14km to Satulung. Three kilometres south of Satulung, take the unmarked turning on the left opposite Cabana Stejarul to Finteuşu Mare and continue for 5km until you reach the village of **Posta**. At the top of the hill towers a small wooden church dating from 1675.

Şomcuţa Mare, 24km south of Baia Mare, is home to the annual Stejarul ('oak tree') festival held in July, which attracts bands and choirs from all over the region. The small **Vălenii Şomcuţei Cave** (Peştera de la Vălenii Şomcuţei), 4km away, is signposted from the centre of the village.

Nine kilometres south of Şomcuţa lies **Valea Chioarului**, the most southern village in Ţara Chioarului. Its delightful, tall church stands next to the bus stop in the centre of the village. Beside the church is a bust of Mihail Viteazul, erected by the village in 1994.

From Şomcuţa a minor road winds its way to **Remetea Chioarului**, 12km northeast. Its tiny church, dating from 1800, is the highlight of Ţara Chioarului. It stands majestically beside the village's extraordinarily ugly, seven-spired, modern church, built in 1996.

Culcea, some 5km north-west of here, has an unremarkable plastered church built in 1720 and extensively renovated in 1939. **Săcălaşeni**, 2km farther north, has a small church built in 1442, but sadly a modern church dominates the village.

From **Catalina**, just north, head west 2km to the predominantly Hungarian village of **Coltău** (Koltó in Hungarian). Hungary's most celebrated poet, Sándor Petőfi (1823–49), lived in the village in 1847, prior to leading the revolution against Habsburg domination of Hungary (1848–49). There is a small memorial house in the centre of Coltău where the poet spent a few months. In the garden stands the giant, 300-year-old cypress tree under which Petőfi sought inspiration.

Places to Stay & Eat

The rambling old *Motel Două Veveriţe*, 11km south of Baia Mare on the road to Cluj-Napoca, has an excellent terrace restaurant. At the time of writing, it was closed for renovation. The motel is 3km off the main road amid pine trees; the turn-off is signposted. Many campers pitch their tents for free next to the lake beside the main road, opposite the motel turn-off.

In Valea Chioarului, *Popasul Mesteacăn* (☎ 062-483 295) has double and four-bed wooden cabins for $10. Its large terrace restaurant and bar are also open 24 hours.

MARA VALLEY

The Mara Valley (Valea Mara) lies in the heart of Maramureş proper. It takes its name from the Mara River which runs south-west through the valley from Sighetu Marmaţiei to Baia Mare. Villages here are famed for their spectacular churches.

Giuleşti & Around

Heading south from Sighetu Marmaţiei, you pass through the tiny village of **Berbeşti**,

---

Roadside Tradition

At the northern end of the village of Berbeşti is a traditional *troiţă* ('crucifix'), a large, Renaissance-style cross, over 300 years old, carved with solar emblems, which stands by the roadside. Traditionally, travellers prayed by the cross to ensure a safe journey, crossing themselves as they passed in their horse-drawn carts. During the 16th and 17th centuries, a troiţă was planted by most roadsides, a tradition most evident today in rural areas. The belief that travelling is dangerous remains; even in cities it is common for passengers to cross themselves for protection as the bus or train pulls out of the station.

MARAMUREŞ

MARAMUREŞ

6km south of Vadu Izei (see Izei Valley, later). Continuing south, bear right after Fereşti to Giuleşti, the main village in the Mara Valley. It was to Giuleşti, in 1918, that the revolutionary poet Ilie Lazăr summoned delegates from all over Maramureş, prior to their signing Transylvania's Union agreement with Romania. Ilie Lazăr's house is preserved and open to tourists as a memorial museum. During the communist crackdown in the early 1950s, Ilie Lazăr was arrested and imprisoned at Sighet prison.

Delightfully untouched by the 20th century, Giuleşti is notable for its crumbling wooden cottages adorned with 'pot trees' in their front yards, on which a colourful array of pots and pans are put out to dry.

Traditional sheepskin waistcoats, and jackets, handwoven rugs, saddlebags and tablecloths are sold at house No 9 (the small house adorned with the most pots and pans), tucked in the first bend on the right as you enter Giuleşti from the north.

Sat-Şugatag & Around

Seven kilometres south of Giuleşti is Sat-Şugatag, home to a church dating from 1642. The church is famed for its fine, ornately carved wooden gate. Sat-Şugatag was first documented in 1360 as the property of Dragoş of Giuleşti.

Mănăstirea is 1km east of Sat Şugatag. The church here was built by monks in 1633. By 1787 just one monk and four servants remained, and during the reign of Austro-Hungarian king Joseph II the monastery was closed. The original monks' cells lie on the northern side of the church. Several 18th-century icons on glass and wood have been preserved, as have some of the frescoes on the outside western wall of the church.

Three kilometres south of Mănăstirea is the small spa resort of **Ocna Şugatag**, built on top of a hill in 1321. The village is named after the former salt mine in the village which was exploited until the 1950s (ocnă means 'salt mine'). Nine kilometres south-east of Ocna Şugatag is **Hoteni**, famed for its Tânjaua de pe Mara Festival (see the accompanying boxed text).

Tânjaua de pe Mara Festival

Hoteni's Tânjaua de pe Mara Festival is a traditional folk festival held yearly on 1–14 May to celebrate spring's first ploughing. Twelve to 16 young men, known as *flăcăi*, put on their finest clothes then decorate the village bulls with flowers, leaves, ribbons and bells. They then lead them to the village's chosen ploughman whose duty it is to plough the first field. Once completed, the flăcăi take the ploughman home from the fields on their shoulders, circling his house three times before taking him to the *dărasca* – the nearest river or well – where they ritually bathe him. This is believed to stimulate the earth's fertility and ensure a good crop. The partying continues for two weeks.

Hărniceşti

Four kilometres south of Ocna Şugatag is Hărniceşti, home to a marvellous Orthodox church dating from 1770. A footpath, signposted 'Spre Monument', leads from the primary school in the centre of the village to the hillside church.

Deseşti

This village is just a few kilometres southwest of Giuleşti on the road to Baia Mare. Its tiny Orthodox church, built in 1770, was struck by lightning in 1925, destroying much of the outer walls and the steeple. It has since been repaired (and fitted with a lightning conductor). Its interior paintings, by Radu Munteanu, date from 1780.

Close to the church is an oak tree, hundreds of years old and measuring 6m in diameter. It has been preserved as a monument to the extensive oak forest that once covered the area before people felled the trees to build their homes.

Mara

Just a couple of kilometres south of Deseşti, Mara is best known for its elaborate wooden fences. These porches – architecturally unique to the Maramureş region – were originally designed to protect the

Lipovani fisherman and reed huts near Uzlina, Danube Delta

Old and new religions, Oradea

Oradea's elegant architecture

Moisei's Festival of St Maria, eastern Maramureş

Vişeu de Sus' forestry steam train refills its tanks.

Religious procession gathers, Rozavlea

Wooden church in Bârsana's Orthodox Monastery

dwellers of the house from evil. Positioned a short distance away from the house on the roadside, the porch marked the boundary between the sacred space of the house and the untidy public space. The pillars of the gate are carved with solar images and the tree of life *(pomul vieţii)*, ensuring the house dwellers a long life.

In more recent times, the spiritual importance of the outside porch has been overridden by the increasing social status attached to it. In Vama, older porches dating from the 1770s are evident, but plenty of brashly decorated, modern gates have been built in the last 10 years. The tradition of carving the construction date, as well as the sculptor's name, into the gate still remains today.

Eastern Mara Valley
Heading south from Sighetu Marmaţiei, bear left at **Fereşti** along the dirt track leading to Maramureş' least accessible villages. From Baia Mare, you can approach this area through Cavnic, across the Neteda Pass.

Corneşti, the first village along this stretch, has a small 18th-century church with interior paintings by Hodor Toador.

Călineşti, 7km farther south, is where in 1862 archaeologists uncovered a cache of bracelets and ankle chains, believed to date from Roman times. Călineşti has two churches, known as Susani (*sus* meaning 'up') and Josani (*jos* meaning 'low'). Susani church (1683) is on the left side of the road as you enter the village from the north. But the 'lower' church, built 20 years previously, is more spectacular. To get to the church, turn right at the road for Bârsana and continue until you reach house No 385. A small path opposite this house twists and turns its way to the church; follow the upper path when you come to the fork.

From Călineşti a mud track leads to **Sârbi**, inhabited since 1402. Its two churches are built from oak, as are most churches in Maramureş. The Susani church dates from 1667 with interior paintings by Al Ponehachile. Sârbi's Josani church dates from 1665.

Budeşti, 4km south of Sârbi, is one of the most beautiful villages in Maramureş. Its

Romania's Robin Hood

Grigore Pintea Viteazul ('the brave') is Romania's most famous *haiduc* (brigand). The unscrupulous outlaw who prowled the country's highways in the 17th century was a nobleman by birth who accumulated his wealth by robbing the poor. But he fell in love with a simple peasant woman, and following her tragic death he was so broken-hearted he gave away all his riches, and henceforth stole only from the rich to give to the poor.

In 1701 Austrian king Leopold I issued a reward for the capture of Pintea, dead or alive. But the cunning outlaw continued to slip through the authorities' fingers, until 1703 when he was shot in Baia Mare by nobles who, on the advice of a local witch, used a gold coin cut in quarters as bullets.

Romania's Robin Hood died instantly, leaving nothing but his undershirt, now housed in a simple Maramureş church in Budeşti, as testimony to his wilful ways.

Josani church, built in 1643, features four small turrets surrounding the main steeple. Inside the church is a small collection of icons on glass and wood, dating from 1766. Its prize piece, however, is the 18th-century painting of the *Last Judgment*, preserved in its entirety. The church also houses the undershirt of its most famous 17th-century inhabitant, Grigore Pintea Viteazul (see the boxed text 'Romania's Robin Hood'), allegedly purchased from the local Romanian community in Budapest for 1000 forint.

Places to Stay & Eat
Ocna Şugatag is the ideal base for exploring the Mara Valley. The large *Hotel Ocna Şugatag* (☎ 062-374 034), on the right as you enter the village from the north, has double rooms with shared bath (no hot water) for $10.

Better value are the modern, beautifully carved wooden bungalows in the centre of Ocna Şugatag at *Camping Trust Miron*. A four-bed bungalow is $6.50. The camping ground also has a restaurant and summer garden. The same company also runs the modern *Trust Miron Restaurant & Motel* (☎ 062-436 015), signposted some 200m farther along the road. It has a swimming pool, sauna, restaurant and six comfortable doubles with private bath for $10.

Agro-Tur-Art arranges accommodation in private homes in the area for around $12 a night, including a breakfast of eggs, jam, and milk straight from the cow; see under Vadu Izei, later.

SIGHETU MARMAŢIEI
☎ 062 • postcode 4925

Sighetu Marmaţiei is the northernmost town in Romania, lying on the confluence of the Tisa, Iza and Ronişoara Rivers. Its name is derived from the Thracian and Dacian word *seget*, meaning 'fortress'.

Sighet (as it is known locally), a couple of kilometres from the Ukrainian border, is famed for its vibrant winter festival, and its colourful peasant costumes. Its dusty streets bustle with markets, tucked beneath church domes of all denominations.

Sighetu Marmaţiei's former maximum-security prison is now open as a museum. Although little evidence remains today of the true horror it housed, it is a definite highlight of any visit to northern Romania.

Information
Tourist Offices The official tourist office (☎ 312 815, fax 315 484), Piaţa Libertăţii 21, runs a currency exchange and can rent you a car (price negotiable); open 8 am to 4 pm weekdays, and 9 am to 1 pm Saturday. For information about the area, however, the office is pretty useless.

Your best bet is to head 6km south to Vadu Izei to the excellent Agro-Tur-Art office, run by a young, dynamic and extremely knowledgeable team.

Post & Telephone The post and telephone office is opposite the Maramureş Museum on Str Ioan Mihaly de Apşa.

Email & Internet Access You can access the Internet from the privately run Sighetu Business Centre (☎/fax 313 887, 📧 lazin@

sintec.ro) in an apartment block at Str Independenţei, Block 2, Stairway A, Apt 23. It costs $2 to send an email or an expensive $10 per hour for online access. The centre opens 7 am to 7 pm weekdays, and 8 am to 2 pm weekends.

Money There is a currency exchange inside the tourist office which is generally besieged by black-market moneychangers. Ignore them. The Banca Comercială Română, Str Iuliu Maniu, offers a better exchange rate, gives cash advances on Visa and has an ATM; it's open 8.30 am to 2.30 pm weekdays.

Piaţa Libertăţii & Around
Sighet, first documented in 1328, was a strong cultural and political centre, being the birthplace of the Association for the Romanian Peoples' Culture, founded in 1863. On Piaţa Libertăţii stands the **Hungarian Reformed Church**, built during the 15th century. Close by is the 16th-century **Roman Catholic Church**.

Off the square at Str Bessarabia 10 is Sighet's only remaining **synagogue**. Before WWII there were eight synagogues serving a large Jewish community which made up 40% of the town's population. Jews first settled in Sighet in the 17th century.

Next door is the **Jewish Community Centre** (☎ 311 652), open 10 am to 4 pm Sunday to Friday, where you can purchase tickets to visit the **Jewish Cemetery**, a couple of blocks south of the centre on Str Szilagyi Istvan (follow Str Eminescu south then turn left into Str Szilagyi Istvan). The cemetery isn't hard to find – just look for the 6m-high stone wall. The cemetery's caretaker, who only speaks Romanian, lives opposite at No 47.

Elie Wiesel, the Jewish writer and 1986 Nobel peace prizewinner who coined the term 'Holocaust', was born in (and later deported from) Sighet. **Elie Wiesel's house** is on the corner of Str Dragos Vodă and Str Tudor Vladimirescu. His autobiography, *La Nuit* (The Night), was the first account ever published of the horrors of the Nazi concentration camps in WWII.

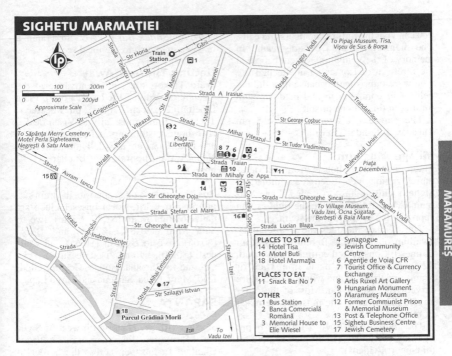

SIGHETU MARMAŢIEI

PLACES TO STAY	4 Synagogue
14 Hotel Tisa	5 Jewish Community
16 Motel Buti	Centre
18 Hotel Marmaţia	6 Agenţie de Voiaj CFR
	7 Tourist Office & Currency
PLACES TO EAT	Exchange
11 Snack Bar No 7	8 Artis Ruxel Art Gallery
	9 Hungarian Monument
OTHER	10 Maramureş Museum
1 Bus Station	12 Former Communist Prison
2 Banca Comercială	& Memorial Museum
Română	13 Post & Telephone Office
3 Memorial House to	15 Sighetu Business Centre
Elie Wiesel	17 Jewish Cemetery

On Str Gheorghe Doja is a **monument** to the victims of the Holocaust.

Off Piaţa Libertăţii at Str Bogdan Vodă 1 is the **Maramureş Museum**, an ethnographic museum in which colourful folk costumes, rugs and carnival masks are displayed; open 9 am to 5 pm Tuesday to Sunday ($0.25).

For contemporary handmade crafts visit the small **Artis Ruxel** art gallery at Piaţa Libertăţii 21. (Serious art lovers should also visit the private collection displayed in the **Pipaş Museum**, 2km east of Sighet in Tisa village.)

Sighet Prison

In May 1947 the communist regime embarked on a reign of terror during which thousands of Romanians were imprisoned, tortured, killed or deported. While many leading prewar figures were sent to hard-labour camps, the regime's most feared intellectual opponents were interned in Sighet's maximum-security prison. Between 1948 and 1952, about 180 members of Romania's academic and government elite were imprisoned here.

Today four white marble plaques covering the barred windows of the prison list the 51 prisoners who died in the Sighet cells, notably the academic and head of the National Liberal Party (PNL), Constantin Brătianu; historian and leading member of the PNL, Gheorghe Brătianu; governor of the National Bank, Constantin Tătăranu; and Iuliu Maniu, president of the National Peasants' Party (PNŢ). Eight more plaques, reading like a 'Who's Who' of the former republic, list those who survived the torture.

The prison, housed in the old courthouse on Str Corneliu Coposu, was closed in 1974. In 1989 it re-opened as a private **Museum of Arrested Thoughts & International Study Centre of Totalitarianism** (Muzeu al Gândirii Arestate şi Centru Internaţional de Studii asupra Totalitarismului;

☎ 314 224). Photographs are displayed and you can visit the torture chambers and cells. The memorial plaque outside reads 'In memory of the young, intelligent people at the forefront of Romanian intellectual life who were imprisoned because they did not believe in communism and died, through torture, in this odious prison'.

The museum is open 10 am to 5 pm Tuesday to Sunday (free).

Village Museum

Traditional peasant houses from the Maramureş region have been reassembled in Sighet's outstanding open-air Village Museum (Muzeul Satului), on the right as you approach the town from the south.

The display includes the 17th-century dwelling of the noble Berciu family from Călineşti. Constructed entirely from wood, the main structure is made from wide fir beams and the door and window frames are carved from ash wood. Most of the other houses displayed in the museum are made from oak.

The museum is open 10 am to 6 pm Tuesday to Sunday ($0.50 plus $1.50/2.50 for cameras/videos).

Places to Stay & Eat

Sighet's one central hotel, *Hotel Tisa* (☎ *312 645, Piaţa Libertăţii 8*), has 43 doubles, most recently renovated. One with private bathroom, TV and telephone costs $22, including breakfast.

Excellent value is *Motel Buţi* (☎/*fax 311 035*), on Str Ştefan cel Mare. Its rooms are small but spotlessly clean. Singles/doubles with shared shower cost $11/20, including breakfast.

A short walk from the centre, overlooking Eminescu Park, is *Hotel Marmaţia* (☎ *512 241, 511 540, fax 515 484, Str Mihai Eminescu 54*). It was closed for renovation at the time of writing.

The upmarket, three-star *Motel Perla Sigheteama* (☎ *310 613, fax 310 268, Str Avram Iancu 65a*), just out of town on the road to Săpânţa, has doubles with private bath, TV and telephone for $25, including breakfast.

Cheap snacks and light meals are served at the fun *Snack Bar No 7* on Str Traian, a real eye-opener into the local scene.

Getting There & Away

Train Tickets are sold in advance at the Agenţie de Voiaj CFR (☎ 312 666), Piaţa Libertăţii 25; open 7 am to 2 pm weekdays. There are four trains daily to Vişeu de Jos (two hours), stopping at Petrova, Bocicoi and Tisa. There are also daily trains to Cluj-Napoca (six hours) and Bucharest (12 hours).

Bus The bus station is opposite the train station on Str Gării. Local buses include six daily to Baia Mare ($1.40, 65km), two to Satu Mare ($1.85, 122km) and Borşa ($0.65), five to Budeşti ($0.65) and Călineşti ($0.60), two to Vişeu de Sus ($1.15), and one to Bârsana, Botiza, Coştiui, Glod, Ieud, Mara, Onca, Săpânţa and Târgu Lăpuş.

SĂPÂNŢA
☎ 062

Săpânţa village, 12km north-west of Sighetu Marmaţiei, lies just 4km south of Ukraine. Locals pop across the border to shop but this border crossing is not open to foreigners.

The history of this strongly Orthodox village is brilliantly illustrated in the church cemetery, unique for the colourfully painted wooden crosses that adorn the tombstones. Săpânţa's crosses, shown in art exhibitions in London and Paris, attract coachloads of tourists every year. Yet this peasant village remains untouched by its fame. Villagers sit outside their cottages, fenceposts strung with colourful rugs and handwoven bags for sale.

Merry Cemetery

Săpânţa's Merry Cemetery (Cimitirul Vesel) was the creation of Ioan Stan Pătraş, a simple wood sculptor who, in 1935, started carving crosses to mark graves in the church cemetery. He painted each cross in blue – the traditional colour of hope and freedom. On top of each he inscribed a witty epitaph to the deceased.

Prior to his death in 1977, Pătraş carved and painted his own cross, complete with a portrait of himself and a lengthy epitaph in which he speaks of the 'cross' he bore all his life, working to support his family since his father's death when he was 14 years old. Pătraş' grave is directly opposite the main entrance to the church.

Every cross tells a different story, and the painted pictures and inscriptions illustrate a wealth of traditional occupations. Shepherds tend their sheep, mothers cook for their families, barbers cut hair, and weavers bend over looms. Newer crosses in the cemetery are distinguished by illustrations of car accidents.

Since Pătraş' death, Dumitru Pop, his apprentice, has carried on the tradition. He lives and works in Pătraş' former house and studio, using the same traditional methods. He makes about 10 crosses each year, depending on the mortality rate in the village.

The house where Pop lives and works is also a **museum** ($0.25). In one small room, various pictures carved in wood and painted by Pătraş are displayed. These include portraits of members of the Executive Committee of the Communist Party, and a portrait of Nicolae and Elena Ceauşescu carved in honour of Ceauşescu's visit to Săpânţa in 1974.

Places to Stay

Camping Poieni, 3km south of Săpânţa, has two-bed wooden cabins for $2.50 per person a night, including breakfast. Tents can also be pitched. The camping ground is only open during summer.

IZEI VALLEY

The Izei Valley (Valea Izei) follows the Iza River eastward from Sighetu Marmaţiei to Moisei. Unlike other rural areas in Maramureş, tourism is gradually developing in this region, providing tourists with ample opportunity to indulge in some traditional cuisine, or try their hand at wood carving, wool weaving and glass painting.

In mid-July, Vadu Izei, together with the neighbouring villages of Botiza and Ieud, hosts the Maramuzical Festival, a lively four-day international folk music festival. Guests stay in local homes or in tents.

Vadu Izei

Vadu Izei is at the confluence of the Iza and Mara Rivers, 6km south of Sighetu Marmaţiei. Its museum is in the oldest house in the village (1750). If you visit a private home in this region, you'll quickly realise that little has changed since the 18th century.

Vadu Izei has been supported since the early 1990s by the Belgian charity Opération Villages Roumains, which originally started out as an international pressure group against Ceauşescu's systemisation program. More recently, the village gained financial backing from the EU's Phare program to develop infrastructure.

The highly efficient village tourism society, Fundaţia OVR Agro-Tur-Art (☎/fax 062-330 171, ℮ OVRAgro.TurArt@mail .alphanet.ro), sells maps and guides of the region and can also arrange a French- or English-speaking guide for $10 a day. It also sells local crafts. Its office is house No 161 at the northern end of the village. If it's closed, contact Denisa Covrig (☎ 062-330 076) at house No 58 (English- and French-speaking).

Agro-Tur-Art also arranges guided tours of Maramureş' wooden churches; picnics in the countryside; wood-carving, icon-painting and wool-weaving workshops; traditional folk evenings; and fishing trips.

Places to Stay & Eat Agro-Tur-Art arranges accommodation in some 20 *private homes* which offer bed and breakfast for $12 a night (half/full board is $15/17). Bookings can be made either through the Agro-Tur-Art office (see the previous paragraph) or directly at the homes involved; some homes are clearly signposted. The foundation also operates a 40-seat *restaurant* serving traditional Romanian meals.

Bârsana

Continue for 12km through the village of Onceşti to Bârsana (formerly spelt Bîrsana). Dating from 1326, the village acquired its first church in 1720, the interior paintings of which were done by local artists Hodor Toador and Ion Plohod.

The Orthodox **Bârsana Monastery** (Mănăstirea Bârsana) is a popular pilgrimage spot in Maramureş. It was the last Orthodox monastery built in the region before Serafim Petrovai – head of the Orthodox Church in Maramureş – suddenly converted to Greco-Catholicism in 1711.

Rozavlea

Continue south through Stâmtura to Rozavlea, first documented under the name of Gorzohaza in 1374. Its fine church, dedicated to the archangels Michael and Gabriel, was constructed between 1717 and 1720 in another village then erected in Rozavlea on the site of an ancient church destroyed by the Tartars.

Botiza

From Rozavlea continue south for 3km to Şieu, then take the turn-off right for Botiza. Botiza's old church, built in 1694, is overshadowed by the giant new church constructed in 1974 to serve the 500 or so devout Orthodox families.

The Sunday service (9 am) is the major event of the week in Botiza. The entire village flocks to the church to partake in the religious activities which continue well into the afternoon.

In the church calendar, however, Orthodox Easter witnesses the most important feast of the year. In the pitch-black darkness of Easter Sunday morning, villagers file through the village to the church, each bearing a lit candle which burns until dawn breaks.

Places to Stay & Eat Villagers in Botiza, with the help of Opération Villages Roumains, have formed their own agro-tourism scheme. Half/full board in a local home is $15/17 a night. Bookings can be made through the local representative, *George Iurca* (☎ *062-334 233*) at No 742.

He also arranges French- or English-speaking guides for $10 a day, hires out mountain bikes for $5 a day and organises fishing trips.

Poienile Izei

From Botiza a track leads west to Poienile Izei, home to the most dramatic **frescoes** of hell you are ever likely to encounter. The church, with its thatched roof, was built in 1604. Its interior frescoes, dating from 1783, depict hell, symbolised by a ferocious bird waiting to swallow up sinners. Aboriginal-style paintings depict the various torments inflicted by the devil on sinners who fail to obey the extensive set of rules represented in the frescoes. To visit, ask for the key at the priest's house – a large wooden house in the centre of the village with an ornately carved terrace. Four kilometres farther north along the same dirt track is the village of **Glod**, the birthplace of the popular Maramureş folk-singing duo, the Petreuş brothers.

Places to Stay For a bed for the night ask for the home of *Ion Petreuş* (not a band member) who heads the local agro-tourism group. Alternatively, approach the agro-tourism group in Botiza, staffed by French speakers who have details of the Poienile Izei scheme.

Ieud

The oldest wooden church in Maramureş (dating from 1364) is in Ieud, 6km off the road south from Şieu. Century-old customs are still firmly intact in this fervently Orthodox village. Abortion is forbidden and divorce is rare. Between 1787 when the first marriage was registered and 1980, there were no divorces in the village.

Ieud was first documented in 1365 but evidence suggests the village was inhabited as early as the 11th century by Balc, Dragoş Vodă's grandson and later prince of Moldavia. In 1364 Ieud's fabulous Orthodox 'Church on the Hill' (Biserica de Lemn din Deal) was built on the castle ruins. Made from fir wood, it housed the first document known to be written in Romanian (1391–92), in which the catechism and church laws pertaining to Ieud were coded. The *Zbornicul de la Ieud* is now in the National Museum in Bucharest. The church is generally locked but you can get the key from the porter's house, distinguishable by a simple wooden gate opposite the *textile incălţă-minte* in the centre of the village.

Ieud's second church (Biserica de Lemn din Şes), today Greco-Catholic in denomination, was built in 1717. The church is unique to the region as it has no porch. The church, at the southern end of the village, houses one of the largest collections of icons on glass found in Maramureş.

Places to Stay Opération Villages Roumains runs a small agro-tourism scheme in Ieud. You can make advance bookings through the tourist office in Vadu Izei (see earlier) or go straight to the local representative, *Vasile Risco* (☎ 062-336 100), who lives at house No 665. A bed for the night starts at $12, including breakfast.

Bogdan Vodă

Just to the south, the former village of Cuhea was renamed Bogdan Vodă in 1968 in honour of the Moldavian prince (r. 1359–65) from Maramureş who marched south-east from Cuhea to found the state of Moldavia in 1359. Some of the interior paintings in the village church, built in 1718, draw upon the traditional method of painting on linen, while others are painted directly on wood.

The church, dedicated to St Nicholas, is on the left as you enter the village from the north.

Dragomireştx

Four kilometres south of Bogdan Vodă lies the village of Dragomireşti, whose church (1722), in fine Maramureş fashion, was uprooted in 1936 and moved to the Village Museum in Bucharest.

The villagers have since built a new wooden church, on the same site, immediately on the left as you enter the village.

A further 4km east is **Săliştea de Sus**, first documented under the name Keethzeleste in 1365. It has two old churches, dating from 1680 and 1722, along with two new multispired, concrete churches.

Places to Stay At *Cabana Popasul Izei*, 2km east of Săliştea de Sus, there are 14

rooms and a camping area. A bed in the main building is $8 a night. Rooms have a shared bathroom and there is no hot running water.

VIŞEU & VASER VALLEYS

The Vişeu Valley (Valea Vişeu), which tracks the Vişeu River on its journey south, is considered among the most picturesque in Maramureş. A railway line links this stretch, from Rona de Jos in the north to Borşa in the south, making it more accessible for travellers without private transport.

The twin villages of **Rona de Jos** and **Rona de Sus**, 19km south-east of Sighetu Marmaţiei, lie just a couple of kilometres apart. Both boast churches, dating from 1793 and 1685 respectively. Continue south through the unremarkable **Petrova** and **Leordina**, and you eventually come to the spectacular logging village of Vişeu de Sus.

Vişeu de Sus

Vişeu de Sus is the main gateway to the Vaser Valley through which the Vaser River flows. First chronicled in 1363, the town has always had a strong logging tradition.

Since the 1940s, following the construction of a **narrow-gauge railway** from Vişeu de Sus into the Vaser Valley, wood was brought down the mountain by steam train. Today, however, most of the 4000 cubic metres of fir wood *(brad)* felled each month by the Vişeu de Sus logging plant is lumbered down the mountain by diesel locomotives instead. Each day at 6 am, a team of burly men is transported 43km up the valley to the logging camp in the forests at **Comanu**, close to the Ukrainian border. The felled wood is carted down the mountains by animals, then loaded onto the train.

Special **steam train tours** are possible but these are costly and need to be arranged well in advance. Prices range from $600 to $700 per person for groups of 30 to 70 people. The Biroul de Turism (☎ 062-352 285, ⓔ proviseu@mail.alphanet.ro), Str Libertaţii 1, arranges tours. Its Web site is at www.viseu.mmnet.ro.

It is still possible to ride with the lumberjacks along the forestry line. The forestry train (diesel or steam) departs from the

MARAMUREŞ

depot at Gara CFR Vişeu on weekdays at 6 am and returns with its load at around 9 pm. It stops at Făina, 32km north of Vişeu de Sus; Halta Valea Babii, 6km farther along the line; and Comanu.

Tickets costing $0.50/0.75 to Făina/Comanu or Valea Babii are sold, an hour before departure, from the ticket office next to the bright-green building at the Station CFR Fabrica, some 200m down the tracks from Gara CFR Vişeu. Photo passes valid for one week are also sold here for $10.

To get to the wood factory (*fabrica de lemn*) and train station (☎ 052-353 533), turn left opposite Hotel Brad on the corner of Str 22 Decembrie and Str Iuliu Maniu and continue along this stone road for 2km. The wood factory and train station are on your left.

Places to Stay Vişeu de Sus' only hotel, *Hotel Brad* (☎ 062-352 999), offers simple singles/doubles for $14/25. The Biroul de Turism also arranges accommodation and there are basic cabanas where you can spend the night in Făina and Valea Babii.

Moisei

Moisei lies 9km south-east of Vişeu de Sus, at the foot of the Rodna Massif. Known for its traditional crafts and customs, Moisei gained fame in 1944 when retreating Hungarian (Horthyst) troops gunned down 31 people before setting fire to the entire village.

In 1944, following the news that the front was approaching Moisei, villagers started to flee, including those forced-labour detachments stationed in the village. Occupying Hungarian forces organised a manhunt to track down the deserters. Thirty-one were captured and detained in a small camp in Vişeu de Sus without food or water for three weeks. On 14 October 1944, Hungarian troops brought the prisoners to a house in Moisei, locked them inside, then shot them through the windows. Before abandoning the village, the troops set it on fire, leaving all 125 remaining families homeless.

Only one house in Moisei survived the blaze; the one in which the prisoners were shot. Today it houses a small **museum** (Expoziţia Documentar – Istorică Martirii de la Moisei 14 Octombrie 1944), in tribute to those who died in the massacre. Photographs of the 29 who died as well as the two who survived the bloodbath adorn its walls ($0.40).

Opposite, on a hillock above the road and railway line, is a circular **monument** to the victims. The 12 upright columns symbolise the sun and light. Each column is decorated with a traditional carnival mask, except for two decorated with human faces based on the features of the two survivors.

The museum and monument are at the easternmost end of the village. If the museum is locked ask for the key at the pink house next door.

Borşa

Ore has been mined at Borşa, 12km east of Moisei, since the mid-14th century. The area was colonised in 1777 by German miners from Slovakia; eight years later, Bavarian-Austrian miners moved to Baia Borşa, 2km north-east of the town, to mine copper, lead and silver.

The **Complex Turistic Borşa**, a small ski resort and tourist complex 10km east of Borşa town proper, is a main entranceway to the **Rodna Mountains**, part of which forms the Pietrosul Rodnei Nature Reservation (5900 hectares). For information on the hiking trails leading into the massif, talk to the staff at the two-star *Hotel Cerbal* (☎ 062-344 199), behind Hotel Ştibina. Single/double/triple rooms here cost $16/20/27, including breakfast.

In winter, you can ski down the 2030m-long ski run in the complex. The ski lift (☎ 062-343 703, 344 442), at Str Brădet 10, is open 7 am to 6 pm daily; ski hire is not available.

PRISLOP PASS

Famed for its remoteness, the Prislop Pass is the main route from Maramureş into Moldavia. Hikers can trek east from Borşa across the pass. From Moldavia you can head north-east to Câmpulung Moldovenesc and on to the monasteries of southern Bucovina; or south to the natural mineral waters of Vatra Dornei and through to the fantastic Bicaz Lake (see the Moldavia chapter).

At 1416m a roadside monument marks the site of the last Tartar invasion prior to their final flight from the region in 1717. Nearby is the Hanul Prislop, site of the Hora de la Prislop, the major Maramureş festival, held yearly on the second Sunday in August. The festival has its origins in a *nedeie*, a traditional sheep market. The hora dancers stamp their feet, swing their upper body, and clap vigorously to the rhythm of a *ţâpurituri*, a chanted rhyme drummed out by three musicians on a traditional *zongora* (a type of viola), a *cetera* (shrill violin) and a *doba* (bongo made from fir or maple wood, covered with goat or sheep hide).

Moldavia

With its forest-clad hills and tranquil valleys, Moldavia rivals mighty Transylvania when it comes to rich folklore, natural beauty and turbulent history. Prince Bogdan won Moldavian independence from Hungary in 1359, after which the central part of the medieval principality, tucked away in the Carpathian foothills, became known as Bucovina ('beech wood'),

Only the southern part of Bucovina belongs to Romania today. It is famed for its fantastic medieval painted monasteries and attracts lots of tour groups.

History

Moldavia was the second medieval Romanian principality to secure independence from the Hungarians, providing refuge during the 18th century for thousands who were persecuted in Hungarian-ruled Transylvania.

In 1359, Maramureş prince Bogdan of Cuhea, after years of conflict with the Hungarians, moved his centre of resistance to this region east of the Carpathians. A bloody battle against Hungarian forces in 1364–65 further secured Moldavian autonomy.

From Suceava, Ştefan cel Mare (Stephen the Great), called the 'Athlete of Christ' by Pope Pius VI, led the resistance against the Turks from 1457 to 1504. This prince and his son, Petru Rareş, erected fortified monasteries and churches throughout Bucovina. Many have miraculously survived centuries of war and weather. Only with the defeat of Petru Rareş by the Turks in 1538 did Moldavia's golden age wane. Moldavia regained a measure of its former glory after it was united with the principality of Wallachia by Prince Alexandru Ioan Cuza in 1859 – when the modern Romanian state was born, with Iaşi as its capital.

Medieval Moldavia was much larger than the portion incorporated into Romania in 1859. Bessarabia, the area east of the Prut River, was conquered and claimed by Russia in 1812. Despite being recovered by Romania from 1918 to 1940 and again between

Highlights

- Trail the homes and meeting places of Romania's greatest literary heroes in Iaşi
- Hike through the Bicaz Gorges; beware the 'neck of hell'
- Watch Nicolae Grigorescu's eyes watching you at Agapia Monastery
- Marvel at the *Last Judgment* fresco at Voroneţ Monastery, famed for its vibrant blue
- See how salt miners live and work in Cacica

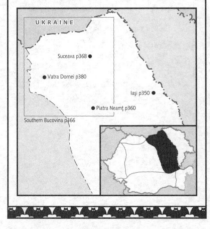

1941 and 1944, Bessarabia is now split between Ukraine and the republic of Moldova.

Confusingly, many Romanians refer to Moldavia as Moldova (the Slavic form of Moldavia), a legacy of the Stalinist era. They always refer to Moldova as the republic of Moldova.

IAŞI

☎ 032 • postcode 6600 • pop 347,000

Iaşi ('yash'), the capital of Moldavia from 1565, is a university city steeped in history. From 1859, Iaşi served as the national capital until it was replaced by Bucharest in

MOLDAVIA

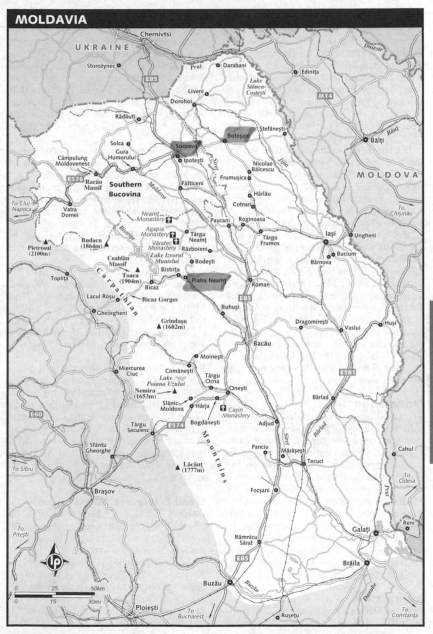

MOLDAVIA

1862. This illustrious history accounts for the city's great monasteries, bust-lined streets and parks, churches and museums. During WWI the seat of the Romanian government was briefly moved back to Iaşi. King Ferdinand and Queen Marie also sought refuge here during the war. During this period Iaşi's notorious history of anti-Semitism took root with the birth of the League of National Christian Defence – the predecessor of the fascist Iron Guard.

Iaşi has a great cultural tradition: the linden tree under which poet Mihai Eminescu meditated, the memorial houses of the city's most prolific writers, and the wine cellars of the 19th-century Junimea literary society of which Eminescu, Creangă and Caragiale were members, remain powerful reminders of this city's literary past. Romania's first university was founded here in 1860.

Modern Iaşi is Romania's third-largest city and its streets bustle with student life, restaurants, bars and hot night spots. Each year the university hosts the National Mihai Eminescu Symposium. If you are coming to or from the republic of Moldova, Iaşi is an ideal place to break your journey en route to the monasteries of southern Bucovina or south to Galaţi and the Black Sea coast.

You will need at least two full days to see the main sights.

Orientation

To reach Piaţa Unirii from the train station, walk north-east along Str Gării two blocks, then turn right onto Str Arcu. From Piaţa Unirii, Blvd Ştefan cel Mare şi Sfânt runs south-east past the Moldavian Metropolitan Cathedral to the Palace of Culture.

Maps *Hartă Municipliului Iaşi* (Info-Turism, 1998) is the best city map. It lists restaurants, museums and theatres giving phone numbers and addresses. It is sold for $1.50 from most bookshops. Also good is the 1:13,000 *Iaşi* city map (Amco Press) available from bookshops for $1.20.

Information

Tourist Offices Iaşi has no official tourist office but the tourism department

(☎ 135 060) at Iaşi County Council plans to open an Info-Turism centre. In the meantime, visitors are welcome to call into the department's office, inside the Civic Centre at Blvd Ştefan cel Mare şi Sfânt 69; open 9.30 am to 4 pm weekdays.

The Automobil Clubul Român (ACR; ☎ 112 345), two blocks from the train station at Str Gării 13–15, assists motorists and sells a small selection of road maps of the region.

Money The IDM exchange inside Restaurant Select on Str Cuza Vodă gives cash advances on Visa/MasterCard and cashes travellers cheques. It also has another outlet at Blvd Independenţei 6. Both are open 8 am to 8 pm weekdays, and 9 am to 1 pm Saturday.

There's a 24-hour currency exchange inside the Scala Restaurant complex (see Entertainment).

Banca Comercială Română, at Blvd Ştefan cel Mare şi Sfânt 6, cashes travellers cheques, gives cash advances on Visa/MasterCard and has an ATM; open 8.30 am to 12.30 pm weekdays. BCIT, at Blvd Ştefan cel Mare şi Sfânt 12, offers identical services and is open 8.30 am to 1.30 pm weekdays.

Post & Telephone The main post office, close to Hotel Continental on Str Cuza Vodă, was closed at time of writing for renovation. But another post office at Str Costache Negri, opposite the Civic Centre, is open 7 am to 8 pm weekdays, and 8 am to noon Saturday. Phonecards are sold at the telephone centre, at Str Alexandru Lăpuşneanu; open 8 am to 8 pm weekdays, and 8 am to 3 pm Saturday.

Email & Internet Access For email and Internet access, DNT Iaşi (☎ 252 936, fax 252 933, e info@dntis.ro), a computer and communications centre set up by the Open Society Foundation (☎ 252 920, fax 252 926, e office@sorosis.ro), is at Str Moara de Foc 35, 7th floor, to the west of the centre. It costs $1 for one hour online.

Travel Agencies Prospect Meridan (☎/fax 211 060), Scara B, Apt 3, Str Arcu 25, an agent for Antrec, arranges rural accommodation, city tours around Iaşi and trips to Cotnari and the Bucovina monasteries.

ATT (π/fax 142 017), inside Hotel Orizont at Str Grigore Veche 27, is open 8 am to 6 pm weekdays. Icar Tours (π 216 319, fax 217 160, e icar@icar.ro), Str Costache Negri 43, sells tickets for buses to Western Europe (departures only from Bucharest) and is an agent for Air Moldova International. Its friendly staff speak English and French.

Bookshops The top bookshop in Iaşi (and Romania?) is the Junimea bookshop, Piaţa Unirii 4. It stocks an excellent range of maps, dictionaries and novels in English and French. It also sells Romanian history books and English-language journals covering social, political and cultural issues in Romania published by the Romanian Cultural Foundation.

Libraries & Cultural Centres The main building of the Mihai Eminescu University Library (Biblioteca Centrală Universitară Mihai Eminescu) is on the corner of Str Păcurari and Blvd Copou. At Str Păcurari 4 is the British Council library (π/fax 116 159, e radut@bcu-iasi.ro).

The French Cultural Centre (Centre Culturel Français de Iaşi; π 147 900, fax 211 026, e equipe@ccf.tuiasi.ro), Blvd Copou 26, arranges film evenings, theatre workshops, and musical evenings. Its library is open from 1 to 6 pm Monday to Thursday, 10 am to 6 pm Friday, and 10 am to 1 pm Saturday. Opposite, at Blvd Copou 21, is the German Cultural Centre (π 214 051, fax 217 075, e kulturzentrum@mail.dntis.ro).

A World Trade Centre was due to open on Str Anastasie Panu in late 2000.

Piaţa Unirii to Piaţa Palatul Culturii

Start your city tour on Piaţa Unirii, the main square, with a trip to the 13th floor of **Hotel Unirea** for a bird's-eye view of Iaşi. On a good day you can see the three monasteries across the valley in the Nicolina district to the south. Walk back down onto Piaţa Unirii. In front of Hotel Unirea stands a bronze **statue of Prince Alexandru Ioan Cuza** (1820–73) who achieved the union of Wallachia and Moldavia. The statue marks the spot where the Union Hora (traditional Romanian dance) was danced in 1859 to celebrate the amalgamation.

Opposite is **Hotel Traian** (1882), a neoclassical building designed by French engineer Gustave Eiffel, father of Paris' Eiffel tower. Walk up the pedestrian street beside Hotel Traian to Cuza's former residence, a large neoclassical building (1812) at Str Alexandru Lăpuşneanu 14. King Ferdinand and Queen Marie stayed here between 1916 and 1918. In 1948 it was transformed into the **Museum of the Union** (Muzeul Unirii). At the time of writing, the museum was closed for renovation but will reopen in early 2002.

Continue north along Str Alexandru Lăpuşneanu then bear right along Blvd Independenţei. The 18th-century Roset house at Blvd Independenţei 16, which served as the seat of the Physicians and Naturalists' Society in 1844, is now a **Natural History Museum** (Muzeul de Istorie Naturală). Alexandru Ioan Cuza was elected prince here in 1859. The museum is open 9 am to 3 pm Tuesday, Thursday and Saturday, and 9 am to 4 pm Wednesday, Friday and Sunday ($0.20). Opposite the museum at Str Universităţii Vechi 16 is the baroque **Costache Ghica House**; the first university in Romania was founded here in 1860. From 1934 until his death, the poet Mihail Codreanu (1876–1957) lived one block north of the old university at Str Rece 5.

East at Blvd Independenţei 33 is the **St Spiridon's Monastery** (Mănăstirea Sfântul Spiridon; 1804). The beheaded body of Grigore Ghica III lies inside a tomb in the church in the monastical complex. His head was sent to the Sultan after the Turks killed him in 1777.

Back-track west along Blvd Independenţei and turn left down Str 14 Decembrie 1989 to Piaţa Unirii. The poet Vasile Alecsandri lived in the house at No 3. Today it is a **Theatre Museum** (Muzeul Teatrului). No 6 was built in 1920 to house the literary group Viaţa Românească. At No 8 is the **Lascăr**

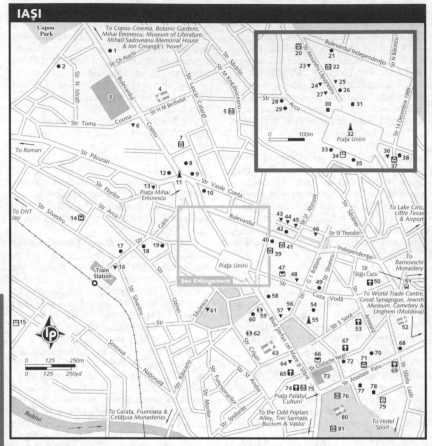

IAŞI

Copou Park

To Copou Cinema, Botanic Gardens, Mihai Eminescu, Museum of Literature, Mihail Sadoveanu Memorial House & Ion Creangă's 'hovel'

To Roman

To DNT Iaşi

To Galata, Frumoasa & Cetăţuia Monasteries

To the Odd Poplars Alley, Trei Sarmale, Bucium & Vaslui

To Hotel Sport

To Lake Ciric, Little Texas & Airport

To Barnovschi Monastery

To World Trade Centre, Great Synagogue, Jewish Museum, Cemetery & Ungheni (Moldova)

Piaţa Unirii

Piaţa Mihai Eminescu

Piaţa Palatul Culturii

Train Station

See Enlargement

Bahlui

Cantacuzino-Paşcanu House where a printing press operated from the 18th century onwards. No 13 housed the printing press and bookshop of the Junimea literary society.

The broad, tree-lined Blvd Ştefan cel Mare şi Sfânt leads directly south-east from Piaţa Unirii to the monumental Palace of Culture. Along this way is the giant **Moldavian Metropolitan Cathedral** (Mitropolia Moldovei). With a cavernous interior painted by Gheorghe Tattarescu, it was built between 1833 and 1839. In mid-October thousands of pilgrims flock here to celebrate the day of St Paraschiva, the patron saint of the cathedral

and of Moldavia. Inside the cathedral lies a coffin said to contain the bones of St Friday.

Opposite is the central park, lined with bronze busts of eminent literary figures, where local artists sell their masterpieces. At the north-eastern end of the park is the **National Theatre** (built 1894–96). In front of it is a majestic statue of its founder Vasile Alecsandri (1821–90), a poet who single-handedly created the theatre's first repertoire with his Romanian adaptation of a French farce. The theatre was built according to the designs of Viennese architects Helmer and Fellner.

PLACES TO STAY		8	Voievodes Statuary	14	Bus Station
30	Hotel Traian	11	Statue of Mihai Eminescu	15	Dacia Cinema
31	Hotel Unirea	22	Museum of the Union	17	Toros Excursii
38	Hotel Continental	32	Statue of Prince Alexandru	18	Automobil Clubul Român
77	Hotel Moldova		Ioan Cuza		(ACR)
78	Hotel Orizont; ATT	39	Theatre Museum	19	Prospect Meridian
		40	House of Vasile Alecsandri	20	Telephone Centre; Farmacon
PLACES TO EAT		41	Natural History Museum	21	IDM Currency Exchange
6	Casa Universatarilor	42	Costache Ghica House	26	Cinema Republica
13	Club RS	50	Golia Monastery	28	Rodex Supermarket
16	McDonald's	52	Bărboi Monastery	29	Tarom
23	Terasa Corsu	53	Armenian Church	33	Agenţie de Voiaj CFR
24	Grădină Iaşul & Brasserie	55	Statue of Vasile Alecsandri	34	Cinema Victoria
25	Ad Hoc	63	Moldavian Metropolitan	35	Junimea Bookshop
27	Iaşul		Cathedral	37	Taxi Rank
36	Restaurant Select; IDM	65	Roman Catholic Church	47	Main Post Office
	Exchange	67	St Sava's Monastery	49	Philharmonic
43	Fast Food Tania	74	Church of the Three	51	Bus to Lake Ciric
44	Warda Fast Food Oriental		Hierarchs	54	Vasile Alecsandri National
45	Summertime	75	Iaşi School Museum; Statue		Theatre
46	Casa Bolta Rece		of Gheorghe Asachi	58	Central Supermarket
48	El Paso	76	Dosoftei House; Museum of	59	Banca Comercială Română
56	EuroParadis		Old Moldavian Literature	60	Agenţia de Opera
57	Cofetăria Opera	80	St Nicolas' Royal Church	62	Banca Comercială Ion Ţiriac
61	GinGer Ale Restaurant & Bar	81	Palace of Culture		(BCIT)
64	Metro Pizza			66	Post Office
		OTHER		68	Club Rosu si Negru
THINGS TO SEE		1	French Cultural Centre	69	Scala Restaurant Disco;
3	Alexandru Ioan Cuza	2	German Cultural Centre		24-Hour Currency Exchange
	University	9	Student Cultural House	70	Central Market
4	Forty Saints Church	10	University Library (Corpus B)	71	Taxi Rank
5	Mihail Kogălniceanu Museum	12	Mihai Eminescu University	72	Icar Tours
7	Pogor House Literary		Library; British Council	73	Civic Centre; Mayor's Palace
	Museum; Club Junimea		Library	79	Luceafărul Theatre

Continuing along Blvd Ştefan cel Mare şi Sfânt, you pass the fabulous **Church of the Three Hierarchs** (Biserica Sfinţilor Trei Ierarhi; built 1637–39), unique for its rich exterior which is covered in a wealth of intricate patterns in stone. In its original form, the exterior was covered in gold.

The Three Hierarchs' church, built by Prince Vasile Lupu, was badly damaged by Tartar attacks in 1650 but later restored. Inside the church are the marble tombs of the Prince Vasile Lupu and his family (to the left), Prince Alexandru Ioan Cuza (to the right), and Moldavian prince Dimitrie Cantemir.

Inside the Gothic hall – reconstructed beside the church – is a **museum of 17th-century frescoes**. In 1994 the church reopened as a monastery.

Nearby, outside the **Iaşi School Museum** is a **statue of Gheorghe Asachi** (1788–1869), a teacher of algebra and geometry at the Greek academy from 1812. The house at Str Theodor Codrescu 2 in which he lived from 1846 is now a **memorial museum**, dedicated to his life and works. Asachi's tomb is inside the 18th-century **Forty Saints Church**, opposite the university on Str Henri Matthias Berthelot.

At the southern end of Blvd Ştefan cel Mare şi Sfânt stands the giant neo-Gothic **Palace of Culture** (Palatul Culturii), built between 1906 and 1925, formerly the administrative seat of the town. The palace was built on the ruins of the **old princely court**, founded by Prince Alexandru cel Bun (ruled 1400–32) in the early 15th century. Some remains of the ruined princely court have been preserved underneath the concrete flooring of what is now the Summer Theatre.

The main attraction of the 365-room building today, however, is the **Gheorghe Asachi library** and the four first-class museums it houses: the **Ethnographic Museum** (Muzeul de Etnografie), one of the best in the country, has exhibits ranging from agriculture, fishing and hunting to wine making, as well as traditional costumes and rugs from Romania's different regions. The **Art Museum** (Muzeul de Artă) is split into two galleries – the Galeria de Artă Românească containing works by Romanian artists including Nicolae Grigorescu and Moldavian-born Petre Achiţemie, and the Galeria de Artă Universală, exhibiting works by foreign artists.

Highlights of the **History Museum** (Muzeul de Istorie) include portraits of all of Romania's rulers from AD 81. Various mechanical creations and musical instruments are displayed in the less colourful **Technical Museum** (Muzeul Ştiinţei şi Tehnicii).

The Palace of Culture is open 10 am to 5 pm Tuesday to Sunday. Admission to all four museums and temporary exhibitions costs $2/1 for adults/concession.

In front of the palace on Piaţa Palatul Culturii is an **equestrian statue** of Ştefan cel Mare, unveiled in 1883. A **memorial** to Iaşi's heroes who died in 1989 stands by the entrance to the palace grounds. Opposite is the **Museum of Old Moldavian Literature**, housed inside the 17th-century Dosoftei House (Casa Dosoftei). Dosoftei, the metropolitan of Moldavia between 1670 and 1686, was responsible for printing the first church liturgy in the Romanian language (1679). The museum is open 10 am to 5 pm Tuesday to Sunday ($0.25).

Behind Dosoftei House is **St Nicolas' Royal Church** (Biserica Sfântul Nicolae Domnesc), founded by Ştefan cel Mare in 1492. Little remains of the original church, restored and extended by Prince Antonie Roset in 1677, only to be rebuilt by French architect André Lecomte de Noüy in 1884.

Monasteries & Churches

A few blocks north, past the central market, is the fortified **Golia Monastery** (Mănăstirea

Golia), built in late-Renaissance style on Str Cuza Vodă. The monastery's walls and the 30m-tall Golia tower at the entrance shelter a 17th-century church, noted for its vibrant Byzantine frescoes and intricately carved doorways. The bastions of the surrounding wall were added in 1667 by Prince Gheorghe Duca (r. 1668–72). The monastical complex was damaged by fire in 1822 and by 1863 was practically in ruins. Between 1900 and 1947 it was closed. It regained monastery status in 1992.

Inside the Golia tower is a Turkish fountain. East of the tower is a **memorial house** to writer Ion Creangă (1837–89), renowned for his short stories based on Moldavian folklore, who lived here between 1866 and 1871. There is a museum dedicated to his life and works in his dwelling close to the university on Ţicău Hill (see the following section).

From Golia Monastery, head south along Str Armeană. On the right at No 22 you pass a small stone-and-brick **Armenian Church** (Biserica Armeană; 1395), considered the oldest church in Iaşi. Extensive renovations have meant that little of the original Armenian architecture remains today. At the southern end of Str Armeană, turn right to **St Sava's Monastery** (Mănăstirea Sfântul Sava), a small red-washed church (1625) at Str Costache Negri 41. If you turn left along Str Costache Negri you come to the 19th-century **Bărboi Monastery** (Mănăstirea Bărboi). The church was built in 1841 on the site of a 17th-century Bărboi church. Its trompe-l'oeil painted interior is worth a look. A block south at Str Grigore Ghica Vodă 26 is **Barnovschi Monastery** (Mănăstirea Barnovschi), dating from the rule of Prince Miron Barnovschi-Movilă (r. 1626–29).

University & Around

From Târgu Cucu (formerly Tîrgu Cucu), just east of Golia Monastery, take bus No 35 westbound and get out when you see a building marked 'Stadionul Emil Alexandrescu' on the left. Iaşi's 80-hectare **Botanic Gardens** (Grădină Botanică), on the far side of Parcul Expositiei, are Romania's largest by far. Dating from 1856, they have 21km of

Voroneţ Monastery, 'the Sistine Chapel of the East'

Exterior fresco on Suceviţa Monastery

Corn harvest, Suceviţa Monastery

Picturesque southern Bucovina landscape

Traditional transport in Suceava

A sunny afternoon in Ştefan cel Mare Park, Chişinău

Chişinău's All Saints Church, built in 1830

shady lanes to explore, and rose and orchid gardens as well as numerous greenhouses.

Follow the bus route back a few blocks to **Copou Park** which was laid out between 1834 and 1848 during the princely reign of Mihail Sturza. It is famed as being a favourite haunt of poet Mihai Eminescu (1850–89), who allegedly wrote some of his best works beneath his favourite linden tree in this park. The tree still stands, behind a 13m-tall **monument of lions** opposite the main entrance to the park. A bronze bust of Eminescu stands in front of it.

Right of the lion monument is the **Mihai Eminescu Museum of Literature** (Muzeul Mihai Eminescu – Muzeul Literaturii Române), housed in an ugly, white, modern building. The museum recalls the life of Eminescu who was born in northern Moldavia; open 10 am to 5 pm Tuesday to Sunday ($0.15). His great love, Veronica Micle, lived in Iaşi (at Str Nicolae Gane 4 with her vicar husband Ştefan). A bust of Veronica faces the bust of her lover and his favourite lime tree at the end of **Junimea alley** in the park.

Walk back down Blvd Copou, past the huge neoclassical **Alexandru Ioan Cuza University** at No 11, where the founder of the fascist Iron Guard, Corneliu Codreanu (1899–1938), once studied. Just before the statue in the middle of the street, turn left to the 1850s mansion at Str Vasile Pogor 4. It was here in the house of Junimea founder Vasile Pogor (1833–1906) that meetings of the literary society were held from 1871. Today it houses the **Pogor House Literary Museum** (Casă Pogor; ☎ 145 760). A statue of Pogor is outside the main entrance which is on the left of the building. In its grounds stand **rows of busts** of some of the more eminent members of the society, including dramatist Ion Luca Caragiale (1852–1912), poet Vasile Alecsandri (1821–90) and historian Alexandru Xenopol (1847–1920).

The foundation stone of the house (1850) is exhibited in the **Club Junimea** (☎ 112 830), an outbuilding in the grounds. If you want to know the real inspiration behind Romania's greatest poets, ask for a tour of the recently restored wine cellars beneath the club. They're vast!

One block south of the Pogor house, behind the **Student Cultural House** on Piaţa Mihai Eminescu, is the Students' House park, the centrepiece of which is the **Voievodes Statuary**. These fantastic, crumbling statues of Moldavia's princes were moved here from the university courtyard in the 1960s. In pairs stand Moldavia's first prince, Dragoş (r. 1352–53) and Alexandru cel Bun (r. 1400–32); Moldavia's greatest prince, Ştefan cel Mare (r. 1457–1504), and Mihai Viteazul (r. 1600); Petru Rareş (r. 1527–38) and Ion Vodă cel Viteaz (r. 1572–74); and Vasile Lupu (r. 1634–53) and Dimitrie Cantemir (r. 1693).

North of the university at Aleea Mihail Sadoveanu 12 is the 19th-century **Mihail Sadoveanu Memorial House** (Casă Memorială Mihail Sadoveanu). The storyteller lived here between 1918 and 1936.

The attractive **Ţicău district** rises to the east of Blvd Copou. At Str Simion Bămuţiu 4 is the *bojdeucă* ('hovel'), built in 1842, where writer Ion Creangă (1837–89) lived with his close friend and mentor Mihai Eminescu.

The politician Mihail Kogălniceanu (1817–91) lived for a short time in the 19th-century mansion at Str Mihail Kogălniceanu 11. Today it houses a **museum** devoted to the life of this Moldavian activist who published numerous papers on the Moldavia National Party during the 1848 revolution; open 9 am to 5 pm Tuesday to Sunday ($0.40).

Close by at Str Henri Matthias Berthelot 18 is the house where the French general Henri Matthias Berthelot lived in 1916–17. The intervention in October 1916 of the 1500-strong French military mission led by Berthelot clinched Romania's survival in WWI. The general was later awarded Romanian citizenship. Iaşi was also the birthplace of the Romanian biologist, explorer and speleologist Emil Racoviţa (1868–1947). He was born at Str Lascăr Catargiu 36, in the west of the Ţicău district.

South of the Centre

Heading out of town along Şoseaua Bucium (DN 224) towards Vaslui, you pass the **Odd Poplars alley**, lined with 25 poplar trees

Jewish Iaşi

Under 17th-century Turkish rule, the head-quarters of the Hacham Bashim was in Iaşi and in the 19th century the city was one of the great centres of Jewish learning in Europe. The world's first professional Jewish theatre opened in Iaşi in 1876. A **statue** of its founder, Polish composer and playwright Avram Gold-faden (1840–1908), stands in the central park on Blvd Ştefan cel Mare şi Sfânt. More than one-third of the city's population at this time was Jewish, served by 127 synagogues.

Only one synagogue remains today – the **Great Synagogue** (1671), no longer used, and barely visible amid the concrete apartment blocks surrounding it at Str Elena Doamna 15. There is a small museum inside the synagogue but you have to contact the Iaşi Jewish community (☎ 114 414) in advance to visit it. In front of the synagogue is a **monument** to the victims of the 1941 pogrom.

Many of the victims of the Iron Guard's pogroms were buried in four concrete bunkers in the **Jewish Cemetery** (Cimitirul Evreiesc) on Mountain Hill (Dealul Munteni), east of the centre off Str Păcurari.

marking the spot where poet Mihai Emi-nescu also sought inspiration.

South-west of the centre in the Nicolina district are three of Iaşi's most tranquil monasteries, which make for a pleasant day's hike. Perched on top of Miroslavei Hill is the 16th-century, fortified **Galata Monastery** (Mănăstirea Galata), founded in 1582 by Prince Petru Şchiopul, who is buried in the church. The ruins of the monks' living quarters and a Turkish bath are all that remain today. The new church was built in 1847.

East of Galata at the northern end of Str Cetăţuia are the ruins of **Frumoasa Monastery** (Mănăstirea Frumoasa; built 1726–33). Built by Prince Grigore Ghica II, it served as a royal residence in the 18th century. From here, go south along Str Cetăţuia and follow the steep, narrow road to the top of Dealul Cetăţuia and the impressive **Cetăţuia Monastery**. Founded by Prince

Gheorghe Duca in 1669, it is preserved in its original form. Between 1682 and 1694 a Greek printing press was housed here.

Places to Stay

Camping There is budget accommodation at Lake Ciric, 6km north-east of town. *Baza Sportivă şi de Agrement Civic* (☎ 176 669), across the dam and to the right, offers simple cabins for $5, and is open mid-May to August. To reach the lake, take a tram to Târgu Cucu, just east of Golia Monastery, and then wait for bus No 25 to Lake Ciric, which leaves hourly from the stop opposite the building marked 'Complexul Târgul Cucului'.

Private Rooms Prospect Meridian (see Travel Agencies, earlier), an agent for Antrec, arranges private rooms in villages around Iaşi. A bed is between $10 and $15 a night, including a home-cooked breakfast. Hosts charge an extra $4 to $6 for an evening meal.

Hotels Most of Iaşi's hotels are within spit-ting distance of each other in the centre of town. Best value for backpackers is *Hotel Continental* (☎ 114 320, Piaţa 14 Decem-brie 1989). Single/double rooms with a squeaky-clean shared bathroom are $13/18. Rooms facing the street are noisy. The hotel has a small cafe and currency exchange on the ground floor.

Similar prices are charged at the grotty *Hotel Sport* (☎ 232 800, fax 231 540, Str Sfântu Lazăr 76), south of the centre in the Nicolina district.

Behind the Moldova is *Hotel Orizont* (☎ 112 700, fax 215 037, Str Grigore Ure-che 27). Rooms with a balcony are $17/25 and doubles without a balcony are $22. The hotel's disco-bar is open 10 am to 4 am daily.

Reception staff at the elegant *Hotel Traian* (☎ 143 330, fax 212 187), on Piaţa Unirii, will offer you the most expensive room if you're a foreigner. The cheapest rooms are on the top floors where water pressure is at its lowest. Singles/doubles/triples with a private shower on these floors cost $18/26/39.

The characterless, three-star *Hotel Unirea* (☎ *142 110, fax 117 854, Piaţa Unirii 2)* has mid-range singles/doubles with private bathroom for $27/36, including breakfast. It has a restaurant and panoramic cafe on the 13th floor.

The 14-storey, three-star *Hotel Moldova* (☎ *142 225, fax 117 940, Piaţa Palatului 1)*, one of the few hotels in Romania to have wheelchair access, is overpriced at $28/51 for rooms with private bath. The hotel has an adjoining indoor swimming pool, sauna and tennis court, open to nonguests too.

Places to Eat

Restaurants Traditional Romanian food is served at *Casa Bolta Rece* (☎ *212 255, Str Rece 10)*, which dates from 1799. Try the *caşcaval* (fried cheese) for $1, or the house speciality, *feteasca neagră* (black pudding served with *mămăligă* and topped with salty sheep's cheese).

Also popular is *Trei Sarmale* (☎ *132 832, Str Bucium 42)*, inside a 17th-century inn south of town. Check before you head out here as the restaurant is often booked by tour groups. Take bus No 30 or 46 from Piaţa Mihai Eminescu and get off at the Bucium bus stop, directly outside the restaurant.

The grey old days are more evident at *Iaşul*, on Str Alexandru Lăpuşneanu. Typical Romanian dishes are served and there is a live folk band some evenings. Opposite Hotel Continental is *Restaurant Select* (☎ *216 440)*, favoured mainly for its bingo hall and casino.

In recent years internationally themed restaurants have sprouted across the city. The not-very-Mexican *El Paso* (☎ *112 007)*, on Str Cuza Vodă, dishes up a rather poor imitation of nachos for $1.75. Its tacos are marginally better at $1.50. For more authentic Mexican fare try the reasonably priced *Little Texas* (☎ *216 995)*, on Str Moara de Vînt just east of the centre.

For a touch of Ireland check out *GinGer Ale* (☎ *276 017, Str Săulescu 23)*, a fun restaurant-bar. Well-portioned meals cost around $4.

Metro Pizza (Blvd Ştefan cel Mare şi Sfânt 18) serves excellent, 26cm-round pizzas for $1.15 to $2. The 'metro special', topped with cheese, salami, mushrooms and a fried egg, is particularly satisfying. It also has a take-away counter.

Cafes There's an abundance of outside cafes along Str Anastasie Panu. More fun are the cluster of summer cafes-bars spilling out onto the pavements around Piaţa Mihai Eminescu. Students run a good cafe outside their cultural house at the northern end of Piaţa Mihai Eminescu.

Favoured by Iaşi's student community is the Greek cafe-restaurant-bar *Club RS* (☎ *213 060, Str Fătu 2)*. It has a great terrace and traditional Greek music spouts from speakers. A four-course set menu will set you back $3.80; discounts are available for students. The attached disco rocks from 11 pm to 6 am daily.

The *Grădină Iaşul & Brasserie*, on Str Alexandru Lăpuşneanu next door to the Iaşul restaurant, and *Terasa Corsu*, opposite the Museum of the Union, are other hot spots on sunny days. For an indoor cup of coffee, try the glittery, modern *Ad Hoc*, next door to the Museum of the Union.

The terrace at the popular *Casa Universatarilor* (☎ *140 029, Blvd Copou 9)* is packed from June onwards, if only for the wonderful scent of its many lime trees. A meal here costs about $1; getting high on lime is free.

Numerous outside cafes are also dotted along Blvd Ştefan cel Mare şi Sfânt. Overlooking the park is *EuroParadis* (☎ *216 664, Str Brătianu 30)* and nearby is *Cofetăria Opera (Str Brătianu 32)*.

Fast Food For pizza delivery, call the other *Metro Pizza* outlet (☎ *276 040, Str Silvestru 10)*.

McDonald's (Piata Garii 4) is to the right as you exit the train station. The restaurant is open 7 am to 1 am daily; the drive-through is open 24 hours. Brilliant-yellow *Nest* fast-food kiosks, open 24 hours and serving hot dogs and more hot dogs, are dotted all over town.

The city's kebab alley runs alongside the eastern side of the Medical University. *Warda Fast Food Oriental (Str Sfânt*

Teodor 20) serves up hamburgers ($1) and fries from 8 am to 1 am daily. For $0.55 worth of falafel, pop into *Fast Food Tania (Str Sfânt Teodor 24)* a few doors down; open 24 hours. Lebanese fast food is dished up with care at *Summertime (Str Sfânt Teodor 30)* in the former Armanda building; also open 24 hours.

Self-Catering The indoor *central market* is great for fresh fruit and vegetables. It has entrances on Str Costache Negri and Str Anastasie Panu.

The *Central Supermarket*, at the northern end of Blvd Ştefan cel Mare şi Sfânt, is open 8 am to 8 pm daily except Sunday. An excellent range of imported and local products is sold at the 24-hour *Rodex Supermarket*, next door to the Tarom office on Str Arcu.

Entertainment

Cinemas The latest box-office hits are screened in English with subtitles in Romanian. Try the *Victoria (☎ 112 502, Piaţa Unirii 4)*, *Republica (☎ 114 327, Str Alexandru Lăpuşneanu 12)*, *Dacia (☎ 164 740, Piaţa Voievozilor 14)* or *Copou (☎ 145 738, Blvd Copou 48)*.

Discos Iaşi's best student disco is *Extazy* at the Complexul Studenţească 'Tudor Vladimirescu' east of town (five stops from Piaţa Unirii on tram No 8); it's closed Monday and Tuesday and from July to mid-September.

Club Roşu şi Negru ('Red & Black'), on the corner of Str Anastasie Panu and Str Sfantu Lazăr, is the popular spot to dance the night away. Diagonally opposite is the cheap and tacky *Scala Restaurant Disco*.

Theatre & Classical Music On the eastern side of Blvd Ştefan cel Mare şi Sfânt is the neobaroque *Vasile Alecsandri National Theatre* (Teatrul Naţional Vasile Alecsandri; ☎ 115 108). More alternative shows and performances are held in the smaller studio hall *(sală studio)* upstairs which has its entrance on Str Cuza Vodă. For advance bookings go to the Agenţia de Opera (☎ 116 070), Blvd Ştefan cel Mare şi Sfânt 8; open 9 am to

1 pm, and 3 to 5 pm weekdays. Tickets cost around $0.80; half-price for students.

Massively popular are the concerts held inside the *Philharmonic (Filarmonica; ☎ 114 601, Str Cuza Vodă 29)*. The box office inside is open 10 am to 1 pm, and 5 to 7 pm weekdays. Tickets are $2.50; students half-price.

There is a youth theatre – the *Luceafărul Theatre* on Str Grigore Ureche. Performances are rarely held at the *Summer Theatre (Teatrul Vară; Str Palatului 1)* inside the Palace of Culture. When they are, details are advertised in the local press.

Getting There & Away

Air Tarom operates a daily flight on weekdays between Iaşi, Suceava and Bucharest ($44, 1.50 pm Monday, Tuesday, Wednesday and Friday, and 3.20 pm Thursday). Tarom (☎ 115 239) has an office at Str Arcu 3–5, open 8 am to 6 pm weekdays, and 8 am to noon Saturday.

Train The Agenţie de Voiaj CFR (☎ 147 673), Piaţa Unirii 4, is open 8 am to 8 pm weekdays. Express train tickets to Bucharest and Timişoara are sold from window Nos 3, 6 and 8. International train tickets are sold from window Nos 11, 14 and 15 on the 2nd floor.

The left-luggage office (open 24 hours) is on platform 1, to the right as you enter the station; ($0.50/1 for small/large bags).

Iaşi is on the main line between Bucharest and Kyiv, which goes via Chişinău. The Ungheni border crossing is only 21km away. Reservations are required on the three daily trains from Iaşi to Chişinău.

For Galaţi you may have to change trains at Bârlad or Tecuci. If you are planning to visit the monasteries in southern Bucovina, take a train to Suceava then change trains, or take a train bound for Vatra Dornei or Oradea and get off at the Gura Humorului stop. To get to Târgu Neamţ from Iaşi you often have to change at Paşcani.

Bus The central bus station (☎ 146 587) is at Şoseaua Arcu. Buses leave daily for Chişinău in the republic of Moldova ($4) at

7 am, and 2 and 5 pm. Tickets for the daily private bus to Istanbul are sold at the Toros Excursii office (☎ 276 339), Str Gării 18, one block from the bus station ($26, 8 am).

Getting Around

To/From the Airport Tarom operates a free shuttle bus service between its office at Str Arcu 3–5 and Iaşi airport (☎ 271 590). It leaves the office 1½ hours before flight departures.

Bus, Tram & Trolleybus Public transport tickets ($0.25 for a two-journey ticket) are sold at the kiosks next to bus stops, news kiosks, and most of the canary-yellow Nest fast-food kiosks. Bus No 35 runs between Piaţa Eminescu and Copou Park, stopping outside the university en route. Tram No 3 runs between the bus and train stations and the centre.

AROUND IAŞI

Rolling hills, lush vineyards and pretty villages surround Moldavia's 'town of seven hills'. At the **Bucium winery**, 7km south of Iaşi, you can taste a variety of sweet wines as well as Bucium champagne. At weekends, Iaşi residents picnic in **Bârnova forest**, 16km south of the city and accessible by train.

Cotnari

Cotnari is 54km north-west of Iaşi. Its **vineyards**, dating from 1448, are among the most famed in Romania, producing four to six million bottles of sweet white wine a year. Legend says Ştefan cel Mare described it as 'wine given by God'. Cotnari wine is also known as the 'flower of Moldavia'.

There was a Geto-Dacian stronghold on Cătălina Hill (280m) in Cotnari from the 4th century BC. In 1491 Ştefan cel Mare built a small church in the village and in 1562 a Latin college was founded. During this period French monks arrived bringing grape stocks which they planted in the village, and by the end of the 19th century Cotnari wine had scooped up prizes at international exhibitions. King Michael I started building a small **royal palace** here in 1947, abandoning it half-complete the same year. It was restored in 1966 and today house... ministration of the Cotnari Winery.

Following the fall of communism, ... hectares of the winery's 2000-hectare esta... were returned to local farmers whose land had been confiscated under Ceauşescu.

The winery's most popular wines include white table wines such as *frâncuşa* (classified as dry but more on the medium side) and *cătălina* (semisweet), and the sweet, golden *grasă* and *tămâioasă* dessert wines.

The Cotnari Winery (☎ 032-730 393/396, fax 730 205/303) arranges wine-tasting sessions and tours of its cellars and factory. Every year on 14 September, wine connoisseurs flock to Cotnari to celebrate the harvest.

To get there, continue past the village shop on the road towards Botoşani and Hârlău. The factory is 200m farther on the left.

Places to Stay & Eat Antrec (see Travel Agencies under Iaşi) arranges *private rooms* in Cotnari – in the home of the general director of the Cotnari factory, next door to King Michael's palace! From the centre of the village, turn left at the shop and continue up the hill until you reach the palace on your left. The Bilius family, next door, offer beds in beautifully furnished rooms from $10 to $15 per person, including breakfast.

Getting There & Away Local trains from Iaşi to Hârlău stop at Cotnari (54km, 1¾ hours). They leave Iaşi at 5.40 am, 4.53 and 9 pm daily. Return trains leave Cotnari at 3.46 am, and 3.06 and 7.30 pm.

Botoşani, Ipoteşti & Liveni

Botoşani is 50km north of Cotnari, with Ipoteşti a further 8km north-west. Poet Mihai Eminescu (1850–89) was born in Ipoteşti. His family home is today a **Memorial House** (Casa Memorială). In the centre of Ipoteşti is a **Mihai Eminescu National Centre of Studies** (Centrul Naţional de Studii Mihai Eminescu; ☎ 031-517 602) housing a library and museum.

Bucovina Estur (see Travel Agencies in the later Suceava section) arranges accommodation in homes in Ipoteşti. There are a handful of run-down hotels in Botoşani:

Hotel Rapsodia Park Hotel (☎/fax 031-518 054, Str
Cuza Vodă 4), *Hotel Rareş* (☎ 031-512 667,
Calea Naţională 315) and *Hotel Tineret*
(☎ 031-525 725), on Blvd Mihai Eminescu.

To get to Ipoteşti (called Mihai Eminescu
on some maps), head north out of Botoşani
on the road to Dorohoi. At the northern end
of Cătămareşti-Deal village turn left at the
signpost for Ipoteşti.

The composer George Enescu (1881–
1955) was born in **Liveni**, 35km north of
Ipoteşti. His childhood home is now a
Memorial House. Liveni is marked as
George Enescu on many maps.

Getting There & Away There are three
daily buses to Botoşani from Iaşi (117km),
and seven daily from Suceava (40km) in
southern Bucovina.

TÂRGU NEAMŢ
☎ 033

Târgu Neamţ (literally 'German Market
Town') offers tourists little except the ruins
of a 14th-century citadel and a cluster of
pre-1989 museums which are always closed.
However, it serves as a stepping stone to the
Neamţ, Agapia and Văratec Monasteries.

Orientation & Information
The bus station (☎ 663 474) is at the end of
Str Cuza Vodă 32. Turn right out of the bus
station, then right along Blvd Mihai Eminescu to Blvd Ştefan cel Mare. The hotel and
citadel are signposted from here. The train
station is signposted from the bus station.

There is a currency exchange centre inside
the Bancapost on Piaţa Mihai Eminescu;
open 8 am to noon weekdays. The post and
telephone office is at Blvd Mihai Eminescu
154; open 7.30 am to 8.30 pm weekdays.

Things to See
Neamţ Citadel, (Cetatea Neamţului), considered Moldavia's finest ruined fortress, is
on a hill above the town. Attacked by Hungarians in 1395, by Turks in 1476, and
conquered by Polish forces in 1691, it fell
into ruin in the 18th century.

Follow the signs for the 'Cetatea
Neamţului' along Blvd Ştefan cel Mare. At

No 37 there is a **History and Ethnographic
Museum** (Muzeul de Istorie şi Etnografie),
seemingly always closed. Opposite is the
Memorial House to Veronica Micle (1850–
89), always closed too.

A **statue** of writer Ion Creangă stands on
Piaţa Mihai Eminescu. The storyteller attended secondary school in Târgu Neamţ.

Places to Stay & Eat
Casa Arcaşului (☎ 662 615), at the foot of
the citadel, offers doubles/triples for $18/
23. The similarly priced *Hotel Oglinzi*
(☎ 663 590) is 4km north of Târgu Neamţ
on the Suceava road.

Pizza Orient (☎ 661 297), in Piaţa Mihai
Eminescu park, slaps out pizza for about $1.

Getting There & Away
Train From Târgu Neamţ take one of four
daily local trains to Paşcani (50 minutes)
from where you can get trains to Iaşi,
Suceava and other cities in Moldavia. There
is one direct train daily from Târgu Neamţ
to Iaşi (2½ hours).

Bus Six buses depart daily from Târgu
Neamţ bus station to Piatra Neamţ (43km).
There are buses to Agapia (listed as Complex Turistic Agapia; 11km, 6.30 and 11.30
am, and 1.15 pm) and to Văratec (7.30 am,
and 2.30 and 6.30 pm).

There is a daily bus to Bacău (93km),
Braşov (280km), Durău (61km), Gheor-
gheni (160km), Miercurea Ciuc (217km),
Radăuţi (258km), Sfântu Gheorghe (315km),
Slănic Moldova (164km) and Suceava
(71km). There are also two daily buses to
Iaşi (100km).

AROUND TÂRGU NEAMŢ
Târgu Neamţ is ringed by monasteries
which are noted not for their outstanding
artistic treasures but rather as Romania's
most active religious centres. Agapia and
Văratec are called monasteries even though
they house nuns.

Neamţ Monastery
Neamţ Monastery (Mănăstirea Neamţ) is
Romania's largest and oldest monastery. In

the fortified compound are a **medieval art museum** and a **memorial house** to novelist Mihail Sadoveanu (1880–1961). It was built during the same time as Neamţ Citadel as a fortified refuge for local people. Just one of its original frescoes dating from 1497 remains intact today.

The monastery, 15km west of Târgu Neamţ, is not served by public transport. Hitch a ride west along the road to Ceahlău and Topliţa.

Agapia Monastery

Heading 4km south from Târgu Neamţ towards Piatra Neamţ, you hit the turn-off for Agapia Monastery (Mănăstirea Agapia) in the Topliţa Valley. Within the confines of the monastery walls live 400-plus nuns who toil in the fields, tend vegetable gardens and weave carpets and embroideries for tourists.

Agapia comprises two monasteries: the upper 'monastery on the hill' (Agapia din Deal) was founded by Lady Elena, the wife of Petru Rareş, in 1527. The more spectacular 'monastery in the valley' (Agapia din Vale) was built by Gavril Coci (brother of Vasile Lupu) between 1642 and 1644. It was badly damaged by the Turks in 1821; its current neoclassical facade dates from 1823. Between 1858 and 1860, the young Nicolae Grigorescu (1838–1907) painted the interior of the church, with a fantastic mural of eyes which stare at you whichever way you turn. The collection of icons inside the monastery dates from the 16th and 17th centuries.

It is occasionally possible for tourists to stay at the monastery (☎ 033-244 618).

Getting There & Away All buses between Târgu Neamţ and Piatra Neamţ stop in Săcăluşeşti village, from where it is a 3km hike along a narrow road to the lower monastery; the upper monastery is a further 30-minute walk uphill.

There are also three direct buses from Târgu Neamţ to the lower monastery, listed on bus timetables as 'Complex Turistic Agapia'. Some people visit Agapia from Piatra Neamţ, from where there are two buses daily to the complex (40km).

Vǎratec Monastery

Six hundred nuns live at Vǎratec Monastery (Mănăstirea Vǎratec), 7km south of the Agapia turn-off. The complex houses an **icon museum** and a small embroidery school. The **grave** of poet Veronica Micle, Mihai Eminescu's great love, lies within the monastery walls. She committed suicide on 4 August 1889, two months after Eminescu's death.

You can hike to Vǎratec from Agapia (1½ hours) and to the tiny **Secu**, **Sihǎstria** and **Schitu Sihlei** Monasteries, founded in the Secu Brook Valley by Moldavian boyars between 1602 and 1813. Trails are clearly marked.

Getting There & Away There are buses daily from Târgu Neamţ to Vǎratec, departing from Târgu Neamţ at 7.30 am, and 2.30 and 6.30 pm (11km). If it's sunny, you might prefer to walk.

PIATRA NEAMŢ
☎ 033 • postcode 5600 • pop 126,000

Piatra Neamţ ('German Rock'), 43km south of Târgu Neamţ, is a picturesque town, sunken in a valley and surrounded on all sides by sheer mountain faces. Perched above the town to the east is the rocky Pietricica Mountain. To the south-west stands the Cernegura Mountain, flanked by the artificial lake, Lacu Bâtca Doamnei, at its westernmost foot. The Cozla Mountain which towers over Piatra Neamţ to the north is a national park. Ştefan cel Mare founded a princely court here in the 15th century.

Every year at the end of May, Piatra Neamţ hosts a week-long international theatre festival, attracting theatre companies from all over Europe.

Orientation

The Bistriţa River runs south-west to east along the southern edge of the town. The train station is on the north bank of the river at Piaţa Mareşal Ion Antonescu 50. The bus station is next door at Str Bistriţei 1.

Blvd Republicii leads north from Piaţa Mareşal Ion Antonescu to Piaţa Ştefan cel Mare where most facilities are. The old

MOLDAVIA

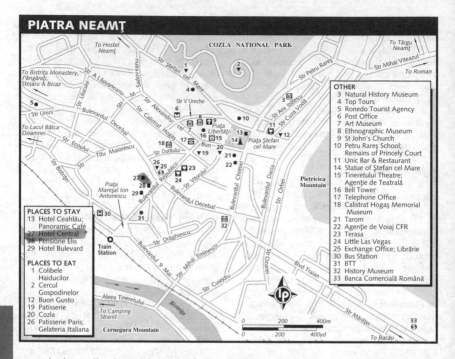

PIATRA NEAMŢ

PLACES TO STAY
13 Hotel Ceahlău;
    Panoramic Café
27 Hotel Central
28 Pensione Elis
29 Hotel Bulevard

PLACES TO EAT
1   Colibele
    Haiducilor
2   Cercul
    Gospodinelor
12 Buon Gusto
19 Patisserie
20 Cozla
26 Patisserie Paris;
    Gelateria Italiana

OTHER
3   Natural History Museum
4   Top Tours
5   Ronedo Tourist Agency
6   Post Office
7   Art Museum
8   Ethnographic Museum
9   St John's Church
10 Petru Rareş School;
    Remains of Princely Court
11 Unic Bar & Restaurant
14 Statue of Ştefan cel Mare
15 Tineretului Theatre;
    Agenţie de Teatrală
16 Bell Tower
17 Telephone Office
18 Calistrat Hogaş Memorial
    Museum
21 Tarom
22 Agenţie de Voiaj CFR
23 Terasa
24 Little Las Vegas
25 Exchange Office; Librărie
30 Bus Station
31 BTT
32 History Museum
33 Banca Comercială Română

town is immediately north-west of this square, at the foot of Cozla Mountain.

Information

Tourist Offices All the hotels have tourist offices which arrange trips to the monasteries. The Ronedo Tourist Agency (☎ 231 870, fax 231 306, ⓔ ronedo@decebal.ro), 1km west of the centre at Apartment 1, Blvd Decebal 59, specialises in steam-train adventures around Romania (see the Exploring the Carpathian Mountains special section).

Tarom (☎ 214 268) is opposite Hotel Ceahlău at Piaţa Ştefan cel Mare 1. It doesn't operate any flights from Piatra Neamţ.

Money The exchange office inside the Librărie, opposite Hotel Central on Blvd Decebal, offers the best rates. Get cash advances on Visa/MasterCard, and change travellers cheques at Banca Comercială Română, Blvd Traian 19; open 8 am to 6 pm weekdays, and 8 am to 2 pm Saturday.

There are also two ATMs which accept Visa/MasterCard.

Post & Telephone The post office is on Str Alexandru cel Bun, open 7 am to 8 pm weekdays and 8 am to noon Saturday. The telephone office on Blvd Republicii is open 7.30 am to 8 pm weekdays, and 7.30 am to 2 pm Saturday.

Things to See & Do

Walk along Blvd Republicii to the central square, Piaţa Ştefan cel Mare. On the square's western side is a small **park**, with a **statue** of Ştefan cel Mare in its centre. Steps from the park lead to Piaţa Libertăţii, a small pedestrianised square where the remains of Piatra Neamţ's historic heart lie.

The quaint **Princely Court Museum complex** (Muzeul Curtea Domnească), founded in 1497 by Ştefan cel Mare, comprises a 10m-tall **bell tower** and **St John's Church** (Biserica Sfântu Ioan; 1498). Some ruined foundations of the princely court have been unearthed in the courtyard of the Petru Rareş school (Liceul Petru Rareş), opposite the pedestrianised square on Str Ştefan cel Mare. An **Art Museum** (Muzeul de Artă) and small **Ethnographic Museum** (Muzeul de Etnografie) are next to the bell tower. Both are open 10 am to 4 pm Tuesday to Sunday.

The local **History Museum** (Muzeul de Istorie), Str Mihai Eminescu 1, is open 9 am to 5 pm Monday to Saturday. There is a **Natural History Museum** (Muzeul de Ştiinţe Naturale) at the northern end of Str Petru Rareş.

Lacu Bâtca Doamnei, 3km west of the centre of town, is a popular spot during summer. It is possible to swim in the lake and you can rent paddles and rowing boats.

Places to Stay

Camping Overlooking the Bistriţa River, *Camping Ştrand (☎ 217 835, Str Aleea Tineretului 1)* offers tent sites/wooden huts for two for $7/8. From the train station, turn right along Blvd 9 Mai and walk 50m until you come to a small bridge on the right. Cross the bridge and turn right along Aleea Tineretului.

Private Rooms Staff at the BTT tourism agency (☎/fax 214 686), opposite Hotel Bulevard at Block 2A, Blvd Republicii, do not speak English but can find you a private room if you can get the message across; open 8 am to 4 pm weekdays.

Top Tours (☎/fax 234 204), Str Ştefan cel Mare 17, takes bookings for Antrec for accommodation in private rooms in villages around Piatra Neamţ, in Durău and Ceahlău.

Hostels Piatra Neamţ's only hostel is the small YHR *Hostel Neamţ (☎ 237 596, Str Ştefan cel Mare 67)*, just north of the centre. A bed for the night in one of its clean two- or six-bed rooms is $6 per person. The hostel is open during July and August only.

Hotels The cheapest place to stay in town is *Pensione Elis (☎ 217 940)*, on Blvd Republicii, five minutes' walk from the bus station. Spacious doubles/triples with a shared bath are $11/16; breakfast not included.

The 11-storey *Hotel Ceahlău (☎ 217 770, fax 215 540, Piaţa Ştefan cel Mare 3)* towers in all its ugliness beneath the picturesque Pietricica and Cozla Mountains. Two-star singles/doubles cost $16/25, including private bathroom, TV and breakfast.

Next door to Pensione Elis, the one-star *Hotel Bulevard (☎ 235 010, fax 218 111, Blvd Republicii 38)* offers cramped rooms for $22/28, including breakfast. Bring your own toilet paper.

Close by is the expensive, 132-room *Hotel Central (☎ 216 230, fax 214 532, Blvd Republicii 26)*. The huge concrete tower is as dreary inside as it is outside. Rooms are $30/39, including breakfast. Staff speak some French, English and German.

Places to Eat

The restaurant *Cozla*, on Piaţa Ştefan cel Mare, is a large, glass-domed building, its interior smothered with hanging ivy and other green plants. Meals are passable at around $4.

A 15-minute hike, but worth it, is *Colibele Haiducilor (☎ 213 909)*, in a traditional old Romanian house halfway up Cozla Mountain. Strictly local cuisine is served here. Steps lead up to the restaurant from Str Ştefan cel Mare; alternatively, from Str Ştefan cel Mare turn on to Str Ion Creangă and continue up the stone road. Farther up the mountain is *Cercul Gospodinelor (☎ 223 845)*, on Str Ion Creangă, another Romanian restaurant located inside a more modern building, favoured for its panoramic views. Expect to pay around $5 for a meal at either restaurant.

Numerous cafes and bars are dotted along Piaţa Ştefan cel Mare. Particularly popular are *Panoramic Café* outside Hotel Ceahlău, and *Buon Gusto*, a 24-hour snack bar and cafe at the square's eastern end.

Patisserie, on the corner of Blvd Republicii and Str Calistrat Hogaş, is a pleasant, airy cafe serving good cakes and coffee. Adjoining each other on Blvd Decebal are the internationally inspired *Patisserie Paris* and *Gelateria Italiana*.

Entertainment

Bars & Discos Risk all in a round of computerised American poker at *Little Las*

Vegas (Blvd Republicii 9), open 10 am to 10 pm daily.

For the cheapest local brew in town, try a pint of homemade beer for $0.25 at the very local *Terasa*, a few doors away from Little Las Vegas. It is constantly filled with a flow of veteran drinkers from 10 am to 6 pm daily.

Unic (Str Ştefan cel Mare 1) bar and restaurant has a large courtyard where bands play and an open-air disco is held; open 6 am to 1 am daily.

Theatre Performances in Romanian are held at 7 pm on Friday, Saturday and Sunday at the *Tineretului Theatre (Teatrul Tineretului; ☎ 211 472, fax 217 159, Piaţa Ştefan cel Mare 1)*. Tickets (around $1) are sold in advance at the Agenţie Teatrală adjoining the theatre.

Getting There & Away

Train The Agenţie de Voiaj CFR (☎ 211 034), at Piaţa Ştefan cel Mare 10, is open am to 7.30 pm weekdays. Daily services include five to Bicaz (26km) and seven to Bacău (60km).

Bus The bus station (☎ 663 474) is next to the train station, at Str Bistriţei 1. Buses run hourly to Târgu Neamţ (43km) between 9 am and 6.15 pm (one bus also at 5.30 am). Buses leave for Agapia at 8 am and 8 pm daily.

BICAZ & THE BICAZ GORGES

Bicaz, on the confluence of the Bicaz and Bistriţa Rivers, is 26km west of Piatra Neamţ. The town is famed for **Bicaz Lake** (Lacu Izvorul Muntelui, or 'Mountain Spring Lake') which sprawls over 3000 hectares north of Bicaz. The hydroelectric dam *(baraj)* at the lake's southern end was built in 1950, with several villages being submerged and relocated in the process. Taking photographs of the footbridge crossing the dam wall is forbidden.

On the eastern side of the lake is **Grozăveşti**, a village with a wooden church typical of those in Maramureş. The church was built during the 20th century after the old church fell into the lake. Apparently the

day the church drowned, the local village priest received a postcard from Maramureş. The postage stamp featured a wooden Maramureş church, thus inspiring him to build his new church in that style.

Boat hire is available at the Munteanu port (☎ 033-671 350) on the western side of lake. Turn right immediately after the bridge at the *Port Munteanu* sign. Paddle boats cost $1 per person an hour. Boats can also be hired on the eastern side of Bicaz Lake from the Boatel Libada (☎ 033-254 036; see Places to Stay). Rowing and paddle boats cost $1 per person an hour, and to hire a cruising boat for up to 50 people costs $25 an hour.

From the southern end of Bicaz Lake you can follow the road north along the lake shores to Vatra Dornei, or continue west to Lacu Roşu and Gheorgheni into Transylvania, via the Bicaz Gorges. Hot tip: both routes are among the most remarkable in Romania!

The **Bicaz Gorges** (Cheile Bicazului) are 21km from Bicaz town. The gorge steeply twists and turns uphill for 5km, cutting through sheer, 300m-high limestone rocks on its journey through the mountains. Around the 'neck of hell' (Gâtul Iadului), the narrow mountain road runs directly beneath the overhanging rocks. Dozens of artisans sell locally made crafts from stalls set up beneath the rocks. This entire stretch is protected under the Hăşmaş–Bicaz Gorges National Park (Parcul Naţional Hăşmaş–Cheile Bicazului). Continuing along this road, you cross into Transylvania.

Places to Stay

Campers can pitch their tents for free outside *Cabana Bicaz Baraj* (430m) at the foot of the dam wall. The cabana has no rooms but serves snacks in its small cafe. *Cabana Izvorul Muntelui* (797m), 12km from Bicaz town on the eastern side of the lake, has a few basic rooms.

Around Bicaz Lake the cheapest spot to stay is aboard *Boatel Libada (☎ 033-254 036)*, moored at the southern end of the lake. It has 13 double/triple cabins costing $9/13 with a shared shower. Str Barajului leads from the main road to the boatel.

Although a little noisy, *Motel Gara* (☎ 033-253 382), right beside the train station in Bicaz, has clean, reasonably priced doubles for $15, not including breakfast.

Next to the Str Barajului turn-off on the main road is *Motel Complex* (☎ 033-671 456), which has double rooms in its main building for $17 with shared bath and two-bed huts for $6 per person a night.

A couple of kilometres farther north on the eastern side of the lake in Potoci village is the two-star *Motel Potoci* (☎ 672 236). Doubles with private bath cost $28 and a cabana is $6 per person.

Getting There & Away
Bicaz is on a branch line between Bacău (1½ to 2¼ hours) and Piatra Neamţ (25 to 40 minutes). There are five trains daily in each direction, most of which stop at Bicaz.

DURĂU & THE CEAHLĂU MASSIF
From the south-eastern end of Bicaz Lake, a road leads north through pine forests to the mountain resort of Durău (800m), a convenient base for hiking in the Ceahlău Massif, Moldavia's most spectacular mountain range. The story goes that Ceahlău's 'magic mountain' spells eternal friendship for those who hike up it together.

Various hiking trails lead from Durău and Ceahlău into the Ceahlău Massif; see the Exploring the Carpathian Mountains special section for details.

From here you can head east into Transylvania or north to Vatra Dornei (see the later Southern Bucovina section). The Vatra Dornei road closely follows the Golden Bistriţa River (Bistriţa Aurie) for much of the way and is one of the country's great scenic delights.

Durău & Ceahlău
In the 19th century, climbers sought shelter at **Durău Monastery** (Mănăstirea Durău; 1830), a complex comprising two churches and quarters for 35 nuns who inhabit it today. Visitors are welcome.

The annual **Ceahlău Folk Festival** takes place in Durău on the second Sunday in August. Shepherds come down from the mountains and locals don traditional dress.

In **Ceahlău** (550m), 6km north of Durău, there are the remains of a princely palace built between 1639 and 1676 and an 18th-century wooden church. The museum is in the centre of the village, 500m up a dirt track off the main road.

Places to Stay The nuns at *Durău Monastery* (☎ 033-678 383) still take in the weary and blistered. The monastery has six modern cabanas where travellers can stay for $7 a night.

Cabana Paulo, the first cabana you pass on the main road to Durău, has 16 places in a wooden, chalet-style house costing $10 per person a night. Some 50m farther is the *family home of Igor Ghinculor* (☎ 033-256 503). He has five double rooms with shared bathroom and hot water heater for $7 per person, and can arrange accommodation in private homes elsewhere in Durău and Ceahlău.

Cascada Pelerinul (☎ 033-256 583), opposite the monastery, is a large, concrete block with singles/doubles for $14/21.

Hiking up the hill by the side of the Cascada, you come to Durău's main cluster of hotels: the 20-room *Hotel Bistriţa* (☎ 033-256 578) is the smallest and friendliest of the lot. Bathrooms are shared and hot water is limited to a couple of hours in the morning and evening. The two-star *Hotel Durău* at the top of the hill has a bowling centre and disco. Doubles in both cost $18.

At *Cabana Dochia* (mobile ☎ 092-235 503), atop Dochia peak, a bed for the night in a dorm room starts from $2 per person. Basic meals can also be provided for an additional $3 per person.

INTO THE DANUBE DELTA
From Moldavia, travelling to northern Dobruja and the Danube Delta involves a short ferry crossing across the Danube River (Râul Dunărea); there is no through road. The alternative is to head south towards Bucharest then head east and cross the Danube at Cernavodă's bridge (see the Northern Dobruja chapter).

MOLDAVIA

Galaţi

Galaţi ('ga-lahts'), on the confluence of the Danube, Siret and Prut Rivers, is Moldavia's main gateway to the Danube Delta. It is home to Romania's largest steel mill with shabby shipyards scattered for kilometres along the riverside. During WWII, Galaţi was heavily bombed. Massive housing complexes fill the centre and cover entire hillsides of this ugly, industrial town today.

A funky **sculpture park** lies on the western outskirts of the town, on the road to Brăila. Farther west are the **Galaţi Steel Works**, inaugurated in 1968 as part of Ceauşescu's grand five-year plan to transform Romania into a great, heavy-industrial machine.

Today the works, which employ thousands of people, are just one of the many thorns in the government's side. The plant continues to make a loss yet its closure would have a devastating economic effect on Galaţi's population, not least because the town's entire heating system is generated by the plant. In a desperate bid to save the struggling, debt-ridden company, the government is attempting to privatise it, but investors have been hard to find.

In May 2000 the government announced plans to merge Sidex Galaţi with the national public utility company Termoelectrica. But this proposal has been slammed as unrealistic and uneconomic.

Since mid-1997, part of Galaţi has been declared a ZLG (Zona Liberă Galaţi) – free trade zone – by the Romanian government, in an attempt to lure foreign investors.

The NATO bombings of Yugoslavia in late 1999 had a devastating impact on local industry in Galaţi. Prior to the Danube becoming blocked with debris from destroyed bridges, Navrom Galaţi was the biggest shipping operator on the Danube, transporting more than 700,000 tonnes of cargo monthly. Bombings brought operations to a grinding halt. As a result the company has been forced to dismiss approximately 87% of its 3000-strong workforce. With debts of some $15 million, it is trying desperately to restructure its business and offload assets.

Romania's naval fleet is paraded in Galaţi in all its glory every year on Marine Day, the second weekend in August.

Orientation & Information Galaţi has two ports; the main port is at Str Portului 34. To get to the centre from here, exit the main port building and turn left along Str Portului, continue for 1km, then turn right onto Str Domnească – the main street. Galaţi's main hotels are 200m north on this street.

From the smaller port, little tug boats – suitable for cars and lorries – cross the Danube to the small village of IC Brătianu (formerly called '23 August') on the river's southern banks. The boat landing is 2.5km east of the centre along Str Portului.

The bus and train stations are adjacent to each other on Str Gării. Exit either station and head straight up the hill along Str Gării. Turn left along Str Domnească, past the university, until you reach the hotels. Continue south along Str Domnească to get to the main port.

Change money in one of the hotel currency exchanges, or head 1.5km west along Str Brăila, past Hotel Dunărea, to the Banca Comercială Română where you can change travellers cheques and get cash advances on credit cards.

Places to Stay & Eat Galaţi has two main hotels – **Hotel Galaţi** (☎ 036-460 040, fax 418 854, Str Domnească 12), and **Hotel Dunărea** ('Danube'; ☎ 036-418 041, fax 461 050) immediately opposite on the corner of Str Domnească and Str Brăila. The Galaţi charges from $26/30 to $37/42 depending on which storey the single/double rooms are on. The Danube's rooms, with private bath, are $33/40.

The towering **Hotel Sofin** (☎ 036-468 362, fax 468 528, Str Gheorghe Coşbuc 1), 2.5km west of the centre, has rooms for $19/25 a night, including breakfast. To get to the hotel, turn right off Str Domnească along Str Brăila, then turn right after passing the Banca Comercială Română.

Str Domnească is clustered with eating places, including the large **Restaurant Olympic**, with a terrace, and the funky **Sydney Restaurant**.

Getting There & Away Daily buses include one to Iaşi (255km) and one to Bucharest (212km).

The Agenţie de Voiaj CFR (☎ 036-472 420) is at Str Brăila, Block 1. Daily train services from Galaţi include 12 trains to Brăila (30 to 40 minutes), and five to Bârlad (three hours) where you can change for Iaşi.

Two small tug ferries depart for IC Brătianu every hour from the eastern boat landing, which is signposted 'Trecere Bac' from the centre ($1.50/0.15 per car/foot passenger).

Southern Bucovina

Southern Bucovina embraces the northwestern region of present-day Moldavia; northern Bucovina is in Ukraine. In 1775 the region was annexed by the Austro-Hungarian empire. It remained in Habsburg hands until 1918 when Bucovina was returned to Romania. Northern Bucovina was annexed by the Soviet Union in 1940 and incorporated into Ukraine.

The painted churches of southern Bucovina are among the greatest artistic monuments of Europe – in 1993 they were collectively designated a World Heritage Site by Unesco. If your time is limited, the Voroneţ and Moldoviţa Monasteries, both quite accessible by bus and train, provide a representative sample of what Bucovina has to offer. To do a complete circuit on your own will require three days. You can save time by renting a car in Suceava for around $60 per day – travelling the rugged mountain road between Moldoviţa and Suceviţa alone is worth the expense.

Apart from the religious art and monasteries, southern Bucovina is well worth visiting for its folklore, picturesque villages, bucolic scenery and colourful inhabitants, all as good as anything you'll find elsewhere in Romania.

SUCEAVA
☎ 030 • postcode 5800 • pop 118,000
Suceava, the capital of Moldavia from 1388 to 1565, was a thriving commercial centre on the Lviv-Istanbul trading route. By the end of Ştefan cel Mare's reign in 1504, Suceava had some 40 churches. In 1675 the Suceava fortress was blown up by the Turks, signifying the decline of the town as a commercial centre.

During the Ceauşescu regime in the 1980s, Suceava became notorious for its toxic pulp and paper works (still in operation) which churned out 20 tonnes of cellulose and fibre waste a day. By 1990 hundreds of local people were reported to be suffering from respiratory and nervous disorders known as 'Suceava syndrome'.

Today it's the seat of Suceava County and gateway to the painted churches of Bucovina. Its few old churches and historic fortress are easily seen in a day.

The colourful Moldavian Furrier Fair is held here every year in mid-August.

Orientation
Piaţa 22 Decembrie is the centre of town. Suceava has two train stations, both a few kilometres north of the city centre and easily reached by trolleybus. Trains which originate or terminate in Suceava arrive/depart at Gara Suceava Nord. Trains which transit Suceava arrive/depart from Gara Suceava.

The department store (magazinul universal) is close to Hotel Bucovina, south of Piaţa 22 Decembrie, on Str Ştefan cel Mare. In front of it is a small flower market.

Maps The Hartă Turistică şi a Municipiului Suceava ($0.30) includes a city map of Suceava as well as information on places of note, but is only available in Romanian. The Bucovina şi regiunea înconjurătoare county guide (1999) has good historical and cultural information in English, French and German and is sold for $2 at the Bucovina History Museum.

Information
Tourist Offices The Agenţia Bucovina Turism (☎ 221 297, fax 214 700) is inside Hotel Bucovina on Blvd Ana Ipătescu 5. Staff speak French and a little English. It arranges monastery tours, guides for $18 a day, and rents chauffeur-driven cars; open

MOLDAVIA

SOUTHERN BUCOVINA

7 am to 7 pm weekdays, and 8 am to noon Saturday.

For service with a smile from people who are as much in love with their work as they are with their country, head straight for Bucovina Estur (see Travel Agencies). Nothing is too much effort for staff here.

The ACR (☎ 516 800), Str Nicolae Bălcescu 8, sells road maps; open 8 am to 4 pm weekdays, and 9 to 11 am Saturday.

Money The currency exchange office inside Hotel Bucovina is open officially 7 am to 8 pm weekdays, and 8 am to 3 pm Satur-

day. However, you can change money at reception 24 hours. There is also an ATM outside.

BCIT, on Piaţa 22 Decembrie, gives cash advances on Visa/MasterCard, changes travellers cheques and also has an ATM; open 9 am to 4 pm weekdays. The Banca Comercială Română, Str Ştefan cel Mare 31, offers the same services 8.30 am to 1.30 pm weekdays.

Post & Telephone The telephone centre is on the corner of Str Nicolae Bălcescu and Str Firmu, and the post office is nearby at

Str Dimitrie Oncul. Both are open 7 am to 9 am weekdays, and 8 am to 4 pm Saturday.

Email & Internet Access Get connected or just relax over a coffee while emailing friends at the very modern Assist Internet Café & Computer Store (☎ 521 100, fax 520 303, e assist@assist.ro), opposite McDonald's, at Blvd Ana Ipătescu 7. Internet access costs $0.75 per hour. Web site: www.assist.ro.

Travel Agencies The well-informed Bucovina Estur (☎/fax 522 694, e bestur@assist.ro), Str Ştefan cel Mare 24, arranges private rooms and has a variety of monastery tours. It also rents out cars, for $60 a day with driver; a minibus is $100. The office is open 9 am to 6 pm weekdays, and 9 am to 1 pm Saturday.

Another goodie is the small Central Turism (☎/fax 523 024, e central@suceava.iiruc.ro), inside Hotel Suceava at Str Nicolae Bălcescu 2. Staff here will happily arrange monastery tours and organise English, French, German or Italian-speaking guides; open 8 am to 4 pm weekdays, and 8 am to 1 pm Saturday.

BTT (☎/fax 520 438), at Str Meseriaşilor 10, arranges monastery tours and accommodation in private homes in Câmpulung Moldovenesc, Vama and Humor; open 8 am to 5 pm weekdays, and 8 am to noon Saturday. The staff here do not speak English.

Things to See
The **Casa de Cultură** (House of Culture) is at the western end of Piaţa 22 Decembrie. North of the bus stop along Blvd Ana Ipătescu lie the foundations of the 15th-century **Princely Palace**. To the west is **St Dimitru's church** (Biserica Sfântu Dimitru; 1535), built by Petru Rareş in a clubbed Byzantine style typical of 16th-century Moldavian churches. Traces of the original exterior frescoes can still be seen.

West of Piaţa 22 Decembrie, at Str Ciprian Porumbescu 5, is **Hanul Domnesc**, a 16th-century guesthouse that now houses an **Ethnographic Museum** with a good collection of folk costumes; open 9 am to 5 pm Tuesday to Sunday ($1).

Close by at Aleea Simeon Florea Marian 2 is the **Simeon Florea Marian Memorial House** (☎ 227 297), dedicated to the life and works of the folk-song poet Simeon Florea Marian (1847–1907) whose bust stands in the small park opposite; open 9 am to 5 pm daily. If the door is locked, knock and someone should answer.

Next to the post office on Str Dimitrie Onciul is the town's only surviving **synagogue** (1870). Prior to WWII, some 18 synagogues served the local Jewish community. There is an **old Jewish Cemetery** on the corner of Str Ştefan Tomşa and Str Alexandru cel Bun (you can only enter it by the backyard of a private house). The **new Jewish Cemetery**, on the opposite side of the road to the central Orthodox cemetery, close to the citadel on Str Parcului, is a lavish affair in contrast.

Return to Piaţa 22 Decembrie and follow Str Ştefan cel Mare south past **Parcul Central** (Central Park) to the surprisingly informative **Bucovina History Museum** (Muzeul Naţional al Bucovinei) at No 33. The presentation comes to an abrupt end at 1945 and old paintings now hang in rooms that formerly glorified the communist era; open 10 am to 6 pm Tuesday to Sunday ($0.65).

Backtrack to the park and take Str Mitropoliei south-east to the **Monastery of St John the New** (Mănăstirea Sfântu Ioan cel Nou; 1522). The paintings on the outside of the church are badly faded, but give you an idea of the church frescoes for which Bucovina is famous.

Continue on Str Mitropoliei, keeping left on the main road out of town, till you see a large wooden gate marked 'Parcul Cetăţii' on the left. Go through it and, when the ways divide, follow the footpath with the park benches around to the left to the huge **equestrian statue** (1966) of the Moldavian leader Ştefan cel Mare. Twenty metres back on the access road to the monument another footpath on the left descends towards the **Cetatea de Scaun** (City of Residence; 1388), a fortress that in 1476 held off Mehmed II, conqueror of Constantinople (Istanbul). The original fortress, known as Muşat's fortress, was built by Petru I Muşat. It had eight square towers and was

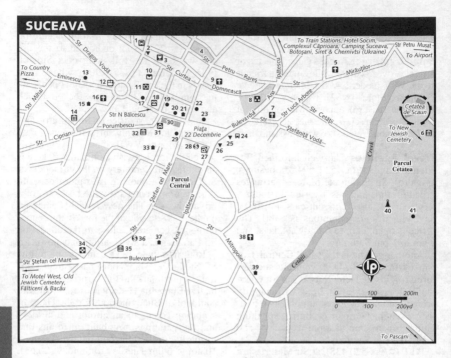

SUCEAVA

surrounded by defensive trenches. Ştefan cel
Mare developed it further, building 4m-thick,
33m-tall walls around it so it was impossible
to shoot an arrow over. From 1775, following the occupation of Bucovina by the Austrians, the fortress was dismantled and the
stones used to build houses in Suceava town.
Restoration work started on the fortress in
1944. It is open 7 am to 6 pm daily ($0.25).

At the southern end of the fortress, work is
progressing on the open-air **Muzeul Satului**
(Village Museum). The houses in the village
are traditional Bucovinan style and are being
decorated with folk art of the region. The
museum should be complete by early 2002.

On the hillside opposite the fortress is
Mirăuţi Church (1390), the original Moldavian coronation church, which was rebuilt
in the 17th century. It was to this church
that Petru I Muşat moved the Metropolitan
cathedral in the 16th century. Get here by
taking the path down through the park on
the west (left) side of the fortress.

Places to Stay

Camping Near the Suceava River, between
Gara Suceava Nord and Suceava, is the privately run *Camping Suceava* (☎ 214 958),
on Str Cernăuţi. A bed in a dusty two-bed
wooden hut costs $3 a night.

Private Rooms Bucovina Estur (see
Travel Agencies) arranges rooms in private
homes in Suceava and surrounding villages
for $15 per person.

Hotels By making bookings through the
tourist offices, in most cases the price will
be cheaper.

The seediest and dodgiest joint in town,
only recommended for groups of die-hard
backpackers, is *Autogară Suceava* (☎ 216
089), on Str Armenască above the bus-
station ticket hall. A simple, smelly double
with bathroom is $8. Reception? The bus-
station information booth. Cleaner is the
five-storey *Hotel Socim* (☎/fax 522 662, Str

SUCEAVA

PLACES TO STAY	9	St Dimitru's Church	12	Cinema Modern
15 Hotel Arcaşul	11	Synagogue	13	Eurostela 24-Hour Shop
21 Hotel Suceava; Restaurant	14	Simeon Florea Marian	17	Automobil Clubul Român
Suceava; Central Tourism		Memorial House		(ACR)
33 Hotel Gloria	16	St Nicholas Church &	18	Telephone Centre
37 Hotel Bucovina; Agenţia		Monument	19	BTT
Bucovina Turism	32	Hanul Domnesc;	20	Agenţie de Voiaj CFR
39 Hotel Balada		Ethnographic Museum	22	Supermarket
	35	Bucovina History Museum	23	Tarom
PLACES TO EAT	38	Monastery of St John the New	24	Buses to/from Train Station
2 Markiz Patisserie & Cofeterie	40	Statue of Ştefan cel Mare	27	Assist Internet Café &
25 Poftă Bună Patisserie	41	Cemetery		Computer Store
26 McDonald's			28	BCIT
		OTHER	29	Bucovina Estur
THINGS TO SEE	1	Bus Station; Autogară	30	Casa de Cultură; Xtreme
5 Mirăuţi Church		Suceava		Disco
6 Muzeul Satului	3	Club Amsterdam	31	Taxi Rank
7 Domniţelor Church	4	Central Market	34	Universal Department Store
8 Princely Palace Ruins	10	Post Office	36	Banca Comercială Română

Jean Bart 24), 200m up the street from Gara Suceava. A bed in a double/triple room with shared shower and toilet costs $3.50 a night per person. Breakfast is not included and hot water is only available from 6 to 9 am and 4 to 9 pm.

Better value for the comfort and security it offers is the central *Hotel Gloria (☎ 521 209, fax 520 005, Str Mihai Vasile Bumbac 4)*. Singles/doubles are $20/25, breakfast included.

The two-star *Hotel Suceava (☎ 521 079, fax 521 080, Str Bălcescu 2)* is a modern four-storey hotel in the centre of town. Rooms with bath are an overpriced $25/35, breakfast included. If you book through Central Turism, you'll find the prices will be cheaper.

Hotel Arcaşul (☎ 520 785, fax 227 598, Str Mihai Viteazul 4–6), close to the Simeon Florea Marian Memorial House, charges $32/44, breakfast included.

Make bookings through Bucovina Estur and get a 10% discount for the 10-storey *Hotel Bucovina (☎ 217 048, Blvd Ana Ipătescu 5)*. Singles/doubles with bath are $33/48, breakfast included (without discount).

The privately run *Hotel Balada (☎ 223 198, fax 520 087, Str Mitropoliei 1)* has rooms with direct-dial phones and cable TV

for $45/49. Book through Bucovina Estur and get a 10% discount.

Out of Town Eight kilometres north, in a forest on the road to Dorohoi, is the *Complexul Căprioara* ('Deer Complex'; ☎ 520 681, fax 520 708), a private motel, disco and bar which draws a large crowd. A bed in one of its six double rooms is $7. There are also a dozen wooden camping huts on the complex which cost $6 per person a night. Tents can be pitched for $2.

Some 4km from the city centre on the road to Humor Monastery is *Motel West (☎ 512 199, Str Humorului 11)*, a member of Youth Hostels Romania. A bed in a double room is $7.50 per person.

Places to Eat

Eating options in Suceava are limited. The soups served at *Restaurant Suceava (Str Nicolae Bălcescu 2)* are greasy and salty, though cheap; a bowl of vegetable soup *(Ciorbă de legume)* is only $0.50.

Favoured locally is *Country Pizza (☎ 218 428, Str George Enescu 27)*, west of the centre. Its small selection of pizza slices, with a variety of generous toppings ranging from salami to seafood, start from $1.20.

Markiz Patisserie and Cofeterie on Str Alecsandri – look for the big blue marquee

MOLDAVIA

opposite the bus station – serves heavenly cakes and pastries as well as hot dogs and hamburgers. Also delicious are the cakes and pastries at *Poftă Bună Patisserie*, on Piaţa 22 Decembrie next to the bus stop. It has a stand-up counter where you can drink juice or dunk your pastry in your coffee.

McDonald's, on Blvd Ana Ipătescu opposite the Assist Internet Café, is open 7 am to midnight daily.

Self-Catering There is a *supermarket* opposite Restaurant Suceava on Str Ştefan cel Mare; open until 11 pm daily. *Eurostela*, opposite St Nicholas Church on Str Mihai Eminescu, opens 24 hours. The *central market* is close to the bus station, on the corner of Str Petru Rareş and Str Avram Iancu.

Entertainment

Cinemas Films are screened in their original languages at *Cinema Modern*, facing the roundabout at the western end of Str Bălcescu. There's also a small cinema inside the Casa de Cultură on Piaţa 22 Decembrie.

Bars & Discos The private *Club Amsterdam*, on Str Curtea Domnească, charges a hefty $3 for entrance to its cheap-thrills nightclub. A cheaper alternative is the *Xtreme* disco inside the House of Culture; open 10 pm to 4 am Thursday to Saturday.

The top spot in summer is the outside disco at the out-of-town *Complexul Căprioara*, surrounded by forests 8km north of Suceava (see Places to Stay).

Getting There & Away

Air Tarom has one flight on Monday, Tuesday, Wednesday and Friday from Suceava to Bucharest ($44). The office (☎/fax 214 686), at Str Nicolae Bălcescu 2, is open 8.30 am to 5 pm weekdays.

Train Tickets for trains can be bought 24 hours or more before departure at the Agenţie de Voiaj CFR (☎ 214 335) at Str Nicolae Bălcescu 8, open 7.30 am to 8 pm weekdays.

The left-luggage office (open 24 hours) is at the information window on the main platform.

Express trains to Bucharest (seven hours), Iaşi (1½ hours) and Cluj-Napoca (6½ hours) are fairly regular. Local trains go to Gura Humorului, Putna, Câmpulung Moldovenesc and Vatra Dornei.

Bus The bus station (☎ 216 089) is in the centre of town at Str Armenească. Tickets for international destinations are sold at window No 4. Six buses run daily, except Monday, between Suceava and Chernivtsi (Cernăuţi) in Ukraine ($4, 90km).

Buses to Romanian destinations include nine daily to Gura Humorului (47km), five to Rădăuţi ($1.20), seven to Botoşani ($1.20, 42km), one to Iaşi ($2.80, 141km) and three daily to Târgu Neamţ (71km).

Getting Around

To/From the Airport Suceava airport is 16km east of the centre in the Salcea district. Tarom operates a free shuttle bus from its office at Str Nicolae Bălcescu 2 to the airport, departing one hour before flights.

Bus & Trolleybus Buses and trolleybuses run between 5 am and 11 pm. The central bus and trolleybus stop is at the western end of Piaţa 22 Decembrie from which all buses and trolleybuses to/from the two train stations arrive/depart. Trolleybus Nos 2 and 3, and bus Nos 20 and 26 run between the centre and Gara Suceava. To reach Gara Suceava Nord, take trolleybus No 5 or bus No 1, 10, 11 or 28. The buses and trolleybuses for both train stations stop directly outside the station.

Local buses to villages within a 15km radius of the city depart from the Autogară Burdejeni, a small building close to Gara Suceava at Str Nicolae Iorga 24. Take trolleybus No 4 or bus No 5 from the central bus stop.

AROUND SUCEAVA

Interesting if time allows are the sights around Suceava: Dragomirna Monastery can be easily incorporated into any trip north to Arbore and Putna. The villages of Ilişeşti and Ciprian Porumbescu are en route to Humor and Voroneţ Monasteries.

Dragomirna Monastery

Dragomirna Monastery (Mănăstirea Drago-mirna), 12km north of Suceava in the village of Mitocul Dragomirna, was founded in 1608-9 by the scholar, calligrapher, artist and bishop Anastasie Crimca who joined the Putna Monastery as a novice monk in his teenage years.

The intricate rope lacing around the side of the main church (1627) represents the unity of the Holy Trinity and the short-lived unification of the principalities of Moldavia, Wallachia and Transylvania in 1600. The church tower is 42m tall.

Dragomirna's treasure, displayed in the **museum of medieval art** in the monastery grounds, includes a beautifully carved candle made by Bishop Crimca, ornamental carved cedar crosses mounted in silver-gilt filigree, and a large number of missals and religious scripts.

Dragomirna remained inhabited during the Habsburg and later communist purges on the Orthodox Church. Crimca's dying wish was that a day should not pass without prayers being said in his monastery. Thus seven elderly nuns defied communist orders and remained alone at the monastery throughout the 1960s and '70s. Today some 60 nuns live here; it's open 8 am to 8 pm daily ($0.25).

It is sometimes possible for travellers to stay at the monastery. Bucovina Estur (see Suceava's Travel Agencies section) can provide more information.

Getting There & Away Buses from Suceava to Dragomirna depart at 7, 8.30 and 11.45 am ($0.45, 45 minutes) from Suceava bus station.

Ilişeşti & Ciprian Porumbescu

Ilişeşti, 20km south-west of Suceava, was home to a wealthy evangelist priest who had a daughter called Berta. In the neighbouring village of Ciprian Porumbescu, 6km south, lived the Romanian composer Ciprian Porumbescu (1853–83) who fell wildly in love with the priest's beautiful daughter. Being poor and of the Orthodox faith, however, the composer was not considered a suitable match for Berta, inspiring him to compose the well-known *Ballad of Ciprian.*

In 1873 Porumbescu was imprisoned in Austria for alleged antistate activities. Until his sudden death in 1883, he taught music in Braşov where he composed Romania's first operetta, *Crai Nou* (The New Moon).

The **Memorial House** (Casa Memorială) to Ciprian Porumbescu, in which the composer lived, remains in the village of Ciprian Porumbescu. The key for the house is available from the **Ciprian Porumbescu Museum** (Muzeul Ciprian Porumbescu), at the western end of the village. On display are various relics from Porumbescu's life. The bed in which Berta slept is also exhibited. The museum is open 9 am to 6 pm Tuesday to Sunday ($0.25/0.15 for adults/students).

To get to Ciprian Porumbescu from Ilişeşti, continue for 4km west along the Suceava–Gura Humorului road, past Hanul Ilişeşti. Turn left at the signpost for Ciprian Porumbescu and continue for 6km along the forest road until you reach the village. At the southern end of the village the road forks; turn left for the memorial house or right for the museum complex.

Places to Stay & Eat Wild *camping* is permitted in Ilişeşti forest which surrounds the village to the west. You can buy fresh milk and cheese from the shepherds who live in small wooden huts in the valley of the Stupca brook.

Doubles/triples with private shower at *Hanul Ilişeşti* (☎ *214 725*), 3km west of Ilişeşti on the road to Gura Humorului, cost $7/11 a night. A bed in an unheated cabana is $3.50. Hot water can be arranged if you call in advance.

Getting There & Away Eleven buses daily, departing from Suceava between 8.15 am and 7.20 pm, stop at Ilişeşti village, from where it is a good 6km hike through forest to Ciprian Porumbescu.

Local trains depart daily from Gara Suceava to Ciprian Porumbescu (40 minutes, 8.30 am, 3.54 and 7.33 pm).

Bucovina's Monasteries

The painted churches of southern Bucovina were erected at a time when northern Moldavia was threatened by Turkish invaders. Great popular armies would gather inside the monasteries' strong defensive walls, waiting to do battle. To educate, entertain and arouse the interest of the illiterate soldiers and peasants who were unable to enter the church or understand the Slavic liturgy, well-known biblical stories were portrayed on the church walls in cartoon-style frescoes.

Most amazing in these vast compositions are the realistic portrayals of human figures against a backdrop not unlike the local landscape (the forested Carpathian foothills). Some frescoes have been damaged by centuries of rain and wind, but more often than not the intense colours have been duly preserved, from the greens of Suceviţa to the blues of Voroneţ and the reds of Humor. Natural dyes are used – sulphur for yellow, madder for red, and cobalt or lapis for blue.

All Orthodox monasteries face the east, in keeping with the traditional belief that the light of God shines in the image of the rising sun. An outside porch, likewise tattooed with frescoes, is typical of the Bucovina monasteries. Within, they are divided into three rooms – the *pronaos* (first chamber), the tomb room, and the *naos* (altar room). Women are not allowed to enter the altar, shielded from public view by an iconostasis – a beautifully sculpted, gilded partition in the naos. The church domes are a peculiar combination of Byzantine pendentives and Moorish crossed arches with larger-than-life paintings of Christ or the Virgin peering down.

Each monastery is dedicated to a saint, whose patron day is among the most important feast days for the monastery's inhabitants. The nuns or monks are required to fast – no meat, eggs or dairy products – for several days leading up to any religious feast. Wednesday, Friday, Lent, the six weeks after Easter, and the days preceding Christmas are likewise fast days.

Novices are required to serve three to seven years in a monastery before being ordained. Numerous penances have to be observed during this training period; many have to stand motionless in the street for several consecutive days, bearing a plaque indicating that they are 'waiting' for cash donations towards the 'spiritual furthering' of their monastery.

Following the Habsburg occupation of Bucovina in 1785, most monasteries were closed and their inhabitants forced to relinquish their spiritual lives for a civilian one. The monasteries were equally persecuted under communism, and it is only since 1990 that the inner activity of these holy sanctuaries has matched the dynamism of their outer facades.

Most monasteries are open 8 am to 6 pm daily and provide free guided tours in English or French. An additional entrance fee is charged for cameras/video cameras. Smoking and wearing shorts are forbidden and women are required to cover their shoulders.

GURA HUMORULUI
☎ 030

This small logging town, 36km west of Suceava, on the main railway line to Cluj-Napoca, is an ideal centre for visiting the monasteries. Most trains stop here and the adjacent train and bus stations are a seven-minute walk from the centre.

The post office is on the corner of Str Bucovinei and Str 9 Mai. The CFR office is at Str Republicii 10 opposite the old cinema. The **Ethnographic Museum**, Blvd Bucovina 21, east of the post office has been closed indefinitely.

You can hike 4km south to Voroneţ Monastery through beautiful farmland or a 6km hike north to Humor where you can stay the night before visiting the monastery. If you plan to bus it from Gura Humorului to Voroneţ and Humor Monasteries, check the bus schedule immediately when you arrive in town; bus times change fairly regularly.

From Gura Humorului you can continue on the main Suceava-Vatra Dornei road west to Câmpulung Moldovenesc and the Rarău Mountains, turning off the main road 16km before Câmpulung Moldovenesc at

Vama where a road leads north to the Moldoviţa and Suceviţa Monasteries.

Alternatively you can head directly north from Gura Humorului to the Solca and Arbore Monasteries making a small detour to the Cacica salt mines en route; from Arbore you can then continue north to Rădăuţi and to Putna Monastery or head west to Suceviţa and Moldoviţa.

Places to Stay
Private Rooms Families in Gura Humorului are organising their own *agro-tourism* scheme, inviting guests to stay in their homes for around $15 a night. The Bolac family at Str Ana Ipătescu 13 are excellent hosts, as are the Andrian family (☎ 238 863) at Str Câmpului 30 who have three modern double rooms for $25 a night in high season, including breakfast. Guests share a bathroom which has a hot water boiler.

Bucovina Estur (see Suceava's Travel Agencies section) takes bookings for rooms.

Hotels You can *camp* for free by the Moldova River 1km south of town at the foot of the wooden hills. Otherwise try the unappealing *Hotel Carpaţi (☎ 231 103, Str 9 Mai 3)*, beside the post office, with single/double rooms with communal showers (no hot water) for $5/8 per person.

Places to Eat
Basic plates of pork and soup are served at *Restaurant Moldova*, on the left just after the bridge as you come from the stations.

Better is *Restaurant Select (Str Bucovinei 1)*, with a Romanian-French-English menu. Next door is a *Mini Market* for supplies if you'll be hiking to the monasteries.

Getting There & Away
Train Gura Humorului is on the main railway line between Suceava and Ilva Mica, with some eight daily trains covering this route which continues west to Cluj-Napoca in Transylvania. From Gura Humorului there are three trains daily to Iaşi (2¾ hours).

Bus From Gura Humorului bus station (☎ 230 707), Str Ştefan cel Mare 37, there is a daily bus to Arbore (36km); two a day to Rădăuţi (40km) and Piatra Neamţ (261km); three a day to Solca (21km), Cacica (15km), Voroneţ (4km) and Botoşani (64km) via Illişeşti (15km); and seven to Humor Monastery (6km), Câmpulung Moldovenesc (33km) and Suceava (47km). On weekends the service is greatly reduced. If you have limited time, bargain with taxi drivers here for monastery tours.

VORONEŢ
The *Last Judgment* fresco, which fills the entire western wall of the Voroneţ Monastery (Mănăstirea Voroneţ) is perhaps the most marvellous Bucovine fresco. At the top, angels roll up the signs of the zodiac to indicate the end of time. The middle fresco shows humanity being brought to judgement. On the left, St Paul escorts the believers, while on the right Moses brings forward the nonbelievers. Below is the Resurrection.

On the northern wall is *Genesis,* from Adam and Eve to Cain and Abel. The southern wall features another tree of Jesse with the genealogy of biblical personalities. In the vertical fresco to the left is the story of the martyrdom of St John of Suceava (who is buried in the Monastery of Sfântu Ioan cel Nou in Suceava). The vibrant blue pigment used throughout the frescoes is known worldwide as 'Voroneţ blue'.

In the narthex likes the tomb of Daniel the Hermit, the first abbot of Voroneţ Monastery (see Putna, later, for more on Daniel). It was upon the worldly advice of Daniel, who told Ştefan cel Mare not to give up his battle against the Turks, that the Moldavian prince went on to win further victories against the Turks and then to build Voroneţ Monastery out of gratitude to God.

In 1785, occupying Austrians forced Voroneţ's monks to abandon the monastery. Since 1991 the monastery has been inhabited by a small community of nuns.

In summer it is open to 8 pm daily ($0.55 plus $1/2.50 for cameras/video cameras).

Places to Stay & Eat
Double rooms at the *Nistru family home (☎ 030-230 551)* cost $25/21 a night in

summer/winter, including breakfast. There are two bathrooms, each with an electric water heater. To reach the house from the monastery, continue past the main entrance, turn right along a dirt track, and continue for 50m.

Casa Elena, (☎ 030-230 651), 2km from Gura Humorului on the main road to the Voroneţ Monastery, has 10 rooms at $24/30 for a single/double, including breakfast. The hotel also has a billiard room and a 24-hour restaurant.

Getting There & Away
There are buses on weekdays from Gura Humorului to Voroneţ, departing at 7 am, and 12.10 and 2.45 pm. A sunny option is to walk the 4km along a narrow village road to Voroneţ. The route is clearly marked and it is impossible to get lost.

HUMOR
Of all the Bucovina monasteries, Humor Monastery (Mănăstirea Humorului) has the most impressive interior frescoes. It was founded by Chancellor Theodor Bubuiog in 1530 under the guidance of Moldavian prince Petru Rareş. Unlike the other monasteries, Humor has no tower and is surrounded by ramparts made from wood; its traditional Moldavian open porch was the first of its kind to be built in Bucovina.

Its exterior frescoes, dating from 1535, are predominantly red. Paintings on the church's southern exterior wall are devoted to the Holy Virgin, the patron saint of the monastery. There's a badly faded depiction of the 1453 siege of Constantinople, with the parable of the return of the prodigal son beside it to the right. St George is depicted on the northern wall. On the porch is a painting of the *Last Judgment*: the long bench on which the 12 apostles sit, the patterned towel on the chair of judgment, and the long, horn-like bucium used to announce the coming of Christ, are all typical Moldavian elements.

Humor shelters five chambers, the middle one (the tombs' room) has a lower ceiling than the others. This hides a treasure room (*tainiţa*) where the riches of the monastery were traditionally kept safe. On the right wall

as you enter the tombs' room is a votive painting depicting the founder, Toader Bubuiog, offering, with the help of the Virgin Mary, a miniature replica of the monastery to Christ. The tomb of Bubuiog, who died in 1539, and his wife, lie on the left side of the room; a painting of his wife praying to the Virgin Mary is above her grave.

The paintings in the first chamber (*pronaos*) depict various scenes of martyrs. Above the decorative border, which runs around the base of the four walls, is a pictorial representation of the first three months of the Orthodox calendar (*synaxary*). Unlike the other interior paintings which were restored by Unesco in the early 1970s, the paintings in the altar room (*naos*) have never been restored.

Admission to the monastery is $0.55; a $1/2.50 fee is charged for the use of cameras/video cameras. Nuns provide free guided tours in French.

Places to Stay & Eat
Don't be deceived by the sign advertising 'rooms free' at the *Maison de Bucovine* (☎ operator 991; ask for ☎ 172 Mănăstirea Humor), 50m from the monastery; free simply means available. The $12 nightly fee, includes a hearty breakfast cooked up by host Maria Albu. Shared bathrooms in a separate outbuilding are clean and have hot water heaters. Maria cooks evening meals for an additional fee.

Private homes offering accommodation include those of the Butucea and Gheorghiţă families; ask in the village for directions. Bucovina Estur and BTT travel agency in Suceava also arrange accommodation in private rooms in Humor. Nightly rates through both start at $15; including breakfast.

It is possible to stay at the monastery (☎ operator 991; ask for ☎ 140 Mănăstirea Humor) but it cannot be arranged in advance. Nuns providing the guided tours will occasionally invite you to spend a night or two at the monastery.

Getting There & Away
There are daily buses from Gura Humorului to Humor, departing from Gura bus station at

7.40 and 11 am, and 12.30, 2.30, 4 and 5 pm (check first). You can also hike the 6km north from Gura Humorului to Humor or hitch a ride on a horsecart (forget cars – few pass by).

MOLDOVIŢA

Moldoviţa Monastery (Mănăstirea Moldoviţa) is in the middle of a quaint village. Moldoviţa consists of a fortified quadrangular enclosure with towers and brawny gates, with a magnificent painted church at its centre. The monastery has undergone careful restoration in recent years. Its frescoes are predominantly yellow.

The fortifications here are actually more impressive than the badly faded frescoes. On the church's southern exterior wall is a depiction of the defence of Constantinople in AD 626 against Persians dressed as Turks, while on the porch is a representation of the *Last Judgment*. Inside the sanctuary, on a wall facing the original carved iconostasis, is a portrait of Prince Petru Rareş, the monastery's founder, offering the church to Christ. All of these works date from 1537.

In the monastery's small museum is Petru Rareş' original throne; open 10 am to 6 pm Tuesday to Sunday. Admission to the monastery is $0.55.

Places to Stay & Eat

Mărul de Aur (☎ 030-336 180), between the train station and the monastery, has tired double/triple rooms for $7.50 per person. Downstairs is a smoke-filled restaurant serving basic meals and beer 24 hours. The complex also operates a *camping ground*, 3km out of town on the road to Suceviţa. Cabins are $3.50 and camping is free.

Vama This small village is 14km south of Moldoviţa, between Gura Humorului and Câmpulung Moldovenesc on the main Suceava–Vatra Dornei road. *Cabana Vama* (open summer only) is signposted on the left as you enter the village from the east; follow the dirt track for 1km. In the centre of the village is the *family home of Lucan Viorel (Str Victoriei 7);* doubles are $11 per person including breakfast, or $17 per person full board. Ask for some fresh milk from their

cow during your stay. The *Mihai Nicorescu family (Str Victoriei 5),* next door, also has rooms to let for $15 per person full board.

The agro-tourist agency Opération Villages Roumains also arranges rooms in private homes in Vama and around, for $10 to $17 a night. It has a small 'biroul de informaţii' signposted in the centre of Vama village, open 1 May to 1 October, where you can arrange a bed for the night. Staff can arrange English- and French-speaking tour guides – price negotiable.

Bucovina Estur and the BTT travel agency in Suceava both arrange accommodation in private rooms here. Nightly rates through both start at $15, including breakfast.

Getting There & Away

Moldoviţa Monastery is right above Vatra Moldoviţei's train station (be sure to get off at Vatra Moldoviţei, not Moldoviţa). From Suceava there are seven daily trains to Vama (1½ hours), and from Vama three trains leave daily for Vatra Moldoviţei (50 minutes) at 7.29 am, and 2.58 and 11.09 pm.

SUCEVIŢA

Suceviţa (Mănăstirea Suceviţa) is the largest and finest of the Bucovina monasteries. The church inside the fortified monastic enclosure, built between 1582 and 1601, is almost completely covered with frescoes. Mysteriously, the western wall of the monastery remains bare of any impressive frescoes. Legend has it that the artist fell off the scaffolding while attempting to paint the wall and was killed, leaving artists of the time too scared to follow in his footsteps. The exterior frescoes – predominantly red and green – date from around 1590.

As you enter you first see the *Virtuous Ladder* fresco covering most of the northern exterior wall, depicting the 30 steps from Hell to Paradise. The frescoes inside the arches above the open porch depict the apocalypse and the vision of St John.

On the southern exterior wall is the Jesse tree symbolising the continuity of the Old and New Testaments. The tree grows from the reclining figure of Jesse, who is flanked by a row of ancient philosophers. To the left is the Virgin as a Byzantine princess, with angels holding a red veil over her head.

Inside the church, in the second chamber, the Orthodox calendar is depicted. The tombs of the founders, Moldavian nobles Simion and Ieremia Movilă, lie in the tombs' room. The last of the painted monasteries to be built, this is the only one not to have been built by Ştefan cel Mare or his family. Ieremia Movilă, who died in 1606, appears with his seven children on the western wall inside the naos.

Sucevita Monastery was first inhabited by monks in 1582. During the communist era, only nuns over 50 were allowed to stay at Sucevita.

Apart from the church, there's a small museum at Sucevita Monastery in which various treasures and art pieces from the monastery are displayed. It is open 8 am to 8 pm daily ($0.55, cameras and videos $0.55 each). The nuns offer free guided tours of the complex in French.

Places to Stay & Eat

It's worth spending a night here and doing a little hiking in the surrounding hills. Wild *camping* is possible in the field across the stream from the monastery. Otherwise the renovated *Hanul Sucevita*, about 1km north-east towards Rădăuti, has double rooms with bath in the main two-storey building for $20. The hotel also has a restaurant which serves OK meals and is open year-round.

Popas Turistic Bucovina (☎/fax 030-565 389), 5km south of Sucevita on the road to Vatra Moldovitei, has two charming villas and an excellent Moldavian restaurant. Singles/doubles with private bath cost $20/28, including a delicious ham and egg breakfast. There are also 10 wooden double huts for $8 per hut.

Getting There & Away

Sucevita is the most difficult monastery to reach on public transport. There are buses from Rădăuti (17km) at 6.30 am and 3 pm daily. At the time of writing, the bus service between Sucevita and Moldovita (36km) had ceased.

The road connecting the two monasteries winds up over a high mountain pass (1100m), through forests and small alpine villages. The drive is stunning and offers unlimited wild-camping opportunities, but you need a car to explore it fully (hiking up would be madness). It's possible to hike the 20km north to Putna in about five hours.

CACICA SALT MINE

The small village of Cacica, 15km north of Gura Humorului on the road to Solca, is home to Moldavia's largest salt mine (Salină Veche Cacica). The mine, discovered in 1445, was not exploited until 1791 under the Habsburg regime. By the end of the 19th century, the Cacica mine was a thriving enterprise with hundreds of miners from Bulgaria, Hungary, Poland, Yugoslavia and Ukraine. The village was nicknamed 'little Austria', for its harmonious, multi-ethnic population.

It was during this same period that the miners discovered a large salt cross in one of the galleries 26m underground. In 1904 the miners dug by hand a small Orthodox church in the mine, lit by oil lamps when it first opened. They dedicated it to St Varvara, the traditional protector of miners. To this day, the miners still celebrate 9 December – their patron saint's day – with a church service followed by merrymaking in the village. The church is still in use today.

On the right wall as you enter, there is an icon of the Holy Virgin to which believers come to pray, light candles and plead for their troubles to be resolved. Locally, it is believed that this icon is miracle-working.

Every year on 15 August, the Holy Virgin's Assumption, Roman Catholic pilgrims from all over Romania flock to Cacica to celebrate the holiday. The parish priests from the three churches in the village are invited to the chapel in the salt mine where an ecumenical Mass is celebrated. A congregation of thousands gathers for this unique religious event.

The mine's other features include a natural salt 'lake of wishes', a dancing hall and a vast array of fantastic salt sculptures. The history of the mine is explained in the small **Salt Museum** (Muzeul Salinei Cacica), next to the main entrance. Guided tours of the mine in Romanian are available. The mine and museum (☎ operator 191; ask for Salină Veche Cacica) are open 9 am to 5 pm daily ($0.30/0.15 for adults/students).

Getting There & Away
From Gura Humorului there are buses daily to Cacica (30 minutes, 6.30 and 11.45 am, and 4.30 pm). Get off at the main bus stop in the village, opposite the red-brick Roman Catholic Church; the old salt mine (Salină Veche Cacica) is immediately opposite the church. If you're driving ask for the 'old' salt mine; the 'new' salt mine, is some 9km from Cacica village. From Suceava there are five local trains daily to Cacica (45 minutes).

SOLCA & ARBORE MONASTERIES
Few tourists make their way to the tiny monasteries of Solca and Arbore; those who do leave disappointed. Arbore has a handful of scarcely visible frescoes on its outside walls while Solca has none at all. Neither monastery is inhabited today and both are often closed; tracking down the person in the village who has the key can prove problematic.

Solca Monastery
The walled monastery of Solca, 21km north of Gura Humorului, is today little more than a village church and rarely used. The monastery was built in 1612 as a defence for the village as well as for religious worship. Following the occupation of Bucovina by the Austrians, it was stripped of its monastic status. The iconostasis inside the church dates from 1895.

A beer factory next door was opened by the monks in the 17th century. In 1810 the Austrian administration opened a larger factory on the same site. This factory – the present-day Solca Beer Factory (Fabrica de Bere Solca) – still uses the gunpowder cellars of the monastery for storing beer kegs.

Getting There & Away Getting to Solca by public transport can be rather tiresome. Theoretically there are buses on weekdays from Gura Humorului to Solca (6.30 and

11.45 am, and 4.30 pm). At Solca, buses turn around and head back to Gura, making it difficult to see much else except Solca in one day. From Rădăuți there is one bus daily to Solca, via Arbore (6 pm).

Arbore Monastery
Arbore Monastery is 15km east of Solca and 33km north of Suceava. It was built in 1503 by Suceava's chief magistrate, Luca Arbore (he owned the entire village), who raised the small church next to his private residence as a family chapel and cemetery. His Gothic-style tomb lies inside the first chamber (pronaos) of the church, beneath a beautiful carved-stone canopy.

The village cemetery across the street from the monastery is adorned with colourful wreaths and flowers.

Arbore's predominantly green frescoes date from 1541. Bad weather has left most of the walls bare, and it is only the impressive frescoes protected by the protruding walls and overhanging eaves on the western wall that are of any interest: scenes from the *Lives of the Saints* and Genesis run along the wall in eight registers and faint traces of the *Last Judgment* are evident in the upper right-hand corner.

Getting There & Away From Gura Humorului there is one bus daily departing at 4.30 pm, which makes it practically impossible to get to Arbore and back in one day. Arbore is easier to access from Suceava if you are prepared to hike the final couple of kilometres from the main bus stop next to the Arbore turn-off on the main Suceava-Siret road. Take any bus from Suceava heading to Siret or Rădăuți (see the following section). From Rădăuți to Arbore, buses leave daily at 6.30 am, noon, and 3.30 and 6 pm.

RĂDĂUȚI
☎ 030
Rădăuți ('rah-dah-oots') is a large and boring market town. The only reason to come is to catch a train to Putna or a bus to the monasteries in Arbore, Solca and Sucevița.

The bus station is on Blvd Ștefan cel Mare, a block north from Rădăuți's train station on Str Gării. From the bus station, head east along Blvd Ştefan cel Mare until you reach the central square, Piaţa Unirii. The left-luggage office at the train station is open 24 hours.

Nine kilometres west from Rădăuţi towards Suceviţa, you pass through the village of **Marginea**, famed for its black earthenware and pottery. Some 12km south of Rădăuţi on the main Suceava-Siret road, you pass through **Grăniceşti**, a completely systemised village.

The 16-room *Hotel Azur* (☎/fax 564 718, *Calea Cernţi 29*), a 10-minute walk from Rădăuţi's centre, has doubles/triples with shared bath for $10/14 a night. Breakfast is $1 extra.

Getting There & Away

Train There are direct trains from Suceava to Rădăuţi (1½ hours) at 8.41 am and 12.10, 2 and 5.58 pm daily. Six trains go daily from Rădăuţi to Putna (one hour) and nine to Dorneşti (11 minutes). From Dorneşti there are direct trains to Suceava (1½ hours) and other stops along the Suceava-Bucharest line.

Bus Buses from Rădăuţi include six a day to Suceava (62km), and two to Suceviţa (17km) and Guru Humorului (55km). Oddly there are none to Putna. Double-check the times posted in the bus station with a ticket clerk. Bus tickets are sold one hour before departure.

From Rădăuţi, there are also two daily buses to Chernivtsi (Cernăuţi) in Ukraine.

PUTNA

Legend has it that Ştefan cel Mare, to celebrate his conquest of the fortress of nearby Chilia against the Turks, climbed to the top of a hill overlooking Putna village, 28km northwest of Rădăuţi, and fired his bow and arrow. Where the first arrow landed in the valley below became the site of Putna Monastery's holy well, the second arrow decided the site of the altar and the third landing was the site of the bell tower. As you approach Putna Monastery (Mănăstirea Putna), you can see the spot where Ştefan cel Mare stood, marked by a large white cross. The monastery, built between 1466 and 1481, is still home to a

very active religious community with groups of monks chanting Mass just before sunset.

The emblem of Moldavia – an auroch's head with the sun between its horns and the moon and stars either side – rests above the entrance to Putna Monastery. In the large building behind the monastery is the **Putna museum** where a wealth of treasures from the monastery and surrounding regions are displayed, including medieval manuscripts, the Holy Book that Ştefan cel Mare carried when he went to battle, and a miniature bronze bell brought in commemoration of the 486th anniversary of his death.

Ştefan cel Mare himself is buried in the tombs' room of the church. Below is the grave of his third wife, Maria Voichiţa. On the left is the grave of their two children, Bogdan and Petru. Above the children's grave is that of Ştefan cel Mare's second wife, Maria of Mangop from Greece.

Outside the church are three bells inscribed in Slavic. The largest of the three, dating from 1484 and reserved strictly for heralding royal deaths, was among the many treasures of the monastery that were stashed away in its tower and thus never plundered during the continuous attacks on Putna in the 16th and 17th centuries. Following the Austrian occupation in 1775, the Roman Catholic creed was imposed on the monastery, and various restoration works during this time reflect Putna's conversion to Catholicism at this time.

Some 60 monks live at Putna today. Under communism the monastery was condemned by the authorities with 75% of its inhabitants being forced into secular life. The monks today practise icon painting, shepherding, wood sculpting as well as agriculture.

In Chilia, 2km from the monastery, is **Daniel the Hermit's cave**. Inside is a humble wooden table and memorial plaque to the hermit Daniel Dimitru, born in a village near Rădăuţi in the 15th century. He became a monk at the age of 16 and later moved to Chilia where he dug himself a cave in a rock. In 1451 Ştefan cel Mare came to Chilia to seek advice from the wise hermit. Daniel told him he would rule Moldavia one day. Ştefan again sought his advice in 1476 at Voroneţ Monastery where Daniel told him to continue

Ştefan cel Mare (Stephen the Great) erected many of Bucovina's monasteries and churches.

his fight against the Turks. Following the building of Putna Monastery, Daniel moved to Voroneţ Monastery where he died in 1596.

To get to Chilia from the monastery, turn right off the main road following the sign for Cabana Putna. Bear left at the fork and continue until you reach a second fork in the road; turn right here, cross the railway tracks, and continue over a small bridge, following the dirt road until you see the rock, marked by a stone cross on its top, on your left.

Places to Stay & Eat
Some people *camp* freelance in the field opposite Daniel's cave at Chilia near the train station.

Cabana Putna, signposted 50m off the main road through the village leading to the monastery, has three- and four-bed cabins with shared bathrooms for $5 per person, including breakfast.

Getting There & Away
Local trains go to Putna from Suceava four times daily (two hours). The large monastic enclosure is at the end of the road, nearly 2km from the station. From Putna there is also one direct train a day to Iaşi (5¾ hours).

You can hike the 20km from Putna to Suceviţa Monastery in about five hours. Follow the trail marked with blue crosses in

white squares that starts near the hermit's cave. About 4km down the road you turn off to the left.

VATRA DORNEI
☎ 030 • postcode 5915
A fashionable spa resort during Habsburg times, Vatra Dornei today is a study in decaying elegance. Grand baroque-style buildings stand neglected and forlorn either side of the Dorna River (Râul Dorna) which cuts across the town from east to west. Treatment 'bases' *(baza de tratament)*, once all the rage, now struggle to sell their array of mud, electric and other types of 'baths'. Today the town is home to Romania's largest sparkling mineral water bottling plants, namely *Dorna*.

Hikers still frequent this quiet, unassuming town nestled at the confluence of the Dorna and Bistriţa Rivers in the Dornelor depression (Ţara Dornelor). Between December and March, skiers come to the snow-topped Dealul Negrii (1300m).

Orientation & Information
The train station is in the centre of Vatra Dornei, on the main street, Str Republicii (it can be reached by Str Dornelor). The post office, cinema and some museums are on the north bank of the Bistriţa, accessible by bridge from Str Republicii.

Vatra Dornei has no tourist information office but hotel staff can answer simple questions. The post and telephone office is in the old centre at Str Mihai Eminescu 1; open 8 am to 8 pm weekdays. You can change money and get cash advances on Visa at Banca Agricolă, on the river's southern bank at Str Vladimirescu 10; open 8.30 am to 12.30 pm weekdays.

Things to See & Do
Vatra Dornei's **park** (Parcul Staţiune) is beautifully laid out with sprawling avenues, well-groomed lawns and neatly arranged flower beds. Bronze busts of national poet Mihai Eminescu, and composers George Enescu and Ciprian Porumbescu gaze out from beneath the trees.

You can taste Vatra Dornei's natural **spring waters** at the drinking fountain in the

MOLDAVIA

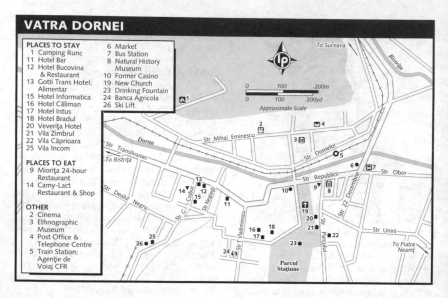

VATRA DORNEI

PLACES TO STAY
1 Camping Runc
11 Hotel Bar
12 Hotel Bucovina & Restaurant
13 Gotti Trans Hotel; Alimentar
15 Hotel Informatica
16 Hotel Căliman
17 Hotel Intus
18 Hotel Bradul
20 Veverița Hotel
21 Vila Zimbrul
22 Vila Căprioara
25 Vila Incom

PLACES TO EAT
9 Miorița 24-hour Restaurant
14 Camy-Lact Restaurant & Shop

OTHER
2 Cinema
3 Ethnographic Museum
4 Post Office & Telephone Centre
5 Train Station; Agenție de Voiaj CFR
6 Market
7 Bus Station
8 Natural History Museum
10 Former Casino
19 New Church
23 Drinking Fountain
24 Banca Agricola
26 Ski Lift

basement of the fairy-tale single-turreted castle in the west of the park. The bicarbonated water is good for curing stomach ills but not recommended for those with heart and liver problems, stomach ulcers or high blood pressure. Adjoining the park on Str Republicii is a grandiose, baroque mansion, once home to a bustling **casino** in Habsburg times but now empty. At Str Parcului 3 a small **Natural History Museum** (Muzeul de Științe Naturale și Cinegetică) displays flora and fauna from the surrounding Căliman and Rarău Mountains; open 10 am to 6 pm Tuesday to Sunday.

North of the river, opposite the post office on Str Mihai Eminescu, is an **Ethnographic Museum** (Muzeul de Etnografie); open 10 am to 6 pm Tuesday to Sunday.

There is a **ski lift** (*telescaun*) at the south end of Str George Coșbuc which takes you to the top of Vatra Dornei's main 1300m-high slope on Negrii Hill (Dealul Negrii). Steps lead to the telescaun station from the street; open 10 am to 5 pm Tuesday to Sunday. Bring your own boots and skis.

Places to Stay

Camping The clean, private *Camping Runc* (☎ 371 892) is in a forest-covered hill overlooking the town from the north-east. It has 43 wooden double cabins with communal showers and toilets for $4 a night; and you can pitch your tent here too. There is a restaurant and bar on the site. To get there, go west along Str Mihai Eminescu until you see a sign on the right for 'Camping Runc'.

Villas The friendly *Vila Zimbrul* (☎ 372 405, Str Parcului 5) overlooking the park is highly recommended. First-class doubles with lots of space are a bargain $10 a night both with and without private bath. Backpackers seeking some good old-fashioned home pampering should head straight here.

Just as homely is *Vila Căprioara* (☎ 372 643, fax 373 844, Str Parcului 29). The villa, which is managed by a pleasant German-speaking couple, has good, clean singles/doubles costing $8/$15, including breakfast.

The very basic *Vila Incom* (☎ 372 343), on Str George Coșbuc, is located next to the steps leading up to the telescaun station. The villa offers 50 places in dorm-style rooms with shared facilities for $4 per person a night.

MOLDAVIA

Hotels A bed at *Hotel Informatica (☎ 373 534, Str George Coşbuc 6)* costs $9 in a musty two-, three- or seven-bed room.

Round the corner is *Gotti Trans Hotel (☎ 371 261, Str Republicii 33)*. Single/doubles are $8/15, not including breakfast. The hotel has a 24-hour restaurant and an adjoining Alimentar.

Next door is the smarter *Hotel Bucovina (☎/fax 375 005, Str Republicii 35)*. It has 49 rooms, many with wooden balconies overlooking the main street. Single/double/triple rooms are $15/20/24, including breakfast.

Farther east is the cheap five-room *Hotel Bar (☎ 375 379, Str Republicii 10)*. Double rooms are good value at $15 but the place is rough and solo women should avoid it.

Just east, off Str T Vladimirescu, is a trio of two-star concrete block hotels where tour groups generally stay. *Hotel Căliman (☎ 371 150, fax 371 778)* has 155 rooms with hot water from 7 to 9 am, 1 to 2 pm and 7 to 9 pm. The six-storey *Hotel Bradul (☎ 371 150, fax 371 778)* has 140 rooms, a sauna, swimming pool and nightclub. Doubles in both hotels cost $15 with breakfast. Marginally cheaper is *Hotel Intus (☎ 375 021, fax 375 025)*, the last in line, with doubles for $10, including breakfast.

Bang in the park, *Veveriţa Hotel (☎ 371 251, Str Parcului 1)*, still sporting a two-tier pricing system, charges foreigners $20 for one of its nine doubles and Romanians $16.

Places to Eat

Vatra Dornei has few eating places, but those it does have offer quality Romanian cuisine at unbeatable prices. *Camy-Lact (Str George Coşbuc 1)*, adjoining the shop of the same name, specialises in dairy products (the shop stocks a wonderful array of homemade cheeses, yogurts etc). Meat is served in its restaurant, as well as delicious chocolate pancakes *(clătite cu ciocolată)* for $1.

The crispiest-on-the-outside, runniest-on-the-inside *caşcaval pané* (breaded cheese) in the whole of Romania is served at the 24-hour *Miorița*, on the corner of Str Parcului and Str Republicii. Other specialities include soups and salads.

There is an *Alimentar* adjoining the Gotti Trans Hotel which stocks most of your basic supplies; open 6 am to 10 pm daily.

Getting There & Away

The bus station (☎ 371 252) is at the eastern end of town on Str 22 Decembrie. There are daily buses to Bistriţa (83km), Iaşi (237km), Botoşani (155km) and Bacău (219km).

Train services are slightly more useful. Tickets are sold in advance at the Agenţie de Voiaj CFR (☎ 371 039), inside the train station (☎ 371 197) at Str Republicii 1. There is one direct daily train to Iaşi (4¾ hours).

AROUND VATRA DORNEI

Vatra Dornei stands in the middle of Romania's most dramatic mountain passes, steeped in legend and famed for their wild beauty and savage landscapes. If you head south-west into Transylvania you cross the **Bârgău Pass**, otherwise known as the Tihuta Pass or, if you've read Bram Stoker's *Dracula*, the Borgo Pass! (See the Bârgău Valley section in the Transylvania chapter.)

In Dorna Candrenilor, 8km west of Vatra Dornei, you can access the **Căliman Mountains**. The highlight of these volcanic mountains is the anthropomorphic rocks which form a nature reservation called the **12 Apostles Nature Reservation** (Stâncile Doisprezece Apostoli). A trail (marked with blue triangles then red circles) leads from Vatra Dornei to its peak at 1760m. Only tackle this tough climb if you are experienced and have a map and the right gear!

A less challenging route if you have a car is to drive to Dorna Candrenilor, turn left along the road to Poiana Negrii and continue for 14km along road and dirt track until you reach Negrişoara. From here it is a three-hour walk (4km) along a path to the foot of the geological reservation.

Heading north you cross from Moldavia into the Maramureş region via the **Prislop Pass** which peaks at 1416m (see the end of the Maramureş chapter).

The road north-east from Vatra Dornei leads, via Câmpulung Moldovenesc, to Gura Humorului from where the trail to southern Bucovina's monasteries begins.

MOLDAVIA

CÂMPULUNG MOLDOVENESC
☎ 030

This small logging town and 14th-century fair town is tucked in the Moldavia valley at an altitude of 621m. Câmpulung Moldovenesc is a good access point for hiking in the **Rarău Mountains**, 15km to the south (see the Exploring the Carpathian Mountains special section). In winter, Câmpulung attracts cross-country skiers. There is also a short 800m ski slope served by a chairlift at the foot of the resort. Between 1786 and 1809 many German miners settled in the region at the invitation of the Habsburg authorities.

A winter sports festival takes place in Câmpulung Moldovenesc every year on the last Sunday in January.

Orientation & Information
The main street, Calea Transilvaniei, which runs into Calea Bucovinei, cuts across the town from west to east. The train station is a five-minute walk west of the centre at Str Gării 8. To get to the centre from the main Câmpulung Moldovenesc train station (don't get off at Câmpulung Moldovenesc Est train station), turn left along Str Gării and then right along Str Dimitrie Cantimir until you reach the post office on the corner of Calea Bucovinei. Câmpulung Moldovenesc's main hotel, the Zimbrul, is a couple of blocks from the post office on Calea Bucovinei. The bus station is at Str Alexander Bogza. From here cut through the market to the left of the station as you exit where you'll see the sign for Hotel Zimbrul. Follow that to reach the centre.

The Banca Română pentru Dezvoltare, next to Hotel Zimbrul on Str Calea Transilvaniei, gives cash advances on Visa; open 8.30 am to 4.30 pm weekdays. The Agenţie de Voiaj CFR is opposite the hotel at Calea Bucovinei 2.

Things to See
The highlight of Câmpulung Moldovenesc is its bizarre **wooden spoon collection**, displayed in a small house at Str Gheorghe Popovici 3. Love spoons, jewellery made from spoons and a host of other cutlery delights collected by Ioan Ţugui are exhibited in the museum. Other fun wooden objects are displayed at the **wood carving museum** at Calea Transilvaniei 10. Both museums are open 9 am to 4 pm Tuesday to Sunday. If either museum is locked, ask around until you find someone who has a key.

Places to Stay & Eat
There is no hot water in the town between 9 am and 3 pm. Bucovina Estur and the BTT travel agency (see Suceava's Travel Agencies section) arrange accommodation in *private rooms* in Câmpulung Moldovenesc. BTT charges $18 a night including breakfast; Bucovina Estur $10 a night.

Complex Turistic Semenic (☎ 311 714, Str Nicu Dracea 6) is a small, family-run hotel with simple doubles for $15, most of which have old ceramic stoves for added warmth in winter. The restaurant, serving local dishes including wild mushrooms from the forest, is open 8 am to 8 pm daily.

Hotel Zimbrul (☎ 314 356, fax 314 358, Calea Bucovinei 1–3) is your typical state-run, 10-storey concrete block. Characterless singles/doubles with private bath are $26/33 a night, including breakfast.

RARĂU MOUNTAINS
The Rarău Mountains, part of the Eastern Carpathians, boast plenty of hiking trails as well as the Slătioara Forest Reservation and the Todirescu Flower Reservation. See the Exploring the Carpathian Mountains special section for details of these reservations and for hiking information.

Places to Stay & Eat
In the heart of the Rarău Massif is *Cabana Rarău (1400m; mobile ☎ 094-320 496)*, the main base for hikers. It has simple doubles for $10, including breakfast. It only has hot water when it is full. There is a small restaurant and shop selling basic provisions.

If you plan on accessing the mountains from Chiril in the south, then *Cabana Zugreni (☎ 030-373 581)*, 4km from Chiril on the Vatra Dornei road, is a good option. It has doubles without/with private bath for $7/15. There are also cheaper wooden huts for $4 per person. The adjoining restaurant serves traditional Moldavian meals.

Moldova

Moldova

The former Soviet republic of Moldova, independent since 1991, is a country in limbo. Historically it is part Romanian, part Russian, united by force under the Soviets to form one country, but not one people. After the demise of the USSR, the question of reunification with neighbouring Romania was raised, fuelling ethnic tensions in the predominantly Russian-speaking regions. Moldova's ethnic tensions exploded into civil war in 1992, killing more than 500 people.

While in 1997 the country seemed to be on the brink of de facto federalisation, today this idea has been all but abandoned. An April 2000 treaty between Moldova and Romania, formally recognising each other's sovereignty, was, at the start of 2001, still awaiting approval by both countries' parliaments.

A sliver of land jammed between Romania and Ukraine, Moldova is roughly bounded by the Prut River on the west and the Dniestr River on the east.

Despite being one of the most densely populated areas in the former USSR, Moldova has few cities. Its capital city, Chişinău, was heavily bombed during WWII but has made a comeback in recent years. Funky bars and fun eating places are sprouting as the country gets back on track towards a market economy.

Take a step into provincial realms and there's no escaping the tremendous poverty that prevails, with battered buses rumbling along dusty streets, while many employees aren't paid for months at a time.

On the eastern banks of the Dniestr lies the self-proclaimed republic of Transdniestr, the last bastion of Soviet socialism in Eastern Europe. Transdniestr's mainly Russian-speaking population yearns for the revival of the Soviet Union. While their attempts to win independence from Moldova have yet to yield results, their efforts at recreating Soviet life have produced USSR-style rampant inflation, hellish bureaucracy and curfews.

Highlights

- Stroll Chişinău's tree-studded avenues and discover a touch of the Orient in its colourful markets
- Tour the Cricova underground wine town if your wallet can take the pinch
- See how 13th-century monks lived by visiting caves at Orheiul Vechi
- Visit the self-styled republic of Transdniestr, the only place in the world where the Moscow *putsch* succeeded

CHIŞINĂU (KISHINEV) p399
Central Chişinău p400

Tiraspol p416

Tighina (Bendery) p418

UKRAINE

Southern Moldova is populated by one of the world's smallest ethnic minorities, the Gagauz (pronounced ga-ga-ooz). Although declaring a Gagauz Soviet Socialist Republic in 1991, the 153,000 Turkic-speaking population settled for large autonomy in regional affairs in 1994 and enjoy parliamentary representation in Chişinău today. The Gagauz even have their own university in their capital, Comrat.

In both Gagauz and Transdniestr, the Organisation for Security and Co-operation in Europe (OSCE) is closely monitoring the respect of minority rights and administering conflict control.

MOLDOVA

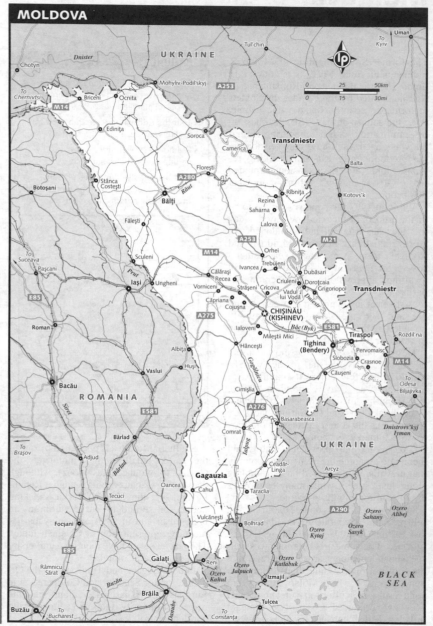

MOLDOVA

Facts about Moldova

HISTORY
Bessarabia & Transdniestr

Moldova today straddles two different historic regions divided by the Dniestr River. Historic Romanian Bessarabia incorporated the region west of the Dniestr, while tsarist Russia governed the territory east of the river (Transdniestr) after defeating the Turks in 1792.

Bessarabia, part of the Romanian principality of Moldavia, was annexed in 1812 by the Russian empire. In 1918, after the October revolution, Bessarabia declared its independence. Two months later this newly formed Democratic Moldavian Republic decided to unite with Romania, angering Moscow. Russia never recognised this union.

In 1924 the Soviet Union created the Moldavian Autonomous Oblast on the eastern banks of the Dniestr, incorporating Transdniestr within the Ukrainian Soviet Socialist Republic (SSR). A few months later the Soviet government renamed the Oblast the Moldavian Autonomous Soviet Socialist Republic (Moldavian ASSR). In 1929 it moved the capital from Balta (in present-day Ukraine) to Tiraspol.

WWII

In June 1940 Romanian Bessarabia was occupied by the Soviet army in accordance with the secret protocol attached to the Molotov-Ribbentrop Pact. The Soviet government immediately joined Bessarabia with the southern part of the Moldavian ASSR – namely, Transdniestr. This newly united territory was named the Moldavian Soviet Socialist Republic (Moldavian SSR). The remaining northern part of the Moldavian ASSR was given back to the Ukrainian SSR (present-day Ukraine). Bessarabia' experienced terrifying Sovietisation, marked by the deportation of 300,000 Romanians. In June 1941, 5000 families from Bessarabia were deported to Siberia.

In 1941 allied Romanian and German troops attacked the Soviet Union. Bessarabia and Transdniestr fell into Romanian hands. Thousands of Bessarabian Jews were rounded up in labour camps in Transdniestr, from where they were deported to Auschwitz.

In August 1944 the Soviet army reoccupied Transdniestr and Bessarabia. Under the terms of the Paris Peace Treaty of 1947, Romania had to relinquish the region and Soviet power was restored in the Moldavian SSR.

Sovietisation & Nationalism

The Soviet authorities continued where they had left off in 1940. An immediate Sovietisation program was enforced in the Moldavian SSR. The predominantly Russian and Ukrainian population in Transdniestr – in Romanian hands between 1941 and 1944 – was relatively unaffected.

Ethnic Moldovans (Romanians) in Bessarabia suffered worse. In July 1949, 25,000 Moldovans were deported to Siberia and Kazakhstan. The Cyrillic alphabet was imposed on the Moldovan language (a dialect of Romanian) and Russian became the official state language. Street names were changed to honour Soviet communist heroes, and Russian-style patronymics were included in people's names. In 1950–52 Leonid Brezhnev, then first secretary of the central committee of the Moldovan Communist Party, is said to have personally supervised the deportation of a quarter of a million Moldovans. Ethnic Russians and Ukrainians were encouraged to settle in the region in order to dilute the Moldovan population further.

Gorbachev's policies of *glasnost* (openness) and *perestroika* (restructuring) from 1986 onwards paved the way for the creation of the nationalist Moldovan Popular Front in 1989. Under the leadership of communist Mircea Snegur as chairman of the Moldova's Supreme Soviet, Moldovan written in the Latin alphabet was reintroduced in August 1989 as the official state language. In February-March 1990 the first democratic elections to the Supreme Soviet (parliament) were won by the Popular Front with an overwhelming majority. In April 1990 the Supreme Soviet reinstated the Moldovan national flag (the Romanian tricolour with the Moldavian coat of arms in its centre). In Transdniestr, local councils refused to adopt the new state symbols and stuck to the red banner.

In June 1990 the Moldovan Supreme Soviet passed a declaration of sovereignty. Following the failed coup attempt against Mikhail Gorbachev in Moscow in August 1991, Moldova declared its full independence.

Romania was the first country, quickly followed by the USA in December 1991, to recognise Moldova's independence.

In December 1991 Mircea Snegur was democratically elected president. The same month he signed the Alma-Ata Declaration to become a member of the newly established Commonwealth of Independent States (CIS). Moldova's full CIS membership was only ratified by the Moldovan parliament in April 1994.

Moldova was granted 'most favoured nation' station by the USA in 1992, qualifying for International Monetary Fund (IMF) and World Bank loans the same year. In March 1994 Snegur signed NATO's Partnership for Peace agreement. Moldova's neutrality is inscribed in its constitution, meaning it cannot join NATO and is not a signatory to the CIS collective security agreements.

In August 1999, eight years after the collapse of the Soviet Union, a treaty between Moldova and Ukraine was finally signed, confirming their borders. The treaty in effect sticks to the Soviet division of territory. Under the agreement, Moldova gains control of a 100m strip of land along the Danube River, earmarked by the Moldovan government for the construction of an oil terminal.

Moldova took a step forward in its bid for a place in the EU when Deputy Prime Minister Ion Sturza signed a Partnership & Co-operation Agreement with the EU in May 1999. The agreement paves the way for improved economic, financial and social relations between the two. But while Moldova is keen to join the ranks of the EU, two major obstacles still block its path: the country's mounting foreign debt and its inadequate economic growth.

Ethnic Tensions

Moldova's race along the road to independence in the late 1980s sparked off nationalist sentiments among ethnic minority groups. In the Russian stronghold of Transdniestr, the Yedinstvo-Unitatea (Unity) movement was formed in 1988 to represent the interests of the Slavic minorities. This was followed in November 1989 by the creation of the Gagauz Halki political party in the south of Moldova, where the Turkic-speaking Gagauz minority was centred. Both ethnic groups' major fear was that an independent Moldova would reunite with Romania.

Following the pursuit of nationalist policies by the Supreme Soviet from early 1990, the Gagauz went on to declare a separate Gagauz Soviet Socialist Republic in August 1990. Their nationalist claims were silently backed by the Turkish government and by Russians in Transdniestr sympathetic to their ethnic brothers. A month later the Transdniestrans also declared independence from Moldova, establishing the Dniestr Moldovan Republic on the eastern banks of the Dniestr River.

Both self-declared republics went on to hold presidential elections in December 1991. Igor Smirnov came out as head of Transdniestr, Stepan Topal of Gagauzia.

Sporadic outbursts of violence ensued as the Moldovan government categorically refused to accept separatists' claims. In March 1992 President Mircea Snegur declared a state of emergency in the country. Two months later full-scale civil war broke out in Transdniestr when Moldovan police clashed with Transdniestran militia in Tighina (Bendery), on the western bank of the Dniestr. The Moldovan army initially succeeded in pushing separatist forces back across the Dniestr but Transdniestran troops, with help from Russia, fought their way back across Tighina Bridge to take control of Tighina. An estimated 500 to 700 people were killed and thousands wounded.

A cease-fire was signed by the Moldovan and Russian presidents, Snegur and Boris Yeltsin, in July 1992. Provisions were made for a Russian-led, tripartite peacekeeping force comprising Russian, Moldovan and

Transdniestran troops to be stationed in the region. Troops remain here today, maintaining an uneasy peace.

Russia continues to play a pivotal role in the Moldovan-Transdniestran conflict. Its 14th army, headquartered in Tiraspol since 1956, covertly supplied Transdniestran rebels with weapons. The continued presence of the 5000-strong Russian 'operational group' in Transdniestr today is seen by local Russian-speakers as a guarantee of their security.

In October 1994 Russia and Moldova signed an agreement for the withdrawal of the Russian army from the region. Troops have not been pulled out despite their presence undermining Moldova's constitution. At the 1999 OSCE summit in Istanbul, Russia agreed to withdraw its troops from the region by the end of 2002. But Transdniestr, keen to keep the Russians close by, has continually blocked the army's withdrawal.

In 1997 representatives of Moldova and Transdniestr signed a memorandum in Moscow agreeing to resolve their conflict 'within the framework of a single state'. This agreement has yet to become a reality.

At a CIS summit in Chişinău in October 1997, Transdniestr formally asked (in vain) to be accepted as a fully fledged member. And there was no breakthrough in peace talks because Igor Smirnov failed to show up for his prearranged meeting with the presidents – Moldova's Petru Lucinschi, Russia's Boris Yeltsin and Ukraine's Leonid Kutchma.

Again in October 2000, scheduled peace talks between Russia, Ukraine, Moldova and Transdniestr failed to take place, as Transdniestr refused to take part in the Moldovan negotiating team.

GEOGRAPHY
Landlocked Moldova covers an area of 33,700 sq km, consisting almost entirely of gently rolling, partially wooded plains cut through with rivers and streams. Some 75% of land is rich in chernozem (black) soils, making it among the most fertile lands in the former Soviet Union. Wine and sunflower production are large industries here.

The centre of the country is more forested and home to Moldova's highest mountain, 430m Mount Balaneşti.

Moldova's western boundary with Romania is marked by the Prut River, a tributary of the Danube. The Dniestr River lies within a few kilometres of its eastern border with Ukraine, crossing the country from north to south on its way to the Black Sea. Moldova also shares northern and southern borders with Ukraine.

CLIMATE
Moldova has a continental climate, with four distinct seasons. Summers are lengthy and warm, with moderate rainfall, and winters are short and cold.

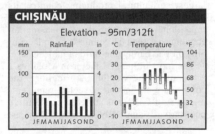

GOVERNMENT & POLITICS
Moldova's parliament was locked in a bitter presidential battle at the time of writing (January 2001). Despite three elections since late November, neither of the frontrunning candidates, the chairman of the Constitutional Court, Pavel Barbalat, nor Communist Party leader Vladimir Voronin, had won the 61 votes needed to become president of the 101-seat parliament – although the communists, who control 40 of the parliamentary seats, were sensing victory as Voronin's votes inched higher with each round of voting. A planned fourth election was boycotted.

In a final bid to end the dispute over his successor, incumbent president Petru Lucinschi (whose term ended in January 2001) announced that he would dissolve the parliament and set early parliamentary elections for February 2001. Lucinschi, a former Soviet Communist Party functionary who has been at constant odds with parliament

MOLDOVA

ever since coming to power in 1997, would continue to run the country until a successor is named.

In June 2000 Moldova's parliament had passed a constitutional law, virtually unopposed, to end the country-wide popular vote for president and instead have the president elected by the assembly. It was hoped that this law would bring a end to the disharmony between the president and parliament.

Moldova's presidential elections are held every four years (the next in 2004), as are the parliamentary elections. The prime minister at the start of 2001 was Dumitru Braghis.

ECONOMY

In the Soviet Union, Moldova was the sixth-largest agricultural producing country, its main export being wine and champagne. Its transition from a centralised to a market economy has seen the country's overall economy drop to barely one-third of its 1989 size.

The most influential factor in Moldova's economy is the weather. Agriculture, the country's main industrial sector, representing 46% of GDP, has suffered consecutive poor harvests since 1996. The IMF forecast

Moldova's coat of arms

a slight GDP growth in 1997, but the economy stagnated following the implementation of structural reforms and the GDP fell by half. In 1999 the GDP fell again by 4.4%. Early estimates for 2000 predicted a growth of 2%, but a severe drought in spring 2000 has led to a revised forecast of zero growth.

Annual inflation in 1999 stood at 43.8%, up from 18.3% in 1998 (8% in 1997, 15.1% in 1996...and 1500% in 1992). The Moldovan leu introduced in November 1993 remained stable until 1997, but as a result of the 1998 Russian economic crisis it suffered two sharp drops. Today the leu remains vulnerable.

Heavily reliant on outside financial assistance, Moldova was hard hit in April 2000 when both the World Bank and IMF suspended all promised loans to the country due to its failure to privatise its tobacco and wine industries. The government issued a warning to the people 'not to panic' at what is considered Moldova's most difficult period in modern history. Towards the year's end Moldova's economic woes began to ease slightly. In mid-October, laws passed through parliament finally paved the way for the privatisation of these industries. The World Bank subsequently renewed its financial assistance, and in December 2000 the IMF, while not resuming payments, approved in principle a further $142 million loan to Moldova to help reduce poverty and increase the country's growth.

For the average Moldovan, economic conditions are abysmal. Figures released by the United Nations Development Program (1998) show 90% of Moldova's population earns only $2 a day. In addition, in mid-1998 a quarter of all salaries were in arrears, further fuelling discontent. In June 1999, violent clashes broke out in Chişinău as members of the General Federation of Trade Unions protested the salary arrears. In an attempt to defuse the situation the government pledged to make regular payments towards all salaries and pensions. To date, the government has been unable to eliminate the arrears.

In April 2000, frustrated students clashed violently with police in the streets of

Chișinău after the government cancelled their right to travel free on public transport. The students, numbering over 10,000, also demanded a 50% reduction in the cost of intercity transport and the lifting of the restrictions on the number of scholarships awarded. As a result of the four-day riots, in which 64 people were injured, the government reinstated the students' transport privileges and promised to set up a special commission to consider their demands.

Other social indicators paint a grim future: the population decreased by 1.5% between 1990 and 1998, and the infant mortality rate is an alarming 17.8%.

The economic situation in the rebel republic of Transdniestr, which does not receive any IMF loans, is dismal.

POPULATION & PEOPLE

Moldova is the most densely populated region in the former Soviet Union (29 inhabitants per square kilometre).

The total population is 4.4 million. Moldovans comprise 65% of this, Russians 14%, Ukrainians 12%, Gagauz 2.5%, Belarusians 3%, Roma 2%, Jews 1%, and other nationalities such as Bulgarians and Poles 0.5%. More than two-thirds of Moldovans live in cities.

Most Gagauz and Bulgarians live in southern Moldova. In Transdniestr, Ukrainians and Russians total 53% of the region's population; Moldovans comprise 40%.

RELIGION

Just over 98% of the population is Orthodox. The Moldovan Orthodox Church, subordinated to the Moscow Patriarchate, is the only church recognised by the state.

Even in religious worship Moldova fails to be united! An increasing number of Moldovan Orthodox believers want to switch sides to the breakaway Bessarabian Orthodox Church, set up by dissident priests from the Moldovan Church in 1992, which looks to the Romanian Orthodox Patriarchate in Bucharest for guidance.

In mid-1997 the Moldovan supreme court overturned an appeals court decision to legalise the Bessarabian Church in Moldova. In June 1998 the Bessarabian Church then took its case to the European Court of Human Rights. The court's decision to review the Moldovan government's refusal to register the church was declared 'unwarranted' by the country's cabinet in February 2000.

LANGUAGE

Moldovan is essentially Romanian. It is a dialect politically manufactured by the Soviet regime from 1924 onwards in a bid to create a 'new' language for its newly created Moldavian ASSR and to pave the way for the incorporation of Bessarabia in 1940.

The introduction of the Cyrillic alphabet created a distinction from Romanian and Russified the Romance language. New words were consequently invented by the authorities, lists of Romanian words 'polluting Moldovan' drawn up and circulated, and all words or neologisms of Latin origin decisively scrapped.

Moldovan is the predominant language spoken today, except in Transdniestr where Russian is the main language and where Moldovan continues to be written in the Cyrillic script. Elsewhere it is written in the Latin alphabet.

Facts for the Visitor

VISAS & DOCUMENTS

All Western travellers need a visa to enter Moldova.

To get a visa, everyone (except citizens of the EU, USA, Canada and Israel) needs an invitation from a company, organisation or individual. Unless you already have contacts in Moldova it is *very* difficult to get an invitation.

For travellers coming from Turkey and Arabic and African countries the letter of invitation from a company within Moldova must be authorised by the Moldovan Foreign Affairs Minister. If the invitation is from an individual it must be authorised by the Moldovan Minister of Internal Affairs.

MOLDOVA

When applying for a visa everyone must also have their passport, a photo and fill out an application form.

Only passport-holders from the EU, USA or Canada can buy visas on arrival at Chişinău airport. No invitation is required. It is also possible for these citizens to get a visa at the Albiţa border crossing when travelling by car or bus into Moldova.

An HIV/AIDS test is required for foreigners intending to stay in Moldova longer than three months. Certificates proving that applicants are HIV-negative have to be in Russian and English.

Types of Visa & Costs

A single transit visa is valid for three days and costs $35. You can also get a double transit visa ($55), which enables you to enter the country twice (maximum stay three days each entry).

Single-entry tourist visas costing $55 are valid for one month from the date of issue. Multiple-entry visas valid for one/two/three months cost $85/115/135.

Visas can be processed within a day at the Moldovan consulate in Romania (Blvd Eroilor 8 in Bucharest). Applications must be made between 9.30 am and 12.30 pm weekdays. You can then collect your visa between 3 and 4 pm the same day.

Other Documents

Upon entering Moldova you must declare how much foreign currency you have. Do not lose this declaration form! You must show it when you leave the country. You are not allowed to leave with more money than you declared on arrival. Any excess will be confiscated. Keep all receipts when changing money to prove you obtained it legally.

EMBASSIES & CONSULATES
Moldovan Embassies & Consulates

Moldova has embassies and consulates worldwide.

Belgium
(☎ 02 732 9659, fax 02 732 9660) Ave Emil Max 175, 140 Brussels

Bulgaria
(☎ 02-981 7370) Blvd Patriarh Evtimii 17, 1000 Sofia

Germany
(☎/fax 0228-91 094) Elisabelkirche 24, D-5331 Bonn
(☎ 069-636 4212, fax 636 4220) Kennedyallee 119a, D-60596 Frankfurt

Hungary
(☎ 1-209 1191, fax 209 1195, 186 8373) Str Karinthy Fr ut 17, fsz 5-6, Budapest

Romania
(☎ 01-230 0474, 312 9790, fax 230 7790, e moldova@customers.digiro.net) Aleea Alexandru 40, RO-71273 Bucharest
Consulate: (☎ 01-410 9827, fax 410 9826) Blvd Eroilor 8, Sector 5, Bucharest

Russia
(☎ 095-924 6342, ☎/fax 924 5353, e moldemb @online.ru) 18 Kuznetskii most, RUS-103031 Moscow

Turkey
(☎ 312-446 5527, fax 446 5816) Kaptanpasa Sok 49, 06700 GOP/Ankara

Ukraine
(☎ 044-290 7721) Sichnevkoho Povstanya 6, UA-252011 Kyiv

USA
(☎ 202-667 1130/1131, fax 667 1204, e mold ova@dgs.dgsys.com) 2101 S Street NW, Washington, DC 20008
Web site: www.moldova.org

Embassies & Consulates in Moldova

Countries with embassies or consulates in Chişinău (phone code ☎ 2) include:

Bulgaria (☎ 237 983, fax 237 978) Str 31 August 125

France (☎ 234 510, 237 234, fax 237 283) Str Sfatul Ţării 18

Germany (☎ 234 607, 232 869, fax 234 680) Str Maria Cibotari 37

Hungary (☎ 223 404, 227 786, fax 224 513) Blvd Ştefan cel Mare 131

Romania (☎ 228 126, fax 228 129) Str Bucureşti 66/1
Consulate: (☎ 237 622) Str Vlaicu Parcalab 39

Russia (☎ 248 286/225, fax 248 288, 547 751) Blvd Ştefan cel Mare 151

Turkey (☎ 245 292, 242 608, fax 225 528) Str A Mateevici 57

Ukraine (☎ 232 563, 234 876, fax 232 562) Str Sfatul Ţării 55

USA (☎ 233 772/266, fax 233 044) Str A Mateevici 103

CUSTOMS

Exiting Moldova, you are only allowed to take out 400 cigarettes and 2L of hard liqueur or wine. The customs office in Chişinău (☎ 569 460, fax 263 061) is at Str Columna 65.

MONEY

Moldova introduced its own currency, the Moldovan leu (plural lei), to replace the Soviet rouble in November 1993. One leu is divided into 100 bani. The initial exchange rate to the US dollar was 3.85 lei.

Travellers cheques and credit cards are only accepted at a couple of banks in Chişinău. Banks charge around 4% commission to cash cheques or give cash advances. There are a couple of ATMs in Chişinău.

Note that the Transdniestran republic has its own currency (see Money in the Transdniestr section).

Most hotels still adhere to the old Soviet three-tier pricing system, meaning foreigners pay twice as much as CIS citizens and three times as much as Moldovans for the same room.

Candies are a sweet form of currency at bus and train stations. Ticket prices are never rounded up to a sensible figure, meaning ticket sellers do not give the correct change. Boiled sweets or sticks of gum are doled out instead.

Currency Exchange

At the time of printing, the Moldovan leu was worth:

country	unit		Lei
Australia	A$1	=	7.10 Lei
Canada	C$1	=	8.50 Lei
euro	€1	=	12.05 Lei
France	FF1	=	1.85 Lei
Germany	DM1	=	6.15 Lei
Ireland	IR£1	=	15.22 Lei
Japan	¥100	=	10.90 Lei
Netherlands	f1	=	5.44 Lei
New Zealand	NZ$1	=	5.70 Lei
Romania	10,000 Lei	=	4.90 Lei
UK	UK£1	=	18.85 Lei
Ukraine	1 hv	=	2.32 Lei
USA	US$1	=	12.80 Lei

POST & COMMUNICATIONS

Avoid mailing letters from Moldova; the post is wildly erratic and letters invariably get lost. It costs $0.25 to send a postcard or letter under 20g to Western Europe, Australia and the USA.

In Chişinău there are public cardphones from which international calls can be made. Phonecards costing $2.95 (35 lei) are sold at the central post and telephones offices. Only local and national calls can be made from the old Soviet, token-operated phones. Tokens cost 35 bani and are also sold at post and telephone offices.

To make an international call, dial ☎ 8, wait for a dial tone, then dial ☎ 10, followed by the country code, city code and number.

Outside of Chişinău, you have to book international calls via an operator from telephone centres. Give the operator the name, city and number of the person you want to call, put down a minimum three-minute call deposit, then sit and wait for your number to be announced over a loudspeaker. If no connection is made, a service charge (about $1) is deducted from your deposit.

To call Moldova from abroad dial the international country code ☎ 373, then the city code followed by the six-digit telephone number.

To call Moldova from the former Soviet Union, you can use the former USSR regional code for Moldova which is still intact: dial ☎ 8, then the Soviet regional code (☎ 042), followed by the city code (ie, to call Chişinău from Moscow dial ☎ 8-0422).

Cellular phone service is provided by Chişinău-based Voxtel (☎ 753 809, 575 757) at Str Alba Iulia 75. If you bring your own mobile it must be registered at a cost of around $300. Roaming service outside the capital is limited. See Voxtel's Web site (www.voxtel.md) for details.

Email & Internet Access

Email is available in Internet cafes in Chişinău (see that section for locations). The going rate for access is around $1 an hour. For local connections the popular choice is Relsoft (☎ 245 580) at St Alexandru cel Bun 51A.

MOLDOVA

INTERNET RESOURCES

Yes, even Moldova has made it into the realms of the World Wide Web. For some good general information in English log on to Moldova's official Web site at www .moldova.md. Two other good sources of information are www.ournet.md, which has news and tourist links, and www.ipm.md.

BOOKS

A good reference is the *Historical Dictionary of the Republic of Moldova* (2000) by Andrei Brezianu, as is *Belarus & Moldova Country Studies*, part of the Area Handbook series, edited by Helen Fedor, which gives a comprehensive analysis of Moldova up to 1995.

For the Soviet period try *Nations, Nationalities, People: A Study of Nationalities Policy of the Communist Party in Soviet Moldova*.

Contemporary politics are tackled by *The Nationalities Question in Post Soviet States* by Graham Smith, as well as *Russian Peacekeeping Strategies in the CIS: The Cases of Moldova, Georgia and Tajikistan* (2000) by Dov Lynch. Also good is *Romania After Tyranny* by Daniel Nelson, focusing on relations between Romania and Moldova.

The Moldovans: Romania, Russia, and the Politics of Culture (Studies of Nationalities) by Charles King (1999) takes an indepth look at the national identity versus the cultural traditions of the peoples of Moldova including a section on Bessarabia and Transdniestr.

Unbeatable for its quirky insight into Moldovan life is the thoroughly entertaining *Playing the Moldovans at Tennis* by British comedian/author Tony Hawks. His witty travelogue follows his exploits as he pursues members of the Moldovan football team for a game of tennis – all to win a bet!

Available in Chişinău only is the picture book *Chişinău* (Editura Uniunii Scriitorilor, Chişinău, 1996). It is packed with photographs of the city with captions in Moldovan and Russian and costs $15.

Engleza de gata – Off-Pegged English by Violeta Wăstăsescu and Fuluia Turu (Editura Uniunii Scriitorilor, Chişinău, 1994) is a valuable pocket-size Moldovan-English phrasebook written for Moldovans heading overseas but easy to use the other way round. It costs $0.50 in most bookshops in Chişinău.

MEDIA

Locally, little is published in foreign languages. The English-language magazine *Welcome* ($0.50) provides updated local news and a 'what's on' listing. It's published fortnightly and is available from most bookshops and kiosks.

Radio France International (RFI) can be picked up on 102.3 FM, and the BBC World Service on 68.48 FM. Sun TV is a joint Moldovan-American venture which utilises the best of all the cable channels including CNN, Euronews, and the popular private Romanian channel Pro TV.

A September 2000 court ruling rescinded the licences of one television station and eight Russian-language radio stations owing to the requirement that no less than 65% of broadcast time be in Romanian, the official state language. Sun TV was also ordered to broadcast its Russian-language shows 'Discovery' and 'Eurosport' in Romanian. The stations plan to contest the ruling.

Since Transdniestran militia took over the Moldovan radio transmitter at Grigoriopol, Radio Moldova International has to broadcast from transmitters in Galbeni. The Grigoriopol transmitter remains under the control of the separatists.

ELECTRICITY

Moldova runs on 220V, 50Hz AC. Most appliances that are set up for 240V will handle this happily. Sockets require two-pin Russian plugs, identical to European plugs except the pins are thinner. Some sockets you can jam a European plug into.

TOILETS

In Moldova most toilets bear Russian signs: Ж for women and M for men. Hygiene standards are as low as in Romania (see Health in the Facts for the Visitor chapter).

GAY & LESBIAN TRAVELLERS

Moldova repealed its Soviet antigay law in 1995, thereby legalising homosexuality.

But it is still not a good idea to be too 'out' in Moldova.

DANGERS & ANNOYANCES
Getting an invitation to visit Moldova is a major hassle. In-country, Soviet bureaucracy can be a trial.

Simply getting around is a pain in the neck. Patience, tolerance and a low expectation of service are key factors in keeping down stress levels. Most trams, buses and trolleybuses are fit for the scrapheap.

Don't flash your wealth about, beware of pickpockets, and stick to the same street rules as in any city. Street crime against foreigners has not yet hit the heights it has in Romania. Likewise few beggars plague the streets, simply because there's no market. This will undoubtedly change as more Western travellers make their way here.

Travelling in the self-declared republic of Transdniestr is safe providing you stay away from military objects and installations. If in doubt, check with the Moldovan consulate in Bucharest or abroad, or with the OCSE.

PUBLIC HOLIDAYS & SPECIAL EVENTS
Moldova's national holidays include:

New Year's Day 1 January
Orthodox Christmas 7 January
International Women's Day 8 March
Orthodox Easter March/April/May
Victory (1945) Day 9 May
Independence Day 27 August
National Language Day 31 August

Transdniestrans boycott the Moldovan independence day and celebrate their own independence day on 2 September.

Getting There & Away

Moldova is way off the beaten tourist track. Few trains and even fewer buses come here, while flight routings from the West are still in their infancy. Most flights are eastbound.

AIR
All international flights to Moldova use Chişinău (Kishinev) airport. The only direct flights into Moldova from the West are from Berlin and Paris.

Moldova has three national airlines: Moldavian Airlines (www.mdv.md), a private airline set up in 1994, offers direct flights to Budapest and Moscow, and flights with one stopover to Vienna, Rome and Warsaw. It has no offices abroad but some specialist travel agencies sell tickets for its flights.

Air Moldova International (www.ami.md) is another private airline, dating from 1995. It flies to Amsterdam, Berlin, Frankfurt, London, Paris and Warsaw.

Air Moldova (www.airmoldova.md) is the state carrier for Moldova with direct flights to Istanbul, Larnaca, Minsk, Moscow, Paris, St Petersburg, Sofia and Yekaterinburg.

Be wary of travel agents who try to convince you the *only* way to the republic is by plane via Bucharest: any honest agent will advise you to only fly as far as Bucharest and then get a train from there to Chişinău.

For further information about air travel in the region, see the Getting There & Away chapter at the beginning of this book.

LAND
For information on travelling to Moldova by land, see the Getting There & Away chapter at the beginning of this book.

Getting Around

For general information on travel within the region, see the Getting Around chapter at the beginning of this book.

BORDER CROSSINGS WITHIN MOLDOVA
Since the 1992 civil war, several army control posts have been set up on the Dniestr River, which marks the 'unofficial' border between Moldova and the self-declared republic of Transdniestr. These posts are set up by the Moldovan army, Transdniestr's border guards, and a Russian-led tripartite peacekeeping force.

MOLDOVA

Before entering Tighina from Chişinău, you have to stop at a control post. Vehicles are searched by the Transdniestrans. Spot checks on your car papers and driving licence by all three forces are frequent. Peacekeeping forces are stationed throughout the republic, including across the bridge between Tighina and Tiraspol.

The bridge along the main eastbound road (M21) from Chişinău to Dubăsari (and to Kyiv) is closed to all vehicles. Despite a sign at the western end of the bridge reading 'Stop: Trespassers will be shot', locals cross the bridge next to the hydroelectric power plant on foot. Foreigners are strongly advised not to try this.

To get to Kyiv from Chişinău you have to follow a minor road east to Vadul lui Vodă where the bridge across the Dniestr was open at the time of writing. From Doroţcaia, bear north to Dubăsari and the M21. Before embarking on this route, it is a good idea to check in Chişinău if this is still possible.

If you are crossing into Ukraine at the Pervomaisc border you have to drive through the republic of Transdniestr.

Chişinău & Around

Chişinău (pronounced 'kish-i-now' in Moldovan, 'kish-i-nev' in Russian), is strategically placed in the centre of the country, surrounded by fertile plains, and is renowned as a rich wine-producing region.

North of the capital lie two of Moldova's most unique treasures – the underground wine kingdom at Cricova and the fabulous 13th-century monastery carved in a cliff face at Orheiul Vechi.

CHIŞINĂU
☎ 2 • pop 735,000
Chişinău, Moldova's capital, is a surprisingly green city on the banks of the Bâc (Byk) River. It is circled by a ring of parks and lakes, and its pretty, tree-lined avenue and refreshingly quiet streets bear more resemblance to a provincial town than a nation's capital. Chişinău was first chronicled in 1420. It became a hotbed of anti-

Semitism in the early 20th century: in 1903 the murder of 49 Jews sparked protests from Jewish communities worldwide, and in 1941 during WWII the notorious Chişinău pogrom was executed.

Chişinău was the headquarters of the USSR's south-western theatre of military operations during Soviet rule. Between 1944 and 1990 the city was called Kishinev, its Russian name still used by the few travel agents abroad who actually know where it is.

More than half of Chişinău's population today is Moldovan; Russians comprise 25% and Ukrainians 13%.

Orientation
Chişinău's street layout is a typically Soviet grid system of straight streets.

The train station is a five-minute walk from the centre on Aleea Gării. Exit the train station, turn right along Aleea Gării to Piaţa Negruzzi, then walk up the hill along Blvd Negruzzi to Piaţa Libertăţii. From here the main street, Blvd Ştefan cel Mare, crosses the town from south-east to northwest. At its northern end is the central square, Piaţa Marii Adunări Naţionale (Great National Assembly Square), dominated by the government building, cathedral and Chişinău's very own Arc de Triomphe.

The central bus station (Autogară Centrală) is behind the central market on Str Mitropolit Varlaam. Buses to/from destinations south of Chişinău use the southwestern bus station (Autogară Sud-vest), 2km from the city centre.

Street names have changed and in many cases, both old and new names are used simultaneously. Hence, Str Hânceşti is sometimes signposted as Str Vasile Alecsandri too, for example. The maps of Chişinău in this book use the new street names.

Maps The *Chişinău Map* (1999), published by STRIH, is a good reference although it still lists some old street names. It costs $1.25 in most bookshops.

Information
Tourist Offices The state tourist office, Moldova Tur (☎ 540 301, fax 272 586), is

on the ground floor of Hotel Naţional, Blvd Ştefan cel Mare 4. The office sells maps and arranges city tours by car or minibus for an extortionate $40 an hour. It also arranges day trips to Cricova wine cellars for $46, can get train or plane tickets for a $1 commission, and rents out chauffeured cars for $10 an hour.

The Cricova Tour excursion bureau (☎ 221 419, fax 243 544) is at Str Mitropolit G Bănulescu Bodoni 45.

Romania has a tourist office in town (☎/fax 273 555 ⓔ optro@mdl.net), at Blvd Ştefan cel Mare 4.

Money Moldindconbank gives cash advances in Moldovan lei on Visa/MasterCard. The branch inside the international ticket hall at the train station is open 9 am to 1 pm and 2 to 7 pm weekdays. The city-centre branch, adjoining the Air Moldova office at Blvd Negruzzi 8, cashes travellers cheques; open 8 am to 1 pm and 2 to 6 pm weekdays. There is a 24-hour currency exchange at Blvd Ştefan cel Mare 6.

The Petrol Bank on the corner of Blvd Ştefan cel Mare and Str Ismail gives cash advances on Visa/MasterCard; open 8.30 am to 7.30 pm weekdays.

If you want to get a cash advance in US dollars on Visa/MasterCard, go to the Banca de Export Import a Moldovei, Blvd Ştefan cel Mare 6.

The Victoria Bank, on Blvd Ştefan cel Mare next to Green Hills Nistru Café, gives cash advances on Visa/MasterCard, cashes American Express travellers cheques and has an outside ATM; open 9 am to 5 pm weekdays and 9 am to 2 pm Saturday.

Another ATM can be found on the left-hand side of the Cinema Patria building on Blvd Ştefan cel Mare.

Post & Telephone The central post office (☎ 222 639) is at Blvd Ştefan cel Mare 134, on the corner of Str Vlaicu Picalab; open 8 am to 7 pm daily (to 6 pm Sunday). There is also a post office on Aleea Gării, open 8 am to 8 pm daily.

The central telephone, fax and telegraph office is on the corner of Blvd Ştefan cel

Mare and Str Tighina. Book international calls inside the hall marked 'Convorbiri Telefonice Internaţionale'. Faxes and telegrams can also be sent from here. This hall is open 24 hours but faxes can only be sent between 10.30 am and 6 pm.

Phonecards costing $2.95 (35 lei) can be purchased from the desk marked 'Reţeaua telefoane Chişinău' inside the second hall. Tokens (35 bani) for the token-operated public phones are also sold here. This hall is open 8 am to 7 pm Monday to Saturday and 9 am to 5 pm Sunday.

Email & Internet Access By far the most popular place in Chişinău to log on is the Black Elephant (☎ 491 104), a funky bar-nightclub at Str 31 August 78a. Online access costs $1 per hour.

The Internet Café (☎ 243 292, ⓔ icf2-1@moldova.md), on Str 31 August on the right-hand side of the National Library, charges $1.25 per hour for Internet access; open 10 am to midnight daily.

Travel Agencies The Voiaj travel agency (☎ 546 464, 543 944, fax 272 741, ⓔ tour ism@voiaj.net.md), Blvd Negruzzi 8, sells plane tickets, organises wine-tasting tours and is the most customer-friendly agency in town. For more information visit Voiaj's Web site at www.voiaj.net.md.

Bookshops English-language books – mainly dictionaries and text books – can be found at the Educational Centre (☎ 228 987), Str Mihai Eminescu 64, Apt 5; open 10 am to 6 pm weekdays and 10 am to 3 pm Saturday. Staff speak English.

Local maps are sold at Cartea Universală, Blvd Ştefan cel Mare 54, open 9.30 am to 8 pm daily (to 7 pm Sunday), and at Cartea Academica at Blvd Ştefan cel Mare 148.

Cultural Centres The French Cultural Centre (Alliance Française; ☎ 234 510, 237 236, fax 234 781, ⓔ alfrmd@mdearn.cri.md), inside the Ginta Latina Theatre at Str Sfatul Ţării 18, screens French films, holds French language courses, has an extensive library, and hosts regular cultural events.

There is a small German-language library (Deutscher Lesesaal; ☎ 247 906) on the 2nd floor of the Biblioteca Hasdeu, Blvd Ştefan cel Mare 148; open 9 am to 6 pm Monday to Thursday and 9 am to 5 pm weekends.

Medical Services The pharmacy close to Hotel Naţional on Blvd Negruzzi is open 8 am to 8 pm daily. The Centrală on Blvd Ştefan cel Mare, close to the 24-hour currency exchange, is open similar hours. Farmacie Ninervia, opposite the flower market on Str Mitropolit G Bănulescu Bodoni, is open 24 hours.

Emergency The emergency suite on the 4th floor of Hotel Naţional provides health care. Contact the US embassy for a list of English-speaking doctors. For emergency assistance dial the following:

Fire	☎ 901
Police	☎ 902
Ambulance	☎ 903

Things to See & Do

Chişinău was heavily bombed during WWII and little remains of its historic heart. Walk north-west along Blvd Ştefan cel Mare to the **Arc de Triomphe** (1846). To its east sprawls **Cathedral Park** (Parcul Catedralei), dominated by the city's main **Orthodox Cathedral** (1836). On the north-western side of the park, on Str Mitropolit G Bănulescu Bodoni, there is a colourful 24-hour **flower market**.

The area immediately west of the Arc de Triomphe on Blvd Ştefan cel Mare is dominated by **Government House**, where cabinet meets. The parliament convenes in **Parliament House**, at Blvd Ştefan cel Mare 123. Nearby is the contemporary **Opera & Ballet Theatre** (Opera Naţională din Moldova).

Ştefan cel Mare Park (Parcul Ştefan cel Mare) dominates the western flank of Blvd Ştefan cel Mare. The park entrance is guarded by a statue of Ştefan himself. The medieval prince of Moldavia is Moldova's greatest hero, bearing testimony to the country's pre-Soviet roots. Just outside the park is the large **Cinema Patria**, built by German prisoners of war in 1947.

From the Arc de Triomphe bear south-west along Str Puşkin. The **National Art Museum** (Muzeul de Arte Plastice; ☎ 245 245) is along this street on the corner of Str 31 August; open 9 am to 5 pm Tuesday to Sunday ($0.10). The **National History Museum** (Muzeul Naţional de Istorie al Moldavei; ☎ 226 614, 245 245) is not far away at Str 31 August 121a; same opening hours and cost as the Art Museum.

A **statue** of Lupoaica Romei (the wolf of Rome) and the abandoned children Romulus and Remus stands in front of the museum. At Str 31 August 121 is the **Licurici Puppet Theatre**. Opposite is the **National Library**.

Continue south-west along Str Puşkin to **Galeria L** (☎ 221 975), on the corner of Str Bucureşti and Str Puşkin, which holds temporary art exhibitions. Farther on is the **state university** at Str A Mateevici 6. The **water tower** (Turnul de Apă; ☎ 241 648) outside its main entrance dates from 1892. It was closed for restoration at the time of writing, but is usually open daily except Friday.

Walk north along Str A Mateevici then bear east for one block to the excellent **National Natural History & Ethnographic Museum** (Muzeul Naţional de Etnografie şi Istorie Naturală; ☎ 244 002) at Str M Kogălniceanu 82. The museum's highlights include a life-size reconstruction of a mammal skeleton which was discovered in the Rezine region in 1966. The museum is open 9 am to 5 pm Tuesday to Saturday.

The **Archaeology Museum** (Muzeul de Arheologie; ☎ 222 574), on the corner of Str 31 August and Str Mitropolit G Bănulescu Bodoni, displays reconstructions of traditional houses from Moldova's different regions and has a colourful exhibition of traditional handwoven rugs, carpets and wall hangings; open 10 am to 1 pm and 2 to 6 pm Tuesday to Saturday.

Back at the university, head south along Str A Mateevici, past a small park, to Str Ismail. On the corner is a small **open-air military exhibition**. It displays various models of Soviet-made tanks, fighter planes and other military toys inherited by

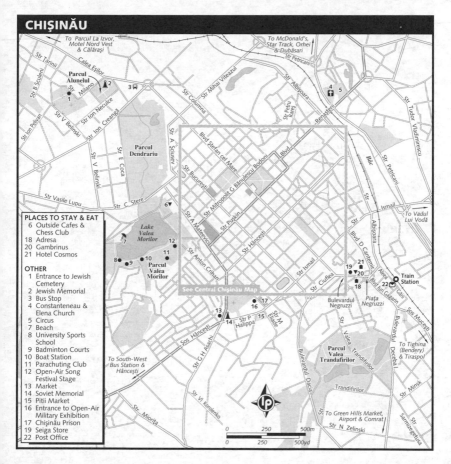

CHIŞINĂU

To Parcul La Izvor,
Motel Nord Vest
& Călăraşi

To McDonald's,
Star Track, Orhei
& Dubăsari

Str Petricani

Str Tărnii

Calea Eşilor

Str B Sculeni

Str Milano

Parcul
Alunelul

Str Albişoara

Str Mihai Viteazul

Str Columna

Str Petru Rareş

Renaştern

Str Tudor Vladimirescu

Str Ion Pelivan

Str V Belinski

Str Ion Neculce

Str Ion Creangă

Str A Sciusev

Blvd Ştefan cel Mare

Str Mitropolit G Bănulescu Bodoni

Blvd

Bâc

Str Petricani

Parcul
Dendrariu

Str V Belinski

Str E Coca

Str Bucureşti

Str Puşkin

Str Vasile Lupu

Str C Stere

Str A Mateevici

Str Hânceşti

Ismail

To Vadul
Lui Vodă

Str Albişoara

Blvd D Cantemir

PLACES TO STAY & EAT
6 Outside Cafes &
   Chess Club
18 Adresa
20 Gambrinus
21 Hotel Cosmos

OTHER
1 Entrance to Jewish
   Cemetery
2 Jewish Memorial
3 Bus Stop
4 Constanteneau &
   Elena Church
5 Circus
7 Beach
8 University Sports
   School
9 Badminton Courts
10 Boat Station
11 Parachuting Club
12 Open-Air Song
   Festival Stage
13 Market
14 Soviet Memorial
15 Pitii Market
16 Entrance to Open-Air
   Military Exhibition
17 Chişinău Prison
19 Seiga Store
22 Post Office

Lake
Valea
Morilor

Parcul
Valea
Morilor

Str Anton Crihan

See Central Chişinău Map

Str Ismail

Str Ciuflea

Bulevardul
Negruzzi

Piaţa
Negruzzi

Alea
Gării

Blvd Iuri Gagarin

Train
Station

To South-West
Bus Station &
Hânceşti

Şos Hânceşti

Str G H Asachi

Str P
Halippa

Str M
Eliade

Bulevardul Dacia

Valea Trandfirilor

Parcul
Valea
Trandafirilor

Bulevardul Decebal

To Tighina
(Bendery)
& Tiraspol

Str Minsk

Str Miorîţa

Str V Korolenko

Trandifirilor

To Green Hills Market,
Airport & Comrat

Str N Zelinski

Sarmizegetusa

Şos Muceşti

0   250   500m
0   250   500yd

Moldova's armed forces. The exhibition is open 10 am to 6 pm Tuesday to Sunday.

Opposite, on the corner of Str Mircea Eliade and Str A Mateevici, is **Chişinău Prison**. The military exhibition is flanked to the south by **Pitii Market**, Str P Halippa.

The small park straddled by Str A Mateevici is dominated by a **victory memorial** to the Soviet army in 1945. An eternal flame burns in the centre in memory of Chişinău's unknown soldiers who died in WWII. Soldiers' graves line the boundaries of the park and there is a small **military cemetery** at its northern end. In the centre of the park is a **memorial** to those who died during the fight for Moldovan independence in 1991.

The entrance to the adjoining **civil cemetery** (Cimitrul Central), known locally as the Armenian cemetery, is on the corner of Str A Mateevici and Str Armenească. The blue and silver-domed **All Saints Church** in the centre of the cemetery dates from 1830.

South of the cemeteries, on the corner of Str P Halippa and Str Hânceşti, is another typically monstrous **Soviet memorial**. There is a small **market** close by on Str Lacului where you can taste the local brew at dirt-cheap prices.

CENTRAL CHIŞINĂU

North of the centre on the corner of Str Anton Pann and Str I Pruncul is the **Pushkin Museum** (Muzeul Puşkin; ☎ 214 138), housed in a cottage where Russian poet Alexandr Pushkin (1799-1837) spent an exiled three months in the 1820s. The museum is open 10 am to 6 pm Tuesday to Sunday ($0.40).

The entire southern end of Str Mitropolit Varlaam is dominated by the huge **central market** which should not be missed. Local traders flog carpets from Turkey while wrinkled pensioners desperately clutch a bizarre collection of bras, T-shirts and not-

so-sexy knickers. Porters scurry around with trolleys to carry goods away, cars honk like crazy as they madly try to squeeze through the bustling crowds, women spit out sunflower seeds and old men huddle in groups haggling for the best bargain.

Close by, opposite Hotel Naţional, is an **Exhibition Hall** (Sala de Expoziţii; ☎ 541 596), which holds regular international exhibitions of paintings and other artworks; open 10 am to 5 pm weekdays and 9 am to 4 pm weekends.

The **Magazin Artă**, inside the hall, has some nice pieces for sale.

MOLDOVA

CENTRAL CHIŞINĂU

PLACES TO STAY
4 Hotel Zarea
6 Hotel Turist
16 Hotel Dacia
19 Hotel Moldova Jolly Alon
34 Hotel Codru
74 Hotel Meridan
82 Hotel Naţional; Moldova Tur
84 Hotel Chişinău

PLACES TO EAT
5 Sănătate
7 Café Fortus
9 Indian Tandoori
14 Belde Company
40 Shaolin
41 McDonald's
55 Green Hills Nistru Café
56 Consar Express
65 La Taifas
67 La Bunel
69 Cactus Café & Bar
76 Cantină
89 Oraşul Vechi; Cafenea & Sala Estivala
90 El Paso

OTHER
1 Russian Embassy
2 Hungarian Embassy
3 Pushkin Museum
8 Jewish Memorial
10 Fedesco Supermarket
11 Victoria Supermarket
12 Opera & Ballet Theatre
13 Presidential Palace
15 Main Entrance to Stadium

17 French Cultural Centre; Ginta Latina Theatre
18 German Embassy
20 Parliament House
21 Cinema Patria; ATM
22 Statue of Ştefan cel Mare
23 Cartea Academica
24 Farmacie Ninervia (24-Hour Pharmacy)
25 24-Hour Flower Market
26 Orthodox Cathedral
27 Yeshiva
28 Chekhov Drama Theatre
29 Arc de Triomphe
30 Government House
31 Black Elephant: The Underground Club; Internet Cafe
32 Archaeology Museum
33 Bulgarian Embassy
35 Republic Palace
36 National Natural History & Ethnographic Museum
37 National History Museum; Pani Pit – Museum Café
38 National Library; Internet Café
39 National Palace
42 Kodak Express
43 Post Office
44 Satirical Theatre
45 La Victor
46 Bookshop
47 Philharmonic Concert Hall
48 Synagogue
49 24-Hour Petrol Station
50 Main Entrance to Market
51 Magazinul de Firm Cricova

52 Bucuria Sweet Shop
53 Ialoveni Sherry Factory Shop & Bar
54 Victoria Bank
57 Kodak Express
58 Mihai Eminescu National Theatre
59 Organ Hall
60 National Art Museum
61 Licurici Puppet Theatre
62 US Embassy
63 Water Tower
64 University
66 Galeria L
68 Luceafărul Theatre
70 Moldindconbank
71 Cartea Universală
72 Central Bus Station
73 Main Entrance to Market
75 Central Telephone, Fax & Telegraph Office
77 Petrol Bank
78 Unic Magazinul Centur
79 Banca de Export Import a Moldovei
80 24-Hour Currency Exchange
81 Centrală Farmacie
83 Air Moldova; Voiaj Travel Agency
85 Exhibition Hall
86 Moldavian Airlines
87 Tarom Airlines; Transaero
88 Dublin Bar & Restaurant
91 Turkish Embassy
92 Entrance to Civil Cemetery
93 University Cultural House; Disco

Parks & Lakes Locals' favoured haunt is **Lake Valea Morilor**, west of the city. Steps lead to the lake and surrounding park from Str A Mateevici (opposite the university).

The beach on the north-western shores gets packed with sunbathers and swimmers at weekends. You can hire canoes, rowing and paddle boats for $1 an hour from the boat station on the lake's southern shores; open 10 am to 9 pm weekdays and 10 am to 8 pm weekends. There are **badminton courts** (☎ 721 753) close to the university sports school on the southern shore. High-flyers should hike up to the **parachuting club** (☎ 515 795, 223 563), above the open-air song festival stage.

Bus No 29a from the city centre stops outside the university entrance to the park.

South of the park is the **Expo-Business Chişinău** (☎ 716 053/864), a free enterprise zone where VAT-exempt goods are sold; open 10 am to 9 pm daily. Locals flock here for cheap alcohol. Next to the entrance stand Chişinău's disgraced heroes – communists Lenin, Marx and Engels.

North-west of the centre on the road to Cojuşna and Ungheni is Chişinău's largest park, **Parcul La Izvor**, on Calea Eşilor. It is dominated by three interconnecting lakes, which you can explore with rented canoes and rowing boats. Opposite the park's southern entrance is a **cable car** station; you

MOLDOVA

Jewish Chişinău

Since independence Chişinău's Jewish community has seen a massive revival. The active community runs an adult education program at its small secondary school, operates a meals-on-wheels service for elderly Jews and prints a newspaper in Hebrew. It also runs a soup kitchen in Chişinău and in Tiraspol.

North of the central bus station is a maze of run-down, dusty streets. Many of these streets formed the **Chişinău ghetto**. On the street leading east from Blvd Renaşterii to Str Fantalului is a **memorial** to the martyrs and victims of the Chişinău ghetto, inscribed in Hebrew, Moldovan and Russian. At Str Rabbi Ţirilson 4 are the remains of a **yeshiva**, Chişinău's Jewish school which functioned until WWII. Chişinău's only remaining working **synagogue** is close by at Str Habad Lubavia 8. Before WWII there were over 70 synagogues in Chişinău, each serving a different trade. Glassblowers worshipped at the one on Str Habad Lubavia.

The city's **Jewish cemetery** is north-west of the centre, next to Parcul Alunelul on Str Milano. Most graves are unkempt and overgrown. There are ruins of an old synagogue next to the cemetery's surrounding stone wall. In Parcul Alunelul there is a **memorial** to the Jews killed in the 1903 pogrom. The remains of the victims were moved here after the cemetery in which they were buried was destroyed by the communists in the 1960s. To get to the park and cemetery take bus No 1 from Blvd Ştefan cel Mare and get off at the Parcul Alunelul stop. Cross the road and walk up the hill and along Str Milano. The cemetery entrance is on the left.

can make a three-minute journey across the valley between 7 am and noon and from 1 to 7 pm Monday to Saturday ($0.25). To get to the park, take trolleybus No 1, 8 or 23 to the last stop. Microbus No 11 runs from Str Studenţilor in the centre to Calea Eşilor.

Places to Stay – Budget
Camping The nearest *camping ground* is 12km north-east of Chişinău in Vadul lui Vodă forest. Open summer only, it is a popular weekend spot for locals. Take the microbus marked Vadul lui Vodă from the central bus station.

Private Rooms The best bet for budget travellers is *Adresa* (☎ 544 392, fax 272 096, Blvd Negruzzi 1), a five-minute walk west of the train station. It rents out apartments and rooms in the city centre for short- and long-term stays. A clean apartment for two people starts from $20 a night. If you stay more than one week you'll get a 10% discount. Most apartments have a well-equipped kitchen and a bathroom with a small water heater. You have to pay in advance and leave a $4.20 deposit for the key. Adresa is open 9 am to 9 pm weekdays and 9 am to 6 pm Saturday. Staff do not speak English.

Hotels Opposite the central bus station is the surprisingly clean *Hotel Meridan* (☎ 270 620, Str Tighina 42). Singles/doubles with TV and private shower are $13/19 and rooms with shared bathroom are $11/15, plus an additional $0.85 registration tax. Hotel staff speak some English. The entrance is through the Foto Express kiosk.

The 120-bed *Hotel Zarea* (☎ 227 625, Str Anton Pann 4) is cheap: a bed in a single/double or triple with shared bathroom is $11, plus $0.75 registration tax. The hotel has a bar and billiard club. Staff are surly.

Hotel Turist (☎ 229 512/639, Blvd Renaşterii 13a), overlooking the giant Soviet memorial to communist youth, has cheap singles/doubles for $20/23 plus $0.75 registration tax. Rooms have a private shower but hot water is unreliable. Reception staff speak no English and are a touch hostile.

The attractive *Hotel Chişinău* (☎ 578 506, fax 578 510, Blvd Negruzzi 7) has pleasant rooms with private bath costing $16/28. The hotel restaurant is reputed to be good for traditional Moldovan cuisine.

Places to Stay – Mid-Range
The towering 17-storey *Hotel Naţional* (☎ 540 305, fax 272 586, Blvd Ştefan cel

Mare 4) is run by Moldova Tur. Singles/doubles with TV cost $38/50, plus $0.75 registration tax. Rooms for Moldovans are cheaper. The hotel has a cafe and restaurant.

Following major renovation in 1996, the *Motel Nord Vest* (☎ *759 828, fax 624 931),* on Calea Eşilor, 3km north-west of the centre on the main Chişinău-Cojuşna highway, is now a pleasant 100-bed motel. Rooms with TV, fridge and shower cost $40/50, plus $0.75 registration tax. The motel has a tennis court, sauna and excellent restaurant and bar.

Places to Stay – Top End
Hotel Cosmos (☎ *572 724, fax 542 747, Piaţa Negruzzi 2),* an ugly concrete block, was undergoing major renovations at the time of writing. Renovated singles with all the mod cons start from a pricey $81 and a two-room apartment costs $190. Unrenovated doubles are significantly cheaper at $48. The staff are friendly and there is a 24-hour bar and a handy left-luggage room (open also to nonguests; $0.25/0.40 for a small/large bag).

Hotel Codru (☎ *225 506, fax 237 948,* e *reservation@codru.dnt.md, Str 31 August 127)* has singles/doubles for $80/120. The hotel decor is dark and gloomy.

The three-star *Hotel Dacia* (☎ *232 251, fax 234 647,* e *info@hotel-dacia.com, Str 31 August 135)* is a large block close to parliament in the heart of the city's 'embassy land'. Foreigners pay a hefty $90/134 for rooms with private bath. See the Web site at www.hotel-dacia.com.

Considered the best in town is the could-be-anywhere-in-the-world *Hotel Moldova Jolly Alon* (☎ *232 875/896, fax 232 870,* e *reservation@ja.moldline.net, Str Maria Cibotari 37),* next to the German embassy. The enticing sofas in the reception are enough to make you want to check in immediately. Single/double rooms go for $135/160, and junior/senior/executive suites are priced at $180/250/295. The hotel has a restaurant and a casino.

Places to Eat
Restaurants The best place to sample authentic Moldovan cuisine is *Sănătate* (☎ *244 116, Blvd Renaşterii 24).* Local delicacies on the menu, written in Romanian, Russian and English, include boiled sturgeon and a huge variety of *mămăligă* (Romanian polenta) dishes for around $1. The adjoining terrace bar overlooking the street hosts live bands on weekends.

Another top choice for traditional Moldovan fare is *La Taifas* (☎ *227 692/693, Str Bucureşti 67).* Here you can sit and watch as bread is cooked the old-fashioned way in a wood-fired oven at the back of the restaurant while you're serenaded by a panpipe player. The menu, written in Romanian, French and English, includes the delicious *ciulama* (chicken in wine sauce) served with *mămăliguţa* for $1.50. Expect to pay around $4.50 for a good bottle of wine.

Gambrinus (Blvd Negruzzi 4/2), next to the Seiga store, is a modern restaurant with a bright decor and even brighter terrace. The menu is in Russian and Romanian and garnishes cost extra. The *Piept de pui la gratar* (chicken baked with apples) for $2.50 is tasty.

For authentic Turkish cuisine look no further than the *Belde Company* restaurant and bar (☎ *233 451, Str Lazo 139)* close to the Dinamo Stadium. The iskender kebab ($3), served on a bed of fried toast and topped with spicy yogurt, is delicious, as is the $1 baclava.

Not particularly authentic is the Indian cuisine served at *Indian Tandoori* (☎ *245 023, Blvd Renaşterii 6).* Expect to pay around $5 to $10 for a main dish. Portions are small and not spicy.

Better value is the Jewish restaurant *La Bunel* (☎ *222 219, Str Mihai Eminescu 50),* whose name means 'at Grandpa's'. Main dishes like chicken fillet stuffed with cheese or *pelmeni* (Russian meat dumplings) in mushroom sauce cost around $1.85; service is impeccable. In summer, bands play outside.

If it's Chinese cuisine you're craving, try *Shaolin* (☎ *227 553, Str Puşkin 26).* Moldovan-Chinese-style dishes start at around $4.

Three of the city's coolest restaurants – in decor and cuisine – are on Str Armenească. *Cactus Café* (☎ *504 094, 224 257),* on the corner of Str 31 August and Str Armenească, is kitted out 'Wild West' style with swinging saloon doors and chairs suspended from the ceiling. Its mind-boggling menu includes turkey with bananas ($2.60) and spicy pork with chicken liver and cheese sauce ($1.75). Its salads are equally adventurous.

El Paso (☎ *504 100, Str Armenească 10*) serves excellent Mexican cuisine. Don't miss the fried pork with chocolate-almond sauce! Book in advance to guarantee a table – especially under the arches on the candle-lit terrace.

Third in line is the elegant *Oraşul Vechi* (*'Old City'; ☎ 225 063, 262 035, Str Armenească 24*). Don't be intimidated by the over-dressed doormen – prices are reasonable and the mix of classical and traditional folk music played is top-notch. Adjoining the restaurant is the cheaper and less exclusive *Oraşul Vechi Cafenea* and the *Sala Estivala* (summer hall).

The perfect place to dine after browsing through the National Art Museum is the adjoining *Pani Pit – Museum Café* (☎ *240 127*), on Str 31 August. Italian and Moldovan dishes are served, including *Costiţa Moldovenească* (pork chops pickled in red wine) at $2.50. The menu is in English.

Cafes When the sun shines, outdoor cafes sprout like mushrooms. Chişinău's top terrace is outside the Opera & Ballet Theatre on Blvd Ştefan cel Mare. There are also some good outside cafes opposite the main entrance to the university on Str A Mateevici and in the opposite courtyard leading to Parcul Valea Morilor. At the northern end of Str A Mateevici is another courtyard filled with outside cafes and chess fiends. The chess club is in the same courtyard.

More permanent fixtures include *Consar Express* (*Blvd Ştefan cel Mare 130*), serving pelmeni, pasties and other light snacks. The video cafe-bar *Café Fortus*, on Blvd Renaşterii, has a terrace and shows videos on two TV screens positioned back to back.

The popular *Green Hills Nistru Café* (*Blvd Ştefan cel Mare 77*), next to the Victoria Bank, serves an amazing array pizzas, salads, pastries and coffee.

A more humble experience is a meal in one of the city's Soviet-style canteens. The best of the bunch is the *Cantină* opposite the telephone office on Blvd Ştefan cel Mare.

Fast Food For fast Turkish food go to *Quickie* (☎ *265 563, Str Ismail 46*); the entrance is on Str 31 August. Tasty *şaşliks* cost $2 and salads start at $0.20. It's open 9 am to 11 pm daily.

The ever-popular *McDonald's* has made it to town, downing a city icon – Wam (which ingeniously used an upside-down copy of the McDonald's logo for its own) – in its wake. There are three outlets: near Kodak Express at Blvd Ştefan cel Mare 134–36, north of the centre at Str Aleco Russo plaza 2 and south of the centre at Blvd Dacia 21.

Self-Catering The *central market* (*piaţa centrală*) is well worth a visit for its glorious choice of fresh food. The main entrances are close to the central bus station on Str Tighina, and Str Armeneasca; open 7 am to 5 pm daily.

The most central supermarket is *Fidesco*, which has an outlet next to Hotel Naţional on Blvd Ştefan cel Mare and one at Str Mitropolit G Bănulescu Bodoni 51. Both are open 9 am to 9 pm daily. A few doors down at No 47 is the *Victoria Supermarket*, open 9 am to 8 pm daily.

Slightly out of town is the *Green Hills Market* on the corner of Blvd Decebal and Blvd Dacia; open 9 am to 9 pm daily (to 8 pm Sunday). It has a bar and restaurant on the 2nd floor and an excellent range of locally produced wines, champagnes and cognacs in the ground-floor shop.

Entertainment

Posters listing what's on where are pasted on the 'teatrul concerte' notice board outside the Opera & Ballet Theatre on Blvd Ştefan cel Mare. The English-language magazine *Welcome* runs a fortnightly calendar of cultural events.

Bars & Clubs A must is the rustic drinking hole in the basement of the *Ialoveni sherry factory shop* on the corner of Blvd Ştefan cel Mare and Str Hânceşti. Swill a tumbler of Moldovan sherry with drunken locals for less than $0.15. Staff speak no English but given they only serve one thing it is easy to make yourself understood! Bottles of the potent sherry, dessert wines and brandies are sold in the shop on the ground floor. It is open 8 am to 2 pm and 3 to 8 pm weekdays, and 8 am to 2 pm Saturday.

The highlight of Chişinău's nightlife is the *Black Elephant: The Underground Club* (☎ 234 715, Str 31 August 78a). Its network of blacked-out, tunnelled rooms play host to jazz nights, live bands and discos. The club also has an Internet cafe and billiard tables. Look for the black door with a large guitar perched above.

The Celtic spirit is alive and well at Irish-inspired *Dublin (Str Bulgară 27)*, an expensive but popular bar-restaurant. A bowl of Irish stew will set you back $5.50 and a pint of Guinness $3.30. Upstairs is a restaurant and billiard table.

Discos Boppy discos are held nightly at *Teresa Nica (☎ 721 736, Str P Halippa 3)*, a disco, bowling and billiard club; ($0.25/1 for women/men on weekdays and $0.50/2.50 at weekends). The billiard and bowling club is open 11 to 3 am daily, the disco 8 pm to 3 am. A calmer teenage disco rocks most weekends inside the *university cultural house* at the southern end of Str A Kogălniceanu.

The flashy *La Victor* dance club and bar (☎ 246 270, Str Mihai Eminescu 55) is frequented mostly by foreign businessmen; open 24 hours.

Located north of the centre on the 1st floor of the Union Building is *Star Track* (☎ 496 207, Str Chievskaia 7), a disco/strip club. Its dark interior sports comfortable sofas and intimate booths where love-struck couples can smooch (admission $3.35/5 for women/men).

Theatre The *Opera & Ballet Theatre* (☎ 245 104), on Blvd Ştefan cel Mare, is home to the Moldovan national opera and ballet company. The box office is open 10 am to 2 pm and 5 to 7 pm daily.

Plays are staged at the *Satirical Theatre (Teatrul Satiricus; ☎ 224 034)* on the corner of Str Mitropolit Varlaam and Str Mihai Eminescu.

Contemporary Romanian productions can be seen at the *Mihai Eminescu National Theatre (☎ 221 177, Blvd Ştefan cel Mare 79)*. The box office is open 10 am to 1 pm and 3 to 6 pm daily.

Plays in Russian are performed at the *Chekhov Drama Theatre (Teatrul Dramatic A Cehov; ☎ 223 362, 228 616)*, on the corner of Str Mitropolit Varlaam and Str Pircaleb, sited where Chişinău's choral synagogue was until WWII.

The Poetic Star youth theatre, *Luceafărul Theatre (☎ 224 121, Str Veronica Micle 7)*, stages more alternative productions.

Productions in Moldovan and Russian are held at the *Licurici Puppet Theatre (☎ 245 273/166, Str 31 August 121)*. Performances start at 11 am daily and the box office is open 9 am to 2 pm Tuesday to Sunday ($0.25).

Various cabarets, musicals and local theatre group productions take place at the *National Palace (Palatul Naţional; Str Puşkin 24)*. Performances start at 6 pm daily and the box office is open 11 am to 5 pm daily.

Classical Music Classical concerts and organ recitals are held at the *Organ Hall (Sala cu Orgă; ☎ 225 404, Blvd Ştefan cel Mare 79)* next to the Mihai Eminescu National Theatre. Performances start at 6 pm and tickets are sold at the box office in the Eminescu theatre.

Moldova's National Philharmonic is based at the *Philharmonic Concert Hall (☎ 224 505, Str Mitropolit Varlaam 78)*.

Circus Bus No 27 from Blvd Ştefan cel Mare goes to the *circus (☎ 486 800, Blvd Renaşterii 33)*, across the river. The box office is open 9 am to 6 pm daily. Performances are held at 6.30 pm Friday, and noon, 3 and 6.30 pm Saturday and Sunday. Tickets cost from $1.25 to $2.95.

Spectator Sports

Moldovans are big football fans and they have two stadiums to prove it. The main

MOLDOVA

Republic Stadium (Stadionul Republican), south of the centre, has floodlighting. The main entrance is on Str Ismail with a smaller entrance at the southern end of Str Bucureşti. The entrance to the smaller Dinamo Stadium (Stadionul Dinamo) is north of the centre on the corner of Str Bucureşti and Str Lazo.

Shopping

Don't leave Chişinău without visiting the Magazinul de Firm Cricova (☎ 222 775), the commercial outlet of the Cricova wine factory, on Blvd Ştefan cel Mare. It stocks 15 types of wine and five champagnes produced in Cricova. The oldest – and most expensive at around $25 – date from 1965; open 10 am to 7 pm daily.

The outlet of the Ialoveni sherry factory is close by on the corner of Blvd Ştefan cel Mare and Str Hânceşti (see Entertainment – Bars & Clubs).

Just a couple of doors down at Blvd Ştefan cel Mare 126 is the heavenly Bucuria sweet shop, open 8 am to 9 pm daily (to 5 pm Sunday).

Chişinău's Soviet-style department store, Unic Magazinul Centru, is at Blvd Ştefan cel Mare 8; open 8 am to 7 pm Monday to Saturday.

Local artists and craftspeople sell their wares in the small plaza next to the Mihai Eminescu National Theatre.

Getting There & Away

Air Moldova's only airport is in Chişinău, 14.5km south-east of the centre. It has only international flights. Airline offices selling tickets include:

Air Moldova
(☎ 525 506) Chişinău airport
(☎ 546 464, 274 009) Blvd Negruzzi 8
Air Moldova International
(☎ 529 791, fax 526 414, e info@ami.md) Chişinău airport
Moldavian Airlines
(☎/fax 525 064, ☎ 529 365) Chişinău airport
(☎ 549 339/340, fax 549 341) Blvd Ştefan cel Mare 3
Tarom
(☎ 542 154) Blvd Ştefan cel Mare 3 (entrance on Str Ismail)

Transaero
(☎ 525 413) Chişinău airport
(☎ 542 454, fax 542 461) Blvd Ştefan cel Mare 4 (entrance on Str Ismail)
(☎ 540 304) Hotel Naţional, Blvd Ştefan cel Mare 4

Train The train station is at Aleea Gării. It's clean and well signposted.

The timetables are outside the station. They are in Moldovan and Russian, and easy to comprehend. You are not allowed on the platform without a valid train ticket. The information booth is in the 1st-floor ticket hall. It costs $0.05 per question (Moldovan and Russian only).

Tickets for international trains for same-day departures are sold at the 2nd-floor ticket office, signposted 'Casă Internationale'. Advance tickets (bought 24 hours or more before departure) are sold at the 'Casă Prealabil' on the 3rd floor, open 8 am to 6 pm Tuesday to Saturday. The ticket hall for local trains is on the 1st floor. For phone reservations call ☎ 250 071 (Russian and Moldovan only).

Moldova's main train line heads east from Chişinău into Ukraine and then north through Belarus into Russia. Another line originates in Tiraspol, passing through Chişinău on its northbound route to Chernivtsi (Cernăuţi) and Ivano-Frankivsk in Ukraine. There are numerous trains from Chişinău to Ukraine, Belarus and on to Russia. Westbound, there are nightly trains to Romania and beyond.

There are two daily local trains from Chişinău to Odesa, which stop at Tighina and Tiraspol. Tighina is always listed on train timetables by its Russian name, Bendery.

There are four local trains daily to Ungheni on the Moldova-Romania border.

Bus Chişinău has two bus stations. Most buses within Moldova depart from the central bus station (Autogară Centrală), behind the central market on Str Mitropolit Varlaam. Tickets for local buses to Străşeni, Căpriana and beyond are sold at ticket window Nos 40 and 41. Window Nos 42 and 43 sell tickets for buses to Orhei and beyond. Tickets cannot be bought in advance.

MOLDOVA

Services from Autogară Centrală include one daily to Recea ($1.12), three daily to Căpriana ($0.65), 11 daily to Străşeni ($0.40), and one every hour to Tiraspol ($3.85) via Tighina ($2.95). There are also daily buses to Bălţi ($2.40), Ediniţa and Briceni, and buses every half-hour between 9.15 am and 10 pm to Orhei ($0.80) and Orheiul Vechi ($1.20).

Bus services to/from Comrat, Hânceşti and other southern destinations use the less crowded south-western bus station (Autogară Sud-vest), 2km from the city centre on the corner of Şoseaua Hânceşti and Str Spicului. Above each ticket window is a list of destinations covered by that ticket-seller. Daily local services include five buses to Comrat ($2.95) in Gagauzia and six to Hânceşti.

Buses to Turkey depart from the train station. Tickets to Istanbul ($34) are sold at the Eskicioğlu Meridian InterTrans office (☎ 549 835, fax 244 336) next to the central bus station. Buses depart at 6 pm Sunday to Thursday. The company also has a weekly service to Berlin at 9.30 am Thursday ($80).

Öz Gülen Turizm (☎ 273 748, 272 591), also at the train station, runs a daily bus to Istanbul ($34, 6 pm).

Getting Around

To/From the Airport
Bus No 65 departs every 30 minutes between 5 am and 10 pm from the central bus station to the airport. Microbus No 65 departs every 20 minutes from Str Ismail, near the corner of Blvd Ştefan cel Mare ($0.20).

Bus & Trolleybus Bus No 45 (and microbus No 45a) runs from the central bus station to the south-western bus station. Bus No 1 goes from the train station to Blvd Ştefan cel Mare.

Trolleybus Nos 1, 4, 5, 8, 18 and 22 go to the train station from the city centre. Bus Nos 2, 10 and 16 go to Autogară Sud-vest. Tickets costing $0.08 for buses and $0.05 for trolleybuses are sold at kiosks or direct from the driver.

Most bus routes in town and to many outlying villages are served by nippy microbuses. These small buses are faster and more expensive than regular buses ($0.10 per trip, pay the driver). Route numbers, displayed on the front and side windows, are followed by the letter 'a' or 't'. Those with the letter 'a' follow the same route as the bus of the same number. Those with a letter 't' follow the trolleybus routes. Microbuses run every 15 minutes between 6 am and midnight.

Car & Motorcycle Car rental does not exist in Moldova as, by law, motorists have to own the vehicle they drive. At the time of writing, it was not even possible to hire a car in Romania and drive it into Moldova.

There is a 24-hour petrol station, Zimbru, north-east of the central bus station on the corner of Str Sfante Gheorghe and Blvd Avram Iancu. A-95 octane petrol (best for Western vehicles) is $0.50 a litre. Lower grade A-92/A-76 (OK for Ladas) is $0.46/0.42.

Taxi The main taxi stand is in front of Hotel Naţional. Drivers here will rip you off. Calling a taxi (☎ 746 565, or dial ☎ 705, 706 or 707) is cheaper. The official rate is $0.20 per kilometre.

CRICOVA
The village of Cricova, 15km north of Chişinău, boasts an underground wine 'town'. The vast cellars are accessed by a labyrinth of underground streets, appropriately named Str Cabernet, Str Pinot etc, stretching for more than 60km. More than one million bottles of fine white wines – 648 types – are stored in the cellars at a constant 12°C.

In Soviet times, Cricova wines and champagnes were considered among the top wines produced in the USSR. Its sparkling white wine was sold under the label 'Soviet Champagne'. Today, demand for its dry white sauvignon, muscadet and sweeter muscats remains high. Some five million bottles are produced each year, 25% of which are exported worldwide. Unique to the Cricova cellars is its sparkling red wine, *kodrinskoie-sparkling*, made from cabernet-sauvignon stocks and marketed as having a

MOLDOVA

'rich velvet texture' and a 'blackcurrant and cherry' taste.

The entrance to the wine factory (☎ 2-444 035, 581 960, ⓔ info@cricova.com) is at Str Ungureanu 1, uphill along Str 31 August from the bus station, then right. Web site: www.cricova-wine.com.

You can only visit the wine factory as part of an organised tour. Travel agencies in Chişinău organise tours including transport to/from Chişinău and wine tasting, as well as souvenir bottles of wine and champagne. Tours have to be booked in advance ($24 per person).

Buy Cricova wine cheaply at the factory outlet shop, opposite the main bus stop in the centre of the village. The 'Cricova Champagne' – white sparkling wine – costs $2.35 a bottle. Note that *demi-dulce* is semisweet, *dulce* is sweet and *brut* is dry. The shop is open 9 am to 10 pm daily.

Next to the bus stop is a memorial honouring local victims of the 1992 Moldova-Transdniestr conflict

Getting There & Away
For visitors not part of an organised tour, bus No 2 from Str Hânceşti in Chişinău runs every 15 minutes to Cricova ($0.15).

COJUŞNA
Cricova's competitors operate 25km northwest of Chişinău in the village of Cojuşna. Sales have dropped since its fabulous distribution network collapsed along with the USSR. Mainstays include 13 different red and white table wines including cabernet, sauvignon and riesling. Cojuşna also produces vodka for Moldova's diehards as well as heavier port wines (*xeres*).

Cojuşna is geared to tourists. Take in the cellars and various wine-tasting halls decked out in different themes. The winery has no land, having reaped the harvests of smaller wineries for the past 30 years.

You can buy wines from the Cojuşna shop on the complex. Expect to pay around $4 for a 1982 bottle of cabernet or $0.87 for a bottle of regular 1994 plonk (still excellent).

Call the Cojuşna wine factory (Fabrica de Vinuri Cojuşna; ☎ 2-624 820, 628 436, fax 639 706) in advance to book a tour. It costs $22 per person and includes a two-hour tasting session of six collection wines. Tours in English are only available in the afternoon. The office is open 8 am to 6 pm weekdays.

In Chişinău, don't let travel agencies con you into paying for an expensive tour to Cojuşna. Expensive perks include transport to Cojuşna from Chişinău, plus souvenir bottles of wine.

Getting There & Away
Bus No 2 runs every 15 minutes from Str Hânceşti (Str Vasile Alecsandri) in Chişinău to Cricova. Get off at the Cojuşna stop. Ignore the turning on the left marked Cojuşna and walk or hitch the remaining 2km along the main road to the winery entrance, marked by a tall, totem-pole-style pillar. You can also take bus No 37 from the bus stop opposite the circus in Chişinău to Stăuceni, where you can pick up any Cricova-bound bus.

STRĂŞENI, RECEA & ROMĂNEŞTI
Străşeni, 12km north-west of Chişinău, is renowned for fine sparkling white wines, which have been produced in the village for the past 35 years. The Străşeni Wine Factory (Fabrica de Vinuri Străşeni; ☎ 2-22 756) produces around 1,250,000 bottles (100,000 decalitres) of wine a year, 80% of which is exported to CIS countries. Vineyards sprawl for 10,000 hectares around the village.

In the isolated village of **Căpriana**, 7km south-west of Străşeni, is a large 14th-century monastery. Daily services have been held here since 1926, and some forty Orthodox monks live here today. Căpriana was one of the few monasteries in Moldova to survive the wrath of the communist regime following WWII.

Recea, 9km north of Străşeni, is a small, family-run wine cellar. The 2000 decalitres of sauvignon wine it yields annually are bottled, labelled and prepared for export at the local cooperative.

The last of the trio is Romaneşti (☎ 2-40 478, 40 230), one of the largest wineries in Moldova and once one of the USSR's leading wine producers. Organised tours flocked here in their droves to taste the red Bordeaux-type wines drunk by Russian tsars. Romaneşti is 7km north of Recea.

You can visit all three wineries on an organised tour. At Recea visitors are welcome all hours; just turn up. At Străşeni and Romaneşti you have to book a tour in advance.

Getting There & Away

Străşeni is in the village centre at Str Oreiului 36. From the bus stop at the northern end of the village, cross the footbridge over the Chişinău-Ungheni highway and continue for 1km until you reach a crossroad. Continue straight, following a dirt drive which leads to the factory. Străşeni train station is 200m south of the bus stop on the main road.

Eleven buses depart daily from Chişinău's central bus station to Străşeni between 8.20 am and 5.40 pm ($0.40, 30 minutes). Microbuses run every hour. There are 10 daily trains to/from Chişinău (30 minutes). Most Ungheni-bound trains stop at Străşeni, as do the daily Chişinău-Moscow and Chişinău-Odesa trains.

From Chişinău there's a daily bus to Recea ($1.12). From Străşeni, the only means of getting to Recea is by taxi ($3). Romaneşti is not served by public transport.

Three buses leave daily, in the morning, from Chişinău to Căpriana. The bus makes its return journey immediately, making a day trip difficult. Forget hitching: few cars or carts pass by.

IALOVENI, MILEŞTII MICI & HÂNCEŞTI

Moldova's wine road sprawls south of Chişinău too. Ialoveni, 10km south of the capital, is a predominantly sherry-making area. Its wine cellars (☎ 268-737 825, fax 737 838), Str Alexandru cel Bun 4, welcome visitors year-round.

The cellars at Mileştii Mici, 15km south of Chişinău, specialise in white table wines. Wine-tasting trips including lunch are arranged by travel agencies in Chişinău. Individuals can call the cellars (☎ 268-68 383) to arrange cheaper tours.

Hânceşti, 35km south-west of Chişinău, is home to a large industrial winery (☎ 234-

22 349) producing some 1.3 million deca-litres of white table wines a year. Wine tasting is offered.

From Chişinău, take bus No 35 from Autogară Sud-vest to Ialoveni. There are no buses between Ialoveni and Mileştii Mici but a local driver will take you there for around $2. There is one direct bus daily at 4.15 pm from Chişinău's Autogară Sud-vest to Mileştii Mici ($1.45), and six buses daily to Hânceşti.

ORHEI

☎ 235 • pop 37,500

The modern town of Orhei, not to be confused with Orheiul Vechi (Old Orhei), is 45km north of Chişinău. It is Moldova's sixth-largest city and was settled on the ruins of 14th-century Orheiul Vechi. Almost decimated during WWII, Orhei has little to offer tourists, but serves as a good stepping stone if you want to visit Orheiul Vechi.

Information

The telephone office is close to the former Catholic church at Str Vasile Mahu 121. The central post office is a few doors down at Str Vasile Mahu 129. You can change money at the Real Currency Exchange, Str Vasile Lupu 33; open 9.15 am to 5.30 pm weekdays and 9.15 am to 3 pm weekends.

Things to See

A statue of Vasile Lupu, reigning prince of Moldavia (ruled 1634–53), stands majestically at the entrance to the city in front of the St Dimitru Church (Biserica Sfântu Dimitru; 1637). The main street, Blvd Ştefan cel Mare, is dominated by St Nicholas' Church (Biserica Sfântu Nicolae).

Behind the Catholic church is a monument to the soldiers killed during the 1992 Moldovan-Transdniestran conflict in Tighina (Bendery) and Dubaşari.

Exhibits at the excellent History & Ethnographic Museum (Muzeul de Istorie şi Etnografie), Str Renaşterii Naţionale 23, trace the city's history from Vasile Lupu's reign through to Moldova's declaration of independence on 31 August 1989. The text is in Moldovan and Russian but is well illustrated

MOLDOVA

with photographs. The museum is open 9 am to 5 pm Tuesday to Sunday.

Places to Stay & Eat

Hotel Codru (☎ *24 821, Str Vasile Lupu 36)* has basic, unheated singles/doubles with shared bathroom and no hot water for $3.50/5.50. Cold water is only available from 6 to 9 am and 7 to 9 pm. The *Codru Restaurant* next door is open noon to midnight daily.

Getting There & Away

Daily buses depart every half-hour from Chişinău's Autogară Centrală to Orhei between 9.15 am and 10 pm ($0.80, two hours). All northbound buses from Chişinău stop in Orhei too, including daily buses to Bălţi, Ediniţa and Briceni. From Orhei there is one daily bus at 12.45 pm to Orheiul Vechi.

All Chişinău-Orhei buses pass 2km west of Ivancea. Get off on the main highway then walk or hitch.

ORHEIUL VECHI

Ten kilometres south-east of Orhei lies Orheiul Vechi ('Old Orhei'; marked on maps as Trebujeni). Ştefan cel Mare built a fortress here in the 14th century but it was later destroyed by Tartars.

The fantastic **Orheiul Vechi Monastery** complex (Complexul Muzeistic Orheiul Vechi; ☎ 235-34 242), carved in a cliff in this wild, rocky, remote spot, is what draws most visitors here. The **Cave Monastery** (Mănăstire în Peşteră), inside a limestone cliff overlooking the Răut River, was dug by Orthodox monks in the 13th century. It remained inhabited until the 18th century, and in 1996 a handful of monks returned to this unique place of worship and are slowly restoring it to its original use.

The central hall of the underground monastery is open to visitors. This served as the main church in the 13th century. Until the 17th century, the monks slept in stone bunks *(keilies)* in an adjacent cave. An earthquake in the 17th century forced them to retreat from these stone cells to smaller caves farther south along the cliff.

In the 18th century the cave-church was taken over by villagers from neighbouring Butceni. In 1905 they built a church above ground dedicated to the Ascension of St Mary. The church was shut down by the Soviets in 1944 and remained abandoned throughout the communist regime. Services resumed in 1996. Archaeologists have recently uncovered remnants of a defence wall surrounding the monastery complex from the 15th century.

A well-presented **village museum** is also included in the monastery complex. The ethnographic exhibits include a traditional 14th-century Moldovan house.

The monastery complex is open 9 am to 5 pm Tuesday to Sunday ($0.20). The 1½-hour guided tour is in Moldovan or Russian only. The ticket office is at the foot of the cliff. Shorts are forbidden and women must cover their heads.

Ten kilometres south of Orhei en route to Orheiul Vechi is **Ivancea**, with a good **ethnographic museum**, housed in a 19th-century stately mansion. Its eight halls are filled with traditional Moldovan costumes, musical instruments, pottery and folk art; open 8 am to 5 pm Tuesday to Sunday ($0.10).

Getting There & Away

Daily buses depart every half-hour from Chişinău's Autogară Centrală to Orheiul Vechi ($1.20). From Orhei, a bus departs daily for Trebujeni at 12.45 pm. Ask to be dropped off by the signposted entrance to the complex. There is a daily afternoon bus back to Orhei from Orheiul Vechi.

A taxi from Orhei to Orheiul Vechi costs around $6.

BĂLŢI, REZINA & LALOVA

Bălţi (population 182,000), 150km northwest of Chişinău, is Moldova's fourth-largest city. A major industrial area, and predominantly Russian-speaking, it offers little beyond being a convenient stopover en route to Ukraine.

Some 60km east of Bălţi on the western banks of the Dniestr River is the small town of Rezina. Seven kilometres south of the town is the Orthodox **Saharna Monastery**.

From Lalova, farther south, you can visit the underground **Ţipova Monastery**, dating from the 13th century when it was fashionable to carve churches and houses in rock.

If you want to stay overnight in this area, *Hotel Basarabia* in Bălţi has doubles with private bath for $14, including breakfast. Next to the hotel is a restaurant and bar. To get to the centre of town from Bălţi bus station, take trolleybus No 1 to Blvd Ştefan cel Mare.

Rezina's only hotel, *Hotel Noroc*, was closed indefinitely at the time of writing.

Getting There & Away
Bălţi is well served by buses. Daily services include one to Tiraspol and Ediniţa, eight to Soroca and seven to Ungheni. There are buses every half-hour to/from Chişinău ($2.40). Daily buses to Iaşi in Romania depart at 7.30 and 8.30 am.

SOROCA
Soroca fortress was part of a medieval chain of military fortresses built by Moldavian princes between the 14th and 16th centuries to defend Moldavia's boundaries. Only its ruins remain.

Strategically placed at (then) Moldavia's most north-eastern tip on the banks of the Dniestr River, Soroca was one of the key military strongholds. The ruins today are from a fortress built by Petru Rareş (1527–38) on the site of an older one.

Moldova Tur in Chişinău arranges tours to the fortress (see Information under Chişinău earlier in this chapter). From Bălţi there are eight daily buses to Soroca.

Gagauzia

Gagauzia (Gagauz Yeri) is a self-governed republic covering 3000 sq km in southern Moldova. It has its own legislative, which is autonomous in regional affairs. On a national level, Gagauzia (population 153,000) is represented by the assembly's elected *başkan* (head), a member of the Gagauz Halki political party who holds a safe seat in the Moldovan parliament.

Comrat is Gagauzia's capital. The republic is divided into three districts – Comrat, Ceadăr-Linga and Vulcăneşti. Wedged between these last two is the predominantly Bulgarian-populated district of Taraclia, which is not part of Gagauzia. Gagauz territory is further broken up by three Bulgarian villages in Ceadăr-Linga and a predominantly Moldovan village in Comrat district, all of which are part of 'mainland' Moldova too.

The Gagauz are a Turkic-speaking, Christian ethnic minority whose Muslim antecedents fled the Russo-Turkish wars in the 18th century. They were allowed to settle in the region in exchange for their conversion to Christianity. Their language is a dialect of Turkish, with vocabulary influenced by Russian Orthodoxy as opposed to the Islamic influences inherent in Turkish. Unlike Moldovans, Gagauz lay no claim to any Latin roots or influences, but rather look to Turkey for cultural inspiration and heritage.

The republic has its own flag, its own police force, its own weekly journals – *Ana sözu* and *Cârlangaci* – written in Gagauzi, and its own university partly funded by the Turkish government. Students are taught in

---

Divine Communication

When Mircea Cerari, the king of Moldova's Roma community, died at the age of 59 in July 1998, it was not his death but his entrance into the afterlife that raised eyebrows. Determined to keep in contact with loved ones from beyond the grave, the king had made arrangements to be buried with his computer, fax and mobile phone.

The lavish funeral, held in Soroca in northern Moldova two weeks after his death, was attended by some 15,000 Roma who had gathered from the far reaches of Europe to pay their respects. Also in attendance was Mircea Cerari's son Arthur, who has since inherited Moldova's Roma crown.

The king's impressive white marble grave contained not only his communication equipment but also a bar stocked with – what else? – vodka!

MOLDOVA

Gagauzi, Moldovan and Russian – the official languages of the republic. Gagauzi is taught in 37 schools throughout Moldova.

Gagauz autonomy was officially recognised by the Moldovan government in December 1994. Unlike the more militant separatists in Transdniestr, the Gagauz forfeited independence for large-scale autonomy. Theirs is a predominantly agricultural region with little industry to sustain an independent economy.

COMRAT
☎ 238 • pop 70,000

Gagauzia's capital, 92km south of Chişinău, is no more than a dusty, provincial town. In 1990 it was the scene of clashes between Gagauz nationalists and Moldovan armed forces, pre-empted by calls from local leaders for the Moldovan government to hold a referendum on the issue of Gagauz sovereignty. Local protesters were joined by Transdniestran militia forces.

Comrat is home to the world's only Gagauz university. Most street signs are in Russian; some older ones are in Gagauzi but in the Cyrillic script. Since 1989, Gagauzi, alongside Moldovan, has used the Latin alphabet.

Orientation & Information
From the bus station, walk south along the main street, ulitsa Pobedy, past the market to ploshchad Pobedy (Victory Square). St John's Church stands on the western side of the square, behind which lies the central park. Prospekt Lenina runs parallel to ulitsa Pobedy, west of the park.

Change money at the Moldovan Agrobank, ulitsa Pobedy 52; open 8 am to 1 pm weekdays. A small currency exchange is inside the entrance to the market. The post office, where you can make international calls via an operator, is next to the bank at ulitsa Pobedy 55; open 8 am to 6 pm weekdays and 8 am to 5 pm Saturday.

Things to See
The regional **başkani** (assembly) is on prospekt Lenina. A Gagauzi flag and a Moldovan flag fly from the roof. The

Gagauzi flag, officially adopted in 1995, comprises three horizontal stripes coloured blue, white and red. Three white stars adorn the blue strip.

Next to the assembly is the **Gagauz Culture House**, in front of which stands a statue of Lenin. West of prospekt Lenina at ulitsa Galatsăna 17 is the **Gagauz University** (Komrat Devlet Üniversitesi), founded in 1990. Mainstream courses are taught in Russian. The main foreign languages taught are English and Turkish. The university has strong links with Turkish universities.

Places to Stay & Eat
Hotel Medelean (☎ 22 572, ulitsa Pobedy 117), on the eastern side of ploshchad Pobedy, is a fairly modern hotel with single/double rooms for $10/15. Its bar serves excellent şaşlik for $1 and crisp, home-grown salads for $0.50.

Getting There & Away
There are five daily return buses from Chişinău to Comrat ($2.95). From Comrat there are two buses daily via Tighina to Tiraspol, and one only as far as Tighina.

Transdniestr

The self-declared republic of Transdniestr (population 700,000) incorporates the narrow strip of land on the eastern bank of the Dniestr River. A predominantly Russian-populated region, it declared independence from Moldova in 1991 sparking off a bloody civil war.

Travellers to Transdniestr will be stunned by a region which is very much an independent state in all but name. It has its own currency, police force, army, and its own (unofficial) borders, which are controlled by Transdniestran border guards.

Its two main towns are Tiraspol, the capital, and Tighina (called Bendery in Russian). Tighina is a security zone in which the peacekeeping forces are headquartered. The Transdniestran and Russian armies are based in Tiraspol. Western travellers can freely travel in the region; Russian is the predominant language, which can make getting around tough. A curfew is still in force in some areas.

Despite all this, visiting Transdniestr provides visitors with a unique opportunity to witness the harsh realities of one of the world's few surviving communist bastions.

Government & Politics

Igor Smirnov was elected president of Transdniestr in 1991 following the region's declaration of independence four months previously. In 1994 the Moldovan parliament ratified a new constitution providing substantial autonomy to Transdniestr in regional affairs.

Two main political organisations dominate the Transdniestran parliament and district administrations: the Working Transdniestr (WTD) emerged from the United Council of Workers' Collectives (OSTK) political party, which was responsible for organising the armed uprising against Chişinău in 1992. The Bloc of Left Wing Forces (BLWF) backs a centrally planned economy and the revival of the USSR, and is opposed to all market reforms. Neither Smirnov's presidency nor the Transdniestran parliament is recognised by the Moldovan government.

In 1993 six ethnic Moldovans were sentenced to life imprisonment for allegedly killing two Transdniestran officials. International human rights groups have since campaigned for their release, claiming they were convicted for being members of the Christian Democratic Popular Front (CDPF), a political party which backs Moldovan reunification with Romania.

On 2 September 2000 Transdniestr celebrated the 10th anniversary of its break from the republic of Moldova. Speaking on the eve of the celebrations, president Igor Smirnov stated that an agreement with Moldova could only be achieved when Transdniestr's independence was fully recognised.

Economy

As a self-declared republic, Transdniestr's economy is disastrous, despite the fact that 40% of Moldova's total potential industrial output is concentrated in Tiraspol. In mid-2000 the rebel republic owed $338 million to the Russian Gazprom.

Inflation is rampant and the local currency, the Transdniestran rouble, is worthless. The average monthly salary is less than $15 a month. State employers are not able to pay their workers, forcing many to earn a living at the flea market.

Population & People

Two-thirds of Transdniestr's population is elderly, impoverished, and yearns for a return to the Soviet Union, under which they had a better quality of life. Ethnic Russians comprise 25% of the population, ethnic Moldovans 40% and Ukrainians 28%.

Language

The official state languages in Transdniestr are Russian, Moldovan and Ukrainian. Students in schools and universities are taught in Russian, and local government and most official institutions operate almost solely in Russian. All street signs are written in Russian, Moldovan in the Cyrillic alphabet and sometimes Ukrainian.

Money

The Transdniestran rouble is a national joke – everyone's a millionaire yet everyone's broke. Most wealth dissolved into an oblivion of zeros long ago.

The only legal tender is the Transdniestran rouble (NH). There are 50, 100, 200, 500, 1000, 5000, 10,000, 50,000 and 100,000 rouble banknotes. The banknotes under 500 roubles have been rendered useless by inflation. There are two types of 50,000 notes – blue and brown. The brown ones featuring the drama theatre on their reverse are actually worth 500,000 roubles

STOP PRESS! Government monetary reforms effective from January 2001 have slashed six zeroes from the currency, with a new 1 rouble banknote worth 1 million roubles in old money. There are new 1, 5, 10, 25, 50 and 100 rouble banknotes. The Transdniestr Republican Bank's Web site (www.cbpmr.net) has a summary of the changes as well as current exchange rates.

MOLDOVA

Funny Money

If a national currency is the symbol of statehood, Transdniestr has a long way to go before achieving real independence. Ever since the republic introduced its own currency, the printing presses have failed to keep up with the breakneck speed of hyperinflation, resulting in a mind-boggling set of unique numismatic specimens.

In 1992–93, following the collapse of the USSR, the Soviet rouble disintegrated into over 15 different currencies. Russia dumped its Soviet Lenin and hoisted the Russian tricolour on its new rouble bills. Chişinău introduced its own Moldovan leu in November 1993.

Transdniestran separatists responded by immediately creating their own currency too. Lacking funding, they stuck a humble postage stamp of Suvorov, the local Russian war hero, on the Soviet rouble bills to create a currency they could proudly call their own. The new Lenin (formerly 1000 Soviet roubles) was worth 100 or 1000 Transdniestran roubles depending on the amount written on the little corner stamp.

In August 1994 this makeshift currency was replaced by the first set of real Transdniestran rouble coupons, issued in denominations of 50, 100, 200, 500, 1000 and 5000. The bills featured Suvorov on one side and the parliament building on the reverse. Smaller denominations of 1, 5 and 10 rouble notes had also been printed at the Moscow press, but they were never circulated: inflation had outpaced the presses.

But they weren't defeated. In 1996, to catch up with galloping inflation, the presses printed four additional zeros on their defunct 1, 5 and 10 rouble notes, upping their face values to 10,000, 50,000 and 100,000 roubles. For some bizarre reason, some fivers missed out on the zero treatment: a flashy silver hologram was stuck on their corners instead to indicate their true 50,000 worth.

The same year, a new brown 50,000 rouble note featuring Chmelnistki and the Chişinău Drama Theatre was printed – only to be traded as a half-million-rouble note (less than US$1) on its release in 1997.

The Transdniestran rouble stood 1:1 with the Russian rouble in 1994. In mid-2000, one Russian rouble equalled 750,000 Transdniestran roubles. Ask the staunchest Transdniestran nationalist to trade you a wad of their funny money for a single greenback and they'll happily agree.

– despite this being printed absolutely nowhere on the banknote.

Not surprisingly, hard currency is desperately sought after by most taxi drivers, shopkeepers and market traders who will gladly accept payment in US dollars – or even Moldovan lei or Ukrainian hryvnia. When changing money, don't change more than $10 at a time, to avoid a stack of banknotes (US$10 currently equals 40 million roubles!).

Black Market Avoid changing money on the black market, even though this is the standard practice of locals and expats alike. If you are caught, you run the risk of being fined or even imprisoned.

Exchange Rates At the time of writing, the exchange rates were:

country	unit		rouble
Germany	DM1	=	NH2,010,000
Moldova	1 Lei	=	NH320,000
Russia	R1	=	NH750,000
Ukraine	1 hv	=	NH750,000
USA	US$1	=	NH4,120,000

Post

Transdniestran stamps featuring Suvorov can only be used for letters sent within the Transdniestran republic and are not recognised anywhere else. For letters to Moldova, Romania and the West, you have to use Moldovan stamps (available here but less conveniently than in Moldova).

Curfew

The curfew imposed in Tighina during the 1992 military conflict is still enforced. You are not allowed to walk in the streets in Tighina between 11 pm and 5 am. You risk being fined by the local police if you do.

Media

The predominantly Russian Transdniestran TV is broadcast in the republic between 9 am and midnight. Transdniestran Radio is on air during the same hours.

The two local newspapers are in Russian. The *Transdniestra* is a purely nationalist affair advocating the virtues of an independent state; *N Pravda* is marginally more liberal.

TIRASPOL
☎ 233 • pop 204,000

Tiraspol, 70km east of Chişinău, is the second-largest city in Moldova. Its population is predominantly Russian (41%), with ethnic Ukrainians comprising 32% and ethnic Moldovans 18% of the population.

The city was founded in 1792 following Russian domination of the region. From 1929, Tiraspol was the capital of the Moldovan Autonomous Soviet Socialist Republic. The MASSR capital was previously in Balta in present-day Ukraine. Today Tiraspol is the capital of Transdniestr.

Registering

All foreign visitors to Tiraspol (but not Tighina) are required to register with the Tiraspol Militia Passport office (☎ 34 169), ulitsa Rosa Luxembourg 2. You have to state which hotel you are staying at, how many nights you intend to stay, and the purpose of your visit. You cannot check into any hotel until you have the scrap of paper dished out by the passport office in return for this information.

If you intend staying in Tiraspol longer than three days, you also have to register with OVIR (Otdel Viz i Registratsii or Department of Visas & Registration; ☎ 61 200), pereulok Rayevskaya 10. If you fail to do so, getting out of Transdniestr could be a costly exercise.

Orientation & Information

The train and bus stations are next to each other at the end of ulitsa Lenina. Exit the train station and walk up ulitsa Lenina, past Kirov Park, to ulitsa 25 Oktober (the main street).

The post office, on ulitsa Lenina, is open 8 am to 6 pm weekdays. The central telephone office is on ulitsa 25 Oktober; open 7 am to 8.45 pm daily. International calls can be booked here; when the recipient answers, dial ☎ 3.

Change money next door at the Transdniestr Savings Bank, open 8 am to 1 pm and 2 to 5.30 pm weekdays.

City maps, regarded as military objects, are not available to humble tourists.

Note that, from 1 April to 30 October, there is no heating or hot water in Tiraspol.

Things to See

Tiraspol has no history museum but the illustrated panels outside the city administration building, **House of Soviets** (Dom Sovetov), trace the city's history from 1792, when it became part of the Russian empire, through to the 1990s.

A **statue of Lenin** is in front of the House of Soviets. Inside the building is a **memorial** to those who died in the 1992 military conflict. Close by at ulitsa Kommunisticheskaya 34 is the **Museum of Headquarters**; open 11 am to 6 pm Monday to Saturday.

On ulitsa 25 Oktober stands a Soviet armoured tank from which the Transdniestrian flag flies today. Behind is the **Tomb of the Unknown Soldier**, flanked by an eternal flame in memory of those who died on 3 March 1992 during the first outbreak of fighting. The inscription in Russian reads 'You don't have a name but your deeds are eternal.' Those who died in the subsequent war are buried in the **city cemetery**, north of the centre, where a special alley has been allocated to the 1992 war victims.

At ulitsa 25 Oktober 42 is the **house museum** of Nikolai Dimitriovich Zelinskogo (1866–1953), the poet who founded the first Soviet school of chemistry; open 9 am to 5 pm Monday to Saturday. Opposite is the **Presidential Palace**, from where Igor Smirnov rules his self-proclaimed republic.

The **Drama Theatre**, pictured on the 50,000 rouble bill, is at ulitsa 25 Oktober. Close by is the **university**, founded in 1930.

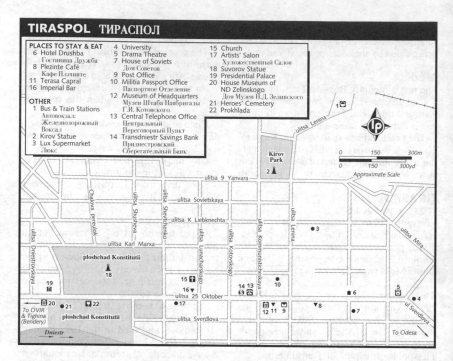

In front is a **statue of Chmelnistki**, pictured on the reverse side of the same bill.

To the side of the Kino Cinema on ulitsa Lenina is a 1918 October revolution **memorial**, erected to mark the 50th anniversary of the Russian revolution. Big plans are being made to celebrate its 100th birthday in 2017.

Places to Stay & Eat

Despite a two-tier pricing system, *Hotel Drushba* (☎ 34 266, ulitsa 25 Oktober 118) is relatively inexpensive. Doubles are $10 for locals and $15 for foreigners. Rooms have private bath, TV and fridge, but toilet paper is not supplied and a hot bath is mission impossible.

The *Plezinte Café (ulitsa 25 Oktober 116)* serves a small selection of lukewarm drinks, fresh cakes and savoury buns. Close by is the cheerier *Terasa Capral (ulitsa 25 Oktober 108)*, easily identifiable by its huge Caribbean-style Sprite and Coke umbrellas outside.

Entertainment

A popular spot is the underground bar-disco *Prokhlada* (☎ 34 642, ulitsa 25 Oktober 50), not far from the Presidential Palace. According to the sign outside you are not allowed to take in hand grenades, guns, gas bottles or alcohol, while doormen adhere to a strict face-control policy. It's open 11 to 3 am daily.

Getting There & Away

Train The train station is on ulitsa Lenina. Tickets for same-day departures are sold in the main train station ticket hall. There is also an information booth – a question about national train services costs $0.05, a question about services to CIS countries costs $0.10, and a copy of the correct timetable is $0.10. Advance tickets (24 hours or more before departure) are sold in the ticket office on the 2nd floor.

All Bucharest-Moscow and Chişinău–St Petersburg trains stop in Tiraspol. Most other eastbound trains from Chişinău to

Ukraine and Russia stop in Tiraspol too (see the Getting There & Away chapter). There is one daily local train between Tiraspol and Chişinău.

Bus Tickets for all buses are sold in the main ticket hall. You can only pay for tickets to other destinations in Transdniestr in the local currency. Bus tickets to Moldova/Ukraine are only sold in Moldovan lei/Ukrainian hryvnia.

From Tiraspol buses go daily to Bălţi at 6.10 and 9.50 am and 2.05 pm, and there are twelve daily to Chişinău ($3.85). There are also four daily buses to Odesa in Ukraine.

Some additional buses not listed on the official timetable depart for Chişinău from outside the train station. These nippy microbuses leave every hour – or when they're full. Tickets are sold at the bus station or direct from the driver.

Getting Around
Bus No 1 and microbus No 3 run between the bus and train station and the city centre. Tickets for regular buses ($0.02) are sold by the driver. Tickets for microbuses cost $0.12.

Trolleybus Nos 1 and 19 cross the bridge over the Dniestr to Tighina. Microbus Nos 1 and 19 also make the 20-minute journey but tickets are more expensive.

TIGHINA
☎ 233 • pop 140,000
Traditionally Tighina (Bendery in Russian), on the western banks of the Dniestr River, has always been an important military stronghold. Russian troops have been stationed here since 1992 but Russia has agreed to their withdrawal by the end of 2002.

During the 16th century, Moldavian prince Ştefan cel Mare built a large defensive fortress here on the ruins of a fortified Roman camp. In 1538 the Ottoman sultan, Suleiman the Magnificent, conquered the fortress and transformed Tighina into a Turkish *raia* (colony), renaming the city Bender, meaning 'belonging to the Turks'. Following the decisive Russian defeat of Sweden's Charles XII and Ukrainian Cossack leader Ivan Mazepa by Peter the Great at Poltava in 1709, it was to Tighina that the Swedish king and Cossack leader fled for refuge. Mazepa consequently died in Tighina's fortress.

During the Russo-Turkish wars in the 18th century, Tighina was seized from the Turks by Russian troops who then massacred Turkish Muslims in the city. In 1812 Tighina fell permanently into Russian hands and the fortress was occupied by Russian troops. USSR forces remained stationed here until 1992 when Tighina was made off-limits to armed forces. Theoretically the fortress has been empty since. Nevertheless it is not open to visitors.

The bloodiest fighting during the 1992 military conflict took place in Tighina and many walls of buildings in the centre remain badly bullet-pocked. Today the city is protected as a security zone by peacekeeping forces who have various military installations and camouflaged personnel carriers at strategic points in the town.

Visitors should note that there is a curfew between 11 pm and 5 am.

Information
Change money at the currency exchange next to the Kolkhoz Market on ulitsa Sovetskaya. International telephone calls can be booked from the telephone office on the corner of ulitsa Liazo and ulitsa Suvorova; open 8 am to 6 pm Monday to Wednesday, 8 am to noon and 1 to 6 pm Thursday and Friday, and 8 am to 4 pm Saturday. The central department store is opposite Hotel Dniestr on the corner of ulitsa Lenina and ulitsa Kalinina.

Tighina's special security zone status enables foreign tourists to stay in the city without having to register with the local militia.

Things to See
At the entrance to the city, close to the famous **Tighina-Tiraspol bridge**, is a **memorial park**, opened in 1996, dedicated to Tighina's 1992 war victims. An eternal flame burns in front of an armoured tank, from which flies the Transdniestran flag.

Haunting **memorials** to those shot dead during the civil war are evident throughout many of the main streets in the centre. The **City Council** building is at ulitsa Lenina 17.

MOLDOVA

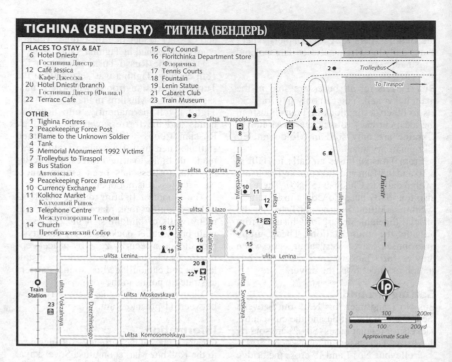

TIGHINA (BENDERY)   ТИГИНА (БЕНДЕРЬ)

PLACES TO STAY & EAT
6   Hotel Dniestr
    Гостиница Днестр
12 Café Jessica
    Кафе Джесска
20 Hotel Dniestr (branch)
    Гостиница Днестр (Филиал)
22 Terrace Cafe

OTHER
1   Tighina Fortress
2   Peacekeeping Force Post
3   Flame to the Unknown Soldier
4   Tank
5   Memorial Monument 1992 Victims
7   Trolleybus to Tiraspol
8   Bus Station
    Автовокзал
9   Peacekeeping Force Barracks
10 Currency Exchange
11 Kolkhoz Market
    Колхозный Рынок
13 Telephone Centre
    Междугородны Телефон
14 Church
    Преображенский Собор

15 City Council
16 Floritchinka Department Store
    Флоричинка
17 Tennis Courts
18 Fountain
19 Lenin Statue
21 Cabaret Club
23 Train Museum

Next to the train station is a **Train Museum**, inside an old Russian CY 06-71 steam locomotive. The museum was closed at the time of writing. Alongside Tighina's only museum is a typically Soviet, over-sized granite mural in memory of the train workers who died in the 1918 revolution.

Places to Stay & Eat

A two-tier pricing system is firmly intact at the central branch of **Hotel Dniestr** (☎ 23 444, ulitsa Kalinina 50). Foreigners pay $8/16 for singles/doubles with shared bath. A luxury double room with fridge, TV and private bath is $18. Adjacent is the **Cabaret Club**. The terrace *cafe* (ulitsa Kalinina 52) next door is also worth a look.

Overlooking the Dniestr River is the main branch of **Hotel Dniestr** (☎ 29 478, ulitsa Katachenka 10). It charges foreigners $11/22 for rooms with TV, fridge and private bath.

Café Jessica, on ulitsa Liazo opposite the telephone office, is the best place to eat in town. Statues of penguins stand outside the funky wooden exterior.

Getting There & Away

The train station is at Privokzalnaya ploschad. The information desk in the ticket hall is open 8 am to noon and 2 pm to 6 pm daily. Questions cost $0.05 each. Printed train timetables in Russian are sold from the main office for $0.10.

There are 16 buses daily to Chişinău and one daily to Comrat. Tickets for Chişinău can only be paid in Moldovan lei.

Trolleybus No 19 for Tiraspol ($0.05) departs from the bus stop next to the main roundabout at the entrance to Tighina. Microbuses clearly marked with their destination on the front also make the 20-minute journey but cost $0.20.

MOLDOVA

Language

Romanian is a Romance language, along with the majority of western European languages such as French, Italian, Spanish and Portuguese. Its origins date back to the 2nd century AD when the Emperor Trajan founded the Roman province of Dacia in the south-west of present-day Transylvania. Romanian is much closer to classical Latin than the other Romance languages, and the grammatical structure and basic word stock of the parent language are well preserved.

Romanian has been influenced considerably by the Slavonic languages of its neighbours (such as Polish, Bulgarian and Serbian), with many words finding their way into the language over the centuries.

Speakers of French, Italian and Spanish won't be able to understand much spoken Romanian but will find written Romanian more or less comprehensible. Moldovan is a very closely related dialect of Romanian.

For a more comprehensive look at the language, get a copy of the new edition of Lonely Planet's *Eastern Europe phrasebook*. If you wish to delve further still, James Augerot's 31-chapter *Romanian/Limba Română – A Course in Modern Romanian* (2000) is recommended. It's published by the Iaşi-based Center for Romanian Studies and is available either in Romania or via the Internet (see Books in Facts for the Visitor for details).

Writing System

Until the mid-19th century, Romanian was written in Cyrillic script. Once the decision was made to adopt a Latin-based alphabet, a long period of debate ensued over whether the alphabet should be phonetically-based or etymologically-based (ie, reflecting the orthography of Classical Latin).

Between 1953 and 1994 elements of Slavic writing systems were introduced as part of the Russification of the country, under which the letter â was replaced by the Slavic î. It wasn't until 1994, however, that the Romanian Academy ruled out the Stalinist î and reverted to the original Latin orthography. Old spellings such as Tîrgu Mureş instead of Târgu Mureş still lurk on the odd map – this book uses the correct â spellings.

The writing system today uses a Latin-based alphabet of 28 letters, some of which bear accents.

Pronunciation

Written Romanian is more or less phonetically consistent, so once you learn a few simple rules you should have no trouble with pronunciation. There are no long variants of vowels, but e, i, o and u form diphthongs or triphthongs with adjacent vowels. At the beginning of a word, e and i are pronounced 'ye' and 'yi', while at the end of a word an i is almost silent. At the end of a word ii is pronounced 'ee'. Word stress generally falls on the penultimate syllable.

a	as the 'u' in 'cut'
e	as in 'tell'
i	as in 'vino'
ă	a neutral vowel; as the 'a' in 'sofa'
â/î	as the 'i' in 'river'
c	as in 'cat' before **a**, **o** and **u**; as the 'ch' in church before **e** and **i**
ch	as the 'k' in 'kit' before **e** and **i**
g	as in 'good' before **a**, **o** and **u**; as in 'gentle' before **e** and **i**
gh	as the 'g' in 'good'
ş	as the 'sh' in 'ship'
ţ	as the 'ts' in 'cats'

Greetings & Civilities

Hello.	*Bună.*
Goodbye.	*La revedere.*
Good morning.	*Bună dimineaţa.*
Good day.	*Bună ziua.*
Good evening.	*Bună seara.*
Please.	*Vă rog.*
Thank you.	*Mulţumesc.*

(the French *merci* is also commonly used)

I'm sorry/Forgive me.	*Iertaţi-mă.*
Excuse me.	*Scuzaţi-mă.*
Yes.	*Da.*
No.	*Nu.*
What's your name?	*Cum vă numiţi?*
My name is ...	*Numele meu este ...*
Where are you from?	*De unde sunteţi?*
I'm from ...	*Sunt din ...*
What work do you do?	*Cu ce vă ocupaţi?*

Language Difficulties

Do you speak English?	*Vorbiţi engleza?*
I understand.	*Eu înţeleg.*
I don't understand.	*Eu nu înţeleg.*
Could you write it down?	*Puteţi să notaţi?*
How do you say ...?	*Cum spuneţi ...?*
What does ... mean?	*Ce înseamnă ...?*
What's it called?	*Cum se cheamă?*

Getting Around

What time does the ... leave/arrive?	*La ce oră pleacă/ soseşte ...?*
boat	*vaporul*
bus	*autobuzul*
train	*trenul*

first	*primul*
last	*ultimul*
next	*următorul*
arrival	*sosire*
departure	*plecare*
bus timetable	*mersul autobuzelor*
train timetable	*mersul trenurilor*

When is the next one after that?	*Când este următorul după acesta?*
How long does the trip take?	*Cât timp durează excursia?*
Where is the bus stop?	*Unde este staţia de autobuz?*
Where is the train station?	*Unde este gara?*
Where is the left-luggage room?	*Unde este biroul pentru bagaje de mână?*
I want to go to ...	*Vreau să merg la ...*

'Street' Romanian

A few useful terms for getting around are:

aleea	avenue
bulevardul	boulevard
calea	road
piaţa	square
şoseaua	highway
strada	street

I'd like a ... ticket.	*Aş dori un bilet ...*
one-way	*dus*
return	*dus-întors*
1st class	*clasa întâi*
2nd class	*clasa a doua*

How do I get to ...?	*Cum ajung la ...?*
Where are you going?	*Unde mergeţi?*
I'm going to ...	*Merg la ...*
Is it near here?	*Este aproape de aici?*
Is it far from here?	*Este departe de aici?*
Can I walk there?	*Pot să merg pe jos până acolo?*
Can you show me (on the map)?	*Puteţi să-mi arătaţi (pe hartă)?*
Go straight ahead.	*Du-te drept înainte.*

left	*stânga*
right	*dreapta*
at the traffic lights	*la semafor*
at the next corner	*la următorul colţ*
behind	*în spatele*
in front of	*în faţa*
opposite	*opus*
north	*nord/miazănoape*
south	*sud/miazăzi*
east	*est/răsărit/orient*
west	*vest/apus/occident*

Accommodation

Where is a ... hotel?	*Unde este un hotel ...?*
cheap	*ieftin*
good	*bun*
nearby	*apropiat*

| youth hostel | *cămin studenţesc* |
| camping ground | *camping* |

Where is there a cheaper hotel?
Unde este un hotel mai ieftin?
What's the address?
Care-i adresa?
Could you write the address, please?
Poţi să-mi scrii adresa, te rog?
Should I make a reservation?
Pot face o rezervare?

I'd like ...	*Aş dori ...*
a single room	*o cameră de o persoană*
a double room	*o cameră dublă*
a private room	*o cameră particulară*
a bed	*un pat*

How much is it ...?	*Cât costă ...?*
per night	*pe noapte*
per person	*de persoană*

Is that the total price?
Acesta este preţul total?
Does it include breakfast?
Include micul dejun?
Are there any extra charges?
Mai este ceva de plătit?
Do I pay extra for showers?
Trebuie să plătesc în plus pentru duş?
Is there hot water all day?
Este apă caldă toată ziua?
May I see it?
Pot să văd?
It's very noisy.
Este foarte zgomotos.
Are there any others?
Mai sunt şi altele?
It's fine, I'll take it.
Este în regulă, îl (o) iau.
Where's the toilet?
Unde este toaleta?

Around Town

I'm looking for ...	*Caut ...*
Where is ...?	*Unde este ...?*
a bank	*o banca*
the ... embassy	*ambasada ...*
the market	*piaţa*
the museum	*muzeu*
the police	*poliţia*

the post office	*poşta*
a public toilet	*o toaetă publică*
the tourist office	*informaţii pentru turism*

open	*deschis*
closed	*închis*

What time does it open/close?
La ce oră se deschide/închide?
Do I need permission?
Am nevoie de aprobare?

Entertainment

Where can I hear live music?
Unde pot asculta muzică în concert?
Where can I buy a ticket?
Unde pot cumpăra un bilet?
I'm looking for a ticket.
Nu aveţi un bilet în plus?
Is this a good seat?
Este un loc bun?

at the front	*în primele rânduri*
ticket	*bilet*
cinema	*cinema*
concert	*concert*
nightclub	*discotecă*
theatre	*teatru*

Shopping

Where is the nearest ...?	*Unde e cel mai apropii at ...?*
bookshop	*librărie*
chemist	*farmacie*
laundry	*spălatorie*
market	*piaţă*
newsagent	*chioşc de ziare*

There is.	*Există.*
There isn't.	*Nu există.*
Where can I buy one?	*Unde aş putea cumpăra?*
How much is it?	*Cât costă?*
That's (much) too expensive.	*Este (mult) prea scump.*
Is there a cheaper one?	*Pot găsi ceva mai ieftin?*
Do you accept credit cards?	*Acceptaţi cărţi de credit?*

LANGUAGE

clothing	îmrăcăminte/haine
condoms	prezervative
sanitary napkins	şervețele igienice
shampoo	şampon
soap	săpun
sunscreen	cremă de soare
tampons	tampoane
toilet paper	hârtie igienică

Food

breakfast	micul dejun
lunch	prânz/dejun
dinner	cină
I'm a vegetarian.	Eu sunt vegetarian.

I don't eat ...	Eu nu mănânc ...
meat	carne
chicken	pui
fish	peşte
ham	şuncă

bread	pâine
cheese	brânză
eggs	ouă
fish	peşte
fresh vegetables	legume proaspete
grocery store	băcănie
hot/cold	cald/rece
ice cream	înghețată
pork	porc
pancake	clătite
salad	salată
self-service cafeteria	autoservire
soup	supă
sugar	zahăr

Drinks

mineral water	apă minerală
milk	lapte
fruit juice	suc de fructe
ice	gheață
tea	ceai
coffee	cafe
black coffee	cafea
coffee with milk	cafea cu lapte

beer	bere
wine (red/white)	vin (roşu/alb)
plum brandy	țuică

Health

Where is the ...?	Unde este ...?
chemist	farmacistul
dentist	dentistul
doctor	doctorul
hospital	spitalul

I'm sick.	Sunt bolnav.
My friend is sick.	Prietenul meu este bolnav.

I have ...	Eu am ...
an allergy	o alergie
anaemia	anemie
a cold	o răceală
constipation	constipație
a cough	o tuse
diarrhoea	diaree
a fever	febră
a headache	o durere de cap
a stomachache	o durere de stomac

antibiotics	antibiotice
antiseptic	antiseptic
aspirin	aspirină
bandage	bandaj
bite	muşcătura
blood pressure	tensiune
contraceptive	contraceptive
medicine	medicament
nausea	greață/rău de mare

Time & Dates

When?	Când?
At what time?	La ce oră?
today	azi
tonight	diseară
tomorrow	mâine
in the morning	dimineața
in the evening	seara
every day	în fiecare zi
day after tomorrow	poimâine

Monday	luni
Tuesday	marți
Wednesday	miercuri
Thursday	joi
Friday	vineri
Saturday	sâmbătă
Sunday	duminică

January	*ianuarie*
February	*februarie*
March	*martie*
April	*aprilie*
May	*mai*
June	*iunie*
July	*iulie*
August	*august*
September	*septembrie*
October	*octombrie*
November	*noiembrie*
December	*decembrie*

Numbers

1	*unu*
2	*doi*
3	*trei*
4	*patru*
5	*cinci*
6	*şase*
7	*şapte*
8	*opt*
9	*nouă*
10	*zece*
11	*unsprezece*
12	*doisprezece*
13	*treisprezece*
14	*paisprezece*
15	*cinsprezece*
16	*şaisprezece*
17	*şaptesprezece*
18	*optsprezece*
19	*nouăsprezece*
20	*douăzeci*
21	*douăzeci şi unu*
22	*douăzeci şi doi*

23	*douăzeci şi trei*
30	*treizeci*
40	*patruzeci*
50	*cincizeci*
60	*şaizeci*
70	*şaptezeci*
80	*optzeci*
90	*nouăzeci*
100	*o sută*
1000	*o mie*
10,000	*zece mii*

one million	*un milion*

Emergencies

Help!	*Ajutor!*
Could you help me, please?	*M-aţi putea ajuta?*
It's an emergency.	*Este o urgenţă.*
There's been an accident.	*A fost un accident.*
Call a doctor!	*Chemaţi un doctor!*
Call an ambulance!	*Chemaţi salvare/ oambulanţă!*
Call the police!	*Chemaţi poliţia!*
I've been raped.	*Am fost violată.*
I've been robbed.	*Am fost jefuit/ă. (m/f)*
Where's the police station?	*Unde este Poliţia?*
Go away!	*Du-te!/Pleacă!*
Thief!	*Hoţii!*
I'm lost.	*Sunt pierdut.*
Where are the toilets?	*Unde este toaleta?*

Glossary

These handy Romanian words can also be used in Moldova. Hungarian (Hun) is included for key words.

ACR – Automobil Clubul Român
Agenția Teatrală – theatre ticket office (Hun: színház jegyiroda)
Agenție de Voiaj CFR – train ticket office (Hun: vasúti jegyiroda)
alimentară – food shop
Antrec – National Association of Rural, Ecological & Cultural Tourism
apă caldă – hot water (Hun: meleg víz)
apă rece – cold water (Hun: hideg víz)
autogară – bus station (Hun: távolsági autóbusz pályaudvar)

bagage de mâna – left-luggage office (Hun: csomagmegőrző)
bandă roșie – red stripe (hiking)
barcă cu motor – motor boat
barcă cu rame – rowing boat
berărie – beer house
biserica – church (Hun: templom)
biserică de lemn – wooden church

cabana – mountain cabin or chalet
cameră cu apă curentă – room with running water
cameră matrimonală – double room with a real double bed
casă de bilete – ticket office (Hun: jegyiroda)
cascadă – waterfall
căsuțe – wooden hut
cazare – room
CFR – Romanian State Railways
cheile – gorge
crap – carp
cruce albastră – blue cross (hiking)

de jos – at the bottom
deschis – open (Hun: nyitva)
de sus – at the top
dispecerat cazare – accommodation office

en detail – retail (shopping)

en gros – wholesale (shopping)

floare de colț – edelweiss

gara – train station (Hun: vasútállomás)
grădină de vară – summer garden
grinduri – sand dune

închis – closed (Hun: zárva)
ieșire – exit (Hun: kijárat)
intrare – entrance (Hun: bejárat)
intrare interzisă – no entry (Hun: tilos belépni)

jos – low

listă – menu
luptă – day

mănăstire – monastery (Hun: kolostor)
muzeul – museum (Hun: múzeum)

noapte – night
notă de plată – bill (Hun: számla)

orar – timetable (Hun: menetrend)

păduri – forest
pâine – bread
piața – square or market (Hun: főtér or piac)
piatra – stone, rock
plecare – departure (Hun: indulás)
popas – camping ground (Hun: kemping)
primarie – town hall
punct galben – yellow circle (hiking)

sală de concert – concert hall (Hun: hangversenyterem)
schimb valutar – currency exchange
scrumbie de Dunăre – Danube herring
sosire – arrival (Hun: érkezés)
spălătorie – launderette (Hun: patyolat)
spălătorie auto – car wash
stufăriș – reed bed
sus – up
systemisation – Ceaușescu's scheme for bulldozing entire rural villages and shifting

inhabitants into purpose-built agro-industrial complexes on city outskirts

ţara – land, country
telecabină – cable car
teleferic – collective term for all ski services
telescaun – chairlift
teleski – drag lift

terasa – terrace
toaleta – toilet (Hun: toalett)
trasee – hiking trail
triunghi roşu – red triangle (hiking)

vamă – customs (Hun: vámkezelés)
vin alba – white wine (Hun: bor fehér)
vin roşu – red wine (Hun: bor vörös)

LONELY PLANET

You already know that Lonely Planet produces more than this one guidebook, but you might not be aware of the other products we have on this region. Here is a selection of titles that you may want to check out as well:

Eastern Europe
ISBN 1 86450 149 9
US$24.99 • UK£14.99

Eastern Europe phrasebook
ISBN 1 86450 227 4
US$8.99 • UK£4.99

Europe on a shoestring
ISBN 1 86450 150 2
US$24.99 • UK£14.99

Read This First: Europe
ISBN 1 86450 136 7
US$14.99 • UK£8.99

Available wherever books are sold

Index

Text

Bold indicates maps.

Boxed Text

MAP LEGEND

CITY ROUTES

Freeway .... Freeway	═ ═ ═ ═ .... Unsealed Road
Highway .... Primary Road	═══➤═══ .... One Way Street
Road ...... Secondary Road	═══════ .... Pedestrian Street
Street .... Street	▭▭▭▭▭▭ ...... Stepped Street
Lane .... Lane	═)═ ═ ═ .... Tunnel
.... On/Off Ramp	═══ .... Footbridge

HYDROGRAPHY

.... River, Creek	.... Dry Lake; Salt Lake
.... Canal	.... Spring; Rapids
.... Lake	.... Waterfalls

REGIONAL ROUTES

═══════ .... Tollway, Freeway	
.... Primary Road	
.... Secondary Road	
.... Minor Road	

TRANSPORT ROUTES & STATIONS

──○── .... Train	─────❑ .... Ferry
┝─┿─┿─┿─ .. Underground Train	─ ─ ─ ─ .. Walking Trail
──Ⓜ── .... Metro	.... Walking Tour
═ ═ ═ ═ .... Tramway	.... Path
┝─┼─┼─┼─ .. Cable Car, Chairlift	.... Pier or Jetty

AREA FEATURES

.... Building	.... Market	.... Beach	.... Campus
.... Park, Gardens	.... Sports Ground	+ + + ... Cemetery	.... Plaza

POPULATION SYMBOLS

✪ CAPITAL .... National Capital	● CITY .... City	● Village .... Village
◉ CAPITAL .... State Capital	● Town .... Town	.... Urban Area

MAP SYMBOLS

♦ .... Place to Stay	▼ .... Place to Eat	● .... Point of Interest

⊞	.... Airfield	🏛	. Church/ Monastery		.... National Park		...... Swimming Pool
✈	.... Airport		.... Cinema	)(	.... Pass		.... Synagogue
	.. Archaeological Site	✚	...... Hospital, Clinic		.... Police Station		.... Taxi Rank
$	.... Bank		...... Internet Cafe	✉	.... Post Office		.... Theatre
	.... Bus Stop	♟	.... Monument		.... Pub or Bar		.... Tomb
	.... Bus Terminal		...... Mountain Hut		.... Shopping Centre	❶	.. Tourist Information
	.... Cathedral	🏛	.... Museum		.... Stately Home		.. Transport (general)

Note: not all symbols displayed above appear in this book

LONELY PLANET OFFICES

Australia
Locked Bag 1, Footscray, Victoria 3011
☎ 03 8379 8000 fax 03 8379 8111
email: talk2us@lonelyplanet.com.au

USA
150 Linden St, Oakland, CA 94607
☎ 510 893 8555 TOLL FREE: 800 275 8555
fax 510 893 8572
email: info@lonelyplanet.com

UK
10a Spring Place, London NW5 3BH
☎ 020 7428 4800 fax 020 7428 4828
email: go@lonelyplanet.co.uk

France
1 rue du Dahomey, 75011 Paris
☎ 01 55 25 33 00 fax 01 55 25 33 01
email: bip@lonelyplanet.fr
www.lonelyplanet.fr

World Wide Web: www.lonelyplanet.com *or* AOL keyword: lp
Lonely Planet Images: lpi@lonelyplanet.com.au